DEVELOPING EXPERT SYSTEMS FOR BUSINESS APPLICATIONS

DEVELOPING EXPERT SYSTEMS FOR BUSINESS APPLICATIONS

John S. Chandler
Ting-Peng Liang

University of Illinois,
Champaign-Urbana

Merrill Publishing Company
A Bell & Howell Information Company
Columbus Toronto London Melbourne

Published by Merrill Publishing Company
A Bell & Howell Information Company
Columbus, Ohio 43216

This book was set in Palatino

Administrative Editor: Vernon R. Anthony
Production Editor: JoEllen Gohr
Cover Designer: Russ Maselli

Library of Congress Catalog Number: 80-62575

International Standard Book Number: 0-675-21102-6

Printed in the United States of America

1 2 3 4 5 6 7 8 9—93 92 91 90

THE MERRILL SERIES IN COMPUTER AND INFORMATION SYSTEMS

BARKER	*Developing Business and Expert Systems with LEVEL5*, 20951–X
BROQUARD/ WESTLEY	*Fundamentals of Assembler Language Programming for The IBM PC and XT*, 21058–5
CAFOLLA/ KAUFFMAN	*Turbo Prolog: Step by Step*, 20816-5
CHANDLER/ LIANG	*Developing Expert Systems for Business Applications*, 21102–6
CHIRLIAN	*Programming in C++*, 21007–0
	Turbo Prolog: An Introduction, 20846–7
	UNIX for the IBM PC: An Introduction, 20785–1
DENOIA	*Data Communication: Fundamentals and Applications*, 20368–6
ERICKSON/ ISAAK	*Easy Ventura: A Guide to Learning Ventura Desktop Publishing for the IBM PC*, 21304–5
GEE	*A Programmer's Guide to RPG II and RPG III*, 20908–0
HOBART/ OCTERNAUD/ SYTSMA	*Hands-On Computing Using WordPerfect 5.0, Lotus 1-2-3 and dBase IV*, 21110–7
HOUSTON	*Looking into C*, 20845–9
INGALSBE	*Using Computers and Applications Software Featuring VP-Planner, dBase III/III Plus, and WordPerfect*, 21097–6
	Using Computers and Applications Software Featuring Lotus 1-2-3, dBase III/III Plus, and WordPerfect, 21179–4
	Business Applications Software for the IBM PC Alternate Edition with VP-Planner, dBase III/III Plus, and WordPerfect, 21000–3
	Business Applications Software for the IBM PC with Lotus 1-2-3, dBase III/III Plus, and WordPerfect, Third Edition, 21175–1
KHAN	*Beginning Structured COBOL*, 21174–3
LETRAUNIK	*MVS/XA JCL: A Practical Approach*, 20916–1
LIPNER/ KALMAN	*Computer Law: Cases and Materials*, 21104–2
MELLARD	*Introduction to Business Programming Using Pascal*, 20547–6

MORGAN — *Introduction to Structured Programming Using Turbo Pascal Version 5.0 on the IBM PC,* 20770–3

MORIBER — *Structured BASIC Programming, Second Edition,* 20715–0

REYNOLDS/ RIECKS — *Introduction to Business Telecommunications, Second Edition,* 20815–7

ROSEN — *Office Automation and Information Systems,* 20557–3

SCHATT — *Microcomputers in Business and Society,* 20862–9

SPRANKLE — *Problem Solving and Programming Concepts,* 20867–X

STARK — *The Complete Textbook of Lotus 1-2-3,* 21103–4

SZYMANSKI — *Computers and Information Systems in Business,* 20905–6

SZYMANSKI/ — *Computers and Application Software,* 20904–8

SZYMANSKI/ MORRIS/ PULSCHEN — *Introduction to Computers and Information Systems,* 20768–1

PREFACE

Expert systems have drawn much attention in the past several years. Because more and more companies are adopting this new technology to sharpen their competitive edge, the demand for expert systems with a business perspective has increased dramatically. Expert systems may have begun as a technical, engineering subject, but now courses on expert systems are offered by many business schools.

Unlike similar courses offered in engineering schools, an expert systems course in a business school should emphasize practical business applications more than the technical details of the technology. Unfortunately, although many recent developments in business domains have been reported, most textbooks are still oriented toward engineering issues, and most examples cited are primarily medical and engineering prototypes. Few textbooks include the application-oriented knowledge that business professionals and students need. This has been a problem for instructors and students alike.

This book aims specifically to alleviate this problem. It has the following objectives:

- To portray the current status of business applications of expert systems;
- To present a current set of readings for business courses on expert systems; and
- To provide background knowledge for future development of expert systems in business by both practitioners and academics.

Underlying all of these objectives is the premise that the presentation of expert systems has to be balanced. Therefore, this book includes not only articles favoring the use of expert systems in business but also articles describing the limitations or questioning the applicability of expert systems. It also covers critical areas not usually presented in other books, including validation, verification, strategic, and legal issues. Such a mix of articles allows for lively discussion in the academic classroom and for healthy skepticism in the corporate boardroom.

In order to ensure the quality of the content, all articles in the book were carefully selected from journals with rigorous refereeing processes. The book is divided into four sections:

1. Overview, providing an introduction to expert systems.
2. The development process, covering issues important in developing expert systems, including project start-up, domain selection, knowledge acquisition, and system validation.
3. Application, including reported business projects in four areas—accounting, financial planning, manufacturing, and management.
4. Perspectives, covering strategic and legal issues and the limitations of expert systems.

This book can be used in several ways. First, it can serve as a supplementary text to provide a broad perspective on expert systems. A primary concept book can be used to teach the technical knowledge of expert systems, and then readings in this book can fill the gap between theory and application. The book fits well, and can be used jointly, with one of the following books:

- Paul Harmon and David King, *Expert Systems: Artificial Intelligence in Business*, New York: John Wiley & Sons, 1985.
- Mike Van Horn, *Understanding Expert Systems*, Toronto, Canada: Bantam Books, 1986.
- Clyde W. Holsapple and Andrew B. Whinston, *Manager's Guide to Expert Systems*, Homewood, IL: Dow Jones-Irwin, 1986.
- Donald A. Waterman, *A Guide to Expert Systems*, Reading, MA: Addison-Wesley Publishing Company, 1986.
- Efraim Turban, *Decision Support and Expert Systems*, New York: Macmillan Publishing Company, 1988.

One of the first four books listed above could be used to cover the first half of the course, and the readings in this book could be used to cover the second half. Alternatively, the overview module could be used concurrently with the first one or two chapters of the four books, and the design process module could then be used to enrich chapters discussing the process for developing expert systems. The articles in the applications and perspectives sections could be used in the second half of the course to help students integrate techniques into business domains.

Turban's book has several chapters covering expert systems development; the reading book can help broaden the coverage. The overview fits well with chapters 10 and 15. The development process section goes with chapter 11. The application module can be used with chapters 13 and 14, and the perspective section suits chapters 16 and 18.

Second, this book could be the main text in an expert systems course, supplemented by a "how-to" book. In the first three or four weeks, the "how-to" book would help students learn basic concepts of expert systems and how to develop one. Then, for deeper knowledge, students would turn to the articles in this book covering issues in the design process and actual business applications. The "how-to" book should be accompanied by an expert systems shell that allows students to gain hands-on experience, or students could be asked to duplicate the project described in the application module of this book. The "how-to" book we suggest is Donald Barker, *Developing Business Expert Systems with Level5* (Columbus, OH: Merrill Publishing Company, 1988).

Third, the book could stand alone as the textbook for an advanced expert systems course. Because it focuses on business applications, it is well suited to courses on expert systems projects and to graduate seminars. The articles in the overview and development process modules provide students with the background they need. The articles in the application module help students identify potential areas of application and understand what issues and problems could arise. The articles in the perspective module help students form realistic expectations.

Acknowledgments

This book depends on the articles included in it for its contribution to the study of the expert systems field. We thank the authors of the articles, as well as the publishers who allowed us to reprint the articles. We received comments and suggestions from several reviewers while we were selecting articles and finalizing the manuscript: Mark S. Silver, University of California at Los Angeles; Jane Carey, Arizona State University; Clay Sprowls, University of California at Los Angeles; George Luger, University of New Mexico; R. Waldo Roth, Amoco Production Company, Tulsa Research Center; and Richard Spillman, Pacific Lutheran University. We also thank Vernon Anthony for his assistance in the editorial process.

CONTENTS

I. OVERVIEW

The goal of this book is to give business readers an understanding and appreciation of the expert systems field and its application to business. Because the reader likely already has some knowledge of expert systems and knowledge-based systems, the book includes only two articles on the fundamentals of expert systems. The first, by Hayes-Roth, gives an excellent overview of the expert systems field, presenting the issues, nomenclature, and problems that will be encountered in any discussion of expert systems. This information supplies a common background for the reader as particular issues are brought up in subsequent articles. The second, by Liang, provides an important bridge to the articles that follow, in that most business decision makers come from a decision aid/decision support environment and need to be shown the relationship between that familiar environment and the expert systems field.

The Knowledge-Based Expert System: A Tutorial

Frederick Hayes-Roth

Knowledge-based expert systems, or knowledge systems for short, employ human knowledge to solve problems that ordinarily require human intelligence.[1] Knowledge systems represent and apply knowledge electronically. In the future, these capabilities will ultimately make knowledge systems vastly more powerful than the earlier technologies for storing and transmitting knowledge, books and conventional programs. These earlier storage and transmission technologies suffer from fundamental limitations. Although books now store the largest volume of knowledge, they merely retain symbols in a passive form. Before the knowledge stored in books can be applied, a human must retrieve it, interpret it, and decide how to exploit it for problem-solving.

Most computers today perform tasks according to the decision-making logic of conventional programs, but these programs do not readily accommodate significant amounts of knowledge. Programs consist of two distinct parts, algorithms and data. Algorithms determine how to solve specific kinds of problems, and data characterize parameters in the particular problem at hand. Human knowledge doesn't fit this model, however. Because much human knowledge consists of elementary fragments of know-how, applying a significant amount of knowledge requires new ways to organize decision-making fragments into useful entities.

Knowledge systems collect these fragments in a knowledge base, then access the knowledge base to reason about specific problems. As a consequence, knowledge systems differ from conventional programs in the way they are organized, the way they incorporate knowledge, the way they execute, and the impression they create through their interactions. Knowledge systems simulate expert human performance and present a human-like facade to the user. Some current knowledge engineering applications are

- Medical diagnosis,
- Equipment repair,
- Computer configuration,
- Chemical data interpretation and structure elucidation,
- Speech and image understanding,
- Financial decision making,
- Signal interpretation,
- Mineral exploration,
- Military intelligence and planning,
- Advising about computer system use, and
- VLSI design.

In all of these areas, system developers have worked to combine the general techniques of knowledge engineering with specialized know-how in particular domains of application. In nearly every case, the demand for a knowledge-engineering approach arose from the limitations perceived in the alternative technologies available. The developers wanted to incorporate a large amount of fragmentary, judgmental, and heuristic knowledge; they wanted to solve automatically problems that required the machine to follow whatever lines of reasoning seemed most appropriate to the data at hand; they wanted the systems to accommodate new knowledge as it evolved; and they wanted the systems to use their knowledge to give meaningful explanation of their behaviors when requested.

This article presents an overview of the field of knowledge engineering. It describes the major developments that have led up to the current great interest in expert systems, then presents a brief discussion of the principal scientific and engineering issues in the field, as well as of the process of building expert systems, the role of tools in that work, how expert systems perform human-computer interface functions, and the frontiers of research and development. But before turning to knowledge engineering, we should consider briefly some background material on the history of artificial intelligence and its relationship to knowledge engineering.

AI Concepts Relevant to Knowledge Engineering

Knowledge engineering is the subfield of AI[2] concerned with applying knowledge to solve problems that ordinarily require human intelligence. Three concepts of AI underlie nearly all work in KE, namely symbolic programming, problem-solving, and search. Symbolic programs manipulate symbols that represent objects and relationships. Generally, these programs exploit expressions with variables to denote classes of objects or relationships among classes of objects. In addition, symbolic programs incorporate conditional expressions that constrain the possible value assignments variables can take, and they exploit inference rules or deductive patterns to determine which variable values derive from others. In this way, symbolic programs can manipulate models of real-world entities, the systems they participate in, and the effects of actual or hypothetical changes in those systems. Finally, symbolic programs usually take the form of lists of symbolic expressions. When these programs are evaluated or interpreted, the programs determine values or produce behaviors as side-effects of their evaluations. These programs are viewed as symbolic data by other programs that can reason about them, modify them, or otherwise manipulate them. Thus, within symbolic programming systems, each program can take on the dual roles of program or data.

Problem-solving programs attempt to achieve goals, often using uncertain and indeterminate methods. In AI, goals correspond to propositions about desired characteristics of some future world. The problem-solving program needs to find a feasible path that leads to a desirable future situation. A significant fraction of all AI systems fit this problem-solving model. A speech-understanding system, for example, tries to discern meaning in an utterance; its goal, abstractly stated, is to identify a sequence of words that could produce the acoustic energy received and provide the most likely interpretation of what the speaker intended. An experiment-planning system, as another example, tries to define a sequence of actions that, if executed, will produce some desired result.

Generally, problem-solving systems must search for solutions. When faced with a problem, they usually cannot access an answer directly. They may use a variety of search techniques, and they may possess a plausible solution generator that enables them to enumerate all possible solutions. Then they can generate and test all possibilities until a solution is found. People call the set of possibilities the *search space* and this approach to search *brute force*. Many ordinary problems, such as repairing a circuit or playing a game, may have search spaces of astronomical size. A problem-solver may improve its efficiency by eliminating from consideration classes of candidate solutions that cannot succeed in the given case. People call this type of search reduction *pruning*. Finally, a problem-solver can employ a variety of rules-of-thumb to improve its search performance. These rules can promote promising candidates, deprecate candidate solutions that have little chance of success, suggest easy tests to perform early that may help eliminate classes of potential solutions from consideration, or notice features of the current problem data that suggest promising directions to pursue. These *heuristic* rules-of-thumb aid problem-solvers in coping with the complexity of difficult problems.

Brief History of AI and KE

AI originated in the 1950's, when several early computer scientists began using computers to write symbolic programs to solve problems. Seminal results in automated deduction and problem-solving produced great excitement and optimism. When the Logic Theorist proved the bulk of theorems in *Principia Mathematica* using heuristic problem-solving methods, it seemed apparent to most people that eventually bigger and faster computers would extend the range of general problem-solvers to all of the world's challenging mental activities.

Many frustrations and failures eventually led people to realize how much other such achievements would require. Throughout the past two decades, AI researchers have been learning to appreciate the great value of domain-specific knowledge as a basis for solving significant problems. Most of the world's challenging mental problems do not yield to general problem-solving strategies, even when augmented with general efficiency heuristics. To solve problems in areas of human expertise such as engineering, medicine, or programming, machine problem-solvers need to *know* what human problem-solvers know about that subject. Although computers have many advantages over humans, including speed and consistency, they cannot compensate for ignorance. In a nutshell, AI researchers learned that high IQ doesn't make a person expert; specialized know-how does. To make a fast and consistent symbol processor perform as well as a human expert, someone must provide it specialized know-how comparable to what a human expert possesses. This need gives rise to knowledge engineering.

Early knowledge engineering applications arose in universities and emphasized matching the performance of human experts. Dendral[3] and Macsyma[4] achieved expert performance first. Dendral identifies the chemical molecular structure of a material from its mass spectrographic and nuclear magnetic resonance data. Macsyma manipulates and simplifies complex mathematical expressions. Both systems evolved over more than 10 years, and in their areas of specialization, both surpass their human creators and all other human professionals.

Beginning in the 1970's, AI researchers initiated several KE applications. By the end of the decade, several projects had accomplished significant results:

- Mycin incorporated about 400 heuristic rules written in an English-like IF-THEN formalism to diagnose and treat infectious blood diseases, but its major impact on the field arose from its ability to explain lucidly any conclusion or question it generated.[5]
- Hearsay-II employed multiple, independent, cooperating expert systems that communicated through a global database called a *blackboard* to understand connected speech in a thousand-word vocabulary.[6]
- RI incorporated about 1000 IF-THEN rules needed to configure orders for Digital Equipment's Vax computers and eliminated the need for DEC to hire and train many new people to perform a task that had resisted solution by conventional computer techniques.[7]
- Internist contained nearly 100,000 judgments about relationships among diseases and symptoms in internal medicine and began to approach a breadth of knowledge and problem-solving performance beyond that of most specialists in internal medicine.[8]

Current Status of Artificial Intelligence

Beginning this decade, many observers decided that AI in general and KE in particular had matured to the point where they belonged in commercial or governmental application programs. This decision accelerated the field's development and specialization within its subfields.

The three primary subfields of AI today include natural language processing, or NLP, vision and robotics, and knowledge engineering. Today, universities and some non-profit laboratories conduct most basic research in AI, regardless of subfield. In the US, DARPA, NIH and NSF have traditionally provided most of the funding for this research. Both Japan and the UK recently have undertaken significant new research programs in AI with government support. Substantial commercial interest has developed in all three subfields. In addition, all three subfields today exhibit commercial applications of the technology and commercial tools to support additional applications. For example, IBM now directly markets the earliest NLP product, called Intellect, from AI Corporation. In addition, several companies have announced NLP products for personal computers. A few companies offer vision systems and integrated hand-eye systems, and a handful of knowledge engineering companies offer specialized end-user expert systems or commercial tools to allow people to build their own expert systems. One company, Teknowledge, builds knowledge systems commercially. It has announced completion of several custom knowledge-system applications undertaken for commercial clients, including a drilling advisor for a major oil company, a computer-software advisor for a data-analysis services company, an order entry and configuration checker for a major electronics company, and an intelligent assistant for the partners in a large accounting firm.

Knowledge engineering faces a long, but promising road. The technology of KE aims to create means for people to capture, store, distribute, and apply knowledge electronically. While the early applications indicate the feasibility and economic importance of this work, they also reveal the enormous size of the field for potential applications. For the foreseeable future, the demand for applications of the current technical capabilities will surely exceed the field's ability to supply them. Moreover, many interesting and important applications lie beyond current technology in this field. Current limitations arise from the small number of workers in the field, the difficulty of building knowledge systems in novel areas, and the breadth and variety of the human knowledge that knowledge engineers now must codify.

Techniques Used in Knowledge Systems

Figure 1 illustrates the primary building blocks of a knowledge system. The base level consists of those techniques which underlie nearly all applications—symbolic programming, propositional calculus, search, and heuristics. Because propositional calculus was not mentioned previously, it deserves consideration.

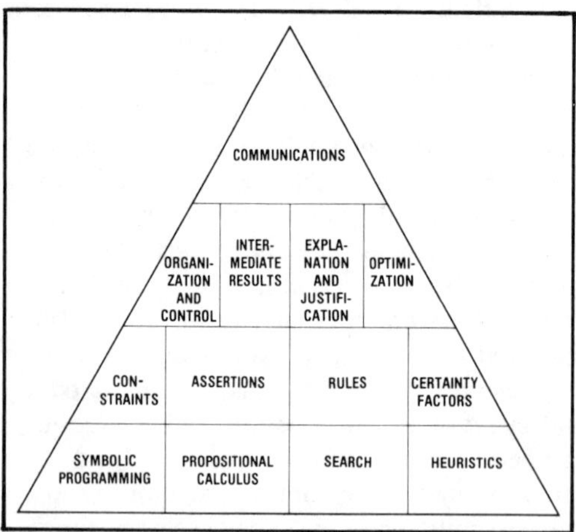

Figure 1. Techniques used in knowledge systems.

Knowledge systems reason to solve problems by generating candidate solutions and evaluating them. Usually, solutions involve applying heuristic rules to given data in order to deduce logical or probable consequences and prove that these consequences satisfy the goal. These actions correspond to the basic propositional calculus mechanisms of inference and proof. Although most knowledge systems today do not actually employ formal logic programs, they achieve the same effects. Propositional calculus provides a formal foundation for their generally more limited inference and proof capabilities.

At the second level of techniques, the figure shows the most frequently used forms of knowledge representation: constraints, assertions, rules, and certainty factors. Examples of constraints are "Two distinct physical objects cannot occupy the same space at the same time" and "Every beneficiary designated in the life insurance policy must have a financial interest in the health of the insured party." A knowledge system incorporates constraints to express restrictions on allowable states, values, or conclusions. In fact, some knowledge systems derive their value primarily through an ability to recognize and satisfy complex, symbolic constraints sets. In this way, KE extends the class of constraint-satisfaction problems amenable to computation. Different from computer systems that focus primarily on linear constraints, knowledge systems address arbitrary symbolic constraints such as requirements on spatial, temporal, or logical relationships.

Assertional databases provide means for storing and retrieving propositions. An assertion corresponds to a true proposition, a fact. Examples of assertions include "The King of Sweden visited my company to explore possible relationships with West Coast high-technology companies," "Morgan is a dog," and "Morgan is my dog's name." Many simple forms of assertions lend themselves to relational database implementations, but more complicated patterns do not. In general, most knowledge systems today incorporate their own specialized assertional database subsystems.

Rules represent declarative or imperative knowledge of particular forms. To illustrate an imperative rule, consider: "If you observe a patient with fever and a runny nose, then you should suspect that the patient has the flu." This rule tells a knowledge system *how* to behave. A related declarative rule would tell the system *what* it could believe, but would leave *how* unspecified: "If a patient has the flu, the patient tends to exhibit fever and a runny nose." Most knowledge systems use one or both of these rule forms. Declarative rules, in general, describe the way things work in the world. On the other hand, imperative rules prescribe heuristic methods that the knowledge system should employ in its own operations.

Certainty factors designate the level of confidence or validity a knowledge system should associate with its data, rules, or conclusions. These certainty factors may reflect any of a variety of different schemes for dealing with error and uncertainty. Some systems employ Bayesian conditional probabilities to estimate certainties. Others use completely subjective systems; for example, where 1.0 implies certainty, -1.0 implies certainty of the proposition's negation and 0.0 indicates either no opinion or no evidence. Many people devote considerable effort to the task of improving the certainty factor technology. To a large extent this may prove fruitless. First, knowledge systems need to estimate the strength of their conclusions precisely because no valid and formal alternatives exist; one cannot eliminate the subjective quality of the decision process by any amount of formalization. Second, many alternative certainty factor schemes work equivalently well. Knowledge systems do well because they can mimic human performance. Humans could not solve problems well if they needed to calculate complex mathematical formulas to determine their own certainty factors. Rather, humans perform well because their knowledge *generally works well enough*. It is efficient, robust, and good enough to solve important problems. Knowledge systems simply exploit those powers of the human's knowledge.

At the third level of techniques, the figure shows organization and control, intermediate results, explanation and justification, and optimization. A knowledge system organizes and controls its activity according to the architectural design principles it embodies. For example, by searching for sufficient confirming evidence, a diagnostic medical expert system might reason backwards from all potential diseases it knows. It might consider first the disease taken a priori to be the most likely. Then it might ask for evidence according to the most likely and characteristic syndromes. Only when it encountered overwhelming amounts of disconfirming data might it begin to consider the next possible disease. An expert system that operated in this manner would exhibit a *depth-first, backward-chaining* control scheme. Each distinct control scheme may require a corresponding organization of the knowledge base and appropriately tailored inferential mechanisms that search it and apply knowledge. Thus control and organization are closely linked.

Intermediate results arise in all systems. Because knowledge systems can face difficult performance requirements, they often need to make effective use of intermediate results. In a backward-chaining system, for example, several possible alternatives under consideration all may require a common bit of evidence. Collecting this evidence may require extensive amounts of computation and inference. Once the knowledge system evaluates that evidence, it has an incentive to save that result so that it can reuse it later. In every organization and control scheme, comparable issues of temporary storage and reuse arise. Most knowledge systems today employ specialized and *ad hoc* methods in these functions.

Because knowledge systems generally explain and justify their results, they have captured the interest of a wide variety of potential users. End-users in many application areas need to trust the recommendations of a knowledge system. By offering to explain how they reached their conclusions, these systems convey to the user an impression of reasonableness. To construct an explanation, they transform the expert, heuristic rules and assertions into lines of reasoning. A line of reasoning shows how a starting set of assumptions and a collection of heuristic rules produce a particular conclusion. End-users generally find these explanations as plausible as the rules themselves. Others who interact with the knowledge system also exploit these explanation capabilities. Knowledge-base maintainers, who may include experts and technicians, continually revalidate knowledge systems by assessing performance on test cases. They validate that the system reaches the right decisions and that it does so for the right reasons.

Optimization techniques play an important role in knowledge systems. Knowledge systems, like other computer applications, must perform their tasks as quickly as needed. Many knowledge systems applications today interact with users so often that they generally are waiting for input. In these cases, knowledge engineers pay considerable attention to assuring that the dialog itself seems expert in terms of which queries the knowledge system generates and in which order it generates them. This verification requires effective ways to optimize the structure of the dialog itself. New tools for building knowledge systems provide improved methods for specifying such imperative knowledge clearly and separating it effectively from descriptive knowledge about the problem domain. The most important area of optimization in complex task domains, however, concerns the knowledge system's problem-solving performance: Does it generate and test candidate solutions in an efficient order? Does it avoid redundant computation? Does it compile the symbolic rules effectively? Does it retrieve assertions efficiently? And does it transform the knowledge base into more appropriate organizations for specialized tasks that can exploit more efficient algorithms? In some applications, optimization of a knowledge system has reduced run-times to as little as one-thousandth of one percent of initial completion times.

The capstone of knowledge-systems techniques is their communication capabilities. Knowledge systems communicate with knowledge engineers experts, end-users, databases, and other computer systems. Just as humans access and interact with these various sources, a knowledge system needs to speak to each in its own appropriate language. Knowledge systems communicate with knowledge engineers through structure editors that allow them to access and modify components of the knowledge base easily. Knowledge systems communicate with experts through sample dialogs with explanations that elucidate their lines of reasoning and highlight for the expert where to make knowledge-base changes.

For end-users, knowledge systems may exploit natural language processes to generate questions and answers or to interpret user responses. Some knowledge systems today use videodisks to retrieve pictures and replay instructional sequences for end-users. Beyond their interactions with people, knowledge systems also interact with other computer systems.

Knowledge systems often need to formulate and execute conventional data-processing applications as a subtask, so, several knowledge systems have evolved, almost like a "new brain" of higher animals that sits piggy-back atop powerful, preexisting, lower-level "old brains." These piggy-back knowledge systems incorporate the scarce expert know-how needed to make effective use of the powerful, but often exceedingly complex computer programs employed today in fields such as structural engineering and seismic analysis. Quite commonly, knowledge systems incorporate the means to access and retrieve information from on-line databases. Then they can apply their knowledge automatically and directly to the vast sources of data that now commonly reside on-line. Frequently, a knowledge system may serve the primary goal of knitting together diverse sources of knowledge that reside in different databases, reflect different formats and coding practices, and require heuristic means to produce a meaningful, integrated interpretation. These needs arise most often in complex organizations, in the order entry and manufacturing systems of large corporations, or in the intelligence and analysis functions of defense departments.

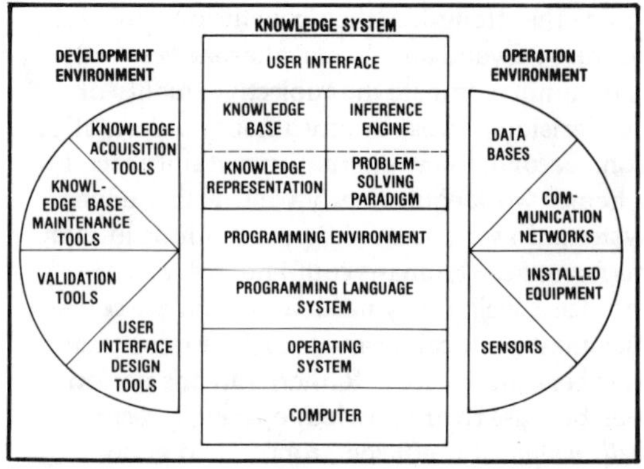

Figure 2. Major components of a contemporary knowledge system. With the development tools on the left, knowledge is acquired and maintained, then put into operation.

Figure 2 illustrates the major components of a contemporary knowledge system and places it in its environmental context. It depicts the knowledge system as a computer application with distinctive development and operational environments. The people who participate in knowledge systems development and extension use the tools shown in the figure—tools for knowledge acquisition, knowledge base maintenance, validation and interface design. With them, they construct knowledge systems that incorporate the three key components shown in the figure: a knowledge base, an inference engine, and a user interface. To do this, the knowledge engineer selects a tool for building the knowledge system whose built-in features fit the problem-solving knowledge in this domain. That goal generally also will embody an approach to organization and control that constitutes the specific problem-solving paradigm the knowledge system will adopt. Once a knowledge system completes development, it enters operation. In that environment, it ordinarily accesses databases, connects to various communication networks, transfers to or integrates with existing installed equipment, and may receive data directly from sensor systems.

Later, this article describes in detail a knowledge system called the Drilling Advisor. At this point, however, it can be used to illustrate the major components and environmental systems.

The Drilling Advisor addresses problems of sticking and dragging that can occur during the process of drilling for oil. In a nutshell, a drill string may encounter tremendous sticking forces arising from friction between geological strata and the drilling pipes, stabilizers, and bit. In operation, the knowledge system needs to access an on-line database of drilling operation reports that describe key parameters. It needs to communicate with regional or central operating management to receive knowledge-base updates and transmit its own reports. It must operate in harsh on-rig environments, which means that it must run on and integrate with special, hardened equipment. And it must also be able to access directly sensors that generate such drilling data as the depth of the bit and the pressure of the drilling mud.

The Drilling Advisor incorporates the knowledge representation and the problem-solving paradigm of Teknowledge's KS300 expert system tool. The knowledge base accessed to avoid sticking includes approximately 300 heuristic rules and descriptions of approximately 50 key drilling parameters. The inference engine conducts an English or French dialog with the user, who is a drilling supervisor. The dialog mimics in its content and sequencing the manner of questioning and analysis of the human expert who served as the model. Each hypothesis is tested by a depth-first, backchaining approach that starts with the most likely sticking problem and proceeds to collect necessary supportive evidence. Each hypothesis, datum, and heuristic rule may reflect uncertainty. The knowledge system combines these uncertain quantities to determine a certainty factor, or CF, between -1 and 1 for each potential diagnosis. For all diagnoses with CFs exceeding 0.2, the Drilling Advisor formulates a plan to resolve the current problem and minimize the likelihood of problem recurrence.

The Drilling Advisor operates currently in a programming environment composed of KS300 and Interlisp, which is its underlying programming system. It operates on Digital Equipment and Xerox computers, under the corresponding operating systems.

The development environment consists of tools provided by KS300, which help the knowledge engineer and expert acquire the expert's knowledge. These include both English language and abbreviated notations for rule display and entry, knowledge-base browsing, structure, editors, case libraries, and automated testing facilities. (During the course of the system development, the expert himself became proficient in using these tools so he could direct late stages of knowledge acquisition and knowledge base maintenance himself.) Each time the expert or knowledge-base maintainer modifies a rule, the KS300 system automatically validates that the knowledge system still performs its test cases correctly. Finally, the knowledge system conducts its interaction with the drilling supervisor in natural language by automatically translating, collecting, and formatting appropriate fragments of text associated with the knowledge-base elements that participate in a line of reasoning. The interface tools make it possible for the knowledge system to produce a sophisticated and intelligible dialog using only the short, descriptive phrases associated with each drilling parameter that the expert provided. The Drilling Advisor also displays graphically several key factors, including the plausible sticking problems, the rock formations, and the drill bit and stabilizers constituting the *bottom hole assembly*. Finally, using standard tools in the KS300 package, it displays dynamically its alternative lines of reasoning, its intermediate conclusions, and the heuristic rules temporarily under consideration.

Fundamentals of Knowledge Engineering

Like most engineering fields, knowledge engineering combines theory and practice. The discipline, as it exists today, involves three main points. First, because knowledge systems solve problems that ordinarily require human intelligence, they exhibit properties common to most intelligent problem-solving systems, whether natural or artificial. Second, organization and design for any particular knowledge system must reflect the type and complexity of the problem and the power and form of the heuristic knowledge available for solving it; although KE has existed for only a very short time, it makes some useful prescriptions for the best way to organize a knowledge system in various situations. Third, knowledge contains a capacity for intelligent action but does not typically carry with it a means for tapping and realizing that potential; thus, in building practical knowledge systems, knowledge engineers always *engineer* knowledge—they convert it to applicable forms. These KE fundamentals are developed in the discussions that follow.

Basic Ideas

When we speak of knowledge in the KE context, we mean those kinds of data that can improve the efficiency or effectiveness of a problem-solver. Three major types of knowledge fit this description: facts that express valid propositions, beliefs that express plausible propositions, and heuristics that express rules of good judgment in situations where valid algorithms generally do not exist. Experts are distinguished by the quality and quantity of knowledge they possess; they know more and what they know makes them more efficient and effective.

Most human professionals perform tasks that require skilled, assertive, and informed judgment. These requirements arise from the complexity, ambiguity, or uncertainty of the available data and problem-solving methods. In contrast to conventional data processing applications, most knowledge systems work in situations that don't admit optimal or *correct* solutions. In such cases, the problem-solver must balance the quality of the answer it produces against the effort it expends. An expert finds the best compromise, usually by seeing a way to find an acceptable answer with a reasonable expenditure of resources.

Given such a pragmatic orientation to performance, intelligent problem solvers benefit directly from improved efficiency. In particular, improvements in speed or selectivity can produce an acceptable solution more affordably, enabling the problem-solver to find better solutions in the time available or take on and solve additional problems. How then does an intelligent problem-solver improve its efficiency?

- It possesses knowledge that applies often, avoids errors, and makes useful distinctions to exploit significant differences among diverse types of situations.
- It eliminates quickly paths of investigation that ultimately will prove useless. It prunes these "blind alleys" early by advancing in time those decisions that can remove fruitless classes of possibilities from further consideration.
- It eliminates redundancy by computing things once and then reusing the results later if needed.
- It accelerates its computation, which, in the case of knowledge systems, means that it increases the quality of its compilation and employs faster hardware.
- It takes advantage of diverse bodies of knowledge that can contribute to the problem at hand. Specifically, it uses independent bodies of expertise to reduce ambiguities and eliminate sources of noise, or it exploits knowledge bases from complementary disciplines to find a solution using whichever techniques or heuristics work best on the given problem.
- It analyzes a problem in different ways, ranging from the high-level and abstract to the low-level and specific.

Most complex problems require the problem-solver to jump around in levels of abstraction; and they can reward an insight at any level by obviating enormous, additional analysis at the other levels. Examples of such insights at various levels include recognizing that the current problem has the same form as one previously solved, detecting that one of the problem requirements rules out all but two candidates, or noticing that a figure incorporates orthogonal, horizontal, and vertical line segments, suggesting that it depicts a man-made object.

The difficulty of problem-solving tasks increases in four ways:

- The problem-solver may not possess accurate data sources or knowledge that performs without errors. These shortcomings cause it to explore many false paths.
- When the data change dynamically, the problem-solver must accelerate its reasoning, base some decisions on its expectations for the future, and revise its decisions when current data disconfirm erroneous prior assumptions.

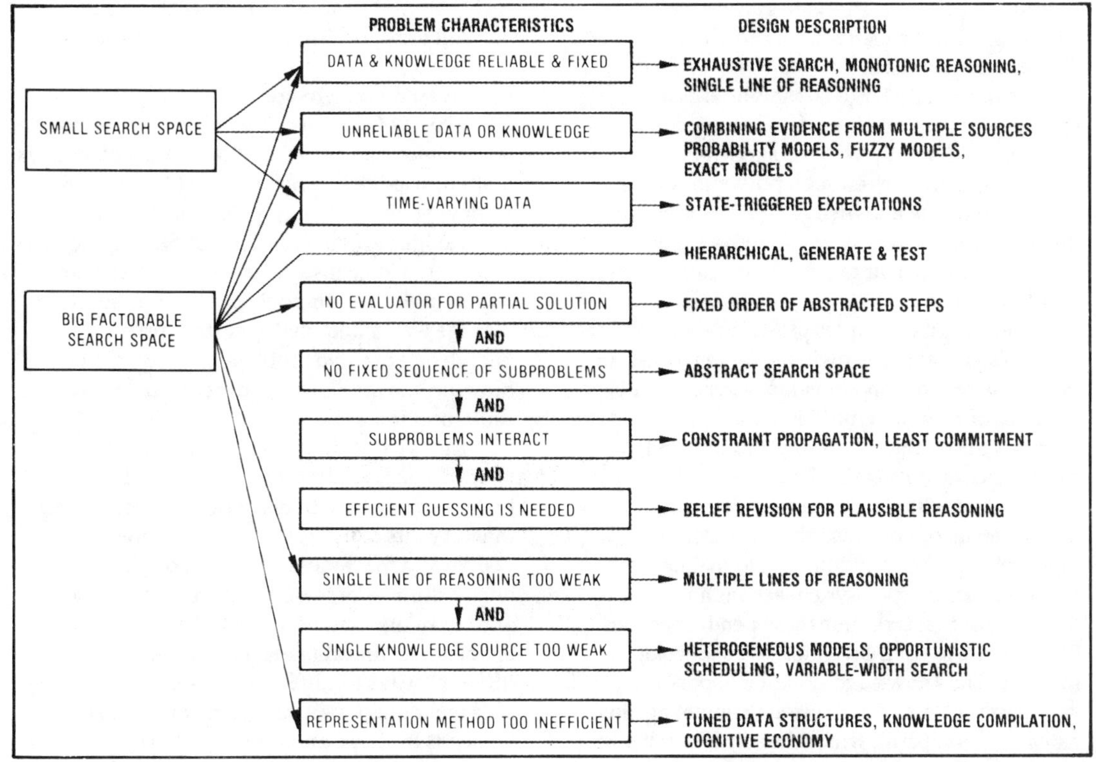

Figure 3. Architectural prescriptions for building knowledge systems.

- Of course, the more possibilities it must consider, the harder the task. However, it is difficult in many applications to quantify the size of the search space and to find alternative formulations of the search space that simplify the problem as much as possible.
- A problem-solver that must use complex and time-consuming methods to eliminate alternatives from consideration works less efficiently than one possessing equally effective but simpler, cheaper measures.

Knowledge System Organization and Design

Unlike data processing applications, current knowledge systems do not fit such specific models as the typical update-master-file or input-process-output forms so common in commercial data processing. Nor does the knowledge engineering field yet have common schemes for characterizing its designs and systems. However, when designing knowledge systems, experienced knowledge engineers do adhere to some general principles that determine high-level architectural properties of knowledge systems and permit them to perform their tasks effectively. To determine an appropriate knowledge-system design, these principles ask questions about the kind of problem-solving complexity involved in a task and the kind of heuristic problem-solving knowledge available. Figure 3 illustrates many of the best understood design principles.

It divides all knowledge systems application problems into two categories, characterized by small and large search spaces. It then elaborates each of these two basic categories by citing additional attributes that also may characterize the problem. For example, in the small space problems, it distinguishes three possibly overlapping subcategories based on the kinds of data the knowledge system must process. When this data seems reliable and permanent and the system knowledge performs reliably, the figure prescribes the most typical knowledge system architecture: one that facilitates exhaustive search and pursues one line of reasoning at a time, such as depth-first backward-chaining. Furthermore, the prescribed system can reason monotonically:

it need not initially formulate guesses that it later might need to retract. At the other extreme, the figure addresses complex problems, such as those with large factorable search spaces* in which one line of reasoning does not perform consistently well, no single body of knowledge provides enough power to solve all the problems the knowledge system faces, and the initial form of knowledge representation proves too inefficient to achieve the needed level of performance.

The design principles prescribe several remedies. First, the knowledge system must immediately explore and develop several promising lines of reasoning until it obtains more certainty about the actual solution. Second, it should incorporate several independent subsystems, each of which contributes to decision-making on an opportunistic basis. That is, the top-level knowledge system should maintain an agenda of pending subsystem actions and schedule for first execution those pending actions that promise to contribute most to the developing solution. The knowledge system will pursue a variable number of simultaneous, competing alternative solution paths, where the actual number at any point reflects the momentary uncertainty about the "best" path. Last, knowledge systems should exploit several advanced techniques for improving efficiency. Generally, these techniques require some kind of transformation to the initial knowledge representation and inference engine. This transformation may include adopting data structures more attuned to the types of inference the knowledge system performs, compiling the knowledge into a new structure—such as a network or tree—that facilitates rapid search, or using dynamic techniques to cache intermediate results and perhaps compile incrementally more efficient methods for frequently repeated inferences that initially require complex chains of compromise.

In short, today's design principles provide high-level guidance to the knowledge-system designer. Like architectural principles in housing and commercial construction, these principles suggest the broad outlines of a construction task without specifying the details. Knowledge systems built in a manner consistent with the principles in Figure 3 will prove similarly well adapted to their environments, but will vary considerably in their fine structure.

Engineered Knowledge

One aspect of knowledge engineering seems both obvious and subtle. What seems obvious is that knowledge engineers extract knowledge from experts and integrate it in an overall knowledge system architecture. Hence, they are engineers who construct systems out of elementary knowledge components. What is subtle is that the way a knowledge system uses knowledge to solve problems directly affects how the knowledge engineer extracts, represents, and integrates it.

Knowledge does not come off-the-shelf, prepackaged, ready for use. In fact, knowledge is the word we use to describe a variety of fragmentary bits of understanding that enable people and machines to perform otherwise demanding tasks reasonably well. As an example, an understanding of technology transfer enables a technical manager to reason in many different ways for different purposes. In setting up a technology transfer program, for instance, he needs to shape and apply the knowledge in a manner different from the way he would review someone else's program, estimate a budget for it, forecast its likely results, or analyze its similarity to previously successful and unsuccessful programs. In short, people seem to possess a general understanding of the way things work and knowledge systems today can incorporate significant quantities of this human knowledge to solve electronically problems that ordinarily require human intelligence. The knowledge systems first adopt a general organization consistent with high-level design prescriptions, then fit the problem-solving knowledge into that framework. To make an expert's knowledge fit, the knowledge engineer molds the knowledge to produce the necessary performance. In this way, he genuinely *engineers* knowledge.

Constructing Knowledge Systems

To build a knowledge system, a knowledge engineer performs the four types of functions identified in Figure 4 as mining, molding, assembling, and refining. These terms taken from the vocabulary of rare-metals mining seem apt for the processes involved in extracting

**If a search space can be broken into smaller subspaces corresponding to independent subproblems, we call it factorable.*

KNOWLEDGE PROCESSING TASKS	ENGINEERING ACTIVITIES	ENGINEERING PRODUCTS
MINING	KNOWLEDGE ACQUISITION	CONCEPTS AND RULES
MOLDING	KNOWLEDGE SYSTEM DESIGN	FRAMEWORK AND KNOWLEDGE REPRESENTATION
ASSEMBLING	KNOWLEDGE PROGRAMMING	KNOWLEDGE BASE AND INFERENCE ENGINE
REFINING	KNOWLEDGE REFINEMENT	REVISED CONCEPTS AND RULES

Figure 4. Key tasks in knowledge systems development.

knowledge and manufacturing knowledge systems. The figure also provides the technical terms for each of the four primary construction activities and identifies the key products of each phase.

Knowledge, like a rare metal, lies dormant and impure, beneath the surface of consciousness. Once extracted, an element of knowledge must undergo other transformations before it acquires commercial value. Extraction involves eliciting from experts or books the basic concepts of the problem domain, i.e., the terms used to describe problem situations and problem-solving heuristics. From this starting point, knowledge extraction—or the acquisition process—continues until enough problem-solving knowledge is elicited to permit an expert performance. Heuristic rules constitute the key product of this activity.

Knowledge system design produces a framework or architecture for the knowledge system, as discussed in the last section. In addition, the knowledge-system designer selects an appropriate scheme for representing the problem-solving knowledge. Representation options include formal logic, semantic networks, hierarchical frames, active objects, rules, and procedures—each of which has supported at least one previous knowledge system development effort. Once knowledge engineers have selected the framework and knowledge representation, programming begins. They then transform human know-how into a knowledge base that will fuel an inference engine.

Generally, people developing knowledge systems today adopt an existing knowledge engineering tool that incorporates a predefined inference engine, so knowledge programming need only produce a knowledge base. The process of refining knowledge into a base continues until system performance is adequate. In transforming an inexact understanding of an expert's behavior into heuristic rules, both the expert and knowledge engineer err. They misunderstand abstract concepts, incorrectly express rules of thumb, and neglect many details needed to insure the validity of knowledge base rules. Generally, a knowledge system performs poorly at the start. This performance does not reflect poorly on engineers' skills; experts do their tasks well because they use lots of knowledge, not because they think about or verbalize it. In fact, KE provides for most knowledge-intensive activities the first practical means for codifying and validating knowledge. Before KE, experts generally could not express their know-how in any effective way, and they could not assess much of it empirically. Knowledge systems make it possible to test directly how well knowledge works and highlight its weaknesses and deficiencies. By correcting these shortcomings, an expert often can improve a knowledge base rapidly. This evolutionary development first approaches human performance levels and then generally surpasses them.

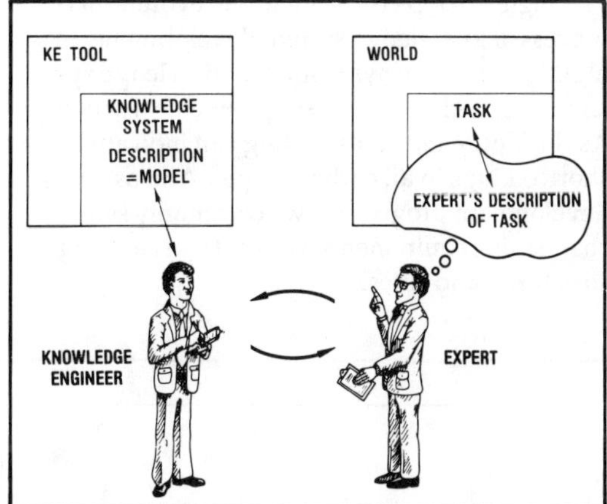

Figure 5. Knowledge acquisition. In consultation with the expert, the engineer develops a knowledge system for solving task-specific problems.

Figure 5 illustrates the transfer of an expert's understanding to a knowledge engineer's knowledge system, a key aspect of knowledge acquisition. This transfer involves two-way communication. At first, the knowledge engineer consults the expert for insight into how he solves particular problems and thinks about the objects and relations of interest (the figure labels these components of understanding *world* and *task* knowledge). The expert reveals some of this knowledge through the problem-solving task descriptions given to the knowledge engineer.

The knowledge engineer listens to the expert's description to hear the problem-solving elements. Unlike a systems analyst, who formulates an algorithm to solve a client's problem, the knowledge engineer seeks to capture the existing problem-solving method. He chooses a knowledge-engineering tool, then tries to fit the fragments of expertise into the structure the tool provides. This requires that he first create a description of the way the expert thinks about and solves problems in the given domain. This description models the expertise of the expert. Then, once implemented as a knowledge system, this model generates problem-solving behaviors that the expert can critique and improve. The process often improves his understanding of his own craft.

Figure 6 depicts the iterative, evolutionary process of knowledge system development, highlighting the ways testing a knowledge system feeds back to earlier stages of construction. As this figure indicates, testing can indicate shortcomings in all earlier stages. And as development progresses, we commonly see changes in requirements, concepts, organizing structures, and rules.

Tools for Building Knowledge Systems

Many software aids simplify knowledge engineering. In fact, most knowledge engineers build knowledge systems by adopting existing tools, then constructing a problem-specific knowledge base. Over the past 20 years, these tools have evolved, bottom-up, from low-level languages to high-level KE aids. Only now are commercial quality software tools becoming available. But what is a knowledge engineering tool?

It is more than software, or put another way, the KE tool software reflects a general-knowledge engineering viewpoint and a specific methodology for building knowledge systems. It involves a high-level problem-solving paradigm. It may, for example, build in an assumption that solutions to diagnostic problems ought to reason from design documents and causal models. Or, conversely, it might reflect a preference for building diagnostic experts by capturing an expert's empirical symptom-problem associations. In short, a paradigm constitutes a high-level strategy for using knowledge to solve a class of problems. Today, different knowledge engineers are investigating diverse paradigms that vary along several dimensions: whether to use empirical associations or reason via first principles from underlying causal models; whether to formulate knowledge in terms of formal logic or in terms of more informal heuristics; whether to aggregate knowledge into relatively large functional units or disaggregate it so it fits a small, grain-size format, etc.

Each paradigm suggests some additional design properties for the knowledge system architecture, and a knowledge engineering tool

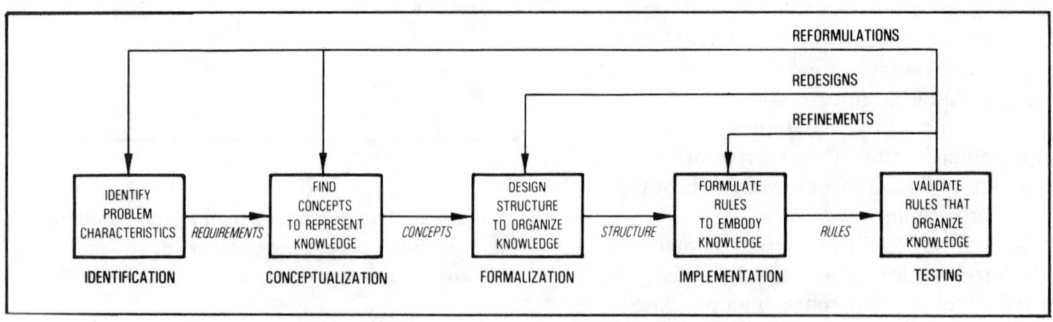

Figure 6. Stages of knowledge system development.

generally builds these properties directly into its knowledge-base structure and inference engine. A tool such as KS300, for example, builds expert systems only with rule-based, backward-chaining, monotonic, and singular line-of-reasoning architectures. Does this sound restrictive? On the one hand, these design constraints surely restrict what a knowledge engineer can do and what the end-user knowledge systems can do. On the other hand, a tool like KS300 exploits its knowledge system design constraints to improve the quality and power of the assistance it gives. Because it knows the form of knowledge in the knowledge base, the detailed operation of the inference engine, and the organization and control of problem-solving, the KE tool can simplify the development tasks considerably.

Each KE tool offers a particular knowledge representation so the engineer must consider the knowledge to be represented when selecting his tool. Some tools emphasize heuristic rules, others emphasize categorical taxonomies, and still others address simulation and modeling. Paired with each kind of knowledge representation, KE tools generally provide one way to apply that knowledge. A tool that builds a backward-chaining knowledge system rarely has the capability to build a forward-chaining system. A tool that helps reason with empirical cause-effect associations generally can not apply systematic search techniques to underlying causal models, and so forth. However, several research-oriented tools aim to provide a mixture of representations and inference techniques and may one day lead to more comprehensive KE frameworks. Examples of these include Xerox's LOOPS, Stanford's MRS and AGE, Yale's DUCK, and Inference's ART.

Tools generally provide some knowledge programming language facilities and knowledge processing utilities. KS300 provides abbreviated forms, allowing experts to express domain rules and browse the knowledge base for rules with arbitrary characteristics, such as those that determine the shear-stress value in a structural engineering knowledge system. ROSIE, another research tool, provides a general-purpose, symbolic programming language and assertional database within the context of a standard sequential, modular programming system, but does not provide problem-solving architecture. As a final example, the research tool RLL[9] provides only a hierarchical, knowledge-base organization and a very general agenda-based control scheme, leaving the knowledge engineer to implement all domain knowledge and problem-solving heuristics directly in Lisp. The low-level symbolic programming languages themselves, notably Lisp and Prolog, provide even less structure. They neither restrict the knowledge engineer nor provide any specific assistance in knowledge acquisition, knowledge representation, or knowledge-system evaluation.

In short, KE tools today span a wide range of software aids that reflect various assumptions about what kinds of knowledge systems to build and how to build them. Some tools, however, have evolved from dozens of related applications covering man-decades of development. The next section discusses these in somewhat greater detail.

Mature KE Tool Classes

Throughout the history of AI, many researchers have focused their efforts on developing tools for building problem-solving systems. Few tools developed in advance of applications offer the needed capabilities—a problem common to explorers of new and uncharted territory.

Several families of applications have given rise, however, to useful paradigms, architectures, and related tools. Three incorporate the Mycin, Hearsay-II, and R1 knowledge systems illustrated below.

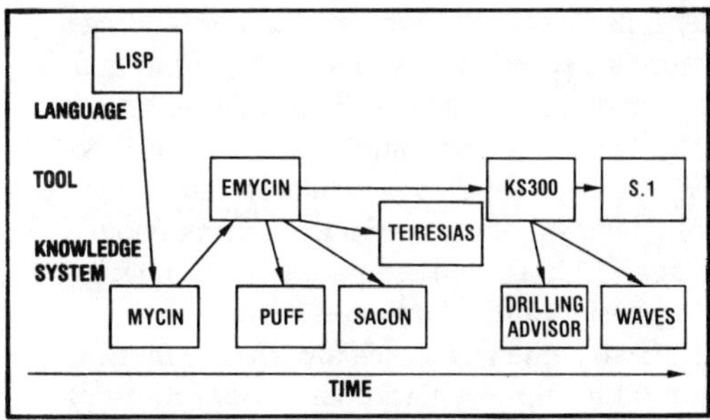

Figure 7. History of Emycin and its descendants.

The Mycin family originated with a rule-based expert system for the diagnosis and treatment of infectious blood diseases. Its general methodology gave rise to a search tool called Emycin and a related system, Teiresias, that could assist the knowledge acquisition process in Emycin. Figure 7 illustrates the history of Emycin and its descendants. Puff, an expert system for interpreting respirometer data and diagnosing pulmonary diseases, was the first actual application built with Emycin. KS300 combined many of the best features of Emycin and Teiresias and has supported numerous commercial knowledge system developments. Two of these—Waves and the Drilling Advisor—illustrate the breadth of systems that can be built with it.Waves is an expert system that assesses a data analysis problem for a geophysicist and prescribes the best way to process the data using selected modules from a million-line, Fortran analysis package. The Drilling Advisor, on the other hand, determines the most likely cause for a stuck oil drill and prescribes expert corrective and preventative measures. S.1 is an enhanced commercial KE tool that encompasses problems in the Mycin family.

The second family with an extensive range of applications incorporates Hearsay-II, one of the first thousand-word, connected-speech understanding systems.[6] Hearsay-II embodies its own general paradigm in a characteristic architecture, as well as the *cooperating experts* paradigm, which represents complex knowledge systems as collections of cooperating expert subsystems. In addition, part of the Hearsay-II paradigm coordinates interaction among cooperating systems through a global database called a *blackboard.* Each independent source of knowledge must read the state of problem-solving on the blackboard and contribute its own ideas by augmenting or modifying decisions on the blackboard. Although Hearsay-II itself solved a problem of understanding connected speech, many other applications and some tools have embraced its paradigm. The HASP and SIAP applications, for instance, used the blackboard approach to interpret sonar signals,[10] and Acronym used it to interpret photo images.[11] Other applications are in learning, planning, design, and information fusion.

Two general research tools have emerged thus far to support blackboard applications of this sort, Hearsay-III[12] and AGE.[13] Hearsay-III provides a very general representation for intermediate results, for independent sources of knowledge, and for flexible control, but it assumes the knowledge engineer will determine the appropriate problem-solving strategy and inference techniques. It also assumes the knowledge engineer will program knowledge directly in Lisp. AGE, on the other hand, facilitates experimentation through modular and customized control algorithms. It too provides a particular representation for intermediate results and asks the knowledge engineer to use Lisp to represent knowledge. Where Hearsay-III expects relatively large modules of knowledge, AGE expects fine-grained rules. Many people believe that the blackboard architecture will become increasingly important as KE takes on more difficult and important tasks. No commercial-quality tools have been announced at this writing.

The R1 family of knowledge systems, recently renamed XCON, configures parts of a Vax computer.[7] R1 solved a problem, which, because it required thousands of heuristic rules to capture the full variety of engineering components and relations, proved intractable to conventional data processing methods. The tool used to implement R1 is called OPS, a tool reflecting the paradigm known as a pure production system. Its underlying principle is that truly intelligent behavior, such as that of humans, consists entirely of many fine-grained, independent, condition-action rules, called productions. OPS makes it easy for a knowledge engineer to write such productions. It also includes an excellent compiler that eliminates many redundant computations and accelerates the selection of the first matching rule on each cycle of computation. OPS provides a simple, but uniform representation method for describing problem-solving state data and for specifying rule conditions that match this state data. To program the action components of rules, OPS expects the knowledge engineer simply to alter the intermediate state data by changing property values or to write specialized Lisp code.

OPS has now been used in a variety of applications, notably XSEL, a DEC sales program for planning the layout for a Vax computer, and Airplan, a knowledge system to plan and schedule flight training on board a US Navy carrier. All applications of OPS exploit its general computational capability specified in relatively independent rules. Each rule provides for a data-driven action, making OPS applications interrupt-driven or data-flow computations. Unlike many other KE tools, however, OPS provides little structure for representing facts, relationships, and uncertain knowledge, and it does not contain a general architecture for problem-solving. Instead, it provides a novel scheme for pattern-directed inference which makes some symbolic programming tasks simple.

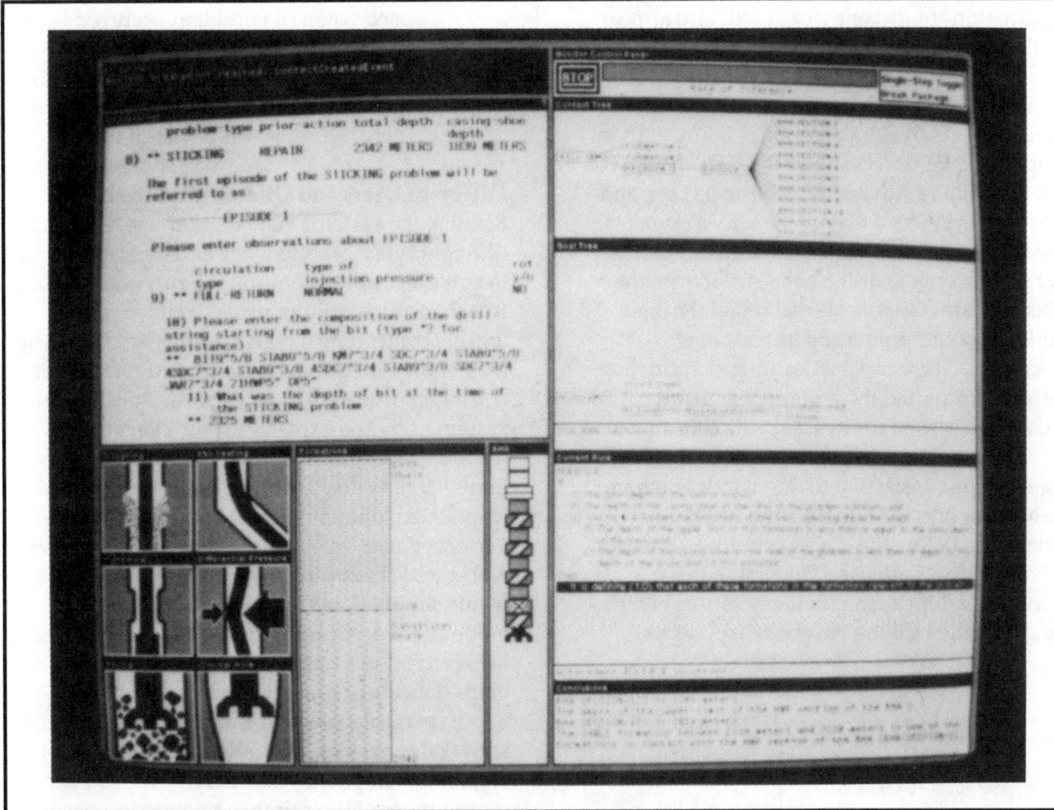

Figure 8a. Drilling Advisor display.

Current Status of Tools
Tools will play a major role in the industrial use of KE. Their power derives from the paradigms, architectures, representations, inference engines, utilities, and programming systems they embody. In complexity and value, they approach the CAD, CAM, and CAE tools used in design, manufacturing, and engineering. Good tools will offer numerous aids to the knowledge engineer but will require considerable work to develop.

We will desire different knowledge engineering tools, however, for different kinds of applications, with different design requirements, different kinds of knowledge, and specialized kinds of inference. Ultimately, KE tools will diversify in form, purpose, and architecture—as did electronic instruments—because knowledge comes in different formats for different uses. We should remember that KE is a very young field. Today's best tools have derived from many years' experience applying the same general kind of research tools repeatedly to a wide variety of applications. Out of that experience comes valid and useful criteria for tool designs. In the next few years, many new kinds of applications will arise, and development of corresponding tools will lag those applications by several years.

Knowledge Systems as a Human-Computer Interface

Knowledge systems interact with humans through the same modalities as other computer programs, but they do different things and use different methods. They carry on meaningful dialogues with users, explain their own reasoning, and generally work to understand a user's problem, then help solve it. Knowledge systems translate their own problem-solving goals into natural language, transform their current lines of reasoning into structures the user can understand, and map the user's description of a problem into a familiar form that they can solve. These capabilities make knowledge systems appear to the user as relevant, intelligent, and helpful. And to the extent a knowledge system gives insightful and credible explanations of its behavior, it will also appear trustworthy to the user.

An Example System

The Drilling Advisor exemplifies many of these properties. Figure 8a shows the CRT display that the Drilling Advisor presents to its user, and Figure 8b provides a map of the screen elements. The left-hand side of the screen shows elements that pertain only to drilling and sticking; on the other side are components that reveal the inner workings of the system and its reasoning processses. These capabilities are generic in that the same forms and methods appear in any knowledge system constructed with the same tools.

The domain-specific elements of the Drilling Advisor consist of a dialog window where the advisor and the supervisor discuss current situations. Below the dialog window, three additional windows appear. The first of these graphically depicts the six likely causes of sticking. Next, the Drilling Advisor displays its

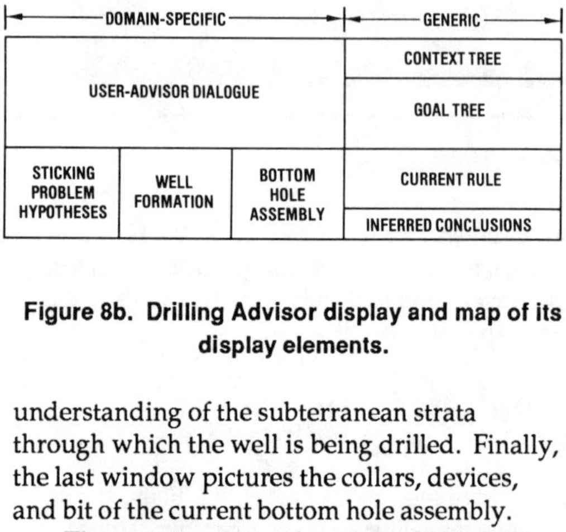

<table>
<tr><th colspan="3">DOMAIN-SPECIFIC</th><th>GENERIC</th></tr>
<tr><td colspan="3" rowspan="2">USER-ADVISOR DIALOGUE</td><td>CONTEXT TREE</td></tr>
<tr><td>GOAL TREE</td></tr>
<tr><td rowspan="2">STICKING PROBLEM HYPOTHESES</td><td rowspan="2">WELL FORMATION</td><td rowspan="2">BOTTOM HOLE ASSEMBLY</td><td>CURRENT RULE</td></tr>
<tr><td>INFERRED CONCLUSIONS</td></tr>
</table>

Figure 8b. Drilling Advisor display and map of its display elements.

understanding of the subterranean strata through which the well is being drilled. Finally, the last window pictures the collars, devices, and bit of the current bottom hole assembly.

The current advisor has about 250 rules representing about 90 percent of the total knowledge required to handle sticking problems and about 10 percent of the estimated total knowledge required to handle all drilling problems the Advisor is designed to cover. Rule 121 illustrates these rules. The box on the next page illustrates a dialog between a drilling foreman and the system.

IF the action being done just prior to the occurrence of the problem is drilling, the formation at the bottom of the hole is a hard formation, the type of bit used when the problem occurred is one of: jet-roller-bit cvl-roller-bit

THEN there is suggestive evidence (0.5) that there is a conical-hole in the well.

Different Users and Different Interfaces

Knowledge systems need to interface to several different types of users. The end-user may want to solve an application-domain problem such as freeing a stuck drilling rig, selecting the best tool, or controlling a high-speed process, and he may want a mixture of graphic and text presentations, clarification of ambiguous questions the system asks, and explanations for surprising results. As he gains familiarity with a knowledge system, verbose interactions with lengthy explanations lose their appeal. The experienced user generally knows how the system works and thinks. In any case, the end-user wants simply data entry, but the preferred modalities vary from user to user. A token recognition/automatic completion function helps data entry considerably.

Experts also need a suitable interface to the knowledge system. For much of the period of system development, they may devote 50 percent or more of their time to knowledge-base development and testing. They want explanations for the system's conclusions, want to know why the system did not reach an alternative conclusion of interest to the expert, want to see all possible ways the system can reason to a particular conclusion, and want to see all rules that reason about specified variables. In addition, they need ways to edit rules and try them out experimentally. Spelling correction and token completion functions help in these activities. In short, they need a very high-level set of programming constructs and knowledge-base utilities, which such lower level symbolic languages as Lisp and Prolog fail to offer.

Knowledge-base maintainers usually have less expertise than the expert but know a little more about the underlying computer and programming components of the knowledge system. They need an interface with editing access to rules and variable definitions, one that also allows them to access and modify a library of stored cases. And they may want tools to provide reports on exceptions that arise when they validate the effect of knowledge-base changes during test cases. We can already expect that commercial tools will provide most of these

Sample Drilling Advisor dialog

Asterisks (**) mark user inputs.

(1) What is the name of WELL-159?
** AGF7-93E

(2) What is the profile of AGF7-93E?
** DEVIATED

The first formation of AGF7-93E will be referred to as:

FORMATION-1

Please enter information about FORMATION-1:

	upper-limit meters	lower-limit meters	main-rock-type	homogeneous/ interbedded
(3) **	747	806	SHALE	HOMOGENEOUS

• • •

PROBLEM-1

Please enter information on PROBLEM-1:

	problem-type	prior-action	total-depth	casing-shoe depth
(13) **	STICKING	REAMING	1111 METERS	747 METERS

The first episode of the STICKING problem will be referred to as:

EPISODE-1

Please enter observations about EPISODE-1:

	circulation type	type of injection pressure	rotation y/n
(14) **	NO-RETURN	OVER-PRESSURE—NON-STABILIZED	NO

(15) Please enter the composition of the drill-string starting from the bit (type ? for assistance):
** BIT 9″⅝ STAPB″⅝ SHORTDC7″¾STAB9″⅝. . . NDP5″

(16) What was the depth of bit at the time of the STICKING problem?
** 1091 METERS

(17) What is the length of the SHORTDC section of the BHA (BHA.SECTION-3)?
** 3 METERS

(18) What was the drilling method employed when the problem occurred?
** ROTARY

(19) Was reaming stopped just prior to the STICKING problem in order to add a single?
** NO

(20) What is the depth of the freepoint?
** UNKNOWN

(21) Is the SHALE formation interbedded with LIMESTONE between 806 meters and 960 meters a creeping formation?
** NO

• • •

The causes of sticking in EPISODE-1 are as follows:
BALLING-UP (.53)

The reason(s) that balling-up was concluded as the cause of sticking in EPISODE-1 are as follows:
The action at the time of sticking was REAMING. There are 4 stabilizers in the BHA. There is evidence of balling-up material in the well. The upspeed of the cuttings is slow.

The list of possible curative treatments for EPISODE-1 are as follows:

You should work on the drill-string both upward and downward, and work on rotation.

Jar both upward and downward, using the jar currently in the BHA.

You may consider squeezing a lubricant and surfactant slug, because the drill-string is now motionless, and some of the non-spiralled elements in the BHA are in front of permeable formations.

Run the freepoint to determine the back-off depth, then (if possible) back-off and run a fishing jar able to work both upward and downward.

If you could not get the pipe free using one of the previous techniques, and depending on the results of the freepoint, you may consider using a cement plug and side-tracking.

The possible preventive treatments for EPISODE-1 are as follows:

If you could get the pipe free, you should now proceed to the following treatments during the next trip down:

Stop at different depths between 917 meters and 1111 meters to circulate complete bottom-up in order to clean the well.

In order to prevent any further problems of that kind, you may consider changing the mud characteristics as follows:

Add products for sticky shales.

You should change the BHA composition according to the following recommendations:

You should incorporate a safety joint in the BHA.

When drilling again, circulate with an increased flow rate around 1925.0 1/mn in order to have a good upspeed of cuttings.

functions without requiring programming in a low-level symbolic language such as Lisp.

Finally, knowledge engineers need access to the knowledge system in ways appropriate for the knowledge-base design and initial knowledge-acquisition tasks. They should be able to build conceptual structures for the key domain concepts and variables, specify the overall problem-solving search and control strategies, and develop ways within the knowledge representation scheme to express the relevant facts and heuristics. Subsequently, they may want to reduce the time and effort required to enter problem data, problem concepts, heuristic rules, and test the system. Once a system operates, they should be able to track the system's reasoning and isolate and patch errors quickly. Tools such as KS300 and S.1 already provide many such facilities.

Interfaces to Knowledge

At the outset, I noted that knowledge systems offer a new approach to knowledge storage and distribution, competing primarily with books and oral communications, alternatives that have evolved over hundreds or thousands of years. As a result, the interfaces to knowledge stored in books and human recollection have evolved considerably. As we look ahead to the future, we can speculate on how interfaces to knowledge systems will need to evolve for this new system of knowledge storage to meet the demands more effectively.

In general, people need interfaces to systems that accommodate their background, skills, and purpose. We cannot say much in general about their backgrounds and skills, but we can characterize with some reliability those purposes that will lead users to seek assistance from knowledge systems. The knowledge system will serve a variety of needs and offer distinct advantages:

- Wider distribution of and access to expert know-how,
- Vigilance in the application of know-how,
- Systematic consistency in the application of knowledge,
- Data reduction and interpretation through analysis,
- Hypothetical reasoning,
- Assistance in problem-solving, and
- Improved control of complex process.

Many specific applications arise in each of these function areas. For example, people need wider access to know-how where education is poor, where expertise is rare, and where professional service is often substandard—in less developed countries, agricultural assistance and medical expertise is lacking or, in this country, the need for legal and accounting advice is great. More characteristic today are the applications of expert systems in large commercial organizations with rapidly changing products, personnel turnover, and highly varied human performance. Each function area and each specific application will benefit from specialized interfaces. Interfaces will need to take into account the local jargon and communication styles of the experts and end-users, the end-user's level of understanding and sophistication, the time-stress on problem-solvers, and many related factors.

Knowledge has the power to solve problems, do work, save costs or save lives. In essence, it is an alternative form of energy. People may one day think of contacting a knowledge system first when they need help. These systems may become the appliances of a new industry based on the power of knowledge to provide such help. Such appliances will need to listen well and speak carefully.

The State of the Art

To assess the state of the art in KE, we can attempt to place the boundary between the practical and the impractical, between the capabilities

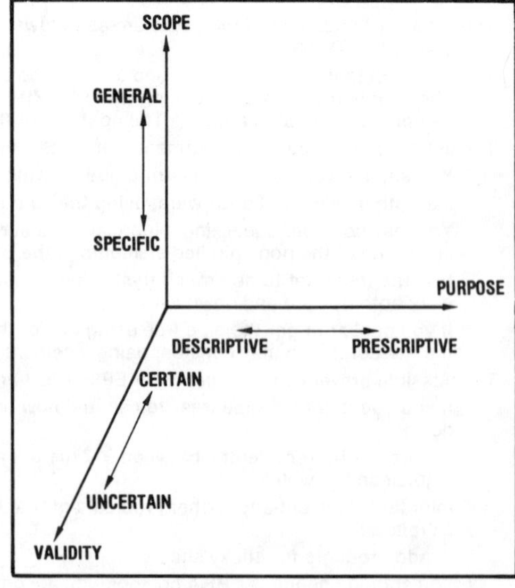

Figure 9. The three dimensions of knowledge.

of today's engineers and the visions of current researchers. To do this, let us focus first on the essence of knowledge engineering, namely knowledge itself, and delve somewhat more deeply into the properties of knowledge to distinguish between kinds of knowledge that engineers can and cannot apply today.

What Knowledge Can We Engineer?
Figure 9 displays three dimensions of knowledge:

- The scope of knowledge, ranging from the general and widely applicable to the specific and narrowly applicable;
- The purpose of knowledge, ranging from descriptive purposes to prescriptive ones; and
- The validity of knowledge, ranging from certain to uncertain.

Although one can generate other ways to classify knowledge, these three dimensions can help assess the role any particular element of knowledge proposes to play in an overall system.

Kind of Knowledge	Knowledge
Specific, descriptive, certain	A dog is a mammal.
Specific, descriptive, uncertain	A dog has 4 legs.
Specific, prescriptive, certain	To conclude x is a dog, confirm that x's parents are dogs.
General, prescriptive, certain	To conclude P(x), show that ~ P(x) is impossible.
General, descriptive, uncertain	Real things are observable.

Table 1. Examples of types of knowledge in three dimensions.

Table 1 illustrates some points in the knowledge space. "A dog is a mammal" is true by definition and has a relatively limited range of applications. Hence, the table characterizes it as a specific, descriptive, and certain bit of knowledge. However, although "A dog has four legs" is true by definition and has a relatively limited range of applications, the table characterizes it differently. Why? Having four legs is not a defining characteristic of dogs, although nearly all dogs are quadrupeds. Some dogs are not, so the fact is uncertain. One certain way to classify an object conclusively as a dog would be to state that its parents are also dogs. This specific prescription appears next in the table. A more general prescription is then to conclude some proposition *P(x)* is true, for any *x* and, show that its negation is impossible. This kind of rule can apply wherever the method is finite, practical, and effective. How hard is it to prove something is impossible? The last table entry illustrates the kind of general knowledge that many humans exploit in spite of its uncertain validity. For example, many scientists consider unobservable phenomena uninteresting intellectually and nonexistent for all practical purposes.

Today, when knowledge engineers build systems, they employ almost exclusively specific knowledge of either certain or uncertain types. Most descriptive knowledge finds its way into a knowledge base, while the prescriptive knowledge is generally distributed over the problem-solving architecture itself, the knowledge base, and the inference engine.

A. *Currently practicable*	B. *Not Available*
Definitions and taxonomies	General problem-solving knowledge
Discrete descriptions	Analogues
Simple constraints and invariants	Naive physics
Empirical associations	Meta-representation knowledge
Perceptual structures	Meta-knowledge
Deductive methods	First principles
Simple inductive methods	Compiling and decompiling know-how
Very simple physical models	
Very simple search heuristics	

Table 2. Possible types of engineered knowledge.

Table 2 shows several more specific categories of knowledge which contemporary knowledge engineers do and do not apply effectively. The elements listed in the right-hand column attract the bulk of KE attention today, while those in the left-hand column attract less attention—most from researchers. Although most of the terms in column A are self-explanatory, those in column B, which involve general problem-solving knowledge, probably require additional explanation. Knowledge engineers build that kind of knowledge directly into the architecture and inference engine of the knowledge system itself.

Although people seem to use analogies frequently, knowledge systems do not. *Analogues* do not play a role in knowledge systems, because no one has yet developed any effective means of exploiting analogies to aid problem-solving. As a topic of research interest, analogy has a long and relatively fruitless history, but it continues to draw low levels of attention.

When people speak of *naive physics*, they mean the common, nonverbal understanding of physical operations and events that even very young children demonstrate. When I hold a glass of water over my tiled kitchen floor and let it drop, you know what will happen. In fact, you involuntarily simulate the event from the moment the glass slips free, while it falls toward the hard floor, until the glass shatters and flies about the room and the water spreads across the floor's surface. Knowledge systems today don't incorporate such knowledge or simulate such effects. It appears that giving knowledge systems these capabilities will require enormous amounts of effort. No single application will justify the expense, but the electronic form of such knowledge should prove useful in countless applications.

Meta-representation knowledge prescribes the best ways to represent knowledge. Determining the best way to represent various kinds of knowledge today requires heuristic reasoning on the part of knowledge engineers. At this point, no clear expertise stands out in this area and certainly none has been reduced to implementable heuristic rules.

Meta-knowledge describes knowledge and prescribes what to do with it. Most meta-knowledge today enters a system by influencing the architectural design of the system, rather than as rules that enter the knowledge base. Many researchers today want to increase the ability of knowledge systems to reason about their own knowledge, their own problem-solving methods, and their own resource allocation problems. These all require meta-knowledge and meta-reasoning.

First principles in any field of study constitute a core set of ideas that generally enable a skilled person to recreate many special cases. For example, physicists pride themselves on how their fundamental theories reduce myriad physical phenomena to special cases of general phenomena. However, studies of human professionals show that they excel in their work largely because they can recognize current problems as examples of problems they solved once before. For the student of physics, this means learning requires solving many specific problems that illustrate the general rules, rather than memorizing the general rules, then applying them variously to differing problems. Knowledge systems do not exploit first

	KNOWLEDGE ACQUISITION	SYSTEM ARCHITECTURE	KNOWLEDGE PROGRAMMING	KNOWLEDGE REFINEMENT
GENERALLY OBSOLETE CONCERNS	Statistical learning Perceptrons Holography Self-organizing systems Neural nets	Associations General systems theory Unordered production theory Cybernetic control systems Transformational systems	Post productions Markov Models Decision Trees Discrimination nets Blind search Unconstrained backtracking	Reinforcement Clustering Unsupervised learning
REPRESENTATIVE CURRENT CAPABILITIES	Expert debriefing Thinking-aloud protocols Case libraries Intelligible formalisms for rules and taxonomies Generalizing rules from examples	Backchaining v. Data-Driven v. Slot filling v. Blackboard Consultation paradigm Intelligent agent paridigm	Lisp/Prolog Frames Rules Fuzzy logic Procedures Relations Constraints Propositions Demons	Parameter tuning Tracing Explanation Consistency checks Syntactic/semantic editors
KEY NEAR-TERM OBJECTIVES	Tools for experts Use of design documents Generic knowledge systems	Improved commercial tools and organizing frameworks	Flexibly integrated KE utilities Commercial quality programming systems	Aids for: Consistency checking Testing Maintaining knowledge bases
KEY LONG-TERM OBJECTIVES	Text understanding Learning by being taught	Multirepresentation systems Model-based reasoning Knowledge compilers and decompilers	Automated transformation of what to how Deep modeling languages Meta-knowledge systems	Learning from experience Learning by conducting experiments

Table 3. State of the art in knowledge engineering.

principles because we do not know how to specialize them efficiently and because experts can provide more specialized rules that work well.

Human engineers exhibit *compiling know-how* when they transform high-level forms of programs into lower-level forms that run faster and consume fewer resources. They exhibit *decompiling know-how* when they can read a program and tell you what it does. Systems that want speed must compile their knowledge. Systems that want to understand their knowledge must maintain a high-level form of that knowledge or decompile compiled knowledge. Researchers have done very little work in this research area to date. Knowledge systems today tend to employ only fairly low-level, moderately compiled forms of knowledge.

State of Technology

Knowledge engineering technology breaks into the four areas characterized by Table 3: knowledge acquisition, system architecture, knowledge programming, and knowledge refinement. For each of these areas, the table summarizes the past, present, and future. To characterize the past, the table lists some old concerns and approaches to KE that have lost their relevance generally. To characterize the present, the table shows a number of capabilities that current knowledge systems generally exhibit. To characterize the future, the table lists the major near-term and long-term research and development objectives.

Knowledge engineering arose as a specialized subfield of AI because general problem-solving methods did not work well enough to solve important problems. Computing speed could not compensate for weak approaches to search in complex tasks. The emphasis on knowledge-intensive expertise grew out of an observation that experts excelled at their work because they knew more than inexpert people did. Their knowledge enabled them to generate better candidate solutions and to prune unattractive candidates more quickly.

Today, knowledge engineers construct two different kinds of systems, those that perform as human experts do and those that perform simpler tasks that normally require human intelligence, though not expertise. Expert systems incorporate real human know-how garnered from experts. The knowledge in expert systems evolves incrementally as systems grow to simulate the human problem-solver. Knowledge systems, in general, do not necessarily mimic human experts. Rather, they provide electronic means to collect, store, distribute, reason about, and apply knowledge. They replace books or manuals and grow more rapidly than expert systems. The examples in this article focused primarily on expert systems because they have been more familiar in the past—a reflection of the academic orientation of most initial applications. In the future, I expect knowledge systems to increase more rapidly. Because expert systems are a special case of the more general category knowledge systems, it is desirable to refer to the entire class of knowledge-based systems simply as knowledge systems.

Most of the world's work requires human knowledge, and KE aims to support knowledge-intensive work with machines. The rate of knowledge development and transfer to application directly affects the rate of cultural development. These factors create a significant demand for technological improvements in knowledge processing. And because knowledge systems actually work, we should expect great support for the future development of this technology.

KE represents a set of methods, approaches and tools. A few hundred teams around the world are now using them to construct or field knowledge systems. However, KE is not a panacea. Today, the technology makes a wide variety of constrained problems tractable, but most problems do not admit of simple KE solutions. The technology faces obstacles as it tries to expand the breadth, depth, and scale of its systems. Against these obstacles, we should expect to see continued, steady technological advances.

Inexpensive computer hardware and maturing software created the conditions in which KE has emerged. With hardware prices plummeting, computer power skyrocketing, and KE software tools entering the commercial era, we should expect to see many dramatic pay-offs as initial knowledge systems address ripe problems. In fact, many applications afford annual savings exceeding $10,000,000 and may pay back a development cost in a few months. Most such analyses are confidential, but DEC spokesmen confirm that figure for one of their knowledge systems, R1.

Economic imperatives will pull knowledge engineering in several directions as they preserve otherwise perishable human expertise; distribute otherwise scarce expertise; reduce the costs of mediocre or poor human performance;

and provide help to humans trying to access information and employ computers. Today the field is growing at a moderate rate. The primary factor that limits growth is an underdeveloped infrastructure of trained people, commercial tools, and easily understood application categories. To accelerate the rate of development, many people with KE experience focus on incorporating their methods into tools that others can apply. This approach follows similar development patterns in circuit design and automated manufacturing. Also, many significant parties have just begun to invest in the field or have significantly increased their level of involvement. Notable among these are the Japanese through MITI, the British through the Alvey Commission, the European Community through the Esprit programs, and the US government through its Strategic Computing Program.

References

1. F. Hayes-Roth, D. A. Waterman, and D. B. Lenat, *Building Expert Systems*, Addison-Wesley, Reading, Massachusetts, 1983.
2. A. Barr and E. A. Feigenbaum, *The Handbook of Artificial Intelligence*, William Kaufman, Menlo Park, California, Vol. 1, 1981, Vol. 2, 1982.
3. R. K. Lindsay et al., *Applications of Artificial Intelligence for Organic Chemistry: The Dendral Project*, McGraw-Hill, New York, 1980.
4. W. A. Martin and R. J. Fateman, "The Macsyma System," *Proc. Second Symp. Symbolic and Algebraic Manipulation*, 1971, pp. 59-75.
5. E. H. Shortliffe, *Computer-based Medical Consultation: Mycin*, American Elsevier, New York, 1976.
6. L. D. Erman et al., "Hearsay-II Speech-Understanding System: Integrating Knowledge to Resolve Uncertainty," *Computing Surveys*, Vol. 12, No. 2, 1980, pp. 213-253.
7. J. McDermott, "R1: An Expert in the Computer Systems Domain," *Proc. First Annual Nat. Conf. Artificial Intelligence*, 1980, pp. 269-271.
8. H. E. Pople, J. D. Myers, and R. A. Miller, "Dialog Internist: A Model of Diagnostic Logic for Internal Medicine," *Proc. IJCAI4*, 1975, pp. 849-855.
9. R. Greiner and D. Lenat, "A Representation Language Language," *Proc. First Annual Nat. Conf. Artificial Intelligence*, Vol. 1, 1980, pp. 165-169.
10. H. P. Nii et al., "Signal-to-Symbol Transformation: HASP/SIAP Case Study," *AI Magazine*, Vol. 3, No. 2, 1982.
11. R. Brooks, R. Greiner, and T. Binford, "The Acronym Model-based Vision System," *Proc. IJCAI 79*, 1979, pp. 105-113.
12. L. D. Erman, P. E. London, and S. F. Fickas, "The Design and an Example Use of Hearsay-III," *Proc. IJCA17*, 1981, pp. 409-415.
13. H. P. Nii and N. Aiello, "AGE: A Knowledge-base Program for Building Knowledge-based Programs," *Proc. IJCAI 6*, 1979, pp. 645-655.

Expert Systems as Decision Aids: Issues and Strategies

Ting-Peng Liang

Expert systems (ES) designed to mimic and replace human experts have drawn considerable attention in the past several years. Although most of the early applications were developed in medical or engineering domains, business applications have become more and more popular (Blanning, 1984; Ernst & Ojha, 1986; Lin, 1986; Michaelsen & Michie, 1983). Articles presenting existing prototypes have increased dramatically. Many potential benefits have been reported (Fried, 1987). They include:

- Improved decision making,
- More consistent decision making,
- Reduced design or decision making time,
- Improved training,
- Operational cost saving,
- Better use of expert time,
- Improved products or service levels, and
- Rare or dispersed knowledge captured.

These potential benefits, coupled with research conducted in the decision support systems (DSS) area, have strongly encouraged an integration of ES and DSS technologies. For example, Scott Morton (1984) stated that "DSS as we know them may become obsolete in the foreseeable future. They are being supplanted by expert decision support systems—EDSS. The next generation of DSS will combine existing DSS technology with the capabilities of AI." Luconi et al. (1986) argued that "for many of the problems of practical importance in business, we should focus our attention on designing systems that support expert users rather than on replacing them." Turban and Watkins (1986) discussed how to integrate ES programs into a DSS in order to create even more powerful and useful computer-based systems.

Developing EDSS that take advantage of both ES and DSS technologies is certainly promising. Its implementation, unfortunately, is not without problems. ES and DSS have different objectives, different design philosophies, and different architectures (Ford, 1985; Turban & Watkins, 1986). These differences make this integration difficult. Furthermore, unlike engineering domains, behavioral considerations usually play an important role in the business arena. For a system that focuses on importing outside expertise, the risk of failure would be high. Therefore, before joining the bandwagon of using ES as decision aids, we need to carefully examine potential applications of this technology and to develop a framework that provides guidelines for employing various types of computer-based decision aids. In the remainder of this article, we shall discuss the issues involved in using ES as decision aids and develop strategies for using this technology.

Issues in Integrating ES and DSS

The basic premise of ES is that in some areas a small group of people (called experts) can perform a particular job significantly better than most of the rest. Since the knowledge (called expertise) of these people is rare and expensive, developing ES that capture and disseminate this expertise will be able to improve the decision performance of non-experts (Waterman, 1986). The basic premise of DSS, however, is that for some semi-structured problems the decision maker can improve performance by conducting "what-if" type of analysis that takes advantage of the power of computers to speed up data

Reprinted with permission from *Journal of Information Systems*, vol. 2, no. 2, Spring 1988, 41-50.

analysis and mathematical calculation. Therefore, the integration of these two technologies has the following problems.

First, ES and DSS have different objectives. DSS focus on supporting decision makers in semi-structured or unstructured problems, whereas ES concentrate on replacing human decision makers in structured and narrow problem domains. This difference has resulted in two completely different design philosophies. In designing a DSS, the designer must always have the user in mind and adapt the system to meet user requirements (Keen & Scott Morton, 1978; Sprague & Carlson, 1982). In designing an ES, however, the designer (or called knowledge engineer) must focus on acquiring knowledge from domain experts who are usually not the user of the system. In other words, the quality of knowledge is the primary concern, users are second. The designer of an integrated system must compromise these two philosophies.

Second, it is not clear whether the focus of integration should be the rule-based approach adopted by ES or the concept of including expert judgment in a system. ES and DSS have different functional capabilities. A typical DSS performs data analysis (called a data-oriented DSS) or model execution assistance (called a model-oriented DSS) for the user. The user is responsible for determining the data to be analyzed and the model to be used. A typical ES, however, further makes judgment based on its built-in knowledge and value systems. Figure 1 illustrates this difference. If an integrated EDSS only takes advantage of the rule-based techniques and still leaves the judgment to the user, then, just like rewrite a COBOL program in PASCAL, there will be no functional difference between EDSS and DSS. The resulting system will not have the anticipated power because it does not have the desired knowledge.

If an EDSS is designed to provide not only data analysis and model execution assistance

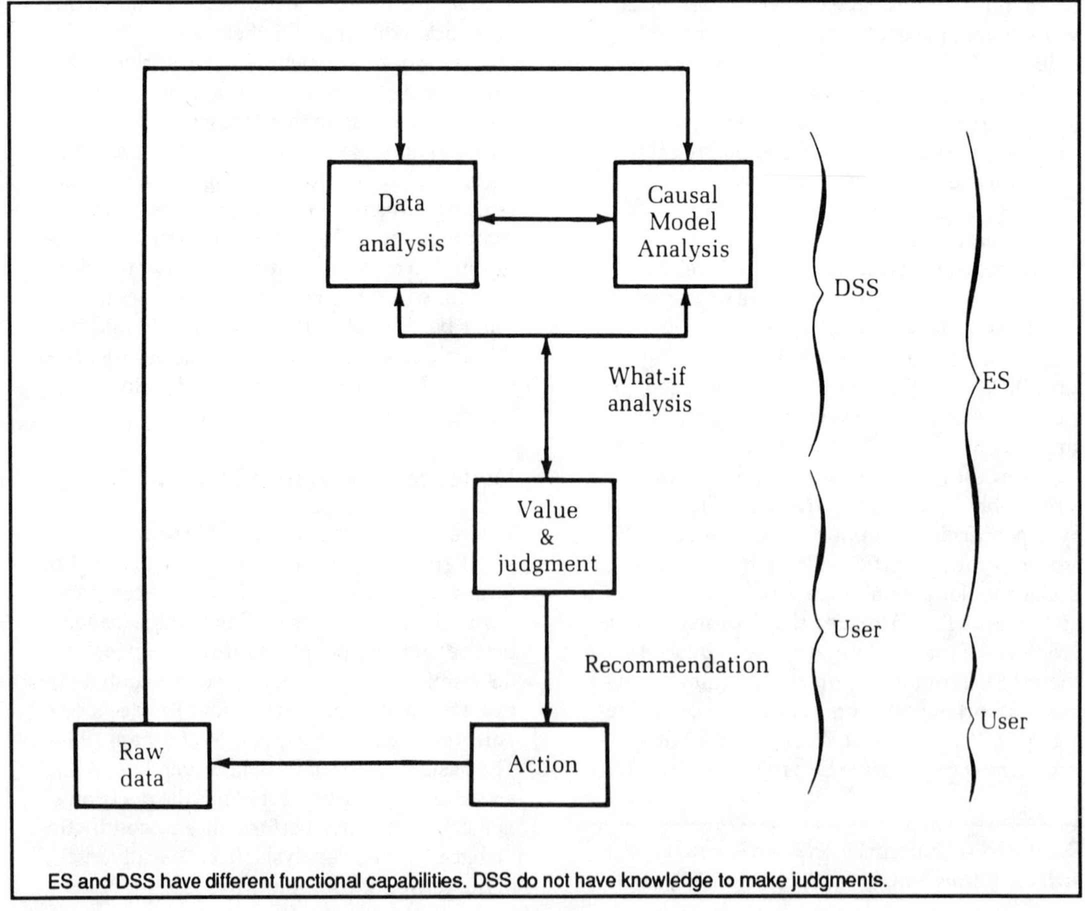

ES and DSS have different functional capabilities. DSS do not have knowledge to make judgments.

Figure 1.

	TPS	DSS	ES	HE
• System-user interaction	Rare	User-directed	System-directed	B-directional
• Reasoning model	Quantitative & causal	Quantitative & causal	Qualitative & judgmental	Qualitative & judgmental
• System guidance in the decision process	Low	Medium	High	High
• System restriction	High	Medium	High	Low
• System customization	Low	High	Low	High
• Performance consistency	High	High	High	Medium
• Common sense reasoning	No	No	No	Yes
• Providing judgment	No	No	Yes	Yes

Transaction processing systems (TPS), decision support systems (DSS), expert systems (ES), and human experts (HE) are four types of decision aids. They are different in many aspects.

Figure 2.

but also its expert judgment, then the next issue is whose value and judgment functions should be coded into the system? From the DSS perspective, the user's judgment function should be used. Since the user may not be an expert, this approach could result in a useless rule-based system. Even if the user is an expert, duplicating the expertise may provide little assistance. From the ES perspective, judgment functions elicited from a small group of selected experts are more appropriate. The problem with this approach is that it may generate high resistance—one of the major reasons for DSS to adopt user-oriented design.

Finally, even if the designer successfully implements an EDSS that provides expert judgment, there are chances that in a given situation the EDSS and the user may draw conflicting conclusions. In this case, whose judgment should be adopted? How can we determine whose judgment is correct? Should we bring in another human expert or expert system to make recommendations? If the user's expertise has been proven better than the system's, then why should the user be bothered by the EDSS? If the system is proven better, then how can we allow the user to overwrite the system's judgment?

All these issues suggest that using ES as decision aids is not as simple or as exciting as it seems to be. We need to know where it can be applied and how it can be used appropriately.

Selection of Decision Aids

From a broad perspective, all systems, including human expert consultants, are decision aids, because nothing can replace the role of a decision maker who takes full responsibility for the outcome. Different types of decision aids have different characteristics. For example, a human expert has both common sense and professional knowledge in a particular area but is usually less consistent in performance. An ES provides a strong guidance in the decision process but has high restriction because it lacks common sense. A DSS provides customized support to decision makers but cannot make its own judgment. Figure 2 shows a comparison of four types of decision aids: transaction processing systems (TPS), DSS, ES, and human experts (HE).

With these differences in mind, we must consider at least four factors to select and use a decision aid properly: the task, the nature of knowledge, the system, and the user. The first two factors determine what kind of decision aids is appropriate and the latter two factors determine the strategy for using a selected decision aid.

Selecting a Decision Aid

The first factor that affects decision aid selection is the nature of task. There are many ways to

Knowledge \ Task	Structured		Unstructured	
	Repetitive	***Ad hoc***	**Repetitive**	***Ad hoc***
Qualitative reasoning	Expert systems	Human experts	Human experts	Human experts
Quantitative reasoning	Transaction processing systems	End-user computing	Decision support systems (institutional)	Decision support systems (*ad hoc*)

Selecting decision aids must consider the problem structuredness, decision frequency, and reasoning method. When qualititive reason is requred, expert systems are appropriate for structured and repetitive decision and human experts must be hired for the rest. When quantitative reasoning is used, transaction processing systems are appropriate for structured and repetitive decisions, end-user computing is appropriate for structured and *ad hoc* decisions and decision support systems are appropriate for unstructured decisions.

Figure 3.

differentiate decision problems. Three of them are particularly important:

- Availability of expertise,
- Structuredness of the problem, and
- Decision frequency.

If the expertise required for solving the problem is not available, then developing a good decision aid is impossible. If the required expertise exists, then we consider whether the problem is structured or unstructured and whether the decision occurs repetitively or only once. The problem structuredness affects the division of labor between the system and the user. In a semi-structured or unstructured decision making, only the structured portion can be automated because a computer system cannot process a job which human beings do not know how to do. The decision frequency is important is determining whether a particular decision aid is cost-effective. For a decision that occurs only once, developing a sophisticated expert system may not be justifiable in terms of development time and costs.

The second factor to be considered is the nature of knowledge processed by the decision aid. It could be qualitative or quantitative. A qualitative reasoning process usually involves judgmental models, whereas a quantitative computation process uses causal models. Transaction processing systems (TPS) and traditional DSS focus on quantitative computation, whereas ES and human experts solve problems by qualitative reasoning.

Taking all these factors into consideration, we find that there is no decision aid that fits all cases. Figure 3 shows the situations where the following decision aids are applicable.

- *Expert systems.* In a structured domain where qualitative reasoning is crucial to problem solving and expertise is available, developing an ES (or EDSS) to support a repetitive decision in the domain may be appropriate. For example, loan evaluation is a repetitive decision for most banks. Except some special cases, the loan evaluation process and evaluation criteria are clearly defined. Therefore, an ES can reduce the workload of a loan officer and allow the officer to focus on special cases.
- *Human experts.* If the decision is structured but *ad hoc* or unstructured by nature, then the assistance an ES can provide is very limited. In this case, human experts must be hired if a support is desired.
- *Transaction processing systems.* If the desired support is quantitative by nature, and the decision is structured and repetitive, then a traditional transaction processing system

that focuses on standard procedures and large amount of data will be sufficient. For example, providing monthly inventory report is a repetitive, structured and quantitative task, a good TPS will make this process much easier.

- *End-user computing.* When the decision is structured, *ad hoc* and quantitative, one technology called end-user computing that encourages decision makers to develop their own *ad hoc* applications by taking advantage of user friendly fourth generation languages (4GLs) is very useful. The key in this case is to provide the user with a powerful 4GL with which an *ad hoc* application system can be built.
- *Decision support systems.* For an unstructured domain that needs quantitative support, DSS technology is appropriate. The system performs data analysis or executes proper models and the user makes judgments. If the decision is repetitive, then an institutional DSS may be developed. Otherwise, the user may develop an *ad hoc* DSS with a DSS generator and discard the system after successfully making the decision.

From this discussion, we find that ES can support only a small set of decisions. Furthermore, proper use of a particular technology may also be affected by characteristics of the system and the user. This is particularly true when ES are used. As discussed in the previous section, from the same set of facts, ES and the user may draw conflicting conclusions. Therefore, strategies for resolving the conflict are required.

Developing these strategies, we must consider the expertise of the user and the quality of the system. Users who use ES may have different levels of expertise varying from beginner to expert. The quality of ES may also vary from a rule-based toy to a real expert. There are many ES that do not demonstrate the desired expertise; but there are also systems that outperform human experts. For example, MYCIN, one of the earliest ES designed to diagnose infections and to recommend appropriate treatment, has been reported better than human physicians (Yu et al., 1979). In the experiment, MYCIN had a 65 percent success rate in prescribing correct medication, while physicians had an average success rate of 55.5 percent (ranging from 62.5 percent to 42.5 percent).

By comparing the quality of the system and the expertise of the user, four strategies for using ES technology can be developed: ignore, revise, follow and synthesize (Figure 4).

- *Ignore.* If only a toy ES is available and the user is also not an expert, then the contribution of the system is virtually none and it should not be used.
- *Revise.* If the system is a toy but the user is an expert, then the user may want to improve the system by revising its knowledge base. This strategy is appropriate only when the user has an intention to disseminate expertise. In other words, the enhanced system can be a good decision aid to other non-expert users. The resulting system may also work as a checklist for the user to avoid mistakes caused by ignorance in the decision process.

		Quality of User	
		Non-expert	**Expert**
Quality of System	Toy	Ignore	Revise
	Expert	Follow	Synthesize

Quality of user and quality of system determine the strategy for using EDSS. If neither the user nor the system has adequate expertise, then the system must be ignored. IF the user is an expert but the system is not, then the user can revise the system to improve its knowledge base. If the system has expertise but the user is a beginner, then the user should follow the system's recommendation. If both are experts, then the best strategy is to synthesize two judgments to find synergy.

Figure 4.

- *Follow.* The follow strategy applies when the user is not an expert but the system has a real expertise. In this case, the user must trust the system and take actions based on the expert system's recommendation. For example, when consulting with MYCIN, a patient should not overlook the system's prescription.
- *Synthesize.* When both the user and the ES are at the expert level, the best strategy is to find synergy. The ES must be treated as an independent consultant. The decision process will be similar to a group decision making process. Potential benefits in this case include: reducing obvious mistakes and expanding the scope of consideration by complementing with each other.

In summary, we have presented various strategies for selecting and using ES as decision aids in this section. To avoid misapplication of this powerful technology and to alleviate the problems addressed in the previous section, the following general guidelines must be followed:

- Focus on appropriate applications,
- Set up realistic objectives,
- Validate expert knowledge,
- Implement evolutionary design, and
- Control system risk.

Guidelines for Developing EDSS

Selected application. One of the obvious dangers involved in using EDSS is called the law of the hammer—give a child a hammer and he will use it on everything encountered (Hopple, 1986). Therefore, to use ES technology constructively, we must carefully evaluate every application. We have known that an ES is appropriate only when the problem domain is structured, the decision is repetitive and the knowledge involves qualitative reasoning. In addition, there are several functional categories appropriate for this technology. These include interpretation, prediction, diagnosis, design, planning, monitoring, debugging, repair, instruction, and control (Hayes-Roth et al., 1983). As long as an application falls into one of these categories, ES may be considered.

To further evaluate an application, the following questions must be asked:

- Does the application have a clear boundary? Current ES technology does not allow the system to have much creativity. Therefore, unless the application needs only a finite set of known knowledge, the support an ES can provide will be limited. For example, tax advising is a bounded domain, but new product development is not.
- Does the application have standard cases from which knowledge can be derived and validated? If these cases do not exist, then knowledge acquisition will be very difficult and the resulting system may not be reliable.
- Is there any expert who can provide knowledge in the domain? The expert must have expertise and also have the willingness and time to cooperate with knowledge engineers in the knowledge acquisition process. If such an expert is not available, developing an ES for the application will not be possible.
- Is the size of the knowledge base reasonable? The complexity of the system is an exponential function of the size of the knowledge base. Therefore, developing a system that needs a huge amount of knowledge may be too costly and error-prone.
- Is a conventional system adequate for this application? Because ES technology is still in its infancy, using a conventional approach may solve the problem quickly and at a lower cost.

Realistic objective. If ES technology is found appropriate for an application, then a realistic objective for system development must be established. This can help us avoid the danger of omniscience that expects an ES to do something we don't know how to do. There are many unsolved (or unsolvable) problems in developing and using DSS. Unfortunately, using ES as a substitute is not the solution. ES are not super-DSS or super-humans. They are just other types of systems focusing on other types of problems. An ES cannot do anything that no one else knows how to do. In most domains, ES cannot perform even close to a real expert. Therefore, attention should be focused on strong economic benefits or knowledge dissemination, rather than unrealistic expectations.

Validated knowledge. Another important fact about ES is that the power of an ES is derived from the knowledge it possesses, not from the particular formalisms and inference schemes it employs. Therefore, thorough validation of the knowledge base is essential to the reliability of the system. The validation should start from the selection of experts and continue throughout the system development and utilization process.

- Before developing the system, qualified experts must be located. Those experts must have the expertise and also have time to work with knowledge engineers. They may not be the user of the system.
- Knowledge acquired from the experts must be validated before coding into the system. Standard cases may be used at this stage to find inconsistency, and indicate incomplete knowledge.
- A complete validation must be connected before applying the system to any real world problem.
- During system utilization, the knowledge base must be continuously revised to meet the changing environment.

If the system is purchased from a third party vendor rather than developed in house, then the system must be evaluated by a group of experts. In addition, it is important to make sure that the knowledge contained in the system can be either revised by the organization or updated by the vendor.

Evolutionary design. Since the user usually does not trust a decision aid until it shows reliable performance, an evolutionary approach that requires the designer first to develop a simple system and then to revise the system under the guidance of the user, has been a major approach for DSS design. In order to support the user with an ES, a similar approach must be adopted. This process will include three major steps.

First, when a system is developed or is purchased from a software vendor, the knowledge base already contains a set of basic knowledge. However, it may not have the specific knowledge that is useful only in that particular organization. Therefore, the system must be considered as a rule-based checklist, the user's judgment still plays a major role in the decision process. The user evaluates the reliability of the system and asks experts to revise the knowledge base if appropriate. The system at this stage may be called a rule-based DSS.

After the first stage, the user has found the strengths and offset the limitations of the system. The reliability of the system increases and the user starts trusting the system. In this case, the system makes judgments, but the user still keeps an eye on the system and overwrites the system's judgment. This system is called a human-aided ES.

Finally, the system becomes very reliable after a certain time period. At this time, the system makes most of the judgment and the user only focuses on special cases that cannot be handled by the system. If the system and the user draw conflicting conclusions for a particular problem, a careful examination of the conflict may be required. Unless there is a good reason, the user should avoid changing the system's recommendations.

This process allows a system to evolve from a rule-based DSS, human-aided ES to a valuable ES. It can reduce the possible resistance from the user and also gradually improve the reliability of the system.

Risk control. In addition to the technical issues, another important consideration is to control risks. Both financial and technological risks may occur if EDSS are used.

- *Financial risks.* Developing ES is very expensive and time consuming. A recent survey indicated that the average cost for developing a system was $700.00 per rule—excluding the costs of hardware, software tools, and the time experts contributed to the knowledge base (Fried, 1987). Therefore, an ES project could be a financial disaster unless the management is fully aware of this fact.
- *Technological risks.* Because current ES technology is pretty young, it is very likely that a system developed today will be obsolete in a few years. In addition, it is sometimes difficult to know who is the real expert in a domain. Knowledge acquired from a nonexpert may mislead the user. For example, some lawyers also provide tax advising service usually provided by accountants. It would be difficult to determine whether they are qualified experts. Finally, no reliable tool for knowledge acquisition is currently available. The development of ES is still more an art than a science. This may significantly restrict the reliability of the system.

Concluding Remarks

The term "expert system" has been controversial. On the one hand, it creates high expectation and has been used as a buzzword for funding and a flag to wave for all sorts of projects (Bobrow et al., 1986). On the other hand, many people have criticized its feasibility. For example, Dreyfus and Dreyfus (1986) stated that "we believe that trying to capture more sophisticated skills within the realm of logic—skills involving not only calculation but also judgment—is a dangerously misguided effort and is ultimately doomed to failure."

In fact, ES are neither the solution to all problems, nor the solution to none. We need to understand where it can be applied and how to use it appropriately. This has been the main focus of this article. In summary, we have first examined the problems involved in using ES as decision aids. Then, strategies for using various types of decision aids have been addressed. Finally, five general guidelines for developing EDSS have been presented.

References

1. Blanning, R. W. 1984, "Management Applications of Expert Systems," *Information & Management*, 7, pp. 311-316.
2. Bobrow, D. G., S. Mittal and M. J. Stefik 1986, "Expert Systems: Perils and Promise," *Communications of the ACM*, 29:9, pp. 880-894.
3. Dreyfus, H. L., and S. E. Dreyfus 1986, "Why Expert Systems Do Not Exhibit Expertise," *IEEE Expert*, 1:2, pp. 86-90.
4. Ernst, M. L. and H. Ojha, 1986, "Business Applications of Artificial Intelligence Knowledge Based Expert Systems," *Future Generations Computer System*, 2, pp. 173-185.
5. Ford, F. N. 1985, "Decision Support Systems and Expert Systems: A Comparison," *Information & Management*, 8, pp. 21-26.
6. Fried, L. 1987, "The Dangers of Dabbling in Expert System," *Computerworld*, June 29, pp. 65-72.
7. Hayes-Roth, F., D. A. Waterman and D. B. Lenat 1983, *Building Expert Systems* (Reading, MA: Addison-Wesley).
8. Hopple, G. W. 1986, "Decision Aiding Dangers: The Law of the Hammer and Other Maxims," *IEEE Transactions on Systems, Man, and Cybernetics*, 16:6, pp. 834-843.
9. Keen, P. G. W. and M. S. Scott Morton 1978, *Decision Support Systems: An Organizational Perspective* (Reading, MA: Addison-Wesley).
10. Lin, E. 1986, "Expert Systems for Business Applications: Potential and Limitations," *Journal of Systems Management*, July, pp. 18-21.
11. Luconi, F. L., T. W. Malone and M. S. Scott Morton 1986, "Expert Systems: The Next Challenge for Managers," *Sloan Management Review*, Summer, pp. 3-14.
12. Michaelsen, R. H. and D. Michie 1983, "Expert Systems in Business," *Datamation*, November, pp. 240-246.
13. Scott Morton, M. S. 1984, "Expert Decision Support Systems," Paper Presented at the Special DSS Conference, Planning Executive Institute and Information Technology Institute, New York, NY, May 21-22, pp. 12.
14. Sprague, R. H., Jr. and E. D. Carlson 1982, *Building Effective Decision Support Systems* (Englewood Cliffs, NJ: Prentice-Hall).
15. Turban, E. and P. R. Watkins 1986, "Integrating Expert Systems and Decision Support Systems," *MIS Quarterly*, 10:2, pp. 121-136.
16. Waterman, D. A. 1986, *A Guide to Expert Systems* (Reading, MA: Addison-Wesley), pp. 24-31.
17. Yu, V. L., et al. 1979, "Antimicrobial Selection by Computers: A Blinded Evaluation of Infectious Disease Experts," *Journal of the American Medical Association*, 242:21, pp. 1279-1282.

Review Questions

I. Overview

Hayes-Roth

1. What are the major differences between conventional programs and knowledge-based systems? Why do we need knowledge-based systems?
2. What is the relationship between artificial intelligence (AI) and knowledge engineering? Describe the AI concepts underlying knowledge engineering and discuss why these concepts are essential.
3. What are the basic techniques used in developing knowledge-based systems? Choose a business domain with which you are familiar and describe how these techniques can be used to develop a knowledge-based system in that domain.
4. Summarize the process for constructing a knowledge-based system; discuss the major problems involved in this process and suggest how these problems can be alleviated.
5. Obviously knowledge-based systems have strengths and limitations in handling various types of knowledge. Choose a business domain to illustrate the type of knowledge that can or cannot be handled by knowledge-based systems.

Liang

1. Discuss how the different premises of expert systems (ESs) and decision-support systems affect the potential for integrating the two approaches.
2. From the discussion of Figure 3, rank order the five types of decision aids from the most potential decisions to support to the least. Justify your ranking.
3. Discuss the author's statement, "An ES cannot do anything that no one else knows how to do." Do you agree or disagree? Why?
4. Suppose you built a software system to support a manager who had to decide which decision aid to use. Categorize the system as one of the five identified by the author and justify your reasons for choosing it. How would you develop it?

II. THE DEVELOPMENT PROCESS

The users of an expert system participate in system development in a different way than do users of traditional information systems. The intended object of the expert system, i.e., the expert, must be intimately involved throughout the entire development process. The intended object of a traditional information system, the decision maker, is not usually so involved. It is therefore important that the presentation of business applications of expert systems be preceded by the details of expert systems development. The development process represents the real cost of the system, which must be weighed against the benefits promulgated in the application articles. In other words, the experts should know what they are letting themselves in for.

In order to be a successful member of the development team, the business expert must know how the expert systems development process works. This is the gist of the three articles in the Design section. Freiling et al., Prerau (1985), and Prerau (1987) present the insights they have gained in expert systems development projects. Freiling et al. approach the development process straightforwardly. Although the authors are in the engineering domain, their comments can be applied to most disciplines, especially business. The first Prerau paper gives a checklist of requirements for selection of a domain, although Prerau does not offer much justification for each requirement. The second Prerau article leads the reader through the difficult and critical knowledge acquisition process. Guidelines, with examples, are highlighted for successful passage through the much-publicized "bottleneck" in expert systems development. All three of these articles cover areas that businesses and experts need to be aware of throughout the development process, providing a collection of pitfalls and pointers for development.

The area of validation and verification (V/V) is just as important to expert systems development as it is to traditional information systems development. The difference is that the application of V/V to expert systems is not as well developed and understood as it is for other systems. Each of the articles in the V/V section sets out criteria for evaluating an expert system and offers insights into how to apply them. The different sets of criteria present a good opportunity for comparison. Nguyen et al. take a practical approach, describing a computer program that does consistency and completeness checks, automatically, on a knowledge base. O'Leary applies a theoretical framework, looking at expert systems as continuous experiments in cognitive psychology. O'Keefe et al. take a scientific, engineering approach, attempting to define an objective general battery of V/V techniques. The bottom line, however, is that the businesses for which the expert system is being built must establish their own criteria. These articles provide a good foundation for defining such criteria.

Starting a Knowledge Engineering Project: A Step-by-Step Approach

Mike Freiling, Jim Alexander, Steve Messick, Steve Rehfuss, and Sherri Shulman

Getting started on a new knowledge engineering project is a difficult and challenging task, even for those who have done it before. For those who haven't, the task can often prove impossible. One reason is that the requirements-oriented methods and intuitions learned in the development of other types of software do not carry over well to the knowledge engineering task. Another reason is that methodologies for developing expert systems by extracting, representing, and manipulating an expert's knowledge have been slow in coming.

At Tektronix, we have been using a step-by-step approach to prototyping expert systems for over two years now. The primary features of this approach are that it gives software engineers who do not know knowledge engineering an easy place to start, and that it proceeds in a step-by-step fashion from initiation to implementation without inducing conceptual bottlenecks into the development process. This methodology has helped us collect the knowledge necessary to implement several prototype knowledge-based systems, including a troubleshooting assistant for the Tektronix FG-502 function generator and an operator's assistant for a wave solder machine.

One fundamental assumption we make is that knowledge is more valuable than inference strategies. Often a company may have only one chance to acquire the knowledge, but can work on it later at leisure. A second assumption is that a knowledge engineering project must provide adequate documentation of its progress. At any stage in the process, knowledge engineers must be able to show some fruits of their labor.

Reprinted with permission from *AI Magazine*, vol. 6, no. 3, Fall 1985, 150-164.

The Need for Knowledge Engineering Methodologies

In any large organization it is quite common to find "pockets of knowledge" or "knowledge bottlenecks." Pockets of knowledge occur when knowledge crucial to the success of an organization is possessed by only one or a few individuals. Knowledge bottlenecks are pockets of knowledge that impede an organization's progress because the knowledge needs to be more widely distributed.

For example, if knowledge about how to keep an important manufacturing process running smoothly resides in the head of only one or two process engineers, we have a pocket of knowledge. If the company now wants to build several similar plants in different international locations, we have a knowledge bottleneck, because the knowledge cannot be distributed as easily as can the material used to build a factory. The lore of manufacturing processes includes stories of engineers who were shuttled by plane between factories in an effort to keep them all running.

It is clear that knowledge pockets and bottlenecks are undesirable and should be eliminated if possible. Pockets of knowledge can quickly become serious bottlenecks if the individuals retire or decide to leave the organization.

Expert system technology has been offered as a means for removing knowledge pockets and bottlenecks. But despite some notable successes, the path to expert system implementation is fraught with difficulties. Among these difficulties are

- *The "AI Mystique."* Terms like "artificial intelligence" or "knowledge engineering" give the impression that there is something magical and/or mystical involved in building expert systems. Despite our claims about making it clear how everyone else does their job, we have had some difficulty making it clear how we do our own. As a result, knowledge engineering is often considered a technology that is far too difficult to attempt.
- *The management problem.* How is it possible to manage the progress of an expert system project? The common wisdom is to build a prototype as quickly as possible. But what can be done to manage the project while the first prototype is being built?
- *Choosing the right tool.* A number of knowledge engineering tools are available on the market today. They range from simple backward chaining inference engines similar to EMYCIN (Van-Melle, 1984) to sophisticated object-oriented environments that permit a number of different inference strategies to be implemented (Kunz, 1984). Assess the problem to be attacked before deciding which tool to use or whether a tool is needed at all.
- *The acceptance problem.* How people will react to using knowledge-based consultants is a big question mark. Even in the prototyping stages, it is important to plan systems with acceptance in mind and to build an acceptance-oriented interface for the first prototype.

Several tools and methodologies have been developed to help manage the early phases of a knowledge engineering project. ETS is a knowledge acquisition system developed by Boeing Computer Services that acquires knowledge via a dialogue with the user and can actually build rule bases for several expert system tools (Boose, 1984).

Stefik et al. (1982) have articulated a variety of inference strategies, along with problem characteristics that dictate one choice or another. For instance, strategies which completely exhaust the possible answers and pursue a single line of reasoning are recommended only for problems where the number of possible solutions is small, the data is reliable, and the knowledge is also reliable. Complex search methods, such as opportunistic scheduling, are recommended when a single source of knowledge or line of reasoning is insufficient.

At a more abstract level, Clancey (1984) has examined the inference structure of many classification systems and articulated two different types of inference step in these problems.

The first type of step involves actions of abstraction and refinement which accomplish those parts of the problem-solving process that are fairly well-understood and automatic. Examples of abstraction steps include qualitative abstraction of numeric values, such as classifying a voltage of 4.67 to be "high" and generalization of a particular collection of symptoms into a relevant general class of patients, like "heavy smoker." Examples of refinement steps include selection of a particular component fault to account for some failure mode when the relevant faults can be exhaustively enumerated and checked, and the selection of some specific disease from the category of diseases known to be causing the patient's illness.

The second type of step involves heuristic associations which make intuitive leaps that cannot be deductively justified and may require reconsideration. Examples of heuristic associations include the association between symptom classes and disease categories that may be responsible, or between measured values in a circuit and failure modes that may be responsible.

In a similar vein, Brachman and Levesque (1982) have identified rules related to terminology and rules related to the problem and argued that separate inference strategies (or *process structure* in Clancey's terms) are needed for each.

The methodology we will discuss here is not intended to replace any of this previous work. Rather, our approach provides a step-by-step approach to building familiarity with a knowledge engineering problem that makes it possible to use techniques such as knowledge level analysis with a better understanding of what is involved in the problem.

Requirements for a Knowledge Engineering Methodology

Before we get into answering the above question, let us step back a minute and ask, "What would we wish from a knowledge engineering methodology?"

- *The methodology must be simple.* We all know knowledge engineering is a hard business, and there are many problems that exceed our ability right now. But there are also lots of small problems for which knowledge engineering in its present form is adequate. A methodology for attacking today's doable problems should be easy to apply and should lend itself to a wide variety of problems.
- *The methodology must be gradual.* The people who need a knowledge engineering methodology most are those who do not have much prior experience with knowledge engineering. Experience has shown that these people often encounter a conceptual bottleneck in attempting to formalize what initially appears to be an amorphous mass of knowledge.
- *The methodology must aim at getting the knowledge first.* As we have seen, there are lots of cases where knowledge acquisition is the time-critical component. A methodology must help with this stage.
- *The methodology must provide measurable milestones.* It is important to communicate a sense of progress in any project. If possible, there should be clear "deliverables" either on paper or in a working program to mark the progress towards a completed expert system.

Origins of the Step-by-Step Approach

Our approach had its start about two years ago when we began designing expert systems for troubleshooting Tektronix instruments. The project team consisted of an AI researcher, a cognitive psychologist, a software engineer, and an electronic engineer. The first problem we had to deal with was to establish a means of communication among such a diverse group. From work on the SIDUR project at Oregon State University (Freiling, 1983; Kogan, 1984), we had had some experience using formal grammars of English fragments as a documentation and communication tool. We decided to use a formal grammar to document the progress of our knowledge engineering efforts.

In order to build a grammar, however, we needed something to start with. So we sat down with several electronic engineers and technicians, and a schematic for the Tektronix FG-502 Function Generator, which we chose for its simplicity. A function generator is an instrument that generates waveforms of known shape and frequency as stimuli for testing electronic equipment. We asked these experts to tell us how they would go about troubleshooting the FG-502. We taped several hours of conversation and transcribed the troubleshooting knowledge onto paper. At this point, of course, the knowledge was in the form of English sentences.

As we collected more of the knowledge, we began to notice regularities. For example, the engineers would frequently mention the temporal relationship between two signals. The behavior of one signal would be considered important only when some other signal was at a particular value, such as low, or had already exhibited some event, such as crossing zero. Noticing that temporal comparisons were haphazardly scattered throughout many types of observations, we scheduled a couple of intensive sessions to define a systematic collection of comparisons between signals.

Gradually, our collection of example statements took the form of a grammar. During the transition, our document had a hybrid form which was part grammar and part examples. Finally, the grammar was at the point where we had enough to start the next phase of the knowledge engineering process. We christened the grammar GLIB (General Language for Instrument Behavior) (Freiling, 1984). Figure 1 shows a simplified fragment of the GLIB grammar for expressing the temporal relationships mentioned above. The semantics of these expressions are roughly the same as those used by other researchers in more general representations of time (Vilain, 1982; Allen, 1981).

At this stage, GLIB was not "complete" in any formal sense. GLIB is still undergoing modifications and extensions, as we learn new subtleties of the knowledge that electronic engineers and technicians possess. But the knowledge representation structures captured by GLIB at that point were sufficient to permit further progress.

We used GLIB as a guide to expressing the rules for our first prototype, the FG-502 troubleshooting assistant (Alexander, 1985). Although we did not then have a framework for rigorously enforcing GLIB syntax in our rule formats, the presence of the GLIB grammar greatly shortened the effort expended on acquiring

```
<temporal predicate> ::=
        <interval expression> BEFORE <interval expression> |
        <interval expression> DURING <interval expression> |
        <interval expression> AFTER  <interval expression> |
        <interval expression> WHENEVER <interval expression> |
        <ordinal integer> TIME THAT <interval expression> |
        <ordinal integer> OCCURRENCE OF <interval expression> |
        FROM <interval expression> UNTIL <interval expression>

<interval expression> ::=
        <interval adjustment> |
        <atomic interval expression>

<interval adjustment> ::=
        <interval expression> DELAYED BY <temporal value>

<atomic interval expression> ::=
        <signal> BECOMES <qualitative state> |
        <signal> ATTAINS <property> OF <value> |
        <signal> CROSSES <signal> |
        <signal> CROSSES <signal> GOING <polarity> |
        <signal> CROSSES <amplitude value> |
        <signal> CROSSES <amplitude value> GOING <polarity> |
        THE INTERVAL WHEN THE <property> OF <signal> <comparator> <value>

<polarity> ::= POSITIVE | NEGATIVE

<qualitative state> ::= HIGH | LOW  | ZERO | NEGATIVE

<property> ::= AMPLITUDE | FREQUENCY

<signal> ::= SIGNAL-<unsigned integer>

<value> ::= <amplitude value> | <frequency value>

<amplitude value> ::= <number> VOLTS

<frequency vlaue> ::= <number> HERTZ

<temporal value> ::= <number> SECONDS

<comparator> ::= IS | = | < | > | <= | >= | ~=
```

Figure 1. Fragment of GLIB grammar defining temporal relations between signals.

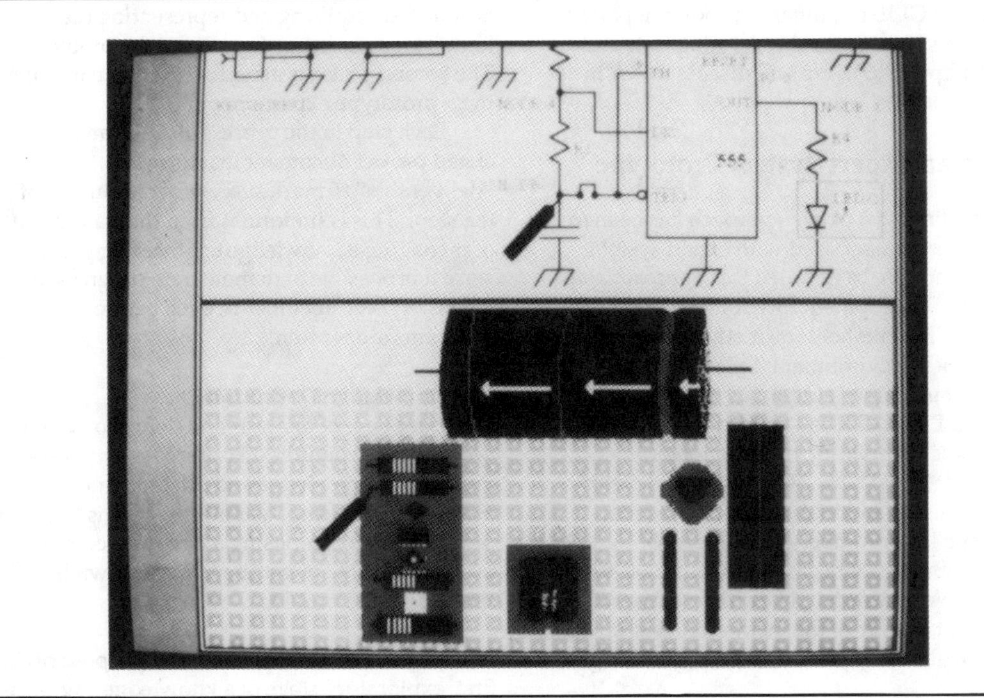

Figure 2.

actual rules, since we now had a collection of well-defined formats for expressing the knowledge acquired.

The primary focus of our prototype troubleshooting assistant for the FG-502 was on another aspect of the expert system implementation process, the development of a credible interface for technicians to use (Freiling, 1984a). As we mentioned earlier, the problem of acceptance of expert system technology requires serious consideration. From many discussions with technicians, we found that they were much more likely to be enthusiastic about expert systems if it offered them some personal added value.

Our clues to what this added value might consist of came by asking technicians what parts of their job were a needless waste of time. Several replied that leafing through the manual to find where a part is located was a distracting and frustrating task. Using these clues, we designed an interface for the FG-502 troubleshooting assistant which eliminates the need to consult a manual for part locations during the troubleshooting and repair process. Our use of Smalltalk (Goldberg, 1983), with its rich environment of graphics primitives, made it possible to implement this interface in a matter of weeks.

Using the interface, technicians can point to the location of a part in either a parts list, a schematic diagram, or a map of the actual circuit board, and retrieve the location and parts data automatically. This interface is also a great help during the troubleshooting process itself. Nodes which must be measured are indicated using icons that represent an oscilloscope probe, and parts to be removed are highlighted by reversing their color. Figures 2 and 3 show examples of this interface in use. The use of this type of interface, even (or perhaps, especially) in the first prototype, can have a major impact on the acceptance issues that every knowledge engineering project must face.

In helping others build their own expert system applications, we became aware of the wider applicability of this step-by-step approach to developing an expert system prototype. Communicating this approach to others has helped to minimize both development times and the level of external consulting required by other projects within Tektronix.

Our experience in developing these prototypes has encouraged us to build tools that support this approach to developing expert systems. One such tool is INKA (IN-glish Knowledge Acquisition), a knowledge acquisition system that uses the GLIB grammar to produce a parser that captures specific troubleshooting facts and rules (Phillips, 1985). We will discuss INKA in more detail later.

Steps to an Expert System Prototype

The overriding goal of our approach has been to reduce the costs associated with expert system development. We have called this approach the DETEKTR (Development Environment for TEKtronix TRoubleshooters) methodology, after a development environment (DETEKTR) we have been building to support it. We originally envisioned DETEKTR as a collection of domain-specific tools for building troubleshooters (Alexander, 1985a) because the costs of developing the grammar and interface could be amortized over a large number of troubleshooting assistants. But as we began to use our tools to support projects around Tektronix, we discovered that aspects of the methodology are relevant to almost any knowledge engineering problem.

Our methodology is divided into six steps, which fall into two general phases of the knowledge engineering project. The first phase is aimed at acquiring and representing the knowledge necessary for solving the problem. The second phase is aimed at actually constructing a prototype expert system.

Each step in the process also has an associated project document that forms a "deliverable" to mark successful conclusion of the step. This is important from the standpoint of managing a knowledge engineering project, since it is possible to demonstrate progress by means of these documents, even before programs are written.

The Knowledge Definition Phase

This is a phase of analysis and definition of the knowledge structures that precedes actual acquisition of knowledge and implementation of a prototype. The emphasis at this stage is to make progress on decomposing a large and complex problem, while not getting bogged down in the specifics of the problem.

Step 1: Familiarization. The purpose of the first, exploratory stage of a knowledge engineering project is to determine the scope and complexity of the task. Experienced knowledge engineers often know how to initiate this

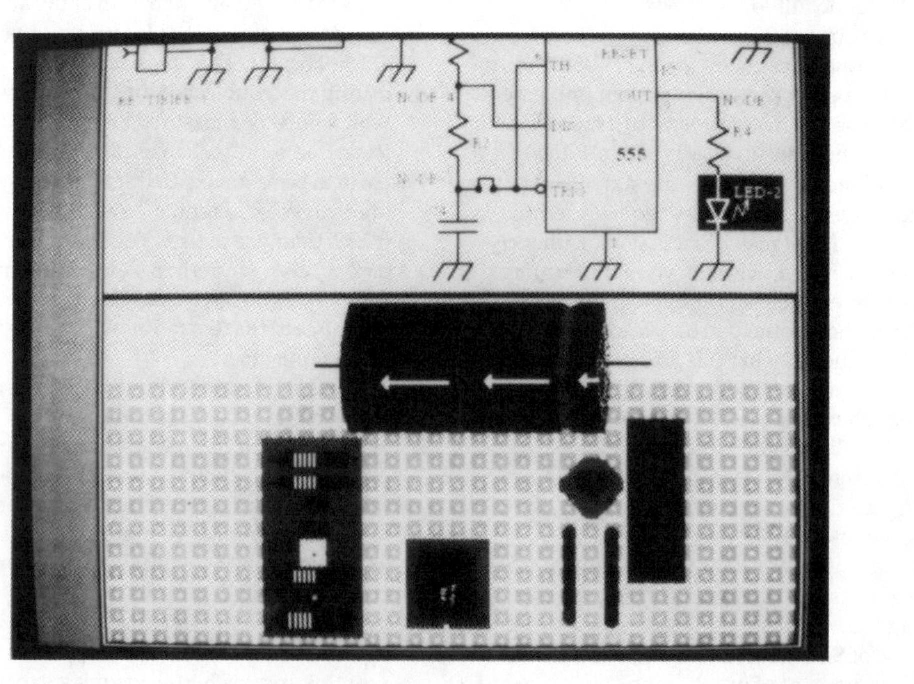

Figure 3.

KNOWLEDGE DEFINITION PHASE		
NUMBER	**STEP**	**PROJECT DOCUMENT**
(1)	Familiarization	Paper knowledge base
(2)	Organizing knowledge	Knowledge acquisition grammar
(3)	Representing knowledge	Internal knowledge base formats
PROTOTYPE IMPLEMENTATION PHASE		
NUMBER	**STEP**	**PROJECT DOCUMENT**
(4)	Acquiring knowledge	Knowledge base
(5)	Inference strategy design	Inference engine
(6)	Interface design	Interface

Table 1.

process by a combination of relatively unstructured interviews and observation sessions. Aspiring knowledge engineers, however, often get stymied at this point.

We have found it helpful to add structure to the initial interviews. The first thing to do is to pick a sample problem to work on that is more or less representative of the task for which you wish to build an expert system. It helps if this first example is on the simpler end of the complexity scale. It is possible to conduct the first sessions by either watching an expert solve the problem or talking to the expert about how the problem is most easily solved. Although experienced knowledge engineers might prefer the former approach because it is less intrusive, the more verbal approach is usually easier to start with.

A record of the sessions is made by taping them or by taking notes. After the session is over, the tape and the notes should be combed to produce a "paper knowledge base" consisting of English sentences that are representative expressions of the facts and rules the expert has given you. They do not, of course, need to be direct quotes from the expert. But they do need to be sentences that the expert can recognize as clear and unambiguous descriptions of relevant knowledge.

Figure 4 shows a fragment of the actual paper knowledge base produced in developing the FG-502 troubleshooting assistant. Notice that the paper knowledge base may employ highly stylized formats to make the knowledge structures clear. Also notice that at this stage of the knowledge engineering process, it is useful to store explanations for every single rule.

It may require many sessions with the expert to review and clarify the paper knowledge base before it reaches a stable form. The documentation of this stage of the project is the paper knowledge base itself.

Step 2: Organizing knowledge.
As the paper knowledge base collected in step 1 gets larger, it becomes unwieldy. At the same time, it should begin to exhibit some regularity in the sense that expressions of similar form reappear frequently in the document. The next step is to capture these regularities by building a knowledge acquisition grammar to express the facts and rules in the paper knowledge base. We are not suggesting that the grammar must be built along linguistic lines, which would require the use of grammatical categories like "prepositional phrase" and "relative clause." It is easier to build a "semantic grammar" (Burton, 1976), especially if the personnel involved do not

have a background in linguistics. In a semantic grammar, the grammatical categories are derived from concepts related directly to the problem under consideration. For example, the GLIB syntax for the category <rule> is

<rule> ::=IF <observation> THEN <conclusion>

and one grammar rule defining the category <observation> is

<observation> ::= <signal> HAS <property> OF <value>

Figure 1 shows a fragment of the syntax of GLIB. The documentation at this step of the project is the syntactic definition of this knowledge acquisition grammar.

Step 3: Representing knowledge. Once the English-like knowledge acquisition grammar has been specified, it is then used to guide the process of deciding how the knowledge is to be represented in a prototype expert system. The simplest way to do this is to begin with the categories of the semantic grammar. Nearly all these categories will be meaningful from the standpoint of a representation. It is necessary to determine a specific form for storing instances of the category. Assuming the target inference engine will run in Prolog, a corresponding syntax for the rule about observations might be

<observation> ::= <property>(<signal>, <value>)

which produces structures like

voltage (signal-3, high)
frequency (signal-3, 5000)

The documentation at this stage the definition of internal knowledge base formats as they relate to the acquisition grammar syntax. We have used lexical functional grammar constraints (Kaplan, 1982) to accomplish this, but any appropriate mapping technique will suffice. Lexical functional grammar constraints will be discussed later. Figure 11 shows an example of these constraints, attached to a fragment of the GLIB grammar.

The Prototype Implementation Phase

Once the external and internal knowledge base formats have been defined, they can be used to guide

```
RULE-BL-4
IF       (1) V(N20) is not equal to V(N24),
THEN            (1) the source follower block is FAILED.

         EXPLANATION: Under correct behavior, a triangle voltage is being
         generated at N20 and N24, in phase with each other. Disruption of
         the loop causes voltages to converge to DC values, because the
         loop itself is required for alternating behavior.

RULE-BL-5
IF       (1) V(N24) is HIGH,
   AND   (2) V(N20) is HIGH,
   AND   (3) V(N19) is HIGH,
THEN            (1) the triangle wave comparator block is FAILED.

         EXPLANATION: Under correct behavior, the voltage at N19 acts as
         a "terminating condition" for the ramp being generated. Normally,
         then, it should be opposite in sign from the voltage at N20. When
         this does not occur, the comparator block is not generating the
         correct voltage at N19.

RULE-BL-6
IF       (1) V(N24) is LOW,
   AND   (2) V(N20) is LOW,
   AND   (3) V(N19) is LOW,
THEN            (1) the triangle wave comparator block is FAILED.

         EXPLANATION: All three of rules BL-3, BL-5, and BL-6 are
         needed to deduce failure in the triangle wave comparator
         block, because all three conditions are manifestations of
         various failure modes for that block.
```

Figure 4.

the implementation of a prototype expert system. The implementation process consists of acquiring the knowledge base, building an inference engine, and building an appropriate interface.

Step 4: Acquiring knowledge. Once a semantic grammar and a mapping to internal rule formats have been defined, it is possible to make a wholesale effort to acquire knowledge relevant to a particular task. This can be accomplished in several ways. The most convenient is to use a tool that allows the expert to generate English expressions conforming to the knowledge acquisition grammar and translates these automatically into the target formats.

Figure 5 shows some sample external and internal rules captured by the INKA knowledge acquisition tool for troubleshooting the simple circuit shown in Figure 6. We will discuss INKA in more detail later.

```
THE CIRCUIT CONTAINS OSCILLATOR-1 AND POWERSUPPLY-1.
has_component(block(circuit), block(oscillator(1))).
has_component(block(circuit), block(powersupply(1))).

RESISTOR-1 IS PART OF OSCILLATOR-1.
has_component(block(oscillator(1)), component(resistor(1))).

IF LED-2 IS NOT FLASHING AND THE VOLTAGE OF NODE-2 IS EQUAL
TO 15 VOLTS THEN OSCILLATOR-1 HAS FAILED.
rule(and(not(state(led(2), flashing))),
        comp(voltage(node(2)), 15)),
   status(block(oscillator(1)), failed),
   []).

IF LED-1 IS DIM AND LED-2 IS OFF THEN RESISTOR-1 HAS FAILED.
rule(and(state(led(1), dim),
        state(led(2), off)),
   status(component(resistor(1)), failed),
   []).
```

Figure 5. Internal and external formats for INKA rule base.

The documentation of this step is a prototype knowledge base, containing facts and rules specifically relevant to the prototype under construction. The prototype knowledge base will exist in two forms, an external knowledge base consisting of rules as acquired from the expert in English and an internal knowledge base, ready to be processed by some inference engine.

Step 5: Inference strategy design. Once a partial knowledge base has been acquired, it is time to build or select an inference engine to process the knowledge base. This is the point at which the work by Stefik et al. (1982) becomes relevant. Because of their prior exercises in acquiring and building the knowledge base, the project team has a much better familiarity with the requirements of the problem and are able to make a more educated choice of inference strategies. Ideally, choices about the knowledge representation would enlighten this decision, but to date we have not found any method to improve on Stefik's informal analysis. We have found in some simple cases, however, that the same knowledge base can be reused with progressively more sophisticated inference engines.

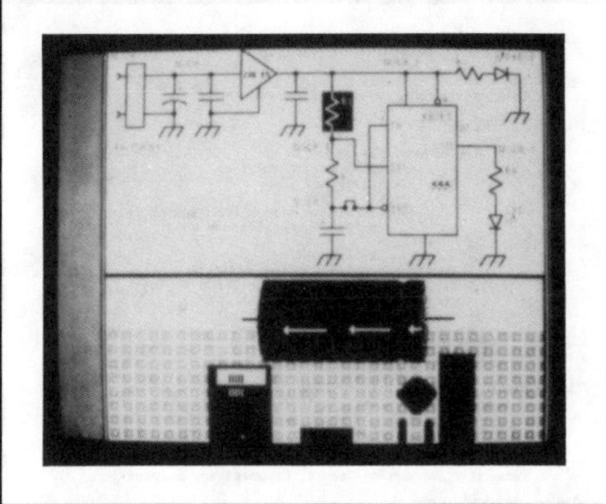

Figure 6. Sample circuit display in INKA.

These findings partially confirm our hypothesis that extracting and articulating the knowledge is the most important phase of the expert system development process. Figure 7 shows simplified Prolog code for two different inference strategies for troubleshooting an electronic instrument. The first is called top-down localization and is similar to the engine used in INKA. The second uses a strategy of direct hypotheses to make educated guesses about where to look for failures. Although additional knowledge (in the form of heuristics) is required to make the hypothesis-based engine work, the actual tests are determined by the same knowledge as used by the first strategy.

The documentation at this stage of the project is a running inference engine.

Step 6: Interface design. As we mentioned before, the design of an effective interface is extremely important in delivering acceptable expert systems. Generally this involves trying to discover what parts of the task are routine and can be handled in an effective interface. In the FG-502 troubleshooting assistant, for instance, we found that helping the technicians locate parts could save them time in troubleshooting instruments. Similar techniques have been used in managing graphical service documents at Brown (Feiner, 1982) and also on the Steamer project at BBN (Hollan, 1984). The number and quality of available primitives can have a large effect on the quality of an interface that can be produced in some fixed period of time. The documentation at this point in the project is a prototype interface.

```
TOP-DOWN LOCALIZATION:
A SIMPLE INFERENCE MECHANISM

RULE FORMAT:
        diagnostic_rule_exists_for(Module, Unit).

PRIMARY INFERENCE LOOP:

        diagnose(Module, FailingUnit) :-
                is_replaceable_unit(Module),
                Module = FailingUnit.

                        ; terminate search when search leads to
                        ; a failing replaceable unit.

        diagnose(Module, FailingUnit) :-
                choose_subsystem(Module, SubUnit),
                diagnostic_rule_exists_for(SubUnit, Test),
                performs_successfully(Test),
                diagnose(SubUnit, FailingUnit).

HYPOTHESIS-BASED STRATEGY:
A MORE POWERFUL MECHANISM

RULE FORMATS:
        diagnostic_rule_exists_for(Module, Unit).

                        ; identical to previous rule,
                        ; same interpretation as before.

        heuristic_connection(Module, Observation, Suspect).

PRIMARY INFERENCE LOOP:

        diagnose(Module, FailingUnit) :-
                is_replaceable_unit(Module),
                Module = FailingUnit.

                        ; terminate search when search leads to
                        ; a failing replaceable unit.

        diagnose(Module, FailingUnit) :-
                heuristic_connection(Module, Observation, Suspect),
                performs_successfully(Observation),
                diagnose_hypothesis(Module, Suspect, FailingUnit).

                        ; this rule tries to find hypotheses for
                        ; a failure if no hypotheses are available.
                        ; failures occuring at a particular module.

        diagnose(Module, FailingUnit) :-
                choose_subsystem(Module, SubUnit),
                not(tested(SubUnit)),
                diagnostic_rule_exists_for(SubUnit, Test),
                performs_successfully(Test),
                diagnose(SubUnit, FailingUnit).

                        ; this rule provides a backup when no
                        ; hypotheses are applicable, that performs
                        ; identically to top-down localization.


        diagnose_hypothesis(Module, Suspect, FailingUnit) :-
                assert(tested(Suspect))
                diagnose(Suspect, FailingUnit).

                        ; this rule establishes that a suspect
                        ; has been tested (so it is only tested once)
                        ; and attempts to diagnose a failure in the
                        ; suspected module.
```

Figure 7. Two troubleshooting inference machines.

Features of the Methodology

As we mentioned before, one major advantage of a methodological approach to knowledge engineering is that it provides a basis for communicating about the progress of a knowledge engineering project. All too often, knowledge engineering projects become a black hole, and managers have difficulty perceiving signs of progress. With a clear sense of stages and documentation which can be delivered at each milestone, it becomes possible to say "We've completed the knowledge organization phase and we're now defining the representation," rather than "We're working on it."

The major question that arises about our methodology is whether it is possible to define the forms for representing knowledge before understanding the uses to which the knowledge will be put. It has been observed by many researchers that knowledge engineering is very much a chicken and egg phenomenon (Buchanan, 1983). The types of knowledge that will be useful and the forms in which this knowledge should be represented depend on the inference strategies to process the knowledge. On the other hand, determining an appropriate inference strategy requires knowing something about the knowledge required to solve the problem.

How can this loop be broken? Our experience is that the knowledge as elicited from the expert consists primarily of references to objects, relations, observations, and events which are well known in the problem world. Only at the final level of grammatical processing do these references aggregate into heuristic connections, say between an observation and a conclusion. The part of GLIB that relates to specific assumptions about the inference strategies to be used, for instance, amounts to probably less than 1% of the total.

This knowledge is likely to contain much in the way of qualitative descriptions and categories which the expert finds useful in discussing the problem. To a first approximation, it is precisely these hints as to the correct levels of abstraction that we want to acquire from the expert in the first place.

If an expert instrument troubleshooter uses a rough qualitative characterization of voltage levels, such as "high" and "low" in describing how to troubleshoot the device, this qualitative categorization of the rules represents an abstraction that the expert finds useful. Whatever inference strategies we may utilize to heuristically connect behavior and its interpretation, it is quite likely that the underlying knowledge will be most effectively processed at this level of abstraction.

Of course, the problem still remains as to how to characterize the qualitative distinctions between "high" and "low" when measurements are made that do not automatically correspond to the expert's categorization. Brown et al. (1982) have discussed techniques for performing this particular qualitative abstraction. We are currently working on an analytical technique for defining these abstractions and their effects in any knowledge engineering problem.

With respect to the interpretation of specific heuristic associations, we note that these connections tend to appear only at the highest level of aggregation of an expert's knowledge. For example, particular troubleshooting rules might be captured from an expert in the form

IF <observation> THEN <conclusion>

These rules might be interpreted as defining rigorous tests that guarantee the conclusion or heuristic associations that relate symptoms to their causes. Distinguishing between these possible interpretations is not possible on the basis of the syntactic expression alone.

In either case, the syntactic structure shown above is likely to be used. It is therefore possible to build the syntax for an expert's expressions without needing immediately to assign an interpretation to them. Herein lies the usefulness of having an external knowledge base, because these associations can even be captured without specific commitment to their interpretation in a particular inference strategy. When interpretation finally becomes inevitable, the external knowledge base provides a store of expressions for processing under whatever assumptions about interpretation are most appropriate. Even when changes are made to these interpretations, the knowledge need not be re-acquired. Even in extreme cases where a dialogue with the expert is necessary to make the correct interpretation, the syntactic structures of the external rule base provide a convenient means for discriminating those expressions that will require close analysis from those that will not.

Variations on the Methodology

The methodology we have presented is, in fact, quite detailed. There are many examples of simple knowledge engineering applications where it does not make sense to follow this approach rigidly. Steps can be skipped or combined, depending on the common sense of the project team and its management.

An example of how this methodology may be varied to suit particular needs is provided by the history of development of a Wave Solder Machine Operator's Assistant, being built by Sal Faruqui and Bill Barton in Tektronix' Lab Instruments Division.

Figure 8 shows a sample dialogue with the program. This program is not especially complicated. The wave solder machine operator checks boards as they are soldered for obvious defects like bridges or holes. When a defect is noticed, the operator must adjust one or more operating parameters of the soldering machine.

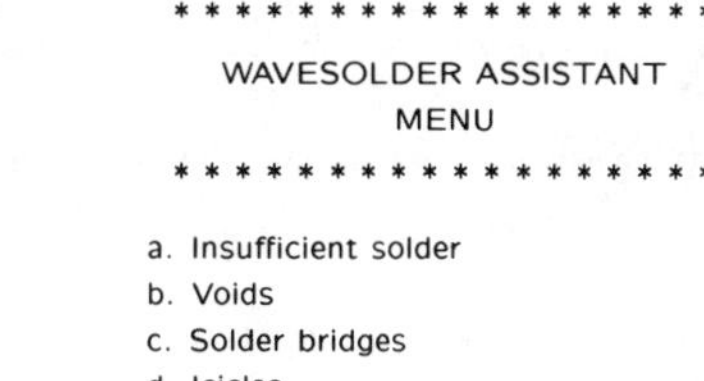

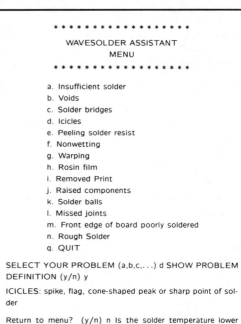

```
*****************
WAVESOLDER ASSISTANT
MENU
*****************

a. Insufficient solder
b. Voids
c. Solder bridges
d. Icicles
e. Peeling solder resist
f. Nonwetting
g. Warping
h. Rosin film
i. Removed Print
j. Raised components
k. Solder balls
l. Missed joints
m. Front edge of board poorly soldered
n. Rough Solder
q. QUIT

SELECT YOUR PROBLEM (a,b,c,...) d SHOW PROBLEM DEFINITION (y/n) y

ICICLES: spike, flag, cone-shaped peak or sharp point of solder

Return to menu? (y/n) n Is the solder temperature lower than 450 degrees? (y,n) n Is the flux density higher than 850? (y/n) n Is the preheat temperature lower than 730 degrees? (y/n) y Increase the preheat temperature to 730 degrees.
```

Figure 8. Sample dialogue with Wave Solder Machine Operator's Advisor.

The important thing about the wave solder operator's assistant is that, though simple, it is typical of many small problems that can be profitably attacked with a knowledge engineering solution, provided costs can be kept acceptably low.

A variation on the DETEKTR methodology was used to manage development of this system. Because of the simplicity of the problem and the fact that it was to be a one-of-a-kind system, it was not necessary to formally define a knowledge acquisition grammar. Instead, the paper knowledge base was transcribed directly to Prolog.

Figure 9 shows an example of the paper knowledge base as it migrated into Prolog. The wave solder machine operator's assistant has passed preliminary testing by an expert on the insufficient solder (holes not full, or poor wicking, or several leads not soldered; affecting the integrity of solder joints)

decrease conveyor speed :- several leads not soldered, or holes not full, and conveyor speed high (5)

increase flux level :- holes not full, or poor wicking, or several leads not soldered, and flux level low (3)

increase preheat temperature :- several leads not soldered, and preheat temperature low (4)

increase solder wave :- holes not full, and solder wave low (4)

VOID (blowhole, or pinhole, or hollow area; poor bond affecting the integrity of solder joints)

decrease flux density :- popping rosin beads exist, and flux density high (5)

increase preheat temperature :- preheat temperature low (4)

recycle boards :- process ok, and voids exist after first pass (4)

decrease conveyor speed :- conveyor speed high (3)

increase solder temperature :- solder temperature low (4)

isolate boards and contact manager :- contamination exists (4)

solder bridge (deposit of solder that short circuits an electrical connection)

increase solder temperature :- solder temperature low [4]

decrease flux density :- flux density high [4]

increase preheat temperature :- preheat temperature low [5]

rotate board 90 degrees :- problem leads are lined up in the direction of travel

isolate boards and contact manager :- leads are longer than 3/16

icicle (spike, or flag, or cone-shaped peak, or sharp point of solder over 3/16)

increase solder temperature :- solder temperature low [5]

decrease flux density :- flux density high [3]

increase preheat temperature :- preheat temperature low

Figure 9. Wave Solder rule base in transit to Prolog clauses.

solder machine's operation. Operational testing is scheduled for June 1985.

Tools for Knowledge Engineering

The DETEKTR methodology provides a view of the knowledge engineering process that emphasizes acquisition and analysis of the knowledge prior to construction of a prototype. The inference strategy to be employed is considered only after much work has already been done.

This view dictates a concrete approach to the idea of a development environment for expert systems. Inference mechanisms are only one of the tools needed to support the progress from interview transcripts to prototype. The knowledge engineering environment to support a methodology like this will also need tools to

- Support the mapping from paper knowledge base to grammar.
- Support analysis of the grammar and definition of the internal knowledge base formats.
- Permit selection from a catalog of inference strategies.
- Build natural language and graphical interfaces.

DETEKTR is designed as a prototype development environment for expert systems that consists of a collection of tools of the form described. These tools have been specialized in our case to support development of expert systems for troubleshooting electronic instruments. The principles behind the tools, however, apply to other problem worlds as well.

INKA is a tool that supports the acquisition of troubleshooting rules for electronic instruments. Using the INGLISH interface (Phillips, 1984), INKA translates expressions from GLIB into Prolog clauses, which are processed by a specialized troubleshooting inference engine written in Prolog. INKA could easily be modified to provide a knowledge acquisition system for other problems as well. The input to INKA is a semantic grammar representing the external knowledge base format, and a mapping to an internal format. INKA acquires troubleshooting rules in the external format and passes them to a prolog inference engine for processing. Figure 10 shows INKA in operation.

The mapping to an internal format is accomplished by supplying lexical functional constraints (Kaplan, 1982) that map categories from the GLIB grammar to internal forms.

Figure 11 shows a fragment of the GLIB grammar that has been annotated with the necessary lexical functional constraints.

When a rule has been parsed, as shown in Figure 12, the constraints act to propagate functional attributes, like FORM, STATE, and IND, from lower grammatical categories to higher ones. Referring to Figure 12, for instance, the constraint above the category <condition>,

$$(\uparrow \text{COND}) = \downarrow$$

governs propagation of all functional attributes (including one called FORM) to the level of the category <rule>, to be stored under the

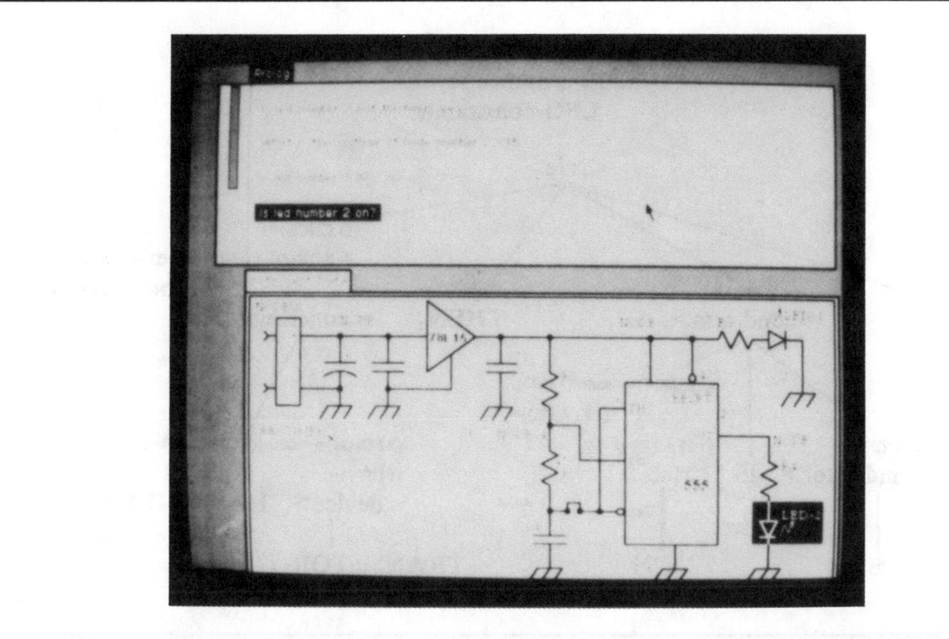

Figure 10.

functional attribute COND. In like manner, the first constraint above <conclusion>

(↑ CNCL) = ↓

governs propagation of all attributes to the CNCL property of the <rule> category. Then the second constraint above <conclusion>,

(FORM) = (<rule ((↑ COND FORM), (↑ CNCL FORM))>

retrieves these two attributes, COND and CNCL, and combines their FORMs to build a FORM for the category <rule>. The final rule constructed, then, resides in the FORM attribute of <rule> and is passed on to Prolog as

rule(state(led-2,on),status(transistor-17,failed)).

These lexical functional constraints are the sole definition of the Prolog-based internal

```
                                         (↑ CNCL)=↓
                   (↑ COND)=↓            (↑ FORM)=<rule((↑ COND FORM), (↑ CNCL FORM))>
<rule>      --> IF <condition> THEN <conclusion>

                                  (↑ FORM)=<state((↑ IND), (↑ STATE))>
                   (↑ IND)=↓          (↑ STATE)=↓
<condition> --> <indicator> IS <state>

                 (↑ FORM)=<status((↑ DEV), failed)>
                 (↑ DEV)=↓
<conclusion>--> <device> HAS FAILED
```

Figure 11. Fragment of GLIB grammar with LFG constraints.

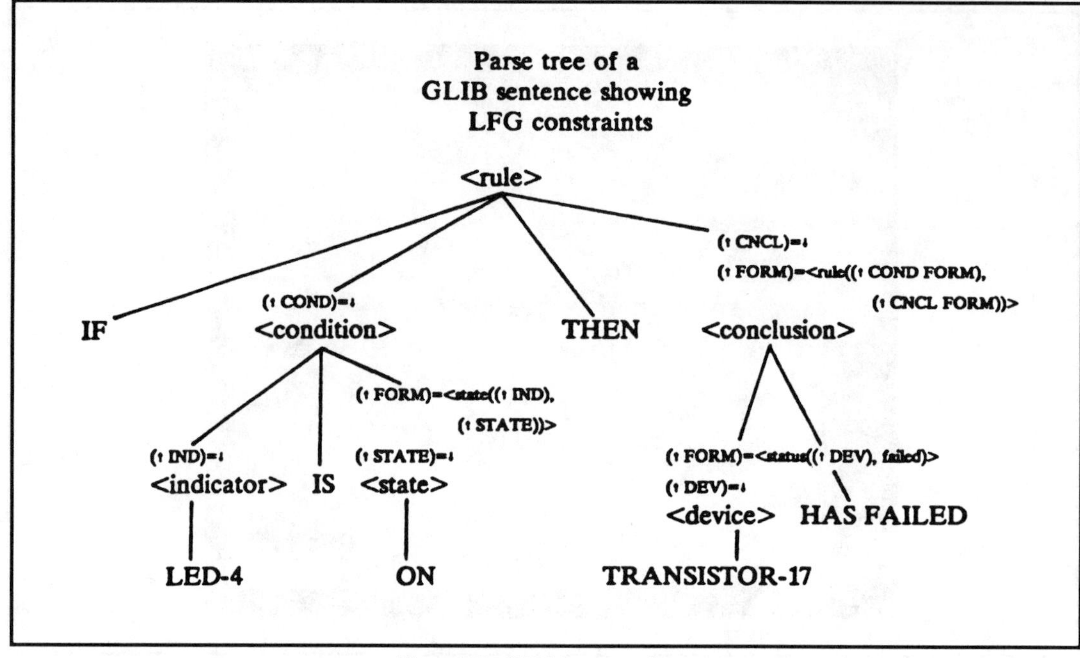

Figure 12. INKA in operation.

knowledge base formats. The GLIB grammar itself depends in no way on the choice of Prolog as a target representation. The rules acquired could be as easily compiled into Lisp, or some other format.

INKA combines the semantic acquisition grammar and internal format definitions to build a parser that acquires rules in the grammar and translates them into the proper internal forms. The rules can then be tested by an inference engine running in the background.

Several features make this a convenient interface to use. When typing a rule, menus can be selected to guide the user (Figure 13). The system also supports phrase completion and spelling correction.

PIKA (Pictorial Knowledge Acquisition) is a graphics editor that produces as its output not a simple picture, but a collection of structured graphical objects. The structure is important to facilitate their use for pointing to and cross-referencing components of the diagram. These structured objects can be assembled to support a multi-level display interface.

Figure 14 shows an example of PIKA being used to create a circuit schematic.

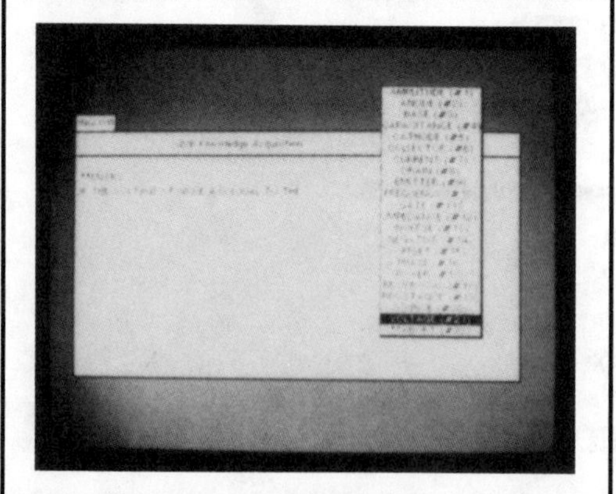

Figure 13. Using menus in INKA to express rules.

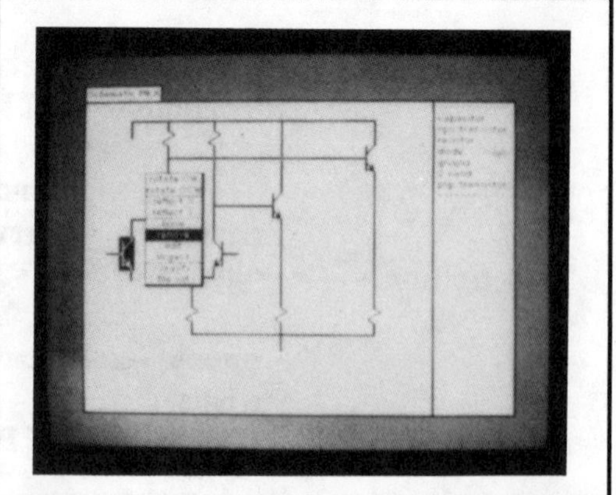

Figure 14. Using PIKA to build a schematic diagram.

A third tool—still in the design stages—is CHEKA (Checker for Knowledge Acquisition). CHEKA accepts a collection of integrity constraints developed during the analysis of a problem and checks new rules being added by INKA for consistency with these constraints. CHEKA will use techniques developed at the Japanese Institute for New Generation Computer Technology (Kitakami, 1984; Miyachi, 1984) that relies on explicit statement of constraints to determine consistency of a particular set of facts and rules.

In a complete development environment to support our methodology, some tools would be general purpose, while others might be specifically tuned to a particular problem world. People using the tools would choose problem-specific tools when available and general tools when specific tools did not exist. The important thing is that the collection of tools support a step-by-step approach to knowledge engineering, always providing some way to keep making progress on the problem at hand.

Conclusions

From our experience in teaching the knowledge engineering process to software engineers at Tektronix, we have discovered that the most important need for expert system prototype development is the need for techniques to examine a problem and begin to turn its amorphous shape into something concrete enough so that a prototype system can be created.

We have demonstrated one approach to this problem that uses formal grammars as a documentation technique in managing these early stages of development. Much more work needs to be done, however, to provide a gradual and step-by-step approach that does not require years of training before it can be used. Tools which support these steps of familiarization, definition, and acquisition of an expert's knowledge will doubtless form the backbone of future expert system development tools.

References

Alexander, J. H. & Freiling, M. J. 1985. Smalltalk-80 aids troubleshooting system development. *Systems and Software* 4, 4.

Alexander, J. H., Freiling, M. J., Messick, S. L., & Rehfuss, S. 1985a. *Efficient expert system development through domain specific tools.* Fifth International Workshop on Expert Systems and their Applications.

Allen, J. F. 1981. *An interval-based representation of temporal knowledge.* IJCAI-7.

Boose, J. H. 1984. *Personal construct theory and the transfer of human expertise.* AAAI-84.

Brachman, R. & Levesque, H. 1982. *Competence in knowledge representation.* AAAI-82.

Brown, J. S., Burton, R. R., & deKleer, J. 1982. Pedagogical, natural language, and knowledge engineering techniques in SOPHIE I, II, and III. In D. Sleeman & J. S. Brown (Eds.), *Intelligent Tutoring Systems.* New York: Academic Press.

Buchanan, B. G., Barstow, D., Bechtal, R., Bennett, J., Clancey, W., Kulikowski, C., Mitchell, T., & Waterman, D. A. 1983. Constructing an Expert System. In F. Hayes-Roth, D. A. Waterman, & D. B. Lenat (Eds.), *Building Expert Systems.* Reading, MA: Addison-Wesley.

Burton, R. R. 1976. Semantic Grammar: An engineering technique for constructing natural language understanding systems. Tech. Rep. 3453 Bolt, Beranek, and Newman, Cambridge, MA.

Clancey, W. J. 1984. *Classification problem solving.* AAAI-84.

Feiner, S., Nagy, S., & Dam, A. Van 1982. An experimental system for creating and presenting interactive Graphical Documents. *ACM Transactions on Graphics.* Vol. 1, No. 1.

Freiling, M. J. 1983. SIDUR—an integrated data model. IEEE Compcon, IEEE Computer Society.

Freiling, M. J. & Alexander, J. H. 1984a. *Diagrams and grammars: tools for the mass production of expert systems.* First Conference on Artificial Intelligence Applications. IEEE Computer Society.

Freiling, M. J., Alexander, J. H., Feucht, D., & Stubbs, D. 1984. GLIB—a language for describing the behavior of electronic devices. Applied Research Tech. Rep. CR-84-12 Tektronix, Inc., Beaverton, OR.

Goldberg, A. & Robson, D. 1983. *Smalltalk 80: the language and its implementation.* Reading, MA: Addison-Wesley.

Hollan, J. D., Hutchins, E. L., & Weitzman, L. 1984. STEAMER: an interactive inspectable simulation-based training system. *AI Magazine* Vol. 5, No. 2.

Kaplan, R. M. & Bresnan, J. W. 1982. Lexical-functional grammar: a formal system for grammatical representation. In J. W. Bresnan (Ed.), *The Mental Representation of Grammatical Relations.* Cambridge, MA: MIT Press.

Kitakami, H., Kunifuji, S., Miyachi, T., & Furukawa, K. 1984. *A methodology for implementation of a knowledge acquisition system.* 1984 International Symposium on Logic Programming. IEEE Computer Society.

Kogan, D. D. & Freiling, M. J. 1984. *SIDUR—a structuring formalism for knowledge information processing systems.* International Conference on Fifth Generation Computer Systems. Institute for New Generation Computer Technology (ICOT). Tokyo, Japan.

Kunz, J., Kehler, T., & Williams, M. 1984. Applications development using a hybrid AI development system. *AI Magazine* Vol. 5, No. 3.

Miyachi, T., Kunifuji, S., Kitakami, H., Furukawa, K., Takeuchi, A., & Yokota, H. 1984. *A knowledge assimilation method for logic databases.* 1984 International Symposium on Logic Programming. IEEE Computer Society.

Phillips, B. & Nicholl, S. 1984. INGLISH: A natural language interface. Applied Research Tech. Rep. CR-84-27, Tektronix, Inc., Beaverton, OR.

Phillips, B., Messick, S. L., Freiling, M. J., & Alexander, J. H. 1985. INKA: The Inglish knowledge acquisition interface for electronic instrument troubleshooting systems. Applied Research Tech. Rep. CR-85-04, Tektronix, Inc., Beaverton, OR.

Stefik, M., Aikins, J., Balzer, R., Benoit, J., Birnbaum, L., Hayes-Roth, F., & Sacerdoti, E. 1982. The organization of expert systems: A prescriptive tutorial. Xerox PARC Tech. Rep., Palo Alto, CA.

VanMelle, W., Shortliffe, E. H., & Buchanan, B. G. 1984. EMYCIN: A knowledge engineer's tool for constructing rule-based expert systems. In B. G. Buchanan & E. H. Shortliffe (Eds.), *Rule-Based Expert Systems.* Reading, MA: Addison-Wesley.

Vilain, M. B. 1982. *A system for reasoning about time.* AAAI-82.

Selection of an Appropriate Domain for an Expert System

David S. Prerau

This article discusses the selection of the domain for a knowledge-based expert system. In particular, it focuses on selecting an expert system domain for a corporate application. The choosing of the domain is a critical task in the development of an expert system, and thus a significant amount of effort should go into the selection process.

Background

Interest in artificial intelligence by the corporate business community has been growing dramatically in the last few years, and many corporations have set up AI groups or are in the process of doing so. One of the prime areas of corporate interest is expert systems. Though the number of expert systems actually functioning in a corporate environment is still relatively small, the number of projects looking into expert system development is growing rapidly.

The knowledge engineering project team working on an expert system development must investigate possible application domains. In some cases there is a very specific application, chosen by management, for which an expert system is to be developed. In this situation, it is likely that those who selected the application area had little technical knowledge of artificial intelligence or expert systems. Thus, the project team must decide whether the selected application is one that is best suited to solution by present expert system technology, or if there might be a better way (or, possibly, no way) to attack the problem.

In other cases, the project team is asked to select one of several corporate problems or to survey corporate concerns to find a good application of expert system technology. Here, the project team must not only decide if an application is suited to present expert system technology, but must also rank potential domains and select the best available application.

To evaluate the potential of a possible application, it has proven very useful to have a set of the attributes desired in a good expert system domain. This article provides such a set of attributes. The set includes technical attributes as well as attributes related to non-technical corporate issues.

An Application Domain Evaluation Process

The set of desired expert system domain attributes was developed as part of a major expert system development project at GTE Laboratories. It was used recurrently (and modified and expanded continually) throughout an extensive application domain evaluation and selection process. Over 50 corporate managers and "experts" were interviewed, and over 30 extremely diverse possible expert system applications areas were considered, at least briefly. This list was narrowed to eight major possibilities, and these were further analyzed and ranked. Two primary candidate areas were studied in great detail. Finally, one application area was chosen, and our system development was begun.

Reprinted with permission from *AI Magazine*, vol. 6, no. 2, Summer 1985, 26-30. The material in this paper has been expanded by Dr. Prerau into a full chapter of his book, *Developing and Managing Expert Systems: Proven Techniques for Business and Industry*, Addison-Wesley Publishing Company, 1990.

At each stage of the selection process, the set of attributes proved very useful. In initial interviews, a discussion of the attributes was an excellent way to give our interviewees, who usually knew nothing about artificial intelligence or expert systems, some quick idea of the sort of application area for which we were looking. As each potential application surfaced, a brief check through the desired attribute list enabled us to identify possible problems related to the candidate area, and then to focus our further questions. When the set of major possibilities was determined, we were easily able to highlight the good and bad points of each potential application. Finally, when the actual application area was decided upon, we used the attribute list to justify the decision. One further point: at each step, the list proved very useful to justify the dropping of politically favored candidate areas.

Desired Properties of the Domain

This section presents a set of desired attributes for the domain of an expert system for a corporate application. Though many of these attributes are applicable to all expert systems, there are some that are specific to the development of an expert system in a corporate environment. These involve, for example, the likelihood of corporate acceptance of a system, the support for the system development by corporate management, etc. There are probably analogous points that apply to an academic or other environment, but these are not addressed here.

The attribute set was developed from the perspective of providing a real working expert system to solve a corporate problem, using state of the art expert system techniques. The discovery of new or better methods for expert system development was not an objective—in fact, a domain that requires a major breakthrough in expert system methodology is probably not a good domain to choose if the goal is to maximize the likelihood of success. Yet, any project that is the first to attack a particular domain is likely to find some unique properties of the domain that may require new approaches.

There may be a degree of commonality among some of the attributes listed in this section. However, to encourage consideration of the different aspects of domain selection, these commonalities were not eliminated.

Very few of these desired attributes are absolute, and it is unlikely that any domain will meet all of them completely. Furthermore, in each different situation the weighting of the factors will be different, and additional factors may apply. This set does provide, however, a fairly extensive list of aspects to consider in domain selection.

Basic Requirements

- *The domain is characterized by the use of expert knowledge, judgment, and experience.* The goal of the project is to extract a portion of an expert's knowledge, judgment and experience, and put it in a program.
- *Conventional programming (algorithmic) approaches to the task are not satisfactory.* If a conventional approach will work well, there is usually less technical risk to using it rather than an expert system approach. Note, however, that expert system methodology may offer some additional advantages over conventional techniques, such as the expected ease of updating and maintaining a knowledge base and the ability to explain results.
- *There are recognized experts who solve the problem today.* If an area is too new or too quickly changing, there may be no real experts. However, these are often the areas that are suggested for expert system developments.
- *The experts are probably better than amateurs in performing the task.* Thus, the task does require expertise.
- *Expertise is not or will not be available on a reliable and continuing basis,* i.e., *there is a need to "capture" the expertise.* Thus, there is a need for the expert system. For example: (1) expertise is scarce, (2) expertise is expensive, (3) there is a strong dependence on overworked experts, and/or (4) expertise is available today, but will be unavailable, or less available, in the future.
- *The completed system is expected to have a significant payoff for the corporation.*
- *Among possible application domains, the domain selected is that one that best meets overall project goals regarding project payoff versus risk of failure.* For example, a conservative approach would be to attempt to develop a system that would meet some criterion for minimum payoff if successful, and that seems to offer the best chance of success.

Type of Problem

- *The task primarily requires symbolic reasoning.* For a task that primarily involves numerical computation, consideration should also be given to other programming approaches.
- *The task requires the use of heuristics,* e.g., *rules of thumb, strategies, etc. It may require consideration of an extremely large number of possibilities or it may require decisions to be based upon incomplete or uncertain information.* A strength of expert systems is their ability to handle heuristics. Problems with very large numbers of possibilities or with incomplete or uncertain information are difficult to attack by conventional approaches, but may be amenable to expert system methodologies.
- *The task does not require knowledge from a very large number of areas.* If it did, the amount of knowledge needed for the expert system would probably be beyond acceptable limits. Also, there are difficulties in combining very heterogeneous knowledge.
- *The system development has as its goal either to develop a system for actual use or to make major advances in the state of the art of expert system technology, but does not attempt to achieve both of these goals simultaneously.* Doing both simultaneously is laudable, but more difficult.
- *The task is defined very clearly: At the project outset, there should be a precise definition of the inputs and outputs of the system to be developed.* This is a good attribute of any task. However, it is not necessary that the task definition be fixed for all time. As the system evolves and as situations change, it should be possible to change the task definition accordingly.

The Expert

- *There exists an expert to work with the project.* This is the source of expertise.
- *The expert's knowledge and reputation must be such that if the expert system is able to capture a portion of the expert's expertise, the system's output will have credibility and authority.* Otherwise, the system may not be used. (This may not be necessary in a domain where an accepted test for "goodness" of result exists.)
- *The expert has built up expertise over a long period of task performance.* Thus, the expert has had the amount of experience necessary to be able to develop the insights into the area that result in heuristics.
- *The expert will commit a substantial amount of time to the development of the system.* This is often a problem. The best experts, in the most important corporate areas, are usually the ones that can be least spared from their usual position.
- *The expert is capable of communicating his knowledge, judgment, and experience, and the methods used to apply them to the particular task.* It is important to find an expert who has not only the expertise, but also the ability to impart it to the project team, whose members probably know little or nothing about the subject area. The expert should be able to introspect to analyze his reasoning process, and then should be able to describe the reasoning process clearly to the project team, and to discuss it with them.
- *The expert is cooperative.* The expert should be eager to work on the project or, at worst, nonantagonistic.
- *The expert should be easy to work with.* The project team and the expert will be spending a lot of time together.
- *The expertise for the system, at least that pertaining to one particular sub-domain, is to be obtained primarily from one expert.* This avoids the problem of dealing with multiple experts whose conclusions or problem-solving techniques do not agree. However, there may be some advantages to using multiple experts—*e.g.*, strength of authority and breadth of expertise in sub-domains.
- *If multiple experts contribute in a particular sub-domain, one of them should be the primary expert with final authority.* This allows all the expertise to be filtered through a single person's reasoning process. (Note that some techniques have been developed, in disciplines such as economic modeling and technological forecasting, to allow combining inputs from multiple experts.)

Problem Bounds

- *The task is neither too easy (taking a human expert less than a few minutes) nor too difficult (requiring more than a few hours for an expert).* If the task is too easy, the development of the system may not warrant the effort, if too difficult, the amount of knowledge needed may be beyond the state of the art in knowledge base size.

- *The amount of knowledge required by the task is large enough to make the knowledge base developed interesting.* If it is too small, the task may be more amenable to another approach—*e.g.*, a decision tree.
- *The task is sufficiently narrow and self-contained: the aim is not for a system that is expert in an entire domain, but for a system that is an expert in a limited task within the domain.* This more tightly bounds the task, which should help keep the size of the knowledge base bounded.
- *The number of important concepts* (e.g., *rules*) *required is bounded to several hundreds.* This is a reasonable size for an expert system, though the number can go into the thousands.

Domain Area Personnel

- *Personnel in the domain area are realistic, understanding the potential of an expert system for their domain, but also realizing that thus far few expert systems have resulted in actual production programs with major industrial payoff.* The system recipients should not be overly optimistic nor overly pessimistic. The project team may have to educate them to understand what are reasonable expectations.
- *Domain area personnel understand that even a successful system will likely be limited in scope and, like a human expert, may not produce optimal or correct results 100% of the time.* The expert system will probably be no better than a limited version of the expert—this must be enough.
- *There is strong managerial support from the domain area, especially regarding the large commitment of time by the expert(s), and their possible travel or temporary relocation, if required.* This should all be agreed upon up front.
- *The specific task within the domain is jointly agreed upon by the system developers and the domain area personnel.* This helps ensure that the system, if successful, will be useful and will be used.
- *Managers in the domain area have previously identified the need to solve the problem which the system attacks.* This is strong evidence that the system is needed and makes managerial support more likely.
- *The project is strongly supported by a senior manager, for protection and follow-up.*
- *Potential users would welcome the completed system.* If not, will the system ever be used? The project team should consider how to make the system unthreatening to the users and welcomed by them.
- *The system can be introduced with minimal disturbance of the current practice.* This will make the users' acceptance of the system more likely.
- *The user group is cooperative and patient.*
- *The introduction of the system will not be politically sensitive or controversial.* If not, the potential resulting problems should be considered in advance. One typical problem: The control or use of the system goes across existing organizational boundaries.
- *The knowledge contained by the system will not be politically sensitive or controversial.* For example, there may be certain practices, embodied in heuristics, which may prove embarrassing if written down, such as how certain customers are treated relative to other customers.
- *The system's results will not be politically sensitive or controversial.* If there will be corporate parties who will challenge the system if its results do not favor them politically (*e.g.*, on appropriation of funds), then it will be much harder to gain system acceptance.

Other Desirable Features

- *The system can be phased into use gracefully: Some percentage of incomplete coverage can be tolerated (at least initially), and the determination of whether a sub-problem is covered by the present system is not difficult.* If the system does not have to do everything in order to do something, it can be put in place much sooner. The more difficult problems can be resolved later, if at all.
- *The task is decomposable, allowing relatively rapid prototyping for a closed small subset of the complete task, and then slow expansion to the complete task.* This makes development much easier.
- *The task is not all-or-nothing: Some percentage of incorrect or nonoptimal results can be tolerated.* The more toleration for incorrect results, the faster the system can be deployed and the easier it will be to win system acceptance. For example, in a domain where even the best experts are often

wrong, system users will not be as upset by an incorrect result from the system.

- *The skill required by the task is taught to novices.* Thus, the task is not "unteachable," and there is some experience with teaching the domain knowledge to neophytes, such as the project team (and, ultimately, the system). Furthermore, this usually means that there is an organization to the knowledge that can prove useful (at least initially) in building the system.
- *There are books or other written materials discussing the domain.* If this is true, then an expert has already extracted and organized some of the domain expertise. As in the previous point, this organized knowledge might prove useful (at least initially) in building the system. Note, however, that one benefit of capturing an expert's domain knowledge might be to make a step toward formalizing a domain that has not been treated in a formal manner before.
- *The task's payoff is measurable.* If not, it is harder to demonstrate success to skeptics.
- *Experts would agree on whether the system's results are good (correct).* If not, the system's results are open to challenge, even if the system accurately embodies the expert's knowledge.
- *Test cases are available.* This makes development much easier.
- *The need for the task is projected to continue for several years.* The need must exist enough beyond the period of system development to generate the payoff.
- *The domain is fairly stable. Expected changes are such that they utilize the strengths of expert systems* (e.g., *ease of updating or revising specific rules in a knowledge base), but will not require major changes in reasoning processes.* An unstable domain may yield a situation where a large number of previously developed knowledge structures (*e.g.,* rules) are no longer valid but cannot easily be changed without redoing the entire development process.
- *The effects of corporate developments that will significantly change the definition of the task can be foreseen and taken into account.*
- *No alternative solution to the problem is being pursued or is expected to be pursued.* However, if a project goal is to compare expert system technology to other technologies, this may be just what is desired.
- *The project is not on the critical path for any other development, and has no absolute milestones for completion.* The use of expert system technology for real corporate applications is still relatively new, and so any development has some risk. Thus, the less dependent other activities are, the better.
- *At the outset of the project, the expert is able to specify many of the important concepts.* This gives good promise of project success.
- *The task is similar to that of a successful existing expert system.* This also makes success more likely.
- *Any requirement for real-time response will not involve extensive effort.* Though it is certainly possible to develop a system for a problem with a real-time requirement, the considerations involved divert effort from the primary task: knowledge acquisition.
- *The user interface will not require extensive effort.* As with a real-time requirement, if the work required is excessive, it could divert effort from knowledge acquisition.

References

d'Agapeyeff, A. 1983. *Preparing for Fifth Generation Computing.* Fifth Generation World Conference, London, U.K.

Davis, R. 1982. Expert Systems: Where Are We? And Where Do We Go From Here? *AI Magazine* Vol. 3, No. 2:3-22.

Gevarter, W. 1983. Expert Systems: Limited but Powerful. *IEEE Spectrum* Vol. 20, No. 8:39-45.

Hayes-Roth, F., D. Waterman, & D. Lenat. 1983. *Building Expert Systems.* Reading, MA: Addison-Wesley.

McDermott, J. 1981. R1: The Formative Years. *AI Magazine* Vol. 2, No. 2:21-39.

McDermott, J. 1984. R1 Revisited: Four Years in the Trenches. *AI Magazine* Vol. 5, No. 3:21-32.

Roberts, S. 1983. Computers Simulate Human Experts. Micro-Mini Systems 16/9.

Smith, R. 1984. On the Development of Commercial Expert Systems. *AI Magazine* Vol. 5, No. 3:61-73.

Knowledge Acquisition in the Development of a Large Expert System

David S. Prerau

Knowledge acquisition is the process by which expert system developers find the knowledge that domain experts use to perform the task of interest. This knowledge is then implemented to form an expert system. The essential part of an expert system is its knowledge, and therefore, knowledge acquisition is probably the most important task in the development of an expert system.

In this article, several effective techniques for expert system knowledge acquisition are discussed based on the techniques that were successfully used at GTE Laboratories to develop the Central Office Maintenance Printout Analysis and Suggestion System (COMPASS) expert system. Knowledge acquisition for expert system development is still a new field and not (yet?) a science. Therefore, expert system developers and the experts they work with must tailor their knowledge-acquisition methodologies to fit their own particular situation and the people involved. As expert system developers define their own knowledge-acquisition procedures, they should find a description of proven knowledge-acquisition techniques and an account of the experience of the COMPASS developers in applying these techniques to be useful.

The next section of this article is a discussion of the COMPASS project. The major portion of the article follows, with over 30 points on knowledge acquisition that were found to be important during the work on COMPASS. Initial points cover the knowledge-acquisition considerations in selecting an expert and an appropriate domain for the expert system. The remaining points highlight techniques for getting started in knowledge acquisition, documenting the knowledge, and finally, actually acquiring and recording the knowledge. Each point is followed by a general discussion and then by a description of how the point specifically applied to the COMPASS project.

COMPASS

COMPASS is a multiparadigm expert system developed by GTE Laboratories for telephone switching-system maintenance (Prerau et al., 1985b; Goyal et al., 1985). COMPASS accepts maintenance printouts from telephone company central office switching equipment and suggests maintenance actions to be performed.

In particular, COMPASS accepts maintenance printout information from a GTE Number 2 Electronic Automatic Exchange (No. 2 EAX). A No. 2 EAX is a large, complex telephone call switching system ("switch") that can interconnect up to 40,000 telephone lines. Such a switch generates hundreds or thousands of maintenance messages daily. The current manual procedure of analyzing these messages to determine appropriate maintenance actions takes a significant amount of time and requires a high level of expertise. COMPASS uses expert techniques to analyze these messages and produce a prioritized list of suggested maintenance actions for a switch-maintenance technician.

COMPASS is implemented on Xerox 1108 Lisp machines using the KEE™ system (Fikes

Reprinted with permission from *AI Magazine*, vol. 8, no. 2, Summer 1987, 43-51. The material in this paper has been expanded by Dr. Prerau into a full chapter of his book, *Developing and Managing Expert Systems: Proven Techniques for Business and Industry*, Addison-Wesley Publishing Company, 1990.

and Kehler, 1985) from IntelliCorp. The COMPASS implementation utilizes multiple artificial intelligence paradigms: rules, frame hierarchies, demon mechanisms, object-oriented programming facilities, and Lisp code.

COMPASS is a large expert system: the COMPASS "knowledge document" (Prerau et al., 1986), which contains a succinct English-language record of the COMPASS expert knowledge, is approximately 200 pages long. The COMPASS implementation consists of about 500 Lisp functions, 400 KEE rules, and 1000 frames with a total of 15,000 slots. The system (COMPASS, KEE, and Interlisp-D) requires about 10 megabytes. COMPASS alone requires about 5 megabytes, and is growing larger as data are analyzed.

In its initial field uses, COMPASS has displayed performance comparable to (and, in some cases, better than) that of domain experts and significantly better than that of average No. 2 EAX maintenance personnel (Prerau et al., 1985a). COMPASS is probably one of the first major expert systems designed to be transferred completely from its developers to a separate organization for production use and maintenance. COMPASS has been put into extensive field use by GTE Data Services (GTEDS) of Tampa, Florida (Prerau et al., 1985d). It has been run on a daily basis for about a year to aid maintenance personnel at 12 No. 2 EAXs in four states. These switches service about 250,000 telephone subscribers. COMPASS is currently being put into production use by GTE telephone companies.

Because COMPASS is designed to be maintained by a group completely separate from its developers, major consideration during development was given to the potential maintainability of the final COMPASS system. The COMPASS project team developed a set of software engineering techniques for expert system implementation (Prerau et al., 1987). These techniques were utilized for COMPASS and are being used in other expert system developments.

Selecting an Expert

A domain expert is the source of knowledge for the expert system. Therefore, even before the actual process of knowledge acquisition begins, a decision crucial to its success must be made: the choice of the project's expert (or experts). Because of the significance of this decision, among the important criteria for selecting an appropriate expert system domain are considerations related to the choice of a domain expert. These considerations primarily relate to the degree that the expert will function well in the role of knowledge source.

Importance of Expert Selection

- Significant time and effort is needed to select an expert.

The selection of an expert is an important element in knowledge acquisition, and knowledge acquisition is critical to the overall expert system.

Early in the COMPASS project, an extensive set of criteria for selecting an expert system domain were developed (Prerau 1985). This set included criteria for selecting a project expert (of these criteria, only those related to knowledge acquisition are discussed here). We then spoke with several contacts in the domain area and explained our need for a project expert and our criteria for selecting one. The discussions yielded a small list of potential No. 2 EAX experts for our project. The most promising of these experts were asked to come separately to GTE Laboratories for two days of meetings. At these meetings, we discussed the project, expert systems in general, and the potential participation of the expert in our project. At the same time, we tried to see how the potential expert met our selection criteria. Based on these meetings, we selected the COMPASS expert.

An Expert's Capabilities

- Select an expert who has developed domain expertise by task performance over a long period of time.

The expert must have enough experience to be able to develop the domain insights that result in heuristics (rules of thumb). These heuristics most distinguish the knowledge in an expert system from that in a conventional program and are the main goal of the knowledge-acquisition process.

Our COMPASS expert, W. (Rick) Johnson, is a switching-services supervisor in the electronic operations staff at General Telephone of the Southwest (GTSW). He has been working in telephone switching for 16 years, including about 5 years specifically on the No. 2 EAX.

- Select an expert who is capable of communicating personal knowledge, judgment, and experience and the methods used to apply these elements to the particular task.

An expert should not only have the expertise but also the ability to impart this expertise to the project team, whose members probably know little or nothing about the subject area. Experts should be introspective, able to analyze their reasoning processes; and communicative, able to describe those reasoning processes clearly to the project team.

The COMPASS expert was an excellent communicator in teaching the COMPASS knowledge engineering team the basics of the No. 2 EAX and in discussing and explaining the methods he used to analyze No. 2 EAX maintenance messages.

- An expert should be cooperative.

An expert should be eager to work on the project or at worst be nonantagonistic. It is a hard job to be a project expert and to have to examine in detail the way you have been making decisions. If the expert is not interested or is even resentful about being on the project, then the expert might not put in the full effort required. One way to ensure a cooperative expert is to find a person who is interested in computers and in learning about expert systems (and possibly in becoming a local "expert" on expert systems and AI when the project is completed). Also, an expert who sees a big potential payoff in the expert system being developed might want to be involved with it.

The COMPASS expert was very interested in, and enthusiastic about, the project, and the effort he put in was more than what was expected. He learned a good deal about AI and expert systems during his work on the COMPASS project and became familiar with the Lisp machines being used. Also, he received considerable visibility with his local management and eventually shared in a major award for COMPASS.

- Select an expert who is easy to work with.

A domain expert in an expert system project spends a lot of time with the project team.

In COMPASS, we had an excellent working relationship with our expert.

An Expert's Availability and Support

- Select an expert who is able to commit a substantial amount of time to the development of the system.

Because knowledge acquisition requires long hours, days, and weeks of discussions between experts and knowledge engineers, an expert for an expert system project must be willing and able to commit the significant time and effort required by the project.

One important factor in the COMPASS project was that our expert was willing and able to make a major commitment to the project.

- Strong managerial support is needed for an expert's commitment to the project.

Because knowledge acquisition for a major expert system can require many weeks or months of discussions with an expert, ample time should be set aside in the expert's schedule for meetings. Available time is often a problem. The best experts in the most important corporate areas are usually the ones who can least be spared from their usual position.

We were very fortunate in the COMPASS project to be able to obtain from GTSW management a commitment of one week per month of our expert's valuable time for the duration of the project (over two years). Any smaller commitment of time would have significantly affected the speed of the project development, and a major cutback would have made it almost impossible to achieve the results that we did.

Selecting the Domain

In addition to the selection of the expert, criteria for the selection of an appropriate domain for expert system development (Prerau 1985) directly relate to the ease of knowledge acquisition.

- The domain should be such that the expert system does not have to perform the entire task to be useful: some degree of incomplete coverage can be tolerated (at least initially).

If this statement is true, the expert system development project can begin by developing a system to cover one subdomain and then expand by adding other subdomains. This method of development allows the knowledge acquisition for a large domain to be focused on one subdomain at a time.

For COMPASS, we spent almost the entire first year concentrating on one class of No. 2 EAX error messages (albeit the most important and most complex message class)—the "network recovery 20" messages. Our knowledge-acquisition sessions did not even consider the analysis of any other message types until our first system was completed. The subsequent expansion of COMPASS added the capability of handling every other No. 2 EAX message type that requires detailed expert analysis.

- The task should be decomposable, allowing relatively rapid prototyping for a closed small subset of the complete task and then slow expansion to the complete task.

This approach allows knowledge acquisition to focus on a subset of the task rather than the entire task at once. Combined with the previous item, the knowledge acquisition can then be directed at any one time to one subtask for one subdomain.

In COMPASS, we (including our expert) did not know at first that the task was decomposable; so we started by finding rules and procedures for the entire initial task (analysis of network recovery 20 messages). After some time, it became clear that the task could be decomposed into five major phases: Input, Identify, Analyze, Suggest, and Output (Prerau et al., 1985b). Then, we were able to concentrate our knowledge acquisition at any one time on one particular phase, thus focusing our attention.

- The domain should be fairly stable.

An unstable domain can yield a situation where a large number of knowledge structures (for example, rules) found early in the knowledge acquisition are no longer valid but cannot easily be changed without redoing a major part of the knowledge-acquisition process.

For COMPASS, the No. 2 EAX domain that we selected was very stable. Through the entire development, no rule was ever altered because of a change in the No. 2 EAX architecture or control software.

Getting Started

Before discussing the major techniques for acquiring, recording, and documenting the expert knowledge (see the next two sections), let us consider some points related to getting started: how to set up the knowledge-acquisition meetings, what the first knowledge-acquisition meetings should cover, and what knowledge-acquisition techniques can be used at these initial meetings.

Knowledge Acquisition Meetings

The planning and scheduling of knowledge-acquisition meetings are important practical concerns.

- Organize knowledge-acquisition meetings so as to maximize access to the expert and to minimize interruptions.

As mentioned, the best experts often are the ones who can be least spared from their usual position. If an expert is consulted frequently for major and minor crises, knowledge-acquisition meetings held near the expert's location are likely to have many interruptions. It might be desirable to hold the meetings at a site remote from the expert's place of business. However, knowledge acquisition at the expert's site might allow observing the expert performing tasks in a usual environment, and this experience can be advantageous (see Starting Knowledge Acquisition).

We held our COMPASS knowledge-acquisition meetings at our Waltham, Massachusetts site, and our expert flew from San Angelo, Texas, to attend them. By having scheduled meetings in Massachusetts, we minimized—but did not completely eliminate—the times when our expert was called upon to help in crises, necessitating a rescheduling of our knowledge-acquisition meetings. However, once the expert was in Massachusetts, we could count on his availability except for occasional telephone calls.

- Knowledge-acquisition meeting attendees should have access to the implementation machines.

Several reasons exist for running the developing expert system program during a knowledge-acquisition session: to check parts of the developing program, to examine results of new knowledge that was acquired and implemented during the session, and to use the output of a part of the program as test input for knowledge acquisition of a succeeding part of the program. Thus, it is important to have access to the implementation during knowledge acquisition. This access can be achieved by having the knowledge-acquisition meetings at the location of the knowledge engineering team. Meetings at this location might offer additional benefits, such as decreased travel expenses and better access to knowledge-acquisition aids, but it might also increase interruptions for other business.

Having COMPASS knowledge-acquisition meetings at our Waltham site gave us immediate access to the COMPASS program for the purposes described. We also minimized travel expenses because one expert, rather than two to four knowledge engineers, had to travel. Work at our site facilitated use of our knowledge-recording and documentation-updating mechanisms. A negative aspect was that the knowledge engineers were sometimes called away to attend various meetings, delaying knowledge acquisition. However, because our primary job was developing COMPASS (as opposed to the expert's primary job: his work at GTSW), we were able to schedule other meetings so that we were rarely called away for long periods.

Getting Background Domain Knowledge

The knowledge engineers developing an expert system are often completely unfamiliar with the domain of the system. Thus, as part of the knowledge acquisition, they must be provided with some background in the domain.

- An initial period of the knowledge acquisition should be devoted to the expert giving the knowledge engineers a tutorial on the domain and the domain terminology, without any actual knowledge acquisition going on.

Although there is a natural impatience to get right into the "real" knowledge acquisition, domain concepts and terms will occur over and over in the knowledge-acquisition meetings. Thus, it is useful to invest some time up front discussing the domain in general without focusing on the specific task to be performed by the system.

In COMPASS, we devoted the entire first week of knowledge-acquisition meetings with our expert to a tutorial on telephone switching in general and on the No. 2 EAX structure. During this week, no mention was made of the specific task of COMPASS—the analysis of maintenance messages. Instead, the knowledge engineers learned a lot of basic telephone-switching ideas and No. 2 EAX jargon that would prove very useful during the remainder of the knowledge acquisition.

- Preparation of a tutorial document on the domain is useful.

This document can be used during the initial tutorial period and can then be available to knowledge engineers who join the project at later stages.

In COMPASS, the expert prepared a tutorial document that consisted of a package of pertinent excerpts of several existing No. 2 EAX reports and publications. This document provided the knowledge engineers with a useful reference during and after the tutorial week. Also, a copy of the document was given to each of the three new project members who eventually joined the COMPASS project. The expert also gave the new individuals private minitutorials as needed, based on the document.

Starting Knowledge Acquisition

Once the knowledge engineers have some basic background in the domain, it is time to start the actual knowledge acquisition.

- References such as books or other written materials discussing the domain can form the basis of an initial knowledge base.

In a book, an expert has already extracted and organized some of the domain expertise. This organized knowledge might prove useful (at least initially) in building the system.

As mentioned, in COMPASS, we used the existing No. 2 EAX reports and publications to help us gain general knowledge about the No. 2 EAX. However, no written materials explained the kind of analysis our expert went through to find and repair problems in the switch; therefore, we could not get any initial rules directly from books or reports.

- Begin the knowledge acquisition by having the expert go through the task, explaining each step in detail.

If possible, the expert should slowly work through the task for some test cases, explaining each step in detail. This task, however, is usually very difficult for the expert. An alternative is to have the expert perform the task at close to normal speed, verbalizing whenever possible, and record the process on audio or videotape. Another alternative is to record the expert at the location where the expert actually performs the task. In either of these cases, the tape of the task performance can be played back one short segment at a time, with the knowledge engineers attempting to find out from the expert exactly what is being considered and what decisions are being made at each point. A briefly considered decision by the expert often actually involves a very large amount of information that must be put into the expert system.

We initially used audiotapes in COMPASS, with our expert going through the task at close to normal speed. We obtained some initial idea of his domain techniques using this method. However, after a brief time, it became clear that our expert was able to slowly step through his analysis while we interrupted him at each step to probe for his methodology. Thus, we stopped taping after just a few days and relied upon this alternative.

Documenting the Knowledge

In order to fully discuss the techniques that can be used to elicit the knowledge, it is important to describe first what this knowledge will look like and what techniques can be used to document it.

- Use some form of quasi-English if-then rules to document expert knowledge whenever possible; use quasi-English procedures when rules cannot reasonably be used.

Utilizing if-then rules for documenting the knowledge acquisition allows the knowledge to be acquired in independent chunks, in a way that might become a basis for implementation. An expert should be able to understand this method of knowledge representation more easily than other AI paradigms and after some exposure might be able to relate some of the knowledge to the knowledge engineers by utilizing this paradigm. Other experts should be able to read and understand the documentation in this form for verification or technology-transfer purposes.

In the COMPASS knowledge acquisition, we used quasi-English if-then rules almost always. Occasionally, other forms of knowledge documentation were used. For example, when a complicated looping procedure was found, a procedure in English was documented. Additionally, when a large amount of data was found related to some items, data in tabular form were utilized. Our expert could easily read and refer to the rules. Later in the development, other No. 2 EAX experts were asked to evaluate COMPASS. They were able to read the rules and procedures in the knowledge document and understand the knowledge inside the system. Also, we were often able to implement a knowledge-acquisition rule by one or more implementation rules in KEE (usually with associated Lisp functions). When this implementation could be done, it allowed a nice isomorphism between the knowledge and the implementation that would not have been possible if the documented knowledge were not in rule form.

- Keep rules and procedures in a "knowledge document."

As the rules and procedures are found, keep them in a knowledge document. The knowledge engineers and the expert will be using the knowledge document frequently. It can be given to other experts for system verification purposes. It can also be considered a "specification" for the knowledge implementation. Finally, the knowledge document should become part of the final documentation of the project (possibly part of, or generated from, the corresponding implementation). The COMPASS knowledge documents (Prerau et al., 1985b, 1986), were used extensively throughout the project for all these purposes.

- Develop conventions for documenting the knowledge-acquisition rules in order to add clarity.

Because the knowledge document can be used for many purposes, clarity is important.

A rule from the COMPASS system documentation (Prerau et al., 1986) is shown in figure 1. Note the use of capitalization and indentation to make the rule readable. The four points that follow highlight some of the other conventions we used.

NR 20 XY ANALYSIS RULES
BC DUAL EXPANSION ONE PGA DOMINANT LARGE NUMBER MESSAGES ANALYSIS RULE

IF There exists a BC Dual Expansion One PGA Dominant Problem
AND
The number of messages is five or more
THEN
The fault is in the PGA in the indicated expansion (.5)
AND
The fault is in the PGA in the silent expansion (.3)
AND
The fault is in the IGA (.1)
AND
The fault is in the Backplane (.1)
BECAUSE
Most messages are in one expansion, so the problem is probably in that PGA.

Figure 1. A COMPASS rule.

- The rules and procedures in the knowledge document should use standard domain jargon that the expert and other domain practitioners can understand; any special conventions should be clearly specified in the document.

This practice allows the document to be used for all the purposes mentioned.

The COMPASS rule shown in figure 1 uses No. 2 EAX domain jargon (for example, "PGA" and "expansion"). Also, the COMPASS knowledge document makes clear (though this point is not evident in the figure) that a number in parentheses in the rule represents the likelihood that the fault is in the cited location.

- Group the documented rules in reasonable divisions.

Organizing the rules aids the user in finding them in the document. It also puts related rules together, which often facilitates document editing. If possible, the implementation should follow this grouping, but grouping the documented rules is a useful procedure to follow even if the implementation cannot correspond to the grouping.

In figure 1, NR 20 XY ANALYSIS RULES refers to a set of analysis rules (Analysis is one major phase of COMPASS) for network recovery 20 messages that deal with problems of the switch which the expert would group under the term "XY."

- Give the knowledge-acquisition rules unique descriptive names (lengthy if necessary) rather than numbers.

The rule name should be descriptive enough to ensure that it is unique. If a rule name is descriptive, it can be utilized as part of the explanation facility of the expert system. If possible, it can also be used to identify the corresponding part of the implementation. Rule numbering should be avoided because of the problems it can cause. The set of rules changes continually during knowledge acquisition (and later in program maintenance). Rules are regrouped; new rules are added; and old rules are deleted, combined, or split. If rules are numbered, they must be renumbered continually. Lengthy names are cumbersome, but they clearly define the rule and remain constant as the rule set changes.

In figure 1, the COMPASS rule name BC DUAL EXPANSION ONE PGA DOMINANT LARGE NUMBER MESSAGES ANALYSIS RULE identifies the expert rule to be applied in the analysis phase of the task under the following specific situation: the system has narrowed the problem to the BC portion of the switch, there are two expansions, the number of messages for one of the two PGAs is significantly more than (dominates) the number of messages for the second PGA, and the total number of messages is large (defined in this rule as "five or more"). The very long rule name can stay with the rule no matter how other rules change. In the COMPASS implementation, the KEE rule that implements this knowledge rule is given the same name (within allowable rule-name syntax).

- Include an explanatory clause as a part of each rule.

An explanatory clause (for example, a BECAUSE clause) appended to an if-then rule provides additional information on the expert's justification for a rule (Kyle, 1985). Although this clause has no effect on the operation of the expert system, it can help the expert and the knowledge-acquisition team remember why they defined certain rules as they did and can clarify these decisions for other experts and the maintainers of the system. The explanatory clause might also be used in a justification part of the system.

The COMPASS rules originally did not have an explanatory clause. We found that occasionally when we examined a knowledge rule which we hadn't looked at in a while, we could not remember exactly why something was done one way rather than another. We wasted valuable time reconstructing the arguments that were used previously. Furthermore, we found related problems occurred when the COMPASS rules were read by persons outside the COMPASS development team (for example, an outside expert who is examining the COMPASS knowledge base or someone involved with COMPASS maintenance). These people sometimes found it difficult to understand the reasoning behind certain parts of COMPASS. The addition of BECAUSE clauses to COMPASS knowledge rules that were not self-explanatory minimized these problems and should help reduce future problems.

Acquiring and Recording the Knowledge

The major work in the knowledge-acquisition process is the lengthy time spent with an expert eliciting, modifying, and recording the domain knowledge.

Acquiring the Knowledge

- Follow a basic cycle of elicit, document (or document and implement), and test.

An effective method of knowledge acquisition is to use the following basic cycle:

- Elicit knowledge from the expert;
- Document and, if possible, implement the knowledge; and
- Test the knowledge by comparing the expert's analysis against hand simulations of the documented knowledge or against the implementation (see figures 2 and 3).

We used this method for the COMPASS knowledge acquisition. We found hand simulations best for examining each small step of reasoning, while comparisons against the implementation were most useful when a large section of knowledge had been completed.

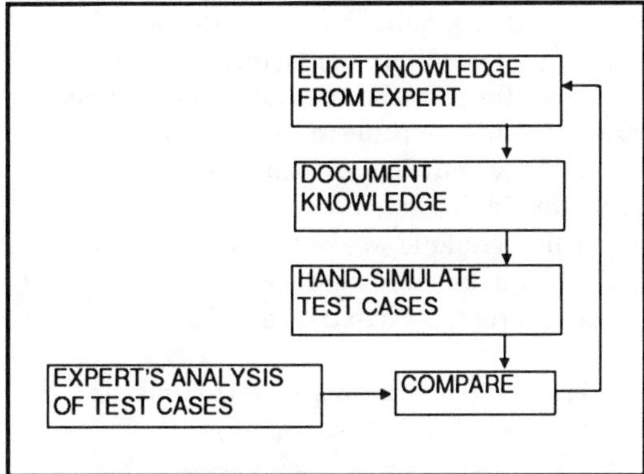

Figure 2. Knowledge-acquisition cycle with hand simulation.

- Use test cases to elicit expert techniques.

When initially considering a new area of the domain, go through several test cases. For each test case, formulate and document the rules and procedures the expert used to perform the task.

We went through each test case with the COMPASS expert. He tried to explain each substep in as much detail as he could, and we formulated knowledge-acquisition if-then rules or procedures to document each substep. We discussed each rule with the expert and modified it until he was satisfied. Because he knew each rule was to be considered just an initial version of the rule and would be subject to much change in the future, he did not feel that accepting a rule was a major decision requiring a great deal of thought.

- Use a large number of additional test cases to expand and modify the initial knowledge.

Go through numerous additional test cases. For each test case, attempt to use the existing rules and procedures to perform the task for the test case. Do this process by hand, or, if the pertinent rules and procedures have already been implemented, by machine. In each case, have the expert examine the reasoning of the system step by step. Find all points of disagreement between the expert and the system, and modify and expand the existing rules and procedures so that they work correctly, that is, they agree with the expert. As the system gets bigger and the implementation grows, you can compare the expert's final results with those of the system and examine in detail only those cases where there is disagreement.

We went through numerous test cases with the COMPASS expert. Rules and procedures were continually changed. At some points fairly early in the process, we (including the expert) thought that we were almost finished. Subsequently, we would find test cases that opened up completely new areas which hadn't been considered, and we would find other test cases that pointed to major required changes and expansions to the existing rules and procedures. The expert made many subtle decisions and checks in his analysis that he did not realize he was making until a test case pointed them out.

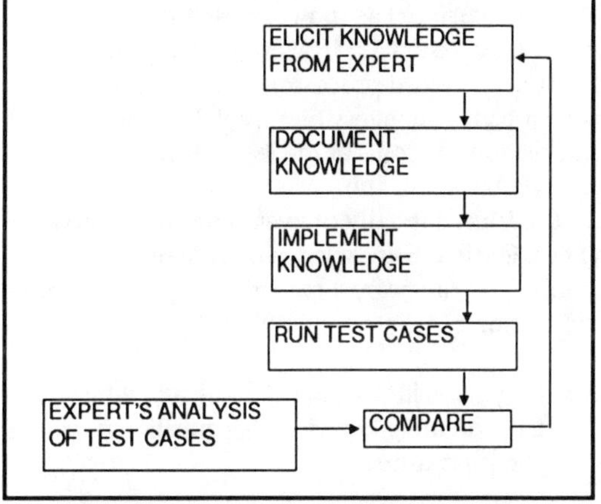

Figure 3. Knowledge-acquisition cycle with program runs.

- Have the expert define the domain reasoning in terms of knowledge-acquisition rules and procedures if possible.

Explain to the expert the ways the knowledge will be documented. As the knowledge-acquisition process continues, an interested expert will begin to understand the use of if-then rules and other AI concepts (just as the knowledge engineers will begin to understand some of the deeper concepts of the expert's domain). This understanding might help the expert describe the domain knowledge by directly using the knowledge-acquisition formalisms, thus speeding the knowledge-acquisition process. In addition, it helps the expert interpret the knowledge base being built and provides a foundation for the expert to eventually participate in the maintenance of the expert system implementation.

As the knowledge-acquisition process continued, the COMPASS expert became increasingly familiar with the rule formalism we used and often was able to formulate his domain expertise in this form. (At the same time, the COMPASS knowledge engineers slowly became No. 2 EAX miniexperts.)

- As knowledge is acquired and updated, generate and continually update the knowledge document.

During the knowledge-acquisition sessions, each knowledge engineer and expert should have an up-to-date copy of the knowledge document. When knowledge is being acquired and modified rapidly, new versions of the document should be printed as soon as possible.

We had our COMPASS knowledge document in our word processor. We updated and reprinted it after every one-week knowledge-acquisition session—at the least. When knowledge acquisition was rapid, we updated and reprinted it daily or even more frequently. (The COMPASS knowledge document was time-stamped to the nearest second—only a slight exaggeration of what was required.)

- Be general in wording, if necessary, when initially defining knowledge-acquisition rules and procedures.

Use general phrases in the rules each time the expert has trouble detailing or quantifying a specific knowledge item. This procedure avoids getting the knowledge-acquisition session bogged down in minor details before the important problems are solved. Later in the knowledge-acquisition process, the general phrase can be replaced by a specific quantity if possible, or techniques for dealing with uncertainty can be used.

During COMPASS development we used this technique several times. For example, the phrase "a sufficient number of messages" was used as a part of several rules for several months. A rule might state, "IF X is true AND there is a sufficient number of messages, THEN conclude Y." The phrase was given a working definition (=5) for a time to allow initial rule implementation and only after several months was the phrase replaced in the rules by a specific number. The number turned out to be different for different rules.

- Use each test case to generate many additional test cases.

When a test case has X = 5 and a rule is formulated, ask the expert whether the rule would be the same if X were 1, X were 10, and so on. By going through this process in the middle of the discussion of the original test case, the entire context of the test case does not have to be rediscussed in order to come to the point at issue. Several new knowledge rules are often quickly generated in this manner.

This technique worked very well in COMPASS, frequently allowing us to examine several different situations based on a single test case.

- Use the generated test cases to find the "edges" of each rule.

If a rule applies for X = 10 and another applies for X = 20, ask the expert which rule applies if X is 15, 17, and so on. Such questioning might make the expert uncomfortable because the rules of thumb often do not have sharp boundaries. However, after some thought, the expert might be able to pick a reasonable cutoff point. Note that if the expert is unsure which of two rules applies for a certain situation, the expert system might not be too far wrong if it uses either one; so, the expert's selection might not be critical. Again, this technique worked very well in COMPASS.

Recording the Knowledge

The final documentation of the knowledge was previously discussed. Here, let us consider techniques for initially recording the knowledge as it is acquired during the knowledge-acquisition sessions.

- Record acquired knowledge in a flexible manner at the knowledge-acquisition sessions.

The method in which the acquired knowledge is initially recorded at the knowledge-acquisition sessions should allow for frequent changes in rules while they are being discussed. It also should facilitate the transfer of the knowledge to the knowledge document when the discussion is completed. It would be efficient if the initial knowledge recording could be immediately and automatically transformed into the knowledge documentation (and even better if the documentation could then be transformed into the implementation). However, if this transformation cannot take place easily, it is wise to use the recording technique best suited to the knowledge acquisition rather than to delay the knowledge-acquisition sessions while the documentation and implementation are being produced.

In the COMPASS knowledge-acquisition sessions, we wrote the knowledge-acquisition rules and procedures on a whiteboard, and after a rule or procedure had been agreed on, we took an instant photograph of the board. The knowledge document was updated as soon as possible after a day's knowledge-acquisition session using the photographs (which were kept on file for reference). This technique proved very useful in COMPASS, but it did require that a project member spend a significant amount of time transcribing the information from the photographs.

- Use suitable conventions for knowledge recording.

To speed the knowledge recording process, develop some reasonable recording conventions.

In COMPASS, we found that adopting a color code for different categories of information (for example, new rules, revisions of old rules, comments, and so on) was initially a help. After several months as we became familiar with our knowledge-recording and -transcribing process, we abandoned the color coding.

- Use reminders to defer overly detailed or secondary items.

During knowledge acquisition, you sometimes come upon topics to discuss or actions to take that are beyond the scope of the current discussion. For example, one obscure case might be complicated enough to require a significant amount of knowledge acquisition. Rather than diverting the knowledge-acquisition session into a very detailed area or, alternatively, neglecting the topic, it is useful to have a formal mechanism to record "reminders" that can trigger a knowledge-acquisition session at a later date.

In the COMPASS knowledge-acquisition meetings, reminders were treated as an outcome of knowledge acquisition, similar to the rules and procedures. These reminders were updated, deleted, or added to in the same manner as the other knowledge. Every so often, the group would go through the reminder list to see if any reminder should be treated immediately or if any could be deleted as no longer necessary.

A Related Implementation Convention

- Implement knowledge acquisition rules by a corresponding implementation rule(s) with the same name if possible.

Using the same name for a knowledge-acquisition rule and its corresponding rule(s) in the implementation helps keep the knowledge acquirers from worrying about the details of the implementation, yet it preserves the correspondence between the acquired rules and the implemented rules. It greatly aids technology transfer and maintenance because it makes a clear correspondence between the knowledge document and the implementation. Use of this technique also facilitates implementation.

As mentioned earlier, COMPASS is implemented using multiple AI paradigms (rules, frames, demons, object-oriented programming, and Lisp), making use of all the facilities of KEE. However, to maximize the maintainability of COMPASS we tried to use KEE rules to implement knowledge-acquisition rules whenever possible. Furthermore, when possible, we tried to have a one-to-one correspondence between the knowledge rules and the KEE rules. Although it might have been more efficient in many cases to use a different paradigm (for example, Lisp code), we feel that the use of KEE rules to implement knowledge-acquisition rules makes COMPASS much easier to understand and maintain, which was a priority for us (Prerau et al., 1987). Each KEE rule used was given the same name as the corresponding knowledge-acquisition rule. When a knowledge-acquisition rule was implemented by multiple KEE rules, then the implementation rules were given the same name as the knowledge rule but with a number added. Thus, the COMPASS knowledge rule F-SWITCH ANALYSIS RULE is implemented by two KEE implementation rules named F-SWITCH ANALYSIS RULE #1 and F-SWITCH ANALYSIS RULE #2.

Conclusions

This article presented several effective techniques for knowledge acquisition and some of the details of a real expert system knowledge-acquisition process. It is doubtful that every point discussed will be usable or even pertinent to the knowledge-acquisition task for another project. However, until some general theories of knowledge acquisition become accepted, it is important for expert system developers to describe successful techniques they have used in order to allow others to glean what they can. Some of the principal techniques that were found to be beneficial in knowledge acquisition are:

- Considering knowledge acquisition when selecting the domain,
- Considering knowledge acquisition when selecting an expert,
- Using test cases to elicit knowledge,
- Using generated test cases to multiply the effectiveness of test-case analysis, and
- Using good knowledge-recording and -documentation practices.

References

Fikes, R., and Kehler, T. 1985. The Role of Frame-Based Representation in Reasoning. *Communications of the ACM* 28(9):904-920.

Goyal, S.; Prerau, D. S.; Lemmon, A.; Gunderson, A.; and Reinke, R. 1985. COMPASS: An Expert System for Telephone Switch Maintenance. *Expert Systems: The International Journal of Knowledge Engineering* 2(3):112-126. Also published in Proceedings of the Expert Systems in Government Symposium, 112-122. New York: Institute of Electrical and Electronics Engineers.

Kyle, T. 1985. Expanding Expertise by Use of an Expert System. In Proceedings of the 1985 Conference on Intelligent Systems and Machines, 244-247. Rochester, Mich.: Oakland University.

Prerau, D. S. 1985. Selection of an Appropriate Domain for an Expert System. *AI Magazine* 4(2):26-30.

Prerau, D. S.; Gunderson, A.; Reinke, R.; and Goyal, S. 1985a. The COMPASS Expert System: Verification, Technology Transfer, and Expansion. In Proceedings of the Second International Conference of Artificial Intelligence Applications, 597-602. Washington, D.C.: IEEE Computer Society.

Prerau, D. S.; Lemmon, A.; Gunderson, A.; and Reinke, R. 1985b. A Multi-Paradigm Expert System for Maintenance of an Electronic Telephone Exchange. In Proceedings of the Ninth International Computer Software and Applications Conference (COMPSAC-85), 280-286. Washington, D.C.: IEEE Computer Society.

Prerau, D. S.; Lemmon, A.; Gunderson, A.; Reinke, R.; and Johnson, W. 1985c. COMPASS-X Rules and Procedures, Technical Note, TN-85-176.2, Computer Science Laboratory, GTE Laboratories Incorporated.

Prerau, D. S.; Schipper, S.; and Janis, J. 1985d. Artificial Intelligence Technology Transfer Related to the COMPASS-X Expert System, Technical Note, TN-85-176.6, Computer Science Laboratory, GTE Laboratories Incorporated.

Prerau, D. S.; Gunderson, A.; Reinke, R.; Adler, M.; Johnson, W.; and Schipper, S. 1986. COMPASS-II Knowledge Document, Vols. I to IV, Technical Notes, TN86-176.8 to TN86-176.11, Computer and Intelligent Systems Laboratory, GTE Laboratories Incorporated.

Prerau, D. S.; Gunderson, A.; Reinke, R.; and Adler, M. 1987. Maintainability Techniques in Developing Large Expert Systems. Forthcoming.

Knowledge Base Verification

Tin A. Nguyen, Walton A. Perkins, Thomas J. Laffey, and Deanne Pecora

Hayes-Roth (1985) describes several features of rule-based systems that would help to make such a system suitable as a general computing approach. He points out that one of the key features these systems lack is "a suitable verification methodology or a technique for testing the consistency and completeness of a rule set." It is precisely this feature that we address here.

LES is a generic rule-based expert system building tool (Laffey, Perkins, and Nguyen, 1986) similar to EMYCIN (Van Melle, 1981) that has been used as a framework to construct expert systems in many areas, such as electronic equipment diagnosis, design verification, photointerpretation, and hazard analysis. LES represents factual data in its frame database and heuristic and control knowledge in its production rules. LES allows the knowledge engineer to use both data-driven and goal-driven rules.

One objective in the design of LES was to make it easy to use. Thus, many debugging tools and aids were added to the LES program. One aid is a syntax checker that examines each rule for syntactic errors such as unbalanced parentheses or misspelled names. Another of these aids is the knowledge base completeness and consistency-verification program called CHECK. Its purpose is to help a knowledge engineer check the knowledge base for existing and potential problems as it is being developed. CHECK analyzes the knowledge base after the rules, facts, and goals have been loaded into LES.

Reprinted with permission from *AI Magazine*, vol. 8, no. 2, Summer 1987, 69-75.

Related Work

Surprisingly enough, little work has been reported on knowledge base debugging. The TEIRESIAS program (Davis, 1976) was the first attempt to automate the knowledge base debugging process. It worked in the context of the MYCIN (Shortliffe, 1976) infectious disease consultation system. TEIRESIAS examined the "completed" MYCIN rule set and built rule models showing a number of factors, including which attributes were used to conclude other attributes. Thus, when a new rule was added to MYCIN, it was compared with the rule model for the attributes found in the IF conditions. The program then proposed missing clauses if some attributes found in the IF part of the model did not appear in the new rule. TEIRESIAS did not check the rules as they were initially entered into the knowledge base. Rather, it assumed the knowledge base was "complete" (or close to it), and the knowledge transfer occurred in the setting of a problem-solving session.

Suwa, Scott, and Shortliffe (1982), on which our work is based, wrote a program for verifying knowledge base completeness and consistency. The program was devised and tested within the context of the ONCOCIN system, a rule-based system for clinical oncology.

Unlike TEIRESIAS, ONCOCIN's rule checker is meant to be used as the system is being developed. It examines a rule set as it is read into the system. Knowledge base problems are found by first partitioning the rules into disjoint sets based upon what attribute is assigned a value in the conclusion. It then makes a table, displaying all possible combinations of attributes used in the IF conditions and the corresponding values that will be concluded in the THEN part of the rule. The table is then checked for conflicts, redundancy, subsumption, and missing rules. Finally, a table is displayed with a summary of any potential errors that were found. The rule checker assumes there should be a rule for each possible combination of values of attributes that appear in the antecedent. It hypothesizes missing rules based on this assumption. Such a process can result in the system hypothesizing rules that have semantically impossible combinations of attributes. Also, if the number of attributes is large, the system can suggest a very large number of missing rules. Nevertheless, the developers of the ONCOCIN system found the rule checker extremely useful in helping them to debug their evolving knowledge base. ONCOCIN uses both data-driven and goal-driven inferencing. Although the rule checker checks the rule set used in the ONCOCIN system, its design is general so that it can be adapted to other rule-based systems.

The intelligent machine model (TIMM) (1985) is an expert system shell that generates its rules from examples (that is, induction). TIMM™ has some capability for checking rules. In its method, inconsistency is defined as

- Those rules with the same IF conditions but with different conclusions,
- Those rules with overlapping IF conditions but with different conclusions, and
- Single rules with more than one conclusion.

The first condition is equivalent to logical conflict, but the other two conditions are peculiar to the way the system generalizes its rules. TIMM checks for completeness by searching for points (that is, combinations of attribute values) in the state space that have low similarity to the existing training cases. It does this check by randomly selecting combinations of attributes and finding the situation that is least similar to any training case. This situation is then presented to the user along with a similarity measurement that tells the user how similar the situation is to the closest training case in the knowledge base.

Knowledge engineering system (KES)™(1983) is an expert system shell that has a support tool called INSPECTOR. INSPECTOR identifies all recursive attributes that have been directly or indirectly defined. An example of a recursive attribute is an attribute that occurs in both the antecedent and the consequent of a rule (this definition is similar to that of circular rules, which we discuss later). INSPECTOR can also identify all unattached attributes. An unattached attribute is one that is not contained in the antecedent or conclusion of any rule. However, this situation might not be an error if the knowledge engineer put the attribute in the knowledge base for future use or is using it to contain some type of reference information.

The work described in this article is an extension of the rule-checking program used in the ONCOCIN project. Our work differs from the ONCOCIN effort in that CHECK is applied to the entire set of rules for a goal, not just the subsets which determine the value of each attribute. Because of this global view of the knowledge base, CHECK includes several new rule-checking criteria, including unreachable conclusions, dead-end IF conditions, dead-end goals, unnecessary IF conditions, unreferenced attribute values, and illegal attribute values. Furthermore, CHECK produces dependency charts and detects any circular rule chains. This rule-checking system was devised and tested on a wide variety of knowledge bases built with a generic expert system shell rather than on a single knowledge base as in the ONCOCIN project.

Potential Problems in the Knowledge Base

A static analysis of the rules can detect many potential problems that exist in a knowledge base. First, we identify knowledge base problems that can be detected by performing an analysis of goal-driven rules and then give definitions and examples of such problems. Later in this article, we look at how these definitions must be modified for data-driven rules.

Knowledge base problems can only be detected if the rule syntax is restrictive enough to allow one to examine two rules and determine whether situations exist in which both can succeed and whether the results of applying the two rules are the same, conflicting, or unrelated. In rule languages that allow an unrestricted syntax, it is difficult or impossible to implement the algorithms described in this article.

Checking for Consistency

By statically analyzing the logical semantics of the rules represented in LES's case-grammar format, CHECK can detect redundant rules, conflicting rules, rules that are subsumed by other rules, unnecessary IF conditions, and circular-rule chains. These five potential problems are defined in the subsections that follow.

Redundant Rules. Two rules are redundant if they succeed in the same situation and have the same conclusions. In LES this statement means that the IF parts of the two rules are equivalent, and one or more conclusions are also equivalent. The IF parts of two rules can be equivalent only if each part has the same number of conditions, and each condition in one part is equivalent to a condition in the other part. Because LES allows variables in rules, two conditions are equivalent if they are unifiable.

Formally, with the notation from predicate calculus, rule p(x)—> q(x) is equivalent to the rule p(y)—> q(y), where x and y are variables, and p and q are logical relationships.

For example, consider the two rules that follow:

IF ?X has a hoarse cough, AND
?X has difficulty breathing

THEN type-of-disease of ?X is CROUP

IF ?Y has difficulty breathing, AND
?Y has a hoarse cough

THEN type-of-disease of ?Y is CROUP

?X and ?Y represent variables that will be instantiated to a person in the database. These two rules would be redundant even if they used different variables and their IF conditions were in a different order.

As reported by Suwa, Scott, and Shortliffe (1982), redundancy in a knowledge base does not necessarily cause logical problems, although it might affect efficiency. In a system where the first successful rule is the only one to succeed, a problem will arise only if one of two redundant rules is revised or deleted, and the other is left unchanged. Also, unless the system uses some type of scoring scheme (for example, certainty factors), redundancy should not cause a problem.

Conflicting Rules. Two rules are conflicting if they succeed in the same situation but with conflicting conclusions. In LES this statement means that the IF parts of the two rules are equivalent, but one or more conclusions are contradictory.

Formally, with the notation from predicate calculus, the rule p(x)→ not (q(x)) is contradictory to the rule p(x)→q(x).

For example, consider the two rules that follow:

IF ?X has a hoarse cough, AND
?X has difficulty breathing

THEN type-of-disease of ?X is CROUP

IF ?X has a hoarse cough, AND
?X has difficulty breathing

THEN type-of-disease of ?X is BRONCHITIS

These two rules are conflicting (assuming the attribute type-of-disease is single-valued) because given the same information, one rule concludes that the disease is croup, and the other concludes bronchitis.

NOTE: It is possible that rules with similar premises might not conflict at all, especially when they are concluding values for a multivalued attribute. (A multivalued attribute can assume multiple values simultaneously. For example, a person can be allergic to many different drugs or can be infected by numerous organisms.)

Subsumed Rules. One rule is subsumed by another if the two rules have the same conclusions, but one contains additional constraints on the situations in which it will succeed. In LES this statement means one or more conclusions are equivalent, but the IF part of one rule contains fewer constraints or conditions than the IF part of the other rule.

Formally, with the notation from predicate calculus, the rule (p(x) and q(y))→r(z) is subsumed by the rule p(x)→r(z). Whenever the more restrictive rule succeeds, the less restrictive rule also succeeds, resulting in redundancy.

For example, consider the two rules that follow:

IF ?X has flat pink spots on his skin, AND
?X has a fever

THEN type-of-disease of ?X is MEASLES

IF ?X has flat pink spots on his skin

THEN type-of-disease of ?X is MEASLES

In this case, we would say that rule 1 is subsumed by rule 2 because rule 2 only needs a single piece of information to conclude "measles." Whenever rule 1 succeeds, rule 2 also succeeds.

Unnecessary IF Conditions. Two rules contain unnecessary IF conditions if the rules have the same conclusions, an IF condition in one rule is in conflict with an IF condition in the other rule, and all other IF conditions in the two rules are equivalent. With our notation from predicate calculus, if we have the rule (p(x) and q(y))→r(z) and the rule (p(x) and not (q(y)))→r(z), the condition involving q(y) in each rule is unnecessary. These two rules could be combined into (p(x) and (q(y) or not (q(y)))→ r(z). The condition (q(y) or not (q(y))) resolves to TRUE; thus, the rule becomes p(x)→r(z). In this case, the unnecessary IF condition actually indicates that only one rule is necessary.

For example, consider the two rules that follow:

IF ?X has flat pink spots on his skin, AND
?X has a fever

THEN type-of-disease of ?X is MEASLES

IF ?X has flat pink spots on his skin
?X does not have a fever

THEN type-of-disease of ?X is MEASLES

In this case, the second IF condition in each rule is unnecessary. Thus, the two rules could be collapsed into one.

A special case occurs when two rules have the same conclusion, one rule containing a single IF condition that is in conflict with an IF condition of the other rule which has two or more IF conditions. With our notation from predicate calculus, if we have the rule (p(x) and q(y))→r(z), then the second IF condition in the first rule is unnecessary, but both rules are still needed and can be reduced to (p(x))→r(z) and not (q(y))→r(z).

Circular Rules. A set of rules is circular if the chaining of these rules in the set forms a cycle. With our notation from predicate calculus, if we have the set of rules p(x)→q(x), q(x)→r(x), and r(x)→p(x), and the goal is r(A), where A is a constant, then the system enters an infinite loop at run time unless the system has a special way of handling circular rules. Also, this definition includes the possibility of a single rule forming a circular cycle (for example, p(x)→p(x)).

For example, consider the following set of rules:

IF temperature of ?X>100 (in Fahrenheit)

THEN ?X has a fever

IF ?X has a fever, AND
?X has flat pink spots on his skin

THEN type-of-disease of ?X is MEASLES

IF type-of-disease of ?X is MEASLES

THEN temperature of ?X> 100 (in Fahrenheit)

Given a goal of
type-of-disease of patient is MEASLES,

this set of rules would go into an infinite loop if one attempted to backward chain them together because the goal would match the conclusion of rule 2, the first IF condition of rule 2 would match the conclusion of rule 1, the IF condition of rule 1 would match the conclusion of rule 3, and the IF part of rule 3 would match the conclusion of rule 2, thus completing our circular chain.

Checking for Completeness

The development of a knowledge-based system is an iterative process in which knowledge is encoded, tested, added, changed, and refined. Knowledge flows from the expert into the knowledge base by way of a middleman (the knowledge engineer). This iterative process often leaves gaps in the knowledge base that both the knowledge engineer and the expert have overlooked during the knowledge-acquisition process. Furthermore, as the number of rules grows large, it becomes impossible to check every possible path through the system. In our research, we have found four situations indicative of gaps (that is, missing rules) in the knowledge base: (1) unreferenced attribute values, (2) dead-end goals, (3) unreachable conclusions, and (4) dead-end IF conditions. Any one of these four conditions might indicate that there is a rule missing.

In the ONCOCIN system, the rule checker assumes there should be a rule for each possible combination of values of attributes that appear in the antecedent. In practice, we found this criterion causes the system to hypothesize a very large number of missing rules and chose to leave it out of our checking process. This problem was not serious in the ONCOCIN project because the checker was only tested on a single application.

LES (and EMYCIN) allows the knowledge engineer the feature of strong typing the defined attributes, thus facilitating the detection of gaps. For each attribute, one can define a set of properties for it, including whether the user can be queried for the value, and a set of values the attribute can take on (that is, its legal values). This method has long been recognized in software engineering as an excellent programming practice. In fact, the newer programming languages (for example, Pascal and Ada) have type-checking capabilities along these lines.

LES allows the knowledge engineer to define properties about each slot in its factual database, including the set or range of acceptable attribute values, system ability to query the user for the attribute, and the attribute's type (single valued or multivalued). In the subsections that follow, we describe how LES uses these properties to aid it in finding gaps and errors in the knowledge base.

Unreferenced Attribute Values. Unreferenced attribute values occur when some values in the set of possible values of an object's attribute are not covered by any rule's IF conditions. In other words, the legal values in the set are covered only partially or not at all. A partially covered attribute can prohibit the system from attaining a conclusion or can cause it to make a wrong conclusion when an uncovered attribute value is encountered at run time. Unreferenced attribute values might also indicate that rules are missing.

For example, suppose we have the attribute TEMPERATURE with the set of legal values (high, normal, low). If the attribute values high and normal are used in the IF conditions of rules but not low, CHECK alerts the knowledge engineer that low is not used. The knowledge engineer would then have to decide if a rule is missing or if the value low should be removed from the set of legal values.

Illegal Attribute Values. An illegal attribute value occurs when a rule refers to an attribute value that is not in the set of legal values. This error is often caused by a spelling mistake. No extra work is required to check for this condition because it is a by-product of checking for unreferenced attribute values.

Suppose we have the attribute TEMPERATURE with the set of legal values (high, normal, low). If a rule has a condition such as

IF temperature of ?X is very high...or
...THEN temperature of ?X is medium

CHECK alerts the knowledge engineer that the values "very high" and "medium" are illegal attribute values for temperature.

Unreachable Conclusions. In a goal-driven production system, the conclusion of a rule should either match a goal or match an IF condition of another rule (in the same rule set). If there are no matches for the conclusion, it is unreachable.

For example, suppose we have the following rule:

IF temperature of ?X > 100 (in Fahrenheit)

THEN ?X has a fever

If the condition ?X has a fever does not appear in the IF part of any rule and is not part of the goal, CHECK alerts the knowledge engineer that this conclusion is unreachable.

It is possible that such a rule is merely extraneous, in which case it might affect efficiency but not the outcome because it will never be triggered. It is also possible that the conclusion does not match a goal (or subgoal) because of a terminology error. For example, a rule might exist with an IF condition of the form

IF ?X has an elevated temperature

THEN ...,

where the terms "elevated temperature" and "fever" are synonymous to the expert but not to the expert system.

Dead-End IF Conditions and Dead-End Goals. To achieve a goal (or subgoal) in a goal-driven system, either the attributes of the goal must be askable (user provides needed information), or the goal must be matched by a conclusion of one of the rules in the rule sets applying to the goal. If neither of these requirements is satisfied, then the goal cannot be achieved (that is, it is a dead-end goal). Similarly, the IF conditions of a rule must also meet one of these two conditions, or they are dead-end conditions.

For example, suppose we have the following as a goal (or subgoal):

type-of-disease of patient is MEASLES.

If the attribute type-of-disease is not askable, and there are no rules that conclude this fact, then this goal would be labeled dead-end goal.

Dependency Chart and Circular-Rule-Chain Detection

As a by-product of rule checking, CHECK generates two dependency charts. One chart shows the interactions among the data-driven rules, and the other shows the interactions among the goal-driven rules and the goals. An example of a dependency chart for a small set of rules is shown in Figure 1.

An * indicates that one or more IF conditions or a goal condition (GC) matches one or more conclusions of a rule. The dependency chart is useful when the knowledge engineer deletes, modifies, or adds rules to the rule base because it is a means of immediately seeing the dependencies among the rules.

List of Rules

R1: IF A and X then Z
R2: IF B and C then A   R2a: IF A and B and C then A
R3: IF D then C   R3a: IF A and D then C
R4: IF R then X
R5: IF S then X

Goal

GC1: determine Z

Then

If	R1	R2	R3	R4	R5
R1		•		•	•
R2		•^{2}	•		
R3		•^{3}			
R4					
R5					
GC1	•				

Figure 1. A simple rule set and its dependency chart.

Note that in Figure 1 the asterisks (*) indicate the dependencies for the original rule set. (For example, the * in row R1, column R2 indicates that an IF clause of rule R1 is concluded by rule R2.) Adding a condition to rule R2 (see rule R2a) caused the *2 dependency to appear. Note that rule R2a now references itself (that is, it is a self-circular rule). The addition of one condition to rule R3 (see rule R3a) caused the *3 dependency to appear. This addition also causes the rule set to be circular because a condition of rule R3a is matched by the conclusion of rule R2, and a condition of rule R2 matches the conclusion of rule R3a.

Circular rules should be avoided because they can lead to an infinite loop at run time. Some expert systems, such as EMYCIN, handle circular rules in a special way. Nevertheless, the knowledge engineer will want to know which rules are circular. CHECK uses the dependency chart to generate graphs representing the interactions between rules and uses a cyclic graph-detection algorithm to detect circular-rule chains.

Checking Data-Driven Rules

To this point, we have only considered goal-driven rules, but as discussed earlier, LES also supports data-driven inferencing. The data-driven rules are called WHEN rules. A WHEN rule consists of one or more WHEN conditions (similar to IF conditions) and one or more conclusions.

Checking a data-driven rule set for consistency and completeness is very similar to checking goal-driven rules. The detection of conflicting rules, redundant rules, subsumed rules, circular-rule chains, dead-end IF conditions, unreferenced attribute values, and illegal attribute values is done in the same manner as described earlier for checking goal-driven rules. However, the detection of unreachable conclusions is not applicable in checking a data-driven rule set because there are no goals to match to the conclusions.

Implementation of the Rule Checker

In solving a problem with LES, the knowledge engineer partitions the rules into sets, where each set is associated with a subject category. (In LES one can have multiple goals, and each goal has zero or more rule sets associated with it.) The set of rules for each goal can then be checked independently. To check a set of rules, the program performs five steps, as described in the following paragraphs (note that the phrase IF part of a rule means the entire set of antecedent clauses, and the phrase THEN part of a rule means the entire set of conclusions).

First, each IF and THEN clause of every rule in the set (and each goal clause) is compared against the IF and THEN clauses of every other rule in the set. The comparison of one clause against another results in a label of SAME, DIFFERENT, CONFLICT, SUBSET, or SUPERSET being stored in a two-dimensional (2-D) table maintaining the interclause relationships. The comparison operation is not straightforward because variables and the ordering of clauses must be taken into consideration.

Second, the IF part and the THEN part of every rule (and the goal) are compared against the IF and THEN part of every other rule to deduce the relationships. This process is done using the 2-D table of interclause relationships, together with the number of clauses in each part, to determine how an IF or THEN part (or goal) is related to another IF or THEN part. The possible relationships resulting from the deductions are the same as described in the first step.

Third, the part relationships of each rule are compared against the part relationships of every other rule to deduce the relationships among the rules. These comparisons are then output to the user; the possible relationships are SAME (redundant), CONFLICT, SUBSET (subsumption), SUPERSET (subsumption), UNNECESSARY CLAUSES, or DIFFERENT.

Fourth, gaps are checked for using the 2-D table of interclause relationships. Unreachable conclusions are identified by finding those THEN clauses which have the DIFFERENT relationship for all IF clauses and goals. Dead-end goals and IF conditions are identified when the DIFFERENT relationship exists for all conclusions, and the attribute these goals and conditions refer to is not askable.

Fifth, the dependency chart is also generated from the 2-D table of interclause relationships. A rule is said to be dependent on another rule if any of its IF conditions have the relationship SAME, SUBSET, or SUPERSET with any of the other rules' conclusions. The actual algorithms that used to do the checking appear in Nguyen, et al. (1985). (Since the publication of these algorithms, we have added the capability to check for unnecessary IF conditions. We have also revised our definition of missing rules.)

How Certainty Factors Affect the Checking

LES allows the use of certainty factors in its goal-driven and data-driven rules. Certainty factors are implemented in the same manner as in the EMYCIN system, with a value of +1.0 for meaning definitely true, 0.0 for unknown, and -1.0 for definitely false. The presence of certainty factors further complicates the process of checking a knowledge base. Allowing rules to conclude with less than certainty and allowing data to be entered with an associated certainty factor affects our definitions, as shown in the following paragraphs.

A conflict—when two rules succeed in the same situation but with different conclusions—is a common occurrence in rule sets using certainty factors. Often, given the same set of symptoms, the expert might wish to conclude different values with different certainty factors.

In reference to redundancy, rules that are redundant can lead to serious problems. They might cause the same information to be counted twice, leading to erroneous increases in the weight of their conclusions.

Subsumption is used quite often in rule sets with certainty factors. The knowledge engineer frequently writes rules so that the more restrictive rules add weight to the conclusions made by the less restrictive rules.

In regard to unnecessary IF conditions, IF conditions that are labeled as unnecessary when rules conclude with absolute certainty might be necessary when dealing with certainty factors. The knowledge engineer might wish to conclude a value at different certainty factors. If the rules conclude with the same certainty factor, then the IF conditions are still unnecessary.

Certainty factors do not affect our definition of or the way we detect unreferenced attribute values. The same is true with our definition of illegal attribute values.

Finding dead-end IF conditions (or dead-end goals) becomes complex with certainty factors. LES, like EMYCIN, allows the user to specify a threshold at which point the value becomes unknown. (In MYCIN this threshold is set at 0.2.) Thus, a dead-end goal could occur if there is a THEN clause that concludes with a certainty factor less than the threshold (or a chain of rules that when combined produces a certainty factor less than the threshold). For example, suppose there is a linear reasoning path of three rules (R1, R2, and R3), where A is to be asked of the user and D is the initial goal which initiated this line of reasoning

```
      R1           R2            R3
A---------> B ---------> C---------->
      0.4          0.7           0.7
```

If A is known with certainty, D would only be known with a certainty factor of (0.4)(0.7)(0.7) = 0.19. This factor is less than the threshold used in MYCIN, and, thus, D would be a dead-end goal. If D is an IF condition rather than a goal, then D would be a dead-end condition if it were not askable, and there were no other lines of reasoning to determine it.

Detecting unreachable conclusions in a rule set with certainty factors also becomes complex. A conclusion in a rule could be unreachable even though its IF part matches a conclusion in another rule. This situation might occur if the conclusion that matches one of the IF conditions cannot be determined with a certainty factor above the threshold. For example, suppose we have the following two rules:

R1: IF A THEN B (certainty factor = 0.1)

R2: IF B THEN C (certainty factor = 1.0)

If the only way to determine B was with rule R1, then the conclusion of rule R2 would be unreachable because even if A were known with certainty, C could not be determined with a certainty factor above the threshold of 0.2.

The detection of circular-rule chains is not affected by certainty factors. However, it should be noted that certainty factors might cause a circular chain of rules to be "broken" if the certainty factor of a conclusion falls below the threshold of 0.2

From this discussion, we can see that certainty factors only introduce minor extensions to the checking process, but the knowledge engineer should be aware of these differences. (The program CHECK does not look at certainty factors when checking a knowledge base.)

Summary

In this article we described CHECK, a program whose function is to check a knowledge base for consistency and completeness. The program detects several potential problems, including redundant rules, conflicting rules, subsumed rules, unnecessary IF conditions, and circular rules. CHECK also attempts to verify completeness in the knowledge base by looking for potential gaps, including unreferenced attribute values, illegal attribute values, missing rules, unreachable conclusions, dead-end IF conditions, and dead-end goals. We extended and applied the verification method for consistency and completeness of Suwa, Scott, and Shortliffe (1982) to a variety of knowledge bases built with the generic expert system shell LES with excellent results. We showed a general algorithm that efficiently performs the checking function in a single pass through the rules. We also built a version of CHECK that works with knowledge bases built with the Automated Reasoning Tool (ART™)(Nguyen,1987).

Finally, as a by-product of the rule-checking process, CHECK generates a dependency chart that shows how the rules couple and interact with each other and the goals. These charts can help the knowledge engineer visualize the effects of deleting, adding, or modifying rules.

From our experiences with constructing different knowledge bases, we found that many changes and additions to the rule sets occur during the development of a knowledge base. Thus, a tool such as CHECK that can detect many potential problems and gaps in the knowledge base should be very useful to the knowledge engineer in helping to develop a knowledge base rapidly and accurately.

As the field of knowledge-based systems matures, large expert systems will be fielded in critical situations. Because it will be impossible to test all paths beforehand, one must be assured that deadly traps such as circular rules and dead-end clauses do not exist in the knowledge base. Thus, a checking capability similar to the one described in this article is essential.

References

Davis, R. 1976. Applications of Meta-Level Knowledge to the Construction, Maintenance, and Use of Large Knowledge Bases. Ph.D. diss., Dept. of Computer Science, Stanford Univ.

Hayes-Roth, F. 1985. Rule-Based Systems. *Communications of the ACM* 28(9):921-932.

KES General Description Manual. 1983. Software Architecture and Engineering , Inc., Arlington, Va., p. 33.

Laffey, T. J.; Perkins, W. A.; and Nguyen, T. A. 1986. Reasoning about Fault Diagnosis with LES. *IEEE Expert, Intelligent Systems and Their Applications* 1(1):13-20.

Nguyen, T. A. 1987. Verifying Consistency of Production Systems. In Proceedings of the Third Conference on Artificial Intelligence Applications, 4-8. Washington, D.C.: IEEE Computer Society Press.

Nguyen, T. A.; Perkins, W. A.; Laffey, T. J.; and Pecora, D. 1985. Checking an Expert System's Knowledge Base for Consistency and Completeness. In Proceedings of the Ninth International Joint Conference on Artificial Intelligence, 374-378. Menlo Park, Calif.: American Association for Artificial Intelligence.

Shortliffe, E. H. 1976. *Computer-Based Medical Consultations: MYCIN.* New York: Elsevier.

Suwa, M.; Scott, A. C.; and Shortliffe, E. H. 1982. An Approach to Verifying Completeness and Consistency in a Rule-Based Expert System. *AI Magazine* 3(4):16-21.

TIMM User's Manual. 1985. General Research Corporation, Santa Barbara, Calif., pp. 46-49.*

Van Melle, W. J. 1981. *System Aids in Constructing Consultation Programs.* Ann Arbor, Mich.: UMI Research Press.

Note

*TIMM™ is a registered trademark of General Research Corporation.

*ART™ is a registered trademark of Inference Corporation.

Validation of Expert Systems—With Applications to Auditing and Accounting Expert Systems

Daniel E. O'Leary

In addition to the processes of designing, developing, and implementing expert systems (ESs), validation is important to the decision-making success of a system and to the continued use of an ES. An ES that has not been validated sufficiently may make poor decisions. This can lead to a loss of confidence in the particular ES or in other systems, resulting in discontinued use and financial loss.

A number of different approaches to validating *particular* auditing and accounting ESs [16][17][18][38][39] and medical ESs [52][8][7] have been reported. Validation of general ESs [21][33] and potential bases for the validation of ESs [4] also have been discussed. This paper presents a theory-based framework that is useful not only for guiding the validation of an ES, but also for eliciting other validation research issues.

Validation of ESs

Developing, designing, and implementing systems for making expert decisions requires analyzing the knowledge base and the decision-making capabilities of the system. That process, referred to as validation, requires

- Ascertaining what the system knows, does not know, or knows incorrectly;
- Ascertaining the level of expertise of the system;
- Determining if the system is based on a theory for decision making in the particular domain;
- Determining the reliability of the system.

Reprinted with permission from *Decision Sciences*, vol. 18, Summer 1987, 468-86.

Once these concerns have been satisfactorily addressed, the system is updated to reflect the findings and may be revalidated. The process should be performed in an environment designed to provide an objective and cost-effective validation.

Validation *ascertains what the system knows, does not know, or knows incorrectly*. For example, when the expert system R1 (a system for configuring computers used by Digital Equipment [36]) was validated, errors and omissions in the knowledge base were identified. These errors and omissions were corrected before the system was placed in service [21].

Validation *ascertains the level of decision-making expertise of the system*. The types of problems a system can solve and the quality of its solutions define the level of expertise. For example, in education it is common to define an individual's level of accomplishment based on the types of problems that the individual can solve and the quality of the solutions produced.

Validation *determines if the ES is theory based.* Davis [12][13] argued that basing an expert system on a theory is an efficient approach to developing such a system. Lack of a theory base has resulted in the failure of at least one system [48].

Validation *analyzes the reliability of the ES*. Given similar inputs, the ES should produce similar outputs. In addition, before and after revalidation a system generally should give similar responses to similar sets of test problems.

Validation Process

Previous analyses of ES validation have stressed the importance of periodic informal validation rather than a single, formal validation at the end of a project [44]. This validation will not be the same in each situation but will differ in formality and in the extent to which the validation process is implemented. As suggested by software engineering [44] and ES validation [21], formal acceptance testing may be appropriate. (A formal acceptance test might consist of a test where the user formally signs off on the quality of the decisions made by the system.)

ES Assessment

Although the focus of this paper is on ES validation, other issues addressed in developing, designing, and implementing ESs do not relate to decisions that the system makes; nevertheless, these other issues do contribute to the overall success of a system. The assessment process involves analyzing the user interface and supporting the quality of the development effort. For example, it involves

- Ascertaining the quality of the user interface [31];
- Evaluating the documentation of the system (a typical weakness of most systems, with good reason; since ESs are evolutionary, the documentation does not evolve at the same rate as the rest of the system);
- Determining what language or shell should be used to develop the system;
- Analyzing the quality of the system programming.

Paper Objectives

This paper has four primary objectives: to propose a set of definitions for the concepts "validation" and "assessment" applied to ESs; to develop a framework for the validation of ESs; to demonstrate that framework on some previously published auditing and accounting ESs; and to use that demonstration to elicit some of the research issues involved in ES validation.

The paper proceeds as follows. The objective of developing a framework is to take advantage of the unique aspects of ESs. Therefore the next section discusses some unique aspects of ESs in general and of auditing and accounting ESs in particular. Using a research methods approach, these unique characteristics are incorporated into a framework for ES validation. The framework is demonstrated on accounting and auditing ESs and that demonstration is used to elicit some of the research issues involved in the validation of ESs.

Unique Characteristics of Auditing and Accounting ESs

If ESs are like other computer systems, then validating an ES should be the same as validating any other computer system. However if ESs are different, then their unique characteristics can be used to develop a specific framework for their validation. A number of technical, environmental, design, and domain characteristics distinguish ESs from other computer-based systems.

The *technical* aspects which distinguish ESs include the following. First, ESs process symbolic information (e.g., "If...then" rules) rather than just numeric information [1][43]. This ability to process symbolic information allows ESs to solve nonnumeric-like problems, which generally are less precise than numeric problems. Second, experience with representing knowledge shows that a fraction (less than 10 percent) of this knowledge escapes standard representation schemes and requires special "fixes" [19] to make it accessible. Since other systems do not use knowledge representation, they do not face this problem. Third, ESs often are developed using either artificial intelligence (AI) languages or ES shells [25]. An AI language is a computer language aimed at processing symbolic information (e.g., Prolog [11] or Lisp [5]). An ES shell is software designed to aid the development of an ES by prespecifying the inference engine and making it easier to input knowledge into the system. Some of the first ES shells were EMYCIN [7] and AL/X [15]. More recently developed shells include Texas Instrument's Personal Consultant Plus, Teknowledge's M.1, and Inference Corporation's ART. The characteristics of ES shells and AI languages (e.g., their ease of examination by nonprogrammers) can be made a part of an ES validation framework.

Environmental characteristics which distinguish ESs include the following. First, ESs directly influence or make decisions [1][25][49]. Other systems (e.g., decision support systems (DSSs)) simply support decision making or have an indirect impact on decisions. Second, the expertise being modeled by an ES generally is in short supply, is an expensive resource, or is not readily available at a particular geographic location [20]. This is in contrast to other computer systems (e.g., accounting systems) where generally a number of personnel understand what the system is designed to accomplish.

In addition to these characteristics that differentiate ESs from virtually all other types of computer systems, the dominant *design* methodology for both ESs and DSSs differentiates them from traditional computer systems. First, ESs (and DSSs) often are developed using a "middle-out" design rather than the traditional data processing approach of top-down or bottom-up design. A middle-out design philosophy starts with a prototype and gradually expands the system to meet the needs of the decision [27]. Second, like DSSs, ESs evolve over time—the system changes as the decision-making process gradually is understood and modeled [28]. As a consequence, traditional validation models based on other design philosophies are not likely to meet the needs of an ES.

Finally, some *domain* characteristics of auditing and accounting decisions (and other business-based decisions) often distinguish these decisions from decisions made in other domains. First, in contrast to some scientific decisions that have a unique solution (such as those represented by the ES DENDRAL [1]), auditing and accounting decisions generally do not have a single solution. Second, the decision reached often can be evaluated only by how similar it is to decisions other decision makers develop (i.e., by consensus); there may be no way to rank the decisions a priori. Third, different schools of thought may represent alternative knowledge bases. This means experts may not agree on a recommended solution. (This can apply to other disciplines as well.) Fourth, a "good" decision does not necessarily result in "good" consequences. Decisions are based on information available at the time they are made; this does not guarantee desirable consequences at a later time. Fifth, in contrast to some disciplines where a decision has no direct dollar value, the decision modeled by an ES can have substantial monetary value.

Validation Framework

Software engineering encompasses the general set of tools and techniques that aid programmers in software development. Since ESs are computer programs, software engineering might appear to be a likely candidate to supply a framework for ES validation. However, the unique characteristics of ESs in general, and of accounting and auditing ESs in particular, indicate that such a framework will not be appropriate.

An examination of one such approach [44] supports this view. First, in software engineering the focus of validation is on finding errors in the program. The validation of ESs is more than just a process of finding errors. Here the validation process meets the development needs of defining the level of expertise of the system, identifying what the system can and cannot do, understanding the quality of the decisions produced by the system, and describing the theory on which the system is based. Because software engineering generally is not concerned directly with human expertise, it is not directly concerned with these issues.

Second, the unique characteristics of ESs indicate they are different from other computer programs. Since ESs process symbolic information, use ES shells and AI languages, and require special fixes in their knowledge bases, they also require different validation approaches than other computer programs. Further, ESs directly affect decisions and they model expertise that is in short supply; the environment in which they operate is different from that of other computer programs.

Third, the domain-based decisions of auditing and accounting ESs often are not well enough understood to use traditional software engineering approaches. While software engineering generally uses structured top-down or bottom-up approach in the design and evaluation of software, ESs are evolutionary and often are developed using a middle-out approach.

One alternative to the software engineering approach is a research methods approach. This approach views the development of ESs as experimental representations of human expertise, that is, as research designs. Kerlinger defined research design as "the plan, structure and strategy of investigation conceived so as to obtain answers to research questions and to control variance" [30, p. 300]. In a similar sense, validation can be defined as the plan, structure, and strategy of investigation conceived so as to obtain answers to questions about the knowledge and decision processes used in ESs and to control variance in that process.

Kerlinger also noted, "research designs are invented to enable the researcher to answer research questions as validly, accurately, objectively, and economically as possible" [30, p. 301].

He also noted that accuracy consists of four concepts: reliability, systematic variance, extraneous systematic variance, and error variance.

We use these characteristics of research design (validity, objectivity, economics, and accuracy) to formulate a framework (Table 1) for the validation of ESs. Since Kerlinger noted the existence of three types of validity in research methods (content validity, criterion-related validity, and construct validity), each will be treated separately.

Content Validity

"Content validity is the representativeness or sampling adequacy of the content—the substance, the matter, the topics" [30, p. 458]. In validating ESs, content validity refers to ascertaining what the system knows, does not know, or knows incorrectly. This can be operationalized in at least two ways: by direct examination of the system components or by testing the system.

1. Content validity
   a. Direct examination of the system by the expert
   b. System test against human experts (Turing test)
      (1) Intraexpert test
      (2) Interexpert test
   c. System test against other models
2. Criterion validity
   a. Definition of the level of expertise of the system
      (1) Human evaluation criteria
      (2) Test problems to define the level of expertise
      (3) Quality of responses defined
   b. Knowledge-base criteria
   c. Clarification of evaluation criteria
3. Construct validity
4. Objectivity
   a. Programmer validation
   b. Independent administration of validation
   c. Sponsor/end-user validation
   d. Biasing and blinding
   e. Different development and test data
5. Economics (cost-benefit)
6. Reliability
   a. System test against itself (sensitivity analysis)
   b. Test probiems for revalidation
7. Systematic variance (experimental variance)
   a. Problems reflecting range of problems encountered
   b. Variation in the test problems
   c. Number of test problems
   d. Type I and Type II errors
8. Extraneous variance
   a. Complexity of the system
   b. ES's location in the system life cycle
   c. Recognition, examination, and testing of special fixes
   d. Location of judges during testing
   e. Learning on part of judges
9. Error variance

Table 1. Summary of validation framework.

Direct Examination of the System Components. An ES is based on the knowledge of experts. Accordingly, it is important that these experts know what is contained in the system. The expert can examine the knowledge base directly in one of two ways. First, the ES could develop, for example, a list of the rules in its knowledge base for periodic review or a summary of the process it uses for the inference engine. Second, the expert could examine the storage of the information by the ES directly.

The first solution might produce reports that could be read easily but, being an intermediate step, it also would require validation. As a result, it would be preferable if the expert could examine the knowledge base directly. In the second case, the primary concern is the format of the knowledge to be reviewed. If the system were built using an ES shell or an AI language such as Prolog, direct review likely is feasible.

A knowledge expert might not be able to investigate the inference engine to see whether it is correct because of the complexity of the computer code. However, if an ES shell is used, the inference engine normally would be prespecified.

The direct examination of the components has some limitations. First, fear of computers [21] may generate hostility toward the system. Second, human information processing is limited. Direct examination may not correctly process the links between parts of the knowledge base; also, the breadth of information contained in the knowledge base could limit the success of a direct investigation. Third, the direct approach may require substantial resources. If the expertise is scarce, purchasing expertise may be costly. Fourth, direct examination may be a tedious job that could lead to errors in the validation. Fifth, if the knowledge base is large or complex, examination could prove very time consuming and complex and lead to information overload. Sixth, current technology is not designed to facilitate direct examination.

Further, any direct analysis of the knowledge base is limited to looking at the pieces of the base and not at how they interact.

In addition, translation of the computer code makes any direct analysis of the heuristics in the inference engine difficult. Accordingly, the best solution is to test the system as a whole.

System Test Against Human Expert. If the system is designed to perform as an expert, it should be tested against an expert(s). To ensure that the ES has captured the expertise of the expert it was designed around, its decisions should be compared to that expert's.

However, such an intraexpert test procedure has the potential to introduce bias into the validation process through the acquisition of information from memory or the manner in which information is processed [26]. In terms of ESs, this means that the knowledge base or the relationships between sets of rules or the heuristics in the inference engine all may contain bias. This suggests that the ES also must be tested against *other* experts from the same "school" as the original expert but who are not biased or invested in the particular ES.

Since such interexpert tests when conducted using experts from *alternative* schools may yield contradictory decisions, this type of comparison is not recommended. However, alternative views of the world might produce additional knowledge for the system.

System Test Against Other Models. System tests against human experts may be preferred to tests against other models. However, tests against human experts can be expensive. Experts also face time constraints [7]. Since the system is a model, one important characteristic should be its relationship to other models. An ES should

- Perform in a similar or better fashion than other models for the same problem;
- Be able to solve problems that are not amenable to other solution methodologies.

One type of model used to analyze decisions is regression analysis [6][32] where independent variables represent the variables used by a decision maker. Other types of models may be used, but the model used largely is a function of the problem and previous recommended solutions to the problem. In particular, the preferred model would be the one that has provided the best solution to the problem so far. For example, an ES for production scheduling would be tested against an existing operations research model.

Unfortunately, in some cases comparison of the ES to regression or to other approaches may not be feasible because of the structure of the ES knowledge base (e.g., if "If...then" statements are present). It may be very difficult to translate such rules into numeric variables. However, simulation generally is a feasible alternative [9][10].

Criterion Validity

"Criterion-related validity is studied by comparing test or scale scores with one or more external variables, or criteria, known or believed to measure the attribute under study" [30, p. 459]. In ES validation, this refers to the criteria used to validate the system, for example, to ascertain the level of the system's expertise.

The primary criterion for system validation is the relationship between the decisions developed by the system and decisions developed by human experts. In AI this is referred to broadly as a Turing test. However, this sort of relationship is not evaluated easily. Difficulties arise for a number of reasons: differing definitions of the level of expertise, differing knowledge-base criteria, and lack of clarity about what is to be evaluated.

Definition of the Level of Expertise. One way to define and measure the level of expertise the ES has attained is to use the same criteria identified for defining expertise in human experts [7]. Where feasible, this is a good option. However, in many auditing- and accounting-based decision-making situations specific criteria are not available for specific decisions. Instead, a portfolio of decisions is subject to a set of criteria. For example, managers may be evaluated on their monthly profit and loss statements. These statements reflect a portfolio of decisions.

An alternative approach is to evaluate the system's performance on a set of test problems. There are at least two possible ways to do this. First, in analyzing a human's knowledge, the problems that the person can solve determine his/her level of accomplishment. Similarly, the difficulty of test problems that a system can solve defines the system's level of expertise. Second, in analyzing a human's knowledge, the quality of the solutions also helps determine the level of accomplishment. Similarly, the quality of the responses to test problems defines the level of expertise of an ES. Quality, of course, is a difficult concept to measure; its definition often is situation-based. However, with humans the number of correct responses obtained often is used to measure quality. This criterion also has been used to validate ESs.

Knowledge-Base Criteria. There are three generic knowledge-base criteria that suggest what to test: consistency, accuracy, and completeness. Consistency refers to the relationship between the information in the knowledge base and the ability of the inference engine to process the knowledge base in a consistent manner. Accuracy refers to the correctness of the knowledge in the knowledge base. Completeness refers to the amount of knowledge built into the knowledge base.

Clarification of Evaluation Criteria. Although general approaches may be developed to test the above generic criteria, a particular application also may require specific evaluation criteria [21]. For example, when evaluating an automobile a number of criterion (such as luxury, economy, and sportiness) might be developed. Particular measures then must be developed to characterize these concepts. For example, "miles per gallon" can be used to measure economy. Because many measures are possible, researchers suggest that the specific criteria and characterizations to be used be established and agreed on before validation begins.

Construct Validity

Construct validity refers to those constructs or factors that the test is designed to discover. "The significant point about construct validity that sets it apart from other types of validity is its preoccupation with these [and] theoretical constructs" [30, p. 461]. In terms of ESs, this type of validity indicates the importance of the existence of a theory on which the system is based. Construct validity suggests that a purely empirical approach may be inappropriate. Davis [12][13] suggested that an empirical approach is not as efficient as an approach based on a theory (or at least on an understanding of the problem at hand) when developing an ES. He suggested instead the use of systems that reason from first principles, that is, from an understanding of causality in the system being examined. McDermott (see [48]) indicated that a primary reason ES development may fail is the lack of a theory on which the knowledge encoded in the ES is based.

One problem with using construct validity as a criterion is that conflicting or alternative theories or first principles may be available. This can lead to difficulties in establishing inter-expert validation tests.

Objectivity

In variance terms, objectivity refers to minimizing observer variance [30, p. 491]. Accordingly, in validating an ES any judgmental variance should be minimized. This includes eliminating expert bias by administering the test independently, and using blinding techniques [7].

Programmer Validation. Because of the programmer's knowledge of the system and the nature of the development process, the system programmer generally will perform periodic informal validation on the system. If the programmer does not have a vested interest in the ES, this can be a way of developing an independent validation. However, programmers typically do not perform all the validation processes required. They may have a vested interest in the system, or they may not understand the problem being addressed by the system. This suggests using a combination of programmer and other validation.

Independent Administration of Validation. The importance of independence is recognized generally in research design. It also is recognized in accounting when a CPA performs an external audit or when internal auditors perform audits for internal purposes. If the model builder also validates the model, conflicts of interest can arise.

Sponsor/End User Validation. Software engineering uses an acceptance test by the sponsor or the end user as the final step in validating the computer program. Gaschnig, Klahr, Pople, Shortliffe, and Terry [21] suggested a similar type of formal test for an ES. That is, the user must "sign-off" on the system. If the end user has expertise in the area, then this acceptance test can be a critical test of user acceptance. However, if the sponsor or end user does not have sufficient expertise to judge the quality of the system, he or she may not be an appropriate judge.

Blinding Techniques to Eliminate Bias. Buchanan and Shortliffe [7] reported that some human expert validators are biased against computers making certain kinds of decisions. In order to minimize this limitation, the validation of MYCIN used a "blinded" study design to remove that source of bias.

Using Different Development and Test Data. Test problems often are used when developing systems to ensure consistent and reliable performance. However, it is important that the problems used to test the system not be limited to those problems used in developing the system; otherwise, these are not true test problems.

Economics (Cost-Benefit)

Cost-benefit decisions permeate research methods. For example, Simon noted "you will want to invest your time and energy in the work that will be the most valuable" [46, p. 100].

A key aspect of any economic activity is cost-benefit analysis. Since auditing- and accounting-based ESs are developed and validated using resources and may make decisions that have economic consequences, cost-benefit analysis is a major concern in their validation.

One important factor used to determine system benefit is how the system ultimately will be used. The system may be used for commercial purposes or it may be a prototype designed to investigate the feasibility of developing a system for a particular purpose. In either case, benefit may be difficult to measure.

Two of the main factors that determine the cost of validating a system are the formality and extent of validation required. Formality indicates the breadth of application of the validation—for example, is there an independent validation of the system? Extent indicates the depth of validation of the system—for example, how many test problems are used? Thus a prototype ES designed to determine whether a particular process can be represented as an ES will not receive a validation that has the same formality or extent as a commercially based system.

Cost-benefit affects not only the scope of validation but also the development of the system because the amount of validation defines the extent to which, for example, it can be determined if the knowledge in the knowledge base is correct or complete.

Reliability

One synonym for accuracy is reliability. "Reliability is the accuracy of precision of a measuring instrument" [30, p. 491]. In ES validation, the stability of the system and the ability of the system to generate identical solutions given identical inputs measures the reliability of the system.

System Test Against Itself (Sensitivity Analysis). One possible validation procedure is the analysis of a program's sensitivity to slight changes in the knowledge base or in the weights[7]. That is, the model can be tested against itself for stability. If the system produces several solutions over minor parametric shifts, the system may be unstable. Alternatively, in certain environments a highly sensitive ES may be required. In this case it can be difficult to differentiate instability from an appropriate model response.

Standard Test Problems. Standard test problems may be used in the revalidation process. These problems should be designed to test standard system responses to ensure, for example, that additions to the knowledge base do not result in contradictions. The limitations of standard problems are discussed in [21].

Systematic Variance (Experimental Variance)

"If the independent variable does not vary substantially, there is little chance of separating its effect from the total variance of the dependent variable, so much of which is often due to change" [30, p. 308]. In validating an ES's performance, the test problems used need to allow the validator to distinguish between systematic variance and chance. This can be accomplished in a number of different ways.

Test Problems Reflect the Range of Problems Encountered. Test problems should be representative of problems the expert encounters in practice. Problems should reflect not only common "middle of the road" situations, but also some of the more unusual occurrences [8].

Variation in Test Problems. Validation success is based to a large extent on the test problems used in the validation process. Variation in the problems must exist if the entire set of parameters in the model and the range of the parameters is to be tested. If the problems are not varied enough in terms of the set and range of the parameters, the validation process and the test of any variations in the system's behavior will be too limited.

Number of Test Problems. A sufficient number of test problems must be used to ensure the statistical significance of the model. A test of only a few problems will not adequately test the knowledge base or range and set of parameters nor will it provide statistical significance [8].

Type I and Type II Errors. A Type I error occurs when we incorrectly reject a null hypothesis. A Type II error occurs when we accept a null hypothesis that is false. Both types of errors need to be considered when validating an ES. In some decision problems (e.g., bankruptcy-no bankruptcy) a large majority of the test problems will result in null hypotheses being accepted (and only a few rejected) because of the nature of the process itself. In these cases, there is a large possibility of Type II errors. In such a decision setting, there may be few test problems that actually test the abilities of the system. Accordingly, the test problems must be chosen carefully in light of this concern.

Extraneous Variance

"The control of extraneous variance means that the influences of independent variables extraneous to the purposes of the study are minimized, nullified or isolated" [30, p. 309]. At least five extraneous variables can influence the quality of system output; complexity of the system, location in the system life cycle, special fixes, location of the judges, and learning by the judges.

Complexity of the System. Complexity of the system is one of the most important variables in determining how difficult the validation process will be in software engineering. Software engineering uses a classification schema to measure the complexity of a computer program [44]: a simple program is one with fewer than 1,000 statements, written by one programmer, with no interactions with any other systems; an intermediate program is one with fewer than 10,000 statements, written by one to five programmers, with few interactions with other systems.

These criteria are not reasonable standards to use for evaluating ESs. Traditional software engineering computer programs do not use a knowledge base or an inference engine. In addition, in software engineering problems the process being modeled generally is well defined. Therefore, these software engineering classification schema cannot be used to evaluate ESs.

The criteria, however, can form the basis for other measures of complexity. Unfortunately, a ready replacement for general evaluation is not available. Some suggest the number of rules in the knowledge base as a standard, but this ignores connections between the rules and the inference engine. In spite of a lack of clear criteria, complexity remains an important variable in determining how difficult the validation process will be.

ES's Location in the System Life Cycle. Gaschnig et al. [21] suggested that the ES's current position in the development cycle is critical in determining the extent of validation desired. Validation is less critical in the early stages of development (but also less expensive and less difficult) than it is in later stages. In the early stages, a system is not very knowledgeable. Accordingly, simple validation tests will determine whether or not the system has an adequate set of working knowledge. In the latter stages, however, the ES may be facing adoption by external users and may require extensive validation. As a result, the ES's location in the life cycle is an important variable in determining the extent of the validation process.

Recognition, Examination, and Testing of Special Fixes. As noted in Fox, "experience with representing large varieties of knowledge show that a small fraction(<10%) escape standard representation schemes, requiring specialized 'fixes'" [19, p. 282]. That is, in order to ensure that the knowledge base is complete, special features (fixes) are added to the system. These special fixes are of concern in ES validation. They need to be summarized so that special validation procedures can be developed to address them. Since these are "special" fixes, it is difficult to generalize any further.

Location of Judges During Testing. A critical distinction is made in research methodology between laboratory and field test settings.

In the laboratory, many variables that may be faced by the judges who will be compared to the ES can be controlled. On the other hand, a field setting offers a richer decision-making environment and a more realistic test of the ES.

Learning During the Validation Process. Although most business-based ESs do not learn from processing decision problems, this is not necessarily true of the judges to whom the system is compared. For human judges, the ability to learn from the decision problems may be an extraneous variable. Learning could occur from the order of the test problems or from the type of test problems used. The amount of the learning due to order can be assessed by changing the order of the test problems. Learning that occurs from the process of making decisions on test problems is a more difficult problem and often is ignored in Turing tests. This problem can be addressed by determining whether an expert who has experience with the test problems makes decisions similar to those made by experts with less system experience.

Error Variance

In a discussion of error variance, Kerlinger noted

> There are a number of determinants of error variance, for instance, factors associated with individual differences among subjects. Ordinarily we call this variance due to individual differences "systematic variance." But when such variance cannot be, or is not identified and controlled, we lump it with the error variance. [30, p. 312]

This kind of variance can be caused by variation in the experts' responses from trial to trial, guessing, momentary inattention, slight temporary fatigue, lapses of memory, transient emotional states, etc. [30]. The validation framework for the ES's attempts to minimize error variance by controlling many of the variables in controlling the extraneous variance is the same as in all experimental designs. However, much of this minimization of error variance occurs by preventing errors and ambiguities, that is, by using proven measurement scales and unambiguous questions.

Relationship of Previous Auditing and Accounting ESs to the Proposed Validation Framework

A limited number of auditing- and accounting-based ESs currently exist. The few that are being used (or are planned for use) on a commercial level (e.g., [50] and [45]) are proprietary. Accordingly, the present analysis is limited to *prototype* auditing- and accounting-based ESs.

The review and analysis of ESs in this paper are limited to those accounting and auditing systems generally available in the literature at the time the paper was written (February 1986) and to information published about the validation processes used in developing and designing those systems.[1] Accordingly, [3], [14], [22], and [24] are not discussed because they are unpublished papers; [3], [14], [20], [23], [29], and [34] are excluded because they contain little or no information about how the systems were validated.

The validation procedures used in those prototype ESs discussed in previous sections offer us a chance to examine the ability of our framework to capture the validation process. These findings are summarized in Table 2. Some framework items (economics and error variance) from Table 1 are not included in Table 2 because of the prototype nature of the systems. *This analysis is not to be considered as critical of these systems—each system was an innovative prototype effort.* The framework also can be used to analyze some of the potential research issues involved in ES validation.

Content Validity

The validators used examined the system's overall behavior rather than individual components. Future research needs to develop cost-benefit tools that allow individual components (such as the knowledge base) to be validated rather than simply comparing the system's overall performance to that of another expert [41].

The system tests analyzed each used human experts (in both interexpert and intraexpert tests) as the basis for validation. However, probably due to the prototype nature of the systems, only a small number of human experts generally were used. In addition, the use of interexpert tests may have introduced variance because the different experts used may have held contradictory views about the subject area.

	Clarkson [9] [10]	Bouwman [5]	Dungan and Chandler [16] [17] [18]	Michaelsen [38]	Steinbart [47]	Meservy [37]
1. *Content validity*						
Direct examination	No	No	No	No	No	No
Human expert comparison	Yes	Yes	Yes	Yes	Yes	Yes
Intraexpert test	Yes	Yes	No (multiple experts)	No (author was expert)	No	Yes
Interexpert test	No	Yes (18)	Yes (2)	Yes (2)	Yes (6)	Yes (3)
Other model test	Yes (random & naive)	No	Yes	No	No	No
2. *Criterion validity*						
Level of system	Expert	Expert	Expert	Expert	Expert	Expert
3. *Construct validity*	Largely empirical	Largely empirical	Weights generated empirically	Books	Audit manuals & textbooks	Prototypic reasoning
4. *Objectivity*						
Independent	No	No	Yes	Yes	Yes	Yes
5. *Reliability*						
Sensitivity	No	No	No	No	No	No
6. *Systematic variance*						
Actual problems	Apparently	NA (experiment)	Yes	Yes	Yes	Experiment similar to actual
Variation	Small range available; funds of 22k-37.5k	Not at extremes	small range; actual $ amounts	Chosen by subjects	Difficult to ascertain (likely)	Sought problems different than development problems
Sample Size	Two sets of four cases	Four sets of one case	11 cases (one company)	Two cases (one company)	Thirteen actual problems	Three sets of one case
Type I and type II errors	No	No	No	No	No	No
7. *Extraneous variance*						
Location of expert	Few controls	Laboratory	Office of expert	Office of expert	Office of expert	Unclear

Table 2. Validation characteristics of selected accounting ESs.

In some cases, the small number of human experts available was supplemented by the use of alternative models or standard tests of validation. Unfortunately, developing an alternative model may cost more than having a human expert serve as a standard by responding to a set of test problems. Perhaps as a result, the comparison models analyzed were relatively unsophisticated. Generally, little research compares the performance of ESs to other sophisticated models.

Criterion Validity

The similarity of solutions proposed by the ES and the human expert(s) was used as the single criterion for success of the model. This standard ignored the possibility that an ES might derive better solutions than those of a human expert. It is not unusual for other types of models to outperform their human counterparts [26]. However, no such comparison has been made with ESs. If ESs can in fact consistently outperform humans, then other criteria will have to be developed to ensure appropriate validation.

Because the developers of these prototypes were involved in their validation, there apparently was little difficulty clarifying the evaluation criteria. However, little research has been done on developing effective evaluation criteria when outside validators are used.

In some cases, identifying the level of difficulty of the test problems established the expertise of the system. For example, AUDITOR [16][17][18] used test problems drawn from the work papers of audits. However, currently there is no general way of determining the system's level of expertise.

The primary knowledge-base criterion used in the studies examined was accuracy of the system. However, little analysis was performed by the validators to ensure completeness or consistency of the system. In part, this may be because few methods for analyzing the completeness or consistency of a system are available. Future research could focus on developing such tools.

Construct Validity

Some of the prototype ESs were tied to a theoretical construct. However, some apparently were designed to discover how decisions are made, without the benefit of a normative decision-making model. The danger in this approach is that the model may be too "expert specific" with no ability to generalize or be compared to other expert systems or humans. On the other hand, of course, one of the primary research benefits of developing an ES is to understand better the nature of the particular decision process being modeled.

Objectivity
Generally, the validation processes used in these studies did not have an independent validator. Since the developers were involved in administering the validation, bias may have been introduced. Commercially developed packages, however, likely will have independent validation or at the least a user acceptance test.

Generally, no blinding techniques were used in administering the validation tests, and this may have affected the results.

Cost-Benefit Analysis
Each of the ESs examined was a prototype system. As a result, validation was minimally cost beneficial. As system development moves away from research-oriented prototypes, however, the cost-benefit relationship favors more validation. Generally, the costs of validation can be specified, but the benefits of validation are not as easily measured. Research could be directed toward measuring the benefits of validation.

Reliability
Since the ESs were prototype systems, there was no need to develop test problems for revalidation. However, for commercial systems, such test problems can be used after revision to ensure that no inconsistent or incorrect information has entered in the knowledge base. Test problems, of course, test only facets of the knowledge base. Research could be directed toward developing other methods to test for reliability.

Further, if revising the ES adds new knowledge to the knowledge base, can tools such as test problems be used effectively? With new knowledge in the system, a test problem may have different correct answers before and after revision.

Systematic Variance
A major recognized problem of auditing- and accounting-based ESs is the small number of test problems used in the sample. In addition, the studies looked at examined test problems from a "middle of the road" viewpoint. While many real-world situations are of this type, such a test does not examine system behavior in extreme situations and may not provide enough variation to test the system's overall behavior. This potential limitation can be overcome by broadening the range of test problem parameters.

Further, validation of the prototypes studied did not take into account the frequency of Type I and Type II errors in developing the test problems, nor did it consider the effect the number of the test problems used would have. Both omissions could produce a false sense of security in the test results for a system.

Extraneous Variance
The researchers in the prototype studies did not account for all extraneous system variables (e.g., complexity) in their validation efforts. Little research elicits or characterizes extraneous variables. Information on the special fixes and the validation of those special fixes also was lacking. This may be because a relatively small number of fixes were required or because the fixes were application specific. However, research into the extent of these special fixes could provide a guide to the amount of effort that should be expended in validating these special fixes.

The effect of learning on the part of the judges apparently was not a concern in validating these prototype ESs. The location of the judges did vary from study to study. The extent to which learning and location affect a judge's decision would make an interesting research question.

Conclusion

This paper has developed a framework for validating ESs. The framework is based on research methods and can be used by ES developers to guide validation efforts. It also can be used to elicit further research topics in validation.

The framework addresses validation in terms of validity, objectivity, cost-benefits, and accuracy. Using previously developed ESs as examples, the framework elicited some directions for future research in validation. Those directions include the development of tools to aid in cost-benefit validation, analysis of intervening variables and their characteristics, and comparison of ESs to other models. In addition, the framework suggests some important validation questions including, "What validation criteria can be used if the ES is expected to outperform a human expert?" and "How can we best identify the system's level of expertise?"

References

[1] Bart, A., & Feigenbaum, E. A. *The handbook of artificial intelligence.* Stanford, CA: Heuristech Press and Los Altos, CA: William Kaufmann, 1981.

[2] Bennet, J. (Ed.). *Building decision support systems.* Reading, MA: Addison-Wesley, 1983.

[3] Biggs, S. F., & Selfridge, M. *GC-X: A prototype expert system for the auditor's going concern judgment.* Presented at the University of Southern California Symposium on Expert Systems, Los Angeles, CA, February 1986.

[4] Blanning, R. W. Knowledge acquisition and system validation in expert systems for management. *Human Systems Management,* 1984, *4,* 280-285.

[5] Bouwman, M. J. Human diagnostic reasoning by computer. *Management Science,* 1983, *29,* 653-672.

[6] Bowman, E. H. Consistency and optimality in management decision making. *Management Science,* 1963, *9,* 310-321.

[7] Buchanan, B. G., & Shortliffe, E. H. *Rule-based expert systems.* Reading, MA: Addison-Wesley, 1984.

[8] Chandrasekaran, B. On evaluating AI systems for medical diagnosis. *AI Magazine,* 1983 4(2), 34-38.

[9] Clarkson, G. P. E. *Portfolio selection: A simulation of trust investment.* Englewood Cliffs, NJ: Prentice-Hall, 1962.

[10] Clarkson, G. P. E. A model of the trust investment process. In E. A. Feigenbaum & J. Feldman (Eds.), *Computers and thought.* New York: McGraw-Hill, 1963.

[11] Clocksin, W. F., & Mellish, C. S. *Programming in Prolog.* New York: Springer-Verlag, 1984.

[12] Davis, R. Reasoning from first principles in electronic troubleshooting. *International Journal of Man-Machine Studies,* 1983, *19,* 403-423.

[13] Davis, R. Diagnostic reasoning based on structure and behavior. *Artificial Intelligence,* 1984, *24,* 347-410.

[14] Dillard, J. F., & Mutchler, J. F. *Knowledge based expert systems for audit opinion decisions.* Presented at the University of Southern California Symposium on Expert Systems, Los Angeles, CA, February 1986.

[15] Duda, R. O., & Gaschnig, J. G. Knowledge-based systems come of age. *Byte,* September 1981, pp. 238-281.

[16] Dungan, C. *A model of audit judgment in the form of an expert system.* Unpublished Ph.D. dissertation, University of Illinois, 1983.

[17] Dungan, C., & Chandler, J. S. *Analysis of audit judgment through an expert system* (Faculty working paper no. 982), University of Illinois, College of Commerce and Business Administration, 1983.

[18] Dungan, C., & Chandler, J. S. Auditor: A microcomputer-based expert system to support auditors in the field, *Expert Systems,* 1985, 2(4), 210-221.

[19] Fox, M. S. On inheritance in knowledge representation. In *Proceedings of the Sixth International Joint Conference on Artificial Intelligence* (Vol 1). Menlo Park, CA: American Association for Artificial Intelligence, 1979.

[20] Fox, M. *Artificial intelligence in manufacturing.* Presented at the CPMS Seminar on Expert Systems, Pittsburgh, PA, December 1984.

[21] Gaschnig, J., Klahr, P., Pople, H., Shortliffe, E., & Terry, A. Evaluation of expert systems. In F. Hayes-Roth, D. A. Waterman, & D. B. Lenat (Eds.), *Building expert systems.* Reading, MA: Addison-Wesley, 1983.

[22] Grudnitski, G. *A prototype of an internal control expert system for the sales/accounts receivable application.* Presented at the University of Southern California Symposium on Expert Systems, Los Angeles, CA, February 1986.

[23] Hansen, J. V., & Messier, W. F. *A knowledge-based expert system for auditing advanced computer systems* (ARC working paper 83-5). University of Florida, Department of Accounting, 1985.

[24] Hansen, J. V., & Messier, W. F. *A preliminary test of EDP-EXPERT.* Presented at the University of Southern California Symposium on Expert Systems, Los Angeles, CA, February 1986.

[25] Hayes-Roth, F., Waterman, D. A., & Lenat, D. B. (Eds.). *Building expert systems.* Reading, MA: Addison-Wesley, 1983.

[26] Hogarth, R. *Judgment and choice.* New York: Wiley, 1980.

[27] Hurst, E., Ness, D., Gambina, T., & Johnson, T. Growing DSS: A flexible, evolutionary approach. In J. Bennett (Ed.), *Building decision support systems*. Reading, MA: Addison-Wesley, 1983.

[28] Keen, P., & Scott Morton, M. S. *Decision support systems*. Reading, MA: Addison-Wesley, 1978.

[29] Kelly, K. P. *Expert problem solving for the audit planning process*. Unpublished Ph.D. dissertation, University of Pittsburgh, 1984.

[30] Kerlinger, F. *Foundations of behavioral research*. New York: Holt, Rinehart & Winston, 1973.

[31] Kidd, A., & Cooper, M. Man-machine interface issues in the construction and use of an expert system. *International Journal of Man-Machine Studies*, 1985, *22*, 91-102.

[32] Libby, R. *Accounting and human information processing: Theory and applications*. Englewood Cliffs, NJ: Prentice-Hall, 1981.

[33] Liebowitz, J. Useful approach for evaluating expert systems. *Expert Systems*, 1986, *3*(2), 86-99.

[34] McCarty, L. T. Reflections on TAXMAN: An experiment in artificial intelligence and legal reasoning. *Harvard Law Review*, 1977, *90*, 827-893.

[35] McDermott, J. *Background, theory and implementation of expert systems, II*. Presented at the CPMS Seminar on Expert Systems, Pittsburgh, PA, December 1984.

[36] McDermott, J. R1 revisited: Four years in the trenches. *AI Magazine*, 1984, *5*(3), 21-35.

[37] Meservy, R. D. *Auditing internal controls: A computational model of the review process*. Unpublished Ph.D. dissertation, University of Minnesota, 1985.

[38] Michaelsen, R. H. *A knowledge-based system for individual income and transfer tax planning*. Unpublished Ph.D. dissertation, University of Illinois, 1982.

[39] Michaelsen, R. H. An expert system for federal tax planning. *Expert Systems*, 1984, *1*(2), 149-167.

[40] Miller, R. K. *The inventory of expert systems*. Madison, GA: SEAI Institute, 1984.

[41] O'Leary, D. *Validation techniques for expert systems*. Presented at the ORSA/TIMS Meeting, Miami, FL, October 1986.

[42] Peat, Marwick, Mitchell & Co. *Research opportunities in auditing*. New York: Peat, Marwick, Mitchell Foundation, 1985.

[43] Rich, E. *Artificial intelligence*. New York: McGraw-Hill, 1983.

[44] Shooman, M. L. *Software engineering*. New York: McGraw-Hill, 1983.

[45] Shpilberg, D., & Graham, L. E. *Developing ExperTAP: An expert system for corporate tax accrual and planning*. Presented at the University of Southern California Symposium on Expert Systems, Los Angeles, CA, February 1986.

[46] Simon, J. *Basic research methods in social science*. New York: Random House, 1978.

[47] Steinbart, P. J. *The construction of an expert system to make materiality judgments*. Unpublished Ph.D. dissertation, Michigan State University, 1984.

[48] Texas Instruments. *The Second Artificial Intelligence Satellite Symposium*. Dallas, TX: Texas Instruments, 1986.

[49] Turban, E., & Watkins, P. Integrating expert systems and decision support systems. *MIS Quarterly*, 1986, *10*(2), 121-136.

[50] Willingham, J., & Wright, W. *Development of a knowledge-based system for auditing the collectability of a commercial loan*. Presented at the ORSA/TIMS Meeting, Boston, MA, 1985.

[51] Winston, P., & Horn, B. *LISP*. Reading, MA: Addison-Wesley, 1981.

[52] Yu, V., Fagan, L., Wraith, S., Clancey, W., Scott, A., Hannigan, J., Blum, R., Buchanan, B., & Cohen, S. Antimicrobial selection by computer: A blinded evaluation by infectious disease experts. *Journal of the American Medical Association*, 1979, *242*, 1279-1282. (See also Buchanan and Shortlife [7, chapter 31].)

Endnote

[1]ESs examined in this paper were found by examining three sources: Peat, Marwick, Mitchell & Co.'s *Research Opportunities in Auditing* (1985) [42], Miller's *1984 Inventory of Expert Systems* [40], and Ph.D. dissertations through calendar year 1984 (listed in University Microfilms). In addition, some systems mentioned in presentations and papers the author was aware of also are included.

Validating Expert System Performance

Robert M. O'Keefe, Osman Balci, and Eric P. Smith

Most definitions of expert systems mention their ability to perform at close to human expert levels. Yet expert system validation — that is, testing systems to ascertain whether they achieve acceptable performance levels — has (with few exceptions) been ad hoc, informal, and of dubious value. This article seeks to establish validation as an important concern in expert system research and development. It discusses problems in expert system validation, and presents both qualitative and quantitative methods for validating expert systems.

Typically, engineers have validated expert system performance by running test cases through a system and comparing results (that is, the classification, final certainty factors, and advice given) against known results or expert opinion. These engineers calculate a percentage for the systems' success rate and use subjective judgment to analyze and explain expert system failures where test results contradict known results or expert opinion. Examples of this simple approach range from MYCIN's early validation[1] to the recently reported validation of Emerge — a chest pain diagnosis system.[2]

However, this simple approach presents several problems. The final percentage obtained hinges on the choice of test cases, and its accuracy hinges on the number of test cases chosen. When we compare a system against the expert on whose knowledge that system was built, as happened with Prospector,[3] the so-called validation is of dubious value.

Since many expert systems began as research prototypes, validation has often been conducted to qualitatively measure system performance, as with Internist-1.[4] Or validation has simply been part of an overall evaluation to assess an expert system's value to a particular domain, as with the medical diagnosis system Casnet[5] and the auditing system EDP-Xpert.[6] However, since expert systems to be used on a regular basis — particularly in critical areas — must be validated carefully, the use of formal validation methods has increased in developing some implemented systems. Both a later validation of MYCIN,[7] and a validation of the chemotherapy adviser Oncocin (like MYCIN, developed at Sanford),[8] used formal methods backed by statistical tests. The VAX configuration system R1/Xcon also underwent some formal validation.[9,10]

Verification, Validation, and Evaluation

We are concerned with validating performance only. Typically, validation is part of evaluation — a broader area seeking to assess an expert system's overall value. In addition to exhibiting acceptable performance levels, expert systems should be usable, efficient, and cost effective. Validation is the cornerstone of evaluation, since highly efficient implementations of invalid systems are useless.

Separating performance validation from other aspects of evaluation can be difficult. For instance, testing is difficult when users balk at using systems that fail to consider human factors; for example, systems with poorly designed interfaces. For this reason, developers must decide at the outset whether or not to separate validation. In ground-breaking applications particularly, an overall evaluation policy may seem more relevant — especially if it is determined at the start that a reasonable performance level will be difficult to attain.

Validation is often confused with verification. Simply stated, validation refers to building the right system (that is, substantiating that a system performs with an acceptable level of accuracy), whereas verification refers to building the system "right" (that is, substantiating that a system correctly implements it specifications). In modeling studies, nobody solves the *problem* — rather, everybody solves the *model* of the problem. Since an expert system represents human reasoning and knowledge, we must justify its representation level through validation.

The purpose of this article is twofold: First, we seek to establish validation and evaluation as important concerns in expert system research and development. Second, we wish to present both qualitative and quantitative methods of formal validation — some taken from other areas of computer-based model validation — that can be applied to expert systems. The work presented here draws upon our experience in

- Developing expert systems[11] and
- Using validation methods in computer-based modeling.

We will examine the problems encountered in validating expert system performance, address basic concepts fundamental to validation, review appropriate qualitative methods, and discuss the use of quantitative methods. We will close with our conclusions regarding the application of validation methods.

Validating Expert Systems

We have encountered the following major problems in validating expert system performance:

- What to validate,
- What to validate against,
- What to validate with,
- When to validate
- How to control the cost of validation,
- How to control bias, and
- How to cope with multiple results.

We encounter all of these, to a greater or lesser extent, in validating any computer-based model. The next section discusses these problems and provides some guidelines.

What to Validate

We can validate any intermediate results, the final result (often called the conclusion), the reasoning of the system, or any combination of these three.[10] Since a poor reasoning process that provides a correct result cannot be scaled up to a larger application domain, or may give a different result when used with an extended knowledge base, we should validate the reasoning process.[12]

What to validate is intrinsically linked to what developmental stage we have reached. At any stage, if part of the system's performance can be measured for a given set of inputs, that part should be validated so as to catch errors as early as possible in the development life cycle. Typically, we may concentrate on validating the reasoning process early on in development, and only be concerned with validating final results when the knowledge base is more complete.

Furthermore, it may be difficult (or impossible) to classify the result of an expert system as right or wrong. In the following excerpt, Kulikowski and Weiss discuss Casnet's validation:

> Classifying conclusions as being merely correct or incorrect is an oversimplification. The program's conclusions are presented not as single unique diagnoses but rather as combinations of judgments about a patient's status.

In such cases, however, one can often get experts to classify intermediate results, conclusions, and reasoning into several categories. For instance, Hickam et al. had chemotherapy protocol experts classify the performance of Oncocin as ideal, acceptable, suboptimal, and unacceptable.[8]

What to Validate Against

Expert systems can be validated against known results as well as against expert performance. For example, consider an expert system that predicts the financial performance of a company. Given the input conditions in 1985, the expert system can be asked (today, that is) to predict that company's known financial performance in 1986. Thus, validity can be assessed by comparing the system's prediction against the company's known performance. It's unfair to expect expert systems to perform at levels close to known results when human experts cannot perform at these levels. Expert systems should be validated against experts, although known results (when available) can provide a useful background for validation.

A problem with known results is that previous expert decisions may precipitate those results. Suppose that a bank uses a performance prediction when deciding whether or not to support company X financially. If an expert had decided a year ago that the financial position of company X would be poor in a year's time and thus implemented withdrawal of financial support, the present poor financial position of company X might be due in part to that previous expert decision.

What to Validate With

In an ideal world, many documented previous cases — representing work from a number of experts on a complete range of problems — would be available for use in validation. In the real world, unfortunately, only a small sample is available — a sample drawn from a single or a few experts. And, in extreme instances, no test cases are available.

Further, the choice of test cases biases the success of any validation. Any test case used in system development should be discarded since (supposedly) the system will have been altered to handle the case successfully. Numerous situations are fairly standard in many domains, and can be handled with limited expertise; for example, suppose we are developing a medical diagnosis system in a domain where 90 percent of the cases are standard and the other 10 percent require considerable skill. A 90-percent success rate for the expert system would not inspire confidence when validated against test cases.

For a fair cross-sectional system validation, test cases should be randomly selected using stratified sampling; that is, randomly selected within each identifiable result type. For instance, if an expert classifies a diagnosis as A, B, or C — and previous histories indicate that these classifications occur respectively 80 percent, 15 percent, and 5 percent of the time — then a collection of 200 test cases should include 160, 30, and 10 instances where A, B, and C resulted respectively. However, the value of a stratified approach is debatable. The ability to handle cases producing infrequent results is an expert trait; frequently, developers devote a disproportionate amount of knowledge and effort to such cases. In many instances, more detailed validation will require testing the system against a small number of obscure or complex cases — cases that even top experts find difficult — and qualitatively assessing how well the system handles these.

Obviously, the number of test cases used affects our confidence in the system. However, the law of large numbers simply does not apply here. The issue is not the *number* of test cases, it is the *coverage* of test cases — that is, how well they reflect the input domain. The input domain is the population of permissible input,[13] and should not be confused with the application domain in which the expert system operates. The larger the input domain, the more difficult validation becomes.

If no historic test cases are available, or if all of them have been used in developing the system, it may be possible to synthesize test cases by having experts randomly create some. But this is problematical because any set of synthesized cases is unlikely to represent a well-stratified sample. Moreover, since experts are unlikely to expend as much time or effort on synthetic as on real problems, their reasoning and the results may well suffer. In some instances, however, this may well be the only means of providing sample test cases.

When to Validate

Little agreement exists regarding when to validate expert systems. In the following excerpt, Bachant and McDermott relate the folly of expecting high performance from a system early in its career:

> To expect anything close to perfection during the first few years a system is being used (especially if the task is significantly more than a toy) is probably a very serious mistake.[9]

On the other hand, Buchanan and Shortliffe believe that

> ... high performance is a *sine qua non* for an expert system and thus deserves separate evaluation early in a program's evolution.[14]

Although these two statements appear contradictory, we believe there is no contradiction. Typically, expert systems must exhibit acceptable performance at some early stage of development. But the level of acceptance may be different for differing systems: With a research prototype, medium performance plus indications that the basic approach is correct may be acceptable. As the system is extended, further validation may be necessary but such validation should concentrate on validating the extensions — indicating areas that need improvement or fine-tuning. With noncritical applications such as R1/Xcon, we can validate the system in the field as it's used. In critical applications where

		State of the expert system	
		System is Valid	System is Invalid
Action	Accept as valid	Correct decision	System user's risk (Type II error)
	Declare invalid	System builder's risk (Type I error)	Correct decision

Figure 1. Types of risk in validation.

lives are at stake or where fortunes are at risk, field-testing is usually impossible (although in certain instances it may be possible to run an expert system in parallel with a traditional system).

How to Control the Cost of Validation
Validation can be time consuming and expensive. Assessing the amount of money and effort that should be applied to validation is difficult. We believe that validation costs can be controlled by designing formal validation methods that are integrated within the development process. Clearly, the value of validation links directly to

- The value of a system to its users, and
- The risk involved in using a poorly validated system.

These ideas will be developed further in a subsequent section.

How to Control Bias
Expert systems may be validated against experts whose expertise is biased when compared with other experts. When judging expert system performance, an expert biased against introducing computer-based systems may unfairly assess the system. Conversely, selecting test cases so as to guarantee good system performance exemplifies developer bias.

We can control expert bias by using blinded evaluation and cross-checking, both employed in Oncocin's validation.[8] When judging performance, experts should not be able to distinguish between human expert and program performance. Using statistical tests, bias between experts can be checked for, as we will discuss later.

Developer bias can be a more difficult problem. Even developers who are honest professionals may be unaware of their biases — while they validate their work thoroughly and objectively, they may be too close to the project to realize broader issues. We can minimize this problem by having a different team validate the expert system; that is, a team replacing the original developers.

How to Cope with Multiple Results
When validating expert system with multiple results, a serious hitch exists — a hitch referred to as the *multiple-response* problem. We cannot appropriately test the validity of a multivariate-response expert system by testing the validity separately for each response variable. Shannon[15] illustrates this problem in validating simulation models (see p. 229). We must use a multivariate approach to incorporate the correlation among results and to test for overall system validity.

In a medical diagnosis system prescribing appropriate drug treatment, for example, two types of drug can be validly prescribed if each is separately considered as a treatment — yet that combination of drugs may be unacceptable. Hence, the overall system response is invalid.

Some Basic Concepts

This section introduces some basic concepts in expert system validation; namely, the acceptable performance range, input domain, validity testing, validation formality, and the expert system builder's/user's risk.

Acceptable Performance Range
The validation concept should not be considered a binary decision variable in which expert

systems are *absolutely* valid or *absolutely* invalid. Since expert systems are representations or abstractions of reality, we cannot expect perfect performance. The performance level acceptable to users is called the *acceptable performance range*, and should be specified during development. In some cases an acceptable performance range can be specified by a government agency, the project sponsor, or a third party.

Suppose that an expert system produces classifications A, B, C, or D. We may be able to specify an acceptable performance range in terms of each result's occurrence. For instance, we may decide that the system should always correctly classify A and B, but that some variation in classifying C and D is acceptable. Further, the probability of a particular incorrect classification may be vital; it may be vital that the system never produces B when the known result is A — that is, *Prob*(B | A) should be shown to be zero.

Frequently, the acceptable performance range will reflect the ability to perform at levels equivalent to human expertise. Bachant and McDermott pointed out that

> ... the people who used R1 did not demand more of it than of its human predecessors.[9]

Thus, we may be able to specify an acceptable performance range with regard to the performance of human experts that the system models.

The Input Domain

Developers should design an expert system for a specific purpose or application, and should assess system adequacy or validity only in terms of that purpose with regard to a prescribed input domain. An expert system can be valid for one input domain, and completely absurd for another.

Validity Testing

An expert system can only be tested for validity under a prescribed input domain and for an acceptable performance range related to the system's intended purpose.

Validation Formality

Validation can range from formal to informal. Formal validation (1) establishes when validation should occur within the development life cycle, and (2) identifies validation methods, input domain specification, the level of acceptance, and (where appropriate) the relevant application of statistical techniques. Informal validation — typically done at the end of development — employs ad hoc methods and is often an afterthought.

Most validation ranges between formal and informal, yet it is generally accepted that validation is too informal — that developers do not consider their approach to validation early enough, and hence do not build it into the development life cycle.

Builder's/User's Risk

Validity testing results in four possible outcomes (see Figure 1), including type I and type II errors. Type I error results if system validity is rejected when it's sufficiently valid. Type II error results if system validity is accepted when it's invalid. We call the probability of type I error *builder's risk*, and the probability of type II error *user's risk*. Balci and Sargent have quantified these risks in using statistical hypothesis testing for the validation of simulation models.[16]

Type I error unnecessarily increases expert system developmental costs; these additional costs may not be negligible and can precipitate abandoning systems that have taken much effort to develop. Type II error, on the other hand, has more dramatic consequences; for example, a medical diagnostic system that incorrectly diagnoses illness can cause patients to suffer through mistreatment. Therefore, we must minimize user's risk in critical applications. Objective consideration of these risk types, their relative importance, and the cost if each should occur, will help provide a basis for validation design.

Qualitative Validation

Qualitative validation employs subjective comparisons of performance. This does not imply that such approaches are informal; we can design highly formal qualitative validation. Where appropriate, qualitative and quantitative methods can be combined. If expert system responses can somehow be quantified (that is, expressed in numbers), then we can employ quantitative (statistical) techniques.

This section reviews seven common qualitative approaches to validation, some of which have been used to validate expert system performance.

Face Validation
Face validation is a useful preliminary approach to validation. Project team members, potential expert system users, and people knowledgeable about the application domain — all using their knowledge and intuition — subjectively compare system performance against human expert performance. They assess at face value, with regard to a prescribed acceptable performance range, the results obtained from an expert system running under a given set of test cases.

A group of six experts validated R1/Xcon, reviewing its performance on fifty orders.[17] Perceived mistakes were rectified prior to installation.

Predictive Validation
Predictive validation requires using historic test cases and either (1) known results or (2) measures of human expert performance on those cases. An expert system is driven by past input data from the test cases, and its results are compared with corresponding results — either known results or those obtained from the human expert. Hudson et al. used this approach to analyze Emerge.[2]

Turing Tests
Turing tests validate expert systems against human experts by evaluating human expert performance and system performance without knowing the subject performer's identity. Assessments of system performance can then be compared with assessments of human performance. Such blind evaluation eliminates any pro or con computer bias — a positive side effect. If assessments can be objectively measured (for example, if experts can conclude that test cases were handled correctly or incorrectly, or can assess performance to be expert, good, fair, or poor), then statistical techniques can be used to test for variation between expert systems and human experts, and for consistency between experts.

Chandrasekaran recommends Turing tests for validating medical expert systems.[12] Such tests have been used to validate both MYCIN[7] and Oncocin.[8]

Field Tests
Field tests place prototypical expert systems in the field, and then seek to perceive performance errors as they occur. From the developer's viewpoint, this offers two considerable advantages: First, it places the burden of testing upon users. Second, acceptable performance ranges are obtained implicitly, since users may cease to report problems when acceptable performance ranges are reached. This may backfire, of course, with users reporting minor problems for the duration of system existence.

Field-testing is possible only in noncritical applications, where users can assess the correctness of expert system performance. Subsequent to its implementation, R1/Xcon underwent considerable field-testing.[9] Incorrect results can be easily observed with R1/Xcon, since the VAX configuration will either not fit together or not work.

Subsystem Validation
Subsystem validation requires that the expert system be decomposed into subsystems, enabling the performance of each subsystem to be observed under given input data. In this approach, subsystems are validated one at a time as they are developed.

Subsystem validation has three significant advantages:

- Validation, incorporated within the development life cycle, is carried out along with development;
- We can validate subsystems more easily since they are less complex and more manageable; and
- Error detection is much easier since errors are localized.

Disadvantages of subsystem validation are

- It may not be possible to observe the input-output behavior of a subsystem, and
- Successfully validating each subsystem does not imply overall system validity since accumulated error tolerances can be significant in overall system performance.

In some instances, we might identify a subsystem in which all possible outputs can be generated for all possible inputs; for example, this could occur in production rule systems where a rule set applies crisp logical inference on a limited discrete input domain. If we gather user's judgments on a continuous scale and use them as certainty factors, we can simulate subsystem performance over the range of permissible input. Langlotz et al. provide a relevant example.[18]

Sensitivity Analysis
We perform sensitivity analysis by systematically changing expert system input variable

values and parameters over some range of interest and observing the effect upon system performance. Consider a system that gives complete satisfaction (that is, if intermediate results, the final result, and reasoning are all assessed to be sufficiently expert) when dealing with case C. If C uses inputs (such as data and user's judgments) $i_1, i_2, ..., i_n$, then sensitivity analysis validation would involve altering each input and assessing the change in system performance. For instance, if i_3 is the patient's temperature and our satisfactory consultation case included a 101-degree temperature — and if, in addition, we know that temperature should have no effect on diagnosing this case — then altering i_3 to any other value (while leaving i_1, i_2, and $i_4, i_5, ..., i_n$ as before) should not alter intermediate results, the final result, or perhaps even the reasoning process.

To our knowledge, expert system developers have not used sensitivity analysis for validation — at least not explicitly. However, sensitivity analysis may be the most powerful qualitative method at hand: It is especially useful where few or no test cases are available. It is also highly appropriate for systems using uncertainty measures and requiring users to provide judgments for premise uncertainty, since these can be altered as desired and the effect on intermediate and final uncertainty measures can be examined.

Visual Interaction

Visual interactive validation provides visual animation of expert system workings and allows experts to interact, altering parameters as desired. In essence, we can view this as an environment for interactive face validation, subsystem validation, and sensitivity analysis. Visual interaction has been successfully employed in validating operations research models — particularly discrete-event simulations.[19]

This validation approach could apply to expert systems, particularly with the appearance of graphical interfaces to knowledge-based systems (Guidon-Watch,[20] for example). Experts studying the reasoning process, rules access, and uncertainty propagation can thereby validate the reasoning process.

Quantitative Validation

Quantitative validation employs statistical techniques to compare expert system performance against either test cases or human experts. We will discuss the applicability of three quantitative methods:

- Paired *t*-tests,
- Hotelling's one-sample T^2 test, and
- Simultaneous confidence intervals.

We will then address consistency measuring between experts — an important issue when performing validation against multiple experts.

Quantitative validation methods generally fall into two categories: Either we construct a *confidence interval* for one or more measures and subjectively compare it with an acceptable performance range, or we use a formal *hypothesis test* to compare measurements with a predetermined acceptable performance range where the hypotheses are

H_0: The expert system is valid for the acceptable performance range under the prescribed input domain.

H_1: The expert system is invalid for the acceptable performance range under the prescribed input domain.

Paired *t*-Tests

Producing a single proportion as a performance measure has limited value. We can use a paired *t*-test more appropriately to compare the difference between observed results. We can measure the difference between expert system performance and human expert performance or known results by D_i where $D_i = X_i - Y_i$, X_i are system results, and Y_i are either known results or results from human expert performance. For n test cases, there will be n observed differences D_i to D_n.

This method covers many types of results. If final judgments are produced on a continuous scale (for example, as is -5 to +5 in Prospector), then X_i can be the system's judgment, and Y_i can be the human expert's judgment. If both known results and expert performance are known, we can have a third-party expert measure the performance of each on a scale of 1 to 10, under blind evaluation, and thus X_i and Y_i will be the absolute performance of the system and the expert, respectively.

For the differences Di, the following confidence interval can be produced:

$$\bar{d} \pm t_{n-1,\alpha/2} S_d / \sqrt{n}$$

where $\bar{d}$ is the mean difference, S_d the standard deviation, and $t_{n-1,\alpha/2}$ the value from the t

distribution with n degrees of freedom. If zero lies in the confidence interval, then we can accept H_o.

Hotelling's One-Sample T^2 Test

A previous section discussed the problems of multivariate responses. While a paired *t*-test is appropriate when systems produce a single final result, simultaneously applying a paired *t*-test to a number of final results is inappropriate since we can expect the final results to be correlated (see the previous section on multiple results). In such cases, Hotelling's one-sample T^2 test should be used.

Consider validating an expert system against human expert performance. We give each exactly the same input. Assuming that we have k responses (measurable results) as the expected output, we determine the differences between corresponding k paired responses. Repeating this for different input values, we construct k vectors of differences, one for each response. Then, the one-sample T^2 test is used to determine if the means of the difference vectors are significantly different from zero simultaneously (or jointly). This method has been used to validate multivariate-response trace-driven simulation models.[21]

Simultaneous Confidence Intervals

To validate multivariate-response expert systems, we can construct simultaneous confidence intervals or joint confidence regions for differences of paired responses. Usually, we compare confidence intervals or regions constructed with a prescribed acceptable performance range. This method has been used to validate simulation models.[22]

Consistency Measures

If we wish to compare an expert system with multiple experts — or to compare multiple experts with a system in a Turing test — then consistency between experts (often called *interobserver reliability*) is a major consideration. The inter-class correlation coefficient, a commonly used consistency measure, has been used to evaluate reliability between legal judges: If a judgment by expert i on test case j is denoted Y_{ij}, then a model for expert reliability is $Y_{ij} = \mu + E_i + \varepsilon_{ij}$ where μ is the mean rating across all experts, E_i is the effect of the ith expert (that is, deviation from the mean μ), and ε_{ij} is the error term. From this model, we can produce and test a correlation coefficient. If Y_{ij} is a categorical variable (such as expert, good, fair, or poor), rather than a continuous variable, then we can use the kappa statistic to measure reliability.[23]

We can use a related statistic to compare joint expert agreement with system agreement.[24] This is appropriate in Turing tests, which aggregate multiple expert judgment; for example, where the system performs a task normally performed by related experts. Fleiss discusses other tests, including confidence interval approaches.[25]

Conclusion

As was once the case with knowledge acquisition, performance validation is seen as a black art. Yet few would disagree that expert systems should exhibit acceptable and reliable performance levels. Validation and evaluation — important concerns for most expert system developers — require considerably more attention than they presently receive. A recapitulation of useful guidelines for validating expert system performance follows.

- We must validate systems only against an acceptable performance range for a prescribed input domain. Previous human performance indicates the acceptable range.
- We should build validation into the development cycle. Often, we must carry out a cross-sectional performance validation prior to implementation, and specific validation tests as the system evolves after implementation.
- We must consider the risks in using invalid systems (user's risk) relative to the risks in not using valid systems (builder's risk).
- We must choose an appropriate qualitative method: Field-testing may be acceptable for noncritical applications. Turing tests are useful for comparing systems against experts in blinded evaluations, and can avoid pro- or anti-computer bias. Subsystem validation and sensitivity analysis are useful for validating specific areas of concern.
- We must use quantitative methods where applicable. We must use them as informatively as possible; for instance, to produce confidence intervals rather than single-point estimates. We must be aware of the multiple-response problem, and use appropriate multivariate techniques.

Of necessity, most of this article has been *descriptive*. But expert system developers need a *prescriptive* methodology; that is, one explaining how to validate expert systems under certain conditions (such as consultative or real-time critical applications) and under certain constraints (such as funding and development time). At present, expert system validation experience is limited. A methodology, or methodologies, will evolve only in the light of future collective experience and critical appraisal of that experience.

References

1. V.L. Yu et al., "Evaluating the Performance of a Computer-Based Consultant," *Computer Programs in Biomedicine*, Vol. 9, No. 1, 1979, pp. 95-102.
2. D.L. Hudson et al., "Prospective Analysis of Emerge, an Expert System for Chest Pain Analysis," in *IEEE Computers in Cardiology*, IEEE Service Center, Piscataway, N.J., 1984, pp. 19-24.
3. J. Gaschnig, "Preliminary Performance Analysis of the Prospector Consultant System for Mineral Exploration," *Proc. Sixth Int'l Joint Conf. Artificial Intelligence*, Morgan Kaufmann, Los Altos, Calif., 1979, pp. 308-310.
4. R.A. Miller, H.E. Pople, and J.D. Myers, "Internist-1, An Experimental Computer-Based Diagnostic Consultant for General Internal Medicine," *The New England J. Medicine*, Vol. 307, No. 8, 1982, pp. 468-476.
5. C.A. Kulikowski and S.H. Weiss, "Representation of Expert Knowledge for Consultation: The Casnet and Expert Projects," in *Artificial Intelligence in Medicine*, P. Szolovits, ed., Westview Press, Boulder, Colo., 1982, pp. 21-56.
6. J.V. Hansen and W.F. Messier, "A Preliminary Investigation of EDP-Xpert," Working Paper 85-6, Accounting Research Center, Univ. of Florida, Gainesville, Fla., 1985.
7. V.L. Yu et al., "Antimicrobial Selection by a Computer," *J. Am. Medical Assoc.*, Vol. 242, No. 12, 1979, pp. 1279-1282.
8. D.H. Hickam et al., "The Treatment Advice of a Computer-Based Cancer Chemotherapy Protocol Advisor," *Annals of Internal Medicine*, Vol. 103, No. 6 (Part I), 1985, pp. 928-936.
9. J. Bachant and J. McDermott, "R1 Revisited: Four Years in the Trenches," *AI Magazine*, Vol. 5, No. 3, 1984, pp. 21-32.
10. J. Gaschnig et al., "Evaluation of Expert Systems: Issues and Case Studies," in *Building Expert Systems*, F. Hayes-Roth, D.A. Waterman, and D.B. Lenat, eds., Addison-Wesley, Reading, Mass., 1983, pp. 241-280.
11. R.M. O'Keefe, V. Belton, and T. Ball, "Experiences with Using Expert Systems in O.R.," *J.Operational Research Soc.*, Vol. 37, No. 7, 1986, pp. 657-668.
12. B. Chandrasekaran, "On Evaluating AI Systems for Medical Diagnosis," *AI Magazine*, Vol. 4, No. 2, 1983, pp. 34-37.
13. W.C. Hetzek, "Principles of Computer Program Testing," in *Program Test Methods*, W.C. Hetzel, ed., Prentice-Hall, Englewood Cliffs, N.J., 1973, pp. 17-28.
14. B.G. Buchanan and E.H. Shortliffe, *Rule-Based Systems: The MYCIN Experiments of the Stanford Heuristic Programming Project*, Addison-Wesley, Reading, Mass., 1984.
15. R.E. Shannon, *Systems Simulation: The Art and Science*, Prentice-Hall, Englewood Cliffs, N.J., 1975.
16. O. Balci and R.G. Sargent, "A Methodology for Cost-Risk Analysis in the Statistical Validation of Simulation Models," *Comm. ACM*, Vol. 24, No. 4, 1981, pp. 190-197.
17. J. McDermott, "R1: The Formative Years," *AI Magazine*, Vol. 2, No. 2, 1981, pp. 21-29.
18. C.P. Langlotz, E.H. Shortliffe, and L.M. Fagan, "Using Decision Theory to Justify Heuristics," *Proc. AAAI 86*, Menlo Park, Calif., 1986, pp. 215-219.
19. P.C. Bell, "Visual Interactive Modeling in Operational Research: Successes and Opportunities," *J. Operational Research Soc.*, Vol. 36, No. 11, 1985, pp. 975-982.
20. M.H. Richer and W.J. Clancey, "Guidon-Watch: A Graphic Interface for Viewing a Knowledge-Based System," *IEEE Computer Graphics and Applications*, Nov. 1985, pp. 51-64.
21. O. Balci and R.G. Sargent, "Validation of Multivariate-Response Trace-Driven Simulation Models," in *Performance '83*, A.K. Agrawala and S.K. Tripathi, eds., North-Holland, New York, N.Y., 1983, pp. 309-323.
22. O. Balci and R.G. Sargent, "Validation of Simulation Models Via Simultaneous Confidence Intervals," *Am. J. Math. and Management Sciences*, Vol. 4, Nos. 3 and 4, 1984, pp. 375-406.

23. J. Cohen, "Weighted Kappa: Nominal Scale Agreement with Provision for Scaled Disagreement or Partial Credit," *Psychological Bulletin*, Vol. 70, No. 4, 1968, pp. 213-220.
24. G.W. Williams, "Comparing the Joint Agreement of Several Raters With Another Rater," *Biometrics*, Vol. 32, No. 2, 1976, pp. 619-627.
25. J.L. Fleiss, *Statistical Methods for Rates and Proportions*, John Wiley and Sons, New York, N.Y., 1981.

Review Questions

II. The Development Process

Design

Freiling et al.

1. At the beginning of the article, the authors speak of differences in developing knowledge engineering systems. Are these differences unique to knowledge engineering projects? Are they any different for non-knowledge-based systems, such as payroll or inventory, when "AI mystique" is replaced by "computing mystique"?
2. Are there other reasons, besides those mentioned by the authors, that make knowledge engineering systems difficult to develop? Discuss.
3. The knowledge acquisition system described in the article has a graphics component called PIKA (Pictorial Knowledge Acquisition). This has obvious applications in engineering designs. Are there business decisions for which graphics input and output would aid knowledge acquisition? Give several examples.

Prerau (1985)

1. Clearly, there are few domains that will contain all of the properties identified in this paper. Beyond the basic requirements, which of the four other general properties—problem type, expert, problem bounds, and domain area personnel—do you consider most important, second most important, and so on? Justify your ranking.
2. Are all of the four general properties necessary? If you had to do without one or more, which would you choose? Why?
3. Compare the properties of the Domain Area Personnel sections with the concerns for organizational support expressed for general systems development projects (for example, see *Information Systems Concepts for Management* by Henry C. Lucas, Jr., or *Systems in Organizations* by Lynne Markus).

Prerau (1987)

1. The knowledge acquisition experience described in the article was for a large, scientific engineering project. Can the "over 30 points" be applied across the board to knowledge acquisition? Do they apply equally to business projects? Why or why not? Which is more important—size or discipline?
2. Of the 35 points of advice in this article, select five that you consider most important and explain their importance. If there are some other important issues not discussed in this article, list them and explain why they should be included.
3. Compare the steps described by the author with the steps for general software systems development (for example, *Systems Development* by Alan L. Eliason) and software testing (*The Art of Software Testing* by L. G. Myers). What are the major differences and similarities? Make a short list of steps that are unique to the knowledge acquisition process.

Validation/Verification

Nguyen et al.

1. Which of the consistency checks ensure logical consistency of the resulting expert system and which ensure efficiency of operation? Discuss.
2. Discuss the relative complexity of checking for the four situations that can lead to incompleteness.
3. Prepare a short list of rules for determining what to have for breakfast. Construct a Dependency Chart for the rules. Are there any circular rule chains?
4. After discussing the impact of certainty factors on checking, the authors state that "CHECK does not look at certainty factors when checking a knowledge base." Does this make their knowledge bases unreliable? Discuss.

O'Leary

1. Of the "unique characteristics of auditing and accounting expert systems," which are unique to expert systems in general? Which are unique to auditing and accounting expert systems? Which are not really unique to either? Discuss.
2. Discuss why the research approach to validation advocated by the author is more appropriate for expert systems than is the traditional software engineering approach.
3. Compare the concept of "systematic variance" to normal testing in software engineering. Is systematic variance unique to expert systems?
4. Locate the original source for two of the six studies identified in Table 2; discuss the overall degree of rigor of validation for each study.

O'Keefe et al.

1. What is the difference between verification and validation? Why is it important to validate expert systems?
2. What issues should be considered in validating expert systems?
3. What qualitative techniques are used to validate expert systems? Compare the techniques' strengths and weaknesses.
4. What quantitative techniques are used to validate expert systems? Compare those techniques' strengths and weaknesses.
5. Suppose you are assigned to develop an expert system for consumer loan evaluation. Prepare a plan that identifies validation procedures at each stage of the system development process.

III. APPLICATIONS

This section presents articles covering a broad spectrum of business applications of expert systems. Of course, all of the reported applications could not be included, but the applications described are a representative sample that will show the applicability and problems of expert systems in business. Prototypes and commercial-level systems are both represented, with prototypes preponderant because of the relative newness of the field.

Accounting was one of the first business disciplines to address the potential of expert systems. Large CPA firms see expert systems as a new area of client service from which substantive competitive advantage can be gained, and the firms have aggressively pursued the technology. In particular, one firm, Peat Marwick Main, has provided funds for pioneering academic research in this new field. Two of the articles (Dungan and Chandler; Hansen and Messier) are direct results of this research.

Dungan and Chandler was one of the first prototypes built in accounting. Although the auditing decision they examined, allowance for bad debt, was not a high-payoff decision, it did allow them to identify many of the problems in building expert systems for real, not simulated, business decisions. Hansen and Messier, with another early prototype, found that the breadth of a decision greatly affects the development process; they also report very interesting attitudinal results. The first commercial, and publicized, successful accounting expert system was ExperTAX[SM] by Shpilberg and Graham. Shpilberg and Graham's article shows the real complications of developing a true expert system in business, and also shows how an innovative organization can meet those challenges. Steinbart rounds out the field with a different application for an expert system, as a tool to understanding expert judgment. Together, the articles in this section present a sense of history, practicality, and theory.

Financial planning is a burgeoning area of development because the payoffs for small improvements in decision making can be extremely lucrative. The articles discuss systems in prototype or pilot stages, several of which are now on the way to commercialization. Analysis of financial situations is the subject of two of the articles, by Mui and McCarthy, and Kastner et al. Significantly, these projects were undertaken by two giants in the field of information systems, Arthur Andersen and IBM; the approaches and results of the projects are important. Urness describes a very competitive area of expert systems application, credit/risk evaluation. His article is notable in that, although there is much activity in this area, little has been published. Braun and Chandler take on a different financial application, stock market behavior, with a different artificial intelligence approach, induction. They were able to learn the rules of an expert area through analysis of the expert's decisions, without having to extract the knowledge from the expert directly. The articles in this section show the breadth of possibilities in financial management.

The manufacturing area is a natural extension of computer integrated manufacturing (CIM) and robotics applications. That is, manufacturing decision makers are already familiar with the potential benefits of artificial intelligence approaches. Bruno et al. are representative of this extension, as they move from CIM to an integrated approach to scheduling. A common yet complex decision, selecting an appropriate truck type, is described by Malmborg et al. Their lucid presentation demonstrates the match between expert systems rules and the realities of practice. The critical analysis by Mertens and Kanet of the potential expert systems applications in production management provides a model for the analysis of any business discipline. The articles in this section show where a discipline can go once it has passed the prototype stage.

The final section covers applications in general management. Steinberg and Plank give the reader an opportunity to examine the boundaries of expert systems application. Project management is an activity common to all management, but as projects grow, coordinating the use of subordinate resources becomes difficult. Sathi et al. describe their efforts to build an expert system to support this activity. Their presentation provides a balanced view of the development process, identifying the problems they faced and the successes they achieved. The general managerial task of problem diagnosis is given theoretical analysis by Courtney et al., who describe a knowledge base to support such managerial tasks. Lemmon presents the results of an expert system developed for cotton crop management. Although the crop management decision itself is rather narrow, the article is important because it describes the generally applicable situation of integrating an expert system with another computer-based tool, a simulation model.

Auditor: A Microcomputer-Based Expert System to Support Auditors in the Field

Chris W. Dungan and John S. Chandler

Decision support systems for implementation on microcomputers are being developed to aid external auditors in the field. Reasons for this development are not hard to find. Increased competition among the major public accounting firms stimulates a search for more efficient and less costly audit procedures. Such procedures can yield not only greater profit from current engagements but can also provide greater flexibility in bidding for new clients. Recent advances in the cost-effective use of microcomputers by auditors in the field opens the door for sophisticated modes of support [1]. The impetus behind much of the published research—including the work reported on here—was initially provided by the Research Opportunities in Auditing program of the public accounting firm of Peat, Marwick, Mitchell and Co. [2].

Auditor is an application of the generic inference engine, AL/X (Advice Language/X) [3]. At the instigation of Donald Michie, AL/X was adapted for use in Pascal systems on microcomputers from the general design principles of Prospector [4]. It separates the domain-specific knowledge from the control program which uses the knowledge. Thus, while AL/X was originally used in one realm of application (oil rig shutdown analysis), its inference structure provides a foundation upon which expert systems in other domains can be built. This is very similar to the relationship of KAS to Prospector and EMycin to Mycin [5]. *Auditor,* however, is implemented on an IBM PC, or compatible, with 256 K.

Reprinted with permission from *Expert Systems,* vol. 2, no. 4, October 1985, 210-221.

This paper describes the development of a microcomputer-based expert system called *Auditor* to aid independent auditors in their estimation of the dollar amount of a client's uncollectible accounts receivable. The task of auditing as an application of expert systems is discussed first. The development of *Auditor* and the mechanics of its inference engine, AL/X, are described next, together with the two validation techniques to which the system was subject. Finally, insights gained during the project are discussed, both as to auditors' decision making and to the implications of decision support for auditors via expert systems on microcomputers.

Auditing as a Task for Expert Systems

Why Expert Systems Are Suited for Auditing

Auditors have not been performing their function unaware of developments in decision support. Regression analysis has been applied to analytic review [6-11] and to sample size determination [12]. Other statistical techniques have been applied to sample size determination and sample analysis [13, 14]. Simulation has been used to analyze potential errors [15]. All of these approaches employ quantitative data to achieve their results. Statistical and operations research software are available for microcomputers so that many of these techniques are now being used in the field by practicing auditors.

Expert systems have been built and used in many fields. Most of these task domains have precisely characterized attributes and objective measurements as inputs to the system: miner prospecting [16,4], computer configuration [17], and chemical structure analysis [18,19]. Medical diagnosis and therapy is commonly driven by a mixture of objective tests and subjectively assessed values [20-29]. In auditing, as in medical diagnosis, although vast amounts of objective data exist (e.g., account balances, confirmation and cash receipts), it is the auditor's subjective interpretation of this data that is used to generate and evaluate alternative solutions. For example, it may be found that a client has a stated, tight credit policy, but it is the auditor's perception of the effectiveness of the credit manager in enforcing that policy that is significant. Thus audit decision making is presented with a mix of objective and subjective inputs and, in general, is an appropriate task domain for expert systems.

There are several expert systems in auditing being developed on or for microcomputers. Hansen and Messier [30] are using the same AL/X used in this project to study auditor evaluations of internal controls in the EDP environment. Braun and Chandler [31] are using ACLS (Analog Concept Learning System), developed by Michie [32], to induce decision rules on bad debt evaluations in the health care industry. The resulting decision rules will then be used as a basis for constructing an expert system. ACLS is the non-commercial version of Expert-Ease. Wright and Willingham [33] are developing an expert system to aid bank auditors in evaluating the collectibility of loans. Their system is based on the M.1 system, developed by Teknowledge, and it is planned to be used in the field by auditors on microcomputers. The initial expert system in accounting, Taxadvisor [34], was built on a mainframe using EMycin. Commercial packages available now could allow Taxadvisor to be built and run on a microcomputer.

The Auditing Task Under Scrutiny

A business enterprise seeks to report its financial performance according to uniform standards called Generally Accepted Accounting Principles (GAAP). A firm which deviates from these official rules finds that its financial statements have lost credibility in the eyes of bankers and stockholders. As a consequence, the ability of the enterprise to raise capital for continued operation or expansion can be seriously hampered. To report its current financial position properly, an enterprise must prepare a Balance Sheet which shows assets and liabilities. One type of asset involves claims against customers, called Accounts Receivable, which arise from credit sales of the firm's product or service. The rules state that the firm must differentiate, however, between those claims against its customer which it can reasonably expect to collect and those which it cannot reasonably expect to collect.

Because of business slowdowns, unemployment, bankruptcy, fraud, or death, some customers will not pay. Such uncollectible accounts (bad debts) cannot be individually identified, *a priori*, with precision. Their aggregate amount, however, must be estimated in order to conform to the accounting rules. The aggregate amount is referred to as the Allowance for Bad Debts (ABD), or the Provision or Reserve for Uncollectible Accounts Receivable. However titled, this is simply an estimate of the dollar value of the accounts which may not be collected.

Certified Public Accountants (CPAs) are hired to examine the enterprise's financial statements in order to enforce the accounting rules. CPAs, or external auditors, are legally liable for their negligence should the Balance Sheet be incorrect. Thus, they are vitally concerned that the Allowance for Bad Debts be estimated correctly. The expert system, *Auditor*, functions as an aid to CPAs in performing judgments as to the adequacy of the ABD.

When the external auditors begin their annual examination of a client's financial statements they are confronted with an ABD which has already been calculated by the client's management team and its in-house accountants. The auditor's responsibility is to give an opinion about the "fairness" of the statements and their adherence to the official accounting rules, including the "fairness" of the Allowance for Bad Debts.

Because of the tremendous volume of transactions entered into by an enterprise, for cost and feasibility considerations, the auditors resort to "test-checking" to accomplish their audit. In the case of the ABD this test-checking consists primarily of a systematic scrutiny of those as-yet-uncollected accounts receivable which are both individually large and delinquent. Delinquent means outstanding and unpaid beyond the credit period normally extended by company policy, usually thirty days but varying with company and industry. The auditor's scrutiny includes sending letters of confirmation to the debtors, examining correspondence between the debtor and the client, making inquiries of the client's management, and investigating economic conditions. Based on these findings, the auditor then makes a professional judgment as to the likelihood of collection of that particular, individually large account. It is this judgment which is supported by the *Auditor* system, using as inputs the external auditor's reports of his findings.

Problems Unique to the Auditing Task
Several facets of the task make it unique. For one, the auditor is not creating from whole cloth an Allowance for Bad Debts. Instead, he is seeking to verify the reasonableness of a judgment already performed, with varying degrees of good faith and competence, by his client. This aspect would seem to tolerate inexactitude on the auditor's part, since he is expected to merely corroborate via test-checks the reasonableness of the primary party's action. An additional facet, however, imbues his decision with a degree of gravity. Although the external auditor may be liable for money damages to anyone who relies upon the accuracy of the financial statements, he is hired and paid by the client whose financial statements he is examining.

Theoretically at least, both parties strive for accuracy and clarity in the statements. There are elements of an adversarial standoff, however, between the two parties. In order to enhance his own financial standing, the client normally will prefer that any doubts as to collectibility be resolved in favor of a showing of a larger asset balance, thus a smaller ABD. Individual employees will also be motivated toward optimistic predictions about the collectibility outcome; the sales manager who approved the sale and the credit manager who extended the credit. Although internal controls exist to restrict the range of their actions, both of these individuals, along with other client employees, enjoy opportunities to manipulate the data examined by the auditor.

Thus, the external auditor must not only search for data but also speculate about its credibility. Hence the need to capture uncertainty in their judgments, which is an attribute of many expert systems. Unfortunately, the ABD judgment, albeit of great importance, is only one of dozens of decisions which must be made by the external auditor in the course of rendering an opinion about a set of financial statements. In all cases, the time available to accomplish the judgment is limited.

Benefits of Using Expert Systems
Quality control within a CPA firm is enhanced through consistency in decision making. The simultaneous conduct by hundreds of auditors in audits of a multitude of clients in locations throughout the world, however, militates against a high degree of consistency despite the firm's dedication of resources to supervision and review. The use of *Auditor* and other microcomputer-based expert systems as decision support tools can underlay a firm's judgment process with a framework of consistent methods which, to a great extent, can be independent of the biases of individual auditors. Additionally, with the aid of these micro-based systems which can carry the knowledge of the firm's experts, the locus of critical judgments can be more safely transferred to less experienced persons operating in the field.

Training in the use of such systems must be provided, which will accomplish two desirable goals as by-products. First, an enhancement of the trainee's personal understanding of the parameters of the critical decision can be expected along with his competence in the use of the system. Second, more consistent, efficient, and less costly audits will be performed by better trained employees.

The Structure and Operation of *Auditor*

Overview of *Auditor* and AL/X
Auditor is a rule-based expert system that applies the knowledge domain of a sub-area of auditing to the generic inference engine, AL/X. In the following discussion of the mechanics of *Auditor*, the details of knowledge representation, uncertainty propagation, hypothesis evaluation, and user interaction essentially describe the functions of AL/X as well. For the sake of clarity, however, we will refer to *Auditor* only. Operationally, *Auditor* interacts with the user; asks for items of evidence, evaluates the new evidence with respect to what the system already knows, and then responds with recommendations or by asking for new evidence. *Auditor* is very similar to Prospector and its shell system, KAS [4].

In *Auditor* knowledge is represented by an inference network of rules, hypotheses, and logical combinations of these rules and hypotheses. The strength of the links within the network (or rule base) is represented by user-defined weights. Uncertainty is handled in two ways by

Auditor. First, each rule and hypothesis has a degree of belief (DB) assigned to it that reflects the likelihood that the evidence is true or false. A DB is a log transformation of probabilities such that a DB of +30 (-30) represents a probability of truth (falsity) of .999 (.001) and a DB of 0 represents a .5 probability. Second, the responses of the user are in terms of "certainty values" (CVs) or scaled responses reflecting the user's belief in the truth or falsity of a query made by the system. A CV of +5 (-5) implies that the statement is absolutely true (false) while any intermediate value requires an interpolation. The initial DB values and link weights are parameters of the system that must be elicited from the user.

The software that controls the operation of the system is called the inference engine. In *Auditor* both backward- and forward-chaining techniques are used. To determine what question to ask, the system searches backward from the goal at hand until it finds that question (i.e., item of evidence) that has the greatest potential impact on the goal. Then, upon receiving the user response, it uses Bayesian revision to update probabilities and propagates them through the network from the goal by forward-chaining.

The Development of *Auditor*

Auditor was built in three stages: initial modeling, refinement, and validation. Initial modeling encompassed the determination of the goal of the system (i.e., what decision to support), interviews with the auditing experts to elicit rules, and polling of the experts to determine the system's internal parameters. In the refinement stage, the experts operated the model interac--tively and presented their suggestions for improvement. These improvements included changes in parameter values, additional interactions among rules, and the rewording of questions. Finally, the completed system was exposed to validation exercises to determine the level of its expertise.

Auditor's single goal is expressed as "the delinquent portion of this account should specifically be reserved for in the allowance for bad debts to a substantial degree." (The internal name of this goal, RESERVE, as well as the names of other rules, will be written in capital letters.) The phrase, "this account," refers to the one individually large account which is under scrutiny by the auditor. "To a substantial degree" means a significant amount is still considered uncollectible. The wording of this goal was modified several times by the auditors themselves until they agreed on this final interpretation.

The rule base was developed from rules accumulated from eight expert auditors on the staff of an international CPA firm. Each auditor was interviewed and asked to identify which decisions they do not allow novice auditors to make and to describe how they make those decisions. From the voluminous notes taken at these interviews an initial set of fourteen rules was made. This list was sent back to the eight auditors for review. At this point four of the eight dropped out of the project. The four remaining auditors included three audit managers and one staff auditor. Their comments expanded the initial list to twenty-five rules, due mainly to the decomposition of compound rules into individual rules. The complete list can be examined in Dungan [35] and is summarized in Table 1.

The four auditors were then polled by mail as to their evaluation of this new rule list. The experts were asked to rank the rules with respect to a scale of "strong," "moderate," "weak," and "no effect." There was a high degree of consensus among the four auditors on each rule. One of the authors, a CPA with auditing experience, translated each set of responses into a set of weights for each rule which reflected the impact of each rule on the goal, RESERVE.

The experts were then allowed to interact with this version of *Auditor* while analyzing previously-prepared sets of audit evidence (called audit work papers) to verify the logic and conclusions of *Auditor*. Because, at that point in time, *Auditor* had to be run on a mainframe, the interactions were made on a hard-copy, portable terminal using a dial-up facility on a CYBER 175. This made testing very laborious because it was run in "full trace" mode which allowed the auditors to observe the sequential and marginal effects of their responses on the goal, RESERVE.

After this round of evaluation, the four auditors added interactions in the form of logical *and* rules to the network. There were many new interactions specified, so many in fact, that the efficiency of the system was threatened. This growing list of rules was pared down by the authors based on their experience and on the implied low impact of certain *and* rules. How these *and* rules affected the goal of RESERVE was also specified. This new version of the system was

Rule name	*Description*
COLLECTED	Account is no longer delinquent by audit completion date.
NO RESPONSE	There was no response to the confirmation request nor to a follow-up request.
NONCONTACT	The confirmation request was returned by the Postal Service as undeliverable.
ACTIVE	Customer continues to be an active customer.
CREDIT MANAGER	The credit manager, or other company official, expresses a strong belief in collectibility.
PROBLEMS	Confirmations revealed serious problems.
CORRESPOND	Recent data in correspondence file supports collectibility.
WORKOUT	Recent collections are proceeding satsifactorily.
LEGAL	Legal action would be fruitless.
ALLBUTONE	All portions have been collected except for a single, large, delinquent transaction.
NOTPAY	Debtors have stated their intention to pay little or nothing of the delinquent balances.
GOOD RECORD	Debtor has a good past record of ultimately paying substantially all delinquent balances.
OUTSTANDING	The outstanding delinquent balance continues to increase.
AVG AVE	The average age of the delinquent portion is increasing.
COLLECT AGENCY	This account has been assigned to a collection agency or lawyer.
CREDITSTOP	The client has stopped credit to this debtor.
NOPAYEVER	No payments have ever been received from this customer.
WRITEOFF	Total writeoff of this account, if required, will represent a material adjustment.
BANKRUPT	The debtor is in bankruptcy-type proceedings.
LAWYER	legal counsel gives poor prospects of any significant recovery from this debtor.
ECONOMICS	Economic factors are hampering this customer's ability to pay.
RIGOROUS	The collection effort being applied by your client is inadequate.
FORMER EMPLOY	This delinquent account is from a former employee.
NEW PAID	Despite the presence of this delinquent item, newer items have been fully paid.
ISSUENOTE	This debtor has issued notes for the unpaid portions of this account.

Table 1. List of rule base.

then again tested by the auditors operating in a "full trace" mode. Further modifications to the internal parameters resulted from this last examination.

How *Auditor* Works

The inference network for *Auditor* is shown in Figure 1. Each arrow represents a logical link between rules. Each of the twenty-five primary rules (e.g., COLLECTED and ACTIVE) have direct links to RESERVE but for the sake of clarity they are not shown in the figure. There are thirteen *and* rules in the inference network, each with its own impact on RESERVE. Thus, a primary rule that is an element in an *and* rule has at least two impacts on RESERVE; one by itself and one from the *and* rule. For example, the primary rule NOTPAY (which means that the customer has stated his intention not to pay the delinquent amount) has five impacts on RESERVE; one by itself and four from associated *and* rules. The actual impact on the DB of the *and* rules is governed by the mechanics of fuzzy logic [36].

The numbers in the parentheses are the user-specified weights associated with the links between rules and the main goal, RESERVE. They indicate how the DB value of RESERVE is to be updated based on a user response to that rule. The first number (called a positive weight or PW) indicates how the DB value of RESERVE is to be updated if the user responds with a positive 5 (absolutely true). The second number (called a negative weight or NW) indicates what

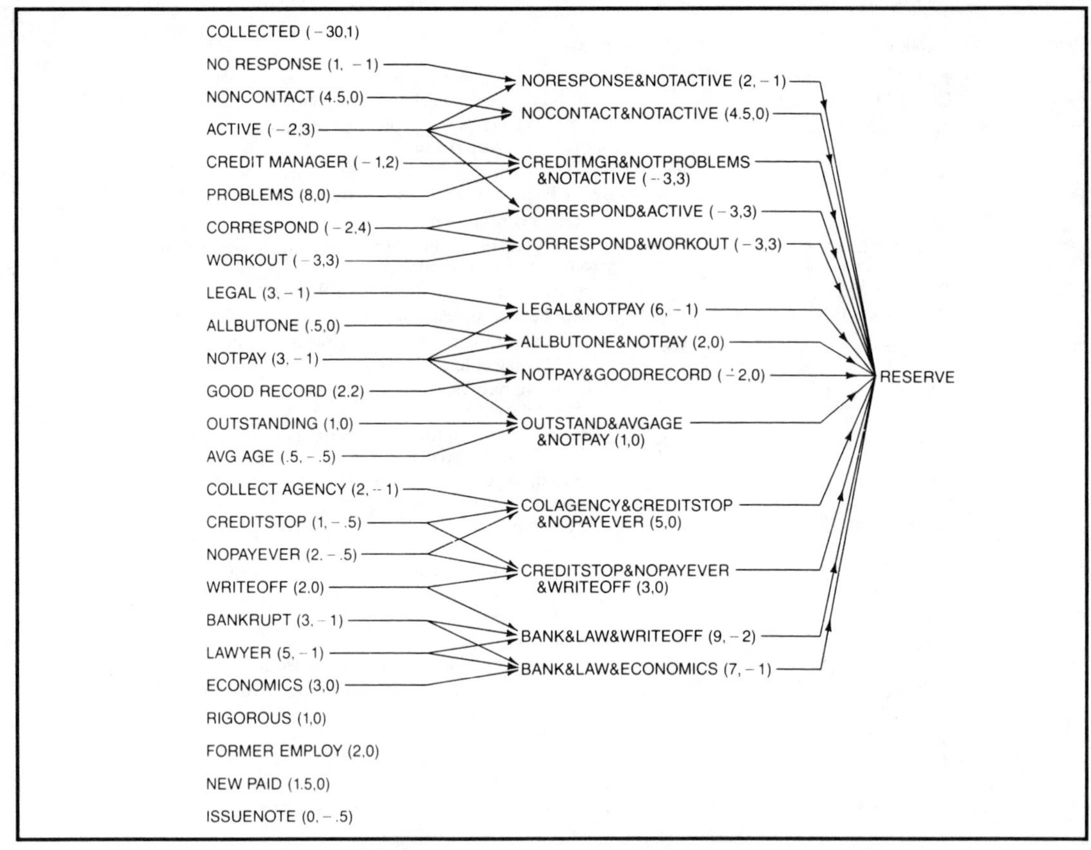

Figure 1. Inference network for *Auditor*.

the impact is if the user responds with a negative 5 (absolutely false). Any response in between, except 0, results in a piece-wise linear interpolation between PW and 0 (if the response is positive) or between NW and 0 (if the response is 0). A response of zero does nothing to the DB or RESERVE. For example, a +5 response to COLLECTED changes RESERVE from DB = 0 to DB = -30, which implies a probability of collection of .001. A -5 response, however, only changes DB of RESERVE to +1 (probability of .56). Note that very few of the PWs and NWs represent symmetrical situations. This is very common in auditing where the presence of negative evidence is much more damning than the absence of positive evidence.

In order to discuss how *Auditor* works from the user's point of view, an annotated trace of an actual interaction is shown in Figure 2. The impacts on the DBs of RESERVE and related rules are shown in Table 2. Several points demonstrated in the trace in Figure 2 deserve comment. First, the questions posed by *Auditor* to the user are in English. Second, the implied IF-THEN rules allow for uncertainty in two ways: the CV and the interpolating function that uses the CV and either PW or NW. Notice also the final ELSE clauses which handle the CV=0 case, i.e., no DB values are changed. Third, the user responses to the CORRES, ACTIVE, and WORKOUT questions are all consistent. Furthermore, although none are absolutely false (-5), the cumulative effect of this type of evidence is to push the probability of RESERVE from .75 to .97.

The propagation of DB values shown in Table 2 also deserves comment. Degrees of Belief have an absolute range of +100 to -100. Besides RESERVE, each rule, primary or *and*, also has a DB associated with it. When that rule is asked, or its component rules in the case of an *and* rule, the CV will affect the DB for that rule as well as the DB for RESERVE. For example, the first question asked, COLLECTED, received a response of -5 (absolutely false) and, as Table 2 shows, its DB went to -100, "absolutely false." Another point shown in Table 2 is the ripple

The current goal is whether or not the delinquent portion of this account should specifically be reserved for in the allowance for bad debts to substantial degree. RESERVE.

[*Auditor* is announcing its goal hypothesis. It has an initial DB = 0.0, i.e., probability of reserve = .5]

How certain are you that your tests of cash receipts indicate that the delinquent portions of the account in question have been collected substantially in their entirety subsequent to the date of the balance sheet?

? -5

[*Auditor* prompts the user for a response with a "?". The user's response of −5 implies that the user is certain that the account is still uncollected. The implied rule is:

```
IF account has been collected (i.e., CV>0)
   THEN DB(RESERVE) = DB(RESERVE) + fn(PW,CV)
  ELSE IF account has not been collected (i.e., CV<O)
           THEN DB(RESERVE) = DB(RESERVE) + fn(NW,CV)
          ELSE DB(RESERVE) = DB(RESERVE)
```

In this case the positive weight (PW) of the rule COLLECTED is −30 and the negative weight (NW) is +1. Thus, the impact of this response is to change the DB(RESERVE) from 0 to 1 (probability of reserve = .56).]

How certain are you that the confirmation request was returned by the postal service as undeliverable and the client for several months has been unable to communicate with the debtor?

? 2

[The user has not firmly established this fact yet but has some indication that it is true, and thus responds with a +2. From the semantic net in Figure 1 we see that NOCONTACT also impacts an AND rule. The implied rule is:

```
IF no contact with debtor (CV>0)
   THEN DB(RESERVE) = DB(RESERVE) + fn(4.5,CV)
           DB(NOCONTACT&ACTIV) =
                   fuzzy(DB(NOCONTACT&ACTIV), CV)
  ELSE IF contact with debtor (CV<O)
           THEN DB(RESERVE) = DB(RESERVE) + fn(0,CV)
                   DB(NOCONTACT&ACTIV) =
                           fuzzy(DB(NOCONTACT&ACTIV), CV)
          ELSE DB(RESERVE) = DB(RESERVE)
               DB(NOCONTACT&ACTIV) = DB(NOCONTACT&ACTIV)
```

In this case, fn(4.5,2) = 3.7 and DB(RESERVE) goes to 4.7 (probability of reserve = .70) and DB(NOCONTACT) = 3.7. Note that fn(0,2) = 0.] and fuzzy (2) for the AND rule is 0.0.

How certain are you that recent correspondence and other data in the customer's credit file supports belief in the collectibility of this account?

? -1

[The user's initial review of this data has found some problems that may need to be investigated but still gives the user the perception of non-support so a response of −1 is given. The semantic net in Figure 1 shows that two other AND rules are effected by a response to CORRES in a non-zero manner. Table 1 shows how the DBs for the AND rules are effected. Thus, RESERVE is updated by three rules, CORRES and the two AND rules and jumps to DB = 10 (probability of reserve = .95). Thus, by asking only three questions so far *Auditor* is already suggesting that the account should be reserved for with a high probability.]

How certain are you that although a portion of this customer's total balance is still delinquent, he continues to be an active customer?

? -1

[This customer is consistent with the CORRES response. The user has evidence indicating the possibility that the customer may not be active anymore. This question is key to the ABD decision as evidenced by its impact on the semantic net. It affects five other rules, its complement NOTACTIVE and four AND rules. In the audit situation as long as the customer remains active there may be still a chance to recover, so the major impact on ACTIVE is justified. The cumulative effect of the −1 response is to increase DB(RESERVE) to 15.2 (probability of reserve = .97)]

How certain are you that recent collections toward the delinquent portions of this account are proceeding satisfactorily?

? -3

[This is a much stronger test of the relationship between the client and the debtor in that money is changing hands, not just correpsondence. Thus, in this case, the user can say with more certainty (i.e., −3) that collections are not proceeding satisfactorily. Again, another AND rule is effected and in this case, its DB changes from −1.8 to −6 (see Table 1). DB(RESERVE) is now at 19.5 which is approximately 99% certain to reserve and the user ended the session with *Auditor*.

Figure 2. Annotated interaction with *Auditor* [annotations are in "[ ]" and user responses underlined].

Rule asked	*COLLECTED*	*NONCONTACT*	*CORRESPOND*	*ACTIVE*	*WORKOUT*
User Response: (in CVs)	−5	+2	−1	−1	−3
Impact on:* (in DB's)					
RESERVE	1	4.7	10	15.2	19.5
COLLECTED	−100	−100	−100	−100	−100
NONCONTACT	0	3.7	3.7	3.7	3.7
CORRESPOND	0	0	−1.8	−1.8	−1.8
ACTIVE	0	0	0	−1.8	−1.8
NOTACTIVE	0	0	0	+1.8	1.8
WORKOUT	0	0	0	0	−6
CORRES&ACTIVE	0	0	−1.8	−1.8	−1.8
CORRES&WORKOUT	0	0	−1.8	−1.8	−6
NONCONT&ACTIVE	0	0	0	1.8	1.8
CR&NPB&ACTIVE**	0	0	0	−1.8	−1.8

* All rules had an initial DB value of 0

** ANDing of rule CREDITMANAGER(CR), NOPROBLEMS(NPB) and ACTIVE

Table 2. Propagation of uncertainty through inference network for actual interaction.

effect of DB through *and* rules. When CORRESPOND is answered it also sets off changes in CORRES&ACTIVE and CORRES&WORKOUT.

Validation of *Auditor*

Auditor was validated with two different procedures: "open-book" and "blind." In both procedures, another external auditor, not involved in the development of *Auditor*, served as validator. His task was to compare the judgment of *Auditor* to that of the actual auditors on the job. In the "open-book" procedure an auditor from a different office of the same CPA firm served as validator. Because the data used by the validator contained the actual judgments made by the auditors on the job, this procedure is called "open-book." The "blind" validation exercise is based on a test proposed by Turing [37]. In this case, the validator was an auditor from a different CPA firm, who, during the validation, did not know the source of the ABD judgment (i.e., whether it was from *Auditor* or a human auditor). Table 3 summarizes the results of both validation procedures.

	Acceptable Auditor judgments	*Unacceptable Auditor judgments*	*Number of cases*
"Open Book"	9(90%)	1(10%)	10
"Blind"	10(91%)	1(9%)	11
Total for all Cases	19(90%)	2(10%)	21

Table 3. Summary of validation exercises.

Conclusions

Insights into Auditing from *Auditor*

In the process of developing *Auditor* several insights into audit decision making were revealed. First, the importance of items of evidence in practice was corroborated through an analysis of the experts' responses in the actual case situations used in the validation procedures. Second, this analysis also suggested that, to some extent, there was an inverse relationship between diagnosticity and availability. Evidence that is commonly gathered in an audit, although inexpensive to obtain, alone provides little aid in making the final decision while high diagnostic evidence is infrequently applied. Third, analysis of the inference network and the expert responses indicated that the auditors in this project formed an efficient sub-hypothesis to distinguish between "slow-pay" and "no-pay" debtors. Because a "slow-pay" does not usually require a reserve, it is more efficient to initially narrow the scope of investigation to the "no-pays" as soon as possible.

Evaluation of AL/X as a Development Tool

There are several built-in features of AL/X that make it a good development environment as well as a supportive, operational environment. AL/X offers several types of traces: debug, full, and partial. The debug trace is unique in that it allows one to follow the logic of AL/X in choosing the next question to ask (see Figure 3). This is very useful in the development stage of an expert system as it allows the knowledge engineer to determine how well the system is matching

```
INVESTIGATING WRITEOFF
INVESTIGATING LAWYER
BEST EVIDENCE FOR BANK&WR&LAW : POS = BANKRUPT   NEG = BANKRUPT
INVESTIGATING ECONOMIC
INVESTIGATING BAN&ECO&LAW
INVESTIGATING BANKRUPT
INVESTIGATING ECONOMIC
INVESTIGATING LAWYER
BEST EVIDENCE FOR BAN&ECO&LAW : POS = BANKRUPT   NEG = BANKRUPT
INVESTIGATING GOODRECORD
INVESTIGATING LEGAL
INVESTIGATING LEGAL&NPAY
INVESTIGATING LEGAL
INVESTIGATING NOTPAY
BEST EVIDENCE FOR LEGAL&NPAY : POS = LEGAL   NEG = LEGAL
INVESTIGATING NPAY&GDREC
INVESTIGATING NOTPAY
INVESTIGATING GOODRECORD
BEST EVIDENCE FOR NPAY&GDREC : POS = NOTPAY   NEG = NOTPAY
BEST EVIDENCE FOR RESERVE : POS = PROBLEMS   NEG = COLLECTED

HOW CERTAIN ARE YOU THAT YOUR TESTS OF CASH RECEIPTS INDICATE
THAT THE DELINQUENT PORTIONS OF THE ACCOUNT IN QUESTION HAVE
BEEN COLLECTED SUBSTANTIALLY IN THEIR ENTIRETY SUBSEQUENT TO
THE DATE OF THE BALANCE SHEET?
```

Figure 3. Portion of a DEBUG trace.

the reasoning of the domain expert. The other trace options provide information on the updated values of the DBs of the main goals and hypotheses of the inference network as a result of user responses. This is also important during development as it allows the domain expert to verify the values of the internal parameters by observing the impact of individual items of evidence on goals.

Another positive feature of AL/X is that it allows the user to volunteer information at any time. Without such an ability the user must wait for the inference engine to select the corresponding question before the user can input the information. In development volunteering evidence is very important to perform localized testing of individual rules efficiently. Otherwise, the tester may have to respond to ten to fifteen meaningless questions to get to the one question that he wants to answer, wasting time and allowing for errors.

In operations, the option of volunteering information has several benefits. First, it provides a more realistic operating environment. In a non-expert-system decision environment, the decision maker does not have to wait to apply known information but can use it immediately. The same situation should apply with an expert system to promote acceptance by the user and gains in efficiency. Second, the diagnostic process of the expert system can be made faster. Because AL/X uses known information to determine what questions to ask next and what conclusions to draw, the more information AL/X has sooner, the better. In some cases, volunteering only a few key items of evidence may allow AL/X to reach a conclusion without asking further questions. And third, if the user discovers that he has made an error in a response, he can rectify it by volunteering the proper response.

One finds that with any expert system, modifications must be made all the time because decision makers change, decision situations change, and evidence changes. Thus, an ability to modify internal parameters and the network structure easily is very important. Because the network structure in AL/X can be coded as a simple text file from any line editor or word-processor, physical changes to the permanent structure can be made easily. But AL/X also provides a mechanism to modify values during a consultation. This can be used in development to perform sensitivity analysis of internal parameter values or the structure of the network.

One key characteristic of an expert system that differentiates it from a decision support system is its ability to explain its reasoning and logic [38]. AL/X offers explanation options by allowing the user to ask "why" a question is being asked and "how" a goal will be proven. Figure 4 shows the response of AL/X to a W(hy) query by the user concerning the WORKOUT

```
. . . THAT RECENT COLLECTIONS TOWARD THE DELINQUENT PORTIONS OF
THIS ACCOUNT ARE PROCEEDING SATISFACTORILY?

? W

TYPE A SPACE NAME, <CR> TO INDICATE WORKOUT, OR ? TO LIST SPACE
NAMES

<CR>

THIS QUESTION IS ASKED TO FIND OUT WHETHER OR NOT
1) THE DELINQUENT PORTION OF THIS ACCOUNT SHOULD SPECIFICALLY BE
   RESERVED FOR IN THE ALLOWANCE FOR BAD DEBTS TO A SUBSTANTIAL
   DEGREE (RESERVE)
   WHICH HAS CURRENT DEGREE 11.0 (PW = -3.0     NW = 3.0)

2) CORRESPOND AND WORKOUT (CORRES&WORK)
   WHICH HAS CURRENT DEGREE -6.0
```

Figure 4. AL/X response to a W(hy) query.

rule. It states that WORKOUT is being asked to help determine the goal RESERVE and the *and* rule of "CORRESPOND & WORKOUT." Figure 5 shows the response of AL/X to a H(ow) query by the user concerning the *and* rule of "CORRESPOND & WORKOUT." It states that the *and* rule will be evaluated by asking about WORKOUT and CORRESPOND.

AL/X is not without its problems, however. A main drawback is that it requires a knowledge engineer to construct the inference network. The actual physical inputting of the network can be done by anybody. But the translation of the user's problem domain into a structure of rules, weights, and degrees of belief requires an intimate knowledge of how AL/X operates. This is especially telling in the current software environment which promotes user-friendly, non-technical interfaces to expert systems (e.g., TI's Personal Consultant).

This technically-oriented interface takes some of the luster off some of the benefits discussed above. To volunteer information one must know the internal name of the associated rule. Although AL/X allows one to list these names, it can still be difficult to select the appropriate one if the rule names are abbreviated or non-associative. The explanation options can be difficult to understand. As Figures 4 and 5 show, the response can be somewhat cryptic unless one knows how knowledge and network information is stored in AL/X.

Finally, one of the intelligent advantages of AL/X can actually be an operational disadvantage. AL/X chooses the next question to be asked based on the greatest potential impact on the goal at hand. This ordering does not take into consideration, however, the cost to the user of obtaining the evidence required to answer the question. Thus, the user may incur a greater cost than needed to use the system or be forced to wade through many questions for which he has no evidence, in order to get to the ones he can answer. In either case, such an ordering of the questions may not match the reality of the user's environment, making acceptance and use less likely.

Evaluation of the Computing Environment

One final benefit of the AL/X environment, not mentioned in the previous section, is that it can be run on a microcomputer. This project is in a unique position in that both a mainframe and microcomputer environment have been used. The original development of *Auditor* was made on a mainframe, a CYBER 175. Onsite (i.e., at the auditors) interactions with *Auditor* had to be handled over long-distance telephone lines with a hard-copy terminal. Busy signals and thirty cps printers made testing very tedious and

```
HOW CERTAIN ARE YOU THAT RECENT COLLECTIONS TOWARD THE
DELINQUENT PORTIONS OF THIS ACCOUNT ARE PROCEEDING SATISFACTORILY

?H

TYPE A SPACE NAME, <CR> TO INDICATE RESERVE, OR ? TO LIST SPACE NAMES

CORRES&WORK

THIS SPACE CONCERNS WHETHER OR NOT:

CORRESPOND AND WORKOUT (CORRES&WORK)

THIS HYPOTHESIS REQUIRES ALL OF THE EVIDENCE:

1) RECENT CORRESPONDENCE AND OTHER DATA IN THE CUSTOMER'S
   CREDIT FILE SUPPORTS YOUR BELIEF IN THE COLLECTIBILITY OF THIS
   ACCOUNT (CORRESPOND)

   WHICH HAS CURRENT DEGREE  6.0

2) RECENT COLLECTIONS TOWARD THE DELINQUENT PORTIONS OF THIS
   ACCOUNT ARE PROCEEDING SATISFACTORILY (WORKOUT)

   WHICH HAS CURRENT DEGREE 0.0
```

Figure 5. AL/X response to a H(ow) query.

awkward. The experts sensed immediately that such an environment was inappropriate for commercial use of any expert system.

Currently, however, AL/X, and thus *Auditor*, can operate on a personal microcomputer. Continued validation and sensitivity analysis can now be made very rapidly. Demonstrations of *Auditor* can and are made anywhere that an IBM PC resides. This has convinced other auditors, who have recently tested *Auditor*, that expert systems provide feasible opportunities for auditing.

The Future of *Auditor*

There are several directions that *Auditor* is now taking. Continued testing of *Auditor* by experienced auditors with actual case situations will result in the refinement of the existing set of rules and inference network. This effort will also aid in the calibration of the use of *Auditor*. Many of the case situations used to develop and validate *Auditor* were all or nothing cases; that is, the decision was to reserve all of the delinquent account balance or none of it. More cases are needed in the middle ground where the delinquent amount is partially reserved for. Practicing auditors have stated that this secondary ABD decision has little consistency across auditors.

Another operational goal of *Auditor* is to develop training applications for novice auditors. The use of an expert system as a simulation environment is one of the by-products of development. Plans are being made to establish an experimental training program with an international CPA firm using *Auditor* as the training vehicle.

References

[1] "Symposium on Decision Support Systems for Auditing," University of Southern California, February, 1984.

[2] Peat, Marwick, Mitchell & Co., *Research Opportunities in Auditing Program Report*, 1983.

[3] A. Paterson, *AL/X User Manual*, Intelligent Terminals Ltd., 15 Canal Street, Oxford, 1981.

[4] J. Gaschnig, "Development of Uranium Exploration Models for the PROSPECTOR Consultant System," Final Report SRI Project 7856, Artificial Intelligence Center, SRI International, Menlo Park, CA, 1980.

[5] D. A. Waterman and F. Hayes-Roth, "An Investigation of Tools for Building Expert Systems," in *Building Expert Systems*, Hayes-Roth, Waterman and Lenat (eds.), Addison-Wesley, 1983.

[6] A. D. Akresh and W. A. Wallace, "The Application of Regression Analysis for Limited Review and Audit Planning," *Symposium on Auditing Research IV*, University of Illinois at Urbana, 1983, pp. 67-128.

[7] W. S. Albrecht and J. C. McKeown, "Towards an Extended Use of Statistical Analytical Reviews in the Audit," *Symposium on Auditing Research II*, University of Illinois at Urbana, 1977, pp. 53-69.

[8] W. R. Kinney, Jr., "ARIMA and Regression in Analytical Review: An Empirical Test," *The Accounting Review*, January 1978, pp. 48-60.

[9] W. R. Kinney, Jr., "Integrating Audit Tests: Regression Analysis and Partitioned Dollar-Unit Sampling," *Journal of Accounting Research*, Autumn 1979, pp. 456-475.

[10] K. W. Stringer, "A Statistical Technique for Analytical Review," Supplement to the *Journal of Accounting Research*, Autumn 1979, pp. 465-475.

[11] W. A. Wallace, "Discussant's Response to 'The Effect of Measurement Error on Regression Results in Analytical Review,'" *Symposium on Auditing Research III*, University of Illinois at Urbana, 1979, pp. 70-81.

[12] E. Deakin and M. Granof, "Regression Analysis as a Means of Determining Audit Sample Size," *The Accounting Review*, October 1974, pp. 764-771.

[13] D. Roberts, M. Shedd, and M. MacGuidwin, "The Behavior of Selected Upper Bounds of Monetary Errors Using PPS Sampling," *Symposium on Auditing Research IV*, University of Illinois at Urbana, 1982.

[14] D. A. Leslie, A. D. Teitlebaum, and R. J. Anderson, *Dollar-Unit Sampling: A Practical Guide for Auditors*, Copp Clark Pitman and Commerce Clearing House, 1979.

[15] D. C. Burns and J. K. Loebbecke, "Internal Control Evaluation: How the Computer Can Help," *Journal of Accountancy*, August 1975, pp. 60-70.

[16] R. Duda, J. Gaschnig, and P. Hart, "Model Design in the PROSPECTOR Consultant System for Mineral Exploration," in *Expert Systems in the Micro-electronic Age*, D. Michie, Ed., Edinburgh University Press, 1979, pp. 153-167.

[17] J. McDermott, "R1: A Rule-based Configurer of Computer Systems," Technical Report CMU-CS-80-119, Department of Computer Science, Carnegie-Mellon University, 1980.

[18] B. G. Buchanan and E. A. Feigenbaum, "DENDRAL and Meta-DENDRAL: Their Applications Dimension," *Artificial Intelligence*, 11, 1978, pp. 5-24.

[19] E. A. Feigenbaum, B. G. Buchanan, and J. Lederberg, "On Generality and Problem Solving: A Case Study Using the DENDRAL Program," *Machine Intelligence*, D. Michie and B. Meltzer, Eds., 6, 1971, pp. 165-190.

[20] W. J. Clancey, "Tutoring Rules for Guiding a Case Method Dialogue," *International Journal of Man-Machine Studies*, 11, 1979, pp. 25-49.

[21] W. J. Clancey, E. H. Shortliffe, and B. G. Buchanan, "Intelligent Computer-aided Instruction for Medical Diagnosis," in *Proceedings of the Third Annual Symposium on Computer Applications in Medical Care*, 1979, pp. 175-183.

[22] L. M. Fagan, J. C. Kunz, E. A. Feigenbaum, and J. Osborn, "Representation of Dynamic Clinical Knowledge: Measurement Interpretation in the Intensive Care Unit," *Proceedings of the International Joint Conference on Artificial Intelligence*, 1979, pp. 260-262.

[23] C. A. Kulikowski, "Artificial Intelligence Methods and Systems for Medical Consultation," *IEEE Transactions on Pattern Analysis and Machine Intelligence*, 1980, pp. 464-476.

[24] S. G. Pauker, G. A. Gorry, J. P. Kassirer, and W. B. Schwartz, "Towards the Simulation of Clinical Cognition—Taking a Present Illness by Computer," *American Journal of Medicine*, 60, 1976, pp. 981-996.

[25] H. E. Pople, Jr., "The Formulation of Composite Hypotheses in Diagnostic Problem Solving: An Exercise in Synthetic Reasoning," *Proceedings of the Fifth Joint International Conference on Artificial Intelligence*, 1977, pp. 119-185.

[26] H. E. Pople, Jr., J. D. Myers, and R. A. Miller, "DIALOG: A Model of Diagnostic Logic for Internal Medicine," *Proceedings of the Fourth Joint International Conference on Artificial Intelligence*, 1975, pp. 848-855.

[27] E. H. Shortliffe, *Computer-based Medical Consultation: MYCIN, American-Elsevier, New York, 1975.*

[28] S. M. Weiss, and C. A. Kulikowski, "EXPERT: A System for Developing Consultation Models," *Proceedings of the Sixth International Conference on Artificial Intelligence*, 1979, pp. 942-947.

[29] S. M. Weiss, C. A. Kulikowski, and A. Safir, "Glaucoma Consultation by Computer," *Computers in Biology and Medicine*, 8, 1978, pp. 25-40.

[30] J. V. Hansen and W. F. Messier, Jr., "Continued Development of a Knowledge-based Expert System for Auditing Advanced Computer Systems," Preliminary Report submitted to Peat, Marwick, Mitchell Foundation, 1984.

[31] H. M. Braun and J. S. Chandler, "Development of an Expert System to Assist Auditors in the Investigation of Analytic Review Fluctuations," Research project for Peat, Marwick, Mitchell Foundation, 1983.

[32] A. Paterson and T. Niblett, *ACLS User Manual*, Department of Computer Science, Class Note 8. CS347/397D, University of Illinois at Urbana, Fall 1982.

[33] W. Wright and J. Willingham, "Development of a Knowledge-based System for Auditing the Collectibility of a Commercial Loan," Research Proposal, 1985.

[34] R. Michaelsen, "An Expert System for Federal Tax Planning," *Expert Systems*, 1, 2, 1984, pp. 149-167.

[35] C. W. Dungan, "A Model of an Audit Judgment in the Form of an Expert System," Ph.D. dissertation, Department of Accountancy, University of Illinois at Urbana, 1983.

[36] L. Zadeh, "A Theory of Approximate Reasoning," *Machine Intelligence*, 9, J. E. Hayes, D. Michie, and L. Mikulich, Eds., Wiley & Sons, 1979.

[37] A. M. Turing, "Computing Machinery and Intelligence," *Mind*, October, 1950.

[38] F. Hayes-Roth, D. A. Waterman, and D. B. Lenat, Eds., *Building Expert Systems*, Addison-Wesley, 1983.

A Preliminary Investigation of EDP-XPERT

James V. Hansen and William F. Messier, Jr.

With the introduction of low-cost computer technology, more organizations have been automating their accounting systems and the automation has been more extensive than in the past. These changes present some serious challenges to auditors in that typical internal controls and traditional audit trails will no longer be present. These challenges will require auditors to make evidential judgment decisions in more complex environments and will therefore require the development of better audit technology (Hansen and Messier, 1982). In this paper, we present the results of a preliminary investigation of EDP-XPERT, an expert system which is intended to assist computer audit specialists (CASs) in making judgments as to the reliability of controls in advanced computer environments.

Because of known human cognitive limitations, tools which help to improve the control reliability judgment process are needed. For example, Einhorn (1972) and Hogarth (1980) point out that psychological research suggests that the best role for individuals in judgment is in *evaluating* the data. The *combination* of the evaluated data, however, is best performed by *mechanical* means. These mechanical means can vary from simple additive models with few variables to expert systems such as the one described in this paper. The basic idea of all mechanical models is to support, and we hope, to improve the judgment process.[1]

In addition to presenting the results of the preliminary investigation of EDP-XPERT, we discuss the issue of evaluating expert systems. Our purpose is to point out the difficulty in evaluating expert systems and to suggest a number of criteria that can be used in the evaluation process. The remainder of the paper is as follows: the first section discusses the evaluation of expert systems; the second and third sections contain the method and results of the preliminary investigation; and the final section contains suggestions for future research and concluding comments.

Reprinted with permission from *Auditing: A Journal of Practice and Theory*, vol. 6, no. 1, Fall 1986, 109-123.

Evaluation of Expert Systems

There may be two different (although not necessarily independent) reasons or motives in constructing computer programs that perform some task (Glass and Holyoak, 1986). In one instance, the motive is to "simulate" one expert. Here the program developers would not only be concerned with the program's ability to reach the same conclusion as the expert, but they would also be concerned with mimicking the expert's reasoning process. This approach takes a cognitive psychology perspective. The second reason is narrower in focus in that it attempts to produce a program that only performs the task as well as the expert with minimum concern for modeling human cognition. This is consistent with the development process for expert systems. The discussions in this paper relate specifically to evaluation of the expert system's conclusions and are not concerned with comparing the program's reasoning process with the cognitive processes of the expert.

The Evaluation Process

There is no single best approach to the evaluation and validation of expert systems. It is apparent from the recent literature (Gaschnig et al., 1983; Buchanan and Shortliffe, 1984, Chapter 30) that the validation process must be undertaken *throughout* the life of the system and that the evaluations should become more formal as the expert system matures. In the early stages of development, the evaluation can be very informal with a demonstration that the initial prototype can be used on simple cases. Next, as the knowledge base is expanded, the evaluation process can begin to include more complex cases and feedback from experts and potential users. This is the stage at which EDP-XPERT is being evaluated in this paper. In later stages, the system can be formally evaluated, perhaps in "blinded" studies (Yu et al., 1979) or actual field studies (McDermott, 1984). (See Chandrasekran (1983) for a detailed proposed evaluation schedule.)

Evaluations typically require a standard by which performance can be measured. Two approaches have been suggested as standards for evaluating expert systems:

- The "correct" answer to the particular case, or
- What a human expert states is the correct answer based on the available information (Buchanan and Shortliffe, 1984, p. 580).

In many of the problem domains where expert systems are built, the "correct" answer is not available. This is particularly true in a number of auditing situations[2] (Ashton, 1983). As a result, the evaluations of most expert systems have been along the lines of the second approach (Dungan and Chandler, 1985). Since a "correct" answer is not immediately known when the reliability of EDP controls is evaluated, the second approach to examining EDP-XPERT's advice was followed.

Suggested Evaluation Criteria

Comparison of the expert's conclusion with that of the expert system is one major criterion for evaluating an expert system. A number of other criteria are also important based upon previous research (Gorry, 1973; Shortliffe, 1976). For example, it is important to assess items such as the wording of the questions posed by the expert system. Poor or unclear wording may cause user uncertainty about what is being asked. Second, the explanation capabilities of the system should include an ability to provide (1) additional explanation for a particular question, and (2) an explanation for why a particular question is being asked. Third, the mechanisms for providing input data (e.g., the response scale for a question) to the system are also extremely important. Finally, the program's reasoning capabilities are another important criterion. Explanation of the reasoning process (i.e., ability to show the user how a conclusion was reached) and reliability of the program's advice are important issues that should be examined as part of the evaluation process. All of these issues were examined during the preliminary investigation of EDP-XPERT.

Our purpose in this section was to elucidate how expert systems might be evaluated and the potential difficulties in such a process. Perhaps Gaschnig et al. (1983, p. 277) summarize this process best: "At this stage of expert systems' evolution, the evaluation process is more of an art, however primitive, than a science."

Method

Development of EDP-XPERT

Our initial work involved determining the feasibility of applying artificial intelligence (AI) techniques to the EDP audit environment. We reviewed the existing literature on the subject including the EDP audit materials of several Big Eight firms. We also conducted interviews with Computer Audit Specialists (CASs) from five Big Eight firms. While some of the firms we examined had structured approaches to dealing with the problem, in many instances the CAS still relied heavily on his or her expertise in advanced computer environments.[3] The initial efforts also involved establishing an appropriate AI structure for representation of the CASs' knowledge. A production system architecture (If-Then rules) was adopted mainly because our interview work indicated the problem domain was not static and that knowledge would have to be continuously updated. Rule-based systems provide easy modification of the knowledge base. Details of this research are contained in Hansen and Messier (1981, 1982). We do not, however, assert that auditors think in a rule-based manner. We do believe that a rule-based approach can capture the thought process in a fashion that will result in an expert system following "lines of reasoning" similar to those followed by the expert. But, as noted earlier, our work does not address the cognitive issues directly.[4]

The second phase of our research was taken in three major steps. First, we conducted a verbal protocol experiment with three senior CASs. Our intent was to examine the decision-making behavior of CASs in some detail and to identify any decision rules (If-Then) that might be appropriate for the knowledge base of the expert system. Second, we identified a software package that would be appropriate for our problem domain. Third, we developed an initial prototype system.

The protocol study (Biggs, Messier, and Hansen, 1986) provided some insight into the decision-making behavior of CASs but it did not provide many If-Then rules appropriate for an expert system in support of auditing advanced computer systems. Two possible reasons exist for this outcome. First, where we did identify a decision rule, it was usually very tentative or not in an obvious If-Then form. Second, the case used in the protocol study had strong user controls. As a result, the CASs used decision rules more appropriate for auditing *around* the computer. (See Biggs et al. (1986) for more detail.) The CASs' *overall* approach to computer auditing did provide general input to our modeling effort and did affect the goal structure used in EDP-XPERT (discussed below).

After examining the software available at the time, we chose AL/X (Advice Language/X) (Paterson, 1984) as our expert system software "shell." AL/X is based on the PROSPECTOR system (Duda et al., 1980) and was originally developed to diagnose the underlying causes of oil platform shutdowns. AL/X was chosen because at the time we started development it was the only software commercially available at a reasonable price. More importantly, however, the system seemed appropriate for the diagnostic-type problem we were investigating. The software does have certain limitations which we discuss in the last section.

The initial EDP-XPERT prototype (Hansen and Messier, 1986) contained approximately 60 rules. Since the protocol study failed to produce usable If-Then rules, we resorted to *reconstructed methods* (Johnson, 1981) to develop this initial knowledge base. Such an approach involves using currently available information (e.g., textbooks, firm materials) to construct the inference network of rules. This initial knowledge base contained a partial set of rules for controls in a distributed processing system[5] and had *one* overall goal (the reliability of the control system). We initially tested this knowledge base using a series of small problem situations. This initial testing, our protocol results (Biggs et al., 1986), and further discussion with our expert pointed out that CASs address the general or supervisory controls *before* looking at the application (input, processing, output) controls. Further, our expert indicated that unless supervisory controls were adequate, there would be no reliance on controls for specific accounting applications. Based on these findings, EDP-XPERT's knowledge base was restructured to include *four* separate goals: the reliability of supervisory, input, processing, and output controls. Additional If-Then rules were added after this restructuring.

We next met with our expert (a senior CAS) for two days to go through the rules in detail to determine if we had appropriate controls, structure, and terminology. The senior CAS also provided the degrees of belief ("weights") for the rules. All of his proposed changes were made to EDP-XPERT's knowledge base. This is the version of EDP-XPERT that was used in the preliminary investigation reported in this paper. The resulting system contained 133 rules. The breakdown of the rules by goals was 66 rules for the supervisory goal, 25 for input, 24 for processing, and eight for the output goal.

EDP-XPERT's Software

AL/X (Paterson, 1984) contains two major components: a knowledge base and an inference engine. The knowledge base contains the inference network of If-Then rules which form the evidence-hypothesis relationships of the problem domain. The inference engine contains the analytical framework for generating and explaining advice to the user. The underlying model in AL/X's inference engine is based on a subjective "Bayesian-like" updating method for rule-based systems suggested by Duda et al. (1976).

We provide a brief overview of AL/X in order to help the reader understand some of the testing. The rules in EDP-XPERT contain degrees of belief (priors) provided by the expert which indicate the strength of the rules. The user chooses which model (goal) to use and AL/X then chooses a question to ask the user. The question chosen is the one that would have the maximum effect on the goal, i.e., the one which causes the greatest shift in the degree of belief of the current goal (Paterson, 1984). AL/X will ask all of the relevant questions related to the goal under consideration. The user normally responds to a question by providing a certainty factor: a number in the range of -5 to 5. This response scale is equivalent in AL/X's inference engine to probabilities ranging from zero to 100. After the user has responded to all questions relevant to a particular goal, the system provides a report on the likelihood of the truth of the hypothesis (goal). The following is an example of such a report:

After considering all significant questions, the degree that supervisory controls are complete and functioning well (supercontrols) initially was 0.0. It is now 9.5.
There are no more significant questions for the current goal. Investigated goals with degree of belief > = 0.0 are:
The supervisory controls are complete and functioning well. Prior degree was 0.0. Current degree is 9.5.

The current degree of belief can be converted to a probability since

$$p = \frac{odds(H)}{odds(H)+1}$$

In this example,

$$degree(H) = 10\log_{10}(odds(H)) = 9.5$$

and p = .90. During the preliminary investigation, the subjects were provided with a table that contained conversion values for the degrees of belief. Significant research exists with respect to the use of "probability-like" rules in expert systems. We do not address these issues in this paper; our interest, as noted earlier, is in developing a problem solver, not an expert emulator. The interested reader is referred to Buchanan and Shortliffe (1984, Chapters 10-13).

Subjects

The 17 subjects who participated in the preliminary investigation of EDP-XPERT were students in an initial CAS training course for a Big Eight public accounting firm. The subjects had an average of 3.3 years of audit experience, ranging from one to eight years. There were two managers, six supervisors, and nine seniors. All but one were CPAs and two subjects had Master's degrees. On average, the subjects had completed 2.5 computer courses in college, ranging from one to ten courses.

Procedure

The test was administered during the second week of the two-week training course. The subjects were required to complete two large case studies during their training. In conjunction with the senior CAS who was assisting us in developing the system, we determined that one of these cases would be appropriate for testing purposes. The case contained the following information on a hypothetical company (approximately 60 pages):

- Audit planning and background information.
- A description of the EDP control environment.
- Documentation of the client's accounts receivable-sales system.
- Information on access controls.
- Various client data file layouts and system's reports.

As part of the training course, the subjects were required to: (1) complete an EDP control environment worksheet; (2) document the accounting system and identify controls; (3) review and evaluate access controls, systems development, program changes, and manual follow-up procedures; and (4) apply computer audit software to test controls in the client's revenue cycle.

The investigation of EDP-XPERT was carried out in five parts. First, the subjects were given a 15-minute presentation on expert systems and an overview of the testing. They were then presented with some audit test results for the case. These results were provided by the senior CAS who was assisting us. Second, they completed the first part of a questionnaire which asked a series of questions about applications of computers in auditing, and in particular, questions about expert systems. This part of the instrument was based on a questionnaire used by Teach and Shortliffe (1981) for assessing physicians' comments on computer-based decision supports. The questions were adapted for an audit setting.[6] Third, the participants assessed the reliability of controls (supervisory, input, processing, and output) for the case company. Fourth, the subjects used EDP-XPERT to assist their assessment of the reliability of the company's controls. Fifth, they completed the final part of the questionnaire which included another assessment of the company's controls, completion of the same questions about expert systems, an evaluation of EDP-XPERT, and some demographic data. The subjects were allowed to use any material that they felt was relevant during the test.

Results

In examining the system at this stage, we realized that the knowledge base was incomplete (i.e., it did not contain all of the rules for an advanced computer system) and that the explanation capabilities of the system were not fully developed. However, we felt it was important to receive some feedback on the system's performance to assist us in further development efforts. We will discuss the results of the preliminary investigation under two categories:

- The subjects' evaluations of expert systems and EDP-XPERT, and
- The subjects' EDP control judgments.

Subjects' Evaluations of Expert Systems and EDP-XPERT

We gathered attitudinal data related to expert systems from the subjects. These data included subjects' responses on: (1) applications of computers to auditing, (2) the subjects' expectations and demands from expert systems, and (3) the subjects' evaluation of EDP-XPERT. Since these data are based on a small sample of auditors from one firm, no statistical tests were performed on these attitudinal questions. The results are shown in Tables 1-4.

Table 1 contains the number of subjects' responses to six areas where computers could be used in auditing. Items 1-4 on this table are current applications in practice. Virtually all of the subjects indicated that these items would be appropriate uses of computers in auditing. Items 5 and 6 were included to elicit the subjects' beliefs concerning expert systems. In particular, 16 of 17 subjects indicated that expert systems would be an appropriate use of computers for *assisting* auditor judgment. On the other hand, only one subject thought that computer-based decision aids should be *substituted* for audit judgment. The subjects who thought that expert systems were appropriate for assisting auditor judgment were also asked to indicate which of nine audit areas might be appropriate for expert systems application. These areas were selected based on areas where expert systems in auditing are currently under development and areas where their use might be applicable.

Tables 2 and 3 present the mean ratings for a series of expectation and demand statements concerning expert systems. Each of the statements was preceded by the following: "Computer-based decision aids (expert systems) when FULLY developed..." The response scales and their corresponding values were: strongly disagree (-2), somewhat disagree (-1), not sure (0), somewhat agree (1), and strongly agree (2). The questionnaire was administered both *prior to* and *after* the use of EDP-XPERT. The second administration was conducted in order to see if the actual use of an expert system would change the subjects' beliefs.

In Table 2 we note that all of the mean values are negative. Thus, the participants disagree to some extent with all the expectation statements and, therefore, do not see a negative impact on themselves as individual auditors or on the profession from the use of expert systems. There is very little difference between the two administrations of the questionnaire. It is interesting to note that the responses by the physicians in the Teach and Shortliffe (1981, p. 549) were positive for 13 of these questions.

Table 3 provides the CASs' mean ratings on a series of questions related to what a user should expect from an expert system. The CASs have some definite views on a number of these statements. For example, there is high agreement that the system should:

- Simulate the auditor's decision processes,
- Be able to explain decisions to auditors, and
- Be portable and flexible.

There is also strong agreement that the system will *not* reduce the amount of technical knowledge an auditor must learn and remember. The strength of these evaluations decreased after the use of the expert system.

Table 4 presents the subjects' evaluation of EDP-XPERT. Nine attributes, based on the previously mentioned criteria, were evaluated on a five-point scale (1=very poor, 2=poor, 3=good, 4=very good, 5=excellent). The overall evaluation of the system (mean responses averaged across all nine attributes) was good (2.98). However, four items (1, 6, 7, and 8) which deal directly with the performance of EDP-XPERT received average ratings less than 3.0. These results show areas in which the EDP-XPERT system needs improvement. Given the current state of development of EDP-XPERT, we view these overall results as encouraging.

Which of the following do you think are appropriate uses of computers in auditing? Mark *all* that apply.

	Number of Subjects (n = 17)
1. Preparing audit workpapers (e.g., replacing conventional paper copies).	17
2. Selecting transactions from client files.	17
3. Testing transactions from client files.	15
4. Monitoring client's internal control systems (e.g., embedded audit modules).	15
5. Computer-based decision aids (''expert systems'') for *assisting* auditor judgment.	16
6. *Substituting* a computer-based decision aid for auditor judgment.	1
If you checked item 5. above, please indicate which of the following areas would seem appropriate for the application of computer-based decision aids (''expert systems'').	
Inherent risk evaluation	10
Auditing accounts receivable	7
Statistical sampling	13
Analytical review	10
Financial modeling	9
Internal control - manual or semi-automated environment	6
Internal control - advanced computer environment	10
Going concern evaluation	6
Audit opinion judgments	5

Table 1. Number of subjects noting applications of computers to auditing.

Subjects' EDP Control Judgments

In Table 5, we present the CASs' overall evaluations of the company's EDP controls. There were two evaluations of the EDP controls made by the subjects:

- Prior to the use of EDP-XPERT (PRE), and
- After the use of EDP-XPERT (POST).

EDP-XPERT's evaluation (SYS) of the reliability of the controls is also shown. Note that EDP-XPERT's evaluation is based on the individual subjects' responses to the questions posed during the interactive session.

Table 6 presents the Pearson correlations of the subjects' judgments (both prior to and after the use of EDP-XPERT) and EDP-XPERT's conclusion.[7] The correlations are calculated by type of EDP control (system goal). An examination of the correlations for the supervisory controls indicates that the subjects' judgments prior to the use of EDP-XPERT (PRE) are not highly correlated with EDP-XPERT's evaluations (SYS), but they are correlated ($p < .10$) with the subjects' POST judgments. Note, however, that the subjects' POST judgments are more highly correlated ($p < .05$) with EDP-XPERT's conclusion.

The results of the correlations for the application controls are mixed. With the input

	Before	After
Will be hard for auditors to learn.	-1.41	-1.12
Will force auditors to think like computers.	-1.29	-1.24
Will result in reliance on cookbook auditing and in time diminish auditor judgment.	- .12	- .12
Will dehumanize audit practice.	- .94	- .94
Will result in serious legal and ethical problems (e.g., increase malpractice suits).	- .29	- .47
Will diminish clients' image of auditor.	- .59	- .71
Will threaten an auditor's self-image.	- .59	- .77
Will depend on knowledge that cannot be kept up-to-date easily.	- .35	- .24
Will reduce the cost of auditing.	- .06	.06
Will result in less efficient use of auditor time.	- .59	- .47
Will alienate auditors because of electronic gadgetry.	-1.12	-1.12
Will reduce the need for specialists.	- .94	-1.12
Will be unreliable because of computer malfunctions.	- .94	- .59
Will be blamed by clients for audit errors.	- .24	- .29
Will threaten personal and professional privacy.	- .82	- .89

Table 2. Mean ratings for expectation statements.

	Before	After
Should respond to voice command and not require typing.	.41	.41
Should simulate auditor thought processes.	1.18	.65
Should never make an incorrect judgment.	- .29	- .06
Should become the standard for acceptable audit practice.	- .47	- .65
Should improve the cost efficiency of audit tests.	.65	.59
Should demand little effort from an auditor to learn or use.	.76	.59
Should significantly reduce the amount of technical knowledge an auditor must learn and remember.	-1.35	- .77
Should display common sense.	.71	.77
Should be able to explain decisions to auditors.	1.59	1.41
Should automatically learn new information when interacting with audit experts.	.82	.65
Should display an understanding of their own audit knowledge base.	.94	.71
Should *not* reduce the need for specialists.	.71	.41
Should be portable and flexible so that the auditor can access them at any time and place.	1.71	1.41

Table 3. Mean ratings for demand statements.

controls, the results follow the general pattern found with the supervisory controls. The correlations of the judgments for the processing controls show similar correlations between PRE, POST, and EDP-XPERT. The output controls show that there was a high correlation between the subjects' PRE and POST judgments and that EDP-XPERT's conclusion was not highly correlated with either the subjects' PRE or POST judgments. This result for the output controls is not surprising since that part of the knowledge base contained only eight rules at the time of the test.

We infer from these results that the subjects' judgments after the use of EDP-XPERT were

Please evaluate the expert system (AL/X) used in this experiment in terms of the attributes listed below:

	Mean Subject Response
1. Wording of questions	2.88
2. Explanation of questions (E command)	3.31
3. Explanation of why a question was asked (W command)	3.08
4. Explanation of program's reasoning (C command)	3.00
5. User response scale (+ 5 to -5)	3.24
6. Program's usefulness	2.77
7. Reliability of program's advice	2.63
8. Program's performance	2.81
9. Educational capability	3.18
OVERALL	2.98

Response Scale:

1 = Very Poor 3 = Good 5 = Excellent

2 = Poor 4 = Very Good

Table 4. Subjects' evaluation of EDP-XPERT.

Controls

SUBJECT	SUPERVISORY			PROCESSING			INPUT			OUTPUT		
NUMBER	PRE	SYS	POST	PRE	SYS	POST	PRE	SYS	POST	PRE	SYS	POST
1	80	15	15	50	95	95	80	0	50	80	65	65
2	65	15	40	60	95	50	60	40	50	60	65	50
3	75	75	75	75	90	75	95	50	95	80	50	80
4	25	10	8	75	95	95	50	90	90	85	60	60
5	40	20	50	40	80	80	40	50	50	40	50	50
6	80	25	60	80	95	80	95	50	90	95	50	90
7	95	5	5	95	90	90	95	30	30	95	55	55
8	75	45	60	85	95	90	85	50	65	85	65	70
9	40	50	40	40	80	50	30	30	30	30	60	30
10	65	20	65	65	70	65	40	50	70	85	65	85
11	75	70	70	80	70	70	90	50	80	85	65	70
12	60	15	40	75	95	60	65	50	50	80	70	50
13	50	10	50	60	95	60	70	20	70	70	50	70
14	75	30	70	75	95	70	80	30	75	80	60	70
15	80	25	80	40	55	40	80	20	80	80	50	80
16	20	10	15	60	90	70	80	20	60	70	65	60
17	40	5	10	70	90	70	70	50	60	65	50	60

Table 5. Subjects' evaluations of EDP controls.

affected by their use of the expert system and its conclusion, and that the subjects' revisions of their control judgments (except for output controls) were in the direction of the expert system's conclusions.

Limitations, Future Research, and Concluding Comments

There are a number of limitations associated with this research which limit the generalizability of the results. First, this work is only a preliminary investigation of EDP-XPERT. As a result, the testing used in this study was not as rigorous as that required for formal testing (e.g., a blinded study). This work is consistent, however, with the suggestions made by Buchanan and Shortliffe (1984) that expert systems be subjected to various types of testing during their development. However, conducting formal tests of EDP-XPERT (and we suspect other expert systems in auditing) will be relatively difficult and costly. For example, the amount of information a subject needs to run *one* case for an interactive session is enormous; basically, all information on the client's EDP system. Additionally, there are only a limited number of CASs and access to them is very costly.

Second, we used a small number of subjects from one firm. Third, these subjects were not as experienced as the intended users (senior CASs) of the system.[8] Our results might have been different if we had used senior CASs. Finally, the expert system software has some built-in capabilities which may have affected the results. For example, the way the system selects the next question to be asked (the question which causes the greatest shift in the degree of belief) may not always appear to be logical. The reader is referred to Kidd and Cooper (1985) for a more detailed discussion of some of the potential difficulties with the AL/X software.

Our future work on EDP-XPERT will involve expansion of the knowledge base to include rules for controls in on-line and data base systems. We are continuing to use reconstructed methods for gathering this knowledge followed by refinement with an expert. After this work is completed, EDP-XPERT will be subjected to two forms of testing. First, we will evaluate EDP-XPERT across a series of case studies using senior CASs. Second, if this previous testing proceeds well, EDP-XPERT will be field tested on a number of actual audit engagements.

In this paper we presented the results of the preliminary investigation of EDP-XPERT. We also provided some insights into how expert systems can be evaluated. It is our hope that this paper will provide useful information to those researchers interested in expert system development.

$* = p < .05 \quad ** = p < .10$

	PRE	SYS	POST
Supervisory Controls:			
PRE	1.0		
SYS	.280	1.0	
POST	.416**	.646*	1.0
Input Controls:			
PRE	1.0		
SYS	-.235	1.0	
POST	.353	.407**	1.0
Processing Controls:			
PRE	1.0		
SYS	.430**	1.0	
POST	.494*	.494*	1.0
Output Controls:			
PRE	1.0		
SYS	.103	1.0	
POST	.711*	-.266	1.0

Table 6. Correlations of subjects' overall EDP judgments and EDP-XPERT's advice by type of EDP control.

References

Ashton, R. H. *Research in Audit Decision Making: Rationale, Evidence, and Implications,* Research Monograph No. 6 (Vancouver, Canada: Canadian Certified General Accountants' Research Foundation, 1983).

Biggs, S. F., Messier, W. F., Jr., and Hansen, J. V. "A Descriptive Analysis of Computer Audit Specialists' Decision-Making Behavior in Advanced EDP Environments," Working paper, April 1986.

Buchanan, B. G. and Shortliffe, E. H. *Rule-Based Expert Systems: The MYCIN Experiments of the Stanford Heuristic Programming Project* (Reading, MA: Addison-Wesley, 1984).

Chandrasekran, B. "On Evaluating AI Systems for Medical Diagnosis," *The AI Magazine* (Summer 1983), pp. 34-38.

Davis, G. B. and Weber, R. *Auditing Advanced EDP Systems: A Survey of Practice and Development of a Theory* (Minneapolis, MN: The Management Information Systems Research Center, 1983).

Duda, R. O., Gaschnig, J. G., and Hart, P. E. "Model Design in the PROSPECTOR Consultation System for Mineral Exploration," in *Expert Systems in the Microelectronic Age,* D. Michie, Ed. (Edinburgh: Edinburgh University Press, 1980).

____, Hart, P. E., and Nilsson, N. J. "Subjective Bayesian Methods for Rule-Based Inference Systems," *AFIPS Conference Proceedings of the 1976 National Computer Conference* (1976), pp. 1075-1082.

Dungan, C. W. and Chandler, J.S. "AUDITOR: A Microcomputer-Based Expert System to Support Auditors in the Field," *Expert Systems* (October 1985), pp. 210-221.

Einhorn, H. J. "Expert Measurement and Mechanical Combination," *Organizational Behavior and Human Performance* (1972), pp. 86-106.

Elliott, R. K. "Unique Audit Methods: Peat, Marwick International," *Auditing: A Journal of Practice & Theory* (Spring 1983), pp. 1-12.

Gaschnig, J.P., Klahr, P., Pople, H., Shortliffe, E., and Terry, A. "Evaluation of Expert Systems," in F. Hayes-Roth, D. A. Waterman, and D. B. Lenat, Eds., *Building Expert Systems* (Reading, MA: Addison-Wesley, 1983).

Glass, A. L. and Holyoak, K. J. *Cognition* (New York: Random House, 1986).

Gorry, G. A. 1973. "Computer-Assisted Clinical Decision-Making," *Methods of Information in Medicine* (1973), pp. 45-51.

Hansen, J. V. "Audit Considerations in Distributed Processing Systems," *Communications of the ACM* (August 1983), pp. 562-569.

____and Messier, W. F., Jr. "The Feasibility of Using Artificial Intelligence Techniques for EDP Auditing," Research Report on Project 80-145 (Peat, Marwick, Mitchell Foundation, December 1981).

____ and ____. "Expert Systems for Decision Support in EDP Auditing," *International Journal of Computer and Information Sciences* (1982), pp. 357-379.

____ and ____. "A Knowledge Based, Expert System for Auditing Advanced Computer Systems," *European Journal of Operations Research* (1986), in press.

Hogarth, R. *Judgment and Choice: The Psychology of Prediction* (New York: John Wiley & Sons, 1980).

Johnson, P. E. "What Kind of Expert Should a System Be?" *Journal of Medicine and Philosophy,* 8(1983), pp. 77-97.

Kidd, A. L. and Cooper, M. B. "Man-Machine Interface Issues in the Construction and Use of an Expert System," *International Journal of Man-Machine Studies* (1985), pp. 91-102.

McDermott, J. " R1 Revisited: Four Years in the Trenches," *The AI Magazine* (Fall 1984), pp. 21-35.

Paterson, A. *AL/X User Manual* (Oxford, England: Intelligent Terminals Ltd., 1984).

Shortliffe, E. H. Personal communications, December 27, 1984.

____. *Computer-Based Medical Consultations: MYCIN* (American Elsevier Publishing Co., Inc., 1976).

Teach, R. L. and Shortliffe, E. H. "An Analysis of Physicians' Attitudes Regarding Computer-Based Clinical Consultation Systems," *Computers and Biomedical Research,* 14(1981), pp. 542-558.

Treisman, A. and Gelade, G. "A Feature-Integration Theory of Attention," *Cognitive Psychology* (1980), pp. 97-136.

Yu, V. L., Fagan, L. M., Wraith, S. M., Clancey, W. J., Scott, A. C., Hannigan, J. F., Blum, R. L., Buchanan, B. G., and Cohen, S. N. "Antimicrobial Selection by Computer: A Blinded Evaluation by Infectious Disease Experts," *Journal of the American Medical Association* (1979) pp. 1279-1282.

Endnotes

[1]Research in expert systems is still in its infancy. Very few systems are being used on an ongoing basis in the field. It may be optimistic at this point to think that expert systems will achieve a performance level greater than an expert.

[2]We initially thought that expert systems researchers in the medical area always had outcome feedback, and therefore, tests of such systems were somehow more objective. However, Shortliffe [1984] points out: "The evaluation of expert systems that deal with medical therapy advice is actually very similar to the situation you describe for computer audit specialists. In the area of treatment, only one decision can be made and applied and it is not possible to back up and try again without having changed the situation. Since there are no gold standards for what is 'correct,' and even experts disagree about the preferred mode of treatment, this situation has presented real challenges in evaluation therapy advice systems."

[3]Our definition of advanced computer systems follows Davis and Weber [1983] and includes three categories: distributed processing systems, data base management systems, and on-line, real-time systems.

[4]No existing expert system that we are aware of claims to make decisions *exactly* the way an expert does, although there is recogniton that a better understanding of *how* experts solve problems may be neccesary before expert systems achieve expert-level performance [Buchanan and Shortliffe, 1984].

[5]We felt it was important to our work to develop an initial prototype. We chose to concentrate our initial efforts on controls in a distributed processing system. See Hansen [1984] for a discussion of audit considerations in a distributed processing system.

[6]The authors would like to thank Professor Edward Shortliffe for allowing us to use and adapt this questionnaire for our study.

[7]After making their POST judgments of the controls, the CASs were asked if they revised their judgments of the company's controls as a result of using EDP-XPERT. Fourteen subjects indicated that they revised their probabilities based on the use of EDP-XPERT. Deletion of the three subjects that did not rely on EDP-XPERT does not significantly change the results reported in Table 6.

[8]The firm that was assisting us with the project has three levels of CASs and there are only a small number of senior CASs (approximately 35) distributed throughout their offices in the United States [Elliott, 1983]. Given the preliminary nature of this investigation, we determined that these less experienced subjects would be adequate.

Developing ExperTAX[SM]: An Expert System for Corporate Tax Accrual and Planning

David Shpilberg and
Lynford E. Graham

Recently, articles about the use of expert systems in accounting and auditing have begun to appear in the audit literature (Longair, 1983; Stoner, 1985), and special audit research conferences focusing on the issue (USC, 1984 and 1986) have been scheduled. These trends are indicative of the growing degree of interest by researchers in the technology of these systems.

Expert systems is a branch of the discipline termed "artificial intelligence," or AI. An expert system may be defined as a system that

- Handles real-world, complex problems requiring an expert's interpretation, and
- Solves these problems using a computer model of expert human reasoning, reaching the same conclusions the expert would reach if faced with a comparable problem (Weiss and Kulikowski, 1984, p. 1).

As additional artificial intelligence software tools for developing expert systems become available at reasonable cost, and the power, speed, and portability of microcomputers increase, more and more audit and professional service tasks become likely candidates for assistance from expert systems. The potential gains in competitive advantage and productivity embodied in the use of this new technology, the ever-increasing complexity and volume of tax, regulatory, and professional accounting and auditing standards, and the increasing sophistication of business environments combine to create a situation in which such systems will be most welcome. Various possible applications to the audit environment have been cited in the literature (Elliott and Kielich, 1985; Dungan and Chandler, 1985).

This paper presents a case study on the development of an expert system in an audit and tax environment. The study points out issues identified in the development process that are of interest to those researchers currently experimenting with expert systems. In addition, the case study may alert researchers to issues and areas of research related to expert systems where their efforts can lead to an advance in knowledge.

This paper describes the key issues surrounding the development of a knowledge-based expert system called ExperTAX. It provides guidance and advice, through issue identification, to auditors and tax specialists in preparing the tax accrual for financial statement purposes. It also identifies relevant issues for tax planning, tax compliance, and tax service purposes.

The Problem

Tax accrual, the process of identifying tax-book differences and explaining differences between statutory and effective tax rates, is an audit task requiring specialized training and considerable time. In connection with tax services provided to most audit clients, the client's tax strategy, timely filing issues, and planning opportunities are also identified during the course of the audit.

Many accounting firms have developed questionnaires, forms, or checklists that facilitate the gathering of information necessary to conduct the tax accrual and tax planning functions. These questionnaires are usually completed by

Reprinted with permission from *Auditing: A Journal of Practice and Theory*, vol. 6, no. 1, Fall 1986, 75-94.

staff accountants in the field and may be brought back to the office or left in the field for analysis. At the client's location, an audit manager conducts the accrual analysis, and a tax manager, either in the office or at the client's location, reviews the analysis and identifies tax planning issues and opportunities. If these issues or opportunities are significant, the case is referred to more experienced personnel for further analysis and/or interaction with the client.

The process, as described, is quite efficient. Knowledge is leveraged to the field by the use of specialized questionnaires. Information is gathered by staff accountants and utilized by audit and tax managers not only to conduct the tax accrual computation, but also to corroborate their tax accounting practices and identify tax planning opportunities. Senior experts are brought in on a timely basis when they are clearly needed.

The problem is that practical realities limit the efficiency of the process. Tax accrual questionnaires are perceived by audit personnel to be long, complicated documents. On the other hand, tax professionals are concerned that such questionnaires attempt to simplify and standardize rather complex situations. Audit staff assigned to the task are concerned primarily with the tax accrual computation, and may not be aware of the detailed tax planning implications of some of the information collected. Other questions clearly address tax issues that are beyond their audit expertise and, while perhaps important to the tax function, may not be directly relevant to the task at hand.

The analysis by both the audit and tax managers of all the required information is a complex task. While the tax accrual computation requires some time, identifying tax planning issues and opportunities is a much more demanding task. Reviewing the issues may necessitate several rounds of on-site information gathering to complete the questionnaires and answer follow-up questions. In the process of this review, the tax and audit reviewers must focus their expert attention on both simple and complex issues. The physical timing of this task creates considerable stress on tax planning efficiency.

The Solution

A tax accrual support system should actively guide the staff accountant through the information gathering process, efficiently directing the individual to the relevant issues and pointing out the specific importance of the information requested. This will motivate the accountant to obtain the data and educate him or her on the potential ramifications of the information requested. Such a system would improve the staff accountant's productivity as well as the quality of the information gathered; it would also accelerate the accountant's training process.

Once the issue of efficient collection of relevant information has been dealt with, processing the information on a timely basis, in adequate depth, and by the appropriate experts becomes the knowledge "bottleneck." Better information does not by itself alleviate the problems associated with the audit and tax managers' reviews. If anything, it increases their need for larger blocks of time near year-end to adequately examine all the known facts and to identify the relevant issues.

Thus, to meaningfully improve the process, the support system should go beyond the efficient collection of information. It should be capable of analyzing and synthesizing the information to identify relevant issues to be brought to the attention of the audit and tax managers. If the support system routinely uncovered and described most of the basic tax accrual and planning issues, so that the attention of the experts could be directed to the higher-level issues, the process would be more efficient. This would effectively eliminate the expert-resource-intensive task of routine information analysis, except for cases in which critical issues require the attention of highly specialized personnel.

In summary, a support system that would significantly enhance the current tax accrual and planning process should include the following features:

- The ability to efficiently guide, motivate, and educate a staff accountant in the process of collecting information.
- The ability to quickly and thoroughly analyze the information collected and identify the relevant issues.

To address those requirements, Coopers & Lybrand has developed ExperTAX, a knowledge-based expert system supporting the corporate tax accrual and planning process. ExperTAX functions as an "intelligent" questionnaire, guiding the user through the information gathering process. It asks only those questions that are relevant to the client situation, is capable of sifting through issues that require clarification, and requests additional information when needed. It is also capable of explaining why a question is being asked and why the response is relevant. In addition to its ability to gather information and identify tax accrual and planning issues, it keeps track of any relevant questions still unanswered and documents all the questions asked, answers given, and user-generated "marginal notes."

ExperTAX's knowledge base consists of over 1,000 frames, rules, and facts derived from knowledge engineering sessions conducted with over 20 senior tax and audit experts at Coopers & Lybrand. ExperTAX has been developed in common LISP and runs on IBM-PC XT, AT, or IBM-compatible personal computers. The following sections describe ExperTAX in greater detail.

Knowledge Engineering: Designing the Product's Environment

Knowledge engineering is defined in this paper as the process of designing the expert system to:

- Facilitate its use,
- Maximize its ability to leverage expert knowledge,
- Facilitate the knowledge acquisition process,
- Optimize system efficiency, and
- Produce a cost-efficient solution.

A process of meta knowledge acquisition should precede the gathering of specific facts and rules. The process encompasses understanding the expert system's tasks, exploring product delivery environments, identifying the experts, defining the structure of the knowledge base, distilling its technical requirements, and selecting the software and hardware for implementation and delivery.

Understanding the Expert System's Tasks

The current operating environment for the tax accrual process and related functions is summarized in Table 1. As can be seen from Table 1, the process consists of a number of phases and involves professionals of differing backgrounds. To aid in the conduct of the process, several supporting instruments are used and interim reports are produced. All these factors and their interactions have to be considered if an effective expert system is to be developed.

The expert system would help improve the tax accrual process if it could reduce the time devoted to specific tasks, reduce the time elapsed from start to finish, maintain the quality of the output, and reduce the time demands and pressures on high-level expertise.

To improve data gathering, the expert system would have to animate the questionnaire functions, asking only relevant questions and explaining the reasons for the required information in the context of the client's situation. The process would allow more specialized questions to be asked, would improve the average quality of the initial responses, and would tend to eliminate the need for additional data-gathering sessions. In terms of input and output requirements, the expert system should allow the user to enter the required information in response to the questions, using a multiple-choice format supported by user-desired or required notes, explanations, and schedules.

The most time-consuming tasks for managers are those associated with the analysis of the completed questionnaires. Over the course of the engagement, identifying and studying tax accrual and tax planning issues may take several days of expert time over several weeks of elapsed time. Since all the information used for these tasks could be captured in the completed questionnaires, the expert system should be able to conduct those tasks more efficiently, utilizing a knowledge base extracted from the experience and know-how of tax accrual and tax planning experts.

Exploring Product Delivery Environments

By their nature, expert systems are serious consumers of computer power. They function more efficiently using specialized hardware (e.g., LISP machines) or fairly large dedicated general-purpose computers. Specialized hardware offers the added advantage of providing user-friendly software environments that are particularly productive in the context of quick prototyping of expert system functions. Several commercially available software environments contribute to making these programming environments even more productive.

When dealing with the issue of a delivery environment for the product, one has to come to grips with the operational restrictions that the environment might impose. For the tax accrual function, the data-gathering task takes place at the client's location and is generally carried out by a senior (in-charge) staff accountant. Only an expert system that can be resident in an easily

Task	Person(s) Responsible	Site	Support Instruments	Duration (Hrs.)	Cumulative Elapsed Time (Days)	Output	Level of Expertise	Type of Expertise
Audit Strategy/Planning								
1. Prepare Tax Strategy Summary	In-charge accountant (ICA) or audit manager	Client/ Office	Prior-year info (summary, questionnaire, tax returns), preliminary financials, client discussion	1	2	Completed Tax Strategy Summary	Medium	Audit and tax
2. Review Tax Strategy Summary and identify alternate tax strategies	Audit and tax managers and partners	Office	Completed Tax Strategy Summary	2	10	Memoranda, possible client discussions	High	Audit and tax
Preliminary Fieldwork								
3. Complete TAX questionnaire	ICA	Client	Prior-year info, preliminary financials, client discussion			TAX questionnaire responses, notes, schedules	Medium	Audit and tax
4. Review data for tax accrual issues	Audit manager	Office	Prior-year info, completed TAX			Memoranda	High	Audit
5. Review data for tax planning/compliance issues and develop alternative tax strategies	Audit manager, tax manager, and audit and tax partners	Office	Prior-year info, completed TAX			Memoranda, client discussions	High	Tax
Year-End Fieldwork								
6. Gather tax accrual data, compute accrual, and update questionnaire	ICA	Client	Memoranda, financial statement data, updated TAX			Financial statement numbers, tax return schedules	Medium	Audit
7. Perform a final review of tax accrual and TAX	Audit manager Tax manager	Client Client/ Office	Tax accrual workpapers, updated TAX			Memoranda	High	Audit and tax
8. Make a final identification of issues and alternative strategies	Engagement managers and partners	Office	Updated TAX questionnaire			Reports to clients, memoranda	Very high	Audit and tax

Table 1. Current tax accrual process.

obtained on-site computer will be feasible for this task. Hundreds of IBM-compatible computers are currently utilized by staff at client sites. If those computers could be used to support the expert system, chances for its successful implementation would be noticeably enhanced.

Identifying the Experts

Typically, very few experts are used while developing an expert system. This occurs for a number of reasons, usually due to the fact that experts are a scarce resource, and in many domains, one expert is all that is needed. In the area of U.S. taxation, there are many areas of expertise. At Coopers & Lybrand this expertise is distributed throughout the firm. ExperTAX used many experts during the construction of its knowledge base, and the knowledge base now represents their collected knowledge.

The task of identifying the professionals whose expertise should be tapped in constructing the knowledge base of the system is significant. These are people who are "experts" in the execution of the process; that is, they know what materials should be gathered, the order in which information should be collected, and the most efficient order in which to answer the various questions. There are other experts who know what questions to ask and why, and what follow-up questions may be required to identify a relevant issue. There is yet another group of experts who are particularly good at summarizing the results and presenting the information for analysis. Finally, there are experts who can construct viable alternative strategies, given the information presented to them. All of those experts have a role in the tax accrual and planning process. Thus, for the expert system to satisfactorily perform its support tasks in the data-gathering, analysis, and planning modes, it will have to incorporate expertise from several sources.

Although most tax managers could do a good job of performing the various tax accrual and planning tasks, they would probably not be as effective in each of the specific areas of the process as some specialized experts would be. Thus, it is conceivable that by bringing together the right experts for the right tasks, the resulting expert system could provide a consistent quality of response in a more efficient manner than would result from the experts acting alone. It is through the integration of the experts' collective specialized knowledge that the tax accrual expert system comes alive.

Defining the Structure of the Knowledge Base

The most difficult task associated with the knowledge engineering function is to determine an adequate structure for the knowledge base. This task requires the most abstract level of knowledge acquisition, since neither the experts nor the knowledge engineer initially has a frame of reference on which to base their discussions.

In early exchanges with the experts, they described their tasks in holistic terms (i.e., "focus on the main issues," "analyze all the relevant data," "base our analysis on experience," "react to the particular characteristics of the client"). They described the process in terms that criticized the shortcomings of questionnaires and emphasized the value of unstructured, yet careful, analysis. However, the evidence clearly suggests that most analysis is based on the information gathered through the existing questionnaires and, on some occasions, through additional requests for specific data.

To bring structure to the process and to facilitate our understanding of the dynamics of the process, a simulation experiment was conducted. An experienced auditor provided a real case for which the tax accrual process had recently been completed. He provided all the basic work-paper and tax return information that had been used to process the case. Two other experienced auditors, one in audit and one in tax, were asked to identify the specific information required to conduct a complete tax accrual process for the client in question.

A conference room with a long table in the middle was divided by a curtain. All the case information was gathered and deposited on the left side of the table, including the forms and questionnaires deemed relevant. A staff accountant with no previous practice experience in the tax accrual process was selected at random and asked to sit at the left side of the table. Two experienced audit and tax people were given blank questionnaires and forms and were asked to sit at the right side of the table, separated by the curtain from the staff accountant and the case data.

The staff accountant was informed that it was his responsibility to conduct a successful tax accrual process for the client. He was told that he currently had all the necessary information in front of him, and most importantly, a panel of experts behind the curtain. The experts were told that it was their responsibility to guide the staff accountant toward the successful completion of the tax accrual process. They were instructed to actively guide him with verbal advice and to answers questions when asked. They were unable to go to the other side of the curtain to explain; only verbal communication was allowed.

The process was videotaped with two cameras and observed by the knowledge engineering team. Several variations of the process were conducted for a total of 12 hours over three days. At the end of the experiment, the knowledge engineering team had a clear picture of the basic structure of the knowledge base and the minimum requirements for the user screen interface. A first prototype of the expert system could then be built.

Distilling Technical Requirements

A careful analysis of the expert system simulation exercise was the basis for distilling the technical requirements of the system.

- The process should be driven by a "smart" questionnaire. The expert system has to continuously probe for information, deciding which questions to ask and in what order. In addition, it has to have the ability to explain why a question is being asked and reveal some of the implications associated with the answers. This was found to be particularly important in motivating and guiding the user to gather the relevant data.
- The data-gathering process should be conducted first. The analysis of the data gathered should be executed only on demand, after part or all of the data have been gathered. The system also needs to produce written reports detailing the information gathered and documenting the accrual process and planning issues raised.
- The knowledge base needs to be organized in frames. The frames are to be classified by the context of the knowledge (e.g., inventory, receivables) and by the type of knowledge they represent (i.e., questions, issues, facts). The knowledge base has to be easy to maintain, since the tax field is in constant flux and the audit and tax planning process may be revised.
- The user interface needs to be highly interactive. Staff auditors will spend considerable time dialoguing with the system and will be highly sensitive to the system's responses. The screen display should be simple and self-explanatory, yet allow the user to control the process at all times, permitting the insertion of free-flow text whenever the user considers it necessary to make a note. The "why" explanations should be easily invoked but only at the user's request, since most auditors do not need to refer to this information for every question. The process sequence should be easily controllable by the user, allowing questions to be skipped for later completion.
- The size of the knowledge base will be substantial, containing over 1,000 frames, rules, or facts. The search structure, however, will tend to be wide and shallow, usually allowing fast conversion on a forward chaining mode. The wide and shallow format follows from such considerations as the system's broad coverage of numerous subject areas and the relatively few questions required in each area to identify an issue. The process is to be controlled by a fact-finding forward chain. Backward chaining will not be a frequently invoked function. It will be required only when changes in previously introduced facts become necessary. The number of text lists to be stored and randomly accessed for display as "why" messages or for the construction of issue reports will be substantial, and they will be components of the frames. However, the length of individual message units tends to be brief, rarely exceeding ten lines of text.
- The findings reported above were used to build the first ExperTAX prototype. It was used interactively during the knowledge acquisition sessions that followed. While the expert system continued to evolve throughout this process, it required only minor modifications to the user interface, inference engine, and knowledge base structure.

Selecting Software and Hardware

The analysis of the product delivery environment strongly suggested an IBM-compatible computer as the recommended hardware for delivery of the ExperTAX system. Based on that requirement, commercially available expert system programming environments for the IBM-PC were carefully evaluated.

Several products, such as ExpertEASE, Exsys, and M.1, ranging in price from $150 to $15,000, were identified and studied. First-cut prototypes were developed on those considered most promising. Several proved easy to use and versatile enough to accommodate some version of the desired prototype. However, they all failed to satisfy the technical specifications deemed essential for ExperTAX. In many cases screen design was not flexible enough to support the level of dialogue interaction required, response time was judged to be unbearably slow, or the facility to explain the system's reasoning was too rudimentary. In some, the size of the knowledge base was severely restricted or the quality of displayed and printed output was unacceptable.

It was decided that the system would have to be custom designed using a suitable programming language. Common LISP was selected because it is relatively mature and versatile and is rapidly becoming the standard LISP dialect for Artificial Intelligence work in the United States (Winston and Horn, 1984). From among the Common LISP implementation vehicles available for the IBM-PC, Gold Hill Computers' Golden Common LISP (1985) was selected for the project. It is a reasonable subset of Common LISP and its code operates very efficiently in the IBM-PC environment.

IBM-PC-AT's were used during the prototyping phase, but the product was designed to run on an IBM PC-XT or compatible unit with 640 kilobytes of memory. The disk storage requirement for the knowledge base is under ten megabytes. To enhance the quality of the user interface, a high-resolution color monitor is supported as optional equipment. A laser printer is the preferred output vehicle for printed reports.

ExperTAX Components

ExperTAX is a rule-based expert system program especially designed to accommodate the requirements of the tax accrual and planning process as conducted at Coopers & Lybrand. While it was designed for a single purpose, the ExperTAX shell has proved to be a flexible programming environment for other kinds of questionnaire-driven expert systems.

ExperTAX consists of four main components:

- The inference engine is responsible for controlling the logic search through the knowledge base, firing the appropriate rules, tracking the inference process, and communicating with the user through the user interface.
- The knowledge base is responsible for harboring all the frames, rules, and facts that constitute the expertise of the system, and for making them available upon request to the inference engine and the user interface.
- The user interface is responsible for the control of the screens and keyboard used by the system to communicate with the user, as well as the generation of all the printed reports. Its operation is controlled by the user. The information it displays comes directly from the knowledge base, and the information it takes in is used by the inference engine to direct its search processes and to enrich the output documentation.
- The knowledge base maintenance system is responsible for supporting the modification of frames, rules, and facts in the knowledge base. It is independent of the other three modules and is designed to facilitate the maintenance of the knowledge base by the designated organization group.

Inference Engine

The ExperTAX inference engine is a forward-chaining, rule-based system. It incorporates a frame manager, a facts data base, and a rule interpreter. Two types of frames are recognized by the frame manager, those associated with questions to be asked (question frames) and those associated with valid issues (issues frames). The frames can also be grouped in sections to be executed one at a time in any prescribed order. Within a section, the frame manager controls the execution of frames. The inferencing from question frames and issue frames takes place at different times.

The actual inferencing process is controlled by the rule interpreter, which uses the facts deposited in the facts data base by the user interface. The rule interpreter focuses on the rules contained in the frames activated by the frame manager. It compares the left-hand side of the rule (the If part of an IF; Then rule) with known facts in the data base. When a match is found, the rule is executed. The execution of a rule, also known as rule firing, consists of implementing the instructions contained in the right-hand side of the rule fired (the Then part). This can result in one of several actions: the set of known facts in the facts data base may be modified, an information string may be sent to the user interface as output, the execution control may be transferred to the user interface, or a fact or documentation string may be requested from the user interface. The rule interpreter will continue to search the same section of frames in the knowledge base until it fires a rule that transfers control to the user interface.

The ExperTAX inference engine keeps track of the inference chain created by the successive firings of rules, allowing for the display of specific reasoning associated with conclusions. The inference engineer permits interruption and resumption of the inference process at any stage, and backtracking of the process for alternative fact evaluation.

November 13, 1985

What is client's bad-debt write-off method for TAX purposes?
S-Specific charge-off
R-Reserve method

Summary: Bad debt write-off method

Precondition: (QZ1 is A): Accrual or Cash Basis IS Accrual

Possible Answers:
S-Specific charge-off
(Clarifying explanation required.)
R-Reserve method
Follow-up Questions:
QA19-Bad-debt reserve method
QA-20-Difference between BOOK and TAX reserve
QA21-Bad-debt recoveries to reserve

WHY Message:
In a typical environment, the Reserve method over time will result in larger tax deductions than the Specific charge-off method.

Figure 1. Coopers & Lybrand question frame ExperTAX knowledge base documentation—question QA17.

Knowledge Base

The ExperTAX knowledge base stores information as "frames." Some information relates to how and when to use the frame, some to what should happen next, and some to what to display or print. A frame can include several rules. There are two types of frames in the ExperTAX knowledge base, question frames and issue frames. They differ in the number and type of attributes (also called slots), procedures, and facts associated with them.

The question frames include the following attributes: Questions, Preconditions (rules), Possible Answers (rules), Marginal Note Instructions, and Why Messages. The attributes include attached procedures that can evaluate facts and fire rules, display information, request additional facts, and transfer control to other frames. Figure 1 presents a typical question frame.

The issue frames are simpler than the question frames. They include only a Rule attribute and a Display attribute. The attached procedures evaluate facts, and fire and issue displays. Figure 2 presents a typical issue frame.

November 12, 1985

The IRS has indicated that it will not allow the taxpayer who is using the Completed Contract method of accounting to also elect LIFO. See proposed long-term contract regulations which is contrary to Peninsula Steel Products and Equipment Co. v. Comm., 78 TC 1029 (1982).

Rule:
(QA2 IS C): LT Contract TAX method IS Completed Contract
AND
(QB14 IS L): Method of accounting for inventory IS LIFO
OR
(QB14 IS B): Method of accounting for inventory IS Both LIFO and FIFO

Issue on PLAN List

Figure 2. Coopers & Lybrand issue frame ExperTAX knowledge base documentation—general rules issue P4.

The frames are further classified by sections, which are groups of frames that share an execution sequence. The number of frames in a section and number of sections in the knowledge base are restricted only by the storage limitation of the hardware and software environment.

User Interface

The user interface of ExperTAX controls the screen display used for communicating with the user and the printer commands necessary for formatting and issuing reports. The screen layout consists of three active horizontal windows. The top window displays information identifying the section being analyzed. The middle window displays long and short forms of the questions being asked, the precondition that fired the current rule, and the valid answers. The lower window is used to present clarification messages (why messages), when requested, and to type in "marginal note" information when requested by the system or the user. Figure 3 presents a sample screen display.

Any Inventory: Yes

Does the client include any of the following items in inventory for TAX purposes?

Real Estate

Materials and supplies not held for sale (e.g., office supplies)

Deferred cost under the Completed Contract method

Consigned goods to which the client does not have title

Summary: Non-inventory items

QB3 Answer one of : (YN)—

The items mentioned above may be treated as inventory items for BOOK purposes, but may not be treated as such for TAX purposes. (Ref. Atlantic Coast Realty v. Comm., Rev. Rul. 59-329, Reg. 1.471-1)

F1-Note F2-Skip F3-Why F5 - Back

Figure 3. Screen display. Coopers & Lybrand tax accrual and planning expert system inventory (section B).

The user interface is operated through a system of nested menus that allows the user substantial control of the inference process. At virtually any point in the process, the user can return to a menu that allows for an orderly interruption of the process or for the resumption of the process at a different session or frame.

The printed reports generated by the user interface include lists of all issues identified by ExperTAX, audit trails of all questions asked and answers received, notes taken during the sessions, and specialized forms issued when additional documentation is required. Figure 4 presents a sample of an issues report.

Knowledge Base Maintenance System

The ExperTAX knowledge base maintenance system is an independent software system designed to update, modify, and expand the knowledge base. The system includes a frame editor, logic evaluator, and rule interaction display.

The frame editor permits the user to state the different components of a frame in simple English. It edits the information entered for consistency and completeness and helps the user correct omissions or inconsistencies.

The logic evaluator checks for possible conflicts in logic between the rules in the frame being edited and the rules contained in currently valid frames. If an inconsistency is discovered, the evaluator suggests editorial actions that would resolve the situation. For example, the system will diagnose the case where a question frame with a structure control rule would transfer to an undefined question, or where a question cannot be asked due to an improper precondition. It will also diagnose the case where an issue frame contains a rule whose antecedent cannot be true (such as "the answer to Q1 is A AND the answer to Q1 is B," and other more complex cases).

The rule interaction display allows the user to dynamically observe all the frames affected by changes in the frame being edited. This permits the user to better visualize the changes in operating procedure that could be implicit in modifications of a frame with several complex rules or follow-up routines.

February 7, 1986

The following planning ideas and issues should be reviewed to determine their applicability to the client. Some may be inappropriate due to immateriality. Others may represent issues which should be examined closely.

- The IRS has indicated that it will not allow the taxpayer who is using the Completed Contract method of accounting to also elect LIFO. See proposed long-term contract regulations which is contrary to Peninsula Steel Products and Equipment Co. v. Comm., 78 TC 1029 (1982).
- Since the client is not determining market value based on bid price, it may not be complying with Reg. Sect. 1.471-4. Under ordinary circumstances, market value means the current bid price prevailing at the current inventory date. If no open market exists, a taxpayer may use such evidence of fair market value as may be available.
- LIFO inventory may not be valued for tax purposes using the lower-of-cost-or-market method!! The IRS may terminate the taxpayer's LIFO election if LIFO inventory is valued at lower-of-cost-or-market. See Rev. Proc. 79-23. In limited situations, a taxpayer may be able to change the Cost method and preclude the IRS from terminating its LIFO election. See Rev. Proc. 87-74. Market writedowns are required to be included in income under the provisions of Sec. 472(d) when LIFO is elected.**
- Items such as real estate, office supplies, consigned goods and deferred costs under the Completed Contract method should not be included as inventory items for TAX purposes and therefore the LIFO inventory method or lower-of cost-or-market method may not be used for these items. Client should consider changing to the proper method for treating these items. Ref. Atlantic Coast Realty Co. v. Comm., Rev. Rule 59-329 and Reg. Sect. 1.471-1.**
- Direct material, direct labor and indirect (overhead) costs must be included in inventory costs!! This will require a change to accounting method which requires prior IRS approval. If request for change is NOT filed, a penalty may be imposed. A voluntary change may not be filed once a taxpayer has been contacted in any manner by the IRS. The spread period for such a change may not exceed three years. See Rev. Proc. 84-74.
- It is normally appropriate to look at the general economic conditions, risk of industry and financial condition of specific customers as judgmental factors in establishing an appropriate level of reserves for bad debts. If the client now wishes to consider these factors in establishing reserve levels, it may constitute a change in accounting...

Figure 4. Coopers & Lybrand issues report ExperTAX planning issues and ideas.

Knowledge Acquisition: Building the Knowledge Base

Knowledge acquisition is defined in this paper as the interactive process of "training" the expert system to the point at which it is capable of delivering a level of performance considered satisfactory for the task to be performed. It is the phase of the project during which detailed gathering of rules and facts takes place. It is a process of careful selection of experts, of exhaustive interactive sessions for knowledge capture, of fine-tuning enhancements to the system shell, and of careful validation of the knowledge base logic, structure, and information.

Selecting the Experts

A careful observation of the current tax accrual and planning process reveals several sources of expertise:

- The audit and tax specialists who design and maintain the support tools (e.g., questionnaires) used in the field.
- The engagement auditors who gather data for the process.
- The managers and partners who review the data and issue recommendations.
- The tax auditors and consultants who specialize in various complex areas of the tax planning process and are regularly used as

expert resources by managers and partners on engagements.

As described earlier, the initial attempt to infer a structure for the knowledge base utilized a simulation experiment. The experts that participated in those sessions came from the four sources mentioned above. This allowed the knowledge engineering team to gain an understanding of the experts' likely role in the detailed knowledge acquisition process.

From those sessions, it was concluded that the existing questionnaires were a good frame of reference for the tax accrual process. They had been carefully designed and incorporated considerable expertise. While they were not as comprehensive as some experts would have liked, and were rigid in their format and a bit cumbersome to administer, they constituted a good frame of reference for the tax accrual process and were being used regularly throughout Coopers & Lybrand. Thus, it was decided that the first source of expertise to be used for the ExperTAX knowledge base would be the existing tax accrual and planning support tools, such as the questionnaire and the audit and tax specialists currently responsible for its maintenance and support.

The expert system simulation sessions also brought home the fact that the knowledge base had several clearly defined subsets or sections dealing with different areas of specialization (e.g., inventory, accounts receivable). Detailed problems related to these areas are routinely supported by different professionals acting as consultants on specific engagements. A variety of specific areas of expertise were identified as being specialized enough to require separate treatment. Since it is always easier to work with narrowly defined knowledge bases, it was decided to address each of those areas one at a time, but only after conducting some general sessions to identify possible interactions between areas.

To implement the process described above, the second source of expertise utilized was the one provided by the generalists. Audit and tax managers and partners who regularly conduct tax accrual and planning processes were consulted on the validity of the basic expertise structure of the questionnaire. These practitioners helped to validate the control process and user interaction features of the system and to identify some areas of cross-correlation between knowledge frames.

The largest pool of experts utilized were specialist tax consultants, who currently serve as expert resources supporting the practice managers and partners. These experts proved to be highly receptive to the structured question framework for knowledge acquisition, since it seems to closely resemble the process they often follow in acquiring information and giving advice over the telephone. By the end of the process, more than 20 experts had devoted over 1,000 hours to the project and had helped transform the prototype questionnaire-based knowledge base into an extensive pool of knowledge capable of efficiently supporting in-depth analysis in many areas of expertise.

The final group of experts asked to participate in the knowledge acquisition process were the staff auditors who currently gather data in the field. Together with the tax and audit managers, they participated in the field validation of successive versions of ExperTAX, comparing and reporting on its performance *vis a vis* reports they had prepared for clients.

Interactive Knowledge Acquisition

Interactive knowledge acquisition is the process of incorporating expert knowledge into an existing expert system at the same time as the knowledge is transmitted by the human expert to the knowledge engineer. The expert system is being "trained" on-site by the expert, with the help of the knowledge engineer, who acts as an information broker. The knowledge engineer ensures that the new knowledge is in phrases that are compatible with the structure of the expert system, elicits explanations and clarifications from the expert, questions the order of or need for the information supplied by the expert, and runs the expert system continuously to let the expert observe the effects of the newly acquired knowledge.

All ExperTAX knowledge acquisition sessions (except for the simulation sessions described earlier) were conducted "live" with the computer. After some initial sessions were completed, a functional prototype of ExperTAX was built. This prototype was then used in all the following working sessions with experts.

The ideal knowledge acquisition session involves one knowledge engineer, a computer with the latest version of the expert system, and one or two experts. The dynamics of these sessions are such that the experts very quickly begin to structure their responses to closely resemble the favored syntax and logic of the expert system structure. The experts become further motivated by observing their suggestions and comments being immediately introduced into the knowledge base. They see how the expert system is "learning" and how the system's advice begins to closely resemble their own. They can also observe when certain rules or facts put into the system affect the behavior of the system in undesirable ways (e.g., when such rules lead to "blind alleys" or attempt to "train" the system beyond the desired level of expertise). Thus, they can correct the mistake immediately, suggesting alternative approaches to address the point.

The net result is a highly efficient knowledge acquisition process in which the quality of the information exchange between the knowledge engineer and the experts is greatly enhanced by the instant feedback provided by the evolving expert system.

Enhancing the ExperTAX Shell

While the final version of ExperTAX closely resembles the original prototype developed, it nevertheless incorporates a few significant changes deemed relevant by the experts as a result of the interactive knowledge acquisition sessions. The friendly and productive programming environment provided by the ExperTAX shell in particular, and LISP in general, made it feasible to expediently modify ExperTAX to accommodate new perceived user needs as the knowledge acquisition process progressed.

When it became obvious that a new feature should be incorporated (e.g., the ability to go back to a previous question, add "why" messages of extended length, or create special forms or schedules to be printed when required), it was added to the system by the knowledge engineering team immediately after the session. The additions were usually available for review at the next scheduled session. The opportunity to observe emerging patterns of use by the experts testing the system permitted the search patterns and knowledge storage and retrieval rules to be designed to minimize system response times, without changing the hardware requirements.

This process of incremental software development yielded a final product closely tailored to the needs of the audit and tax professionals. Only the original prototype was based on a formal software system design. The final product was the result of incremental enhancements of the prototype, which were made possible by the interactive knowledge acquisition sessions and the highly productive programming environment provided by the ExperTAX shell and LISP.

Knowledge Base Validation

The exhaustive validation of an expert system's knowledge base is a difficult task. Logic tests should be run to ensure the consistency of the knowledge base, and the system should be tested against the experts in an extensive array of situations. One way, possibly the best way, to validate a pool of knowledge is for professionals that were not involved in the development process to conduct an independent validation of its performance. There are two potential problems with this approach. First, different professionals might have different approaches to arriving at a specific conclusion. Second, the sheer number of possible combinations of responses that the system is capable of producing makes it difficult to test the system exhaustively.

Our approach to the problem was to select a group of practice partners and managers in different offices and ask them to test the system for a representative set of their clients. A knowledge engineer supervised the process and ensured that all relevant comments made during the sessions were noted. The practice partners and managers familiarized themselves with ExperTAX by running random exercises and evaluating the system's responses. Once they were satisfied with the overall performance, they processed several client cases whose tax accrual and planning process had recently been completed, and compared the system's responses with their personal evaluations of the cases. Some issues were raised as to the clarity of the wording of specific questions, explanations, or recommendations. These issues were brought back to the experts who contributed those areas to the knowledge base and appropriate modifications of the knowledge base were made.

While the knowledge base validation was by no means exhaustive, it did suggest a procedure to be followed for the ongoing monitoring of the system's performance. For example, it is clear that practitioners in the field will continually face situations that might not be directly addressed by the system. In some cases, it will be desirable to enhance the knowledge base to handle the situation. This decision will be evaluated by the group within the organization responsible for maintaining the knowledge base. The knowledge maintenance group will be able to conduct a continuous validation of the knowledge base and an ongoing evaluation of its performance, as well as respond to changes in the environment that dictate modifications to its frames, rules, or facts.

ExperTAX at Work: A Sample Session

The first thing ExperTAX does is to present a menu that allows the user to make a selection from a series of options. While there are several possible choices nested in various menus, they basically deal with the choice between starting to work with a new client or continuing a job for a recurring client. To illustrate, assume we are starting with a new client, Artificial Company, a highly successful manufacturer of smart computers. ExperTAX would start by asking some questions from the preliminary section of its knowledge base. It would quickly discover that Artificial accounts for its transactions on an accrual basis, is a privately held company, and is interested in tax minimization strategies. That general information would help ExperTAX structure its search procedures and access frame sections so as to minimize unnecessary paths, and then load into memory those subsets of the knowledge base that contain rules more likely to be fired.

If we join an ExperTAX session where inventory issues related to the write-down of obsolete goods are being aired, the middle window on the ExperTAX screen displays the following question:

How does the client value these obsolete goods?

C - Cost

S - Selling price less direct cost of disposition

Summary: Net realizable value method

The user always has the option of answering the question, asking why the question is being asked, or skipping it altogether. He elects to answer C. The middle window of ExperTAX changes its display to the following:

Net realizable value method: Cost

Do the obsolete goods include any excess inventory items which are sold under an agreement which allows the client to repurchase the items at a predetermined price?

Summary: Thor Power Sham Transaction

At this point, the user elects to press the "Why" key. The lower window displays the following statement (the middle screen is still displaying the question):

The IRS has held that a sale of items under an agreement to repurchase at a predetermined price is not a sale and thus the excess inventory must be continued to be valued at cost.

Having read the explanation, the user answers the question and continues in a similar manner until ExperTAX finishes with the section and returns to the selection menu.

Once the user has finished the inventory section, he/she might elect to continue with another section, to look at the issues raised so far, or to print those issues and the accompanying documentation. If he/she elects to look at the issues raised, they would appear in the middle window, one at a time, together with the specific answers that triggered them. For example:

LIFO inventory may not be valued for tax purposes using the lower-of-cost-or-market method!! The IRS may terminate the taxpayer's LIFO election if LIFO inventory is valued at lower-of-cost-or-market. See Rev. Proc. 79-23. In limited situations, a taxpayer may be able to change to the Cost method and preclude the IRS from terminating its LIFO election. See Rev. Proc. 84-74. Market write-downs are required to be included in income under the provisions of Sec. 472(d) when LIFO is elected.**

Reasoning:

Method of accounting for inventory: LIFO

Inventory valuing: Lower of cost or market

**These issues require a change in accounting method for which approval must be requested within 180 days of the beginning of the taxable year.

Once the user has answered all relevant sections, a complete printed report can be generated. The report would list all issues raised, segmented by type (e.g., accrual, planning). It would also list all questions asked and responses received during the session and all notes taken by the user, whether voluntarily or because of prompts by the system to further explain an answer.

The ExperTAX report would then be used by the audit and tax managers or partners in charge of the engagement to prepare the final tax accrual and issue their tax planning recommendations to the client. Figure 4 shows part of the Planning Issues section of a typical ExperTAX report.

Issues and Suggestions for Further Research

A number of observations came to mind during the development of ExperTAX that may be of interest to researchers in identifying areas for further scholarly research or to those interested in experimenting with the technology. Some of those issues are discussed further below.

Identifying the Experts

An important element in the development of an expert system is the identification of experts. It is illogical to attempt to develop an expert system if recognized expertise does not exist. The identification of experts in the practice environment is a complicated task, perhaps because so many support mechanisms are used by practitioners for certain tasks (questionnaires, informal and formal consultations, texts, etc.). Together these support mechanisms contribute to the high quality of professional output. However, this may tend to make it difficult to identify a knowledge "czar" whose estimates, processes, or knowledge are clearly superior to what the system and mix of staff, support tools, and consulting skills produce in the rendering of normal client service. Clearly, the delivery of consistent, high-quality service is a primary objective for the practice of public accounting.

The more narrowly technical expertise is defined, the easier it may be to define an expert to begin the knowledge acquisition process. For example, a "LIFO" expert may be easier to identify than an "inventory" expert. But problems may arise if the LIFO expert is unfamiliar with the process being supported by the system. The expert may have little or no knowledge of the tax accrual or planning process and may be more attuned to the special project environment than the audit environment. Thus, identifying the right "expert" may be a critical and difficult task in applying this technology to some types of problems.

Knowledge Base Management

To justify the development of the initial system, knowledge base management and maintenance must be evaluated and considered feasible. From a distant vantage point, the development of an expert system may appear similar to the development process of any other software product. However, the parallels become blurred when one considers the specialized expertise necessary to evaluate or design system shells in a commercial environment, the interactive growth of the system (rather than the detailed design and programming stages), the more complicated issues of quality assurance, and the technical expertise needed to supervise system growth and updating.

Groups such as the national organizations of the functional specializations (e.g., audit and tax), EDP development groups, and decision support groups may all interact in the development process and are candidates for the continuing management and oversight of such systems. It remains an open but important question as to how the maintenance of such systems should be handled. The new technological environment provides an opportunity to reconsider the issue in light of organizational factors and efficiency.

System Distribution and Security

The existence of a competitive environment introduces significant issues into the expert system development process that are not encountered in more traditional software development environments. The handling of those issues may be influenced by whether the system will be sold commercially or will be resident only within the domain of the developer. One such issue that may be raised is whether the client will know (or care) that expert systems technology was applied during the engagement. This issue will affect the distribution process and publicity surrounding product releases.

Security is a heightened concern in expert systems. Such systems are no longer akin to computer software templates with only the capacity to manipulate numbers, but may also contain the accumulated knowledge of a firm. Communicating and distributing the product, protecting the software, and at the same time providing an environment that does not constrain authorized users in its applications is a practical problem. While the value of such a system may diminish over time if not continuously updated and maintained, the implications of the system's misappropriation or unauthorized use or transfer are more significant than with many other software products. Accordingly, organizational and hardware and/or software controls assume increased importance in the design and distribution of such systems.

Other Issues

Some issues, such as the organization and mechanism by which projects are identified, assigned priority, managed, and maintained, are very important to developers of support systems but may yield limited independent research opportunities. Other issues that may have research potential flow from some of the aforementioned topics—for example:

- The need to better understand what is meant by "expertise."
- More tools and techniques to evaluate and simulate real-world environments.
- Continued research into methods of extracting and capturing expertise.

The purpose of this paper has been to describe an application of AI technology (expert systems) to a real-world environment. It has attempted to go beyond a simple recitation of hardware and software options and capabilities, since that would hardly constitute a contribution to the research literature. We hope that the case presented will assist researchers in understanding more of the issues and areas that may be conducive to future research.

Conclusions

The ability to apply expert systems technology to develop audit practice aids is being made more economical and feasible by the increasing power and availability of microcomputers and expert systems tools that operate in that changing microcomputer environment. Since these trends for microcomputers and expert systems tools are likely to continue, increasing numbers and types of solutions to problems that could not cost-effectively be produced or delivered today will become possible in the future.

Once researchers have obtained a sufficient understanding of the mechanics of the technology, attention must be directed to identifying areas for future worthwhile scholarly research. The expert systems area needs this identification to remain a topic of useful research interest.

References

Dungan, C. W. and Chandler, J. S. "Auditor: A Microcomputer Based Expert System to Support Auditors in the Field," *Expert Systems* (October 1985), pp. 210-221.

Elliott, R. K. and Kielich, J. A. "Expert Systems in Auditing," *Journal of Accountancy* (September 1985), pp. 130-131.

Gold Hill Computers. *Golden Common LISP* (Gold Hill Computers, 1985).

Longair, R. "What 'Expert Systems' Will Mean for Auditors," *Chartered Accountant in Australia* (November 1983), pp. 27-29.

Stoner, G. "'Expert Systems': Jargon or Challenge?" *Accountancy* (February 1985), pp. 142-145.

USC, *Symposium on Expert Systems and Audit Judgment* (University of Southern California, 1986).

USC, *Symposium on Expert Systems and Audit Judgment Research* (University of Southern California, 1984).

Weiss, S. M. and Kulikowski, C. A. *A Practical Guide to Designing Expert Systems* (Rowman and Allenhead, 1984).

Winston, P. H. and Horn, B. K. P. *LISP Second Edition* (Addison-Wesley, 1984).

The Construction of a Rule-Based Expert System as a Method for Studying Materiality Judgments

Paul J. Steinbart

Materiality judgments play a fundamental role in the audit process, influencing both the planning of audit procedures and the evaluation of audit evidence. Nevertheless, there are no authoritative guidelines for making those judgments. The Financial Accounting Standards Board (FASB) considered establishing such guidelines and issued a Discussion Memorandum on the topic [FASB, 1975], but eventually decided that "no general standards of materiality could be formulated to take into account all the considerations that enter into an experienced human judgment" [FASB, 1980, para. 131]. Statement on Auditing Standards (SAS) 47 makes a similar claim:

> materiality judgments are made in light of surrounding circumstances and necessarily involve both quantitative and qualitative considerations [AICPA, 1983, para. 6].

The important role played by materiality judgments in the audit process, coupled with the lack of authoritative guidance for making those judgments, has produced a large body of research on the topic. Holstrum and Messier [1982] review that research and conclude, however, that the results do not provide any "definitive comprehensive implications for audit practice or policy formulation" [p. 59]. They point out that previous research has concentrated on materiality judgments for public, industrial companies and suggest that future research needs to investigate the effects that the nature of the client and its industry classification have on materiality judgments. Moreover, they note that most previous studies have examined materiality judgments in the context of evaluating audit evidence and call for future research to address the role of materiality in the planning stages of the audit process.

This paper reports on the construction of a rule-based expert system (RBES) as a means of conducting descriptive research on planning-stage materiality judgments. Researchers in the field of artificial intelligence have long recognized that building such systems is a means for learning more about how particular judgments are made.

> The aim here [in building knowledge-based computer programs such as RBESs] is thus not simply to build a program that exhibits a certain specified behavior, but *to use the program construction process itself as a way of explicating knowledge in the field, and to use the program text as a means of expression of many forms of knowledge about the task and its solution* [Davis and Lenat, 1982, p. 471].

The program text of a RBES consists of a set of If-Then rules that represent the knowledge used to make a particular judgment. The conclusions of the rules specify an action to take or an inference to make; the premises specify the situations in which it is appropriate to use that rule. Thus, the rules used to make a specific judgment describe not only what information was used to reach that decision but also why that particular information was used.

Reprinted with permission from *Accounting Review*, vol. LXII, No. 1, January 1987, 97-116.

The knowledge used by AUDITPLANNER (the name given to the RBES built in this study) to make planning-stage materiality judgments was acquired, in large part, by having an audit partner make those judgments for actual clients. No constraints were placed upon the nature of the information that was used to make those judgments. This ability to study judgment behavior in its natural setting makes the construction of an RBES a particularly attractive method for conducting descriptive research, because of empirical research evidence that seemingly minor changes in either the content or setting of a decision task can significantly affect the observed behavior [Adelman, 1981; Cox and Griggs, 1982; Ebbesen and Konecni, 1980; Einhorn and Hogarth, 1982; Hayes and Simon, 1977; Hoch and Tschirgi, 1983; Kahneman and Tversky, 1979].

The remainder of this paper is organized in four sections. The first section reviews prior research on materiality and provides some background on planning-stage materiality judgments. The second section describes the process followed to build AUDITPLANNER. The third section discusses the judgment model used by AUDITPLANNER. Some of the rules contained in the system are presented to explicitly illustrate how specific information is used to determine materiality. The last section summarizes the findings of this study, discusses its limitations, and explores implications for future research.

Background

SAS 47 states that the auditor should consider materiality "both in (a) planning the audit and designing auditing procedures and (b) evaluating whether the financial statements taken as a whole are presented fairly in conformity with generally accepted accounting principles" [AICPA, 1983, para. 8]. Planning-stage materiality judgments influence decisions about the nature, timing, and extent of audit procedures. The purpose is to ensure that adequate evidence will be collected so that an opinion on the fairness of presentation of the financial statements can be expressed. The evaluation of audit evidence then involves a consideration of materiality to determine the effect on the overall fairness of presentation of any errors that may have been uncovered by the audit tests and procedures.

SAS 47 points out that the two materiality judgments may not be the same, because each is made at a different point in time and, therefore, is based on different information:

> Assuming, theoretically, that the auditor's judgment about materiality at the planning stage was based on the same information available to him at the evaluation stage, materiality for planning and evaluation purposes would be the same. However, it is ordinarily not feasible... to anticipate all of the circumstances that may ultimately influence his [materiality] judgment.... Thus, his preliminary materiality judgment ordinarily will differ from his judgment about materiality used in evaluating the audit findings [AICPA, 1983, para. 15].

One of the more important pieces of additional information available at the evaluation stage is information about the nature of the item that may be in error.

> The answer to that question [Is the item material?] will usually be affected by the nature of the item; items too small to be thought material if they result from routine transactions may be considered material if they arise in abnormal circumstances [FASB, 1980, para. 123].

The results of previous empirical research tend to support the discussions of materiality in the authoritative literature cited above. Both the studies that used controlled experiments and those using questionnaire cases found that the percentage effect of the item on income was the single most important quantitative factor influencing those judgments [Boatsman and Robertson, 1974; Pattillo and Siebel, 1974; Pattillo, 1975, 1976; Moriarity and Barron, 1976; Firth, 1979; Messier, 1983]. Respondents to the surveys, however, indicated that information about the nature of the item (e.g., whether it involved a contingency or an extraordinary item, etc.) was also an important determinant of materiality. Although only one of the studies using controlled experiments varied the nature of the item, the results indicated that that factor was indeed a significant determinant of materiality. Boatsman and Robertson [1974] report that a simple model based solely on a percentage of income rule accurately classified 65 percent of the subjects' judgments; the addition of two more variables — one to represent the nature of the item, the other to represent the degree of perceived risk in the audit — raised the model's predictive accuracy to 84 percent.

Holstrum and Messier [1982] point out another important implication of previous research results:

> [I]n the absence of clear materiality guidelines, auditors' materiality judgments demonstrated considerable diversity and lack of consensus [p. 59].

That result was found when comparing auditors from large national firms with auditors from small firms [Woolsey, 1973; Messier, 1983]; among auditors from different large firms [Firth, 1979; Lewis, 1980; Mayper, 1982]; and even among auditors within the same firm [Moriarity and Barron, 1979].

There is also some evidence that auditors' attitudes toward risk may affect their materiality judgments and may also be partially responsible for a lack of consensus about materiality. Boatsman and Robertson [1974] found that including a variable to represent the perceived degree of risk in the audit improved the predictive accuracy of their judgment model. Ward [1976] found a lack of consensus among auditors concerning the effects of their failure to find a material error. Newton [1977] examined how the uncertainty surrounding the resolution of an item affected materiality judgments; 55 percent of the audit partners in that study were classified as being risk-averse, but 34 percent were classified as being risk-seeking.

The studies reviewed thus far all examined the materiality judgments made when evaluating audit evidence. Moriarity and Barron [1979] conducted the only previous empirical study of planning-stage materiality judgments. Five audit partners from the same public accounting firm were given summarized financial statements for 30 hypothetical companies and were asked to determine the overall materiality level to be used in planning the audit. Five variables were experimentally manipulated:

- Net income,
- Earnings trend,
- Total assets,
- Number of shares outstanding, and
- Debt-to-equity ratio.

Net income was the most important factor for four of the partners, with total assets being most important for one partner. Either earnings trend or total assets were second in importance for each partner. There was also some evidence of a breakeven effect: the importance of net income declined as it approached zero.

Moriarity and Barron did not provide their subjects with background information about the client such as its industry classification, management objectives, and the identity of the prospective users of its financial statements. In post-experimental debriefings the partners complained about the artificial nature of the cases due to the lack of that information. Indeed, discussions of materiality in SAS 47 indicate that such information is important to the determination of materiality:

> The auditor's consideration of materiality is a matter of professional judgment and is influenced by his perception of the needs of a reasonable person who will rely on the financial statements [AICPA, 1983, para. 6].
>
> An amount that is material to the financial statements of one entity may not be material to the financial statements of another entity of a different size or nature [AICPA, 1983. para. 5].

In summary, previous research on materiality indicates that the percentage effect of the item on income is the single most important determinant of materiality when evaluating audit evidence. Similarly, the lone empirical study of planning-stage materiality judgments found the amount of net income to be the most important determinant of those judgments. When evaluating audit evidence, however, information about the nature of the item is also an important factor influencing materiality judgments. Similarly, the comments of the participants in the Moriarity and Barron [1979] study, together with the statements in SAS 47, suggest that information about the nature of the client is an important factor influencing planning-stage materiality judgments. The purpose of this study is to build a model which explicitly illustrates how such information is used. The next section describes the process used to build that model.

Construction of AUDITPLANNER

An RBES consists of three components:

- A knowledge base, which contains the If-Then rules that represent the domain knowledge used to make a particular judgment;

- An inference engine, or control strategy, which guides the application of those rules; and
- A working memory, which serves as a scratch-pad to keep track of the goals being pursued and the progress made toward their attainment. [1]

A number of software tools (called shells) are available to facilitate the construction of an RBES. Those shells consist of an inference engine, an empty knowledge base, and the functions needed to create and maintain the knowledge base. Consequently, the use of one of these shells permits the researcher to concentrate on the acquisition and organization of the knowledge used to make the judgment being studied, rather than on writing the computer code to manipulate that knowledge. The remainder of this section describes the steps involved in the construction of AUDITPLANNER:

- The choice of a particular software tool,
- The selection of a subject, and
- The development and refinement of the knowledge base.

Selection of a Software Tool

The shell program EMYCIN [Van Melle et al., 1981] was used to build AUDITPLANNER. EMYCIN is based on the expert system MYCIN, which was designed to diagnose infectious blood diseases [Shortliffe, 1976; Buchanan and Shortliffe, 1984]. EMYCIN has been used successfully to build a number of RBESs to perform such tasks as

- Diagnosing lung diseases,
- Assisting engineers in the selection of tests to analyze the stress characteristics of physical structures,
- Performing psychoanalysis,
- Interpreting data about the geological characteristics of oil wells, and
- Identifying the causes of telecommunications systems failures [Van Melle et al., 1981].

EMYCIN has also been used in two accounting applications of RBESs that

- Plan for individual estate taxes [Michaelsen, 1982, 1984] and
- Evaluate the quality of internal controls [Gal, 1985].

EMYCIN-based systems function as consultants: the user is asked a series of questions and the RBES makes its recommendations based on the answers to those questions. EMYCIN uses a backward-chaining control strategy which involves reasoning back from the desired goal of the session (in the case of AUDITPLANNER, a planning-stage materiality judgment) to the objective facts that are needed to support that decision (i.e., specific characteristics of the client being audited). Questions are asked to obtain the objective data that would support a particular chain of deductive reasoning; the result is a focused dialogue that is easy to follow and understand. Appendix A presents an example of one session with AUDITPLANNER.

Selection of a Subject

Eleven major accounting firms were contacted and asked to provide those portions of their audit manuals that discuss materiality. Ten of the firms complied with that request. Interviews were arranged with four firms whose audit manuals indicated that

- They regularly made and quantified planning-stage materiality judgments and
- Quantification of materiality resulted from the exercise of the individual auditor's professional judgment and not from the application of a specific mathematical formula to all clients.

During the interviews additional questions were asked about how the planning-stage materiality judgments were made. In addition, the substantial time commitment that would be required of the participant in this research was explained.

An audit partner at one firm agreed to participate in the study, but requested anonymity because of the sensitive nature of materiality judgments and the current litigious environment facing practitioners. The partner had experience in making planning-stage materiality judgments for a wide variety of clients, with particular emphasis on finance companies and health care organizations. Cushing and Loebbecke [1986] develop a taxonomy for classifying audit firms in terms of the degree of structure in their audit methodology. The firm to which the partner belonged would be classified as falling into one of the two more structured categories in that taxonomy.

One limitation of the tools currently available to build RBESs is that they cannot effectively deal with conflicting judgment strategies. Consequently, to ensure consistency the rules contained in AUDITPLANNER were acquired primarily from this one audit partner. After the knowledge base was developed, however, six other auditors in the same firm used AUDITPLANNER and suggested further refinements.

Development and Refinement of AUDITPLANNER's Knowledge Base

The first step in building AUDITPLANNER involved the construction of an initial working version, or prototype, of the system. That prototype contained rules gleaned from the discussions of materiality in the firm's audit manuals. The use of such textbook knowledge, if available, is an efficient means for building the prototype's knowledge base and has been successfully incorporated in previous EMYCIN-based systems [Van Melle et al., 1981; Michaelsen, 1982, 1984].

The working prototype system provided the auditor with a tool that could be used to make, albeit rather crudely, planning-stage materiality judgments for actual clients. The majority of the rules included in AUDITPLANNER's knowledge base were then acquired during interactive sessions with the auditor. The audit partner would use the current version of AUDITPLANNER to make planning-stage materiality judgments (i.e., set an overall materiality level for use in planning the audit) for actual clients that had been dealt with in the past. Such use enabled the auditor to identify areas where AUDITPLANNER was not performing satisfactorily (i.e., it was reaching the "wrong" conclusions or following an inappropriate line of reasoning).

Whenever the auditor disagreed with AUDITPLANNER, EMYCIN's interrogation facilities were then used to identify the rules that were the cause of that disagreement. Those facilities permitted the asking of How and Why questions to determine what AUDITPLANNER was doing, and why, at a particular point in time. Such questions could be asked either during a consultation or after AUDITPLANNER had made its recommendations. Appendix B presents an example of how those capabilities could be used during a consultation.

Once the cause of the disagreement was identified, the researcher asked the audit partner to explain why the particular rules in question were not appropriate in this situation and to explain how the judgment should have been made. The suggested modifications were written down and AUDITPLANNER's knowledge base was modified later. At the next interactive session the audit partner used the revised version of the system on the clients for which it had previously made the correct decisions and also on those for which it had erred, to ensure that the modifications worked correctly and did not

Client	*Characteristics*
Machine tool manufacturer	involved in a major acquisition of a subsidiary
Machine tool manufacturer	a subsidiary of a foreign parent
Insurance company	subsidiary company
Restaurant	normal, profitable company
Automobile dealership	normal, profitable company
School district	nonprofit organization
Boy Scout Council	nonprofit organization
Computer manufacturer	normal, profitable company
Retail supermarket	normal, profitable company
Retail supermarket	suffered a loss for the year
Common carrier—trucking	subject of litigation and also involved in several large acquisitions
Common carrier—trucking	subject of an inquiry by a regulatory agency
Microcomputer retailer	private entity about to go public

Table 1. Characteristics of clients used to evaluate AUDITPLANNER.

Question	*SA*	*A*	*N*	*D*	*SD*
7. AUDITPLANNER is not competent	0	1	0	3	2
22. AUDITPLANNER is competent	0	4	2	0	0
8. Would accept AUDITPLANNER's recommendations	0	3	1	2	0
24. Would approach the materiality judgment in a different manner than did AUDITPLANNER	0	1	0	5	0
6. Would want to use AUDITPLANNER as a decision aid	0	6	0	0	0
14. Would permit subordinates to use AUDITPLANNER as a decision aid	0	5	0	0	1
18. Would not want subordinates to use AUDITPLANNER as a training device	0	0	1	4	1
3. AUDITPLANNER asked irrelevant questions	0	0	0	3	3
19. AUDITPLANNER's logic easy to follow	2	4	0	0	0
15. AUDITPLANNER's logic hard to follow	0	0	0	3	3

Key: SA =Strongly Agree
A =Agree
N =Don't Know or Neutral
D =Disagree
SD =Strongly Disagree

Table 2. Frequency distribution of responses to questionnaire.

have any unintended side effects. The revised system was then used on additional clients.

Each interactive session lasted about four hours and took place about once every four weeks. After five such sessions, involving approximately 20 different clients, the audit partner indicated that AUDITPLANNER was performing satisfactorily. Six other auditors (three managers and three seniors) from the same firm were then asked to use AUDITPLANNER to make planning-stage materiality judgments for some of their clients. Each auditor had at least one and one-half years experience in making such judgments. A representative, rather than random, sample of clients was selected to provide some measure of the breadth of AUDITPLANNER's competence. Table 1 describes the 13 clients that were selected.

Each of the six auditors used AUDITPLANNER to make a planning-stage materiality judgment for the clients he had selected, and then indicated whether AUDITPLANNER's recommendation was acceptable. After they had used AUDITPLANNER for their clients, each auditor was also given a questionnaire to fill out and return later that day. A copy of the questionnaire is included in Appendix C.

AUDITPLANNER's recommendations were considered to be acceptable for eight of the 13 clients that were tested. Table 2 presents the results of the questionnaire items that dealt with AUDITPLANNER's competency.[2]

The responses to the questionnaire indicate that the six auditors generally agreed that AUDITPLANNER was competent. Not all of AUDITPLANNER's recommendations were accepted, however. One reason may be that one of the six auditors indicated that he would definitely take a different approach to determining materiality than that used by AUDITPLANNER. Another factor may be AUDITPLANNER's conservatism: it almost always recommended a materiality level that was lower than that previously selected by the auditors.

In summary, the responses of the six auditors indicate that AUDITPLANNER possesses a general level of competency for making planning-stage materiality judgments, although additional work would be required before it could actually be used as a decision aid.

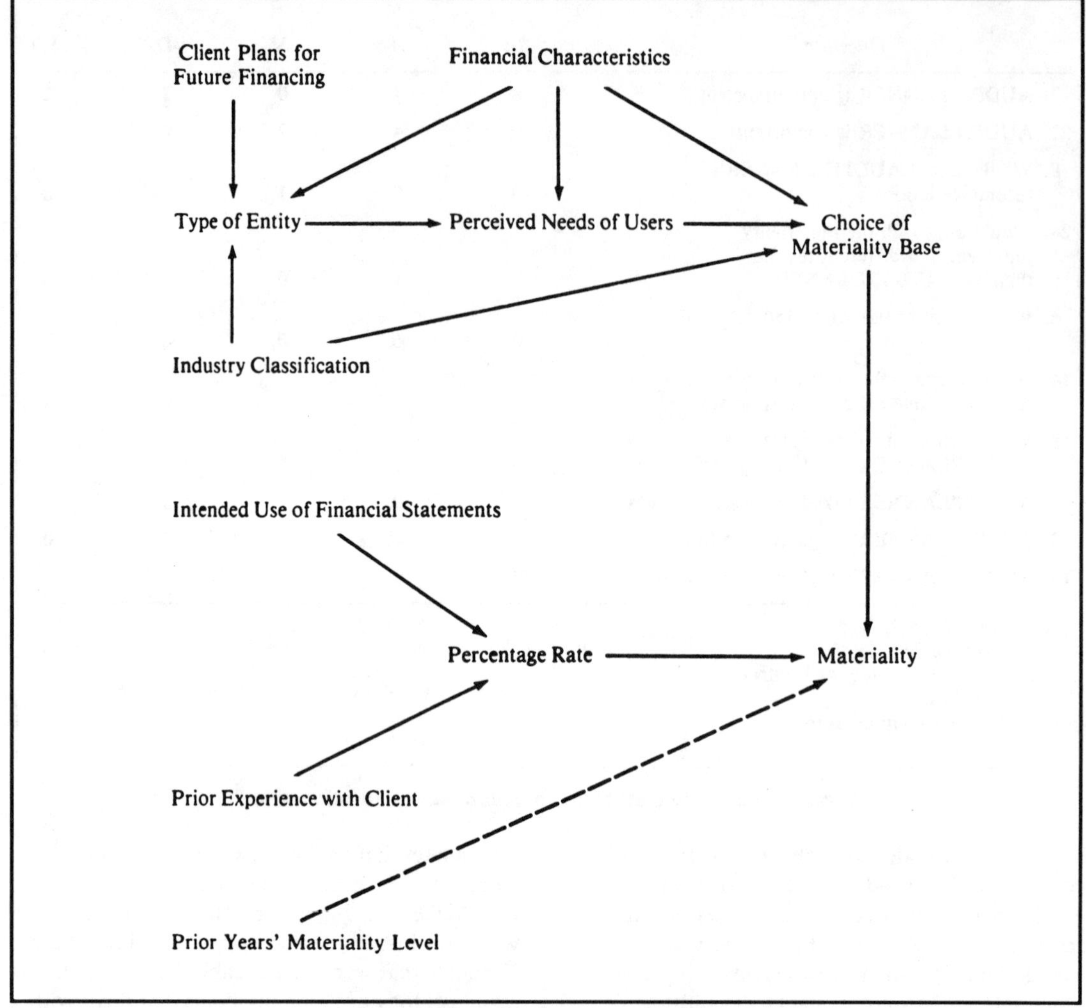

Figure 1. AUDITPLANNER's judgment model.

The purpose of the present study, however, is not to build a decision aid but to build an RBES as a means to learn more about how various types of information affect the planning-stage materiality judgments. The next section does that by describing the judgment model used by AUDIT PLANNER.

AUDITPLANNER's Judgment Model

AUDITPLANNER's knowledge base consists of 95 rules which it uses to make planning-stage materiality judgments. The general strategy followed by AUDITPLANNER is presented in Figure 1. Eight factors were found to influence planning-stage materiality judgments: (1) client plans for future financing, (2) financial characteristics of the client, (3) the client's industry classification, (4) the type of entity that the client is, (5) the perceived needs of the users of the client's financial statements, (6) the intended use of the client's financial statements, (7) prior experiences with the client, and (8) prior years' materiality levels. The first five factors affect the choice of the appropriate base for calculating materiality; factors 6 and 7 influence the selection of a percentage rate to multiply by that base, and the last factor may be used to modify the resulting calculation. The remainder of this section presents some of the rules used by AUDITPLANNER to show explicitly how each of these factors affect planning-stage materiality.

The discussion is organized around the major sub-decisions:

- The choice of a base for calculating materiality,
- The selection of a percentage rate, and
- The actual calculation of an overall planning-stage materiality level.

Choice of Materiality Base
The choice of a materiality base is influenced by decisions that determine what type of entity is being audited and the perceived needs of the users of the client's financial statements. Each of these decisions is discussed in turn.

Type of Entity. Figure 1 shows that information about the client's (1) plans for future financing, (2) financial characteristics, and (3) industry classification are all used to decide what type of entity the client is. The basic rules involve the use of financial characteristics to decide whether the client is a public or private entity:

If 1. the client has publicly traded debt or equity securities *or*
2. the client has restrictive debt covenants that are measured by or depend on periodic financial statement amounts or ratios that involve results of operations,

Then the client is a public entity.[3]

Should neither of the premises be true, AUDITPLANNER concludes that it is highly likely that the client is a private entity. That conclusion, however, is made with less than absolute certainty; information about the client's plans for future financing (if any) and industry classification may indicate that the client should be treated as a public entity for purposes of calculating materiality:

If 1. it is likely that the client is a private entity *and*
2. A: the client is filing with a regulatory agency in preparation for the sale of its securities in a public market *or*
B: the client does intend to go public within the next two or three years,

Then the client is a public entity.

If the client's main line of business or industry classification is insurance,

Then the client is a public entity (for purposes of calculating materiality).

Gibbins and Wolf [1982] found that client plans for future financing were an important factor in planning the audit; the first rule above illustrates how AUDITPLANNER uses that information. The second rule illustrates one way in which AUDITPLANNER uses information about the client's industry classification. Note that both of these rules have an indirect effect on materiality (in fact, both appear quite early in the chain of reasoning that results in a materiality judgment).

Perceived Needs of Financial Statement Users. SAS 47 states that the auditor's perception of the needs of financial statement users is one of the factors that influences materiality judgments. AUDITPLANNER uses information about the type of entity that a client is and about certain financial characteristics of the client to infer the likely interests of the users of the client's financial statements:

If 1. the client is a public entity *and*
2. there is not any significant concern about the client's liquidity or solvency,

Then the principal users of the client's financial statements can be assumed to be interested primarily in the results of current operations.

If 1. the client is a public entity *and*
2. there is significant concern about the client's liquidity or solvency,

Then the principal users of the client's financial statements can be assumed to be interested primarily in measures of financial position.

If the client is a private entity,

Then the principal users of the client's financial statements can be assumed to be interested primarily in measures of financial position.

Choice of Materiality Base. Inferences about the interests of financial statement users guide the choice of a base for calculating materiality. The following rules show how AUDITPLANNER makes that choice:

If 1. the principal users of the client's financial statements can be assumed to be interested primarily in the results of current operations *and*
2. income from continuing operations is greater than zero,

Then the materiality judgment should be based on the amount of income from continuing operations.

If 1. the principal users of the client's financial statements can be assumed to be interested primarily in measures of financial position *and*
2. the amount of current assets is greater than the amount of owners' equity,

Then the materiality judgment should be based on the amount of owners' equity.

If 1. the principal users of the client's financial statements can be assumed to be interested primarily in the results of current operations *and*
2. income from continuing operations is less than or equal to zero *and*
3. last year's income from continuing operations was greater than zero *and*
4. income from continuing operations has been at or below zero no more than once during the preceding three years,

Then the materiality judgment should be based on the trend in past earnings.

The last rule illustrates the breakeven phenomenon reported by Moriarity and Barron [1979]. Note, however, that earnings trend is used as the base for calculating materiality only when there have not been recurring losses. Should either premise 3 or premise 4 not hold, AUDITPLANNER would use another rule that bases materiality on the amount of owners' equity. The rationale is that in the case of continuing losses, financial statement users begin to become concerned about the long-run liquidity of the company. The rather limited situations described by the above rule for using earnings trend probably explain the findings of previous research that it is a secondary factor of only marginal significance for predicting materiality judgments.

The authoritative literature states that the client's industry classification may affect materiality judgments [AICPA, 1979, para. 150.04]. We have already seen one way that AUDITPLANNER uses such information; the following rule illustrates another, more direct, use of that information:

If 1. the client is a financial institution *and*
2. the product of stockholders' equity and the materiality percentage rate is greater than the result obtained by dividing income from continuing operations by the average rate of return on the investment portfolio,

Then set the materiality level for the investment portfolio to be equal to the amount of income from continuing operations divided by the average rate of return on that portfolio.

The rationale for this rule is that investment portfolios of most financial institutions are so large that use of the overall materiality level would lead to too much testing of that item.

Selection of a Percentage Rate

Figure 1 indicates that AUDITPLANNER uses information about the intended uses of the client's financial statements and about prior experience with the client to select the percentage rate for calculating materiality. The following rule shows how the latter information is used:

If 1. this is the first time that we have audited the client *and*
2. A: this is the first time that the client has ever been audited *or*
B: the client's previous auditors left because of a dispute with the client,

Then the materiality level needs to be reduced below what it would otherwise be calculated to be because of the increased risk and uncertainty reflected in this situation.

This rule provides an explicit example of how audit risk and materiality interact. The rationale for this rule is that on initial audits there is no track record to assist in the evaluation of the quality of internal controls. Moreover, if the previous auditors left because of a dispute with the client, that is probably an indication that there may be certain areas which will require special attention.

Certain types of situations represent increased business risk. The audit partner who participated in this study indicated that in such situations additional testing beyond that required by GAAS is appropriate. AUDITPLANNER responds to situations representing increased business risk by reducing its recommended percentage rate for calculating materiality. The following rule shows how information about the intended use of the client's financial statements influences that decision.

If
1. the financial statements are not going to be used in connection with a public offering of the client's securities *and*
2. the financial statements are not going to be used in connection with a transfer of interests in the client *and*
3. the financial statements are not going to be used in connection with a contest for control of the client *and*
4. the financial statements are not going to be used to settle some outstanding litigation in which the client is involved *and*
5. the financial statements are not going to be used in connection with an inquiry by a regulatory agency *and*
6. the client is not in violation of, and is not likely to be found to be in violation of, restrictive debt covenants relating to the results of continuing operations,

Then a percentage rate of five percent should be used to calculate materiality.

Should any of the premises in this rule not hold, it would indicate that there is an increased business risk which may call for the use of a lower percentage rate in calculating materiality.[4]

Calculation of Overall Materiality Level

Figure 1 indicates that the materiality base is multiplied by the percentage rate to establish the overall materiality level for use in planning the audit. Prior years' materiality levels may also influence that calculation. The audit partner indicated that *after* a materiality level has been calculated, it is compared to subjective bounds which represent both an upper and lower limit to acceptable materiality levels. The upper bound represents the auditor's perception of an amount that most users would consider, *prima facie,* to be material; the lower level represents an amount that would result in an uneconomical amount of testing.[5] The following rules illustrate what happens when the materiality level is too high:

If
1. the overall materiality level is deemed to be too high *and*
2. this year's calculated materiality level is greater than that used last year,

Then it is very likely that this year's materiality level should be set at an amount that is 20 percent above the level used last year.

If
1. the overall materiality level is deemed to be too high *and*
2. this year's calculated materiality level is less than that used last year,

Then it is very likely that this year's materiality level should be used as calculated.

Together, these rules show a conservative bias. On the other hand, if the materiality level is deemed to be too low, it is reset at a level equal to the auditor's lower bound for economical testing.

Conclusion

This study demonstrates the feasibility of studying audit judgments in natural settings. An RBES was built as a means of studying planning-stage materiality judgments. Those judgments were seen to involve two separate sub-decisions:

- The choice of an appropriate base for calculating materiality and
- The selection of a percentage rate to multiply by that base.

The rules presented in the previous section illustrate explicitly how various aspects of the decision setting affect each of those decisions and materiality.

The choice of the base for calculating materiality was shown to depend on the perceived needs of financial statement users and objective characteristics of the client. The choice of a percentage rate, on the other hand, was much more subjective. It depended on both the identification of specific situations representing increased risk and the auditor's preferred response to that risk.

One limitation of this study is that AUDITPLANNER's knowledge base reflects primarily the judgment model of one audit partner. This clearly limits the generalizability of the findings. The primary reason for using one subject was the inability of current tools for building RBESs to deal with conflicting judgment strategies, and previous research had indicated a lack of consensus among auditors concerning their materiality judgments. The development of individual-specific models may, however, play an important role in understanding that lack of consensus:

> Since intelligent systems are programmable [i.e., they adapt to the demands of the task environment], we must expect to find different systems (even of the same species) using quite different strategies to perform the same task. I am not aware that any theorems have been proved about the uniqueness of good, or even best, strategies. Thus, we must expect to find strategy differences not only between systems at different skill levels, but even between experts.
>
> Hence, research on the performance of adaptive systems must take on a taxonomic, even a sociological aspect. We have a great deal to learn about the variety of strategies, and we should neither disdain nor shirk the painstaking, sometimes pedestrian, tasks of describing that variety. That substrate is as necessary to us as the taxonomic substrate has been to modern biology [Simon, 1980, p. 42].

The development of a taxonomy of materiality judgment models should identify the commonalities and differences between auditors in their approach to making materiality judgments. This study represents but one step toward developing such a taxonomy. Much additional work is needed. Similar models need to be built for individuals both in the same firm and from different firms. Eventually, such a taxonomy may enable us to identify the bases for establishing general guidelines for determining materiality.

Appendix A

A Sample Session with AUDITPLANNER

This is an example of a session with AUDITPLANNER. Each session begins with an introductory statement which is followed by a series of questions. The same sequence of questions would *not* be asked for all clients, because later questions depend upon answers given to earlier ones. The capitalized entries that follow the double asterisks are the user's responses.

You will be asked a series of questions about a client you are about to audit. On the basis of your answers to those questions, a set of recommendations will be presented about the appropriate materiality level(s) to be used in planning the extent of audit procedures.

1. What is the name of the client?

** EXAMPLE

2. What is Example's main line of business or industry classification?

** MANUFACTURING

3. Is this the first time that we have audited Example?

** NO

4. Have there been any acquisitions which either singly or in total amount to ten percent or more of client's total assets?

** NO

5. Some of the questions that follow will ask you to input dollar amounts from the client's financial statements. Will your answers be in terms of thousands of dollars?

** YES

6. Does Example have any publicly-traded debt or equity securities?

** YES

7. What do you project retained earnings to be?

** 7616

8. What is the amount of current assets?
** 5822
9. What is the amount of current liabilities?
** 3009
10. What do you estimate the annual income from continuing operations to be?
** 3786
11. Are the financial statements going to be used in connection with a public offering of securities?
** NO
12. Are the financial statements going to be used in connection with a transfer of interests in Example?
** NO
13. Are the financial statements going to be used in connection with a contest for control of Example?
** NO
14. Are the financial statements being used to settle some litigation involving Example?
** NO
15. Are the financial statements being used in connection with an inquiry by a regulatory commission?
** NO
16. How much long-term debt does Example have?
** 882
17. Does Example have any covenants on either its long-term debt or existing lines-of-credit?
** YES
18. Does Example have any debt covenants which restrict dividends to a percentage of either current earnings or cash flow?
** NO
19. Do any of Example's debt covenants require it to maintain some level of earnings?
** NO

20. Does Example have any debt covenants which require it to use part of its cash flow to retire its debt?
** NO
The overall materiality level to be used in planning the extent of audit procedures is 189,300.

The reasons for the materiality judgment are as follows:

The calculation of the materiality level was based on the use of income-from-continuing-operations as the base for the materiality calculation. The materiality level was calculated using a percentage rate of .05.

Appendix B

Example of AUDITPLANNER's Explanation Capabilities that Can Be Exercised During a Consultation Session

The following dialogue illustrates how the normal series of questions that AUDITPLANNER asks can be interrupted to find out *why* a particular question was being asked. As before, the capitalized entries following the double asterisks represent the user's responses. The other statements are AUDITPLANNER's responses to the questions.

3. Is this the first time that we have audited Example?
** WHY
[i.e., WHY is it important to determine whether this is the first time that we have audited Example?]
[1.0] Whether this is the first time that we have audited a client is one of the five standard parameters that identify a client. This may be useful later in the consultation. For example, it is relevant in determining whether there is a need to reduce the calculated materiality level due to the increased risk associated with an initial audit of the client and is relevant in determining the percentage rate used to determine the materiality level.
[back to question 3...]
** YES
(Note: Several questions asked by AUDITPLANNER are skipped until the next time the user asks "WHY".)
10. Is Example filing with a regulatory agency in preparation for the sale of its securities in a public market?
** WHY
[i.e., WHY is it important to determine whether Example is filing with a regulatory agency in preparation for the sale of its securities in a public market?]

[2.0] This will aid in determining the type of entity that Example is. It has already been established that

[2.1] it is suspected that the type of entity that Example is is private.

Therefore, if

[2.2] Example is not filing with a regulatory agency in preparation for the sale of its securities in a public market, and

[2.3] Example does not intend to go public within the next two or three years,

Then

it is definite (1.0) that the type of entity Example is is private. [RULE007].

(Note: AUDITPLANNER explains the current rule being followed that causes it to ask question 10 about Example's plans for future financing.)

[back to question 10...]

** HOW 2.1

(Note: Rather than answering the question, the user wants to explore further the line of reasoning being followed by AUDITPLANNER. Here AUDITPLANNER is asked about one of the conclusions that it has already made.)

[i.e., HOW was it established that it is suspected that the type of entity Example is is private?]

[2.4] RULE056 was used to conclude that the type of entity Example is is private (.9).

Thus, it has been established that it is suspected that the type of entity Example is is private.

[back to question 10...]

** HOW 2.4

[i.e., HOW was RULE056 used?]

It has already been established that

[4.1] Example does not have any publicly traded debt or equity securities, and

[4.2] Example does not have restrictive debt covenants that are measured by or depend on periodic financial statement amounts or ratios that involve results of operations, and

[4.3] Example is not controlled by a public entity.

Therefore

there is strongly suggestive evidence (.9) that the type of entity Example is is private. [RULE056]

Appendix C

Questionnaire Used to Evaluate AUDITPLANNER

Read each question and circle the response which best represents your feelings to that statement.

Where SA=Strongly Agree
A=Agree
N=Neutral
D=Disagree
SD=Strongly Disagree

1. I found AUDITPLANNER easy to use.	SA	A	N	D	SD
2. AUDITPLANNER did not provide adequate HELP facilities to make it easy to use.	SA	A	N	D	SD
3. AUDITPLANNER asked too many questions —often about irrelevant information.	SA	A	N	D	SD
4. I think AUDITPLANNER would be useful as a training device.	SA	A	N	D	SD
5. I think AUDITPLANNER would be useful as a decision aid when planning an audit.	SA	A	N	D	SD
6. I would like to use AUDITPLANNER as a decision aid.	SA	A	N	D	SD
7. AUDITPLANNER does not exhibit a basic level of competence in making materiality judgments.	SA	A	N	D	SD

8. I would accept AUDITPLANNER's recommendations.	SA	A	N	D	SD
9. I did not enjoy using AUDITPLANNER.	SA	A	N	D	SD
10. AUDITPLANNER was too slow in making its recommendations.	SA	A	N	D	SD
11. AUDITPLANNER would be more useful as a training device than as a decision aid.	SA	A	N	D	SD
12. I can see no use for a program like AUDITPLANNER.	SA	A	N	D	SD
13. AUDITPLANNER was hard to use.	SA	A	N	D	SD
14. I would not mind my subordinates using AUDITPLANNER as a decision aid.	SA	A	N	D	SD
15. It was hard to follow AUDITPLANNER's flow of logic.	SA	A	N	D	SD
16. I made frequent use of AUDITPLANNER's question answering facilities.	SA	A	N	D	SD
17. AUDITPLANNER's question answering facilities did not adequately explain what it was doing.	SA	A	N	D	SD
18. I would not want my subordinates to use AUDITPLANNER as a training device.	SA	A	N	D	SD
19. AUDITPLANNER's line of reasoning was logical and easy to follow.	SA	A	N	D	SD
20. I enjoyed using AUDITPLANNER.	SA	A	N	D	SD
21. The sequencing of questions in AUDIT-PLANNER was easy to follow.	SA	A	N	D	SD
22. I think that AUDITPLANNER's recommendations and rationale were sound and reflected professional competence.	SA	A	N	D	SD
23. AUDITPLANNER's ability to respond to HOW and WHY questions was very helpful.	SA	A	N	D	SD
24. I would not approach the planning materiality decision the way that AUDITPLANNER did.	SA	A	N	D	SD
25. AUDITPLANNER jumped around from topic to topic.	SA	A	N	D	SD

26. Please write down your overall impression of AUDITPLANNER. Discuss what you think it could best be used for, needed improvements, potential role in an audit, etc. Use as much space as you need, including the backs of the questionnaire pages.

References

Adelman, L., "The Influence of Formal, Substantive, and Contextual Task Properties on the Relative Effectiveness of Different Forms of Feedback in Multiple-Cue Probability Learning Tasks," *Organizational Behavior and Human Performance* (June 1981), pp. 423-442.

American Institute of Certified Public Accountants, *Codification of Auditing Standards Numbers 1 to 23* (Commerce Clearing House, 1979).

——, *Statement on Auditing Standards No. 47: Audit Risk and Materiality in Conducting an Audit* (AICPA, 1983).

Boatsman, J.R., and J.C. Robertson, "Policy-Capturing on Selected Materiality Judgments," *The Accounting Review* (April 1974), pp. 342-352.

Buchanan, B.G., and E. Shortliffe (Eds.), *Rule-Based Expert Systems: The MYCIN Experiments of the Stanford Heuristic Programming Project* (Addison-Wesley, 1984).

Cox, J.R., and R.A. Griggs, "The Effects of Experience on Performance in Wason's Selection Task," *Memory and Cognition* (September 1982), pp. 496-502.

Cushing, B.E., and J.K. Loebbecke, *Comparison of Audit Methodologies of Large Accounting Firms* (American Accounting Association, 1986).

Davis, R., and D. Lenat, *Knowledge-Based Systems in Artificial Intelligence* (McGraw-Hill, 1982).

Ebbesen, E.B., and V.J. Konecni, "On the External Validity of Decision-Making Research: What Do We Know About Decisions in the Real World?", in T.S. Wallsten (Ed.), *Cognitive Processes in Choice and Decision Behavior* (Erlbaum, 1980), pp. 21-45.

Einhorn, H.J., and R.M. Hogarth, "A Theory of Diagnostic Inference: I. Imagination and the Psychophysics of Evidence," Working paper (University of Chicago, 1982).

Financial Accounting Standards Board, *Discussion Memorandum: An Analysis of Issues Related to Criteria for Determining Materiality* (FASB, 1975).

——, *Statement of Financial Accounting Concepts No. 2: Qualitative Characteristics of Accounting Information* (FASB, 1980).

Firth, M., "Consensus Views and Judgment Models in Materiality Decisions," *Accounting, Organizations, and Society* (No. 4, 1979), pp. 283-295.

Gal, G., "Using Auditor Knowledge to Formulate Data Model Constraints: An Expert System for Internal Control Evaluation," Unpublished Ph.D. dissertation (Michigan State University, 1985).

Gibbins, M., and F.M. Wolf, "Auditors' Subjective Decision Environment — The Case of a Normal External Audit," *The Accounting Review* (January 1982), pp. 105-124.

Harmon, P. and D. King, *Expert Systems* (Wiley, 1985).

Hayes, J.R., and H.A. Simon, "Psychological Differences among Problem Isomorphs," in N. Castellan, Jr., D.B. Pisoni, and G.R. Potts (Eds.), *Cognitive Theory: Volume 2* (Erlbaum Press, 1977), pp. 21-41.

Hayes-Roth, F., D.A. Waterman, and D.B. Lenat, *Building Expert Systems* (Addison-Wesley, 1983).

Hoch, S.J., and J.E. Tschirgi, "Cue Redundancy and Extra-Logical Inferences in a Deductive Reasoning Task," *Memory and Cognition* (March 1983), pp. 200-209.

Holstrum, G.L., and W.F. Messier, Jr., "A Review and Integration of Empirical Research on Materiality," *Auditing: A Journal of Practice and Theory* (Fall 1982), pp. 45-63.

Kahneman, D., and A. Tversky, "Prospect Theory: An Analysis of Decision under Risk," *Econometrica* (March 1979), pp. 263-291.

Lewis, B.L., "Expert Judgment in Auditing: An Expected Utility Approach," *Journal of Accounting Research* (Autumn 1980), pp. 594-602.

Mayper, A.G., "Consensus of Auditors' Materiality Judgments of Internal Accounting Control Weaknesses," *Journal of Accounting Research* (Autumn 1982), pp. 773-783.

Messier, W.F., Jr., "The Effect of Experience and Firm Type on Materiality/Disclosure Judgments," *Journal of Accounting Research* (Autumn 1983), pp. 611-618.

Michaelsen, R.H., "A Knowledge-Based System for Individual Income and Transfer Tax Planning," Unpublished dissertation (University of Illinois, 1982).

____, "An Expert System for Federal Tax Planning," *Expert Systems* (October 1984), pp. 149-167.

Moriarity, S., and F.H. Barron, "Modeling the Materiality Judgments of Audit Partners," *Journal of Accounting Research* (Autumn 1976), pp. 320-341.

_____, and _____, "A Judgment Based Definiton of Materiality," *Journal of Accounting Research* (Supplement 1979), pp. 114-135.

Newton, L.K., "The Risk Factor in Materiality Decisions," *The Accounting Review* (January 1977), pp. 97-108.

Pattillo, J.W., "Materiality: The (formerly) Elusive Standard," *Financial Executive* (August 1975,) pp. 20-27.

_____, *The Concept of Materiality in Financial Reporting, Volume 1* (Financial Executives Research Foundation, 1976.)

_____, and J.D. Siebel, "Factors Affecting the Materiality Judgment," *CPA Journal* (July 1974), pp. 39-44.

Shortliffe, E.H., *Computer-Based Medical Consultation: MYCIN* (American Elsevier, 1976).

_____, and B.G. Buchanan, "A Model of Inexact Reasoning in Medicine," *Mathematical Biosciences* (April 1975), pp. 351-379.

Simon, H.A., "Cognitive Science: The Newest Science of the Artificial," *Cognitive Science* (January-March 1980), pp. 33-46.

Van Melle, W., A.C. Scott, J.S. Bennett, and M. Peairs, *The EMYCIN Manual* (Stanford, 1981).

Ward, B.H., "An Investigation of the Materiality Construct in Auditing," *Journal of Accounting Research* (Spring 1976), pp. 138-152.

Waterman, D.A., *A Guide to Expert Systems* (Addison-Wesley, 1986).

Woolsey, S.M., "Approach to Solving the Materiality Problem," *Journal of Accountancy* (March 1973), pp. 47-50.

Endnotes

[1]For a more detailed discussion of RBESs, the interested reader is referred to any of the following general texts: Hayes-Roth, Waterman, and Lenat [1983], Buchanan and Shortliffe [1984], Harmon and King [1985], or Waterman [1986].

[2]The other questions were included in the questionnaire to examine the auditors' reactions to the use of RBESs and to obtain feedback about its future development. Those responses are not discussed here because they are not directly relevant to this study.

[3]Most of AUDITPLANNER's rules have a certainty factor of one associated with their conclusions; that is, the conclusions definitely follow from the premises. Those rules which have a certainty factor of less than one are translated here with the phrase "it is highly likely" in their conclusion, followed by a decimal number representing the degree of certainty that the conclusion follows from the premises. Certainty factors are not Bayesian probabilities, but rather, resemble belief functions. For more information about certainty factors, the interested reader is referred to Shortliffe and Buchanan [1975].

[4]The partner's concern about the sensitive nature of the situations in which a lower percentage rate is used precludes the publication of those rules that specify the exact rates to use in those situations.

[5]The actual levels of these bounds would depend on the types and size of clients normally audited and would, therefore, probably vary from one auditor to another.

FSA: Applying AI Techniques to the Familiarization Phase of Financial Decision Making

Chunka Mui and
William E. McCarthy

Financial decision making consists of a familiarization phase and a reasoning phase. Expert systems requiring users to manually input much original data — data the user has extracted from the environment by observation monitoring, or interpretation — address the reasoning phase by embodying procedures and heuristics transforming that original data into a final classification (or plan) set. Typically, such final interpretations involve decisions like

- Whether or not to invest in certain equity stocks,
- Whether or not to effect corporate restructuring,
- Whether or not to extend loans to certain corporate entities, and
- Whether or not to reevaluate a bond rating for a given entity.

By contrast, this article will demonstrate AI techniques in support of the familiarization phase. More specifically, we will show how relatively free-form financial filings (unstructured financial statements and footnotes, for example) can be captured with natural language processing techniques and interpreted for further use with knowledge representation formalisms such as inheritance hierarchies. We will explain how we used these ideas to design and construct FSA — the financial statement analyzer — an AI system built by Arthur Andersen & Company under contract from the SEC during the pilot phase of the EDGAR project (electronic data gathering, analysis, and retrieval).

Before explaining specific details of FSA's operation, we will discuss financial decision making and the use of financial statements in general. We believe such general discussion will convince readers of the need for widely applicable front-end processing of corporate data such as balance sheets and income statements that, along with other mandated government filings, constitute an invaluable resource for financial analysis. Surveys assessing information sources for individual investors, institutional investors, and financial analysts confirm this view by consistently giving corporate annual filings the highest rankings of importance.[1]

Financial Decision Making

Human information processing theorists hypothesize that decision making divides into a number of phases.[2] The first phase embraces those cognitive activities concerned with explicitly recognizing relevant information in the decision maker's environment, and is referred to by terms like "information acquisition" or "intelligence." This first step can include some preliminary interpretive data processing; however, its primary purpose is to set the stage for later problem-solving activities that process first interpretations into final decisions.

This initial exploratory activity was recently studied in a series of process-tracing experiments.[3-6] Each of these experiments asked experienced subjects to talk aloud while solving a significant financial problem. Protocols transcribed from these recorded sessions showed extensive important use of financial statement data. Figure 1 illustrates Bouwman's explanation of this process.[4]

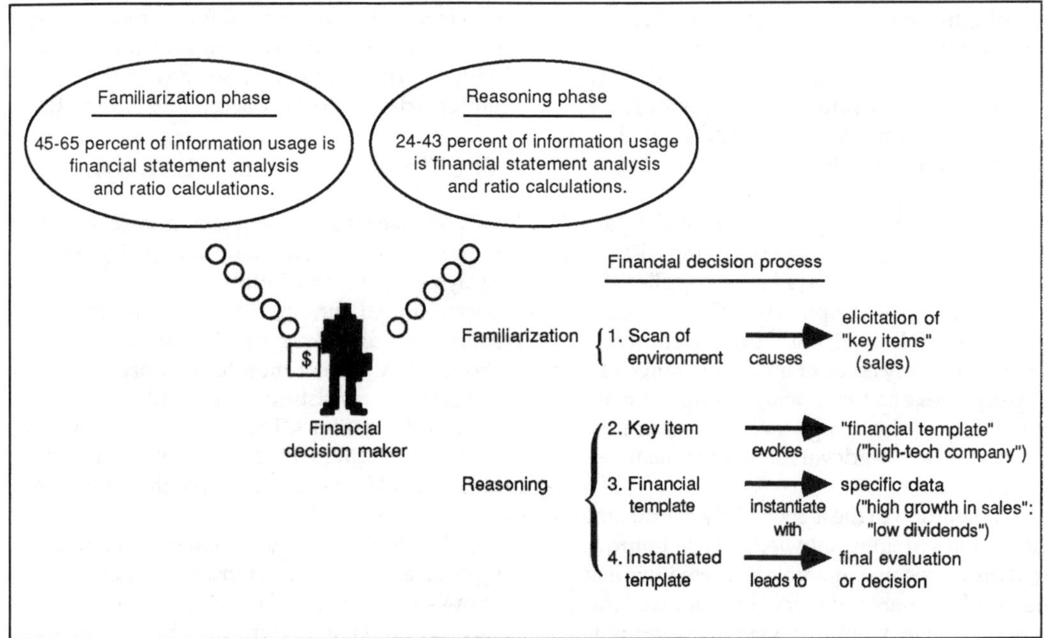

Figure 1. The financial decision process.

Bouwman divided financial decision-making into two phases—familiarizing and reasoning. His subjects included two groups of experts making two types of decisions. Financial analysts evaluating a stock for possible investment formed the first group, while loan officers evaluating a multimillion-dollar participation loan formed the second. As Figure 1's "clouds" illustrate, analyzing financial statements and calculating financial ratios comprised significant information usage in both phases — but in the first phase especially.

According to Bouwman, as Figure 1 portrays, financial decision making consists of the following steps:

- Scanning the environment and background values to identify key items such as "sales" or "net income";
- Evoking financial templates for companies or industries from long-term memory (for example, "high-tech company" or "late recessionary industry");
- Searching for instantiations of these templates with specific information (that is, a more directed reading of initial data); and
- Evaluating, or deciding overall.

In rough terms, the first step corresponds to familiarizing — while the second, third, and fourth accrue to reasoning. The instantiations called for explain the continued use of financial statement and ratio data throughout the entire decision process.

Bouwman developed this description of the decision process after several experimental studies of financial decision-making. We would not attempt to generalize Bouwman's two-phase description to cover most actual users; however, we do believe it constitutes a widely applicable framework for analyzing problems involved in providing automated support for financial problem solving. The next section uses that framework in discussing AI approaches to front-end processing of corporate financial data.

Standardized Processing for Familiarization Purposes

Surveys of financial decision-makers and detailed laboratory studies of those decision-makers in action establish the primacy of financial statement use in investment, loan, and restructuring decisions. However, this primacy leads to an interesting data availability paradox.

On the one hand, the amount of presently available corporate financial data is clearly overwhelming. For instance, the required corporate filings with the SEC exceed four-million pages annually. This viewpoint is best expressed in the following analysis of a previously cited process-tracing study:

> Individuals who, as a result of their professional position, act as proxies for other investors, all felt inundated with [corporate financial] information they felt was of questionable value.[7]

On the other hand, present financial data sources are inadequate in many respects. Research has noted that this judgment applies even to the vast array of computerized financial data services currently available.[8,9] Present sources do not adequately account for a wide range of company sizes and types, and they do not make it possible to aspire to high levels of uniform classification and retrieval for heterogeneous corporations.

The solution to these seemingly contrasting problems lies in some knowledge-based processing of disaggregated and uninterpreted financial data. While present data services work well in many cases, they would do better if their input were made more uniform and interpretive.

Such front-end processing would require considerable accounting knowledge concerning the composition of financial statement numbers, and it would also require the ability to extract those accounting numbers (and related conceptual ideas) from unformatted text-like footnotes and proxy statements. Such interpretive and extractive processing is a formidable task and is difficult to build into a computerized system — which probably accounts for the fact that most present-day financial expert systems aim at decision support for problem solving's reasoning phase rather than its familiarization phase. Such reasoning support systems are not uniform because they attempt to emulate a disparate group of expert decision makers. Support for familiarization can be uniform, however. In fact, the SEC's EDGAR project sought such support.

EDGAR

The EDGAR pilot system enabled volunteer corporations to submit required filings electronically (as opposed to paper submissions). While developing this pilot, the SEC wanted to assess the ultimate feasibility of an automated system that would include some of the types of interpretive and extractive processing discussed above. Because their legislatively mandated goal is to make all filed information on registered corporations available to the trading public, the SEC was exploring the potential for a processing system that would monitor filings for compliance with securities laws and also convert that non-uniform data into easily accessible information.

The Financial Statement Analyzer

FSA represents a first step at applying AI techniques to the familiarization phase of financial analysis. It performs ratio analysis using corporate annual reports (10K) as the information source. Building the system required approximately 18 man-months of effort with a project team consisting of SEC and Arthur Andersen personnel. The development environment was IntelliCorp's KEE running on Symbolics Lisp Machines. Results of this work are on file with the SEC.[10]

An object-oriented system, FSA's structure is modeled after the accounting domain's knowledge structure. Explicit knowledge representation and natural language processing techniques were molded to technical requirements imposed by the problem domain. In order to extract key financial data from corporate annual reports, the system had to systematically interpret tabular financial statements and textual footnotes. FSA explicitly represents accounting knowledge needed to understand financial statements and financial knowledge needed to perform ratio analysis. It incorporates natural language processing techniques to parse textual footnotes.

Analysis is organized using a message-passing control structure. Each financial statement item is a computational object having a local state (composed of slots) and operators (represented as methods) and communicating via message. Each object must find itself within financial documents — a responsibility invoked via message to the object's FIND-YOURSELF method. A ratio (such as QUICK-RATIO) receiving a FIND-YOURSELF message sends a FIND-YOURSELF message to each item in its formula, waits for replies, and then applies these values to the formula. A statement item (such as RENTAL-EXPENSE) receiving a FIND-YOURSELF message would search the company's financial documents for its value. In the case of RENTAL-EXPENSE, the object would search the Income Statement and, if that failed, the textual footnotes. The nature and complexity of this search is completely hidden from the FIND-YOURSELF message sender.

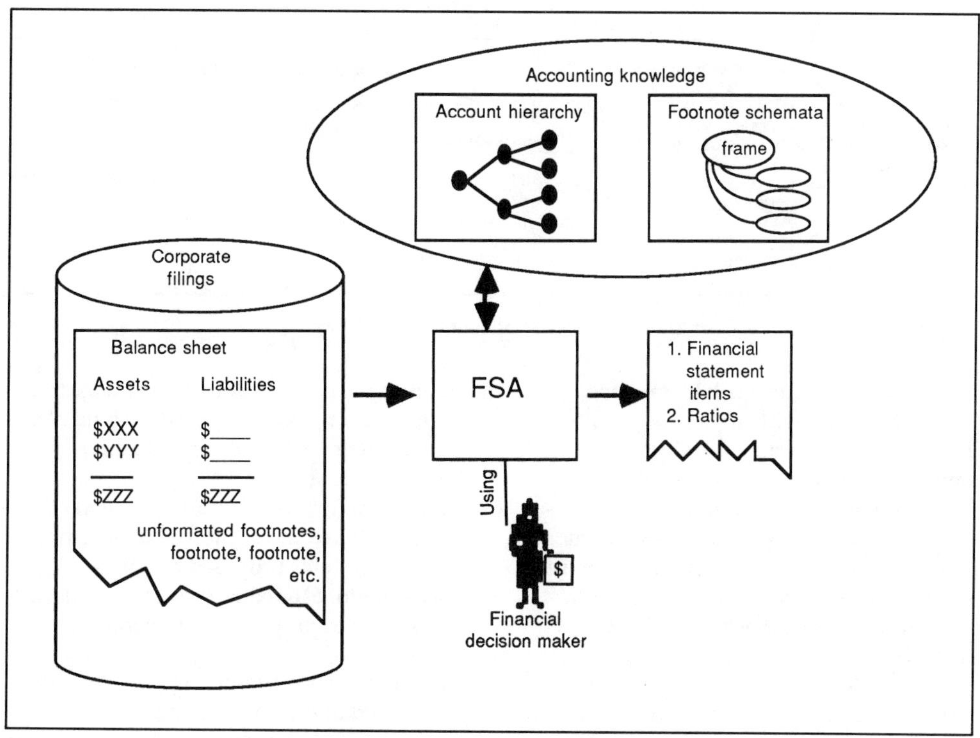

Figure 2. An overview of FSA operation.

This message-passing control structure makes analysis a demand-driven process. Data search must be explicitly invoked via a message to an object. This control structure follows the Actor model.[11] The result is a modular system allowing for easy expansion and maintenance, with FSA's search behavior closely modeling the heuristics of human problem solvers in accounting.

FSA currently understands balance sheets, income statements, and their accompanying footnotes. It can extract necessary data and perform ratio analysis. For example, it uses

- The *quick ratio* to measure a firm's ability to pay off short-term obligations without relying on inventory sale,
- The *current debt to equity ratio* to measure how much a firm has been financed by short-term debt, and
- The *times fixed charges earned ratio* to measure a firm's ability to pay fixed charges.

A System Model

Figure 2 models FSA as it currently exists. The main system input is a company's financial documents, including statements and footnotes. Two knowledge bases support the system: One contains accounting and financial knowledge, and the other contains semantic structures (schemata) that drive footnote processing. Users are financial analysts interacting with the system to initiate queries and resolve ambiguities. For an overall grasp of FSA's functionality, one must understand how the two accounting knowledge bases are used in interpretive and extractive processing. Each is described below.

Account Hierarchy

FSA uses a structured representation of accounting knowledge covering the composition of financial statements and the relationships between statement items. We need this knowledge to interpret loosely structured financial statements and to extract accurate account values from them. FSA models its financial knowledge after chart of account hierarchies used in the accounting profession.[12] Such structures constitute a standard method for organizing financial information, and we found that accounting problem solvers intuitively attempt to

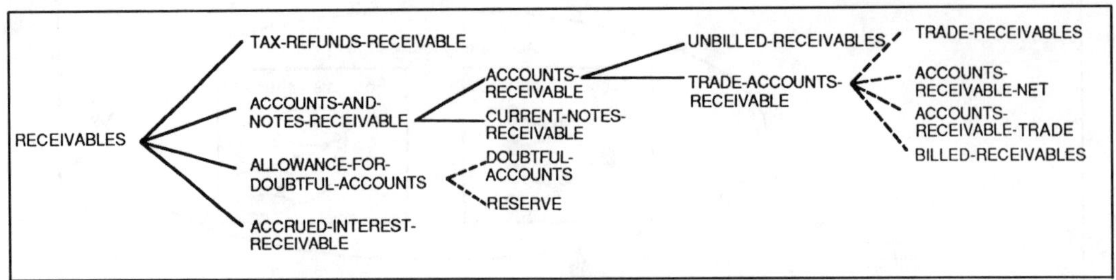

Figure 3. A subset of account hierarchy.

organize financial data into such hierarchies before trying to reason with it.

Charts of accounts lead naturally to taxonomic classification using a semantic network formalism. Figure 3 illustrates a small portion of FSA's accounting semantic network (the actual network is much larger). Each node represents an object corresponding to some financial item. The taxonomic relationships within the network are SUB-ACCOUNT-OF and ISA, corresponding to the canonical SUBCLASS and INSTANCE relationships. Charts of accounts contain many levels of general accounts and subaccounts, as the SUB-ACCOUNT-OF relationship represents. The ISA relationship represents that each account may be designated in different ways. Figure 3 indicates the SUB-ACCOUNT-OF relationship with a solid arrow and the ISA relationship with a dashed arrow. For example, UNBILLED-RECEIVABLES is a subaccount of ACCOUNTS-RECEIVABLE, and RESERVE is an ALLOWANCE-FOR-DOUBTFUL-ACCOUNTS.

We reason within the semantic network via heuristic and algorithmic methods attached to each object. Methods (like FIND-YOURSELF) use the network directly to reason about aggregations and alternative interpretations. The inheritance hierarchy formed by the network enables descriptive and procedural information to move from accounts to subaccounts and instances.

The semantic network's efficacy in representing accounting knowledge was essential for eliciting knowledge from domain experts. The network could be presented in much the same way that a chart of accounts is normally depicted, which in turn maps well to an expert's intuitive image of the domain. Experts could then take direct roles in structuring the knowledge base, thereby lessening problems that arise when knowledge engineers must translate from the expert's domain language to an AI representation language. Experts could also describe their analytical methods directly in chart of account terms.

By design, this application of semantic networks exhibited the desirable qualities of representation systems proposed by Rich — representational adequacy and inferential adequacy.[13] These properties correspond to

- Adequately representing knowledge needed in the domain, and
- Successfully manipulating representational structures to derive new structures — structures replicating human inference of new knowledge from old.

Our representation also displayed acquisitional efficiency — the ability to acquire new information easily. The system's search strategy and representation structure enabled us to easily identify knowledge base deficiencies. Most omissions were new instances for the network. For version control reasons, FSA required that we insert this new information by hand. However, system-controlled acquisition could also have been implemented.

Footnote Schemata

FSA faced financial statement footnotes that significantly challenged automated analysis. Footnotes tend to be unstructured collections of text and tables, with information spread over multiple sentence fragments interwoven with numerical tables. This anomalous syntactic structure foiled our attempts to build a full syntactic parser — a parser using grammar based on systematic formalisms such as augmented transition networks or charts.[14]

Consequently, in conjunction with semantic analysis, we chose to parse footnote syntax

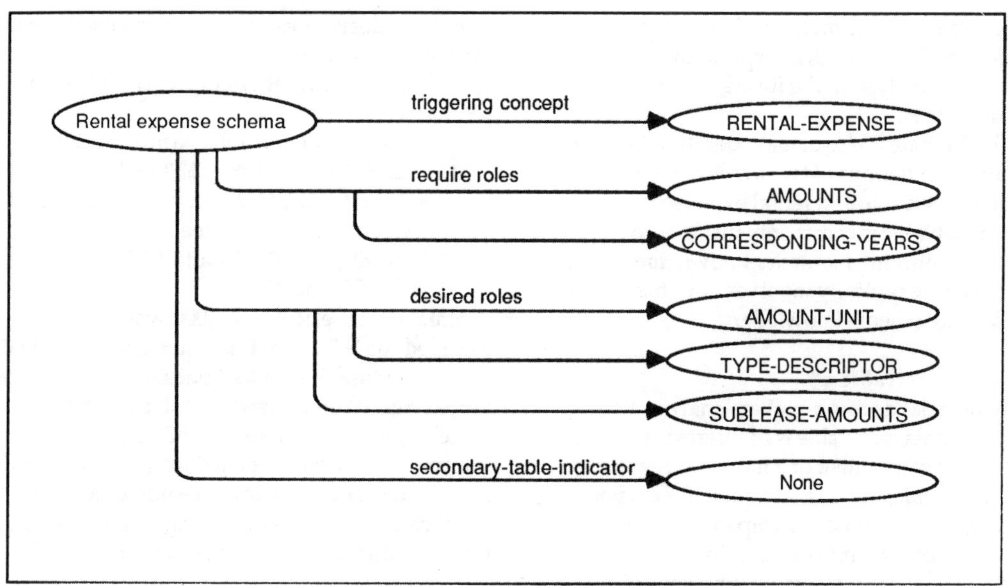

Figure 4. A rental expense schema.

partially. We defined special objects in the semantic network, representing financial items to be found within the textual footnotes. We called these special objects *schemata,* and used them to represent accounting knowledge contained within footnotes. Figure 4 shows a sample schema for RENTAL EXPENSE that we will use in a later example. We designed these schemata directly from our experiences in designing and implementing the earlier SEC prototype ELOISE. ELOISE read corporate proxy statements, looking for certain corporate antitakeover provisions, and was patterned on the semantically driven top-down approach developed by DeJong in FRUMP.[15]

FSA uses DeJong's prediction and substantiation model to interpret footnotes, which integrates with financial statement processing's demand-driven nature. The system activates schemata via FIND-YOURSELF messages, and then invokes methods that *predict* and then try to *substantiate* each schema role. A text analyzer developed specifically to deal with a footnote's loose syntactic structure performs substantiation. FSA's text analyzer relies on weaker methods than its ELOISE and FRUMP counterparts because footnotes have neither the strong grammatical structure found in ELOISE's legal proxy statements nor the simple grammatical clarity found in FRUMP's UPI news stories. Our text analyzer proved sufficient for FSA's domain.

A Typical FSA Scenario

FSA provides a workbench-like user interface giving analysts control over multiple information sources and system functions. In a typical scenario, financial analysts choose a company and year to analyze. FSA can display any company document on the screen. Analysts can initiate ratio calculations at any point. During the calculation, the system may alert users when certain anomalous conditions arise. If the company had no cash assets, for example, analysts would be notified immediately. Results of the calculation are shown beside source documents within 30-60 seconds (further performance statistics are available from the authors). Hardcopy session logs are also available. Analysts control the conditions under which the system will query and the detail level of system responses ranging from alerting on all ambiguous conditions and showing all processing details to never alerting and showing only final ratio values.

Currently, the system is designed to interact with the financial decision maker. However, we believe FSA should ultimately be a background monitoring system. In this monitoring mode, it would support financial decision making's familiarization and (in part) reasoning phases. It would scan all incoming documents for relevant information, perform limited interpretive processing on that information, and channel its results to a more comprehensively interpretive mechanism. Today, such interpretation is done by a human analyst; in the future, an expert system could do it.

To illustrate FSA's actual operation, we will display instantiations of two account elements — accounts receivable and rental expense. Accounts receivable is commonly instantiated through accounting hierarchy knowledge, while rental expense typically involves both hierarchy and footnote schema knowledge.

Accounts Receivable

When financial decision-makers analyze a company, accounts receivable is of interest either by itself or as a component of a more aggregate figure like the quick ratio (a surrogate for corporate liquidity, as it estimates a company's ability to meet short-term financial obligations). Decision makers interested in assessing loan or equity potential can compare such surrogates across companies.

When users opt to see a QUICK-RATIO, FSA sends a message to all numerical components of that formula to find themselves in the financial statements using structures resembling Figure 3's. The search range for that particular ratio's numerator would be defined as CURRENT-ASSETS (not shown in Figure 3) and one of its key components would be ACCOUNTS-RECEIVABLE. If that particular account is not found, FSA will go up or down the knowledge hierarchy and offer either generalization to a parent or combination of subclasses as an alternative. For this particular element, analysts will often accept just TRADE-ACCOUNTS-RECEIVABLE as a substitute because it normally constitutes most of ACCOUNTS-RECEIVABLE.

Rental Expense

Unlike ACCOUNTS-RECEIVABLE, instantiating items like RENTAL-EXPENSE frequently requires digging information out of financial statement footnotes. When this account figure is not found in corporate income statements, the account object issues a message to find itself with the aid of frame-oriented knowledge structures encoded in Figure 4's schema. The account name serves as the "triggering concept" for calling the schema and fills the first slot. The "required roles" slot indicates concept attributes required for instantiation (AMOUNTS and CORRESPONDING-YEARS), while the "desired roles" slot designates optional items used in rent expense calculations.

This schema might interpret the following sentence:

> Gross rental expense amounted to $36,238,000 for 1983, $33,467,000 for 1982, and $29,046,000 for 1981, which was reduced by sublease income of $3,114,000, $3,582,000, and $2,578,000 in 1983, 1982, and 1981.

A rental expense of $29,885,000 would be returned for 1982 after this schema was invoked. We did not use Figure 4's final slot in this example, but we often need that slot when sentence fragments in footnotes indicate that information must be gleaned from tabular data. If such tabular processing is required, footnote interpretation reverts to parsing techniques used for the bodies of the financial statements.

Conclusion

At the outset, we made a case for directing significant AI system building effort towards the front-end or initial phases of financial problem-solving. We based our case on evidence gleaned from empirical laboratory studies and surveys of financial decision-makers. We envision that the somewhat standardized and wide-ranging interpretive processing such systems could accomplish might serve the needs of many different reasoning phase decision-support tools, including some expert systems.

The second part of this article described FSA, focusing on its goal of making familiarization phase information from financial statements more accessible. Our descriptions concentrated on the successful application of AI techniques to codifying specific accounting knowledge structures such as account hierarchies and footnote schemata.

Since the SEC's EDGAR project remains in its pilot phase, no final cost-benefit decisions have been made regarding the ultimate feasibility of fully implementing an FSA-like system. Such a decision would require candid assessment of "the scaling problem" for this particular domain.[16] Judgments would have to be made as to how well techniques used and lessons learned in the pilot would work on larger search spaces involving the following extensions:

- An ability to process additional financial statements and to calculate additional ratios,

- An expanded capability to accommodate both opportunistic and background processing in addition to FSA's present abilities with demand-driven query processing, and
- An augmented accounting vocabulary that includes terminology from a wider variety of industries.

Our experience indicates that AI approaches work well and that a similarly designed operational system in this domain would be successful.

References

1. L. Chang, K. S. Most, and C. W. Brain, "The Utility of Annual Reports: An International Study," *J. Int'l Business*, Spring/Summer 1983, pp. 63-84.
2. H. A. Simon, *The New Science of Management Decision*, Harper Brothers, New York, N.Y., 1960.
3. K. Ericsson and H. Simon, "Verbal Reports as Data," *Psychological Review*, Vol. 87, No. 3, 1980, pp. 215-251.
4. M.J. Bouwman, "Towards Expert Systems: The Analysis of Expert Financial Behavior," tech. report, Dept. of Accounting, University of Oregon, Eugene, Ore., 1985.
5. S.F. Biggs, "Financial Analysts' Information Search in the Assessment of Corporate Earning Power," *Accounting, Organizations and Society*, Vol. 9, No. 3/4, 1984, p. 313-323.
6. M.J. Anderson, "Some Evidence on the Effect of Verbalization on Process," *J. Accounting Research*, Vol. 23, No. 2, 1985, p. 843-852.
7. M.J. Anderson, *The Investment Decision — An Analysis Using Verbal Protocols*, PhD dissertation, Michigan State Univ., E. Lansing, Mich., 1982, p. 85.
8. R. B. McElreath and C.D. Wiggins, "Using the Compustat Tapes in Financial Research: Problems and Solutions," *Financial Analysts J.*, Jan./Feb. 1984, pp. 71-76.
9. G. Foster, *Financial Statement Analysis*, Prentice-Hall, Englewood Cliffs, N.J., 1986.
10. "Final Report on the Financial Statement Analyzer to the Securities and Exchange Commission," tech. report, Arthur Andersen & Company, Chicago, Ill., Dec. 1985.
11. C.E. Hewitt, "Viewing Control Structures as Patterns of Passing Messages," *Artificial Intelligence*, Vol. 8, No. 3, pp. 323-64.
12. B.E. Cushing, *Accounting Information Systems and Business Organizations*, Addison-Wesley, Reading, Mass., 1982.
13. E. Rich, *Artificial Intelligence*, McGraw-Hill, New York, N.Y., 1983, Ch. 7.
14. T. Winograd, *Language as a Cognitive Process: Syntax*, Vol. 1, Addison-Wesley, Reading, Mass., 1983.
15. G. F. DeJong II, *Skimming Stories in Real Time: An Experiment in Integrated Understanding*, PhD dissertation, Yale Univ., New Haven, Conn., 1979.
16. D.A. Waterman, *A Guide to Expert Systems*, Addison-Wesley, Reading, Mass., 1986, pp. 27-28.

A Knowledge-Based Consultant for Financial Marketing

John Kastner, Chidanand Apté, James Griesmer, Se June Hong, Maurice Karnaugh, Eric Mays, and Yoshio Tozawa

This article describes the initial stages of an effort to develop a knowledge-based financial marketing consultant system. The project for Financial Marketing Expertise (FAME) is to produce a system that addresses the area usually referred to as *financial marketing*. This term characterizes the financial decision processes used in the marketing of products and services of such large scale that they can significantly impact a company's financial status. In particular, our project emphasizes financial marketing as it applies to the marketing of computers. For instance, a customer interested in buying computing technology on a large scale is usually concerned that the financing plan being used to acquire the technology is safe, sound, and attractive from a financial investment point of view. Therefore, in making very large sales, financial considerations often become as important as the computing considerations.

We have found financial marketing to be a very interesting and characteristically unique domain. The problem is that of generating a financing plan, and this differs from most expert systems applications, which usually tend to be classificatory in nature. Human financial marketing experts, rather than exhaustively generating an optimal plan (which might not even exist), use their experiential heuristics and domain knowledge to prune the generate-and-test space for efficiently designing a plan that is attractive from the customer's viewpoint. There have been relatively few expert systems that employ such a heuristically guided generate-and-test problem-solving paradigm for designing an acceptable plan. Systems that partially exhibit some of these facets include DENDRAL (Lindsay et al., 1980) for heuristic generate and test and MOLGEN (Stefik, 1981) for plan design.

Another important distinction between this problem and many others addressed by AI researchers is that a typical financial marketing problem frequently has no one solution. There might be no definitive answer to a problem. The issue is not merely a question of computing financial optimality. The importance lies not only in the answer you provide but also in the explanation and justification that you use to back the answer. For this purpose, it is important to generate a convincing financial argument that strengthens the selling of the answer (financing plan). Explanation generation in natural language, for a solution that might be competing with many others has been addressed by very few knowledge-based systems. Some similarity exists, though, between this problem and the one faced by researchers building systems for doing legal reasoning; there, too, a problem exists in presenting a convincing argument for winning one's case (for example, the TAXMAN project) (McCarty and Stridharan, 1981). However, the financial marketing domain contrasts with the legal reasoning domain in that one usually cannot make use of precedents because they are rarely available. For an automated financial marketing problem solver to generate

Reprinted with permission from *AI Magazine*, vol. 7, no. 5, Winter 1986, 71-79.

such convincing arguments, it is crucial to accurately determine what concerns a potential customer and then to use these concerns in the plan and justification generation.

The FAME project was begun in early 1985. The first several months were spent familiarizing ourselves with the domain, characterizing the types of problem solving in this domain, and identifying the different areas requiring expertise. While undergoing this educational process, an initial prototype system was built as a means for communicating to our potential user community the flavor of a knowledge-based approach for solving their problems. The tools used in this effort were chosen on the basis of our group's recent extensive experience in building YES/MVS (Griesmer et al., 1984; Ennis et al., 1986). The initial prototype system consists of over 700 OPS5 rules, about 40 Lisp/VM functions, and the IBM graphical data display manager (GDDM) graphics interface. The system makes full use of the color graphics capability of an IBM 3279 terminal, using a domain-independent window-management package especially developed for use by OPS5 programs.

Financial Marketing: A Vehicle for AI Application and Research

A twofold problem, which seems to require significant expertise, exists for a marketing representative:

- The preparation of a recommendation to a customer of a capacity solution that meets the customer's computing requirements over a period of time and
- A financial solution which outlines a plan for acquiring this capacity under financial terms and conditions that best address the customer's needs and concerns.

In addition, the marketing representative must be able to justify the proposal.

For the sake of illustration, we outline a typical marketing situation—a corporation whose installed processing power will fall short of its estimated growth requirement at a certain time. The corporation management might, therefore, seek solutions to this problem from marketing representatives. A data processing executive might request proposals and forward reasonable recommendations to a financial executive who might make the final decision. The financial executive's concerns, such as the company's outlook on its earnings-per-share ratio, might differ from the data processing executive's budgetary concerns. Given this type of information, the problem is to come up with a solution that can be justified and sold to personalities with diverse criteria and concerns. Considerable expertise lies in generating a set of reasonable plans and then proposing and defending the one that is best based on the criteria and concerns of the customer.

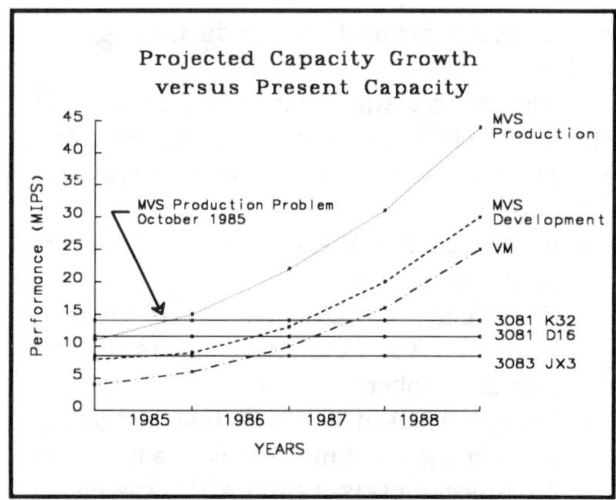

Figure 1. TNW Capacity growth plan. [1]

An Example

As an example, assume that the imaginary TNW Corporation's data processing center has three IBM mainframe processors: a 3081 D16 running MVS development applications, a 3081 K32 running MVS production applications, and a 3083 JX3 running VM interactive applications.

The current date is 1 July 1985. The compound growth rates in processing power requirements through the end of 1988 have been estimated to be 40% for MVS production, 40% for MVS development, and 55% for VM. Figure 1 shows these processing requirements over a four-year period relative to the current install base. The TNW vice-president in charge of information systems, having realized that his current install base will soon run out of power, has requested his marketing representative develop a capacity solution which can be implemented using an attractive financing plan. The VP's key concern is budget; he is committed to spending no more than $4 million on CPU expenditures in 1985. Although his 1986 CPU budgetary expenses have yet to be decided, the 1985 figure and the required growth in computing are fair

[1] *Estimates of processor power are for illustrative purposes only.*

indicators of what his future budgetary figures will be.

Also, let us assume that a competitive situation exists; a third-party leasing company by the name of ABC Leasing has proposed the following four-part solution:

- Install a used 3081 K32 from ABC Leasing on 20 October 1985;
- Remove the 3081 D16 that is currently on lease from ABC Leasing as soon as possible after 20 October;
- Replace the used 3081 K32 (installed on 20 October 1985) in June 1986 with a new 3090 200 processor leased from ABC Leasing at a good rate; and
- Move all MVS production work to the 3090 at that time (June 1986), and move MVS development to the 3081 K32 leased from XYZ Leasing when ABC's 3081 D16 is removed.

In addition to solving the computing needs problem, the marketing representative might also want to develop a financing plan which is better than that offered by the competition. In this way, the marketing representative is addressing the total financial marketing problem faced by the customer and can provide an integrated solution.

Financial marketing problems such as in the TNW case are knowledge intensive. A situation needs to be assessed using a complex collection of case-specific data points in conjunction with databases containing information on product offerings. A situation is specified by information on the customer install base, his projected growth in computing needs, his financial and organizational profile, and the marketing representative's proposed solutions (if any). The offerings database might contain information on a wide variety of subjects, ranging from specific data on processor models and options and their costs to terms and conditions of the various financing options available for acquiring such products. This large amount of situation-specific knowledge in turn requires employing significant problem-solving expertise.

Two major knowledge-intensive tasks have been identified: generating suitable capacity solutions for a customer and generating financially attractive plans for the acquisition of these capacity solutions. In general, a *capacity solution* can be defined as a series of discrete times, each associated with a set of actions (for example, upgrades, replacements, additions, and removals of processors). Each action-time pair needs to be associated with a financing method such that the overall financing plan for a capacity solution is the most attractive possible, both analytically and qualitatively. The goal is to tailor a financially attractive proposal that will solve the customer's computing growth requirement and to generate a convincing argument which will enable the "selling" of this action to the customer.

The balancing of the capacity solution with the financial-acquisition solution is one of the key issues involving expertise. It is because of these two competing goals that the financial marketing problem is not merely one of optimization. The expert in this domain must produce effective arguments for a balance of these competing goals.

Capacity Planning

Given a large customer's install base and the projected growth in processing power requirements, it is possible to generate a vast number of possible capacity solutions based on the availability of a very wide range of processors and their various models and upgrade options. Exhaustive generation of these solutions can be computationally expensive. The search space can be efficiently pruned using heuristics that retain only a moderate number of the best solutions for further financial analysis. A sample of these heuristics follows: avoid upgrading old technology, avoid upgrading processors that are nearing their lease expiration, and consider balancing processor work loads.

Acquisition Method

After arriving at a set of computing solutions to the problem, reasonable financing plans for each of the computing solutions must be determined. Here, too, a computational problem can exist. The vast number of financing options that are available, if applied to each of the computing solutions and their subsolutions (for example, if a computing solution consists of carrying out actions on three processors, then each of these actions can be performed using different financing plans), can result in a very large set of financing plans. Because these plans need to be financially analyzed to examine their impact on the tax and accounting books of the customer, it is prudent to keep the size of this plan set small. Here, too, a number of criteria based on the customer's financial and organizational profile can be used to constrain the number of financing plans generated. A sample of these heuristics follows: If the customer has any identifiable historical trends, he will probably continue following them (for example, always lease short-term solutions and purchase long-term solutions). The customer will probably prefer consistent financing plans for each of the subcomponents of a computing solution.

It is worth noting here that these heuristics also tend to keep the number of generated financing plans down to a moderate number. The major drawback of using heuristics for constraining and pruning the search space is there is no guarantee that you won't overlook a better solution for the specific problem at hand. This shortcoming can be partially compensated in an interactive system by allowing the user the ability to augment a solution set each time this technique is used.

Financial Analysis and Selection

We now have a set of complete solutions (that is, a series of capacity solutions, each associated with one or more acquisition methods). Prior to performing the financial analysis, the monthly cash streams the customer will have to bear over the useful life of the capacity solution are calculated for each capacity-acquisition pair. Cash streams are generated using information in the database on the various purchase and lease rate terms and conditions. Financial analysis is then performed for each of these plans. The analysis indicates how each of these plans will affect the customer's budget, tax books, and profit-and-loss books. The cash stream generation and financial-analysis methods used are fairly conventional accounting methods approved by the Internal Revenue Service (IRS) and the Financial Accounting Standards Board (FASB).

Using numbers from the financial analysis, selections, which are based on two criteria, can be made of the preferred solutions: financial considerations and qualitative considerations. *Financial considerations* dictate that the financing plan which is best from the pure finance point of view should be selected. *Qualitative considerations* go beyond the pure dollar consideration. For example, the customer's business interests might require the selection of a plan even if it is not the most attractive financially. Very often, financial and qualitative considerations can result in the selection of two different plans. The marketing representative thus needs convincing arguments for both, depending upon the person to whom the arguments are addressed as well as the person who ultimately makes the acquisition decision. A sample of these selection heuristics follows: The financial example is, "Propose the solution that has the best discounted after-tax cash flow if the customer contact point is a financial executive who utilizes discounting and is concerned with his cash flow." The qualitative example is, "Propose a lease solution if the key decision maker views his business as cash poor, with a low effective tax rate and a high borrowing rate."

These selections need to be presented in the form of convincing financial arguments, and a system that generates such arguments should be able to conduct a dialogue on the contents of the argument. The user might wish to see further explanation on a point or might require help on how to clarify some concerns. The system should be aware of the user's intentions in order to minimize actions required on the user's part and to maximize the utilization of the limited bandwidth (sales call) available for conducting this explanation process.

Now that we have discussed the domain in general, we describe the implementation of an initial prototype system. In this system, there is special emphasis on a mixed mode of interaction in which the user and the system cooperatively solve problems under the user's control, with guiding and focusing strategies provided by the system. This interactive operation mode, which allows the user complete control over the direction of problem solving but able to draw upon the system's expertise for guidance and planning, has successfully been used before in systems such as expert log analysis system (ELAS) (Apté and Weiss, 1985) and VLSI expert editor (VEXED) (Mitchell, Steinberg, and Schulman, 1985).

Initial Prototype System

The initial prototype system was written as a set of relatively independent OPS5 rule groups. Each rule group contains its own computational expertise and communicates with the other groups through a set of protocols. This grouping of the rules was originally intended to divide the system into small easily maintained subsystems, but as we point out, this grouping led to computational bottlenecks.

In the simplest case, communication between rule groups is accomplished by simply sharing internal memory. For other communication, a rule group generates the data expected by the next group and then creates that group's task, thereby transferring control. For example, access to the product-offering database (products, pricing, and lease rates) is achieved for each routine by creating an incomplete product working memory element:

```
(make db:product
↑product        3083
↑model          JX3)
```

The database rules detect that the prices are missing and fill in the rest of the data. The rules requiring pricing information for the 3083 JX3 do not fire until after the database query on that product is completed successfully.

```
(db:product
↑product        3083
    ; Product number
↑model          JX3
    ; Model/FEA number
↑description    Processor Unit
    ; Description
↑purchase       1975000
    ; Purchase price
↑rental         128310
    ; Monthly rental
↑lease          102650
    ; Monthly lease
↑maintenance    3695
    ; Monthly maintenance
. . .)[2]
```

Alternatively, control can explicitly be passed when the necessary calculations have completed. The following is a rule that passes control from the capacity-analysis rule group to the explanation rule group:

```
(p cp:advance-goal-to-explain
  (dp:waiting ↑status <status>)
    ; If the computing
{<goal>
    ; alternatives have
(cp:goal
    ; all been
↑type calculate)}
    ; generated,
→
(modify <goal>
    ; then proceed with
↑type explain)
    ;   the explanation by
(make xs:start
    ;   setting explanation
↑goal start
    ;   goal. When done,
↑title Computing-Alternatives
    ;   the goal will be
↑return-to-caller explained))
    ;   modified to explained.
```

Figure 2 shows the major rule groups in the initial prototype system along with typical control flow paths.

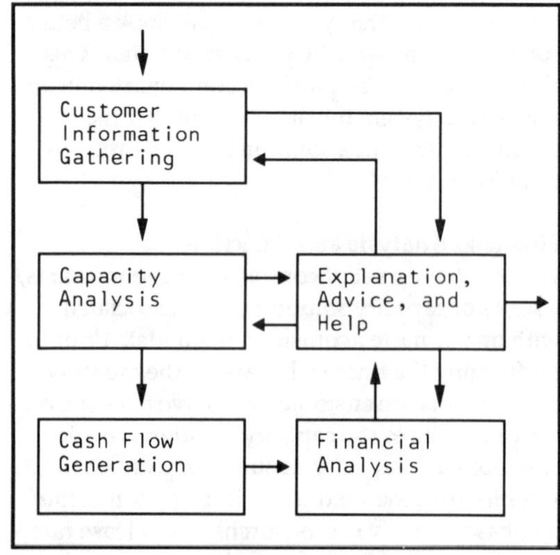

Figure 2. Rule groupings with typical control flow.

The *customer information gathering* rules query the user or database to obtain information about the customer company, its computing needs, and its financial status. This information is then given to the *capacity-analysis* rules that generate all reasonable computing alternatives for the given compound growth rate in computer capacity. This information is then given to the *explanation generation* rules that allow the user to verify, add to, or modify the computing alternatives to be considered in further analysis. Next, the *cash flow generation* rules translate each computing alternative into the monthly cost of that computing environment. This information is then fed to the *financial analysis* rules that provide a ranking of the alternatives. The *explanation generation* rules then use the information provided by the previous rule groups to provide explanations, justifications, and arguments for and against computing and financial

[2] *Prices shown are merely for illustrative purposes and might not reflect actual pricing.*

alternatives. The next subsections describe each rule group in greater detail.

Customer Information Gathering

The first step in analyzing the current situation is the user input of relevant customer information. The system attempts to gather the following types of information: customer identification, analysis period, current install base, capacity planning, customer history, and current financial information.

Typically, the system is able to access either common databases (for example, the sales manual, corporate financial profiles, and current install base information) or databases generated from previous runs of the system to fill in most of the over 40 categories of customer information used in the initial prototype system. Therefore, a typical session requires only the identification of the customer, the period of time for this situation analysis, any recent changes to the customer information, and special constraints or restrictions for this analysis.

The rule group responsible for obtaining customer information is automatically invoked whenever the next stage of the analysis requires some input information that is not available within the system resources. Thus, the user can command the system to proceed with an analysis without first worrying whether the necessary information has been entered.

Capacity Analysis

The next step in a typical situation analysis is the generation of the possible computing options to fit the customer's capacity requirements and growth plan. Figure 3 shows the major steps in this rule group. The computing options rule group (together with the explanation rule group) provides the user with the capability of specifying as much or as little of the computing alternatives as desired. The system then critiques (by way of a one-line message) each user input alternative and generates all "reasonable" unspecified parts of the computing plan. The "reasonableness" criteria are encoded as rules and, hence, are quite flexible. Refer to the Capacity Planning subsection for three examples of such criteria.

For example, the user might provide the input that the 3083 JX3 is to be retained. The system critiques this information and indicates that the JX3 will lack the necessary processing power for its application (VM) on December 1985. However, this input is allowed, and the system proceeds with the analysis. Then the system generates all possible upgrades or replacements for the computers running the other two applications (MVS development and MVS production). The user can then further restrict the alternatives by eliminating some of those generated.

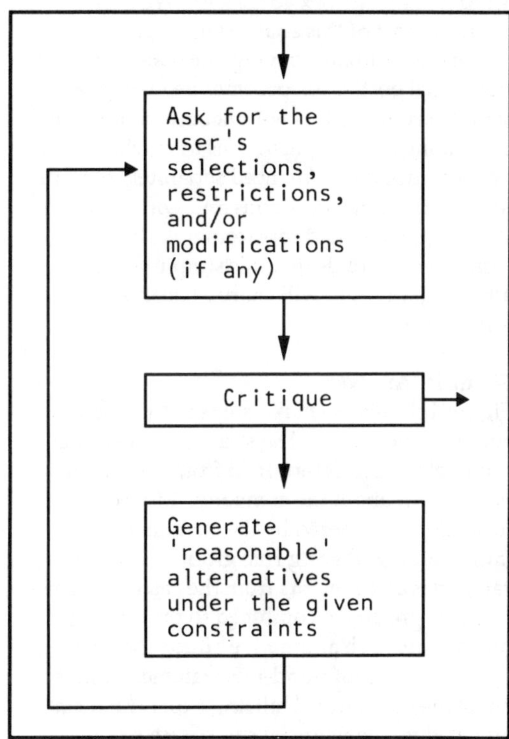

Figure 3. Capacity analysis.

The combination of automatically generated alternatives within user-specified constraints provides a powerful tool for the novice and expert user alike. If the user already knows what options are to be considered, then they merely need to be input. Otherwise, the system is capable of generating what it considers are reasonable alternatives.

Cash Flow Generation

One of the most computationally intensive parts of the initial prototype system is the rule group that calculates the total cost of computing for each computing and financing alternative. This rule group computes month by month the principal, interest, annuity, insurance, maintenance, property taxes, and so forth, where applicable. In addition, these rules ensure that all payment streams start and end on the same dates for each alternative. This rule provides for a fair financial comparison of the alternatives.

For the TNW case, the capacity analysis was able to heuristically prune the list of alternatives to four, which meant that to consider two financing options over a four-year analysis of each of the computers in each alternative required over 1,100 rule firings (2 x 48 x 3 x 4). We later recoded most of this analysis in Lisp.

As the domain coverage increases, this computational bottleneck becomes an even more serious problem. It is not uncommon for a large computing center to have tens of machines, with major components financed separately with different terms and conditions and with multiple viable upgrades and replacements. It has become obvious to us that this simple generate-and-test paradigm will shortly become intractable.

Financial Analysis

Figure 4 shows the major steps in the financial-analysis rule group. The strategic constraints for this analysis are determined from the information known about the company. Most of this information is gathered by the customer information gathering rule group. Next, the categories of payments from the cash flow generator rule group are combined to produce a picture of how each alternative affects the budget, the taxes, the profit-and-loss statement, and so on, of the company. Utilizing expert financial knowledge, the financial rule group strictly ranks each alternative financially (that is, which alternative is the least expensive) and qualitatively (that is, business judgment by the customer and the marketing representative). These rankings are purely heuristic and reflect our experts' opinions of successful marketing practices. The heuristic nature of the advice offered by this rule group demands the support of explanation capabilities in order to provide a useful tool.

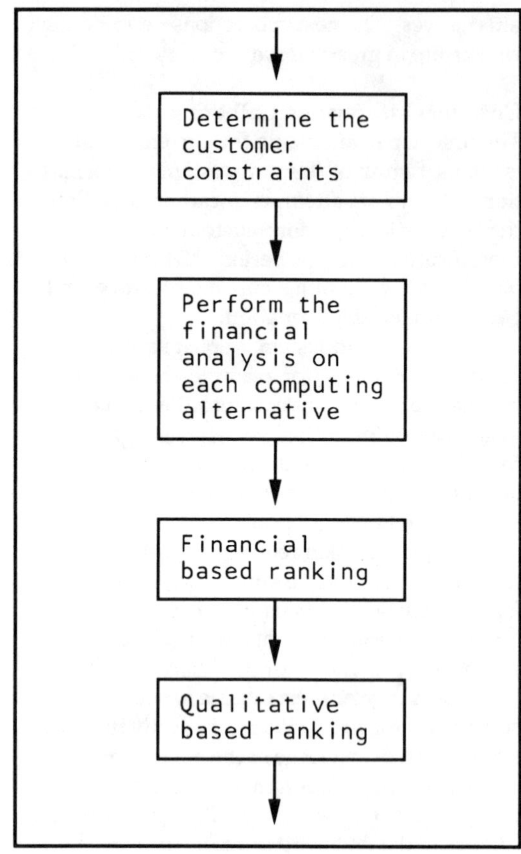

Figure 4. Financial analysis.

Explanation, Advice, and Help

The explanation rule group assumes control of the session after each major step in the analysis. The default output gives a general explanation of the current state of the analysis, prompts for one of several options on how to proceed further with the analysis, and provides advice on the use of these options. The explanation rule group contains user-modeling and session-monitoring capabilities to anticipate the user's intentions, which enables the group to provide defaults for the user. In addition to the screen generation and control rules, the explanation rule group consists of rules for handling user intention, controlling advice, and controlling help.

The user intention handling rules use a set of explanation templates linked in a network by the possible queries on each template. The explanation templates are filled using information left in working memory by the rules that calculated the information being explained. For instance, the generation of computing alternatives includes the critiquing of alternatives that won't be considered in later calculations. This critique is then available in the explanation system so that the user can ask why a particular computing alternative wasn't considered.

The user can question any part of the explanation by merely pointing to its representation on the screen. The interpretation of that questioning is a context-dependent traversal of the explanation network to a new template. This template is then appropriately filled and displayed. In other words, the system is able to estimate the user's intention based on the session history and the part of the screen pointed to. The system can do this because we were able to anticipate potential queries from the user for further information. This user modeling works well for our domain because we were able to effectively determine *a priori* the typical questions.

The rules that control advice use the explanation network to guide the user to the next recommended action: The cursor is placed on the screen at the point of the explanation that (according to our studies) would typically be probed next. The rules that control help also use the explanation network to provide a small pop-up window at the bottom of the screen to indicate what operations might be desirable in addition to what is recommended by the current cursor position.

Each screen displayed by the explanation rule group is represented internally as one OPS5 working memory element. The attribute-value pairs contain information about the various slots in the explanation template. When a screen is being prepared for display, all appropriate slots in the working memory element for that screen are filled by rules which collect information left in working memory by the problem-solver rules. The screen is then displayed, and the user is given the opportunity to place the cursor over any of the filled-in items in the template. When the ENTER key is pressed, the cursor position is read, and the information is placed in the working memory element for that screen. Rules from the explanation rule group then interpret the cursor position as an indication that the user is requesting more information on the item which was under the cursor.

Associated with each selectable item on an explanation template is an ordered collection of pointers to other explanation templates. In other words, each selectable item on the screen points to all of the available screens which could possibly be used to further explain that item. The ordering of the other explanation templates is context dependent. This ordering enables the system to provide one explanation (the most commonly asked for) the first time an item is selected and at a later time provide another explanation. Thus, each time the user places the cursor on an item a different explanation is possible.

```
—Recommendation—
We recommend that on May 1986, TNW take the following action:
upgrade the 3081 K32 to a 3084 Q64 for MVS-PRODUCTION
and finance it using PURCHASE.

The Cumulative Cash Flow After Tax over 48 months resulting from
the above recommendation is $10,000,000, which is the minimum
among possible alternatives.  It is also the best alternative with
respect to Cumulative P&L Impact.

The Cumulative Cash Flow After Tax is $123,400
less than that for the next best alternative, which is to
upgrade the 3081 K32 to a 3084 Q64 for MVS-PRODUCTION on May 1986
and finance it using IBM-LEASE.

→ Go to Financial Analysis
→ Go to next screen.

This recommendation is based on purely financial consideration.
—Advice—
Though the above recommendation seems appropriate for TNW
from a financial point of view, you may wish to take into account
a qualitative consideration.  Press Enter to see the next screen.
Press PF3 to quit, PF2 for help.

Initially the cursor is located on → Go to next screen.
```

Figure 5. An example of the initial screen of explanation.

We provide two examples of the explanation capability. Figure 5 shows a "Recommendation" screen that indicates a recommendation derived as the result of a capacity analysis and a financial analysis.

At this point, the user can press the ENTER key to go to the next screen. In this case, a screen entitled "Recommendation with qualitative consideration" is displayed. Alternatively, the user can position the cursor at any point in the text and press ENTER to provide a detailed explanation based on the particular text. Several areas in the text can be colored to emphasize their importance. For example, if the cursor is placed on the date "May 1986," before pressing ENTER, a screen entitled "Date for Action to be taken" is shown, overlaying the previous screen in the telescoping fashion shown in Figure 6.

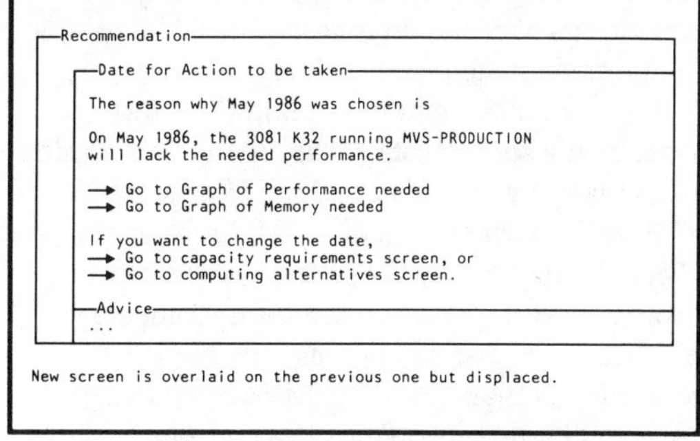

```
—Recommendation—
  —Date for Action to be taken—
  The reason why May 1986 was chosen is

  On May 1986, the 3081 K32 running MVS-PRODUCTION
  will lack the needed performance.

  → Go to Graph of Performance needed
  → Go to Graph of Memory needed

  If you want to change the date,
  → Go to capacity requirements screen, or
  → Go to computing alternatives screen.
  —Advice—
  ...

New screen is overlaid on the previous one but displaced.
```

Figure 6. Telescopic screens.

This explanation facility was quite effective for our initial prototype system because the user was not required to know very much about the domain (every screen includes a pop-up help window), a standard analysis path is always available to the user (the next selection is under the cursor by default), and typing is kept to a minimum. However, the user is always in control of the session because the system is merely providing defaults. It remains to be seen if such a simple facility can be as effective when the domain coverage and complexity increase.

Current Implementation
The initial prototype system was written in OPS5, which in turn was written in Lisp/VM. The system mainly consists of OPS5 rules with supporting Lisp functions for efficient database manipulation, graphics handling, and some numerical calculations. All of the system's control and inference processes are encoded in rules. This makes the system quite flexible. The following is a breakdown of the rule groups:

Number of Rules	Description
7	Top Level Interface and Control
50	Graphic Display Handler and Window Manager
40	System Documentation
16	Database Interface (e.g., sales manual)
120	Financial Analysis
147	Customer Information Gathering
40	Capacity Analysis
18	Cash Flow Generation
337	Explanation, Advice, and Help
775	**Total number of rules**

On the average, there are 4 condition elements (if clauses) in each rule, about 3.5 attributes in each condition element, and 4 action elements (then clauses) in each rule. The TNW scenario analysis requires approximately 3,000 rule firings and uses in excess of 11,000 working memory elements.

The financial marketing initial prototype system rule set consists of slightly more complex rules than our group's previous effort, YES/MVS (Griesmer et al., 1984; Ennis et al., 1986). Unlike YES/MVS, the FAME initial prototype system rules often set up long complex chains of goals requiring substantial numeric calculations. YES/MVS consisted of rules to diagnose problems in a computer center and to perform remedial actions. Thus, many of the rules classified problems into a known set for which there was a fixed set of remedies. The financial marketing initial prototype system, however, consists of rules to generate many possible alternatives (computing and financial) and to provide reasonable explanations for these alternatives. Also, the interactive explanation capability accounts for a substantial portion of the rule set.

Ongoing Research
Using the experience gained in our initial prototyping effort, we are currently developing new representations and algorithms for a complete restructuring of our system. We are attempting to generalize from our early efforts to build a financial marketing knowledge-based consultant for the financial marketing domain in order to provide a set of generally useful mechanisms for similar domains.

Several of the rule groups involved in the generate-and-test paradigm pose a serious computational bottleneck. The use of clever heuristics to prune the search space will probably have limited usefulness with the present representation scheme. We are currently attempting to utilize structured inheritance networks (Mays and Balzac, 1986) to represent the shared structures of the domain, which are so often found during the development of the initial prototype system. The inheritance mechanisms will allow us to share computation by doing computation on abstract aggregate objects rather than on each instance.

The financial calculations performed in the initial prototype system were spread throughout the rules. This style produces a substantial rule maintenance problem. The dynamic nature of the financial world will constantly force changes in the way financial calculations and their results are made and reported. We have begun work on the fundamental modeling of financial equations (Apté and Hong, 1986) so that the system will have one consistent representation from which the various uses can be derived.

The initial prototype system uses a relatively fixed computational sequence. Each rule group works relatively independently on its task. However, we have found that financial marketing experts opportunistically mix the solution of aspects of the capacity-planning and financial-acquisition problems. This mixing is usually driven by customer constraints. We are currently evaluating blackboard models to allow such opportunistic problem-solving planning (Hayes-Roth 1985).

Summary

The initial prototype system solves a small subset of the problems in the financial marketing domain but not in as much detail and depth as the system currently being developed to replace it. At present, the initial prototype's domain coverage is somewhat spotty and severely limited. Currently, it only addresses problems of a selected subset of large mainframe processors, their upgrades, and replacements and can only compute the financial impact of straight lease and outright purchase acquisition methods. Even though severely limited in its scope, the initial prototype system generated an enthusiastic response from our marketing organizations. The domain spectrum will be broadened as we introduce more product lines, such as disk drives, terminals, and other processor and peripheral families, as well as other financing options. Modeling of situations will also become comprehensive and detailed as more assessment data are introduced.

The financial marketing application has revealed itself to be a rich vehicle for working on a number of interesting open problems in AI and expert systems, and the completeness and usefulness of the final system will be impacted significantly by the research in strategy modeling, representation and control in planning, knowledge acquisition, and explanation generation and the development of models of man-machine interaction and of intelligent interfaces to existing analytical tools and databases. The next version of the FAME system, based on the principles and methodologies developed after the initial prototyping effort, will be tested on real cases. Such a productivity tool could have considerable impact on the ability of marketing representatives to market their products effectively in a rapidly changing business world.

References

Apté, C. V., and Hong, S. J. 1986. Using Qualitative Reasoning to Understand Financial Arithmetic. In Proceedings of the 1986 National Conference on Artificial Intelligence, 942-948. Menlo Park, Calif.: American Association for Artificial Intelligence.

Apté, C. V., and Weiss, S. M. 1985. An Approach to Expert Control of Interactive Software Systems. *IEEE Transactions on Pattern Analysis and Machine Intelligence* 7(5): 586-591.

Ennis, R. L.; Griesmer, J. H.; Hong, S. J.; Karnaugh, M.; Kastner, J. K.; Klein, D. A.; Milliken, K. R.; Schor, M. I.; and Van Woerkom, H. M. 1986. A Continuous Real-Time Expert System for Computer Operations. *IBM Journal of Research and Development* 30(1): 14-28.

Griesmer, J. H.; Hong, S. J.; Karnaugh, M.; Kastner, J. K.; Schor, M. I.; Ennis, R. L.; Klein, D. A.; Milliken, K. R.; and Van Woerkom, H. M. 1984. YES/MVS: A Continuous Real-Time Expert System. In Proceedings of the 1984 National Conference on Artificial Intelligence, 130-136. Menlo Park, Calif.: American Association for Artificial Intelligence.

Hayes-Roth, B. 1985. A Blackboard Architecture for Control. *Artificial Intelligence* 26: 251-321.

Lindsay, R.; Buchanan, B. G.; Feigenbaum, E. A.; and Lederberg, J. 1980. *Applications of Artificial Intelligence for Chemical Inference: The DENDRAL Project*. New York: McGraw-Hill.

Mays, E., and Balzac, S. R. 1986. Interactive Reclassification in Structured Inheritance Networks. Forthcoming.

Mitchell, T. M.; Steinberg, L. I.; and Shulman, J. S. 1985. A Knowledge-Based Approach to Design. *IEEE Transactions on Pattern Analysis and Machine Intelligence* 7(5): 502-510.

McCarty, L. T., and Sridharan, N. S. 1981. The Representation of an Evolving System of Legal Concepts II: Prototypes and Deformations, Technical Report, LRP-TR-11, Laboratory of Computer Science Research, Rutgers Univ.

Stefik, M. 1981. Planning with Constraints (MOLGEN: Part 1) and Planning and Meta-Planning (MOLGEN: Part 2), *Artificial Intelligence* 16(2): 111-139, 141-169.

On-Line Underwriter

Kent Urness

Expert systems have received a great deal of media attention in recent months, and insurance underwriting has been identified as one business function that can benefit from this technology. Expert systems generally are defined as computer software programs that capture the skills and knowledge of the most experienced managers and professionals from a given business. Once captured, this expertise can be made available through computer workstations to assist other professionals within the organization.

Last fall The St. Paul completed an 18-month joint development project with Syntelligence, Sunnyvale, Calif., by conducting the first test of a new system for computer-assisted underwriting called the Underwriting Advisor. This test was successful and confirmed the usability of the expert system, while highlighting certain areas where further development is required.

The Underwriting Advisor was designed to operate with a standard IBM mainframe that interfaces with many personal computer workstations on underwriters' desks. It supports commercial insurance underwriting by providing daily, risk-specific assistance to the commercial lines underwriter. It is not a scoring or screening system like those developed for other sectors of the insurance industry. Rather, it is an advisory system that helps guide and inform underwriters throughout the commercial risk evaluation process.

The system helps the underwriter to identify key concerns and factors that an expert underwriter would consider prior to making a particular judgment and to determine which current underwriting guidelines apply to the risk at hand. In contrast to conventional computer systems, the system requires little typing and no memorization of command words. A menu displays appropriate choices at each stage of risk evaluation, and a desktop "mouse" enables the underwriter to make entries and to issue commands by moving the on-screen pointer to a particular menu selection.

When our company's management determined that the potential benefits of an expert underwriting system warranted investment and research, we signed a joint development contract with the vendor and pulled together a team of half-a-dozen commercial property experts who met with the vendor's expert-system developers. Meanwhile, our data processing and field operations people worked with the system designers to devise the system's general screen functions and to determine how the system would operate in the mainframe environment.

Frankly, we were a bit skeptical at first. Could the experts all agree on a single definition of a fire and allied lines underwriting system? Would the result be both comprehensive enough to be useful, yet limited enough to be organized into a computerized form? Finally, could a computer program really be expected to assist a complex underwriting evaluation?

The results reported here are generally positive answers to these questions. Getting there required a team effort which often involved difficult negotiations to resolve disagreements.

We conducted our first test of the system in a home office underwriting group to assess the system's usability and to make any required adjustments before expanding the system to the field. We expected the test to uncover any programming bugs and problems in transferring expert-level underwriting knowledge to the software.

Our Manufacturers Output group was the home office property underwriting environment selected for the test. Besides being a classic environment for fire and allied lines underwriting,

Reprinted with permission from *Best's Review*, vol. 88, May 1987, 32-36.

this group included one of the experts who helped develop the system.

Test participants were given an initial two-day training session that covered both the required computer basics and in-depth training on the system's functions, capabilities and its knowledge base. During a six-week testing period, 45 risks of varying complexity were entered into the system and evaluated by four underwriters, one underwriting trainee and two underwriting assistants. Weekly review meetings allowed the participants and the development team to monitor progress and to resolve conflicts between the time-consuming testing process and the other work of the group.

Remaining in Control

Our test of the underwriting group's use of the system identified several areas of distinct success, some negative experiences requiring improvements to the system and two uncertainties that still need to be resolved. One important overall result was the unanimous agreement of the participants that the system did not force them to change their basic underwriting thought processes. Rather, it provided them with assistance in handling their professional underwriting responsibilities.

By the end of the test period, those underwriters who participated also agreed that the system would not replace them in any way or make any underwriting decisions for them. A most important consideration from management's standpoint was that there was no visible tendency among the participants to let the system think for them. The underwriters quickly learned to use the system's information and advice as appropriate, and to replace the system's recommendations with their own professional judgments when necessary, adding typed footnotes for explanation.

A Few Shortcomings

During testing, several shortcomings were discovered. For example, we found that the format of certain inspection reports complicated the entry of data into the system. This was frustrating for the users, particularly the underwriting assistants who were assigned the task of transferring the data manually.

Also, in a few specific areas of analysis, the system's intermediate-level evaluations were found to be consistently different from the professional evaluations of senior underwriters using the system. However, when we began development, we anticipated a need for an ongoing process of system adaptation, and this system's ability to adapt is one of its strengths.

We also were concerned that we did not have time before this test to develop a capability to help users check the system's logic. This capability would help underwriters to determine whether risk-specific conditions signal a special case in which the underwriter's judgment must take precedence over the system's evaluations.

Two main uncertainties remain after our first test. The first is how efficient the system will be in processing new business, where a considerable amount of information must be entered at each stage of the underwriting evaluation. Underwriting assistants and underwriters spent a great deal of time providing the system with data that normally would be entered into our existing rating/coding system, or which already is resident in loss history and other systems.

The second remaining uncertainty is the system's projected impact on our IBM mainframe under field underwriting conditions and workloads. Although we need to do standard mainframe capacity planning to handle the load effectively, the test has not yet provided us with sufficient information on which to make reliable projections. Current projections regarding the system's impact on mainframe usage are higher than our goals.

One clearly positive result is that the system has demonstrated its value as a training tool for new underwriters and as a resource to improve the knowledge of experienced underwriters. Concerning the system's usability, one of our experienced underwriters reported a distinctly improved ability to underwrite unfamiliar geographical areas of the U.S., while an underwriting trainee with only six months of experience reported increased confidence, since using the system, that he was performing a complete underwriting analysis consistent with our company's standards. Another underwriter noted that since she is not a financial analyst, the system's guidance in assessing the insured from a financial standpoint is "worth its weight in gold" (especially the system's ability to calculate key financial ratios and comparative industry averages).

Breathing in Some Life

Other observations made by underwriters are that in contrast to the big commercial lines underwriting manuals kept on each desk, the system helps to "bring alive" underwriting guidelines by automatically displaying them on the screen where appropriate. Moreover, the distribution of changes to the guidelines will be speedier and more effective than the current paper-based methods. The system also helps to handle some of the underwriting dirty work, such as insurance-to-value calculations and reinsurance line setting. Finally, it was reported that virtually all users quickly replaced their fears of computers with an eagerness to use both this system and other applications, such as the central computer file of loss information.

Feedback from test participants concerning improvements in renewal processing and transferring of accounts is limited, since this was not actually experienced during the test. The following report, therefore, actually is a projection by the underwriters as to the likely result of system use in the field:

> In reference to renewals in particular, too much of the underwriter's time currently is spent finding the right information in the paper file and interpreting previous actions, especially those of another underwriter. The system will consolidate the information automatically in a single display, including typed (not handwritten) notes.

We expected to encounter negative experiences during the test, and we did. One of our findings it that not all of the system's evaluations are perfect—one reason why the underwriter remains firmly in control of the final evaluation, sometimes choosing to override the system's recommendations.

Other issues that need to be resolved are our need to rekey data, the confusion involved in filling out some inspection reports and the initial inefficiency of the inexperienced user. In order to not rekey data and to increase the system's efficiency, we are developing system interfaces to substitute data transfer for much of the routine and repetitive data entry. We also are reworking the format of inspection reports to make data entry less confusing.

The user's efficiency also will increase naturally as the level of familiarity with the system increases. Finally, it is worth noting that the first year's extra work to enter all risks into the system will pay off handsomely in the second year in faster and more effective renewal processing.

Those who participated in the test made the following observations about the system's value as a tool for training underwriters.

- One underwriting trainee appreciated the way in which the system provided useful information and assistance without ever making him hesitant to ask a "stupid" question. In fact, he received the added benefit of tapping into a knowledge base that was compiled from the entire organization, not just from a single underwriter.
- The experienced underwriter who worked closely with this trainee reported that since less time was spent answering routine questions (because they were handled effectively by the system), his discussions with the trainee focused more on this company's underwriting philosophy and included "what if" exercises.
- The underwriting assistants, who were charged with collecting and entering information, reported that the system helped them, too. Once they understood better the importance of the information they entered—as reflected in changes shown by the system's evaluations—they tended to use more initiative to locate important facts that were not immediately accessible.
- A senior underwriter who recently joined our company was pleased with the system's ability to provide on-demand clarification of why a question was being asked or what made a factor important. Because of this, she was able to learn how our underwriting culture is similar to and different from the one she just left.

Further testing is planned to resolve the efficiency and systems capacity questions we have identified. We expect to begin field tests in midyear. Also, we are developing general liability expertise for the system, and we are customizing the "standard" workers' compensation expertise provided by the vendor to include our own guidelines.

Finally, we are working to integrate all lines of business into a combined system that permits system-assisted underwriting of a multi-line risk as a single package. We expect that further refinement of the expert system and the planned field tests will continue to confirm the value of using an "on-line" underwriter.

Predicting Stock Market Behavior Through Rule Induction: An Application of the Learning-from-Example Approach

Helmut Braun and
John S. Chandler

Stock market analysts use many techniques in making their predictions, but most use some form of technical analysis such as trend analysis, cycle analysis, charting techniques, or one of many other types of historical data analysis. Each of these tools provides the analyst with information about how the market will move. However, the reliability of each tool is low. As a result, analysts must use many techniques and then integrate the evidence from all of them to make market predictions. Although many market analysts follow a rigorous program of data analysis and evaluation, they find it difficult to explain how individual data elements are combined to arrive at specific market predictions.

Constructing a model of stock market predictions is very difficult. The various technical analysis procedures produce a mix of categorical and quantitative measures. Some are specific financial ratios while others are general indicators of trends. Statistical techniques such as discriminant analysis and regression analysis can analyze the quantitative measures. Techniques such as logit and probit regression analysis can address the categorical measures. A market analyst, however, employs both in practice.

Each factor reviewed by the analyst is important. Some (e.g., Dow Jones indices) are used in every instance and therefore are of greater relative importance. No factor, however, has zero importance. In fact, the singular anomaly in an obscure measure may provide an analyst with the small edge to beat the competition—it may yield large financial rewards or prevent a major disaster. Modeling approaches that focus on factors that best explain the aggregate behavior of the market may be missing just those factors an analyst wants to see. Thus, a modeling approach that can integrate categorical and quantitative measures and can recognize the importance of individual measures is desirable.

One possible approach to analyzing and modeling the market prediction decision is a process called rule induction. This method is an artificial intelligence (AI)-based technique under the general rubric of learning-from-example (LFE) approaches. In this method, the rule-induction system is presented with examples of a decision (its inputs and outcomes) and attempts to induce a decision model. This is in contrast to learning-by-being-told methods that try to extract the decision model explicitly from the decision maker using extensive interviews.

The goal of this study is to investigate one market prediction situation through the rule-induction approach. A commercially available software system, ACLS (Analog Concept Learning System), is used to analyze past examples and formulate decision rules. Rules are generated to predict not only an expert market analyst's prediction of the market but also to predict the actual market's movement.

Reprinted with permission from *Decision Sciences*, vol. 18, Summer 1987, 415-429.

Validation exercises are performed to demonstrate the effectiveness of the rules generated. Analysis of the rules provides interesting insights into the process of applying an LFE approach to a business environment.

Overview of the LFE Approach

Several steps are involved in applying the LFE approach. First, a source of expertise must be identified (an expert or a panel of experts). Just what constitutes a "most appropriate source" still is debated in the AI literature. As with any AI-based system, the most crucial step in the process is identifying the decision to be analyzed; some decisions are too easily supported while others are too poorly defined. The expert must determine which decision to support and the appropriate set of outcomes for that decision. This may not be as easy as it sounds. Some decisions have a continuum of possible outcomes—such as those in medicine (alternative treatments) or in business (levels of profit)—and these must be quantized into a finite set of outcome ranges for most LFE approaches.

Once a decision environment has been chosen, the expert must identify the relevant cues. This is similar to what takes place in other AI-based approaches (e.g., production systems like MYCIN [17]). In these other approaches, however, the expert also must identify the relative importance of and interrelationships among these cues. Because decision makers, even experts, may not be able to reveal how they integrate evidence [8], AI-based approaches that depend on this task may have difficulty in building their systems. In the particular approach used in this study, these cues can be a mixture of quantitative and categorical variables.

The third step in an LFE approach is to establish the example data base (EXDB). The cues and outcomes identified above set up the structure of the EXDB. What remains is to fill in the EXDB with examples. These may come from many sources. If this decision has been made many times in the past, there may be documented cases to refer to. If there are "holes" in the set of examples, cases may be simulated by assigning values to the cues and then asking the expert what the probable outcomes would be. In either case, knowing the line of reasoning employed by the expert, implicitly or explicitly, is not required.

Previous Research

Rule induction techniques have been successful in many domains. One of the earliest techniques was Winston's [18, 19] system designed to teach toy block constructions. Lenat's [5] AM system developed proofs in elementary mathematics. A more practical application was the Meta-DENDRAL system's [1, 2] analysis of mass spectroscopy data.

Of particular note have been studies on the identification of soybean disease [6] and chess endgames [12, 16]. Michalski and Chilausky [6], using the program AQ11, induced a rule from a set of 290 examples and tested it on 340 cases. Their rule provided the correct diagnosis of soybean disease in every case; its first choice was correct 97.6 percent of the time. The rule then was compared to one generated from interviews with soybean experts. This second rule was tested on the same 340 cases and proved to be correct only 96.9 percent of the time; its first choice was correct only 71.8 percent of the time.

Experiments by Quinlan [12] and Shapiro and Niblett [16] showed that rule-induction methods can be very successful at inducing rules from very small subsets of examples from large data bases. Both experiments involved rules for chess endgames. A complete table lookup was available to verify the correctness of the induced rule. Quinlan showed that a decision rule induced from a set of examples that represented .07 percent of the entire population was 99.67 percent correct. When the example set was expanded to .36 percent of the population, the induced rule was 99.92 percent correct. These results were confirmed by Shapiro and Niblett. Using ACLS, they induced rules using .2 percent of their data base and found these rules to be over 99 percent correct. O'Rorke [10] compared the rule-induction methodologies of AQ11 and ACLS on several criteria but determined no clear advantage of one over the other.

Application of the LFE Approach

The Mechanics of ACLS

ACLS was used in this research as the vehicle for rule induction. The program was written by Paterson, Blake, and Shapiro under the direction of Michie (see [11] for details). It was developed from Quinlan's ID3 (Iterative Dichotomizer 3) program [12, 13] which in turn was developed from Hunt, Martin, and Stone's [4] original work on CLS (Concept Learning System). The induction algorithm of ACLS creates a decision tree that partitions the examples in the EXDB with respect to combinations of cue values. The method for determining the specific branches in the decision tree is based on information theory. Details of the algorithm and an example are given in the Appendix.

Selection and Description of an Expert

This study used a single expert as its source of expertise. The expert was an investment analyst from a medium-sized midwestern city.[1] He owned his own investment firm and had been analyzing the stock market for a period of 12 years prior to this study. For three years prior to this study he had been writing a newsletter in which he gave biweekly recommendations on the stock market. The performance of his recommended stocks was very good over this period (1979 to 1982). Average annual returns exceeded 40 percent for the overall period with returns for 1982 at 41.8 percent. Although his newsletter was not at the top of those ranked by *Barrons*, it was in the upper quartile.

In our initial meeting with the expert the nature of the project and the information that would be required were discussed. The expert was skeptical of computer-based systems. His only previous involvement with computers had been for graphing purposes and the results had been poor. He was not favorably impressed with computers in general. However, he was willing to discuss the details of the methods he used to make his predictions.

Most of the techniques used by the expert would be considered technical analysis. These included using trends and various other charting techniques to determine future market trends. Economic and political factors were considered, but not in any formal manner. The expert's primary tools were charts and graphs of various data for past periods. Some of these had been developed by the expert himself; others were from other analysts such as Joseph Granville, Stan Weinstein, and Robert Farrell.

Definition of Cues and EXDB

The expert explained that the stock market is a complex system with many subsystems operating simultaneously. There are many cycles in the market and some cues work well in the prediction of certain cycles but not well for others. According to the expert, three types of cycles could be selected for study, based on fluctuations in the Dow Jones industrial average (DJI). These were small fluctuations (<10 percent change in DJI), intermediate fluctuations (10 percent-20 percent change in DJI), or large fluctuations (>20 percent change in DJI). We decided to study intermediate fluctuations in the DJI because these probably were the ones most traders used in timing their buy and sell decisions. The DJI, the most commonly quoted indicator of market activity, was used as a reference point in this study.

At the initial meeting with the expert the tools and cues used in making a forecast of market behavior were discussed. A list of these is shown in Table 1. From this initial list of approximately 50 variables, a final list of 20 was selected to be used in the induction of prediction rules by ACLS. We reduced the initial list for several reasons. Some of the cues were not relevant to the intermediate market. Others were described insufficiently by the expert as useful signals of market movement. Several were eliminated because of lack of data. Table 1 indicates these reductions and identifies those cues used to build rules. It should be noted that the expert could use all these cues in making his own predictions.

To construct the example data base a specific time period was determined. Initially this time period was from 20 March 1981 to 24 September 1982. Later it was extended to 9 April 1983 to produce a larger EXDB. Data at closing time on Friday for each of the 108 weeks were accumulated.[2] Most of the data were collected from *Wall Street Journal* microfiche by one of the authors. Some of the cues were interpretations of trend-charting techniques. These presented special problems for the authors in drawing and in interpreting the trend lines. More skill is required to draw the trend lines than the authors could develop. Procedures for interpreting these charts after the lines had been drawn, however, were stated explicitly and were followed easily. Thus, for this study, the expert drew the trend lines; to avoid bias in interpretation, the authors applied the formal procedures for evaluation.

1. Put-call ratio, Chicago Board of Options Exchange (PCCBOE)[a]
2. Put-call ratio, American Options Exchange (PCAMEX)[a]
3. Granville Cumulative Climax Indicator (GCCI), nonconfirmation cumulative climax[c]
4. GCCI, retrogress (GRANRET)[a]
5. GCCI, trend (GRANTRN)[a]
6. Weinstein Last-Hour Activity, volume NYSE index nonconfirmation[c]
7. Weinstein Last-Hour Activity, volume NYSE index trend[c]
8. Weinstein Last-Hour Activity, price DJI nonconfirmation[c]
9. Weinstein Last-Hour Activity, price DJI trend[c]
10. Dow Jones moving average, 10-day cycle (DJI10)[a]
11. Dow Jones moving average, 30-day cycle (DJI30)[a]
12. Dow Jones moving average, conjointly (when DJI10=DJI30)[b]
13. On-balance volume DJI, trend (OBVDOW)[a]
14. On-balance volume DJI, nonconfirmation[c]
15. Cash of DJI, trend (CASHDOW)[a]
16. Cash of DJI, nonconfirmation (NETCDOW)[a]
17. Specialist short sales, ratio vs. odd-lot sales (SSOLS)[a]
18. Specialist short sales, 4-week moving vs. total shorts (SSTS)[a]
19. Market pressure index, 1-day moving average (MPI)[a]
20. Intensity DJI, trend (expert's trend model)[b]
21. Intensity DJI, nonconfirmation (expert's trend model)[b]
22. Dow theory, compare transportation to industrials[b]
23. Dow theory, over-bought over-sold oscillator (OBOSOS)[a]
24. NYSE composite index, trend and field trend (NYSECI)[a]
25. NYSE composite index, nonconfirmation vs. DJI price index[c]
26. Dow Jones Industrial, trend and field trend (DJIFT)[a]
27. Dow Jones Transportation, trends and field trend (DJTT)[a]
28. Dow Jones Transportation, trend breaks (DJTTB)[a]
29. S&P front spread, trend[c]
30. S&P front spread, nonconfirmation[c]
31. Cash of DJI Weekly, trend[b]
32. Cash of DJI Weekly, nonconfirmation[b]
33. Dow Jones figure point objective, 5 points[c]
34. Dow Jones figure point objective, 10 points[c]
35. Optimism-pessimism index, trend[c]
36. Optimism-pessimism index, nonconfirmation[c]
37. Optimism-pessimism index, 10-point figure chart[c]
38. Optimism-pessimism index, 25-point figure chart[c]
39. Wycoff Wave, trend (WWTRN)[a]
40. Wycoff Wave, nonconfirmation (WWREV)[a]
41. Trend barometer, momentum[b]
42. Trend barometer, force[b]
43. Trend barometer, technometer[b]
44. Ratio of ratios, trend of 6-day ratio[b]
45. Ratio of ratios, value of 6-day ratio (RATRAT)[a]
46. Ratio of ratios, trend of 10-day ratio[b]
47. Ratio of ratios, value of 10-day ratio[b]

[a]Variable used as cue to develop rule
[b]Variable primarily for long-term fluctuations
[c]Unable to use because of insufficient data

Table 1. List of potential cues.

Definition of Outcomes

The expert's weekly newsletter contained recommendations, concerning the market as a whole and particular stocks, for specific types of investors (conservative, intermediate, and aggressive). Conservative investors keep their holdings in cash until a long-term bull market is forecast. They never sell stocks short and take advantage of only about one-half of the movement predictions (i.e., those for a bull market).

We therefore decided to study only those recommendations made for intermediate and aggressive investors. Data also were collected from a call-in service available to investors during weeks when no newsletter was published.

Three types of outcomes (predictions by the expert) were used to categorize these weekly recommendations: bullish (forecasting an upward trend), bearish (forecasting a downward trend), and neutral (indicating that either call was too risky). These predictions were interpreted for each of the 108 weeks in the EXDB. Limiting the number of outcomes to three is a simplifying assumption, but may be realistic in that more-accurate calls are correct considerably less often. Data also were collected on the actual movements of the market for each of the 108 weeks. Only the outcomes bullish and bearish applied here. Thus, essentially there were two EXDBs. Both had the same values for the 20 selected cues for each of the 108 weeks, but one had the expert's predictions for each week as the outcomes while the other had actual market movements for each week as the outcomes.

Phase I—Initial Pilot Results

In phase 1 of this study, we used an initial data base of 80 examples of our expert's predictions dating from 20 March 1981 to 24 September 1982. The first test split the examples into two groups of 40 on a random basis. One group was used to induce a rule using ALCS; the other was used to test the induced rule. The induction produced a 29-node rule that used 10 cues from the data base. This rule was then applied to the remaining 40 examples, and the degree of consensus between rule-generated predictions and actual predictions was compared. The rule correctly matched the predictions of our expert in 23 of 40 cases (a hit rate of 57.5 percent).

In an effort to improve these results, the number of examples used to construct the rule was increased to 60. This left only 20 examples on which to test the induced rule. This second induced rule matched the expert's predictions on 13 of the 20 examples (a hit rate of 65 percent).

The last rule induced during phase 1 split the actual-market-movement data base into two groups of 40 and constructed a rule that would predict actual movements of the market. This induced rule had 27 nodes and used 8 of the 20 cues. It had a hit rate of 62.5 percent.

We discussed these results with our expert. He examined the decision rules that had been generated by ACLS and was favorably impressed by the general structure of the decision tree and also by the cues that had been included. Our expert considered most of those cues included in the trees to have higher predictive power than cues that had been excluded. He also was favorably impressed that a rule could be generated that would predict actual market movements correctly more than 60 percent of the time.

Phase II—Validation Exercises

Because the EXDBs contained both quantitative and categorical cues, external validity for the entire decision modeled could not be established by comparing our technique to a standard statistical technique such as discriminant analysis. Therefore, it was decided to establish internal validity through repeated applications of the holdout technique used in phase 1. Each EXDB was expanded to 108 examples. Two situations were replicated: one predicting the expert's predictions and one predicting actual stock market movements. The EXDB was split into two equal subsets five times; five rules were induced for each situation. Table 2 presents the results of these exercises.

Our main question was, "How good is the average 64.4 percent correct prediction of actual market movements obtained using ACLS?" In comparison, for the complete set of 108 examples the expert was correct 60.2 percent of the time. Thus, the induced rules performed slightly better than our expert. (A note is needed here to explain that if the analyst or the rule predicting the analyst called for a neutral condition and the market continued in the same direction as the last call made by the analyst, we considered this a correct call. This is because investors would hold their current positions and thus profit from the decision.)

It also is interesting to note that it was more difficult to predict calls made by the expert than it was to predict actual market movements. This may indicate that our expert was not consistent in making his market calls. Table 2 also shows that predictions of the actual market were less variable. It was learned in later discussions with the expert that some changes had been made in the types of data collected. It also appears that the rules used to classify data to predict the expert's recommendations were more complex than those used to predict the actual market; the average number of nodes was higher (39.0 to

Trial	Nodes	Cues	Number Correct	Percent Correct
A. Predicting the expert's calls				
1	36	8	35	64.8
2	37	9	24	44.4
3	40	11	27	50.0
4	38	7	24	44.4
5	43	9	28	53.8[a]
Average	39	8.8	27.6	51.5
B. Predicting the actual market				
1	20	6	36	66.7
2	23	7	38	70.4
3	22	6	36	66.7
4	20	6	33	61.1
5	26	9	31	57.4
Average	22.2	6.8	34.8	64.4

[a]Two situations not predicted (28/52=53.8 percent)

Table 2. Results of validation exercise.

22.2) and the average number of cues was higher (8.8 to 6.8). These measures are not absolute indicators of greater complexity, but provide general rules of thumb for rule-induction techniques.

Analysis of Results

Predicting Market Behavior

One of our most interesting findings was that predictions of actual market movements were more accurate than predictions of the expert's recommendations. As discussed above, this may have been the result of the expert changing some of his analytical techniques during the data collection period. Over the two-year period of study, certain cues and their associated values may have taken on different meanings for the expert and this may have made a difference in the consistency of his recorded predictions. However, such changes probably take place continually; markets are dynamic and a decision rule effective in one time period may not be effective in other time periods. The implications this has for LFE techniques are discussed later.

It also was interesting to note that the ACLS-generated rule predicted actual market movements better than our expert. This may be somewhat deceiving, however, because the decisions a successful investor needs to make are not as simple as this study made them appear. For example, individual stocks do not always move exactly with the market—they may move ahead or behind the rest of the market by short periods of time. As a result, our expert sometimes is cautious and instructs investors to begin selling before an actual market peak is reached or to begin buying before a trough is reached. Sometimes, when a market move is missed, he advises investors to keep their holdings in cash to protect their capital. These calls were counted against him in his study. The expert might well have been able to call the last two weeks of a three-week rise correctly, but if 60 percent of the move already had occurred during the first week, it would have been too late for investors to make profits. Thus, our expert would have recommended a neutral position and these weeks also would have been counted against him when measuring the accuracy of his predictions.

Furthermore, many of this study's interpretations are somewhat subjective. It is difficult to make absolute statements about market predictions without more-detailed descriptions of market performance. The interpretations made in this study also may be idiosyncratic to our particular expert. An interesting extension of this study would be to analyze the decisions of other market analysts and compare the results.

Rule-Induction and LFE Approaches

The effectiveness of any LFE approach depends on the examples in the EXDB. One crucial aspect concerns the size of the EXDB [3]. One rule of thumb applied by AI researchers is that more examples always are better. However, another perspective is that not the number but the particular content of the EXDB (i.e., positive, negative, and "near misses") is important [18]. The problem is that defining a "near miss" for a stock market prediction problem is not as easy as it was in Winston's [19] toy block problem. Finally, researchers such as Quinlan [12] and Shapiro and Niblett [16] demonstrated outstanding accuracy with a relatively minute EXDB of chess positions. As reported in the section on phase 1, in this study a marginal improvement in accuracy was obtained by increasing the size of the EXDB. It may not, in fact, be valid to compare a highly dynamic decision problem such as stock market prediction to a chess decision problem that can be completely enumerated.

The importance of individual examples to LFE approaches is shown in Table 2. For each of the ten rules induced, a different set of cues resulted. If these results were obtained using a statistical technique, we would question the stability and robustness of the approach. For ACLS, each of these ten cases represents a different set of 54 individual examples. Whereas a statistical approach attempts to build a "straight wall" between outcome groups that minimizes misclassifications, ACLS attempts to build a "meandering wall" customized to each individual example so that none are misclassified. This implies that great care should be taken to include the correct set of examples in the EXDB (i.e., to select a set of examples that covers the spectrum of possible situations). Significant situations not represented in a sample EXDB should be entered with a simulated outcome obtained from interviews with the expert. Anomalies and "holes," whose importance can be diluted in statistical approaches, on the other hand, may receive unwarranted importance in LFE approaches.

This biasing effect can be discussed with respect to the data base of examples in this study. Both positive and negative examples (bull and bear) are needed. If, for example, only cases that produced a bull outcome were analyzed, a simplistic prediction rule would be "the market is always bull" which would be false. In this case, negative (bear) examples are needed to bound the rule for predicting the positive (bull) outcome.

One aspect of EXDB composition peculiar to this study is temporal effectiveness. Decisions on chess endgames and toy blocks do not change over time, but stock market predictions may change daily (or even more frequently). New economic news, a political crisis, or a change in financial status can alter an expert's decisions. To demonstrate this, we split the actual-market EXDB into two groups (one containing first-year data, the other containing second-year data) and examined it sequentially. A rule was generated from the first group to predict actual market movements. We then tested this rule against the second group on a quarterly basis. The percentage of correct predictions per 13 calls per quarter (1st quarter: 77 percent, 2nd quarter: 62 percent, 3rd quarter: 62 percent, 4th quarter: 54 percent) clearly shows how the effectiveness of the rule wanes as the time from rule generation to rule application widens. This suggests that such rules should be monitored constantly and updated to maintain their accuracy.

The question of predicting next year's movements based on this year's activity also was analyzed using discriminant analysis. Of the 20 cues, 7 were quantitative (PCCBOE, PCAMEX, OBOSOS, SSOLS, SSTS, MPI, and RATRAT). A separate data base was constructed for years 1 and 2 with just these cues. The SAS DISCRIM procedure [14] was applied to year 1 to derive a discriminant function which then was tested against year 2. The accuracy results per quarter (1st quarter: 77 percent, 2nd quarter: 46 percent, 3rd quarter: 38 percent, 4th quarter: 54 percent) indicate a generally lower level of accuracy than was obtained by ACLS and an inconsistent trend.

We also compared the characterization accuracy of each method (i.e., the accuracy of the discriminant function when applied to the base examples, in this case, those in year 1). The discriminant analysis method was correct only 70 percent of the time, while ACLS was correct 100 percent of the time. This again emphasizes the importance of individual observations to ACLS. ACLS attempts to build a rule that covers all cases equally, allowing no errors, whereas statistical approaches attempt to minimize the aggregate deviation, allowing for individual errors. This may force ACLS at times to produce an overly complex and idiosyncratic rule that may not be an effective predictor. ACLS (or LFE approaches in general), however, may produce better characterization rules.

One final point concerns what we learn about the decision under scrutiny through an

LFE approach. Analysis of the induced decision rule may help a decision maker improve his or her own decision processes. In this study, for example, a seventh and final random halving of EXDB was made and two rules were generated: one predicting the expert's call and the other predicting actual market movement. The former correctly predicted the test group 50 percent of the time, the latter 59 percent of the time (significant at the .05 level). This difference may partially be explained by examining the cues in each rule.

Market-rule cues: PCCBOE, PCAMEX, MPI, GRANRET, RATRAT

Expert-rule cues: PCCBOE, PCAMEX, MPI, GRANRET, DJTTB, NETCDOW, OBOSOS, DJTT, SSTS, GRANTRN

Notice that the market rule cues form almost a subset of those in the expert rule. This suggests that our expert may have overwhelmed himself with information. It might be better to concentrate on a reduced set of cues.

Conclusion

A rule-induction approach to analyzing the stock market prediction decision has been presented. A particular segment of the market (intermediate fluctuations) and a particular type of investor (nonconservative) were selected for study. The results demonstrate that for this decision environment, a rule-induction technique can produce predictions as good as those of an expert market analyst. Such a tool can be beneficial in developing a decision support system for market analysts or in improving market analysts' own decision-making processes. The dynamics of the stock market make the particular decision environment studied quite different from those previously analyzed using LFE approaches. It should provide a rich test bed for further analysis of the effectiveness of LFE and rule-induction techniques.

Appendix

Description of ACLS Induction Algorithm

This description draws heavily on the reasoning behind the conceptual designs of Hunt et al. [4] and Quinlan [12, 13] and the practical design of Paterson and Niblett [11]. A comparison of induction approaches can be found in Michalski and Dietterich [7] and O'Rorke [10].

ACLS begins with a set of examples, EXDB, to be classified according to a set of classes or categories. These examples ultimately are divided into a decision tree where each leaf node contains examples of the same class or category. The following sequence of steps is used to create this decision tree:

- Create the root node and associate all examples with it.
- If all examples at the current node are of the same class then stop.
- Choose the best attribute to split the examples at the current node. This is done according to an information theoretic measure described below. The attribute chosen may be either logical (categorical) or integer (quantitative). If (it is) logical then the tree splits at this point with one branch for each value of the chosen attribute. If (it is) integer then a binary split is performed by partitioning the integer range about a threshold value. The threshold value is chosen to split the examples at the current node according to an optimality criterion (see below).
- The current node now has two or more branches. The examples at the current node are then associated with the branch nodes according to the value of the split attribute. Examples which have a "don't care" are associated with all branch nodes.
- For each branch node go to step 2 [11, p. 7, reprinted with permission].

The splitting algorithm is based on information theory. Its fundamental premise is that a decision tree can be thought of as a source of information. The decision tree provides information about a collection of examples by classifying them into groups based on attributes or cues [13]. The attribute selection part of ACLS is based on the assumption that the cognitive complexity of the decision tree is strongly related to the information content of the message conveyed by the tree [11]. For example, say a decision tree will be induced to classify two classes of stock market data on several attributes. Let the classes be bearish (*B*) and bullish (*b*). If the probabilities of these are *P(B)* and *P(b)* respectively, then, based on the communication theory view of information developed by Shannon and Weaver [15], the expected information content conveyed by the tree (*ICT*) would be

$$ICT = -[P(B) \cdot log2(P(B))] - [P(b) \cdot log2(P(b))].$$

Given that ICT is the information content of the entire tree, the objective at each node is to choose the attribute that provides the maximum information about the classification being considered. In order to determine this, ACLS evaluates the information content of each of the immediate subtrees formed when each attribute is chosen. The sum of the information content from each of the subtrees, multiplied by the probability of taking the branch attributes that lead to those subtrees, yields the remaining information necessary to complete the tree (*RIC(i)*) at the *i*th attribute of the current node. Thus for each attribute *i*, ACLS determines *IC(i)* as *IC(i)* = *ICT-RIC(i)*, where *IC(i)* = information content of attribute *i* at current node, *ICT* = information content of the entire tree, and *RIC(i)* = remaining information content to complete tree if attribute *i* is chosen for the split. ACLS then selects the attribute that maximizes *IC(i)* as the attribute on which to branch.

The above splitting algorithm works as is for logical or categorical attributes. In the case of integer or quantitative cues, however, the value of *IC(i)* and the integer value on which to split the attribute must be calculated. Assume that attribute *i* has *N* given attribute values labeled *V(1), ..., V(j), ..., V(N)*. Further assume that all *V(j)* are ordered in increasing value. For each *j*, $1 < j < N$, we can split the values into two subsets: {*V(1), ..., V(j)*} and {*V(J+1), ..., V(N)*}. These subsets define a value for *IC(i)*. ACLS chooses *V(j)* such that *IC(i)* is maximized. If *V(j)*+1 = V(j+1), the attribute is split on *V(j)*; otherwise, the split value is *(V(j)+V(j+1))/2*. This ability to handle integer-valued classes separates ACLS from other rule-induction techniques such as NEWGEM [9] which can handle only categorical attributes.

An Example of the ACLS Algorithm

Possible Outcomes: bullish or bearish

Cues:

1. Put-call ratio on the Chicago Board of Options (PCCBOE)
   Values: positive (pos) or negative (neg)
2. On-balance volume of the Dow (OBVDOW)
   Values: positive (pos), neutral (neu), or negative (neg)
3. Granville Cumulative Climax Indicator (GCCI)
   Values: positive (pos) or negative (neg)

The following set of examples contains three situations in the class bullish and five in the class bearish. With a known set of examples, the probabilities can be estimated using the relative frequencies. We can calculate *ICT* as *ICT*= $-[^3/_8 \log 2\ ^3/_8]-[^5/_8 \log 2\ ^5/_8]=.954$.

Set of Examples:

PCCBOE	OBVDOW	GCCI	Outcome
pos	neg	pos	bullish
neg	neg	neg	bearish
neg	neu	pos	bullish
pos	pos	pos	bearish
neg	pos	pos	bearish
neg	neg	pos	bullish
neg	pos	neg	bearish
pos	neg	neg	bearish

If the first attribute is tested, the tree structure begins:

PCCBOE:
  Negative:
    neg,neg,neg,bear
    neg,neu,pos,bull
    neg,pos,pos,bear
    neg,neg,pos,bull
    neg,pos,neg,bear

  Positive:
    pos,neg,pos,bull
    pos,pos,pos,bear
    pos,neg,neg,bear

In the positive branch, one-third of the examples are bullish and two-thirds of the examples are bearish. Thus the information still needed for the positive branch would be $-[^1/_3 \log 2\ ^1/_3]-[^2/_3 \log 2\ ^2/_3]=.918$. In the negative branch, two-fifths of the examples are bullish and three-fifths of the examples are bearish. Thus the information still needed for the negative branch would be $-[^2/_5 \log 2\ ^2/_5]-[^3/_5 \log 2\ ^3/_5]=.971$. The total information content of the remaining subtrees after splitting on the cue PCCBOE, given that three of the eight examples are in the positive branch and the remaining five examples are in the negative branch, would be $[^3/_8 \cdot .918]+[^5/_8 \cdot .971]=.951$. Thus the information gained by using PCCBOE as a branch would be $.954 - .951=.003$.

If the second attribute, OBVDOW, were chosen for the root node, the tree would begin:

OBVDOW:
  Positive:
    pos,pos,pos,bear
    neg,pos,pos,bear
    neg,pos,neg,bear

Neutral:
neg,neu,pos,bull
Negative:
pos,neg,pos,bull
neg,neg,neg,bear
neg,neg,pos,bull
pos,neg,neg,bear

At this juncture, two of the branches (the neutral and positive branches) are complete since all examples at the end nodes are of the same class. Therefore, the remaining information necessary to complete these branches is 0. The other branch (negative) is not complete and, because it has two bullish and two bearish outcomes, the information to complete it would be: $-[^2/_4 \log 2\ ^2/_4]-[^2/_4 \log 2\ ^2/_4]=1.00$. The total remaining information needed to complete the tree if it were split on the attribute OBVDOW would be $[^4/_8 \cdot 1.00]+[^1/_8 \cdot 0]+[^3/_8 \cdot 0]=.500$. Thus the information gained by testing the attribute OBVDOW would be .954-.500=.454.

Performing these same calculations for the attribute GCCI would show that the information to be gained by testing the attribute would be .347. Based on this data, the algorithm would select OBVDOW to become the root node of the tree. It then would continue to follow the algorithm and test nodes at the ends of all branches where more than one class of examples is present (in this case, only the OBVDOW negative branch). The resulting decision tree for this limited example is the following:

OBVDOW:

Negative:	GCII	Neg→	Bearish
		Pos→	Bullish
Neutral:	→		Bullish
Positive:	→		Bearish

References

[1] Buchanan, B. G., & Feigenbaum, E. A. DENDRAL and meta-DENDRAL: Their applications dimension. *Artificial Intelligence*, 1978, *11*(1,2), 5-24.

[2] Buchanan, B. G., Smith, D. H., White, W. C., Gritter, R. J., Feigenbaum, E. A., Lederberg, J., & Djerassi, C. Applications of artificial intelligence for chemical inference XXII. Automatic rule formation in mass spectrometry by means of the meta-DENDRAL program. *Journal of the American Chemical Society*, 1976, *98*, 6168-6178.

[3] Chandler, J. S. *Studies on the limits of rule inductance techniques.* Working paper, University of Illinois, Department of Accountancy, 1986.

[4] Hunt, E. B., Marin, J., & Stone, P. T. *Experiments in induction.* New York: Academic Press, 1966.

[5] Lenat, D. B., *AM: An artificial intelligence approach to discovery in mathematics as heuristic search.* Unpublished Ph.D. dissertation, Stanford University, 1976.

[6] Michalski, R. S., & Chilausky, R. L. Learning by being told and learning from examples: An experimental comparison of the two methods of knowledge acquisition in the context of developing an expert system for soybean disease diagnosis. *Journal of Policy Analysis and Information Systems*, 1980, 4(2), 125-160.

[7] Michalski, R. S., & Dietterich, T. G. A comparative review of selected methods for learning from examples. In R. S. Michalski, J. G. Carbonell, & T. M. Mitchell (Eds.), *Machine learning.* Palo Alto, CA: Tioga Publishing, 1983.

[8] Michie, D. The state of the art in machine learning. In D. Michie (Ed.), *Introductory readings in expert systems.* New York: Gordon & Breach, 1982.

[9] Mozetic, I. *NEWGEM: Program for learning from examples. Program documentation and user's guide.* Urbana: University of Illinois, Department of Computer Science, Artificial Intelligence Laboratory, 1985.

[10] O'Rorke, P. *A comparative study of inductive learning systems AQ11 and ID3* (Intelligent Systems Group Report 82-2). University of Illinois, Department of Computer Science, 1982.

[11] Paterson, A., & Niblett, T. *ACLS user manual.* Glasgow, Scotland: Intelligent Terminal Ltd., 1982.

[12] Quinlan, J. R. Discovering rules from large collections of examples: A case study. In D. Michie (Ed.), *Expert systems in the micro electronic age.* Edinburgh, Scotland: Edinburgh University Press, 1979.

[13] Quinlan, J. R. Semi-autonomous acquisition of pattern-based knowledge. In D. Michie (Ed.), *Introductory readings in expert systems.* New York: Gordon & Breach, 1982.

[14] SAS Institute. *SAS user's guide: Statistics.* Cary, NC: 1982.

[15] Shannon, C. E., & Weaver, W. *The mathematical theory of communication.* Urbana: University of Illinois Press, 1975.

[16] Shapiro, A., & Niblett, T. Automatic induction of classification rules for a chess endgame. In M. R. B. Clarke (Ed.), *Advances in computer chess* (Vol. 3). Edinburgh, Scotland: Edinburgh University Press, 1982.

[17] Shortliffe, E. *Computer based medical consultations: MYCIN*. New York: Elsevier, 1976.

[18] Winston, P. H. *Learning structural descriptions from examples* (Technical report AI-TR-231). Cambridge: Massachusetts Institute of Technology, 1970.

[19] Winston, P. H. Learning structural descriptions from examples. In P. H. Winston (Ed.), *The psychology of computer vision*. New York: McGraw-Hill, 1975.

Endnotes

[1]For reasons of confidentiality the identity of the expert cannot be revealed.

[2]Attribute values for all 108 weeks are available on request from the authors.

A Rule-Based System to Schedule Production

Giorgio Bruno, Antonio Elia, and Pietro Laface

Flexible automation can enhance productivity dramatically—but it does so by increasing the complexity of operations and the difficulty of production scheduling, which often means that human decisions fail quality and timing goals. A flexible manufacturing system (FMS) can process many types of parts produced in lots from the release times of raw materials to the due dates of completed parts.

An FMS requires production scheduling that can handle the changes flexibility demands. Production scheduling—determining a schedule (a sequence) of part lots to be machined in the FMS—must meet the due dates of lots while taking into account several related problems, such as

- Minimizing machine idle times,
- Queues at machines, and
- Work in progress.

Thus, the FMS manager must be provided with adequate software support for two tasks:

- *Production scheduling.* This scheduling takes a medium term horizon (two weeks) and determines the estimated starting times of lots to allocate auxiliary resources, such as manpower for arranging pallets. The scheduling is subject to several constraints, such as planned maintenance periods of machines and raw material availability items.
- *Real-time rescheduling.* This activity is invoked when the planned schedule must be modified because unexpected events occur, for example, when a machine breaks down or raw materials are not available when required.

The rule-based FMS production scheduling system described here is based on an earlier system developed with a traditional programming language (Fortran-77). The original system is now used in a plant that produces several different types of air compressor components.

We chose a rule-based approach because production scheduling is well described by a set of event-driven activities operating on a global database containing the relevant system state variables. Such activities cooperate to solve the complex, ill-structured problem of FMS scheduling, a task that naturally requires a certain amount of reasoning capability and expert knowledge because no direct algorithmic solution is feasible. Bourne and Fox[1] and Fox and Smith[2] have reported other experiences in this field.

Traditional procedural programming languages—such as Fortran and Pascal— have commonly been used to implement these systems. While the efficiency of such implementations is largely acknowledged, they cannot adequately satisfy many other essential requirements (especially transparency, modularity, and flexibility). In procedural languages, the knowledge representation and use turn out to be embedded in the program's control flow. Adding, deleting, or updating the knowledge is time-consuming for even a skilled programmer.

The lot scheduling problem has been extensively studied in the operations research literature, and many results have been obtained with a wide range of constraints and performance measures. Unfortunately, such results cannot be applied to production scheduling in an FMS because the throughput of each lot (the number of lot parts produced by the plant per time unit) depends on the plant loading condition: the mix of lots processed at the same time. Hence, the time required to process a whole lot is not known until the production schedule has been completed.

Building a schedule involves a series of decisions about introducing a new lot into the FMS's current mix of lots. Such a decision is based on estimating the effect that introducing such a lot would have on the system performance: machine uses, queue lengths, and throughputs of the other lots.

A well-established model for performance evaluation is a closed queueing network where a fixed number of customers, such as pallets, are routed according to their processing requirements. The advantage of a model based on the closed queueing network is that good performance measure estimates can be obtained by efficient heuristic algorithms.[3]

The production scheduling system described here combines and exploits two different techniques:

- Expert systems techniques for knowledge representation and problem solving.
- Queueing network analysis for fast performance evaluation.

The Scheduling Problem

An FMS essentially contains a set of machine tools connected by an automated palletized transportation system. The main advantages of an FMS are the ability to work on different part types simultaneously and, consequently, to adapt rapidly to changes in production mix and volume and the ability to ensure a lower but constant production in case of accidental or programmed machine stops.

The components of an FMS are either single-purpose machine tools, such as lathes, boring machines, and milling machines, or multi-purpose machine tools, such as machining centers.

For each operation, machines require the proper tools to be available. Dedicated fixtures accommodate parts on pallets. A computer lets the plant operate automatically by assigning operations to machines, mounting proper tools on machines, and routing pallets.

Production scheduling must satisfy the following constraints:

Production constraints. Each lot cannot be worked on before its release time and should not finish after its due date. Lots are characterized by a sequence of operations, and each operation can be carried out on a given set of equivalent machines.

Resource constraints. Several lots may use the same fixtures, so they cannot be produced at the same time. Moreover, programmed maintenance periods for machines must be taken into account.

Capacity constraints. Machine use and average queue lengths should not exceed predefined limits, otherwise an unacceptable congestion will occur in the transportation system.

Figure 1 shows the FMS described here. It contains a turning center (M1), four machining centers (M2, M3, M4, and M5) equipped with autonomous tool storage, a washing station (M6), a blowing station (M7), a load/unload station (L/U), and a closed palletized transportation system.

Most machines have a one-place input buffer to store parts waiting to be machined and a one-place output buffer to store parts for delivery to the transportation system.

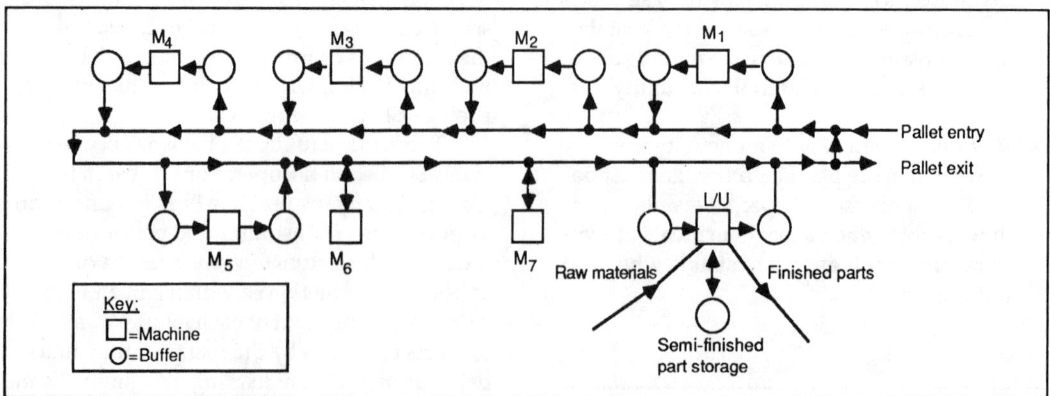

Figure 1. The FMS layout.

Scheduling Guideline
Because of the complexity of the scheduling problem, no optimal solution is sought. Instead, the scheduler follows a simple guideline given by the priority of lots. The priority for each lot is a measure of its urgency and processing effect on the FMS. It is computed as

remaining machine time/(due_date—release_time).

Therefore, a schedule can be built by examining lots according to their priorities and by introducing them into the system as long as their constraints are satisfied. In particular, the scheduler enforces resource constraints by making sure that suitable fixtures and machines are available. It then enforces capacity constraints by estimating the FMS performance if the lot were introduced.

This analysis is carried out by a closed queueing network algorithm. If either the resulting machine use or the resulting average queue lengths at workstations exceed predefined limits, the lot is not introduced, so the scheduler can examine another lot, if there is one.

Production scheduling is an activity that takes place over a period of time because not all lots can be introduced into the FMS at the same time. Thus, the scheduling can be conceived as a discrete event decision-making process since changes in the system can occur only at discrete times (or events). Events are marked by an occurrence time and are given types according to

- *Lot completion.* This lot is removed from the FMS and new lots may be introduced.
- *Machine state change.* When, for example, a machine breaks down or is undergoing maintenance, it is no longer usable. All lots being machined that have no alternative operational machine must be removed from the FMS.
- *New lot release.* From this instant on, the lot can be introduced into the FMS.

The events belonging to the last two types are constraints for the scheduler (that is, they are exogenous). However, the events of the first type depend on the decisions previously taken by the scheduler, so they are determined by the scheduler itself. In fact, the completion times of the lots being processed depend on the current mix of lots (because it influences their throughputs) and on the remaining number of parts to be worked on.

Model Simulation
It turns out that this approach to production scheduling perfectly fits the framework of discrete-event simulation. In fact, discrete-event simulation is characterized by a global simulation clock and evolves with asynchronous timing, since, when an event has been processed, the next one is considered and its occurrence time updates the simulation clock.

In general, the processing of an event will generate other events in the future. An important feature of a simulation model—a feature rarely offered by conventional discrete-event simulation languages—is tentatively scheduling future events and canceling them later if required. This is necessary in production scheduling because the completion times of the lots being processed depend on the current mix of lots, so the insertion or the removal of a lot or even the change of state of a machine will alter the completion times of those lots.

Scheduler Architecture

It is well-known that procedural control is perfectly suited to numerical and algorithmic tasks. However, a nonprocedural approach is more appropriate for those applications in which most of the knowledge can be represented declaratively.

The FMS scheduling activity can be organized so the advantages of the two approaches are exploited by two cooperating modules: the scheduler, which is a knowledge-based module containing a set of rules, and the load evaluation module, which exploits its algorithmic knowledge to provide the scheduler with a set of performance measures to aid decision making.

Activity Scanning
We have adopted the activity scanning approach to discrete event simulation. Such an approach focuses on the activities in which the entities of the system are involved. Each activity is prefixed by a precondition that triggers its execution. By checking the preconditions of all activities, the control of the simulation determines when the next event occurs and advances the simulation clock accordingly. Then all the activities are scanned to establish which can be executed.

This approach could be inefficient because of the need to scan each activity at each time update. However, it is particularly suited for

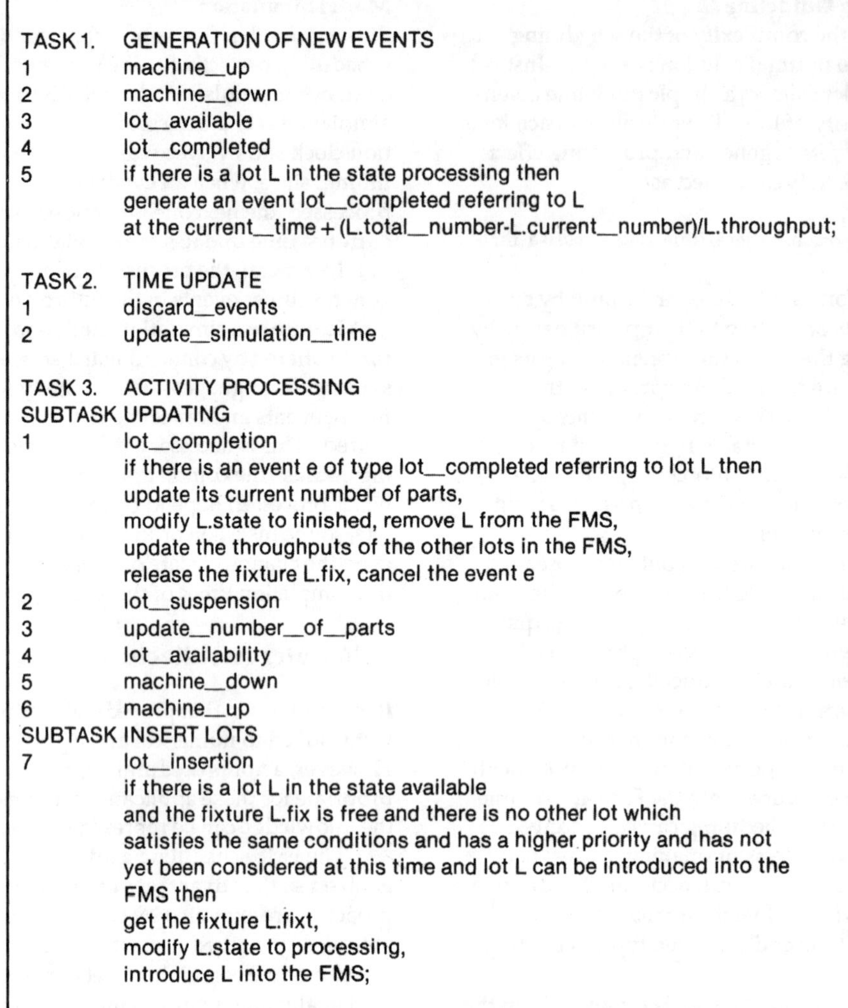

```
TASK 1.   GENERATION OF NEW EVENTS
1         machine_up
2         machine_down
3         lot_available
4         lot_completed
5         if there is a lot L in the state processing then
          generate an event lot_completed referring to L
          at the current_time + (L.total_number-L.current_number)/L.throughput;

TASK 2.   TIME UPDATE
1         discard_events
2         update_simulation_time

TASK 3.   ACTIVITY PROCESSING
SUBTASK UPDATING
1         lot_completion
          if there is an event e of type lot_completed referring to lot L then
          update its current number of parts,
          modify L.state to finished, remove L from the FMS,
          update the throughputs of the other lots in the FMS,
          release the fixture L.fix, cancel the event e
2         lot_suspension
3         update_number_of_parts
4         lot_availability
5         machine_down
6         machine_up
SUBTASK INSERT LOTS
7         lot_insertion
          if there is a lot L in the state available
          and the fixture L.fix is free and there is no other lot which
          satisfies the same conditions and has a higher priority and has not
          yet been considered at this time and lot L can be introduced into the
          FMS then
          get the fixture L.fixt,
          modify L.state to processing,
          introduce L into the FMS;
```

Figure 2. The production scheduler architecture.

situations where the duration of some activities is not foreseeable because they depend on the system's global state. Indeed, this is true for production scheduling. Fishman[4] presents a more general discussion of the main approaches to discrete event simulation.

The scheduler contains the following tasks:

- *Generation of new events.* All the activities are scanned and the events corresponding to the instants at which each activity can start are generated.
- *Time update.* The simulation clock is updated to the earliest occurrence time of the events generated in the first phase. All the events having an occurrence time greater than the selected one are canceled.
- *Activity processing.* The activities for which an event exists are executed. A partial order can be forced on their execution according to the logic of the scheduler. For instance, the events related to the state change of some machine are served before trying to introduce new lots into the FMS.

Such tasks are executed in a cyclic sequence until the stopping condition is reached. The stopping condition occurs when all the lots have been completed or a predefined interval has elapsed.

Structured Implementation

Figure 2 shows the scheduler framework. The rules in the third task are grouped in two

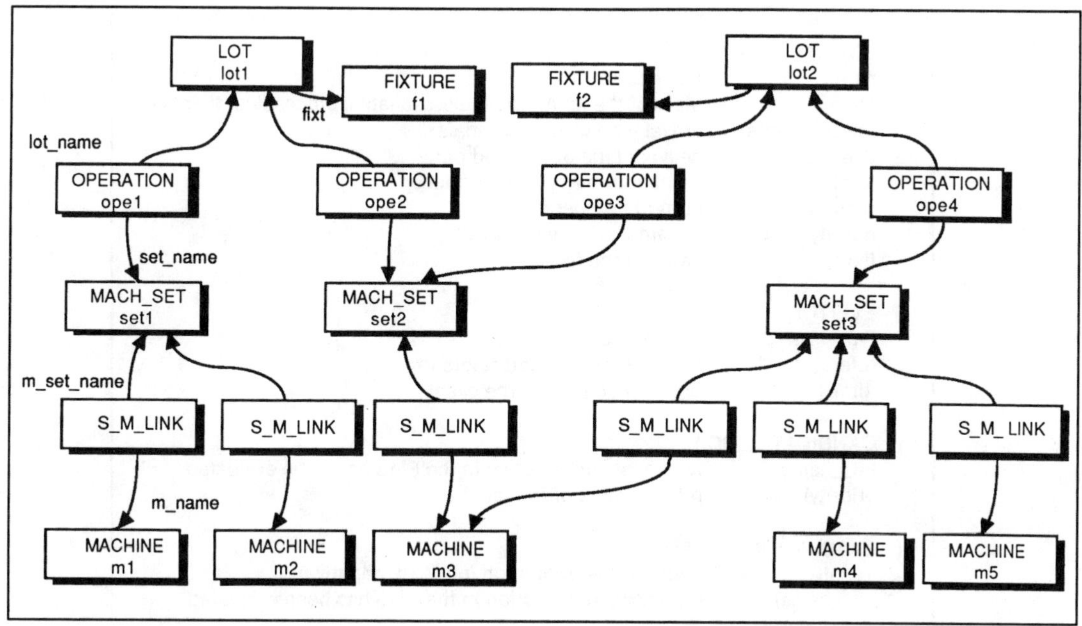

Figure 3. The production scheduler data structure.

subtasks that are activated in sequence. When there are no longer applicable rules in a subtask, the next subtask is activated.

The structure of the scheduler lends itself to a straightforward implementation by using a production system programming language. This programming approach offers the advantages of modularity and flexibility because the data, knowledge, and control are separated. In fact, a rule of a production system represents an independent component of the overall system's behavior and reacts to a specific situation.

This encourages structured development by stepwise refinement that incrementally adds and verifies new features and constraints. Since extensions and updates of the system require relatively little effort, this approach is well-suited for rapid prototyping. Moreover, this approach lets heuristic knowledge be introduced in the form of behavioral rules that can be suggested by a scheduling expert. These rules can take into account quantitative *and* qualitative aspects involved in the decision.

An example of such a rule is the following:

If a lot is available and could be scheduled but it is foreseen that an essential machine must undergo a maintenance period in a short time

Then delay this lot and try to schedule another one.

The load evaluation module basically implements a closed queueing network algorithm that deals with capacity constraints and optimization issues. Its task is quite limited. Well-structured chunks of procedural knowledge are available to it.[3]

The algorithm is based on the assumption that the FMS state is completely determined by the current mix of lots. It implements an efficient heuristic extension to the mean-value analysis technique[5] for closed queueing networks. It receives as input the information about the lots being processed and returns as output the values of machine use, average queue lengths, and lot throughputs.

```
( LOT
^ name            ; name of the lot
^ state           ; state of the lot (unavailable, available, processing, finished)
^ release_time    ; arrival time of raw materials
^ due_date        ; delivery time of finished parts
^ total_number    ; number of parts to be produced
^ current_number; current number of parts
^ priority        ; dynamic priority of the lot
^ fixt )          ; name of the fixture

( EVENT
^ type            ; type of the event
^ refers_to       ; name of the object it refers to
^ time )          ; occurrence time of the event

( CANDIDATE_GOAL
^ lot_name        ; lot whose introduction in the FMS has to be evaluated
^ priority)       ; priority value of the lot

( EVALUATION_GOAL
^ result          ; result of the evaluation (positive, negative)
^ lot_name)       ; lot whose introduction in the FMS has been evaluated

( CONTEXT
^ task            ; ^ subtask  ^ step )
```

Figure 4. Examples of working memory elements.

Scheduler Implementation

The scheduler was written in OPS5, a rule-based, domain-independent production system language.[6] An OPS5 program contains a global database, called *working memory*, and a set of rules operating on it.

Figure 3 illustrates the data structure for production scheduling with a simple and informal graphical notation that shows the system's objects and the relationships between them. Objects are represented by rectangular boxes, while relationships are depicted as labeled arcs.

Objects belong to classes and have attributes. A particular attribute is the name of the object. In the figure, each object is denoted by the name of its class in uppercase and by its name in lowercase. An arc between two objects indicates that a link exists between them. Such a link is carried out by storing the name of the object the arc is directed to into an attribute of the object the arc emanates from. The name of this attribute labels the arc.

As the figure shows, each lot is characterized by several operations that can be performed on a set of equivalent machines. The objects of the class mach set represents such sets.

We chose this data organization because it reflects the entity-relationship approach,[7] a well-known data management method. Furthermore, it fits the structure of the OPS5 working memory well.

A working memory element contains tuples of attribute-value pairs. The attribute names are prefixed by ^, while their values are constants. Some examples of working memory elements are given in Figure 4.

OPS5 Interpreter

In OPS5, each rule has a lefthand side composed of a set of condition elements and a righthand side that specifies actions. A condition element is a pattern containing both constants and variables (denoted by names within angle brackets [< and >]).

The OPS5 interpreter cyclically performs a recognition-action loop, during which the condition elements are matched to the working memory elements. This process binds attribute variables that have the same name to working memory elements that have the same attribute value. When all the condition elements in a rule are satisfied, the production is instantiated and enters the conflict set.

The OPS5 interpreter selects for execution one instantiation of this set with a user-specifiable strategy. For this scheduler implementation, we chose the special-case strategy. According to this strategy, if there are given two instantiations, the one with the greatest number of condition elements is chosen because it is considered more specialized for dealing with the current situation. Figure 5 presents some OPS5 rules that correspond to the organization in Figure 2.

Rules are partitioned into tasks, subtasks, and steps with a working memory element, called *context,* that indicates the active task and any active subtask or step. Tasks and subtasks correspond to those indicated in Figure 2. Steps have been introduced because some of the high-level rules shown in Figure 2 cannot be implemented by a simple OPS5 rule but instead require a sequence of OPS5 rules.

Some rules are devoted to task, subtask, or step switching. In fact, for each context there is a rule containing only the condition sensitive to it. This rule deactivates the current context and activates a new one by changing the attributes of the context element. Since the deactivation rule is a general case of all the other rules sensitive to the same context, it fires only after all the other rules in the context have been satisfied.

Separate Data Structures

The integration of the rule-based system and the closed queueing network algorithm is not straightforward because of the deep differences between the corresponding programming techniques. A major consequence of these differences is that two separate—but consistent—data structures are maintained. Both modules, in fact, must record information about the entire state of the system, but the form in which the information is organized and its contents are different.

To maintain the consistency of such data structures, the modules must communicate. The data structure of the scheduler is loaded, in the initialization phase, by simple actions that create working memory elements. Since it is impossible to address working memory elements from a foreign environment, a parallel data structure is created for the queueing network analysis algorithm to use.

Thus, communication is achieved by a set of production rules in the form of external function calls. The external functions are implemented in Fortran-77 and are referred to in uppercase. The exchange of information between the modules takes place through the following mechanisms:

- *Actions that request some performance index to be externally computed.* For example, the evaluation of the load caused by the introduction of a new lot into the FMS (PERFORMANCE_EVALUATION).
- *Actions that announce a change in the state of some entity.* For example, a lot that must be introduced into the FMS (INSERT_LOT).
- *Rules that monitor external events such as machine failures.* These rules use the VAX/VMS operating system service routines and the related asynchronous system trap mechanism to interrupt the program when a particular event occurs. This proves valuable during real-time rescheduling.

For efficiency, most of OPS5's power relies on its complex and flexible pattern-matching mechanism. The matching process is complicated and could be a major source of trouble, but Forgy has devised a very efficient implementation[8] based on the reasonable assumption that a small number of working memory elements change at every recognition-action cycle. Moreover, the communication between the modules, although rather frequent, involves the exchange of only a few pieces of information.

We have compared the current OPS5 system and the original Fortran-77 version for a few examples. The results show that there is no appreciable increase in the response time of current scheduling with respect to the old one. This can be justified since the procedural approach implies an iterative monitoring of all possible changes that might affect the system state.

An Example

Table 1 summarizes the essential parameters of the simple scheduling problem described here

```
;TASK 3. ACTIVITY PROCESSING. SUBTASK INSERT_LOTS

;RULE 3.7 STEP 1
;A goal is generated for each candidate lot
  ( p candidate_machinable_lot
       ( context            ^ task activity_processing
                            ^ subtask insert_lots ^ step 1 )
       ( lot                ^ name <l>       ^ state available
                            ^ priority <p>   ^ fixt <fix>)
       ( fixture            ^ name <fix>     ^ state free)
  →
       ( make candidate_goal ^ lot_name <l> ^ priority <p> ))

;Switching to the next step
  ( p candidate_machinable_lot_end
       {( context           ^ task activity_processing
                            ^ subtask insert_lots ^ step 1 ) <c>}
  →
       (modify <c>          ^ step 2 ))

;RULE 3.7 STEP 2
;selects the lot with the highest priority and evaluates the effect
;of introducing it into the FMS by calling PERFORMANCE_EVALUATION function
  ( p evaluate_lot
       {( context           ^ type activity_processing
                            ^ subtask insert_lots ^ step 2 ) <c>}
       {( candidate_goal
                            ^ priority <p>   ^ lot_name <l> )<goal>}
       ( lot                ^ name <1>       ^ fixt <fix> )
       ( fixture            ^ name <fix>     ^ state free)
     - ( candidate_goal     ^ priority { <p1> > <p> })
  →
       ( bind <evaluation> ( PERFORMANCE_EVALUATION <l>))
       ( make evaluation_goal
                            ^ result <evaluation> ^ lot_name<l>      )
       ( modify <c>         ^ step 3) ( remove <goal> ))

;RULE 3.7 STEP 3
;If the evaluation is positive, the lot is introduced into the FMS
;by calling the INSERT_LOT function
 ( p define_processing
       {( context           ^ type activity_processing
                            ^ subtask insert_lots ^ step 3 ) <c> }
       {( lot               ^ name <l>  ^ fixt <fix> )<lot> }
       {( fixture           ^ name <fix> )   <fixture> }
       {( evaluation_goal
                            ^ result positive ^ lot_name <l> )<g> }
 →
   ( modify <c>             ^ step 2 )
   ( modify <fixture>               ^ state used )
   ( modify <lot>                   ^ state processing )
   ( bind <reslot> (INSERT_LOT <l>)) ( remove <g> ))
```

Figure 5. Examples of OPS5 rules.

and the methods used to solve the problem. For example, three operations are associated with LOT03: the first one lists 16.06 minutes and can be carried out by machine M4 or machine M5, while the other operations are executed by machine M6 and machine M7, respectively.

We have made further assumptions for the sake of simplicity in the presentation of the results:

- Lots have equal release times and due dates.
- Lots require different fixtures.
- Only one machine, machine M1, undergoes a maintenance period, lasting 500 minutes every 3000 minutes. Its first maintenance period starts 1000 minutes after the lots' release time.

The number of parts produced for each lot at any given time is shown in Figure 6, which

Table 1. A schedule of the machine time needed to carry out each operation associated with a particular lot. Each machine (M1, M2, and so on) that falls within the time span of an operation is capable of carrying out that operation.

	Lot 01 (100 Parts Processed)	Lot 02 (150 Parts Processed)	Lot 03 (200 Parts Processed)	Lot 04 (100 Parts Processed)	Lot 05 (100 Parts Processed)	Lot 06 150 Parts Processed)	Lot 07 (175 Parts Processed)	Lot 08 (100 Parts Processed)	Lot 09 (200 Parts Processed)	Lot 10 (100 Parts Processed	Lot 11 (100 Parts Processed)
M1	8.64 min.				12.94 min.	12.14 min.					
M2							16.33 min.			26.65 min.	19.54 min.
M3						11.38 min.		13.25 min.	18.11 min.		
M4			16.06 min.	15.94 min.							
M5		19.49 min.									
M6	4.22 min.	4.22 min.	4.22 min.	4.22 min.	4.22 min.	4.22 min.	4.22 min.	4.22 min.	4.22 min.	4.22 min.	4.22 min.
M7	4.00 min.	4.00 min.	4.00 min.	3.00 min.	4.00 min.	4.00 min.	4.00 min.	4.00 min.	3.00 min.	4.00 min.	4.00 min.

Table 1. A schedule of the machine time needed to carry out each operation associated with a particular lot. Each machine (M1, M2, and so on) that falls within the time span of an operation is capable of carrying out that operation.

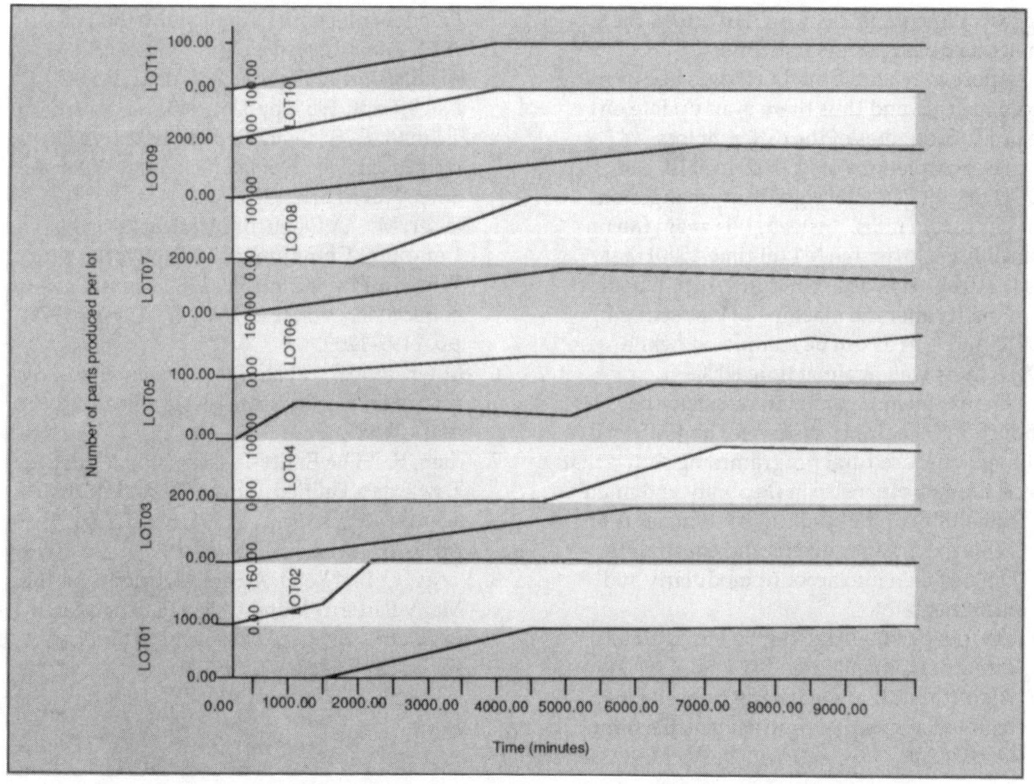

Figure 6. Production rates achieved by following the schedule described in Table 1.

summarizes the main decisions taken by the scheduler.

When the raw materials are released, the scheduler lets only eight of the 11 lots be introduced into the FMS because of capacity constraints. The order in which lots are selected depends on their dynamic priority.

In our example, LOT05, which must produce 100 parts (each of them requiring a relatively long operation performable only by machine M1), is the most urgent. LOT01, LOT04, and LOT08 can be delayed without causing any trouble because it is easier to respect their due dates.

The unavailability of machine M1 at time 1000 for 500 minutes is the next event that compels the scheduler to remove LOT05 and LOT06 because no alternative machine can carry out the job. As a consequence, the production rates for the other active lots increase slightly.

At the end of the maintenance period (at time 1500), LOT01 and LOT06 are scheduled. LOT05 is not rescheduled because LOT01 has gained priority over it because of its greater estimated remaining machining time for completion and because the queueing network analysis suggests these three lots would overload the system if scheduled at the same time.

Another available lot, LOT08, can be introduced instead, and thus there is an update on the production rates of the different lots.

The completions of LOT02, LOT10, and LOT11 do not generate significant changes on the production rates. Instead, it is again the unavailability of machine M1 (at time 4500) that lets LOT04 be scheduled and interrupt LOT01.

Finally, after the machine M1 is repaired, LOT05 and LOT01 can be completed, while LOT06 must wait again at time 8000.

The experience gained in restyling the production scheduling system for an FMS by exploiting nonprocedural programming shows that

- A dramatic increase in flexibility and maintainability of the resulting system has been achieved because events and constraints can be taken into account modularly and incrementally.
- Heuristic knowledge can be introduced to direct decision making.
- Algorithmic knowledge can be easily integrated as external routines callable from OPS5 rules.

We have aimed our current work at improving the scheduler's problem-solving strategy. It is now simply based on the priority of lots, and does not guarantee that due dates of finished parts will always be met. We are implementing a more complex strategy that uses backtracking to explore several schedules in parallel.

Further research will address the integration of this scheduling system into the operating environment to cope with real-time events captured on the field. These asynchronous events are now emulated with the host operating system's real-time features.

References

1. Bourne, D. A., and Fox, M. S. "Autonomous Manufacturing: Automating the Job Shop," *Computer*, Vol. 17, No. 9, Sept. 1984, pp. 76-86.
2. Fox, M. S., and Smith, S. F. "Isis—A Knowledge-Based System for Factory Scheduling," *Expert Systems, the Int'l J. Knowledge Engineering*, Vol. 1, July 1984, pp. 25-49.
3. Menga, G., et al. "Modeling FMS by Closed Queueing Network Analysis Methods," *IEEE Trans. Components, Hybrids, and Manufacturing Technology*, Vol. CHMT-7, No. 3, Sept. 1984, pp. 241-248.
4. Fishman, G. S. *Concepts and Methods in Discrete Event Digital Simulation*, John Wiley & Sons, New York, 1973.
5. Reiser, M. "A Queueing Network Analysis of Computer Communication Networks with Window Flow Control," *IEEE Trans. Communications*, Vol. C-27, No. 27, August 1979, pp. 1199-1209.
6. Brownstone, L., et al. *Programming Expert Systems in OPS5*, Addison-Wesley, Reading, Mass., 1985.
7. Chen, P. "The Entity-Relationship Model: Towards a Unified View of Data," *ACM Trans. Database Syst.*, Vol. 1, No. 1, Mar. 1976, pp. 9-36.
8. Forgy, C. L. "Rete: A Fast Algorithm for the Many Pattern/Many Object Pattern-Match Problem," *Artificial Intelligence*, Vol. 19, No. 1, Sept. 1982, pp. 17-37.

A Prototype Expert System for Industrial Truck Type Selection

Charles J. Malmborg, Marvin H. Agee, Gene R. Simons, and J. V. Choudhry

A compelling match exists between the problem of selecting an industrial truck type and the attributes of the artificial intelligence (AI) approach to decision making. Solving this problem requires extensive knowledge of facts, relationships and rules that are specific to material handling. It also requires consideration of complex equipment characteristics that can suggest many feasible, nondominating alternatives. Finally, the selection process may have to accommodate multiple, possibly conflicting objectives, and a shortage of experts exists.

These features of the industrial truck selection problem suggest the application of AI methodologies. More specifically, an expert system designed to identify a set of feasible industrial truck types, based on an easily formulated generic description of a particular material handling problem, would be applicable.

In fact, one of the most frequently cited advantages of expert systems is that they can make efficient use of the type of extensive domain-dependent knowledge that characterizes the industrial truck selection problem without the need to consult with an expert for every decision.

The purpose of this article is twofold. The first purpose is to show how a knowledge base could be developed to support the problem of selecting an industrial truck type. We define an industrial truck type as a collection of attributes that specify an industrial truck model in sufficient detail that one or more commercially available truck models could be associated with it. An example of such an industrial truck type might include "an electric, cushion tired, counterbalanced, front loading lift truck rated at 4,000 lb or below."

The second purpose of this article is to describe the construction of a prototype expert system to utilize the knowledge base. The expert system is designed to proceed from a simple description of a material handling problem to a truck type alternative using a process known as pattern-directed inference.

The tool used to build the expert system is PROLOG, a conversational, relatively easy to use programming language for expert systems that is implemented on a Prime 750 computer at Rensselaer. The expert system is considered a prototype because it stops short of the final phase of industrial truck selection, which is the association of truck type alternatives with commercially available industrial truck models.

Furthermore, the knowledge base supporting the expert system contains only a limited range of truck types and is by no means a complete treatment of the problem. The prototype system is meant merely to indicate the type of larger scale system that could be constructed to deal with industrial truck selection or other material handling problems.

In the next section, the alternatives and factors involved in the selection of an industrial truck type for a given material handling problem will be discussed. This will include an overview of different truck types and their applications. In the third section, the development

Reprinted with permission from *Industrial Engineering* magazine, vol. 19, March 1987, 58-64.

of the knowledge base supporting the expert system will be described. This will include a review of facts, relationships and rules used by the system, a discussion of the user interface and a description of the actual PROLOG program in the context of the industrial truck type selection problem. The final section will offer a summary and conclusions.

Industrial Truck Selection

The first step in the creation of the knowledge base is a review of the problems associated with selecting a truck type for a given material handling problem. Normally, this step involves interviewing human experts and review of literature that contains expertise on this subject. We begin this process by citing a categorization of industrial trucks that is suggested by Agee (see "For further reading"). These categories include:

- Front-loading counterbalanced trucks.
- Front-loading straddle trucks.
- Side-loading trucks.
- Order-picking trucks.
- Reach trucks.
- Low-lift and no-lift trucks.

In the above list, front-loading counterbalanced trucks can include several variations of engine designs, tire types or capacity ratings. For example, electric cushioned-tired trucks include sit-down center-control units with a four-wheel or three-wheel configuration and stand-up center-control or end-control units. Used mostly for indoor services, they have capacities up to 10,000 lb and 20 ft lift height.

Internal combustion engine-powered, cushioned-tired trucks are mostly sit-down center-control units, with a four-wheel configuration and gasoline, LP-gas or diesel engine. Primarily for indoor use, they handle loads up to 15,000 lb and can lift to heights of 20 ft.

Engine-powered pneumatic-tired trucks are mostly sit-down center control units and are available in a wide range of engines and fuels. These trucks are useful for outdoor service on reasonably flat, smooth surfaces. Indoors they cushion loads and permit high-speed travel. Capacities are up to one million pounds for container-handling trucks, and lifts extend to 20 ft.

Engine-powered rough terrain trucks are sit-down rider trucks suitable for use on rough terrains. These trucks also have a choice of engine and fuel. They generally feature high traction and flotation tires and a high underclearance.

In the second category, front-loading straddle trucks are a type of high lifters. Starting from a small value of 10 ft, the lift range extends up to 40 ft and above. The category includes the straddle, reach and long reach electric trucks. They are primarily designed for unit-load storage in narrow aisles. High-lift platform trucks and fork-over-arm trucks also exist.

Side-loading trucks include three basic types of high lifters: outrigger side-loading trucks, side-loader trucks and counterbalanced side-loading trucks. Such trucks can pick up or tier a conventional-size unit load at the side and carry it without making a right angle turn within a rack aisle. These trucks can provide multi-aisle service, and their range of lift extends to over 35 ft. Swing masts and turret trucks are versatile trucks needing very little aisle space. They are both front and side loaders.

Order-picking trucks generally feature high-lifting capacities. As high-lifters they are especially effective in two ways: They boost the productivity of a picker of less-than-unit-load quantities, and they permit high-level storage in narrow shelving aisles or rack aisles.

Conventional order-picking trucks include the straddle style and the counterbalanced style, among others. They can lift an operator 40 ft and above. Aisle-guided vehicles are special vehicles within the order-picker category that are known to increase picking productivity considerably. There are also dual-purpose trucks that can be used for both unit-loading and order-picking. They are generally straddle-type side-loaders.

Reach trucks can be either straddle or counterbalanced. A counterbalanced reach truck can carry loads of 20,000 lb rising to heights of 20 ft. An outrigger version has a capacity of 4,000 lb and lifts of 40 ft. These trucks are useful in stacking goods in double rows.

Consisting of the pallet and platform types, low-lifts are used for in-plant transportation requiring medium distance trips and frequent local moves. Outrigger-styled and self-loading, they can nearly turn in their own lengths. "No-lift" trucks move loads by pulling or carrying them. Among these are two tractors, burden carriers and personnel carriers.

Application Areas

Given a truck taxonomy, the selection of an industrial truck type must also use knowledge about the various types of material handling applications that are apt to be encountered and what truck types are appropriate for these application areas. Based on a classification suggested by Agee ("For further reading"), the following five application categories are identified for use in constructing the prototype expert system:

- Dock operations.
- Unit load storage.
- Order picking.
- In-process handling.
- Yard operations.

For each of the five application areas, the possible roles of various truck types can be identified. For example, dock operations encompass both receiving and shipping activities. In receiving, materials are unloaded from a carrier and moved to temporary storage (usually short moves). Shipping activities may include removing loads from finished goods storage, moving these to the dock, then loading them into a carrier.

Dock service calls for prompt loading and unloading of railcars and highway trucks and short moves between storage areas (or a staging area). The primary function is to speed material flow, keep the dock free and uncluttered, and cut turnaround time of carriers.

Key selection features for a dock truck are maneuverability, low profile and ramp climbing ability. Typical trucks for dock operations include high-lift, low-lift and no-lift types, high-lift counterbalanced trucks and outrigger platform trucks, low-lift outrigger-style platform and pallet trucks, and the no-lift rider-type burder carriers.

One reason for such a variety in dock trucks is frequent use away from the dock, consistent with overall systems requirements. For example, dock trucks often carry pallet-loads or skidloads to or from an adjacent staging area. A guided-loading capability may also be required to stack or unstack unit loads, or to otherwise position loads using forks or various special attachments. In a similar fashion, the roles of the remaining four applications areas could be elaborated on with respect to the designated truck taxonomy.

Relating Truck Types to Handling Problems

Based on information relating applications areas to truck types, it is possible to develop a preliminary set of rules for relating general handling problems to truck types. The most basic information for defining a material handling problem is a description of the unit handling load. Information such as load length, width, height, form, weight and center of gravity is pertinent to the determination of appropriate truck capacity. In addition, rules must be developed to address questions relating to load stability, stackability and fragility.

The rules must also address environmental factors such as lifting requirements and travel requirements. Truck characteristics that relate to lifting requirements include maximum fork height, overall lowered height of the mast, and the tilt of the mast.

The maximum fork height determines how high loads may be stacked. The overall lowered height must be considered in regard to passing through doors and under pipelines and entering trailers and railroad box cars.

The tilt of the truck mast relates to the pick-up and deposit of loads and whether the load needs to be cradled during travel for load stability. Travel requirements relate to the power source needed and transmission type. Measures of travel requirements include distance, average daily utilization, the frequency and grades of inclines and declines in the travel path, and lift speed requirements.

Other environmental factors that are useful in relating a handling problem to truck types include aisle space restrictions, terrain/floor surface, presence of dockboards/ramps and structural building limitations. Also, adverse operating conditions such as abrasive particle atmospheres may require special bearings, grease seals, filters, etc.

Developing Knowledge Base

The information describing the industrial truck type selection problem must be organized in a form that is usable by a computer code. The creation of the knowledge base follows a systematic process of collecting and categorically listing raw data; establishing a framework of facts, relationships and selection rules; and establishing user knowledge requirements.

Initially, a structure must be established for differentiating truck types. For the prototype expert system, the 17 truck type attributes shown in Table 1 were established based on the limited literature review.

- *Code*: given by the data compiler (and used internally).
- *Fundamental design: Counterbalanced, outrigger, pallets, platforms, tractors, dollies, balanced vehicles.*
- *Functional design*: loading mechanism: front, front-reach, side-loading, order-picking, external loading.
- *Load capacity*: maximum load possible.
- Existence of lifting capacity.
- Maximum lift.
- Lifting mechanism: mechanical, power, manual.
- Aisle size required.
- Type of engine: Electric, ICE, none.
- Type of tires: Pneumatic/cushion/nylon.
- Pallet design: Critical/noncritical.
- Stacking design: Single/double.
- Price of truck.
- Rider/walkie.
- Rider—sit/stand.
- Riding—fixed/moving.
- Ability to accommodate special attachments.

Table 1. Seventeen categories of data used by the prototype expert system to identify truck types.

Truck type alternatives as defined by the prototype expert system consisted of various combinations of levels of these attributes. A total of 49 combinations of attribute levels and/or ranges were identified as *feasible* truck type alternatives. For example, category "1015G" represents four-wheel, electric, counterbalanced front-reach lift trucks with maximum load capacity of 5,000 lb and maximum lift height of 20 ft.

Trucks in this category must also be capable of operating within 154-in. aisle spaces, have pneumatic tires, be sit-down rider trucks capable of double row storage, and be priced below $35,000. Ultimately, the expert system must recommend one or none of the 49 alternative truck types in response to various inputs provided by a user.

Rules for the Expert System

The inputs that the user must provide are based on expert level consideration of the various functions of truck characteristics and material handling problem requirements. This process focuses on the identification of four aggregated truck classifications chosen for their mutual exclusivity.

The classifications include self loading low-lift, nonloading low-lift, non-lift and "other" lift trucks. Specific parameter limitations relating to material handling problems are identified in each classification and used as rules to relate problem descriptions to truck types.

Five sample rules established for use by the prototype expert system for self-loading low-lift trucks and non-loading low-lift trucks are summarized in Tables 2 and 3. For the aggregate classification of "other" lift trucks, a sample of five general rules is shown in Table 4.

In addition, it was found to be advantageous to subdivide this classification into medium- and high-lift trucks and establish separate rules for each of these subclasses. A sample of five separate rules for each of these subclassifications is shown in Tables 5 and 6.

In the case of non-lift trucks, it was determined that selection of a given variation should be based on the load to be carried, the frequency of use, surface conditions, etc. Here, a logic was devised based on a series of "if/then" relationships, a subset of which is shown in Table 7.

- Maximum lift height is approximately six inches.
- Powered versions are electric.
- Required minimum aisle size is about 35 inches.
- Cannot be used where gradients are greater than 5°, utilization is about 30%, or floor surfaces are rough.
- If load weight $<$ the maximum allowable of 8,000 lb but $>$5,000 lb and move frequency is high, powered versions are recommended. If load weight $<$8,000 lb and move frequency is low, mechanical lift varieties may be recommended.

Table 2. Sample of five rules used for self-loading low-lift trucks.

- Can function in ≤ 35 in. of aisle space.
- Load weight should not exceed 3,000 lb.
- For loads < 1,500 lb, hand platform low-lift trucks and mechanical lift mechanism are recommended.
- For loads between 1,500 lb and 3,000 lb, hand platform low-lift trucks and power lift mechnaism are recommended.
- Utilization should be under 20%, and gradients less than 5°.

Table 3. Sample of five rules used for non-loading low-lift trucks.

Developing a Protocol

In order to utilize rules such as those summarized in Tables 2 through 7, an interactive protocol needs to be established. This process must obtain enough information from the user to allow application of a sufficient number of rules to develop a specific truck type recommendation. Thus, a questioning sequence is developed to proceed from a conveniently enumerated problem description to identification of a specific truck type alternative. The questioning sequence includes inquiries relative to factors such as:

- The need for loading capability.
- Required lifting heights.
- Description of the handling load.
- Environmental conditions including surface conditions of flooring, utilization levels, aisle size restrictions and use of ramps.
- Need for specialized applications such as outdoor use, less than unit load order picking and front reach.

The prototype expert system is designed to attempt specification of a truck type following only minimal inquiries of the user. This is accomplished through a technique known as pattern-directed inference. This technique allows the expression of relational and methodological knowledge in the form of "condition/action" pairs.

If the system can satisfy itself that a given condition holds (e.g., through direct or indirect user input), it performs the corresponding action. For example, if the expert system can establish that material handling is over irregular outdoor terrain, it may limit considerationto internal combustion engine trucks with flotation tires, and focus subsequent inquiry on cost or lifting requirements.

After each inquiry, the rules are reexamined until one is found that satisfies the condition part. Then the action part is executed and the recognize/act cycle is repeated.

In most cases, when the action component of a rule is executed, this will satisfy the condition component of another rule and allow for continuation of the recognize/act cycle. However, a conflict or lack of information may occur prior to convergence on a truck type alternative. When this occurs, the system asks the user for

- Maximum lift heights are from 12-45 ft with two likely ranges of <30 ft and 30-45 ft.
- Load length does not exceed the standard 60 in. unless otherwise specified (used to compute aisle size requirements).
- Outrigger versions require pallets with appropriate design.
- Most specialized attachments are available at extra cost.
- Less than unit load order-picking trucks are used only when deemed necessary by the user.

Table 4. Sample of five general rules used for "other" lift trucks.

- For rough terrain, only special trucks fitted with flotation tires are used.
- Rider and walkie trucks are differentiated based on the following: For a walkie to be used there must be:
  (1) Ramps less than 5°.
  (ii) Utilization <20%.
  (iii) Length of each run <200 ft.
- Pneumatic tires are used on a rough terrain surface. However, there should not be sharp metal debris on the floor surface. Pneumatic tires can also be used on smooth ground.
- Cushion tires are used only on smooth surfaces. Sharp metal pieces will not affect the performance.
- Internal combustion engines give more power than electric engines. The effect of this is considered in the load and travel requirements of the truck.

Table 5. Sample of five rules used for medium-lift trucks.

- Aisle requirements are confined to a minimum of 50 in.
- All are outriggers unless otherwise specified by the user.
- Less than unit load carrying is possible.
- Only cushion tires will be used, since high lifters are required to stack components inside buildings with loads <4,000 lb.
- Electric-powered versions are preferable for indoor applications.

Table 6. Sample of five rules used for high-lift trucks.

the information it needs to proceed with program execution.

The system uses a combination of forward and backward reasoning. In forward reasoning stages, the system attempts to deduce a truck type recommendation based on known relationships and user specified information. In backward reasoning stages, the system attempts to establish that each possible truck type is the appropriate one, and asks the user questions as they come up in the course of the attempted proofs.

The expert system utilizes backward reasoning early in the inference schedule to quickly eliminate as many truck type clusters as possible. In the later stages of the inference schedule, more use is made of forward reasoning due to the dependence of factors.

For example, in the final selection of a medium-lift truck cluster, it may be necessary to consider maximum load weight, lift, aisle size and tire requirements. However, for a given lift height, if carrying capacity is to be increased, aisle size requirements may increase. If the user specifies that aisle size is to be kept down, specialized trucks may be required, at higher costs.

In any case, the system is designed to recommend the truck type alternative that meets all user-specified requirements and optimizes flexible criteria specified by the user (e.g., minimum cost).

The prototype expert system is coded in PROLOG, a conversational, relatively easy to use language for building expert systems. Creation of the PROLOG code involves the declaration of facts, relationships, rule definition and inference scheduling. A copy of the actual PROLOG code may be obtained by mailing a stamped, self-addressed envelope to the lead author (Dr. Charles J. Malmborg, Center for Industrial and Management Engineering, Rensselaer Polytechnic Institute, Troy, NY 12180).

Summary and Conclusions

A knowledge base and a prototype expert system were constructed for the truck type selection problem. This was accomplished through a preliminary survey of published materials on industrial truck applications and compilation of the knowledge and recommendations in these sources in the form of facts, relationships and rules.

A prototype expert system was then created to utilize this knowledge base for relating material handling problems to industrial truck type alternatives. This involved construction of an interactive PROLOG code that utilized user-specified inputs along with facts, relationships and rules in a process known as pattern-directed inference to recommend industrial truck types.

The prototype expert system described in this article is by no means thorough enough for most real-world applications. However, it does illustrate the basic process by which such a system is constructed.

If			Then		
Load <lb	Usage frequency	Surface condition	Vehicle	Engine	Type of tire
3,000	high	rough	tow tractor	electric	pneumatic
4,000	high	smooth	ttow tractor	electric	cushion
10,000	high	rough	tow tractor	I.C.E.	pneumatic
50,000	v. high	smooth	AGV	electric	cushion
300	low	smooth	burden car	electric	cushion
6,000	high	smooth	burden car	electric	cushion
1,500	low	smooth	dollies	—	rollers

Table 7. Sample of the if/then relationships used for non-lift trucks.

Basically, facts about alternatives are first accumulated from appropriate sources such as human experts and published literature. Secondly, relationships among these facts are identified and used to construct rules for solving specific problems. Finally, an appropriate expert system building tool is selected that can be used in a process of pattern-directed inference to apply the knowledge base to individual problems.

Industrial truck type selection involves an unstructured and complex decision-making process and, typically, the use of substantial domain-dependent knowledge. Expert systems provide the potential for extensive and economical distribution of expertise for solving this selection problem.

In considering the construction and/or application of an expert system for solving this or any other problem, the user must be aware of the limitations of such systems. First, they are only as good as the information on which they are based. If the knowledge base is invalid or perishable due to technical changes in equipment alternatives, it cannot produce reliable recommendations. An expert system must be updated periodically, since it does not learn through experience like the human expert.

Second, expert systems cannot recognize whether a given problem falls within the domain of its knowledge base. It is generally up to the user to correctly identify whether or not a given problem should be addressed using the expert system. For example, if a conveyor is the appropriate solution to a given material handling problem, it is not possible for an expert system restricted to the domain of industrial trucks to recognize this fact.

Third, expert systems can provide only shallow justifications for their recommendations, since they simply point to the specific rules used in developing a recommendation when explaining their reasoning to the user.

Finally, as was shown, the expert system utilizes more elaborate execution of program statements than simple computer programs. That is, rather that executing statements based on their sequence in the code, as with simple programs, the PROLOG code might execute a given statement many times during the course of a run as it repeatedly attempted to prove the condition part of a condition/action pair.

For a simple code such as the prototype expert system for truck type selection, this was not a significant problem. However, in more elaborate systems, especially those that were microcomputer-based, computational requirements could become a significant limitation.

For Further Reading

Agee, M. H., "Powered Rider Lift Trucks," Internal Report, Department of Industrial Engineering and Operations Research, Virginia Tech, 1984.

Apple, J. M., *Material Handling Systems Design*, John Wiley and Sons, New York, 1976.

Application Analysis, Lift Truck Training Brochure No. CE015082-00, Caterpillar Tractor Co., Mentor, OH.

Fichtelman, M., "The Expert Mechanic," *Byte*, Vol. 10, No. 6, 1985.

Fisher, E. L., "Expert Systems Can Lay Groundwork for Intelligent CIM Decision Making," *Industrial Engineering*, Vol. 17, No. 3, March 1985.

Fisher, E. L., Nof, S. Y., "FADES: A Knowledge Based Facility Design Procedure," Annual International IIE Conference *Proceedings*, Chicago, Illinois, Spring 1984.

Goldenberg, J., "Experts on Call," *PC World*, Vol. 3, No. 9, 1985.

Hayes-Roth, F., Waterman, D. A., Lenat, D. B., *Building Expert Systems*, Addison-Wesley, 1983.

Kulwiec, R., "Lift Truck Specification Chart," *Plant Engineering*, November 11, 1976.

Kulwiec, R., "Material Handling Equipment Guide: Selection, Application and Cost Factors for Basic Equipment," *Plant Engineering*, August 21, 1980.

Tompkins, J. A., White, J. A., *Facilities Planning*, John Wiley and Sons, New York, 1984.

Expert Systems in Production Management: An Assessment

Peter Mertens and John J. Kanet

Over the last several years expert systems (ES) have gained almost sensational interest in many scientific fields. Quite a number of pilot industrial applications have already been described in seminars and periodicals. Production management in a broad sense appears to be an area where expert systems could provide many benefits. Up to now, however, applications have been haphazard. As research and development of expert systems requires considerable effort, an organized assessment seems warranted. It appears worthwhile to identify specific production management functions where an expert system approach is more (or less) appropriate.

We assume the reader is already familiar with the concept of expert systems. For those who are not, the articles by Stefik et al. [15] and Chandrasekaran [3] provide good reviews. Fisher [5] discusses how expert systems differ from other approaches and how they might be applied in computer-integrated manufacturing systems. Our approach here will be to examine the applicability of expert systems in production management by considering the types of generic decisions that often require experts and to see when and if these decision types apply in production management settings.

Expert Decision Areas

Stefik et al. [15] have provided what they claim as a characterization of expert tasks. Their list of expert tasks includes:

- Interpreting (INT)—the analyzing of data to determine their meaning.
- Diagnosing (DIA)—the process of fault-finding in a system (also could include finding out what may be good about a system). Analyzing.
- Monitoring (MON)—the continuous interpreting of signals and the setting-off of alarms as needed.
- Predicting (PRD)—the forecasting of some future event.
- Planning (PLA)—the creating of programs of action that are to be carried out to achieve a goal.
- Designing (DES)—the creating of specifications for objects that satisfy a given set of requirements.

We would add the following tasks to the above list (see Mertens and Allgeyer [8]):

- Consulting (CON)—the recommending of certain actions or behavior in light of a given set of circumstances. Advising.
- Teaching (TEA)—the facilitating of the human learning process. Tutoring.

A Taxonomy for Production Management

Broadly speaking, we can interpret the role of production management as having to produce *what* is wanted by the customer in the *time* and *quantity* that the customer wants. When viewed in this light, production management lends itself to be broken down into two major groups of activities: those having to do with *what* (the technology of what and how to produce), and those having to do with *time* and *quantity* (the

Reprinted with permission from The American Production and Inventory Control Society, *Journal of Operations Management*, vol. 6, no. 4, August 1986, pp. 393-404.

logistical aspects of production). We can then organize all the production management activities into these two groups as follows:

Technological Activities

- Manufacturing Engineering (ME)—determining how products are to be produced.
- Industrial Engineering (IE)—setting production standards, designing facilities, etc.
- Maintenance (M)—assuring that production equipment runs efficiently with minimal downtime.
- Quality Control (QC)—assuring that the product is made to engineering specifications.

Logistical Activities

- Production Planning and Control (PC)—setting the levels of resources that are to be made available as well as scheduling when the resources will be used.
- Materials Control (MC)—physically controlling materials; for example, shipping and receiving, traffic management, and storeroom administration.
- Purchasing (P)—procuring from vendors materials of high quality at a favorable price in the quantities and time required by inventory management.
- Inventory Management (IM)—deciding what, when, and how much to order.
- Forecasting (F)—predicting demand for raw materials, semifinished and finished products, and replacement parts.

An "Applications Map"

The nine production management functions and the eight types of expert tasks are combined in Table 1 to form what we shall call an "applications map" for expert systems in the field of production management.

The numbers contained in Table 1 refer to one of the numbered sections that follow. In each paragraph we discuss examples of existing expert systems that perform the indicated expert task(s) within the given production management function and/or our ideas concerning how an expert system in that case might be of benefit.

1. Process Selection

One important application of planning in manufacturing engineering occurs in connection with the introduction of new products into manufacturing. The task is complicated to the extent that a network of interrelated activities need to be coordinated. The criteria are efficiency (low cost, minimal disruption of production of existing products), reliability (adherence to schedule), and quality (conformance to product design specifications). A major aspect of the manufacturing engineering task is to decide how the new product will be made, that is, to choose the production technology to be employed. This often requires a working knowledge of a large variety of production processes (i.e., the technological capabilities of the process, the costs associated with the process, and the relative availability of the process). For example, a given cylindrical steel part for a new product may be produced in a number of different ways. One choice might be to employ an automatic screw machine to form the part and cut it to length all in the same operation. An alternative approach might be to employ a simple cutoff machine and then do the forming as a secondary operation performed on a turret lathe. The first approach may be less costly from the standpoint of labor hours required, but the screw machine may be pressed to hold the required dimensional tolerances. Assuming existing equipment is to be used, the issue of machine availability also has to be considered. The screw machine approach might well be able to hold the required tolerances but the available uncommitted screw machine capacity might not be adequate to support the production schedule of the new product. The problem is further complicated when the purchase of additional equipment (due to capacity) must be considered as an alternative. Then the financial analysis of possible investment alternatives becomes a necessary part of the overall analysis. An expert system might be employed to help manufacturing engineers with these types of choices. The knowledge base would consist of existing process capabilities, relative costs, and total capacities. Rules in deciding how a process is in fact chosen would have to be "mined" from experienced manufacturing engineering experts. Such a system might also be used for training engineers and production managers.

Researchers at the University of Karlsruhe in West Germany are already working on a system that embodies some of the ideas expressed above. Their focus is on developing an expert

	Expert Task							
	INT	DIA	MON	PRD	PLA	DES	CON	TEA
Decision Area								
Technological:								
(ME)					1	2		1, 2
(IE)						4	3	
(M)		5	5	5	5		5	
(QC)	6		6		6			
Logistical:								
(PC)					7, 11		7	
(MC)						9	8	
(P)							10	
(IM)								
(F)				12				

Table 1. An applications map for expert systems in production management.

system to plan the design of flexible assembly systems. An interesting feature of the proposed system at Karlsruhe is that it will have the capability to recommend product design changes that might simplify the production process. Viewed in this light it is a step towards integration of product and process design. Expert systems are already being used to aid with product design specifications. A good example is the well-known XCON system at Digital Equipment [12].

Rixhon [14] describes an intelligent knowledge-based system whose main role is to support the make-or-buy decision. The system uses eight individual knowledge bases (product quality, patents, skills and materials, long-term considerations, other qualitative factors, opportunity costs, incremental costs, and idle facilities). The advice given by the system combines (through a weighting scheme) the results extracted from the eight knowledge bases. The system begins by gathering data, forming a hypothesis, and then testing it. For example, knowing that a considered piece is patented, the system would first recommend to purchase it. If the user refuses this advice, the system gathers more data to determine whether the potential supplier is a competitor who could prohibit buying or whether the piece could be modified "around" the patent.

2. Process Design

Closely related to the above is the issue of designing the processes of production. Here we assume that a given process has been chosen to produce a given product (or part) and the problem now is to design how this process will in fact be employed. The performance criteria remain efficiency, reliability, and quality. Consider the automatic screw machine process mentioned above. Tool slide arrangements, and machine feeds and speeds all need to be decided in such a way that initial tool costs (and subsequent maintenance), setup times, and dimensional specifications are all given due consideration. For this purpose an "expert process engineer" might be useful. The expert system would have a knowledge base of appropriate feed-speed relations for different materials as well as dimensional capabilities of different types of tooling arrangements. Rules governing how this knowledge base is manipulated to achieve a tool layout would have to be mined (as above) from human experts. The difference between this type of system and the type envisioned in Section I (above) is that in this case the expert system is concentrated on a single production process. As in Section I, such a system might be put to good use as a training device.

Under the theme of process design, the Siemens Company in Erlangen, West Germany, is currently experimenting with an expert system for product assembly. In their application, the system would be used to decide the sequence of assembly operations that a robot would perform to assemble a given product or subassembly. The usual technological precedence data would be considered along with the knowledge of the kinematic restrictions of the robot in order to arrive at an efficient sequence of assembly operations and robot motions.

3. Facility Location

Facility location is a type of industrial engineering planning decision that requires deciding the size and location of new facilities. The problem is complicated because it involves both quantitative (e.g., local labor costs and availability, transportation costs, etc.) as well as subjective factors (local politics, community attitudes, legal considerations, etc.). The decision is not so frequently required, but whenever it must be made, the consequences are usually quite high and have long-term implications to the firm. An expert system might be gainfully employed in helping to decide among competing alternative plant locations. The system, using principles of multi-attribute decision theory, might help the decision maker identify "dominance" situations (enabling the elimination of one or more alternatives from consideration) as well as serving to quickly show the sensitivity of the choice to a change in a given assumption or initial set of preferences. Because this type of decision is made only infrequently by any individual firm, an expert system built for this type of problem would probably have to be useable by many firms (perhaps all in the same industry) to justify its development.

4. Facility Layout

Related to facilities location is the facility layout decision. Here the problem is to decide the arrangement (or rearrangement) of process equipment within a given factory. As with the choice of plant location, the layout decision may not be frequently required, but whenever it is, the consequences can be relatively costly. The criteria in such a decision are usually related to some measure of efficiency (e.g., stated in terms of transportation costs) and flexibility (e.g., can the layout accept a large variety of different product mixes). The knowledge base for such decisions would contain the physical characteristics of the facility and existing equipment as well as any constraints on the relative arrangement of the equipment (e.g., the heat treating furnaces must be located some minimum distance from the paint facility). The rule base might mimic human heuristics in a combinatorial search of alternatives. One approach for augmenting existing layout methodologies with an expert system has been proposed by Nof [11].

5. Maintenance

In this area there are actually several expert tasks. The first is to diagnose equipment malfunctions as early as possible (early warning). The data for this must be collected from a number of sources (production data such as extended processing time, operator-reported data, and machine idle time; process information like above-average heat, noise, vibration, and fluctuations in measures, weights, and chemical consistencies; and quality control of the product—for example, rising scrap rates and growing fluctuations in other quality indicators). Because of the sheer volume of data they would have to be reduced to a few patterns. These patterns would then have to be compared with patterns stored in the knowledge base in order to make a diagnosis. The data reduction and diagnosis would have to be done very quickly to avoid damages to the facility, to the products, or even to prevent dangerous situations for personnel (explosions, etc.).

With new equipment or redesigns, the above patterns or critical values may have to be changed. This is where the feature of expert systems of being able to modify the knowledge base in a flexible manner becomes a real advantage. One can imagine the equipment supplier delivering, together with the change in the physical design, the information on the necessary modifications of the knowledge base in order to minimize the training and programming effort at his customer's site.

After the diagnosis, several planning decisions must be made. Examples of alternatives include taking the facility out of production immediately; shifting the repair until the current production order is completed; waiting until the next period with sufficient excess capacity to make the repair; occupying the facility with products that do not need such high equipment standards; or shifting the repair to the date of next preventive maintenance. Also, the interrelation between unplanned repairs and planned preventive maintenance must be considered—should the rhythm of the preventive maintenance be changed after an unplanned repair? So-called opportunistic strategies may be complicated—among the parts that are not yet worn out, which of them should be replaced during the unplanned repair because the machine is out of production anyway or has to be disassembled?

When making these decisions a great number of restrictions which can be found in the database must be observed, for example, actual machine utilization, availability of a standby machine, availability (waiting line) of the maintenance personnel, availability of replacement parts, buffer stocks at succeeding work stations, the scheduling situation of the affected customer orders, sensitivity of the customer to minor deviations in quality, and the probability of significantly greater repair costs if the repair were further delayed.

An interesting application of an expert system approach to a maintenance problem is provided by Hakami and Newborn [7]. They report on an expert system that is used to diagnose equipment faults in a steel rolling mill of the British Steel Corporation. The system analyzes symptoms (signals collected at various checkpoints within the mill) and can advise the attending manager to conduct additional tests to help diagnose the source of a mill stoppage. Much like a physician, the system weighs the effectiveness of a given test against its attendant costs before making a recommendation. In computing the effectiveness of a test the system uses information about the a priori likelihood that a given fault is present. This highly successful system, in operation since 1982, has also been extensively used by British Steel as a very effective training aid.

6. Quality Control

An important planning decision in quality control is to determine quality layouts (or plans), that is, to specify where, when, and how the production processes are to be monitored. A knowledge of what could go wrong is needed. This means an understanding of the product design as well as the production processes. An expert system might be employed to help with this type of decision. The decision would have to be frequently made (once for each part or product produced). The expert system would use a knowledge base of process capabilities to judge (using a rule base supplied by the experiences of human experts) when and how a given product would be tested during the production process to see if it conformed to engineering specifications.

An interesting implementation of an expert system in the quality control field is the system in use at Standard Elektrik Lorenz (SEL) in Stuttgart, West Germany. SEL employs an expert system to diagnose defects in highly complicated (and expensive) electronic assemblies. An assembly may not function properly but the source of the malfunction may be extremely difficult to pinpoint. The expert system suggests a line of additional tests to be performed on the assembly in order to locate the fault. Akin to the maintenance system at British Steel, the system operates on a store of expert knowledge (which was extracted from the experiences of human experts) that relates symptoms to possible fault sources.

7. Production Planning and Control

Two important planning functions in the area of production control are deciding what level to make a given resource available (in a given period or set of periods) and when to commit a given resource to a given unit of product. Baker [2] has differentiated these two types of decisions and used them to describe the difference between production planning and production scheduling. Production scheduling essentially involves a type of sequencing decision and implicitly assumes that the production (capacity) planning process has already taken place. The scheduling problem is easily defined as a problem of combinatorial optimization. The difficulty is that the sheer size of these types of problems makes finding optimal solutions virtually impossible. An expert systems approach would mimic the heuristic methods that humans currently employ to solve these types of problems. Criteria for scheduling problems include dependability (the schedules produced must adequately meet customer due dates), flexibility (the procedure must be prepared to update schedules rapidly when new information becomes available), and cost (the solution must be sensitive, for example, to the inventory investment that it generates). A key requirement for any expert scheduling system would be a well-developed explanation subsystem. Unless the system is capable of clearly defending why it chose a given schedule, production managers would not be quick to accept its recommendations. A second key to the acceptability of an expert scheduling system is the ease with which the system can accept new rules (or rule changes) from the system user.

For example, in the expert scheduling system ISA (Intelligent Scheduling Assistant) developed by Digital Equipment, users of the system are continually adding new rules and knowledge to the system. Digital's experience in the development of these types of systems is that user acceptability grows as more and more of the person's knowledge is encoded into the system [12].

8. Material Selection

The decision situation here comprises two phases:

- *The Design Phase.* The design engineer should not choose parts based on technological considerations only, but should also consider the availability (or even overstock) of existing parts. When the material is not on hand, purchasing considerations must be observed such as required delivery lead times, etc.
- *The Delivery Phase.* As an example here consider the steel industry. It may be that the exact material that a customer desires is not in stock. But a more valuable material is available. The decision is whether the requested material should be produced (e.g., smelted) leaving a more expensive material in stock. (In this case we have smelting costs and inventory costs.) Or, should the more valuable material be used? Then there may be lost profits if an order for the more expensive material arrives in the near future. Another alternative would be to use material that has the correct physical and chemical properties but is too thick. In this case the available material might be rolled to the required thickness.

The decisions cited above depend on a number of different facts and conditions, for example, on the delivery date requested by the customer, on available storage room, on the supply of cash, on the sales forecast, on the capacity utilization level, and on the sensitivity of the customer.

9. Storeroom Design

Two related problems in materials control are the specification of storeroom layouts and the design of procedures for storage and retrieval decisions. The layout problem is similar in concept to the facility layout application described above. The problem of storage-retrieval in warehouses usually includes the geography of the storage facility as a given. Simply stated, the problem is to decide where to put incoming materials and which locations of materials to retrieve to satisfy a given withdrawal order. In a given storeroom, the problem may have to be solved hundreds of times a day. The consequences of an individual decision might be of negligible impact, but taken in aggregate, consistently good decisions can make a significant difference in the performance of the organization. Humans currently solve this problem by heuristically processing information about pallet/container capacities, distances to storage locations, urgency of orders, anticipated future demand for materials, etc. An expert systems approach would formalize these heuristic rules and possibly combine them with embedded algorithms to arrive at storage/retrieval decisions.

10. Vendor Selection

A typical feature here is that many criteria have to be considered simultaneously, such as price, delivery, time, adherence to due date, and quality level. Furthermore, the individual criteria may have at different times different relative importance. For example, one would not necessarily select the vendor with the lowest price when the material is needed quickly because of an urgent in-house order.

If a vendor gives a rebate on the basis of total annual purchases, one has to check near the year's end whether the rebate limit can be reached by augmenting the last purchase quantity. Moreover, to remain independent, a firm will aim to not concentrate its purchases on a single vendor. In such situations it would be worthwhile to systematically rotate vendors.

In summary, the vendor selection problem alone appears to be not so complex that an expert system would provide significant improvements over simpler procedures such as scoring models or decision tables. An expert systems approach might prove to be more valuable when the vendor selection problem is simultaneously considered with other related problems (e.g., the material selection problem discussed in Section 8 above).

11. Capacity Planning

Capacity planning, in the sense that capacities are adjusted according to current work load, pertains to equipment as well as personnel. Aside from the well-known decisions, for example, between investment, overtime, and subcontracting, the flexible calling-in of employees depending on the current workload may also become an interesting alternative in the future. See for example, the ideas of Glover, McMillan, and Glover [6]. In this case it is not just a question of deploying the right employees (quantity and skill level); there may also be complicated work contracts with the trade union that must be observed. For example, in West Germany there are union agreements that limit the amount of overtime and require the average work week to be 38.5 hours. Some workers could work 40 hours, others 37, and sometimes a lower limit is only valid for workers over fifty-five years old. The average of 38.5, however, must be exactly achieved for every two-month period.

12. Forecasting
An important logistics problem in production management is forecasting. The more recent developments in the literature (e.g., see Armstrong [1] and Mertens and Backert [9]) indicate that a promising area for improvement in forecasting performance might stem from intelligently combining the forecasts obtained from different sources. For example, a sales forecast from an exponential smoothing model might be compared to the forecast provided by a Box-Jenkins technique and, according to some set of rules, the two individual forecasts would be combined to develop a single forecast of the item in question. The rules may involve a simple weighted averaging of the individual forecasts, or perhaps when the individual forecasts are significantly different, a systematic reexamination of the parameters used in the individual methods. This might take the form of a computerized Delphi approach, which would recursively generate new rounds of forecasts until a consensus forecast was reached. An expert systems approach might be used to embody and administer the rules that govern how the individual forecasts would be combined.

An Assessment

Table 2 shows our numerical assessment or "degree of belief" (on a scale of 1 to 5) of the importance, of the potential for improved solutions, and of the ease of development for expert systems in the twelve production management decision situations described in the sections above.

These three criteria are aggregates of single items. Problem importance is the "product" of the importance of a good decision in a single decision case "times" the number of cases per period (the frequency with which the decision has to be made). In this light, facility location receives the moderate score of 3 because it

	Subjective Ratings		
	Problem Importance[1]	Potential for Improved Solutions[2]	Ease of Development[3]
Decision Situation:			
1. Process Selection	3	3	3
2. Process Design	4	3	5
3. Facility Location	3	1	3
4. Facility Layout	3	2	4
5. Maintenance	5	4	3
6. Quality Layouts	3	1	5
7. Scheduling	5	3	3
8. Material Selection	2	2	3
9. Storeroom Design	1	1	3
10. Vendor Selection	2	1	5
11. Employee Scheduling	3	3	3
12. Forecasting	5	3	3

[1] Scale: 1 = (not important), 5 = (very important)
[2] Scale: 1 = (low potential), 5 = (high potential)
[3] Scale: 1 = (easy to develop), 5 = (hard to develop)

Table 2. Assessment of expert systems in decision situations.

	Subjective Rating[1]		
	Problem Importance	Potential for Improved Solutions	Ease of Development
Decision Area			
Technological:			
1. Manufacturing Engineering	9	8	11
2. Industrial Engineering	6	3	7
3. Maintenance	5	4	3
4. Quality Control	3	1	5
Logistical:			
5. Production Planning & Control	8	6	6
6. Materials Control	1	1	3
7. Purchasing	2	1	5
8. Inventory Management	0	0	0
9. Forecasting	5	3	3

[1] All table entries were obtained by adding those entries in Table 2 that correspond to a particular decision area.

Table 3. Consolidation of decision situations to production management functions.

represents a very important problem that is infrequently made. Improvement of the solution has to be seen in comparison with manual procedures as well as with conventional decision support procedures such as simple scoring methods or simulation. For example, the vendor selection problem gains only 1 point because it might be handled by a scoring technique, whereas the facility location decision is influenced by a number of political or other considerations so that it would be made without much computer assistance. Ease of development is a combination of the estimated development costs and the chance to find a straightforward solution.

In viewing Table 2 we find that process design and maintenance seem to be the fields where research and development projects might be most promising, followed by scheduling and forecasting. it is no accident that there are existing expert systems in these areas, such as the Intelligent Scheduling Assistant (see Orciuch and Frost [13] or O'Connor [12]) and the system ICLX (see Hakami and Newborn [7]).

Based on the discussion above, one could imagine that expert systems that helped in the *combined* task of production scheduling and equipment maintenance to be a fruitful area for further investigation. Such a system would help schedule production orders in times when maintenance activities are not required and, conversely, help plan maintenance in times when production orders are not demanded. It would thus see the problem in the simultaneous way it presents itself in reality. But as experience proves, only expert systems with limited scope have a good chance of realization and acceptance. So a combined system might be more of a long-term than a short-term goal.

In Table 3 we have consolidated the twelve situations cited above to the nine production management functions simply by adding up the scores from Table 2.

In the upper half of the table we find the more technical functions and in the lower half the more commercial functions. One should not pay too much attention to the gross numbers. In viewing the *relative* size of the numbers however, the pattern shows that there might be a better chance to build good expert systems in the more technically inclined decision problems than in the more commercially oriented. The breadth of expert task applications appears to be also wider in the technological group of functions. Referring back again to Table 1 we see that for the technological functions each of the eight expert tasks is performed at least once. In the logistical group, however, the tasks appear to be concentrated to the set: planning, designing, and controlling (with the exception of forecasting). One explanation for this may be that the technological functions require a large, broad knowledge base of technical facts, for example, as in quality control or maintenance systems that may have to diagnose system defects. The logistical functions, however, require a "deeper" type of knowledge base that is more skillful at deductive reasoning, for example, as may be the case in scheduling systems where the planning function is to a certain extent a complicated combinatorial problem. It is remarkable that inventory management received the score of zero in Table 3. We found no existing systems nor research proposals applying expert systems to inventory management. It may well be that existing algorithmic procedures sufficiently address this type of problem.

Our investigation here indicates that successful expert systems of the future might well be ones that take a broader perspective, that is, ones that combine technological and logistical knowledge, for as is often the case in practice, both types of information are needed for production decisions. Fox and Smith [4], for example, are using this very principle in the design of their knowledge-based system for factory scheduling. Considering some existing systems such as those developed by Digital Equipment (see McDermott [10]), we could argue that at least part of their success stems from the fact that they combine technical knowledge (e.g., component design characteristics) with logistical data (such as part availability) in arriving at a recommendation.

References

1. Armstrong, J. S. "Forecasting by Extrapolation: Conclusions from 25 Years of Research." *Interfaces*, Vol. 14, No. 6 (Nov.-Dec. 1985), pp. 52-66.
2. Baker, K. R. *Introduction to Sequencing and Scheduling*. New York, 1974.
3. Chandrasekaran, B. "Expert Systems: Matching Techniques to Tasks." *Proceedings of NYU Symposium on Artificial Intelligence for Business*. New York, 1983.
4. Fox, M. S. and S. F. Smith. "ISIS—A Knowledge-Based System for Factory Scheduling." *Expert Systems*, Vol. 1, No. 1 (1984), pp. 25-49.
5. Fisher, E. L. "Expert Systems Can Lay Groundwork for Intelligent CIM Decision Making." *Industrial Engineering*, Vol. 17, No. 3 (March 1985), pp. 78-83.
6. Glover, F., C. McMillan, and R. Glover. "A Heuristic Programming Approach to the Employee Scheduling Problem and Some Thoughts on 'Managerial Robots.'" *Journal of Operations Management*, Vol. 4, No. 2 (February 1984), pp. 113-128.
7. Hakami, B. and J. Newborn. "Expert System in Heavy Industry: An Application of ICLX in a British Steel Corporation Works." *ICL Technical Journal*, November 1983, pp. 347-359.
8. Mertens, P. and K. Allgeyer. "Kuenstliche Intelligenz in der Betriebswirtschaft." *Zeitschrift fuer Betriebswirtschaft*, Vol. 53, No. 7 (July 1983), pp. 686-709.
9. Mertens, P. and K. Backert. "Vergleich und Auswahl von Prognoseverfahren fuer betriebswirtschaftliche Zwecke—Uebersichtsartikel." *Zeitschrift fuer Operations Research*, Vol. 24, No. 2 (March 1980), pp. B1-B27.
10. McDermott, J. "Building Expert Systems." In Reitman, W. (ed.). *Artificial Intelligence Applications for Business*, pp. 11-22, Norwood, N.J., 1984.
11. Nof, S. Y. "An Expert System for Planning/Replanning Programmable Facilities." *International Journal of Production Research*, Vol. 22, No. 5 (1984), pp. 895-903.
12. O'Connor, D. E. "Using Expert Systems to Manage Change and Complexity in Manufacturing." *Proceedings of NYU Symposium on Artificial Intelligence Applications for Business*. New York, 1983.
13. Orciuch, E. and J. Frost. "ISA: Intelligent Scheduling Assistant." *The First Conference on Artificial Intelligence Application*. New York, 1984, pp. 314-320.
14. Rixhon, P. "Intelligent Knowledge-Based Systems: A Tool for Manufacturing Planning and Scheduling," unpublished paper presented at the IFAC Workshop on Artificial Intelligence, Zurich, March 12-14, 1985.
15. Stefik, M., J. Aikins, R. Balzer, J. Benoit, L. Birnbaum, F. Hayes-Roth, and E. Sacerdoti. "The Organization of Expert Systems: A Tutorial." *Artificial Intelligence*, Vol. 13, No. 2 (March 1982), pp. 135-173.

Expert Systems: The Integrative Sales Management Tool of the Future

Margery Steinberg and Richard E. Plank

Recent literature abounds with discussions of the recurring problems faced by sales managers today. Poor utilization of time and planned sales efforts was the number one concern of sales executives cited in a recent study (Dauner and Johnson 1980). Sales productivity and the value of salespersons' time were the focus of the latest McGraw Hill Laboratory Report (*Sales and Marketing Management*, 1986). Substantial performance differences among the typical sales force and the legendary 80/20 rule suggest the need for more effective training of salespersons (Hayes-Roth 1985). High selling costs, reported to be escalating at a rapid rate, are generating a great deal of interest among sales managers to develop effective cost-cutting measures (Hutt and Speh 1986 and Kern 1986).

Obviously, with escalating sales costs, even small increases in productivity can bring about substantial savings and incremental profitability to the organization. The personal computer is the kind of tool that has the potential to generate the desired bottom line results. The advent of microcomputers, the increasing technological advances in reducing their size and portability and the networking concept make possible rapid potential advances in sales employee productivity.

Many examples exist in the practitioner press that describe the use of personal computers in the sales or marketing function. One specific application of computers in enhancing the sales function was demonstrated by Hamel Publication's 25% increase in salesperson productivity (Taylor 1986a). Customized IBM-PC compatible software that integrated telemarketing, tickler files, call reports and sales information from prospecting to closing helped maximize salespersons' time and efforts.

Few examples exist in the academic literature; the most notable is Collins (1985a, 1985b, 1986), whose work is directly applicable to the personal selling process. One article (Collins 1985b) reported on the Dow Jones Prospect Organizer, which is essentially a lead handling system. It appears that few, if any, multipurpose programs have been developed.

The purpose of this paper is to explore in detail the concept of developing an expert system to integrate the sales management function within a useful computer-based decision support system, and to demonstrate how this kind of software will greatly enhance the productivity of the sales function. While the focus of this work is on the problems faced by sales managers, it is important to keep in perspective the relationship of the sales function to the marketing activities and the overall objectives of the entire firm. Traditionally, sales management problems tend to be treated in isolation. An idealized notion is that of a number of expert systems from various functional areas integrated into a comprehensive decision support system. The scenario, perhaps fifteen to twenty years hence, will involve decision support systems as part of the overall marketing information system, consisting of numerous expert systems integrated into one interactive system. The benefit of these kinds of integrated systems will be the greater coordination of company activities with resulting increases in overall productivity.

Reprinted with permission from *Journal of the Academy of Marketing Science*, vol. 15, no. 2, Summer 1987, 55-62.

Following a definition and discussion of the concept of expert systems, two possible frameworks for the development of an expert system for sales management and its integration into a unified marketing expert system will be described.

Expert Systems

One way of defining the concept of expert systems was suggested in *Training* (1986).

> "A computer program that does an intelligent analysis of data that creates a dialog with the user and can generate further analysis based on the data entered."

Seven attributes were defined that distinguish expert systems from other types of computer management systems: expertise, reasoning by symbol manipulation, intelligence, solving difficult and complex problems, reformulation, reasoning about self and task specificity.

Expertise refers to the goal of the system to emulate the performance of a human decision maker. Expert systems use knowledge coded symbolically rather than coded computer routines to imitate the human expert. Problem solving is done heuristically rather than algorithmically. The system is intelligent in that it can solve problems by applying rules to arrive at an acceptable, but not always correct or perfect answer, just like a human expert using rules of thumb.

Thus, difficult problems (i.e., those requiring many rules) are capable of being solved. The actual problem can be formulated and reformulated just as a human expert would. The rules allow the system to explain how it works, thus justifying the answer it gives. Finally, expert systems must be task specific and therefore must be developed especially for each application.

Harmon and King (1985) refer to expert systems as "knowledge-intensive computer programs." They suggest that such technology will enable users to act as experts in defining problems and applying available knowledge to their solutions. The user becomes an expert because the system enables him to access both the data and the rules with which to evaluate the problem and the alternative solutions.

Oxman (1985) has suggested that expert systems, knowledge-based systems, artificial intelligence systems, decision support systems, management information systems and the like are related to each other since their respective goals overlap. He states that:

"Expert systems are computer software systems that use knowledge (rules about the behavior of elements of a particular subject domain) and facts and inference (reasoning) techniques to solve problems that normally require the abilities of human experts."

Figure 1 (Oxman 1985) illustrates the components and linkages of a typical expert system.

The key to any expert system is in the inference engine, the component of the program which uses information from the domain database, knowledge database and system user to derive a conclusion from these inputs in a deductive manner. Based on rules and facts supplied by an expert, a knowledge engineer (programmer) develops the algorithms in computer code which comprise the inference engine. The domain database and the knowledge database form the database management system (DBMS) and are provided by the expert, knowledge engineer and the user. The domain database contains information about a topical subject area. The knowledge database contains the facts and rules about the behavior and the elements of the subject which empower the expert. The domain database has constant input from the user, and the knowledge database can be updated by the knowledge engineer and the expert as the need arises. The user enters facts, usually by answering questions, and receives advice, consultation and justification from the inference engine.

As Konopasek and Jayaraman (1984) note, expert systems are in their infancy with large scale domain-specific systems first developed in the 1960's. Duda and Gaschnig (1981) indicated that knowledge-based expert systems really became prevalent between the late 1970's and 1981.

Carrington (1986) notes the kind of applications that are currently utilizing expert systems. General Electric and United Technologies have many applications including diagnostic manufacturing applications. Coleco has a new toy about to debut which contains an expert system so that it can react to its environment with human-like behavior.

Booker, Kick and Gardner (1986) review the applications of expert systems which are used in accounting for auditing and taxation. They explain that such technology could change the

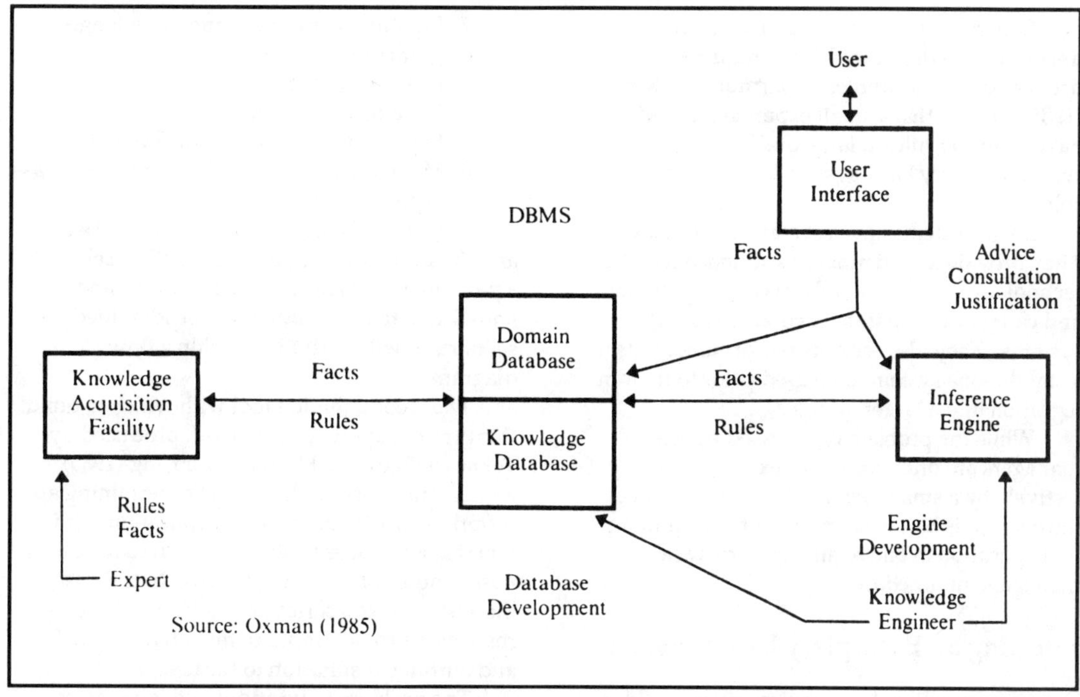

Figure 1. Components and linkages in a typical expert system.

patterns of competition among accounting firms by allowing small firms to provide the kinds of problem-solving expertise that traditionally only large firms could supply.

Marketing functions, however, have not yet been the focus of many efforts to develop expert systems or to integrate such applications across all facets of the marketing function.

An Expert System for Sales Management

Sales management has been defined by Dalrymple (1982) as:

> "the planning, implementing, and control of personal contact programs designed to achieve the sales objectives of the firm."

As such it involves the major managerial tasks of analysis, planning, organization, direction, and control within the framework of the function of personal selling.

Effective problem-solving capabilities evolve from a base of knowledge and experience. In examining the nature of problems faced by sales managers, it becomes clear that such sales force issues as poor utilization of time, lagging productivity, poor performance, escalating selling costs and overall lack of productivity can be effectively addressed by the implementation of an expert system. In addition, through the development of a larger expert system servicing the entire marketing function, the day-to-day and long term operations of an organization can be enhanced, affecting overall profitability. Specifically, the development of a marketing expert system will enable coordination among a company's managers who perform various functions relating to the marketing mix elements. Knowledge and experience can be pooled into a unified knowledge database, controlled by a common inference engine, and draw upon domain specific information. Figure 2 represents a view of the components of an expert system for the marketing function.

All marketing managers, and for that matter, all managers, deal with the same set of tasks, but within their own environments. Thus one would expect a degree of overlap, both in the information used as well as the rules for defining how a particular function is fulfilled. In a normative sense, the environment should be the major factor in differentiating both the use of data and the rule structure. Thus, different rules may be applied to solving different problems within the context of common organizational information and goals.

Expert systems can be small or large, depending on the rules that are required to address a particular problem. Harmon and King (1985) suggest that a small expert system will have 50 to 350 rules, a large one 500 to 3000 rules and a very large system 10,000 or more rules.

Small systems have several roles to play. They provide a preliminary experience with the technology that is relatively easy to implement and can serve as an introduction to the larger systems. They also serve as performance aids in a stand-alone system to be used prior to their integration into a larger system.

While the problems addressed by sales managers are often too complex to be handled effectively by a small system, the introduction of the concept is better exemplified by examining its application in one relatively narrow sales management function.

Building an Exemplary Expert System

Building a small system requires six steps (Harmon and King 1985).

1. Select a tool which commits the user to a consultation paradigm.
2. Identify the problem and knowledge to be included.
3. Design the system.
4. Develop a prototype.
5. Expand, test and revise the system.
6. Maintain and update the system on an as-needed basis.

This paper will deal with steps one, two and three: a tool and paradigm will be selected, a particular problem will be examined, and knowledge to be included will be identified. A set of rules will be drafted within a flow diagram.

The recommended tool with which to build this type of expert system is M.I. produced by Teknowledge, Inc. Harmon and King (1985) demonstrated its application in determining appropriate media for training applications. It is a tool that addresses problems which require diagnosis/prescription consultations. In this case, the system asks a series of questions whose responses provide input to the inference engine and output consultation to the user.

The problem to be addressed is a very complex but somewhat generic one, that of evaluating the performance of a salesperson. Assuming that quarterly sales force evaluation is a key task

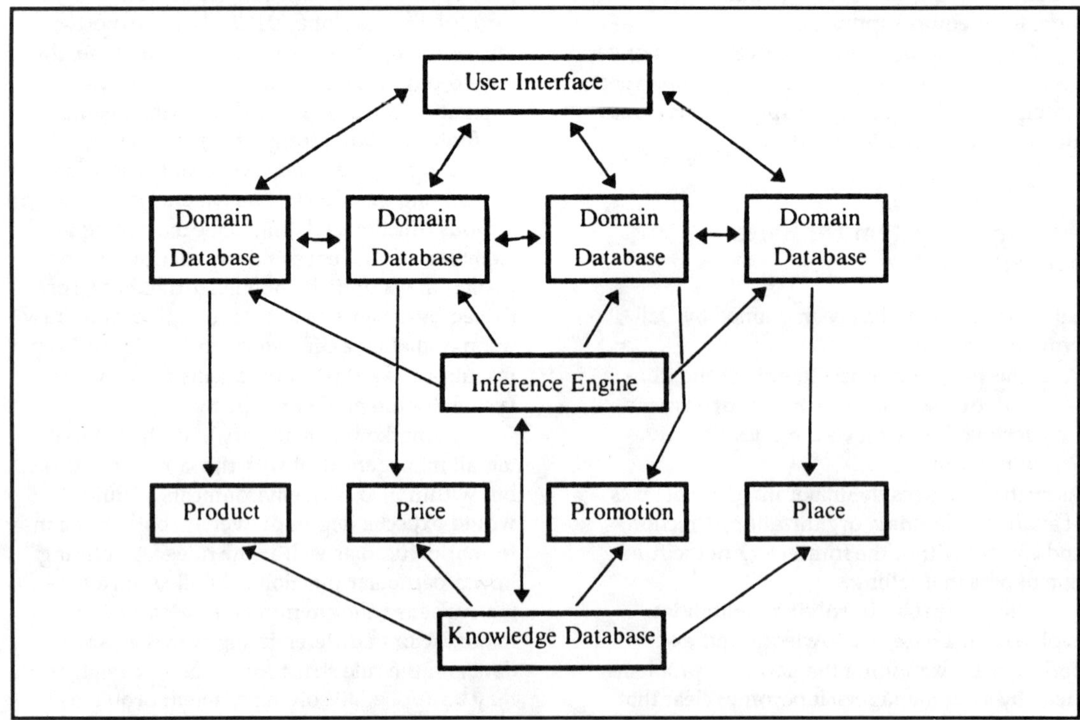

Figure 2. Components of a marketing expert system.

performed by a sales manager, the maintenance and evaluation of information can be invaluable in the planning and diagnostic processes. In developing this kind of system, a typical model-building exercise occurs. The first step requires identification of desired outcomes and data input needs. The next step defines the rules that will manipulate the data and provide the output.

The outcome generates a key numerical variable that will allow the sales manager to distinguish between the performance of one salesperson and another. The necessary data depends upon the company's definition of important selling success factors. The rules determine how the data is to be manipulated or computed to arrive at a rating.

Following the data analysis, the sales manager will be able to utilize the outcomes to prescribe a course of action which will assist in improving the salesperson's productivity. For example, the output may indicate areas in which the salesperson needs more training, or the fact that the salesperson is not achieving his/her fullest potential in the territory.

The following example demonstrates the development of a simplified component of a sales management expert system and its linkages to the larger marketing expert system. Figure 3 itemizes sample information which would be included in the unified domain database servicing this system. As this figure indicates, data from other marketing and planning functions as well as sales force performance data can be combined within the sales domain database, which is only one part of the overall promotional database (see Figure 2). Thus, domain database information comes from a variety of sources and is transferred to be applied as necessary by all decision makers within the marketing function.

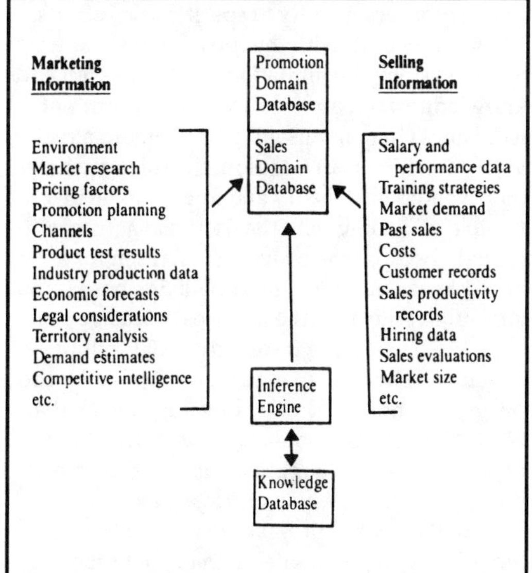

Figure 3. Sample information in unified domain database.

Within the compensation function, one of the most difficult decisions a sales manager must make is how to evaluate the motivational level of a salesperson. This decision might be determined by selected rules stored in the knowledge database. The user asks questions of the inference engine which in turn, combines the rules and the data to report back the outcomes. Table 1 demonstrates a simplified set of rules for making this decision.

In this example, the company has defined expertise in terms of three measures of motivation and the rules assign values to different levels of each measure. In this instance, the information which will contribute to the scoring by the rules is stored by the domain database, and is the result of ongoing customer surveys, quarterly evaluation reports, and other productivity measures. After determining the personal values, the inference engine then combines the categorical values to determine the motivational score.

While this example is intentionally simplistic, it illustrates the potential usefulness of expert systems to sales managers. Planning, training, staffing, scheduling, compensating, supervising, forecasting and other important sales and marketing functions are all potentially serviced by this kind of information system.

Another means of exemplifying the concept of an expert system for sales management is through the examination of two existing microcomputer software packages. One simplistic expert system for personal selling is Sell! Sell! Sell! (Thoughtware, Inc.). One of its major weaknesses is in the database capabilities, which can be improved with the integration of a sales database program, PMS (Datamatics Corp.). The integration demonstrates how a stronger database function will enhance this particular program which, in turn, leads to further improvements in expert systems technology for this application.

IF	THEN
1. New accounts = 0-1 per month	Motivational score = 1
2. New accounts = 1-2 per month	Motivational score = 2
3. New accounts = 3-5 per month	Motivational score = 3
4. New accounts = 6-9 per month	Motivational score = 4
5. New accounts = 10 and over per month	Motivational score = 5
6. Salesperson always late filing reports	Motivational score = 1
7. Salesperson usually late filing reports	Motivational score = 2
8. Salesperson sometimes late filing reports	Motivational score = 3
9. Salesperson rarely late filing reports	Motivational score = 4
10. Salesperson never late filing reports	Motivational score = 5
11. Salesperson provides customer little or no after sale service	Motivational score = 1
12. Salesperson provides customer minimal after sale service	Motivational score = 2
13. Salesperson provides customer adequate after sale service	Motivational score = 3
14. Salesperson provides customer adequate after sale service	Motivational score = 4
15. Salesperson provides customer exceptional after sale service	Motivational score = 5

Table 1. Rules about salesperson's motivational level.

SELL! SELL! SELL!

SELL! SELL! SELL! is an integrated sales training and sales management personal computer software package which attempts to accomplish what was previously the private domain of seminars and management teams. Collins (1986) has discussed the package in some detail from the perspective of a sales training device. It is a three module program that includes sales management, training, and applications. The package's basic components are:

- The assessment program, which enables the user to measure his selling aptitude and his own selling strengths and weaknesses.
- The training program, which teaches and evaluates the user's mastery of basic selling skills.
- The applications component, which provides the structure for creating reports, prospect and customer lists, as well as other sales training tools.

The program functions as an expert system, particularly in the use of its personal assessment and sizing up the customer segments. Analyzing the package according to Oxman's (1985) model, the user interfaces with the program which acts like a sales consultant in questioning and responding to the information entered into the database. The set of questions reside in the domain database and the user's responses enter the knowledge database. The preestablished rules of "good selling strategy" are also part of the expert system and, based on the user's responses to the program's line of questioning, advice is given as to the best approach to the target customers. The user is assisted in planning sales strategy because the database development features of the program keep track of which sales approaches have worked well for certain types of clients.

While each of the package's three component parts is crucial to the selling function, the program treats them as three separate modules and does not integrate them into one system. In addition, the program does not assist the salesperson in making routing decisions, applying past successful sales experiences to current selling situations, or in allocating expenses and other resources directly to specific sales efforts. Thus, while built with the capacity to act as an expert system, the limitations of the domain and knowledge databases reduce the program's effectiveness in many useful planning and supervisory functions. In addition, the rules are based on psychological theory and appear to be inflexible in dealing with the dynamic nature of selling. Because the program is written for a broad-based audience, its knowledge base is too general to adjust for the nuances of each type of customer and each type of individual selling situation. The level of expertise supplied by this program is not sufficiently developed such that SELL! SELL! SELL! may be truly defined as an expert system. As suggested above, the type of domain database which resides in the package does not allow the program to act as a truly integrative selling and sales management tool. The inclusion of a more advanced database such as that exemplified by PMS will demonstrate how a well developed expert system can improve the productivity of the selling function.

PMS

PMS, or Performance Monitoring System, is an interactive MS-DOS operating system based microcomputer software program that was developed for the banking industry. The major advantage of PMS over similar programs is that it was developed as an interactive program in which data entered from a remote location can be assessed at any time and by a controlled number of people. It is not an expert system, but a highly developed database manager which can be used for sales planning as well as providing an electronic supervisory mechanism for management. From the expert system perspective of Oxman (1985) the program provides a knowledge database function.

The program contains four sets of operations arranged into ten modules. Figure 4 is the program's main menu.

Executive Operations
1. Customer/Call Logical Entry
2. Automatic To Do List

Inquiry Modules
3. Customer File Inquiry
4. Call File Inquiry
5. Plans File Inquiry

Data Analysis Modules
6. Consolidated Call/Sale Analysis
7. Consolidated Plans Analysis
8. Department/Service Officer Sales Analysis

Sub-Menus
9. Print Reports Menu
10. Master File Maintenance Menu

Select Option By Number Enter 99 to Exit

Source: Main Menu of PMS by Datamatics Corp., Woodbridge, New Jersey

Figure 4. PMS main menu.

The executive operations function includes modules for entering data and generating automatic "to-do lists." The "to-do list" provides a reminder file which the salesperson or manager can access at any time. It functions as an appointment calendar, but can also be used to record sales leads from various sources, thus directing the salesperson to follow up and maintain a listing in the system.

Inquiry modules allow salespeople and other authorized participants to examine activity in specific accounts, i.e., the calling plans and the entire planning activities of specific salespeople by time, area, account type or other preestablished variable.

The third set of modules provides the data analysis functions of the system. Evaluation can be performed at the plans or results level for units of salespeople, territories, industries or other fields for which information is defined and collected. Thus, aggregation or decomposition of information can be accomplished depending on the needs of the system user.

The final set of modules, sub menus, provides for file maintenance and allows users to design the system to fit their needs and print out reports. The master file maintenance menu allows the user to define the parameters of the system. In most situations, the master file maintenance menu would not be accessed by the users, but only by those personnel who maintain the system.

These four areas thus form an integrative set of functions. Some of the more obvious applications include lead source tracking, sales and territory planning, sales analysis, forecasting, and market analysis.

Integrating PMS and SELL! SELL! SELL!

As noted previously, SELL! SELL! SELL! has several weaknesses. A major weakness, and one which will not be directly addressed here, has to do with the nature of the rules for the inference engine. The program, in attempting to be broad based and appeal to many potential users, suffers from being too general and is unable to handle the complexity of many selling situations. It is difficult to imagine an expert system which can operate in such a complex set of environments and, as such, cover many potential selling situations. Collins (1986) makes this point in his evaluation of SELL! SELL! SELL! Developing an expert system for one company to use in dealing with its particular activities may be problematical in itself. In addition, there are many activities, such as routing, which could be incorporated into an expert system for the selling function, but which are not apparent in SELL! SELL! SELL!

The second major problem is the weakness of the database activities of SELL! SELL! SELL! Kennedy (1984) notes that database manipulation provides some of the more interesting and productive applications of microcomputer based systems. The importance of the database must be underscored when considering the fact that data collected in one particular environment in an organization can be useful to many other areas of corporate decision making. As an example, data collected by salespeople with respect to competitive activities could assist marketing planners, help determine capital outlays and even provide direction for the research and development group.

To date, there is no consensus on what constitutes an ideal decision support system for the selling function. Sales managers are consistent, however, in wishing to increase the productivity of their individual salespeople and thus increase the contribution of the sales function to corporate objectives. The coordination of SELL! SELL! SELL! with PMS provides a starting point for the development of an idealized expert system. This type of system not only offers solutions to sales function problems, but also enhances the sales contribution through its integration with other marketing activities and other corporate functions.

Within the context of the Oxman (1985) view of expert systems the integration of PMS within the framework of SELL! SELL! SELL! improves the capabilities of the domain database. Such advances as increases in factual knowledge provide for more effective use of decision support systems through increases in options to the user. Inasmuch as selling is an integral part of the company's marketing function, coordination of sales force efforts will enhance the overall achievement of company plans. SELL! SELL! SELL! coupled with PMS provides the capability of ongoing training and electronic supervision of the sales force.

The next step in furthering knowledge of expert systems in selling involves the development of a system designed for a specific user. Of course, the extent to which this concept can be implemented depends both on the technology and the willingness of the potential participants to make the effort and resource commitments necessary.

Conclusion

This paper has sought to introduce the concept of expert systems into the context of sales management. An expert system provides a computer-based framework which can assist the user in finding the optimum solution to a problem based on a carefully developed set of rules dealing with that problem. As such, it is the latest in a long line of technological aids to decision-makers.

Expert systems have made their greatest impact in areas concerned with production and/or engineering technology. These functional areas are more driven by physical laws, whereas the marketing area has not developed the scientific rules upon which to make expert decisions. Yet, the lack of lawlike generalizations should not constrain marketers in their search for normative approaches to decision-making. The dynamics of the expert systems approach allows the marketer to search for prescriptive solutions to problems based on integrative stored and updated information.

As demonstrated here, the complex sales management area can be approached from a more informed perspective. Because data and rules specific to the company's needs can be developed, maintained and updated, decisions are evaluated from not only the perspective of the user, but also as they will affect the entire marketing operation.

References

Booker, J., Kick, R., and Gardner, J., (1986) "Expert Systems in Accounting: The Next Generation of Computer Technology." *Journal of Accountancy* 161 (March): 101-104.

Carrington, K., (1986) "Artificial Intelligence: Business Puts Thinking Cap on Computers." *The Hartford Courant Business Weekly* (September 22): 1,24.

Collins, R. H., (1985a) "Microcomputer Systems to Handle Sales Leads: A Key to Increased Salesforce Productivity." *Journal of Personal Selling and Sales Management* 5,1 (May): 77-83.

Collins, R. H., (1985b) "Enhancing Spreadsheets for Increased Productivity." *Journal of Personal Selling and Sales Management* 5,2 (November): 79-81.

Collins, R. H., (1986) "Sales Training: A Microcomputer-Based Approach." *Journal of Personal Selling and Sales Management* 6,1 (May): 71-76.

Dalrymple, J. Douglas, (1982) *Sales Management: Concepts and Cases.* New York: John Wiley and Sons, Inc.

Dauner, J., and Johnson, E., (1980) "Poor Utilization of Time and Planned Sales Efforts." *Training and Development Journal* 34,9 (January): 22-26.

Duda, R., and Gaschnig, J., (1981) "Knowledge-based Expert Systems Come of Age." *Byte* 6 (September): 34-37.

Harmon, Paul, and King, David, (1985) *Expert Systems*. New York: John Wiley and Sons, Inc.

Hayes-Roth, F., (1985) "Discover Expert Selling: Will Machines Be Better." *Direct Marketing* 48,2 (June): 62-65.

Hutt, M., and Speh, T., (1986) *Industrial Marketing Management 2nd ed*. New York: Dryden Press.

Kennedy, J., (1984) "Want Higher Sales Productivity?: Start With a Data Base." *Sales and Marketing Management* 133,8 (December 3): 66-68.

Kern, R., (1986) "Survey of Selling Costs: Onward and Ever Upward." *Sales and Marketing Management* 136,3 (February 17): 12-13.

Konopasek, M., and Jayaraman, S., (1984) "Expert Systems for Personal Computers." *Byte* 9 (May): 137-138, 140, 144, 146, 152, 154.

Oxman, S., (1985) "Expert Systems Represent Ultimate Goal of Strategic Decision Making." *Data Management* 23,4 (April): 36-38.

Sales and Marketing Management 137,1 (1986) "Are Salespeople Gaining More Selling Time." (July): 29.

Taylor, T., (1985) "PC's Used by 1 in 10 Salespeople, Half of Marketing Staffs." *Sales and Marketing Management* 134,8 (June 3): 116.

Taylor, T., (1986a) "Electronic Call Reports Boost Productivity 25%." *Sales and Marketing Management* 136,5 (April): 72-73.

Taylor, T., (1986b) "Marketers and the PC: Steady as She Goes." *Sales and Marketing Management* 137,3 (August): 53-55.

Training 23 (1986) "Expert Systems: Artificial Intelligence in Action ... More or Less." (January): 81-84.

Callisto: An Intelligent Project Management System

Arvind Sathi, Thomas E. Morton, and Steven F. Roth

In the following two subsections, we present a brief discussion of the project management problem and how the Callisto[1] project began.

The Project Management Problem

Innovation is important to the continued vitality of industry. New products and changes in existing products are occurring at an increasing rate, causing product lives to decrease. In order to maintain market share, companies are forced to reduce product development time and bring their products to the market as early as possible.

A major portion of development involves performing and managing many activities. For example, in high-technology industries such as the computer industry, thousands of activities must be performed to design and build the prototype of a new product. Poor performance or management of an activity can result in critical delays. If product development time is to be reduced, better management and technical support are crucial.

The Callisto project was started at the initiative of Digital Equipment Corporation (DEC) with the goal of studying and supporting the management of large projects. The focus has been on large system development *programs* (collections of several projects geared toward the design of a new computer). The following points illustrate the complexity of project management tasks in such programs:

- A large number of activities (possibly greater than 10,000) make it impossible for a manager to acquire current information about all activities.
- A number of departments are involved with different foci, attitudes, and goals.
- A program requires significant cooperation. The engineering department cannot use components that are short on supply and has to interact with the purchasing department to ascertain the supply position. The engineering department also has to interact with the manufacturing department for prototype development. Any changes made by any of these departments have an impact on the entire program.
- The developmental and technological nature of these programs makes it difficult to plan accurately. Changes are frequent and need to be approved by a large number of managerial personnel.

Related project management tasks can be decomposed into three areas:

- Activity management,
- Product-configuration management, and
- Resource management.

Each of these areas can, in turn, be further delineated. Activity management involves four elements:

- *Planning*, which involves definition of activities, specification of precedence, resource requirements, durations, due dates, milestones, and responsibilities;
- *Scheduling*, which is the selection of activities to be performed (if more than one way exists) and the assignment of actual times and resources;
- *Chronicling*, which is the monitoring of project performance, detection of deviations from the schedule, and analysis of deviations for changes to plan (possibly resulting in renewed planning and scheduling); and
- *Analysis*, which is the evaluation of plans, schedules, and chronicled activities for normal reporting and extraordinary situations and involves the study of durations, budgets, and risk projections.

Reprinted with permission from *AI Magazine*, vol. 7, no. 5, Winter 1986, 34-52.

Product configuration management involves two elements:

- *Product management*, which is the management of various versions and variations of the product being designed, and
- *Change management*, which is the management of change proposals and impact evaluations, assignment of personnel for making changes, and installation of product versions.

Finally, resource management involves three elements:

- The projection and acquisition of resources for project needs;
- The assignment of responsibilities to ensure proper utilization of resources; and
- The storage, maintenance, and repair of critical resources to minimize bottlenecks.

Deficiencies in past approaches can be attributed to inadequate modeling techniques, poor scheduling algorithms, and limited analytical tools. Our first and foremost research effort concentrated on modeling how good managers deal with the size, complexity, and changes in large projects and how they foster cooperation given the organizational diversity and loose coupling. The first leg dealt with using rule-based models to build quick prototypes of project expertise. This understanding of point solutions was then used to capture the underlying models of project expertise in the areas of project negotiations and computer-generated explanation of change using comparative analysis. This article describes our exploration into project management needs and the evolution of the resulting models of project management.

The Callisto Project

An initial investigation was encouraged by the vice-president of engineering at Digital Equipment Corporation during fall 1981. It was observed that in many ways the problems encountered in managing large development projects were similar to those associated with managing job shop activities, which was the focus of the Intelligent Scheduling and Information System (ISIS) project at CMU. The focus of the initial investigation was to determine the feasibility of developing an expert system to aid in the management of large system development projects.

It was concluded that a significant improvement could be realized in project scheduling, monitoring, and control through the inclusion of resources and other project management constraints in the project-scheduling algorithms. It was also expected that a knowledge-based project management tool would facilitate the documentation of project management expertise and its reuse from one project to another. The engineering prototype development for large systems was selected as the representative application. No tools existed to monitor and control these projects. Their nature—engineering oriented, volatile, ill structured—was ideal for a test case.

Research goals were established in the following four areas for the Callisto project: In the area of activity modeling, the goal was to generate a model of the activities and the constraints related to these activities. It was hoped that the model would facilitate the manager's ability to create activities and identify problems at creation time. In the area of configuration management, the goals were to generate a hierarchical product representation for various versions and prototypes and a way of representing the changes of these products and to develop a system to support the management of change. In the area of activity scheduling, the goal was to schedule with various hard and soft constraints and goals, which involve dynamic rescheduling and what-if simulation during project monitoring and heuristics to guard against "bad" schedules. Finally, in the area of project control, the goal was to study and model the status updating and activity-tracking procedures and the use of managerial heuristics for reporting, focusing, and diagnosing problems.

A number of factors make engineering prototype development a difficult domain for experimentation with intelligent project management systems. First, building rule-based prototypes for large and dynamic environments is a resource-intensive activity and cannot be justified on its own. Second, such projects involve a mix of economic, engineering, and manufacturing considerations. It is not possible to appreciate the problem-solving process without an understanding of all these areas. Finally, such projects involve a large number of important, yet specialized project management problems. It is difficult to understand all of these problems, isolate important ones, or develop systems that solve everyone's problems. Figure 1 traces the phases of the Callisto project.

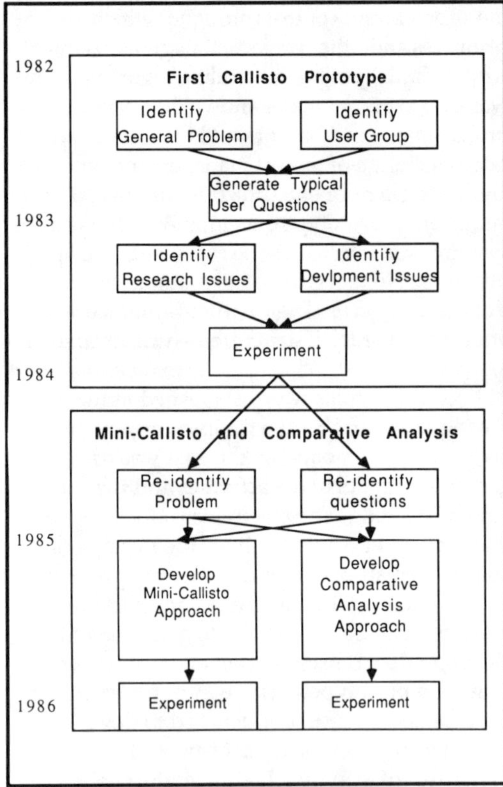

Figure 1. Callisto development path.

The first phase of the project lasted about two years. Its purpose was to develop the first Callisto prototype, which consisted of a model of project knowledge and a rule-based prototype of project expertise to formulate hard-wired solutions to specific problems using production rules. Although the prototype was found to be operationally usable for configuration tracking, a useful subset of the program management problem, its usability was restricted. The information was to be funneled through a group whose responsibility was to maintain the project model. The existence of a committee inevitably causes a reduction in the information recorded, delays in the incorporation of information in the model, and the cleansing of information (for example, project reports might be too optimistic). Another problem was the level of analysis provided by Callisto. Although the model used a set of hard-wired procedures for pattern matching of typical comparisons, it could not intelligently configure the procedures together to decipher real problems.

A toy example project that engineered a fictitious computer named Micro-84 was fabricated for demonstration purposes. All the examples and scenarios in this article refer to this fictitious computer. The following test cases were used for the experiments: the developmental plans (40 activities) and configuration of Micro 84 (9 parts), the project network for Callisto itself (80 activities), a portion of the activity network for an ongoing system development project (125 activities), a random set of activity networks (776 networks with a range of 10 to 200 activities), and the system configuration and changes for a system under development (17 layers of hierarchy with 5000 parts).

The development of the configuration-tracking system (currently under way) uses as a test case a configuration with seven layers of hierarchy and about 10,000 schemata (Lynch, Marshall, and O'Connor 1986). The earlier versions of Callisto used the schema representation language (SRL) (Wright and Fox 1983; Wright, Fox, and Adam 1984), and the current work is being done using Knowledge Craft™ (Carnegie Group 1986).

Two models of project expertise emerged from the experiments. The first model attempts to capture the expertise used by good project managers in developing cooperation among project participants. In distributed project management situations, project participants often carry divergent and possibly conflicting goals and constraints. The plan specification and revision involves considerable negotiation around the constraints in order to formulate contracts to ensure cooperation. The constraint-directed negotiation model captures the expertise used by project managers in specification and revision of plans that satisfy individual constraints and foster cooperation on project goals (see Mini-Callisto for a description of the theory). These negotiations occur iteratively during plan generation, scheduling, monitoring, and repair. This model resulted in explorations with Mini-Callisto[2], a distributed problem-solving approach. Constraint-directed negotiations are examined in this article by exploring a number of negotiation situations.

A second model captures the expertise in comparative analysis of project knowledge. This analysis includes understanding the quantitative, qualitative, and causal relations among activities, people, and resources (for example, the impact of a delay in resource procurement on the risk of meeting a follow-on milestone); how these properties change; how they can be classified, aggregated, abstracted (for example, a common project member responsible for all the delayed activities); and how the result of analysis can be explained using verbal and pictorial means. The purpose of this model is to support automated explanation by providing search and comparison, computation, significance testing, and verbal descriptions of change in project models. The work in this area is still in the formative stage and is the primary focus of current Callisto research.

Section 2 provides a summary of past approaches. Section 3 describes the first Callisto prototype. The experiments and related observations are described in section 4. Section 5 describes the distributed problem-solving architecture and its application to resource, activity, and configuration management. Section 6 summarizes the ongoing experiments with the distributed problem-solving architecture. Section 7 describes the current work on comparative analysis. Finally, section 8 summarizes the achievements and unexplored areas for research.

Past Approaches

The origin of computer-based network analysis for project management dates back to 1959 when two separate but essentially similar procedures were developed: Program Evaluation and Review Technique (PERT) (Malcolm, Rosenboom, and Clark 1959) and Critical Path Method (CPM) (Kelley and Walker 1959; Kelley 1961). PERT involved the use of three separate time estimates for each activity and statistical procedures to produce probability estimates of project completion. CPM used a one-time estimate. Today, both terms are interchangeably used to refer to the common approach of (1) representing the project in the form of a network diagram and (2) performing the necessary calculations on the diagram to determine the "critical path" and start and finish times for each activity.

PERT/CPM was limited to precedence constraints and single projects. A number of researchers in management science were drawn toward the project-scheduling problem. Notable among them are Turban (1976), Pritsker et al. (1966), Crowston (1970), Weist (1967), Lambourn (1963), Davis (1973), and Talbot (1982). Their main agenda for research was the inclusion of resource considerations in the scheduling of project activities. Work has also been conducted in the project measurement area, where the emphasis has been on measuring, forecasting, and reporting project information, for example, cost (DeCoster 1964; Saitow 1969). For a detailed review of project management techniques, refer to Davis (1973, 1976) and Elmaghraby (1977). Despite their versatility, most of these techniques have gained little popularity. In a study of research and development (R&D) projects, Liberatore and Titus (1983) found that managers used very few sophisticated techniques to manage their projects. Gantt charts and project network diagrams were the only notable exceptions. Clearly, real-world project management problems were either different or too complex.

The human planning process has often been scrutinized by researchers in artificial intelligence (AI); their findings are applicable to project management problems. There are three major streams of research efforts that apply to project management:

- Plan representation;
- Plan generation and scheduling; and
- Plan measurement, diagnostics, and explanation.

Research in plan representation explores the semantics of various concepts associated with human planning, such as time (Smith 1983; Allen 1984; Allen and Hayes 1985), process or activity (Hayes 1979; Georgeff, Lansky, and Bessiere 1985; Sathi, Fox, and Greenberg 1985), causality (Rieger and Grinberg 1977), and possession (Fox 1983). The research in this area has led to the development of semantic models of projects that can be used for intelligent reasoning and problem solving.

Research in plan generation and scheduling uses the knowledge about activities and goals to generate a sequence of steps for a plan (Tate 1977; Sacerdoti 1974; Fox 1983). A number of planning techniques have evolved, such as hierarchical planning (Sacerdoti 1974), least commitment (wait and see) approaches (Sacerdoti 1977), script-based planning (Stefik 1981; Wilensky 1983), blackboard architecture (Hayes-Roth 1985), constraint-directed search (Fox 1983), and distributed planning (Corkill 1983).

Research in plan measurement, diagnostics, and explanation interprets the project progress and diagnoses the delays to find problem areas. Many types of research touch this area including model explanation (Kosy and Wise 1984; Wise and Kosy 1985; Weiner 1980), plan recognition (Schmidt 1978), reactive scheduling (Fox and

Smith 1984), vehicle monitoring (Lesser and Corkill 1983), speech interpretation (Erman et al. 1980), and simulation analysis (Reddy 1985).

Hierarchical descriptions of products are common to computer-aided design (CAD) (Freeman and Newell 1971; Latombe 1976; Preiss 1976; Stallman and Sussman 1977; Barbuceanu 1984) and software management systems (Tichy 1980) and draw upon the hierarchical modeling of objects (Winston 1975; Brachman 1979; Hendrix 1979). Refinement and change processes, however, are found less frequently (Tichy 1980; Zdonik 1984).

Tichy designed a software development and maintenance environment with three aspects: representation, interface control, and version control. His model supports multiple versions and configurations. A module family can have three kinds of members: parallel versions, revisions or sequential versions, and derived versions. A system family includes compositions or configurations and derived compositions (Tichy 1980).

The distributed constraint-directed negotiation approach is based on work in three research areas:

- Economic literature,
- Organizational behavior literature, and
- Distributed AI literature.

Economic literature contains modeled agents in n-player game situations. Each player makes a choice whose outcomes (gains) are dependent upon the actions taken by the other agents, and the joint benefits depend upon the level of cooperation (Nash 1950; Luce and Raiffa 1957). The extensions to Nash's model include syndicate theory (Wilson 1968; Demski and Swieringa 1974; Demski 1976), team theory (Marschak and Radner 1972), the demand revelation model (Loeb 1975; Groves 1975; Groves and Loeb 1979), and agency theory (Fama 1980; Harris and Townsend 1981; Baiman 1982).

The work in agency theory deals with a principal and an agent. The principal forms a contract with the agent. Any returns from this contract are shared so as to maximize the returns to the principal, while subject to the constraints imposed by the agent. Agency theory model has been used by economists to study the optimal contract formulation (which would maximize cooperation between the principal and the agent subject to self-interests), admissible action rules for the agents, and the information asymmetry between principal and agent (Baiman 1982).

Organizational behavior literature provides studies in human organizations on the human negotiation process (Pruitt 1981) and on the formation of matrix management in project organization (Galbraith 1973). Although this research is closely linked with project management, we have not yet encountered its impact on project management techniques.

In distributed AI literature, the distributed problem-solving approach conceptualizes a network of intelligent agents or actors (Greif and Hewitt 1975) capable of generating and executing plans and negotiating with other agents (Davis and Smith 1981). These problem-solving agents can be organized in an organizational hierarchy (Fox 1979; Fox 1981a; Fox 1981b) and can dynamically refine their roles (Durfee, Lesser, and Corkill 1985). This problem-solving approach decentralizes the problem solving with a limited communication sufficient for functionally accurate cooperation (Lesser and Corkill 1981) and makes solution generation feasible for large problems (Fox 1979). The approach also provides models of the contract formation process (Smith 1978) and organization designs for optimal flexibility and efficiency (Malone and Smith 1984). It theorizes distributed problem solvers with different beliefs (Fagin and Halpern 1985) negotiating on contracts (Smith 1980) and proposes a calculus of resource ownership (Lee 1980; McCarty and Sridharan 1981).

First Callisto Prototype

This section describes the various components of the first Callisto prototype which was developed to experiment with the emerging semantic model of project management.

Introduction

Consider the following scenario: *The engineering development activity for a central processing unit (CPU) typically involves the development of specifications, design on a CAD tool, and verification of the board on test cases. A committee of hardware engineers develops the specifications and assigns an engineer to design and verify the board specifications. Hence, specification is followed by design and verification. If verification is successful, the CPU is released for prototype development. Otherwise, the bug is located, the board is revised, and the design is performed again.*

Mr. Jones, a project manager in the engineering department, has been assigned the responsibility of designing the Micro-84 CPU board. Because it is not possible to cover all design aspects together, two milestones have been set for developing versions 1 and 2 of the board, respectively, and it is expected that the second version of the board will conform to project goals.

The expected duration of the design activity depends heavily on whether a new technology is used for the design. Because the decision on whether to go with the new technology has not yet been made, two schedules need to be developed, one with the assumption that the design durations will be reduced using the new technology and the other without the new technology.

Although this scenario sounds simplistic from a project management viewpoint, it raises a number of project management system engineering issues that are nontrivial. For an intelligent system that supports the management of such projects, we need to identify the critical components of the project management expertise and project knowledge representation. We need to define how this expertise and knowledge is acquired, maintained, and extended from one domain to another and how it supports the project managers.

The project representation should be complete. That is, the project knowledge should span the application domain and include all the relevant project elements used by expert project managers. For example, it should include activities (such as CPU specification); the durations of the activities; logical and temporal precedence; aggregation and abstraction (for example, how engineering development of the CPU is linked to the three activities of specification, design, and verification); individuation of schedules for the two versions of the board; representation of the two alternate schedules, one with and the other without the new technology; representation of Micro-84 and its component hierarchy, versions, and variations; representation of changes in the product; changes in the start or end dates; and resources required for each of these activities (for example, engineers, CAD tools, simulation software, and test examples). For each resource, one needs to define their availability, capabilities, and ownership. Finally, the project representation should include the representation of constraints that restrict the usage of the resources, for example, the maintenance schedule and previous reservations by other users on the CAD machine and the use of engineers for the next project.

An arbitrary set of data structures cannot be used to capture this knowledge, especially if completeness implies extensibility to include new concepts. The knowledge architecture should have clarity. That is, one and only one representation exists for a given situation. For example, if a new situation involves a new type of resource, say suppliers, there should be a semantic rationale for how this new element is represented in the project knowledge base.

In addition, the knowledge representation should be precise. That is, the project descriptions should be at the appropriate granularity of knowledge. For example, depending upon the type of retrieval, the system should be able to either state that CPU verification is the next activity of CPU design or to specify all the conditions under which one activity can follow another.

The architecture for the first Callisto prototype was comprised of two major components: the knowledge architecture and the interface architecture.

Knowledge Architecture. The project knowledge is organized into layers of representation. For details of the layers and their rationale, refer to Sathi, Fox, and Greenberg (1985). The *domain layer* provides concepts, words, and expressions specific to a domain of application. The *semantic layer* is composed of models of the common primitives, such as the concepts of time, activity, state, possession, agent, ownership, and so on. These concepts are common across domains and can, therefore, be used as building blocks for modeling the domain-specific concepts. The *epistemological layer* provides a way of regulating the flow of information through inheritance. It includes the concepts of set, prototype, and individuals as well as the structural relationships such as classification and aggregation. The *logical layer* defines the blocks or chunks of knowledge, such as concepts, assertions, and relations. Finally, the *implementation layer* provides primitives for machine interpretation of knowledge, such as schema, slot, relation, value, metaschema, and so on. Their specification depends on the knowledge engineering tool used.

Interface Architecture. Callisto was interfaced as a single-writer, multiple-reader system with user-directed commands for activity management, configuration management, and resource management (inventory only) and supported a common (centralized) knowledge base. Through a hierarchical menu, it provided the user with the capability of interactively generating plans, scheduling the project in a simulated world to analyze the project progress under several what-if scenarios (one or more of these schedules could be stored and compared to actual progress), posting project progress, and reviewing project progress. Product configurations could be developed or changed. The user could post inventory transactions or seek status reports. Various expert critics could be activated to analyze plans, schedules, inventory status, and configuration changes. Some functional details of this system are described in the following subsections.

Resource Management

Resource management is concerned with the specification and allocation of resources to support activities. Resources in this context include personnel, work centers, tools, parts, and so on. Semantic and domain layers include the following concepts that relate to resource representation: At the domain layer exist calendars and shifts of work, stocks, vendors, stockrooms, kits, work centers, supervisors, and managers with responsibility for various resources. At the semantic layer exist resources, the time line, temporal relations, possession of resources, agents, objects and their transactions from one agent to another, aggregation of objects, resources, and associated inheritance of ownership and status.

The project-scheduling system included considerations of resource availabilities and capacities. Our initial resource-management system had three components: an inventory management component tracking resource consumption; a resource adjudication component dealing with decision making in resource allocation; and a resource critic documenting managerial heuristics for isolating problems in the utilization of resources.

The inventory management component was a discrete event-based inventory transaction system that was developed to support the activity scheduling and chronicling tasks. For example, "arrival event" increases the quantity of a given part. Events were defined for the loading and unloading of resources and for changes in the inventory. All machines and personnel were treated as resources that were possessed for the execution of activities.

The second component, resource adjudication, was an automated manager that could operate under either of three modes: the mail notification mode, the interactive mode, and the heuristic mode. In the mail notification mode, concerned responsibility centers were informed of conflicts by electronic mail, which were, in turn, resolved manually. In interactive mode, the user was given the conflicts on the screen and resolved them interactively by initiating the important activities. In heuristic mode, conflicts were resolved using a set of predefined managerial rules. A large number (56) of scheduling heuristics were collected from the management science literature, and experiments were conducted to determine their comparative performance (Lawrence 1984).

The third component, the resource critic, was a rule base constructed by acquiring and encoding a number of managerial heuristics related to resources and suppliers. These rules criticized schedules and monitored performance. The rule base was assembled for concept demonstration. No experiments were performed to measure the adequacy or the impact of the criticisms.

Activity Management

Activity management deals with the generation, scheduling, and chronicling of project activities. The three phases are considered distinctly. The knowledge architecture supports these three phases using specific project knowledge at the domain and semantic levels. At the domain level exist knowledge of project activities, associated durations, risks, milestones, average (default) durations, aggregate activities for specification, design, verification, project members, mailing addresses, and responsibilities. At the semantic level exist representation of activities, states, the time line, causal and temporal relations, possession of resources, and agents and their relation to activities (see figure 2) (Sathi, Fox, and Greenberg 1985).

The three phases activity management is comprised of, are:

Concept	Definition	Illustration
State	Fact which holds as of some point in time	*Cpu-specification is comlete Possess CAD tool during cpu-design*
Activity	Basic unit of action Transforms states	*Specification of cpu*
Aggregation	Combine parts to make a whole	*Cpu-engg -network has three activities, spec, design and verification.*
Abstraction	Process of reducing specific information	*Cpu-engg abstracts cpu-engg-network as a single activity*
Instances	Development of individual from universal	*Micro-84-design is an instance of cpu-design activity*
Manifestation	State specific description of individual	*M-cpu-design-1 specifies the schedule for Micro-84-design*
Temporal Relations	Relations to describe relative time	*Cpu-design is after cpu-specification*
Causality	Specifies an order of occurance	*Start-cpu-design (an aggregate state) enables cpu-design*
Relational Abstraction	Abstract relations to summarize complex relationships	*Cpu-design is the next activity-of cpu-verification (abstract)* *It occurs when verification fails (detail)*

Figure 2. Activity representation definitions.

- Plan generation,
- Scheduling, and
- Chronicling.

In the plan generation phase, an activity editor was developed to create and edit hierarchical activity networks. Interaction with the editor was through an English-like interface based on dynamic parser (DYPAR) (Carbonell et al. 1983). A rule-based activity critic was used to criticize the plans generated by the manager using structural (for example, missing precedence constraints) and heuristic (for example, duration estimates) project rules.

We perceived a major difference between the project scheduling of large engineering projects and the job shop scheduling being attempted in ISIS. Such projects involve a large degree of uncertainty and many changes. The accuracy or optimality of scheduling in such an environment is not as important as the development of a rough schedule that can be used for assessing and managing risk. In addition, the plan is typically too big to be developed or scheduled by one individual. Various organizational techniques, such as mutual agreements, internal pricing, and slacks, are used to distribute the scheduling problem and to solve it independently at multiple responsibility centers. A typical schedule might consist of a detailed three-month plan. Every week, or as often as needed, the project managers create a revised plan, implementing only its first week. This type of a procedure is widely used in industry and is termed a *rolling horizon procedure*; it involves scheduling far ahead of time to be sure what to do this week.

There are basically two ways of scheduling: forward or "dispatch" and backward or "reservation." The *dispatch approach* basically simulates the activities working forward in time. At each time point in the simulation, activities whose preconditions have been met are considered for scheduling. When two or more activities require the same resource, priority rules are applied to resolve the conflicts. The strength of the dispatch method is that it gives good control over the schedule in the near future. Compact schedules that make full use of resources are produced. The disadvantage is that there is less control over what happens in the distant future, for example, meeting due dates.

In contrast, the *reservation approach* works backward from the due date, reserving starting and ending times for each activity. First, a reservation is made for the last subactivity of the most important activity, then the next to the last, and so forth. Then the second most important activity is scheduled from its due date, and so forth. The strength of the reservation method is that the distant future is well controlled. Due dates for the most important projects are considered first. The disadvantage is that it provides poor control of scheduling in the near future. Gaps are often left in the schedule, and all activities of a project might not be reservable. These problems must be resolved in a second pass working forward. The reservation approach is typically useful in situations where the environment is stable, and there is a need to push work close to the deadline (for example, to reduce the cost of work-in-process inventory).

Given the level of risk and unforeseen changes, we decided to use a version of the dispatch approach. We simulated forward in time and forecast which projects create the most difficulties. These forecasts were then used to correct the current priorities so that the project with the maximum difficulties was given current priority over other projects.

Now, our principal problem was that slacks and lead times are unknown but must be included in forecasting priority. We recognized four distinct methods: (1) estimate the slacks using simple PERT/CPM; (2) use a historically estimated lead time for each resource to augment the duration of an activity; (3) repeatedly use the actual lead-time results instead of the historical estimates, and input these actual results for a second run, repeating the process until convergence is obtained; and (4) use regression to estimate the lead time for each resource from a set of critical factors, which might include shop dynamic load factor, load composition, and so on.

For multiple projects and multiple resource constraints, the algorithm can be extended by weighting the lead time on each resource by its price. The proper way to calculate prices is an interesting and complex subject. In general, one would have to solve a simpler, aggregate version of the problem with a method that would produce dual prices. These prices could be used in the detailed scheduling procedure. We found the computation of dual prices to be a cumbersome and unstable process and used the following approximation (which is similar to the way expert project managers would schedule): If a resource is, on an average, less than fully utilized, the price is 0. If a large number of activities demand the resource in the near future, the price is the ratio of resource demand to the supply available. For example, if given two engineers, one is required for two full-time activities and the other for two half-time activities, their respective prices are 2.0 and 1.0. Expensive resources are avoided during resource conflict resolution, resulting in less bottlenecking of those higher in demand.

Project chronicling is comprised of three components: progress recording, reporting, and repairing. The first Callisto prototype was restricted to the first two. It provided capabilities of propagating the progress along the activity hierarchy and for generating rate charts, which combines progress from different levels to compute scheduled or actual performance. The structured reports and query system are used for passive reporting, and monitoring rules are used for proactive reporting, such as reporting all the pending activities at least once a week.

Configuration Management

Product configuration management involves maintenance of the configuration status, impact analysis, and installation of changes. The primary emphasis in the first Callisto prototype was on representing the configuration and change knowledge (including their relationship to the resources and the activities).

At the domain layer exist components, versions, variations, basic parts, systems and prototypes, a configuration editor, configuration reports, and the change management system. Micro-84 is composed of hardware and software. The hardware contains two circuit boards: board-h1, which consists of the CPU and the I/O, and board-h2, which contains the memory. There are two versions of board-h1. The first version is composed of a workable CPU with all the proper interfaces; the second version is a speed enhancement of version 1. Variations consist of different specifications for power supply in the U.S. and European models, requiring 60 Hz and 50 Hz power supply, respectively. Basic parts represents generic parts. Each part is defined conceptually; the parts are not connected hierarchically, for example, Micro-84 hardware. Finally, systems and prototypes represent actual physical products as instances of versions. For example, prototype 1 is an instance of Micro-84 version 1.

At the semantic layer exist the physical description, the behavioral description, and the links to activities. The physical description is derived from the work by Hayes (1979): Objects have a number of physical properties, such as mass, volume, momentum, and so on. In addition to the physical description, objects carry a description of how they behave under given conditions. The behavioral description is also the functional view of the object description.

Links to activities refers to objects in the project world that are produced, consumed, and transformed by project activities. Thus, the Micro-84 CPU behavior is defined through specifications, although its structure is defined by the design activity, and is released to the rest of the project organization by the verification activity. The specific activities, such as *revise part definitions*, are called *change orders*.

The configuration description in Callisto is hierarchical (that is, defined at multiple levels of detail). At its highest level of abstraction, Micro-84 is composed of hardware, software, and peripherals. At a detailed level, the hardware can be expanded into board-h1 and board-h2, and so on. Figure 3 is an illustration of the product representation. It shows the relationship between the two versions of Micro-84 and how one is generated from the other. The scope of the activity that acts on Micro-84-50Hz-v1 to produce Micro-84-50Hz-v2 can be reduced or increased by redefining the two versions.

The configuration editor is a semantic editor for specification and revision of product configuration. It can be used for adding or deleting basic parts, revisions, variations, and engineering change orders. The configuration reports can be used for reporting the configuration status or for comparatively analyzing at arbitrary levels of detail. Comparative analysis reports the changes from one version or revision to another and the associated causes for changes.

Finally the change management system can be used for entering a change. The changes can be grouped and used for creating a new version of the configuration. At any level, the system interactively chooses three optional procedures for installing a change: destructive change (the new option supersedes the old), disjunctive (both new and old coexist) or release version (a new version is created for the part, and the procedure is repeated at the next higher level). A rule base is then used to analyze the impact of the change on the existing and scheduled prototypes.

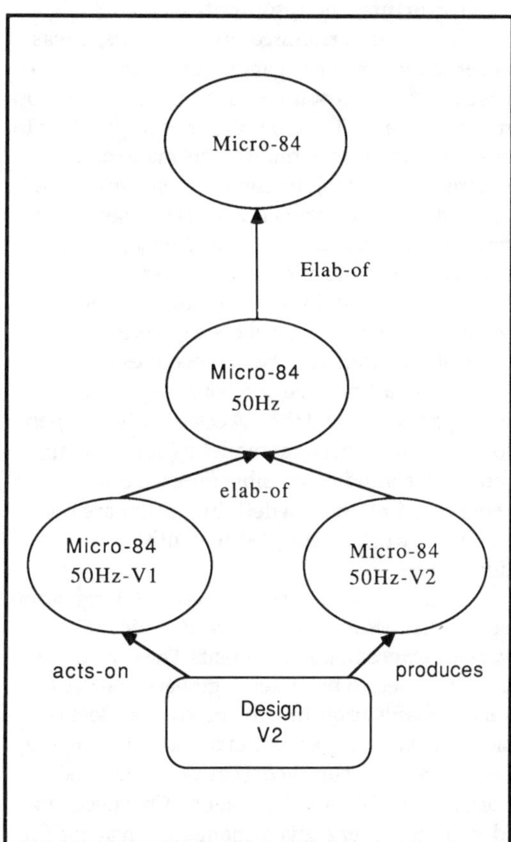

Figure 3. The Micro-84 and changes.

Conclusion

The primary objective of the first Callisto prototype was to explore the knowledge architecture and the rule base prototypes of project management expertise. Although the knowledge architecture addressed some of the issues listed at the beginning of this section, the rule base prototype was inadequate for documenting or utilizing project management expertise. Although the rules matched the point solutions to the problems, they could not be extended to other problems. The project-scheduling approach required tolerance to incompleteness of project knowledge, appreciation for distribution of the plans and resources to various project managers, and the use of change orders in schedule revisions. The next section describes in detail the experiments with the first Callisto prototype and the associated observations.

Observations

The single user system was developed to the proof-of-concept level (that is, having enough functionality to demonstrate concepts but not really usable) and extended for the purpose of experimentation into the areas of activity scheduling and product-configuration management. The Callisto prototype was used in test cases for activity networks with up to 776 activities. The system was augmented with a subroutine written in C for faster number crunching. Our observations developed from the following activities:

- Interviewing key scheduling personnel: Interviews help to determine tasks and information-acquisition strategies.
- Observing review meetings to augment descriptions given by scheduling managers: The observations provided snapshots of actual project progress and problem-solving strategies used by program management personnel.
- Ascertaining commonly asked activity management questions from the project managers: These questions were the primary data points in understanding the difference between needs and available tools.
- Modeling of activities for two test cases using Callisto: These networks involved 80 and 125 activities, respectively, at multiple

levels of detail. The modeling experiments were used to refine the expressiveness of the initial model.

- Interactively developing of the next set of ideas: Continuous discussions, presentations, and concept demonstrations were used to foster idea development.
- Experimenting with scheduling: The purpose of the experimentation was to study and compare project-scheduling heuristics based on knowledge used, time taken for scheduling, and the quality of schedule generated. A random set of activity networks (776 networks with a range of 10 to 200 activities) was created. Fifty-six scheduling heuristics were used individually to schedule the networks using the dispatch approach and the knowledge available for the scheduling (Lawrence 1984).
- Experimenting with product configurations: Callisto was used to model configurations and associated changes for a product under development. The system was used experimentally to assess its interface and problem-solving abilities compared to existing systems being used. The system contained two versions of the configuration, with 17 layers of hierarchy and about 5000 parts. Nearly 15,000 schemata were needed to store the above configuration.

Numerous observations were made in regard to the various aspects of system development. In relation to planning, it was noted that plans evolve through negotiations and are not prespecified. For example, negotiations are often used to allocate slack time. The project support system should model and support negotiations on slack time and associated revisions in the plan rather than assume fixed durations and generate slack time as in PERT/CPM-based models.

Obvious organizational distances in communications were observed. Typically, the activities are not executed in the same department, office, or plant. The lack of face-to-face contact makes it difficult to maintain or analyze activity information in networks of the order of 10,000 activities. The critical paths generated by the PERT/CPM models lose their meaning in such situations because they do not carry or support the justifications and assumptions made during negotiations on the allocation of slack time.

Incomplete plans must be allowed for. Because networks of the order of 10,000 activities cannot be fully specified or maintained, we need tools for planning, scheduling and monitoring that tolerate incompleteness in specification and trigger revisions when more knowledge is made available.

Project knowledge should be used for scheduling. Although a number of scheduling heuristics have been developed, they take a narrow view of constraints as applied to activity scheduling. As the knowledge is increased, the scheduling results improve; however, the time needed for scheduling increases (Lawrence 1984).

In regard to organizational ownership, it was noted that program management brings together a number of plants, divisions, and departments. The program manager seldom has overall control over the resources used by these organizations, and each of these organizations is a fairly autonomous unit with goals (that might not be identical to the program goals), management structure, and resources owned.

In regard to resource commitments, it was observed that these organizations commit some portion of their resources to the product development program. The commitments might have to coexist with other commitments made elsewhere. Very often, the commitments might be relaxed or renegotiated due to unforeseen changes, such as breakdowns, emergency needs, or changes in organizational structures.

Product descriptions need to be diverse. Various project personnel need different descriptions of the product. The perspectives of the supply department person counting the number of chips needed and the CAD simulation expert looking into behavioral modeling are very different. It should be possible for each one of them to maintain local definitions that are not necessarily tightly coupled with others' definitions.

Change needs to be managed. A large number of changes are made to the product at various stages of development. These changes are circulated to the other engineers, the field service staff supporting the product at Beta test sites, the manufacturing personnel building the prototypes, the supply department involved in the purchase of parts, and so on. One needs to identify whether a given change, such as the formation of the two subversions, needs to be communicated outside the negotiating entities and, if so, to whom and when. For example, for a change introduced by the design engineers, the supply department might need to be informed that some of the integrated circuits would be needed earlier than originally specified.

Product configurations are generated for diverse needs. As the needs change, they result in new definitions. The project management system should track the negotiation on definitions and the resulting product configuration.

Mini-Callisto

In this section, we describe the Mini-Callisto approach and illustrate it with resource activity and configuration management applications.

Problem-Solving Architecture

Consider the following scenario: *A new integrated circuits technology was introduced in the engineering design of Micro-84, a new supermicro. While the CAD engineers started designing the CPU using the new technology, the materials department was asked to procure the chips. The materials department informed the program manager that they could not come up with a definite plan unless they knew which chips would be included in the bill of materials. When the program manager asked the CAD group about the exact specifications of the chips, he was informed that they would be ready in about one year when the design was fully finalized. A detailed negotiation mediated by the program manager resulted in a revised plan with a predesign activity: The CAD team would develop rough specifications using high-level designs, and the materials department would purchase the chips using the rough specifications. From the first communication, the entire negotiation took about five months. Project management tools were then used to specify the resulting plan.*

In situations such as this, organizations or individuals initiate negotiations when faced with inconsistent or incomplete project knowledge. Constraints are shared, relaxed, and strengthened among all individuals involved in the negotiations. The negotiations result in plans which satisfy everyone and which, possibly, are much more detailed than the original plans. Existing support systems help the managers in storing the plans but only after the negotiations are complete.

Many project management systems, including the first Callisto prototype, are based on a fundamental assumption. They focus their attention on a plan, which is generated, stored, scheduled, and monitored, for proper project management. Such support systems are likely to fare well in situations involving stable or small project models. In contrast, engineering program management involves a large number of changes that are initiated and cooperatively agreed upon by a large number of participating project members or organizations. The support system in such an environment requires additional emphasis on the specification and revision processes and the need for cooperation, which leads to the concept of Mini-Callisto.

Mini-Callisto is a system capable of supporting the specialized needs of an organizational unit and of communicating with other such systems in a network during specification and revision processes. This system draws upon past research in distributed problem solving. A description of the design of the Mini-Callisto architecture follows.

It is assumed that the project is distributed across a number of organizational entities, such as the program manager, the CAD group, and the materials department, with overlapping, but not necessarily common, goals and associated specialized knowledge. These organizational entities hold agreements with one another to facilitate cooperation on the project. Each organizational entity has a Mini-Callisto that provides a portion of the project management capabilities. Thus, a Mini-Callisto attached to the program manager is capable of working as a scheduling assistant with procedures for critical-path and risk analyses. Each Mini-Callisto has its own local knowledge base that reflects the beliefs of the organizational entity it supports.

These Mini-Callistos are connected together. They use messages to communicate with each other. Each message has an associated action. Messages are used for generating proposals, communicating constraints, proposing constraint relaxations, committing to plans, and querying others' knowledge. The messages are grouped into protocols that describe how a specification or change can be made.

A *constraint* expresses an impediment to plan variables. It can be interpreted in three ways: (1) an elimination rule from the perspective of object selection; (2) a partial description and commitment from the perspective of plan refinement; and (3) a communications medium for expressing interactions among organizational entities, each of which solves a subproblem. A constraint is not only a restriction but also the aggregation of a variety of knowledge used in the reasoning process. In particular, it includes the relative importance of multiple constraints; the possible relaxations and their relative utilities; the obligation to satisfy constraints according to time, context, and source; the interactions among constraints; and the dynamic generation of constraints (Stefik 1981; Fox 1983).

Negotiation is a form of decision making in which two or more parties communicate with one another in an effort to resolve nonoverlapping interests (Pruitt 1981). In the context of project management, the nonoverlapping interests are in the form of constraints faced by each party. A negotiation is initiated if and when an organizational entity faces an inconsistency or an incompleteness in the project knowledge base that can only be resolved with the help of other organizational entities. Negotiation is the process of isolating the constraints, communicating them to the other organizational entities, and jointly relaxing or strengthening them in order to resolve the inconsistency or incompleteness. A variety of negotiation operators, such as cost cutting, trading, arbitration, and mediation, are used for selecting the direction and magnitude of the strengthening or relaxing (see figure 4).

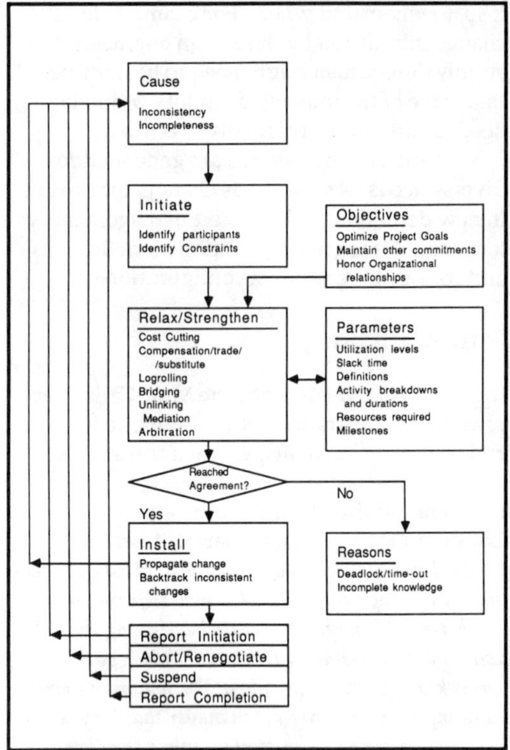

Figure 4. Constraint directed negotiation.

In a centralized algorithm, the constraint-directed search uses global importance for each constraint and global utility for each relaxation. In the distributed case, such global measures are extremely expensive (if not impossible) to compute. Instead, the negotiation needs to accommodate multiple agents, each with a set of constraints and their evaluations. A number of techniques are used by expert negotiators to reach an agreement (Pruitt 1981). The techniques that can be chosen to manipulate constraints in an automated negotiation situation are cost cutting; trade, substitution, and compensation; log rolling; bridging; unlinking; mediation; and arbitration.

Cost cutting involves reducing the cost of a relaxation for the other party by manipulating other parameters, such as the context. For example, an overutilization of a resource for a short duration of time can be made to look like normal utilization by extending the time horizon.

Trade, substitution, and compensation involves the exchange of project objects, such as resource reservations, to reduce the cost of relaxation for all the negotiating parties. The sharing of the losses, if any, should be according to goals shared.

Log rolling involves an exchange of concessions through selective violation of a portion of the constraints. For example, two agents, each contributing three constraints to the negotiation, might decide to violate one constraint each, in order to reach an agreement. Log rolling involves prioritizing constraints by their importance and selectively violating those which are low in priority. Although trading involves bargaining on relative losses, log rolling focuses on the relative importance of the competing constraints.

Bridging occurs when a new option is developed that satisfies both parties' most significant constraints. Such a relaxation is selected even though it violates all the other constraints.

Unlinking occurs when selective concessions are necessary to reach a solution and bridging or log rolling has not worked. It involves removing weak interactions among constraints for the purpose of negotiation (for example, relaxation of a due date that affects organizational stability).

Mediation occurs when the negotiating parties reach a deadlock (that is, are unable to relax any more constraints to reach an agreement). Mediation involves reassessment of the relaxations and the important constraints by a third party with, hopefully, a global perspective.

Arbitration occurs when the negotiation reaches a deadlock and even a third party can not mediate. In such cases, if the need is critical, a third party assigns losses and forces relaxations to the constraints posed by each of the negotiating parties.

Each Mini-Callisto is managed by a program module called an R-object (R stands for responsible). *R-objects* maintain the organizational structure of the project and have mechanisms for generating, filtering, and archiving messages for communicating with other modules as well as mechanisms for generating procedures for solving problems. The R-objects are comprised of ports, views, plans, and local and shared knowledge.

Ports provide the mechanism for communication across R-objects. Messages can be generated by an R-object and directed to the out port where they are preprocessed before the communication. Then the messages arrive at the in port of the receiving R-object where auxiliary communication can take place to resolve any inconsistency and incompleteness before their assimilation into the rest of the local knowledge.

Each R-object carries *views* specifying the other R-objects and their organizational relationships. The views use the organizational information to process a message for inconsistency and incompleteness. For example, in a given incomplete message, a Mini-Callisto can automatically fill in the name of the project if this is the only project common to the Mini-Callisto sending the message.

R-objects also carry *plans* associated with each protocol or message. Given a message in the in port, an R-object executes the associated plan. For example, the plan associated with a query message involves checking whether the query is understandable and whether the source has the authority to make the query and then responding to it (Kedzierski 1983).

Each Mini-Callisto carries two types of objects: those objects which are local to the Mini-Callisto and are thereby owned by the local R-object (*local knowledge*) and those objects which have been moving from one Mini-Callisto to another and are possibly owned by another R-object residing in another Mini-Callisto (*shared knowledge*). Any revisions to an object owned by another Mini-Callisto use *revision protocol,* which involves negotiation and approval before the revision is finalized.

A test bed of the Mini-Callisto network has been created using knowledge craft and its context (alternate world) mechanism (Carnegie Group 1986) in a simulated distributed environment. This network facilitates modeling of distributed knowledge and problem solving on local knowledge. The choice of simulating rather than actually using a distributed environment was made entirely for convenience (a real distributed version was also created but was found too difficult to experiment with). The test bed has provisions for creating several Mini-Callisto nodes; switching from one node to another; sending messages from one node to another; negotiating on project management problems; and gathering associated statistics on the number of messages, the processing load, and the associated changes for each negotiation. The test bed is currently being used for the experiments described under Mini-Callisto experiments. The next three subsections discuss the evolution of constraint-directed negotiation for resource, activity, and configuration management, respectively.

Resource Management

Consider the following scenario: *The printed circuit lab to be used for the design of the Micro-84 CPU belongs to the manufacturing department. The manufacturing department has agreed to the engineering department's use of 40% of the throughput. Jack, the supervisor of the printed circuit lab, schedules its use for the engineering department along with the preventive maintenance requirements and ongoing manufacturing department needs. The engineering department requested from Jack specific reservations for lab use for the next month. A round of negotiation was conducted, ending with a mediation by the plant manager, to provide the needed throughput.*

Although project-scheduling systems have been extended to include considerations of resource availability and capacity (Talbot 1982; Project/2 1981), we have not yet come across any approaches that include resource negotiations based on ownership and commitments in project scheduling. Large projects involve resource sharing between resource owners and project-activity owners (for example, sharing of the printed circuit lab between engineering and manufacturing departments). The sharing is finalized through negotiations, which involve complex agreements resulting from trading, log rolling, or arbitration.

The Mini-Callisto model explicitly brings resource ownership and commitment into the resource-allocation process. Each resource is owned by an agent. Resource sharing needs to be negotiated with the agent owning the resource. Agents are interdependent through organizational links. These organizational links are used for delegating of resource ownership from one agent to another and for adjudicating conflicts at lower levels of the organization. Contracts are formed across two or more agents for the use of a resource. The contracts specify the resource, the contracting parties, and the duration of use. No changes can be made to a contract without the approval of the contracting agents.

The steps for constraint-directed resource negotiation begin with the cause: A Mini-Callisto locates an incompleteness or an inconsistency in the project knowledge that needs to be resolved. As an example, a Mini-Callisto supporting the plan generation for the engineering team recognizes the absence of a contract for the use of the printed circuit lab in the design and verification activities. (Every resource reservation that requires a resource outside the engineering department should be in the form of a contract).

Next, it is necessary for the initiating Mini-Callisto to identify the negotiation participants (that is, those agents whose input or approval is necessary for resolving the inconsistency or incompleteness). Thus, our Mini-Callisto supporting the engineering department locates Jack as the owner of the printed circuit lab.

The third step is to identify the constraints. The agent requiring the resource shares the constraints with the agent owning the resource. The Mini-Callisto that supports our engineering department communicates to Jack's Mini-Callisto of the need to use 40% of the printed circuit lab over the next month.

Jack's Mini-Callisto then searches through the existing reservations for the lab and recognizes that the available capacity is less than 40%. It communicates the constraint to the Mini-Callisto supporting the engineering department. The Mini-Callisto supporting the engineering department responds back, informing Jack's Mini-Callisto that the reservations can not be made in any other time period (because of a due-date constraint).

Any of the negotiation operators can be used to relax the constraints. This negotiation takes into account the importance of the agents, their organizational relationship, and the past contracts. If conflicts cannot be resolved, the negotiation is passed to a higher level for mediation. If mediation at a higher level fails, the proposal is aborted or revised.

Thus, in our example, Jack's Mini-Callisto searches through the existing reservations to find that the contracts are with the manufacturing department and that Jack is unable to assess their importance. In the absence of any other local ways of relaxation, Jack's Mini-Callisto informs the engineering department that the PC lab is not available. The engineering department communicates the negotiation situation to the plant manager (request for mediation). The Mini-Callisto supporting the plant manager searches and finds a contract specifying an overall 40% throughput for the engineering department and decides to trade the reservations (by moving or bumping manufacturing reservations into the future).

Finally, if no conflicts remain, the contract is formalized. The formalization can result in auxiliary proposals for associated changes in contracts with other organizations. For example, the Mini-Callisto supporting the plant manager communicates the changes in existing reservations to the Mini-Callisto supporting Jack. Jack's Mini-Callisto reevaluates the constraints associated with the utilizations and recognizes that the proposed reservations can be granted to the engineering department. It informs the Mini-Callisto supporting the engineering department of the agreement to use the printed circuit lab. The Mini-Callisto supporting the engineering department responds with an acknowledgment, thereby signaling the contract formation. New negotiations are initiated within the manufacturing department to decide when the manufacturing reservations should be scheduled.

The test bed is being used for experiments with the Mini-Callisto model of resource management in various allocation specification and revision situations. In the next two subsections, we explore other types of negotiations and how they are used if and when the resource negotiations fail (or take too long).

Activity Management

Consider the following scenario: *The design engineers were falling behind in their work because of the unavailability of CAD machines. The negotiations between the CAD machine owners and the design engineers resulted in the realization that verification of the first version of the CPU was competing (in the CAD machine utilization) with the design of version 2. It was decided to trade some slack time available in the verification of version 2 to version 1, thereby pushing the design of version 2 into the future.*

Resource management dealt with the specification of resource schedules through negotiations based on ownership and commitment levels. Activity management tasks extend the negotiation to include the constraints related to the activities, such as activity criticality and available slack time. These negotiations often repeat, with the focus changing from resource to activity constraints and back again. In the scenario just described, each of the two versions of the Micro-84 CPU design carry slack time meant to be used in unforeseen situations. The contention for resources, which could not be adequately addressed through resource-commitment negotiations, was retried and resolved through negotiations on the activity slack, thereby "substituting" or "trading" some time available for version 2 to version 1.

The activity negotiation support system involves three activities. The first is the distribution of problem and activity knowledge, which assumes that the project organization is divided into a large number of groups, each possessing the capability to execute a subtask and each having the knowledge of the prototypical activity networks for the subtask. The project goals are divided accordingly and distributed to each group. These goals are translated by each group into a set of activities to meet the goals.

The second activity is a negotiation on plan specification and revision. The groups begin to share a portion of their local plans to define the durations and the performance in accordance with the project objectives or milestones. Extending activities beyond the due dates (as assigned in the milestones) implies additional costs to be incurred. The most common way to eliminate these additional costs is to trade slack time available from one activity to the activity requiring more time. Another strategy, one that is often technically infeasible, is to compensate by providing more resources (that is, activity crashing). Sometimes, it is possible to reduce the costs of delaying the activity beyond the due date. Mini-Callisto supports the sharing of plans as well as the relaxation of constraints (for example, changes to activity durations and related slack times). It provides the support by computing constraint utilities (for example, using critical-path evaluation for the local network) or by using automated interactions for simpler negotiations.

The third activity is the completion of incomplete specifications. The local plans might not be complete for the negotiation with others. Completion of the incomplete portions initiates new negotiations at a future time.

Figure 5 illustrates the negotiation process for the CPU engineering activity. The test bed experiments with the use of activity negotiations to augment resource negotiations and to improve the quality of the final plans (that is, the level to which they satisfy all of the constraints).

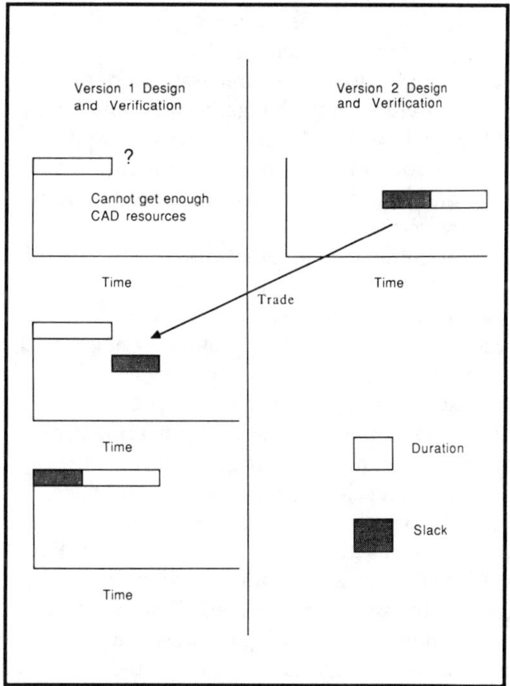

Figure 5. Activity negotiation.

The experiments simulate a set of engineers negotiating on the completion of the overall project using commitments, resource substitutes, and activity slack times.

Often negotiations on resources or activities require consistent understanding of the plan or product definitions, which is especially true when the negotiations fail at the resource or activity level. The next subsection extends the negotiations to include the definitional constraints.

Configuration Management

Consider the following scenario: *Each of the CPU design and verification activities for Micro-84 will take a year. The engineers were told that the engineering development needs to be completed in 1 1/2 years. It became apparent to the engineers that some verification had to take place while design was still being done. Detailed negotiations on the design elements and technological precedence constraints resulted in a plan for verification of a portion of the instruction set while other portions were still being designed. The supply department was informed about the change so that the related purchases were made six months earlier.*

Such negotiations require a good understanding of the components of the CPU and their design, verification, and associated purchase activities. Any changes to the components of the CPU can affect or initiate such negotiations. Also, multiple versions of the CPU can exist, and negotiations can focus on one or more of these versions.

Definitional negotiations use product definitions and generate new definitions in order to resolve project conflicts. These changes have far-reaching consequences for previously negotiated resource allocations or activity networks. The biggest deficiency in conventional project management tools, for use in engineering program management is their exclusion of configuration and change management and their inability to propagate these changes to the rest of the project activities. For example, if a change made to the design activities is not communicated to the supply department, it nullifies the intended effect of finishing the design early. In order to model negotiations and related changes, one needs to model the diverse descriptions, their relationships, and the impact of one specification or revision on another.

The Mini-Callisto approach models product definition and change negotiations as an integral part of the negotiation process. It supports user-initiated change negotiations and identifies and initiates the associated activity management or resource-allocation negotiations. A typical scenario begins with the generation of a change requirement. The design team detects the need for a change in the plan for Micro-84 CPU design. A goal of reducing the engineering time by six months is established.

Change negotiation is the next step. A number of negotiations are attempted to meet the goal. Let us assume that the goal cannot be met through increased resource commitments because they are already 100%. Also, available slack time cannot be decreased any more because no slack time is left. Each of these negotiations involves sharing of knowledge, such as resource commitment, capacities, and slack time available for the entire activity network. Finally, the negotiation is turned toward product definitions. A possible relaxation is found in dividing the CPU into two parts, each complete in itself (that is, no design dependence). The cost of delaying a part of the design is thereby reduced.

Change installation is the final step. The changes lead to two subversions of Micro-84. A search among other activities related to the Micro-84 CPU reveals that the supply department needs to be informed. A subsequent negotiation is initiated with the supply department and results in changes to the project activities.

Figure 6 shows the activity and product knowledge before and after the negotiations. The part definition negotiations are the most difficult to implement and support. As can be seen from this scenario, the negotiations cannot be done unless the model includes design descriptions. A miniature design expert was developed to explore the design knowledge and its use in project negotiations (Glackemeyer 1984), although the related experiments are yet to be designed or conducted.

To summarize, the three components of project management—activity, resource, and configuration management—are interconnected both at the project knowledge and the negotiation levels. Negotiations begin with one type of constraint and are either resolved or continued to include relaxations of other constraints, with possible backtracking if the negotiations fail. The Mini-Callisto system can be used for modeling, supporting, or automating these negotiations.

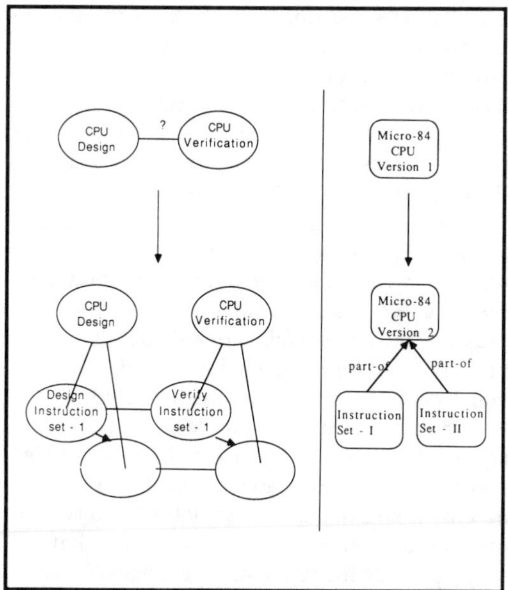

Figure 6. Product definition negotiations.

Mini-Callisto Experiments

We need to validate the constraint-directed negotiation approach on real project situations. The Mini-Callisto experiments initiate the validation process in three ways.

First, Does it work? The constraint-directed negotiation should be able to model various project management situations with activity, resource, or configuration management. Also, the approach should converge to a solution wherever a solution exists. This article demonstrates the applicability of the approach. The experiments involve a number of random situations for each of the three types of negotiation situations. The solutions are tracked for quality (that is, the number of successful negotiations) and negotiation effort (that is, the number and size of communication messages.)

Second, How good is it? A centralized project-scheduling or change installation algorithm can provide an ideal solution to a cooperative problem, that is, the performance of the systems when the goals are identical and when the information is completely available to all the project members. A series of experimental runs compare the distributed project negotiation-based solutions to the upper limit generated by the centralized solution under different distributions of goals to the project members.

Third, Does it use negotiation expertise? Choosing the right goals and constraints for negotiation is important. Choosing incorrect constraints involves additional sharing of information, expensive trade-offs, and additional time spent searching and backtracking.

The third set of experiments will probably be the most difficult and will take the longest time. At the same time, the comparisons and adequacy of the approach (as in the first two experiments) will be affected by the level of negotiation expertise, thereby requiring a reasonable level of negotiation expertise to be captured in the Mini-Callisto test bed. The details of experiments and their results will be the subject of a follow-on article.

The Mini-Callisto concept is being developed with the goal of fulfilling any of the following roles, depending on the objectives, the complexity of the situation, and the negotiation expertise embedded in the system: a support system which documents human negotiations, such as that developed by Marca and Cashman (1985); an enhancement to existing tools, providing minimal negotiation and change management support; an expert system that automatically negotiates in simpler (yet large and dynamic) situations, especially those involving automation of the activities (for example, flexible manufacturing systems (FMS) scheduling); and a test bed for understanding and exploring project management practices. The extension to these areas will trigger a set of experiments to assess the adequacy of the Mini-Callisto approach to problem solving.

Model of Explanation Using Comparative Analysis

We observed that it is inherently difficult to interpret and analyze complex, resource-constrained activity networks (even when graphically illustrated). For example, it requires tremendous effort to identify and understand the effects of changes to some areas of a schedule on other areas. Project managers regularly study project schedules and status information to analyze progress and its effect on related activities. Very often, such analysis is done using unfamiliar tools and graphic aids that offer virtually no assistance other than fancy documentation. Such utilities usually allow users to peruse a project schedule at a single phase of completion and never support comparison of multiple schedules.

By "explanation," we mean the analysis, interpretation, clarification, and report presentation of plans, schedule information, and conclusions produced by activity management systems. The motivation for our work is based on several observations about the task of project management and our attempts to build tools to support it. First, managers must be able to maintain, access, interpret, and act upon information from large and diverse project knowledge bases. Monitoring and managing change in project plans and the status of project activities requires frequent comparisons of lengthy schedules and networks. Managers must know what information is needed, where to locate it, and how to interpret and use it. Equally important is that they be able to do so without great effort.

Our second observation is that with advances in project management research, this task has become more difficult rather than easier. AI and operations research (OR) techniques for project management are increasing the quantity and complexity of knowledge about projects that can be represented and maintained. Decision support systems are using this knowledge to assist or automate many aspects of management decision making. As a result, advances in knowledge representation and inference-making capabilities will greatly expand the need for managers to access and interpret project knowledge and procedures and justifications behind system decision making. Although the process of monitoring the evolution of project plans was complex enough when only activity precedences and durations were represented (for example, with critical path method (CPM) approaches), this process becomes an even greater bottleneck as plans become more knowledge intensive.

Our approach to explanation extends a technique called *comparative analysis* (Kosy and Roth 1986), that has been used successfully in the explanation of change in financial modeling (Kosy and Wise 1984). Although previous work was limited to explaining change in quantitative models, our approach involves identification and interpretation at many levels of understanding, depending on the depth required by the user or the knowledge that is available to the system. These levels include (1) understanding the quantitative relations among the temporal properties of activities and resources contained in PERT networks (for example, knowing statistically how the change in risk in a milestone was produced by changes in delays of prior activities); (2) understanding the qualitative properties of activities, resources, and other project entities and the ways they can be classified, aggregated, abstracted, and summarized in order to help managers find reasons for changes beyond quantitative relations (for example, recognizing that a set of activities contributing to the increased risk for the milestone of a large project is the responsibility of a single subproject); (3) understanding the methods by which changes to a plan are made, including who makes the changes (people or software agents), the types of changes made (for example, precedence, time estimates, detailed breakdowns, or addition of new activities), and (when possible) awareness of other information that might provide the rationale for changes (for example, recognizing the existence of new precedence links and realizing their creation is the result of a Mini-Callisto in response to new commitment information); and (4) understanding other events in a project environment which explain the causes of changes (for example, the process and results of commitment negotiation among people or software agents in a project).

A series of experiments were performed to implement components of comparative analysis within Callisto (Roth et al. 1986). CPM was chosen as the first application because it involves only a single dimension (time) and a single quantifiable constraint (technological precedence) and is therefore analogous to financial spread sheets (costs and algebraic equations) (Kosy and Wise 1984). Although this restriction limits explanation to the identification of change based on quantitative relations (the first level of understanding), it serves as a starting point for explaining complex models of projects.

Explanation is one of the important future areas of research in project management. We intend to expand the necessary expertise in the following ways: (1) to increase the complexity of quantitative models that can be explained (for example, resource-constrained schedules and probabilistic time estimates), (2) to expand comparative analysis to deal with qualitative changes and integrate with quantitative changes, (3) to develop explanatory capabilities for the results of distributed processes for negotiation, (4) to develop an approach to knowledge-based graphics for creating and coordinating multiple text and graphic displays to satisfy the needs of explanation, and (5) to develop a discourse model of human explanations in project management both to support and test our approach to computer-generated explanation.

Conclusions and Future Plans

The Callisto project has made a number of significant research contributions. It has successfully modeled the specification and revision process of project management as a series of constraint-directed negotiations. This model enhances the capabilities of project management tools in dealing with large, complex, and dynamic projects. It has also contributed toward the development of knowledge-based models for project management and similar planning tasks. This model has subsequently been applied to a number of diverse situations ranging from software engineering to manufacturing planning. A configuration-tracking system has been developed out of the first Callisto prototype to be used by Digital Equipment Corporation for the tracking of product configurations. The system is currently being field tested.

The successful implementation of Mini-Callisto requires a set of user interface capabilities that facilitate the use of mixed-mode negotiations. The interfaces are critical for intelligent assistants because the users need to share assumptions, defaults, and decisions with the system. The capabilities include methods for displaying and reporting information contained in various Mini-Callistos as well as tools for their specification and revision. Our efforts in the comparative analysis area need to be extended to include other interface tools required to support mixed-mode project negotiations.

Callisto provides an excellent opportunity for studying distributed problem solving and validating the constraint-directed negotiation approach. We foresee a large number of experiments to validate and extend the Callisto model in project management and similar domains. The approach can be used to solve large real-world problems. The successful applications, though, require a maturing of technologies in the areas of communications, hardware for workstations, and system software for distributed problem solving.

References

Allen, J. F. 1984. General Theory of Action and Time. *Artificial Intelligence* 23(2):123-159.

Allen, J. F., and Hayes, P. J. 1985. A Common-Sense Theory of Time. In Proceedings of the Ninth International Joint Conference on Artificial Intelligence, 528-531.

Baiman, S. 1982. Agency Research in Managerial Accounting: A Survey. *Journal of Accounting Literature* 1:154-213.

Barbuceanu, M. 1984. Object-Centered Representation and Reasoning: An Application to Computer-Aided Design. In SIGART Newsletter, January, 33-39.

Brachman, R. J. 1979. On the Epistemological Status of Semantic Networks. In *Associative Networks: Representation and Use of Knowledge by Computers,* ed. N. V. Findler, 3-50. New York: Academic.

Carbonell, J.; Boggs, M.; and Monarch, I. 1984. DYPAR User's Manual, Computer Science Dept., Carnegie-Mellon Univ.

Carnegie Group. 1986. Knowledge Craft User's Manual, Version 3.1, Carnegie Group.

Corkill, D. D. 1983. A Framework for Organizational Self-Design in Distributed Problem Solving. Ph.D. diss., Computer and Information Sciences Dept., Univ. of Massachusetts.

Crowston, W. B. S. 1970. Decision CPM: Network Reduction and Solution. *OR Quarterly* 21(4):435-452.

Davis, E. W. 1976. *Project Management: Techniques, Applications, and Managerial Issues.* Atlanta, Ga.: American Institute of Industrial Engineers, Inc.

Davis, E. W. 1973. Project Scheduling under Resource Constraints: Historical Review and Categorization of Procedures. American Institute of Industrial Engineering Transactions 5:297-313.

Davis, R., and Smith, R. G. 1981. Negotiation as a Metaphor for Distributed Problem Solving. Technical Report, AI Memo 624, Artificial Intelligence Laboratory, Massachusetts Institute of Technology.

DeCoster, D. T. 1964. PERT/Cost—The Challenge. *Management Services,* May-June.

Demski, J. S. 1976. Uncertainty and Evaluation Based on Controllable Performance. *Accounting Research,* Autumn:230-245.

Demski, J.S., and Swierniga, R.J. 1974. A Cooperative Formulation of the Audit Choice Problem. *Accounting Review* 49 (3): 506-513.

Durfee, E. H.; Lesser, V. R.; and Corkill, D. D. 1985. Increasing Coherence in a Distributed Problem Solving Network. In Proceedings of the Ninth International Joint Conference on Artificial Intelligence, 1025-1030.

Elmaghraby, S. E. 1977. *Activity Networks: Project Planning and Control by Network Models.* New York: Wiley.

Erman, L. D.; Hayes-Roth, F.; Lesser, V. R.; and Reddy, D. R. 1980. The Hearsay-II Speech Understanding System: Integrating Knowledge to Resolve Uncertainty. *Computing Surveys* 12(2):213-253.

Fagin, R., and Halpern, J. Y. 1985. Belief, Awareness, and Limited Reasoning: Preliminary Report. In Proceedings of the Ninth International Joint Conference on Artificial Intelligence, 491-501.

Fama, E. F. 1980. Agency Problems and the Theory of Firm. *Journal of Political Economy* 88(2):288-307.

Fox, M. S. 1983. Constraint-Directed Search: A Case Study of Job-Shop Scheduling. Ph.D. diss., Computer Science Dept., Carnegie-Mellon Univ.

Fox, M. S. 1981a. The Intelligent Management System: An Overview. In *Processes and Tools for Decision Support*, ed. H. G. Sol. Amsterdam, The Netherlands: North Holland.

Fox, M. S. 1981b. An Organizational View of Distributed Systems. In IEEE Transactions on Systems, Man, and Cybernetics 11(1): 70-80.

Fox, M. S. 1979. Organization Structuring: Designing Large Complex Software. Technical Report, CMU-CS-79-155, Computer Science Dept., Carnegie-Mellon Univ.

Fox, M. S., and Smith, S. 1984. The Role of Intelligent Reactive Processing in Production Management. In Proceedings of the Thirteenth Annual Computer Aided Manufacturing International Incorporated Technical Conference, 6-13—6-17.

Freeman, P., and Newell, A. 1971. A Model for Functional Reasoning in Design. In Proceedings of the First International Joint Conference on Artificial Intelligence, 621-640.

Galbraith, J. 1973. *Designing Complex Organizations.* Reading, Mass.: Addison-Wesley.

Georgeff, M. P.; Lansky, A. L.; and Bessiere, P. 1985. A Procedural Logic. In Proceedings of the Ninth International Joint Conference on Artificial Intelligence, 516-523.

Glackemeyer, R. 1984. Behavioral Simulation of Electronic Design. Technical Report, Intelligent Systems Laboratory, The Robotics Institute, Carnegie-Mellon Univ.

Greif, I., and Hewitt, C. E. 1975. Actor Semantics of PLANNER-73. In Proceedings of Association of Computing Machinery, Special Interest Group in Programming Languages-Special Interest Group in Automata and Computability Theory Conference, Palo Alto, Calif.: ACM.

Groves, T. 1975. Information, Incentives, and the Internalization of Production Externalities. In *Theory and Measurement of Economic Externalities*, ed. S. Lin. New York: Academic.

Groves, T., and Loeb, M. 1979. Incentives in Divisionalized Firms. *Management Science* 25: 221-230.

Harris, M., and Townsend, R. M. 1981. Resource Allocation under Asymmetric Information. *Econometrica* 49(1):33-64.

Hayes, P. J. 1979. The Naive Physics Manifesto. In *Expert Systems in the Micro Electronic Age*, ed. D. Michie, 243-270. Edinburgh, United Kingdom: Edinburgh.

Hayes-Roth, B. 1985. A Blackboard Architecture for Control. *Artificial Intelligence* 26(3):251-321.

Hendrix, G. G. 1979. Encoding Knowledge in Partial Networks. In *Associative Networks, Representation and Use of Knowledge by Computers*, ed. N. V. Findler. New York: Academic.

Kedzierski, B. I. 1983. Knowledge-Based Communication and Management and Support in a System Development Environment. Ph.D. diss., Computer Science Dept., Univ. of Southwestern Louisiana.

Kelley, J. E., Jr. 1961. Critical-Path Planning and Scheduling: Mathematical Basis. *Operations Research* 9(3):296-320.

Kelley, J. E., Jr., and Walker, M. R. 1959. Critical-Path Planning and Scheduling. In Proceedings of Eastern Joint Computer Conference, 160-173.

Kosy, D. W., and Roth, S. F. 1986. Applications of Explanation to the Analysis of Schedules and Budgets. Technical Report, Intelligence Systems Laboratory, The Robotics Institute, Carnegie-Mellon Univ.

Kosy, D. W., and Wise, B. P. 1984. Self-Explanatory Financial Planning Models. In Proceedings of the Fourth National Conference on Artificial Intelligence, 176-181. Menlo Park, Calif.: American Association of Artificial Intelligence.

Lambourn, S. 1963. Resource Allocation and Multi-Project Scheduling (RAMPS)—A New Tool in Planning and Control. *Computer J.* 6:300-303.

Latombe, J. C. 1976. Artificial Intelligence in Computer-Aided Design: The TROPIC System. Technical Report, Tech Note 125, Artificial Intelligence Center, Stanford Research Institute.

Lawrence, S. R. 1984. Resource-Constrained Project Scheduling: An Experimental Investigation of Heuristic Scheduling Techniques. Technical Report, GSIA, Carnegie-Mellon Univ.

Lee, R. M. 1980. CANDID: A Logical Calculus for Describing Financial Contracts. Ph.D. diss., Dept. of Decision Sciences, The Wharton School, Univ. of Pennsylvania.

Lesser, V. R., and Corkill, D. D. 1983. The Distributed Vehicle-Monitoring Testbed: A Tool for Investigating Distributed Problem-Solving Networks. *AI Magazine* 4:15-33.

Lesser, V. R., and Corkill, D. D. 1981. Functionally Accurate, Cooperative Distributed Systems. In *IEEE Transactions on Systems, Man, and Cybernetics* 11(1):81-96.

Liberatore, M. J., and Titus, G. J. 1983. Management Science Practice in R&D Project Management. *Management Science* 29:962-974.

Loeb, M. 1975. Coordination and Informational Incentive Problems in the Multidivisional Firm. Ph.D. diss., Graduate School of Management, Northwestern Univ.

Luce, R. D., and Raiffa, H. 1957. *Games and Decisions.* New York: Wiley & Sons.

Lynch, F.; Marshall, C.; and O'Connor, D. 1986. AI in Manufacturing Start-Up. Paper presented at Computer and Automated Systems Association, Society of Mechanical Engineers Ultratech Conference on AI in Manufacturing.

McCarty, L. T., and Sridharan, N. S. 1981. The Representation of an Evolving System of Legal Concepts. In Proceedings of the Seventh International Joint Conference on Artificial Intelligence, 246-253.

Malcolm, D. G.; Rosenboom, J. H.; Clark, C. E.; and Fazar, W. 1959. Application of a Technique for Research and Development Program Evaluation. *Operations Research* 7(5).

Malone, T. W., and Smith, S. A. 1984. Tradeoffs in Designing Organizations: Implications for New Forms of Human Organizations and Computer Systems, Technical Report, CISR WP #112, Sloan WP #1541-84, Center for Information Systems Research, Sloan School of Management, Massachusetts Institute of Technology.

Marca, D., and Cashman, P. 1985. Toward Specifying Procedural Aspects of Cooperative Work. In IEEE Proceedings of Third International Workshop on Software Specification and Design, 151-154.

Marschak, J., and Radner, R. 1972. Economic Theory of Games, Monograph 22, Cowles Foundation, Yale Univ.

Nash, J. F. 1950. The Bargaining Problem. *Econometrica* 18:155-162.

National Air and Space Administration. 1979. Voyager Encounters Jupiter.

Preiss, K. 1976. Engineering Design Viewed as an Activity in Artificial Intelligence, Technical Report SRIN-167, Stanford Research Institute (SRI).

Pritsker, A.A.B.; Watters, L. J.; Wolfe, P. M.; and Happ, W. 1966. GERT: Graphical Evaluation and Review Technique, Part I. *The Journal of Industrial Engineering* 17(5):267-274.

Project/2 User's Manual, Sixth Edition. 1981. Project Software & Development, Inc., Cambridge, MA.

Pruitt, D. G. 1981. *Negotiation Behavior.* New York: Academic.

Reddy, Y. V.; Fox, M. S.; and Hussain, N. 1985. Automating the Analysis of Simulations in KBS. In Proceedings of Summer Computer Simulation Multiconference, 34-40.

Rieger, C., and Grinberg, M. 1977. The Declarative Representation and Procedural Simulation of Causality in Physical Mechanisms. In Proceedings of the Fifth International Joint Conference on Artificial Intelligence, 250-255.

Roth, S. F.; Mesnard, X.; Mattis, J. A.; Kosy, D. W.; and Sathi, A. 1986. Experiments with Explanation of Project Management Models, Technical Report, Intelligence Systems Laboratory, The Robotics Institute, Carnegie-Mellon Univ.

Sacerdoti, E. D. 1977. *A Structure for Plans and Behavior*. New York: American Elsevier.

Sacerdoti, E. D. 1974. Planning in a Hierarchy of Abstract Spaces. *Artificial Intelligence* 5(2):115-135.

Saitow, A. R. 1969. CSPC: Reporting Project Progress to the Top. *Harvard Business Review* 47(1):88-97.

Sathi, A.; Fox, M. S.; and Greenberg, M. 1985. Representation of Activity Knowledge for Project Management. In IEEE Transactions on Pattern Analysis and Machine Intelligence 7(5):531-552.

Schmidt, C. F.; Sridharan, N. S.; and Goodson, J. L. 1978. The Plan Recognition Problem: An Intersection of Psychology and Artificial Intelligence. *Artificial Intelligence* 11(1-2):45-83.

Smith, R. G. 1980. The Contract Net Protocol: High-Level Communication and Control in a Distributed Problem Solver. In IEEE Transactions on Computers C-29(12):1104-1113.

Smith, R. G. 1978. A Framework for Problem Solving in a Distributed Processing Environment. Ph.D. diss., Computer Science Dept., Stanford Univ.

Smith, S. F. 1983. Exploiting Temporal Knowledge to Organize Constraints. Technical Report, CMU-RI-TR-83-12, Intelligent Systems Laboratory, The Robotics Institute, Carnegie-Mellon Univ.

Stallman, R. M., and Sussman, G. J. 1977. Forward Reasoning and Dependency-Directed Backtracking in a System for Computer-Aided Circuit Analysis. *Artificial Intelligence* 9(2):135-196.

Stefik, M. 1981. Planning with Constraints (MOLGEN: Part 1), 111-139; and Planning and Meta-Planning (MOLGEN: Part 2), 141-169. *Artificial Intelligence* 16(2).

Talbot, F. B. 1982. Resource-Constrained Project Scheduling with Time Resource Tradeoffs, The NonPreemptive Case. *Management Science* 28(10):1197-1210.

Tate, A. 1977. Generating Project Networks. In Proceedings of the Fifth International Joint Conference on Artificial Intelligence, 888-893.

Tichy, W. F. 1980. Software Development Control Based on System Structure Description. Ph.D. diss., Computer Science Dept., Carnegie-Mellon Univ.

Turban, E. 1976. The Line of Balance—A Management by Exception Tool. In *Project Management: Techniques, Applications, and Managerial Issues*, 39-47. Atlanta, Ga.: American Institute of Industrial Engineers, Inc.

Weiner, J. L. 1980. BLAH, A System That Explains Its Reasoning. *Artificial Intelligence* 15(1-2):19-48.

Wiest, J. D. 1967. A Heuristic Model for Scheduling Large Projects with Limited Resources. *Management Science* 13(6):359-377.

Wilensky, R. 1983. *Planning and Understanding*. Reading, Mass.: Addison-Wesley.

Wilson, R. B. 1968. The Theory of Syndicates. *Econometrica 36(1): 119-132.*

Winston, P. H. 1975. *The Psychology of Computer Vision*. New York: McGraw-Hill.

Wise, B. P., and Kosy, D. W. 1985. Model-Based Evaluation of Long-Range Resource Allocation Plans, Technical Report, CMU-RI-TR-85-22, The Robotics Institute, Carnegie-Mellon Univ.

Wright, J. M., and Fox, M. S. 1983. SRL: Schema Representation Language. Technical Report, The Robotics Institute, Carnegie-Mellon Univ.

Wright, J. M.; Fox, M. S.; and Adam, D. 1984. SRL/2 User's Manual. Technical Report, The Robotics Institute, Carnegie-Mellon Univ.

Zdonik, S. B. 1984. Object Management System Concepts. In Second Association of Computing Machinery-Special Interest Group in Office Automation Conference on Office Information Systems, 113-119. Toronto, Canada: ACM.

Endnotes

[1]Callisto, only slightly smaller than Ganymede, has the lowest density of all the Galilean satellites, implying that it has large amounts of water in its bulk composition. Its surface is darker than the other Galilean satellites, although it is still twice as bright as our Moon. Callisto is the most heavily cratered

body in the Solar System and, therefore, has the oldest surface of the Galilean satellites, probably dating back to the period of heavy meteoritic bombardment that ended about four billion years ago (NASA 1979).

[2]The word Mini-Callisto was coined to signify that the new Callisto system locally contained a "mini" knowledge base and "mini" problem-solving capabilities which were owned by a suborganizaton or project member.

A Knowledge-Based DSS for Managerial Problem Diagnosis

James F. Courtney, Jr., David B. Paradice, and Nassar H. Ata Mohammed

Problem diagnosis refers to hypothesizing about or searching for causal relationships among variables believed to be associated with the problem at hand. The work described in this paper was motivated by the belief that problem diagnosis is a critical aspect of the managerial decision process, but one that has been neglected by decision support system (DSS) researchers.

Support for the belief that problem diagnosis is critical but neglected is given by several authors [83] [79] [6] [95]. As Mintzberg, Raisinghani, and Theoret put it,

Diagnosis is probably the single most important routine (i.e., subprocess) since it determines in large part, however implicitly, the subsequent course of action. Yet researchers have paid almost no attention to diagnosis, preferring instead to concentrate on the selection routines [83, p. 274].

In two independent surveys, DSS users rated problem diagnosis as one of the most important but least supported decision-making steps [79] [6]. This has led to the conclusion that existing techniques provide adequate support for problem analysis but very limited support for problem diagnosis [95].

The objective of the present authors' work has been to develop intelligent decision support tools for managerial problem diagnosis. In accordance with the perspective adopted in most DSS research, we have approached this problem from a strategic level. A major premise of our work is that to diagnose organizational problems from this perspective it is necessary to have a global representation of the organization's operating environment, both internal and external. We refer to this representation as the structure of the organization's problem domain or the global problem domain. It is important to represent the structure of the organization's problem domain because problems may be caused by any element within that domain—either inside or outside the organization itself. Thus, if problem diagnosis is to be supported at the strategic level, knowledge of the global problem domain must be obtained, represented, and managed by the system.

The next section of our paper describes the problem of managerial problem diagnosis more fully. Artificial intelligence (AI) research on problem diagnosis, reviewed in the third section, indicates that diagnostic systems are more effective when based on causal ("deep") structure. Research on causal structure in management problems is found in the literature on model management systems (MMS) and structural modeling, which also is reviewed to show its relevance to managerial problem diagnosis. Then concepts from these different areas are integrated and an approach that provides computer-based support for managerial problem diagnosis is developed. Finally, some applications are discussed and conclusions are drawn.

Managerial Problem Diagnosis

A number of models describing decision processes have been presented in the literature (see, e.g., [106], [83], [58], [3], [4], [112], and [102]). Work in DSS is concerned with providing computer-based assistance for one or more phases or

Reprinted with permission from *Decision Sciences*, vol. 18, Summer 1987, 373-399.

steps of such managerial decision processes, especially in ill-structured decision situations. Since ill-structured situations are common at the strategic level of an organization, much DSS research has been concerned with support for strategic planning and decision making at the organizational apex.

Most models of the managerial decision process begin with some type of environmental scanning or problem finding activity. Pounds [93] observed that managers "find" problems when observed conditions do not correspond to anticipated or expected conditions.

Once a problem has been located, the next step typically is described as problem structuring [95], problem formulation [5], or problem diagnosis [83]. The terms "structuring," "formulation," and "diagnosis" are used to refer to the same or very similar concepts. For example, problem diagnosis has been defined both as hypothesizing about cause-effect relationships between variables involved in the problem [83] and as "backward inference" from observed symptoms and signs to prior causes [41]. Problem structure has been defined as involving the elements or variables in a problem and how those variables fit together and interact [1]. Problem formulation is similar but may be restricted to a mathematical representation of the problem [102] [5].

Intuitively, problem diagnosis, structuring, and formulation are closely related because each involves the specification of causal relationships among variables. It seems unlikely that a problem can be diagnosed without at least a hypothesis about its structure. Indeed, hypothesizing about cause-effect relationships *is* hypothesizing about structure [78]. Furthermore, mathematical representations of a problem are based on some understanding of the problem's structure. Thus, even though the work in this paper is directed toward problem diagnosis, it is related directly to problem structuring and formulation since improper formulation may arise from incorrect diagnoses [97] [84] [120].

Einhorn and Hogarth [41] discussed causal relationships and diagnosis, emphasizing the fact that diagnosis and prediction are based on the *same* causal structure. Thus, causal structure is useful both in diagnosis and in planning since planning inevitably involves predicting the outcome of possible courses of action.

Einhorn and Hogarth used a 2x2 table as a framework for analyzing how people infer causal relationships between two variables, *X* and *Y*. The rows of their table are labeled *X* and $\overline{X}$ (not -*X*, indicating the assumption that *X* did not occur) and the columns are *Y* and $\overline{Y}$. Six different types of cues are used to determine whether or not a causal relationship exists: temporal order, contiguity in space and time, constant conjunction, number of alternative explanations, similarity, and predictive ability.

Temporal order refers to which of the two variables occurred first, *X* or *Y*. This is used to determine which is the potential cause and which the effect. In the ensuing discussion we will assume *X* occurred before *Y*, so we are attempting to determine whether *X* may have caused *Y*.

Contiguity in space and time refer to the notion that people have a stronger tendency to feel *X* caused *Y* if *X* and *Y* are close together in space and time. If so, then the strength or "frequency" (as Einhorn and Hogarth called it) of the cell corresponding to *X* causing *Y* is greater relative to the other cells.

Constant conjunction is "the degree to which X and Y occur together, holding contiguity in space and time constant" [41, p. 27]. This also relates to the relative strength of cell *X,Y*.

The number of alternative explanations refers to cell $\overline{X}$,*Y* as it asks the question, "Would *Y* have occurred if *X* had not?" The greater the number of ways that *Y* may have occurred in the absence of *X*, the lower the causal relevance of *X* to *Y* and the lower the relative strength of cell $\overline{X}$,*Y*.

Similarity occurs within the context of some metaphorical analogy, such as comparing the human brain to a computer. It is defined as a weighted linear function of confirming evidence (cells, *X,Y* and $\overline{X}$,$\overline{Y}$) and disconfirming evidence (cells $\overline{X}$,*Y* and *X*,$\overline{Y}$).

The final cue, predictive ability, is the correlation coefficient between *X* and *Y*, defined over all four cells. The meaning of the correlation coefficient is *interpreted* in light of information about *other* cues, however. If other cues do not indicate sufficient reason to believe a causal relationship exists, the correlation is spurious.

We refer to these six causal cues when we discuss the experiential knowledge base (EKB) of the diagnostic system we propose and show

how information about cues can be generated. In the next section, we describe research in AI and MMS that relates to diagnosis.

Related Research

Research related to managerial problem diagnosis and problem structuring is found in the AI and MMS literatures.

AI Research on Diagnosis

Stefik, Aikins, Balzer, Benoit, Birnbaum, Hayes-Roth, and Sacerdoti [107] indicated that (nonmanagerial) expert systems have been developed for a wide variety of tasks including planning, design, prediction, diagnosis, monitoring, and interpretation. They referred to systems that perform more than one of these tasks as "control systems." All six tasks occur in the management domain. Our main concern in this paper is with managerial problem diagnosis; however, we later show how this task relates to other tasks as well.

The crux of diagnostic activity is the ability to infer system malfunctions from observed activities and to relate the observed behavioral irregularities to underlying causes [24]. Stefik et al. [107] defined diagnosis as a process of faultfinding in a system based on interpreting potentially "noisy" data. Diagnosis requires understanding the system organization and the relationships and interactions among subsystems. Key problems are

- Faults can be masked by the symptoms of other faults;
- Faults can be intermittent;
- Diagnostic equipment can fail;
- Some data about a system are inaccessible, expensive, or dangerous to retrieve.

There has been a great deal of research related to *nonmanagerial* problem diagnosis in the field of AI. Many expert systems dealing with diagnosis in nonmanagerial domains have been constructed including INTERNIST and CADUCEUS (medicine) [92], MYCIN (medicine) [105], Alven (medicine) [86], PROSPECTOR (mineral exploration) [49], DIPMETER ADVISOR (geologic signals) [35], and an unnamed system for diagnosing grain combine malfunctions [103]. Further, a host of other diagnostic systems generally are known to researchers (see, e.g., [47]) including DART from IBM (computer systems faults) and PUFF from Stanford (lung disorders).

The unique features of these systems include

- Separation of knowledge about the problem domain into a knowledge base that can be manipulated as a separate entity,
- An inference engine that operates on the knowledge base to extract knowledge and make inferences in response to user problem statements,
- The use of probabilistic or quasiprobabilistic factors (certainty factors) concerning relationships or rules in the knowledge base to provide a way of dealing with problems that involve uncertainty, and
- Explanation facilities that are used to describe the reasoning the system uses to arrive at particular conclusions.

Recently, expert systems development has been based on inference engines that reason from "first principles" [33] [34] (the fundamental laws or relationships of the problem domain). Diagnosis from first principles also has been explored in a number of domains including medicine (CASNET [119], ABEL [91], RX [17], computer-aided instruction [25], electronic troubleshooting [36], and physics [37] [69] [48]).

Notably, all these systems have been developed in "deep and narrow" problem domains [13]. A deep and narrow problem domain is one where experts exist and the underlying laws of the problem domain are well formulated and usually static. Management, on the other hand, is a "wide and shallow" domain [13]. Managerial expertise generally is drawn from several sources and the fundamental laws frequently are ill-structured and even changing [39] [88].

Gentner and Stevens [51] confirmed that deep and narrow domains have been the most fruitful areas for research aimed at capturing models of human expertise. For example, recognizing an expert in physics is much easier than recognizing an expert in human relations. Furthermore, an expert's "mental model" [51] in a domain such as physics can be compared to the well-formed laws of the domain; such a comparison for an expert's mental model in a wide and shallow field is very difficult, if not impossible.

Although the management domain is wide and shallow, managerial problem diagnosis shares a fundamental characteristic with approaches taken in other domains. Specifically, causal explanations frequently are used to diagnose problems in managerial domains [5] [15].

Kasper [62], Pracht [95], and Loy [75] demonstrated the effectiveness of supporting the construction of mental models in a managerial problem domain. Paradice and Courtney [88] [90] and Pracht and Courtney [96] showed preliminary ways to capture, organize, and manipulate managerial mental models. The work reported herein seeks to combine recent insights gained in the field of AI with prior efforts in managerial problem formulation to support diagnosis of managerial problems—a significantly different type of problem domain than those addressed in prior studies.

Davis [34, p. 404] argued that models of causal interaction in diagnostic systems are superior to empirically based diagnostic systems. Such models are called "deep models" [53] [81] [28] [29] because they attempt to capture relationships and first principles that are at the basis of expert knowledge. Deep models have the capability to deduce behavior from structure [70] and may be able to build predictive models of future behavior [119].

Chandrasekaran and Mittal [29] observed that the straightforward approach taken by expert systems employing condition-action production rules is not feasible in problem domains of any significant size. Hence, deep models will be necessary in large problem domains. Bouwman's [23] work on financial problem diagnosis and research in MMS provides a partial basis for a diagnostic system for the wide and shallow domain of management, as described next.

Bouwman's Study of Financial Diagnosis

Bouwman [23] is one of very few researchers who have studied managerial problem diagnosis. In what may be regarded as landmark research, he used protocol analysis to study how financial analysts diagnose accounting statements. He then developed a computer program to mimic this diagnostic process in a qualitative manner. Bouwman's analysis revealed problem detection as the first step of the diagnostic process. Five operators were used in the problem detection process: computation of a simple trend, computation of a more complex trend, comparison with other information, comparison with a norm, and application of a heuristic or "rule of thumb." He also established rules for determining which operator to apply in a particular situation. These operators were used to translate the problem into qualitative terms.

The next step was to screen out insignificant findings, which his subjects then excluded from further analysis. Then came actual diagnostic reasoning, which involved integrating new findings with existing knowledge, and forming hypotheses that attempted to explain these findings. Existing knowledge used by subjects involved a model representing "a causal structure that describes the internal model of a typical firm" [23, p. 659]. Bouwman found that causal chains were integrated into "trees of causes," the branches of which represent different problem hypotheses or potential explanations of the problem's causes. Subjects mentally explored the branches of these trees in order to diagnose the problem. Bouwman was able to construct a sophisticated computer program that simulated this complex process very effectively. He even was able to tune his program to simulate the processes used by individual subjects.

From our perspective, one of the most important aspects of Bouwman's program is its reliance on the "internal model of a typical firm" to perform the diagnosis. This model consists of causal relationships among variables in the problem domain and was derived from the protocol analysis. The internal model was used to develop trees of causes (or causation trees, as we shall call them) on which diagnoses were based. Since the internal model is used to drive the construction of causation trees and the diagnostic process, the accuracy of the diagnosis is determined largely by the accuracy of the internal model. Thus, it is critical that the internal model accurately reflect the actual firm being modeled. We illustrate how the causation trees are constructed when our diagnostic system is described.

As in most DSS research, the concern in this work is with the development of tools to assist in formulating and using quantitative models. Bouwman's qualitative system provides an excellent starting point for a quantitative approach. In the next section we describe related work on problem structuring in MMS.

Model Management Systems (MMS)

Work on MMS is relevant to problem diagnosis because it deals with quantitatively oriented problem structuring. MMS seek to support dynamic problem structuring and to facilitate the use of mathematical models in managerial decision making [42] [44] [43]. As Lenard noted, "model management begins with a scheme for representing models and must provide for generating, restructuring, updating, and obtaining results of models" [72, p. 36]. Thus, research in MMS typically has treated models as entities and employed some knowledge representation technique to represent either relationships between variables within models (intramodel relationships) or between the models themselves (intermodel relationships) or both [44] [66] [82] [46].

Another branch of MMS research involves the use of techniques from database systems, often combining these with a knowledge representation scheme [18] [19] [20] [21] [22] [15] [16] [104] [115] [116] [72]. Again, models are the entities on which these approaches are based.

Our concern is with representing the structure of problem domains. Since MMS deal with problem structuring, it appears the MMS approach may be relevant to problem diagnosis. This approach does have shortcomings, however, because of the somewhat limited perspective adopted in MMS work.

Although Elam, Henderson, and Miller [44] suggested that MMS be able to incorporate broad knowledge of the problem domain, virtually all the MMS work cited above is limited to that portion of the domain for which models already exist. Since managerial problems may result from elements that are not contained in existing models, it is necessary to extend the techniques of MMS to the broader concept originally proposed by Elam et al. [44]. The next section describes how concepts from AI, MMS, and structural modeling may be integrated to form a more comprehensive approach to managerial problem diagnosis.

Techniques for Representing System Structure

Techniques for representing and analyzing the structure of problems have been developed in a branch of systems engineering known as structural modeling. The seminal theoretical work on structural modeling is Harary, Norman, and Cartwright's [52] and relies heavily on the theory of directed graphs (digraphs). In structural modeling, problems have both a graphical and numeric (matrix) representation. Kane [61] referred to techniques that deal mostly with structural properties as geometric; those that deal with numeric representations he called arithmetic. For reasons discussed shortly, we chose to use the structural modeling approach to represent the global structure of problem domains.

A rather simple structural model is shown in Figure 1 for purposes of illustration. This model is meant to represent the global problem domain. Causation trees for specific problem instances will be derived from the global

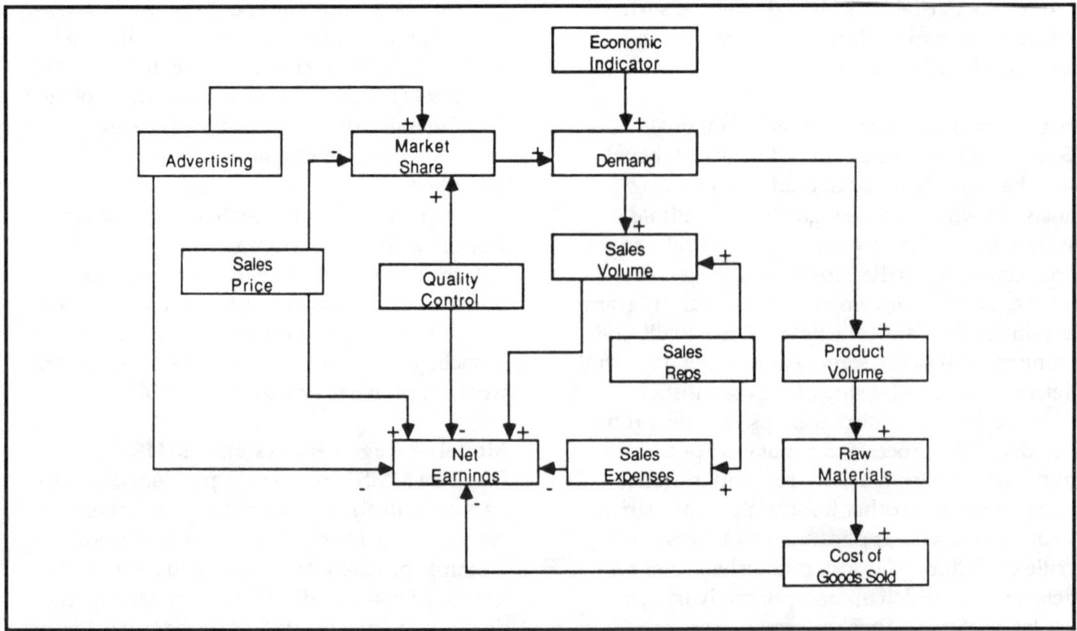

Figure 1. Structural model relating net earnings to marketing and production variables.

structural model. Causation trees have a particular problem variable as the root node, and directly related and indirectly related variables as children. Hence a causation tree is just that portion of a structural model relevant to a given problem.

Information in a structural model such as this is obtained from a person (or persons) knowledgeable in the problem domain—hopefully an "expert" in that domain. The information normally is collected via assertions about the relationship between pairs of variables in the domain. These assertions may take various forms such as

Changes in x_i cause changes in x_j,
Changes in x_i cause increases (or decreases) in x_j, or
A one-unit change in x_i causes x_j to change by c_{ij}.

The information in Figure 1 may be represented in a matrix by forming a row and column for each variable in the problem. The resulting matrix is called a binary connection matrix or adjacency matrix because a 1 is entered in cell i,j if there is a causal relationship from variable x_i to x_j; otherwise a zero is entered. The first form of assertion given above yields a binary adjacency matrix.

Matrix powering may be applied to adjacency matrices to determine paths of various lengths between variables. Specifically, if **A** is the adjacency matrix, then $\mathbf{A}^n$ gives all paths of length n in the matrix. Each element of A^n gives the total number of paths from variable i to variable j. A "total connection matrix" **T** gives the total number of paths between each variable pair and is given by: $\mathbf{T} = \Sigma\mathbf{A}^n$ for $n = 1, 2, ..., p$, where p is maximum power to which **A** is raised.

From the point of view of problem diagnosis, matrix powering and the total connection matrix may be used to determine the paths from problem variables (problem symptoms) to potential problem causes. McLean and Shepherd [77] referred to this as qualitative information in the sense that it gives the *number* of paths between a problem and a cause, but not the *strength* of the cause.

Signs indicating the direction of change in x_j induced by the changes in x_i (the second form of assertion given above) may be added to the adjacency matrix to yield a signed digraph. If changes in x_i lead to increases in x_j then x_i is said to augment [100] or excite [26] [27] x_j. If x_i decreases x_j the relationship is said to be inhibitory. Burns and Winstead [26][27] developed a geometric approach to determine the redundancy of paths in a model based on the excitatory or inhibitory nature of the path. Roberts [99] used signed digraphs to study energy demand.

In managerial problem diagnosis, some paths from causes to symptoms may be excitatory, others inhibitory. Thus the question we are concerned with is the net impact of the excitatory and inhibitory paths. In order to answer this question, information about the strength of the path must be given. Hence McLean and Shepherd's [77] observation that the strength of relationships often is critical is relevant for quantitative managerial problem diagnosis. Paradice and Courtney [90] showed how this information may be used in a managerial context.

If coefficients indicating the amount and direction of change induced in x_i by a one-unit change in x_j are included in the matrix (the third assertion form), then a "weighted adjacency matrix" is produced. Suppose, for example, we have a three-variable problem of the form $x_1 = f(x_2); x_2 = f(x_1, x_3); x_3 = f(x_1)$. Letting

$$C_{ij} = \frac{\partial x_i}{\partial x_j}$$

and writing these in matrix form yields an "interaction matrix" [77]. If each function is linear, each C_{ij} is a scalar; thus a weighted adjacency matrix is produced. Therefore the weighted adjacency matrix represents first-order changes in the relationships among variables in the model.

The arithmetic property of weighted adjacency matrices that we are concerned with is referred to as a pulse process [100] or pulse analysis [77]. This is a form of sensitivity analysis in which input variables are changed and the resulting change (or "pulse") in an output variable is computed over a given period of time.

Roberts [100] assumed discrete time periods and showed that the one-period pulse in variable i at time $(t+1)$ is given by

$$P_i(t+1) = \sum_j C_{ji}P_j(t).$$

He went on to show that *forecasts* of future values may be obtained from

$$\mathbf{V(t) = V(0) + P(0)(A + A^1 + ...+A^t)}$$

where **V(t)** is the forecasted matrix of values at times t, **V(0)** is the initial value matrix, **P(0)** is the matrix of initial pulses, and A is the weighted adjacency matrix. Thus the capability of forecasting is inherent in the structural modeling approach.

This information on structural modeling provides the basis for our approach to managerial problem diagnosis. Other arithmetic techniques related to weighted adjacency matrices are described by Axelrod [11], Kruskal [67], McLean and Shepherd [77], McLean [76], Roberts [100], Waller [114], and Lendaris [73]. As a final remark, we note that several software packages have been developed for various structural modeling techniques. Some of the more popular are KSIM [61] [68], QSIM [113], SPIN [78], ISM [117] [118] [9], SMGS [71], GRIPS [56], and GISMO [94] [95].

The next section of the paper develops an approach to managerial problem diagnosis that integrates the pulse process technique of structural modeling with Bouwman's findings on managerial problem diagnosis. This approach extends Bouwman's approach in several ways.

Proposed Approach

Before describing our system for managerial problem diagnosis, it will be useful to describe the managerial decision-making context within which the system is presumed to operate. We describe a decision-making model that is not intended to be new or novel; it is used to set the context for subsequent discussions.

Our diagnostic approach is designed to support ongoing managerial control activity. The model we present (Figure 2) is similar to several in the literature [106] [83] [102] [58] but most closely approximates that of Ackoff [3]. Note that the model is cyclical in nature, emphasizing the ongoing nature of management control. The terminology of Stefik et al. [107] was chosen specifically to emphasize the relationship of the model to work in AI. Note that all the tasks in the model involve complex cognitive processes, many of which have been studied extensively in cognitive psychology. Some references to that literature are given where appropriate. We begin our discussion of the model with monitoring, the topmost rectangle in Figure 2.

Monitoring involves acquiring information (perhaps via a data-base management system) describing the current state of the organizational system, comparing the current state to the desired (goal) state, and noting significant discrepancies [93] [41]. As Bouwman [23] found, these discrepancies between what is expected or desired and what is obtained constitute a list of significant findings or problem symptoms that is

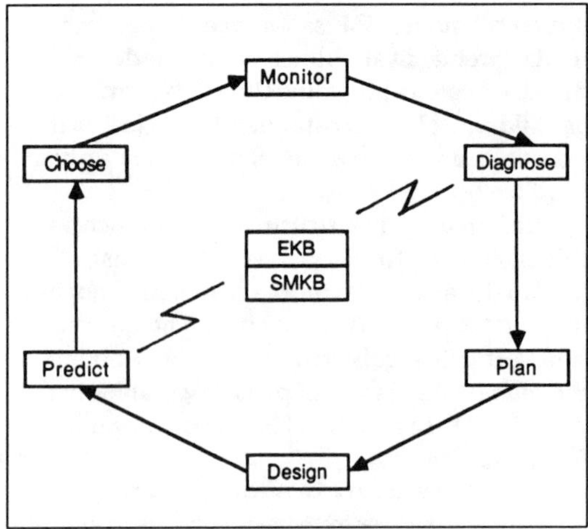

Figure 2. Support for the management control process via a structural modeling knowledge base (SMKB) and an experiential knowledge base (EKB).

passed forward for diagnosis. Hogarth and Makridakis [55] listed six different types of human bias that may occur at this stage of the process. They suggested that a DSS should attempt to control the effect of such biases, some of which we describe briefly later.

Diagnosis is the next step and consists of searching for or hypothesizing about causes of the observed discrepancies or problem symptoms. Mintzberg et al. [83], Ackoff and Sasieni [5], and Bouwman [23] described managerial diagnostic activity. As discussed earlier, Einhorn and Hogarth [41] described how people decide whether or not a causal relationship exists between two variables. At least 10 different types of bias may affect information processing at this stage [55].

The next three steps, *planning, design,* and *prediction,* frequently form a feedback loop within the overall cycle [83]. Stefik et al. [107] described planning as setting new goals in light of the current situation. In our case, the problems confronting the organization are especially important, as are the resources available to attack these problems. Design consists of generating alternative ways of achieving the goals; prediction refers to forecasting the outcomes of each alternative.

Ackoff [4] described the tradeoffs between prediction and planning. That is, if we can predict well, then planning for contingencies is less important. Similarly, if our plans provide for many contingencies, then the need for accurate prediction is reduced. Einhorn and

Hogarth [41] discussed the fact that causal models may be used in both diagnosis and forecasting. They noted that planning often leads to an unjustified "illusion of control" over an uncertain environment.

The final step in this cycle involves comparing the predicted outcomes of the various alternatives, *choosing* an alternative (presumably the one most likely to achieve the planned goals), and implementing it. Then new information is acquired and the cycle is repeated. Several types of bias also are associated with choosing an alternative, and several occur in a feedback process such as the one described [55].

We would like to emphasize that as the cycle is repeated, a learning process occurs within individual managers and the organization as a whole [63] [30] [96]. This learning process relates to gaining an understanding of the organizational problem domain [96]. Learning is another area of study in cognitive science that has been suggested as a "reference discipline" [64] for DSS [54] [65] [57] [102]. Our system includes a module that accumulates knowledge gained from the diagnostic process and thus is a form of experiential knowledge [65]. This is a unique aspect of our system. As illustrated later, it has uses in helping to control biases which may arise during the decision-making process. To emphasize the fact that structural knowledge of causal relations may be used in diagnosing, analyzing, and predicting problems, we have placed a structural modeling knowledge base (SMKB) in the center of Figure 2 with arrows indicating which processes it may support. We also have shown an experiential knowledge base (EKB) that also is useful in these processes.

Architecture of the Diagnostic System

The architecture of a system to support managerial problem diagnosis is illustrated in Figure 3. The full architecture supports both formal and concrete thought processes by including a module for storing the results ("experiences") of formal diagnostic analyses in the EKB, which serves as a memory for problems that have been diagnosed in the past.

Basic elements of the system include

- A user interface,
- A monitor that searches for problem situations,
- A problem processor that searches for a problem's causes,
- A knowledge manager that maintains causal relationships and historical information about successful diagnosis (the EKB),
- A data manager that supplies data to the rest of the system as needed,
- A dictionary manager that maintains information on all data items and variables in the system, and

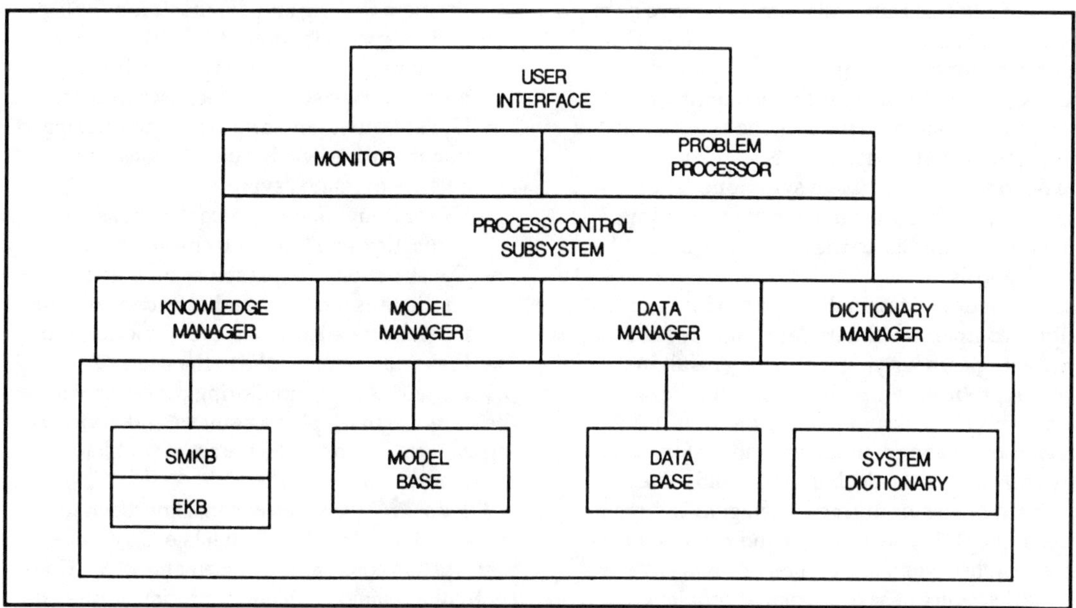

Figure 3. Basic system architecture.

- A process-control subsystem that links various elements of the system together and controls the flow of information.

This paper is concerned primarily with the problem processor and the knowledge bases, which are described in some detail.

The Monitor and List of Problem Symptoms

Since problems must be located before they can be diagnosed, the system includes a module (the monitor) for problem finding. Our approach to problem finding is based on the work of Pounds [93] who found that managers define problems as the difference between the present situation as observed and some expectation or standard. Expectations and standards may be based on recent trends, projections, or the behavior of comparable organizations. They may be the result of formal studies or derived from formal models; or they may be very informal and reside only in the manager's mind.

Since our primary concern is with problem diagnosis and not problem finding per se, our treatment of problem finding is very limited. The problem-finding module itself could be very complex. Sophisticated forecasting models (perhaps based on structural modeling techniques) could be used to predict anticipated values for selected variables (monitored variables) in the problem domain.

We assume the user selects monitored variables from among the variables in the problem domain and that standards somehow have been established for these monitored variables. The monitor's function simply is to compare observed values (the most recent values in the data base) to the standards for each monitored variable. Any variable violating its standards will be referred to as a problem symptom. The monitor prepares a list of problem symptoms and delivers this list to the problem processor for diagnosis.

Since organizational problem domains are highly complex and interrelated, it is possible that a single underlying cause may result in several problem symptoms. For example, a downturn in the economy may result in decreased sales and increases in inventory holding costs due to the declining demand. The problem processor must be intelligent enough to account for this phenomenon and to avoid excessive searches when one or a few causes have led to the discovery of several related problem symptoms.

The Problem Processor: Problem Structuring and Diagnosis

Support for problem diagnosis is based on structural modeling. As described previously, structural models may be based on assertions of the form: "A one-unit change in variable i causes variable j to change by c_{ij}." Such assertions are captured and stored in the knowledge base as a semantic network. Thus, as noted previously, the system begins with relationships between pairs of variables, not complete models as in MMS. As illustrated below, these relationships are combined to form models on which the diagnostic process is based. Relationships are based on changes observed in values between two points in time; thus this is a differential approach.

The following notation will be used to describe the diagnostic process:

$X = [x_1, x_2, ..., x_n]$, the indexed set of elements (variables) in the problem domain,

M = the set of monitored variables and is a subset of X,

S_t = the set of problem symptoms (monitored variables violating standards) at time t and is a subset of M,

$\Delta(x_i)$ = the observed change in x_i between times t - 1 and t,

$\Delta'(x_i)$ = the change in x_i computed using the structural model currently stored in the knowledge base (how $\Delta'(x_i)$ is computed is described later).

Problem finding and diagnosis is a phasewise process involving

- Application of monitoring procedures to determine the set of problem symptoms,
- Use of Bouwman's approach and information in the knowledge base to construct clusters of related symptoms,
- Use of Bouwman's approach to construct a "causation tree" for each cluster,
- Construction of explanatory models based on the causation tree and extraction of data from the data base to test each model, and
- Presentation of results to the user.

Phase 1: Apply monitoring procedures to the elements of M, placing any variables violating their standards on S_t, the set of problem symptoms.

Phase 2: Apply Bouwman's approach to form clusters of related elements of S_t. Notice that clusters consist only of elements of S_t. Conceptually, related problem symptoms form one "problem" with the same underlying set of base causes. Thus a diagnosis will be attempted for each cluster. The following recursive definition of a cluster with symptom x_i as the root node may be implemented easily in a logic programming language such as PROLOG:

x_j clusters with x_i if x_j impacts x_i and $x_i \in S_t$ and $x_j \in S_t$. (1a)

x_j clusters with x_i if x_k impacts x_i and x_j clusters with x_k. (1b)

Phase 3: Apply Bouwman's approach to form a causation tree for each cluster. Causation trees are defined in (2a) and (2b). These are similar to clusters except that only the root node of a causation tree must be on the list of symptoms. Any other element in the problem domain is a candidate for the causation tree for each cluster.

x_j causation tree x_i if x_j impacts x_i and $x_i \in S_t$. (2a)

x_k causation tree x_i if x_k impacts x_j and x_j causation tree x_i. (2b)

Phase 4: Attempt to diagnose each cluster by constructing and testing arithmetic models based on the causation trees formed in Phase 3. A model is constructed for each x_i that is a root node in a causation tree. If the model accurately computes the observed change in the value of the root node, then a diagnosis may be obtained. If not, the model does not represent the problem domain faithfully and an accurate diagnosis is not possible.

Models are based on the structural modeling assumption that changes in x_i are due to changes in the variables that impact x_i. Thus we assume that

$\Delta(x_i) = f(\Delta(x_j) \mid x_j \text{ impacts } x_i)$. (3)

In order to computer $\Delta'(x_i)$, the estimate of $\Delta(x_i)$ given by the current structural model, we must have some information about the form of the function in (3). In the linear case, which will be used for simplicity of exposition, $\Delta'(x_i)$ is computed using

$\Delta'(x_i) = \Sigma(Cji\Delta(x_j))$ (4)

This is a breadth-first approach because all the variables one level below x_i enter into the analysis. It is a one-period pulse process.

If equation (4) is a perfect model for the actual changes in x_i, then no discrepancy will exist between the computed change $\Delta'(x_i)$ and the actual (observed) change $\Delta(x_i)$. Of course, in practice, discrepancies will occur. The accuracy of the model is reflected by the degree of discrepancy between the actual and the computed values. If the difference in actual and computed values is "small," then the model represents the problem domain faithfully and explains the change. That is, the model "explains" or accounts for the observed change, even if the change was not anticipated. (Recall that the diagnosis is attempting to explain unanticipated variances.)

As far as the system is capable of determining, the base causes of the problem lie along the branches of the causation tree. These branches represent different hypotheses about the cause of the problem. Of course, several branches may work together to contribute to the problem, while others may work to mitigate the problem somewhat. Branches contributing most to the problem (excitatory branches) will have an impact that is "large" relative to other branches and in the same direction (+ or -) as the change in the problem variable. Branches offsetting the problem by the greatest amount (inhibitory branches) have relatively large contributions, but in the opposite direction.

Branches causing and mitigating the problem constitute the first level of problem diagnosis. A deeper level of diagnosis is given by searching these branches for base causes, which lie at root nodes. If the causation tree models the problematical area of the domain accurately, then one or more variables at terminal nodes must be causing the problem. These variables have changed in value, thereby triggering changes up the branch to the root node or symptom variable. To discover these, branches of the causation tree are searched in an effort to find variables at terminal nodes that have changed and which lie along a branch whose impact is significant. These variables at terminal nodes constitute the ultimate diagnosis of the problem insofar as the system is capable of determining.

If the model is accurate and the system is able to find such nodes, then explanations such as "Variables x_1, x_2, and x_3 have contributed v_1, v_2, and v_3 to the changes observed in variable z; the problem would have been worse had it not been for variables y_1 and y_2 whose changes have offset the magnitude of the problem" can be offered. It also can provide explanations based on paths from terminal nodes to the root node.

Our discussion so far has assumed that the computed change $\Delta'(x_i)$ is "close to" the observed change $\Delta(x_i)$. If the difference in the computed change and the observed change is "large," the model fails to explain the source of the discrepancy. In this case, the model does not represent the structure of the problem domain accurately and the system is not able to diagnose the source of the problem. A message to that effect is delivered to the user. The process may be terminated at that point, or the model may be revised and retested. This is essentially a "what if..." type of process that helps the user explore and test hypothesized relationships in the problem domain. It is designed to help the user learn about the problem domain and formulate an accurate model of the structure of that domain. The next section describes how a history of successful diagnosis is maintained in the EKB and how this may be used to provide information concerning the causal cues described by Einhorn and Hogarth [41].

The EKB and Causal Cues

The EKB acts as the organizational memory for problem clusters that have been diagnosed successfully in the past, along with their respective diagnoses. It thus consists of structured declarative knowledge about problems and their diagnoses and can be represented in the format of a hierarchical data base (see Figure 4). Since a problem cluster may have occurred on several occasions, a count is maintained of the number of occurrences of each cluster.

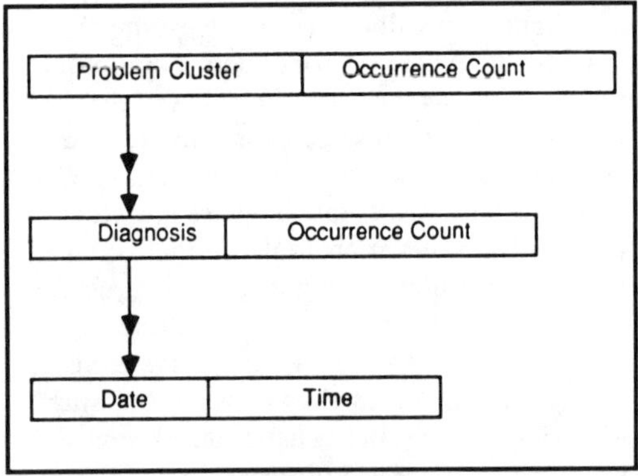

Figure 4. Logical structure of the EKB.

In addition, clusters may have different diagnoses on different occasions, so a count also is maintained of the number of occurrences of each diagnosis, along with the corresponding dates and times. This information is useful in determining whether particular problem clusters have been occurring repeatedly, which may indicate some fundamental problem in organizational policy or strategy that should be addressed by management.

The EKB may be interpreted as simulating experiential human learning [54] [102] [57] [65]. In some cases, the EKB may be used to circumvent the need for a formal diagnosis. Whenever a cluster is formed, the EKB is searched first to determine whether the problem has been diagnosed previously. If so, the previous diagnoses are presented to the user, along with the current data values for variables constituting the diagnosis. If the user believes a previous diagnosis explains the current problem, the corresponding occurrence count is incremented,and the current date/time stamp is inserted. If no previous diagnosis is acceptable, then a formal diagnosis is undertaken as described previously. If the problem is successfully diagnosed, appropriate action is taken to update the EKB.

The EKB, in conjunction with the diagnostic system, also is a potential source of information regarding the causal cues described by Einhorn and Hogarth [41] discussed earlier. The manner in which assertions are captured defines temporal order. The date/time stamp of each diagnosis clearly provides information about the contiguity in time of the cluster and its diagnosis. Since the EKB is for a single organization, contiguity in space is inherent in the system. Information about the number of alternative explanations is given by the number of different paths from terminal nodes to monitored variables. The EKB contains the number of times each of these paths has contributed to diagnoses that have occurred in the past. To generate information about the questions of whether *Y* would have occurred in the absence of *X*, the change in *X* can be set to zero in previous diagnoses and the system can be used to determine whether *Y* would have been on the list of problem symptoms. Finally, predictive ability (correlation coefficients) can easily be computed and similarity can be computed if weights are given for the cells.

We show elsewhere [88] [89] how causal modeling and path analysis, which are based on correlation and regression analysis, can be used to go beyond Einhorn and Hogarth's concept of predictive ability in helping users gain unbiased perceptions of relationships among variables in the problem domain.

Applications

The system as described herein has been implemented and tested in prototype form by Ata

Mohammed [8] as part of the BML/SLIM system used in other DSS research [32] [96] [62] [63]. Monitoring and generating the list of problem symptoms are based simply on changes in observed values from one period to the next and on user-supplied bounds for those values. The problem-structuring and diagnostic modules have been implemented in full, although linearity is assumed in the derived models and cycles are prohibited. The diagnostic process is under user control via menus, rather than being strictly phasewise.

This approach may appear to require very restrictive assumptions, but work already has begun to remove the linearity restriction and provide for automatic updating of impact coefficients by statistically deriving coefficients using data in the data base [88] [89].

Further, a large class of problems (diagnosis of accounting system data) satisfies the restrictions listed above. As illustrated in Figure 5, charts of accounts have an acyclic, hierarchical structure and relationships between levels are known and additive. Moreover, accounting systems (which are one form of organizational model) are found universally in both profit and nonprofit organizations. Thus, even with very restrictive assumptions, the model is applicable to a type of problem common to *all* organizations.

Moreover, it is standard practice in cost accounting systems to maintain standard costs against which actual costs are compared. In the budgeting process, most firms produce a master budget in which budgeted amounts are maintained for some accounts and against which actual costs are compared. Standard costs and budgeted amounts provide excellent vehicles on which the monitoring function and construction of causation trees may be based.

Large organizations maintain thousands of accounts in such systems. It may be exceedingly difficult for one individual to trace a large variance in current assets if the organization inventories thousands of items, has several thousand customers, or has several other current asset accounts. A diagnostic system such as the one we have described should greatly increase the speed and accuracy with which the causes of such variances can be isolated.

As an example, consider the recent emphasis on cost containment in the health care industry. The adoption of the Tax Equity and Fiscal Responsibility Act (TEFRA) of 1982 has caused a significant change in the way hospitals manage their daily operations. Prior to 1982, hospital staff members could order tests and prescribe medications and therapies with little regard for the cost incurred. This was because there frequently was a third party (e.g.,

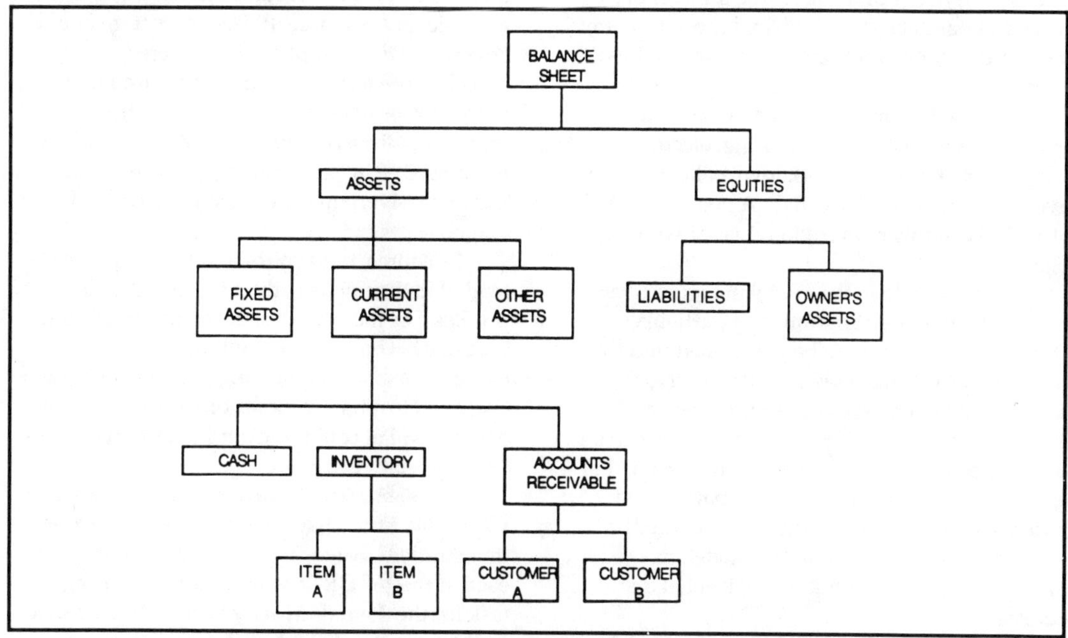

Figure 5. An illustration of the hierarchical nature of accounting systems.

Medicare) available to assume the responsibility for paying the costs.

The adoption of TEFRA has replaced the third-party cost reimbursement system with a cost-per-case payment system [80] [40] [14]. Put simply, each patient's case is classified into one of 467 classes known as diagnosis-related groups (DRGs). Third-party payment for a case is determined by the national average cost (adjusted for area wage differences) based on the case's DRG classification. If the hospital's costs for a particular case exceed the DRG payment, the hospital must absorb the difference. On the other hand, if the hospital's costs are lower than the DRG payment, the hospital enjoys a profit. The concept of ensuring that a profitable outcome is realized is known as "cost containment."

A system can be envisioned based on the methodology discussed above that could be used to support cost containment in hospital management. The decision maker would be the chief administrator in the hospital. The "problem" would be to identify processes (or services) that lead to inefficient handling of aspects of a patient's case.

Within a DRG many variables can be identified that contribute to the total cost of handling the case. For example, the length of the hospital stay is critical. Or the patient's age may necessitate special costly procedures. The number and type of drugs prescribed, the number of sutures and bandages required, and the equipment needed to administer these items also will impact the total cost. Nursing, laboratory analysis, and physical therapy services may be ordered. Finally, other costs such as heating, electricity, and administrative costs—known collectively as overhead costs—are incurred. A generic model of a DRG classification could be as shown in Figure 6.

The root node in the model in Figure 6 represents the payment amount for a particular DRG. This payment can be partitioned into five components (or submodels): special services, length of stay, material cost, service cost, and overhead cost. Each of these components can be partitioned again into finer subcomponents. For example, materials costs could be partitioned into costs for drugs and costs for other medical supplies. As can be seen in the model, this process can be carried out to any level of detail necessary.

By monitoring the variables in the model, the hospital's chief administrative officer would be able to identify areas in which substantial deviations caused hospital costs to exceed the DRG payment. This analysis could be restricted to specific DRG classifications—in which case the chief administrator would learn how well the hospital handles those particular cases —or the analysis could be across a range of DRG classifications. This would permit the administrator to examine how well the hospital functioned in a general area (e.g., in administering drugs). In this way, inefficient practices in the hospital's daily activities could be identified. Once identified, these activities could be studied and improved.

To illustrate, Averill, Kalison, Sparrow and Owens [10] suggested constructing departmental and physician "profiles" as a way of coping with the new era in health care management. A departmental profile based on our approach would examine DRG models such as the one shown in Figure 6 to identify potentially inefficient resource usage. For example, suppose the costs for treating this DRG in an intensive care unit have increased 20 percent. The DRG model for the intensive care unit would identify where the cost increases had occurred.

A physician profile could be developed by examining all DRG models for a physician. By comparing a specific physician's profile against some designated "norm" (possibly constructed from mean or median values for all physicians), a physician's resource utilization pattern could be constructed. If a physician ordered an unusually large number of tests compared to the norm, for instance, a discussion with the physician to verify a need for these tests might be advised. The physician might be unaware of less expensive, equally effective methods of diagnosis.

Of course, this type of analysis could be extended in the opposite direction to hospital profiles. As the market share in the health care industry becomes more dominated by investor-owned "hospital chains" (e.g., Humana Corporation and Hospital Corporation of America), an entire hospital could be examined for overall efficiency relative to costs.

A system such as we describe would provide many immediate benefits to hospital administration. For example, storing a model for each of the 467 DRGs would be an imposing task for the mental capacity of most humans, but could be accomplished easily in a computer-based environment. (Since each patient case

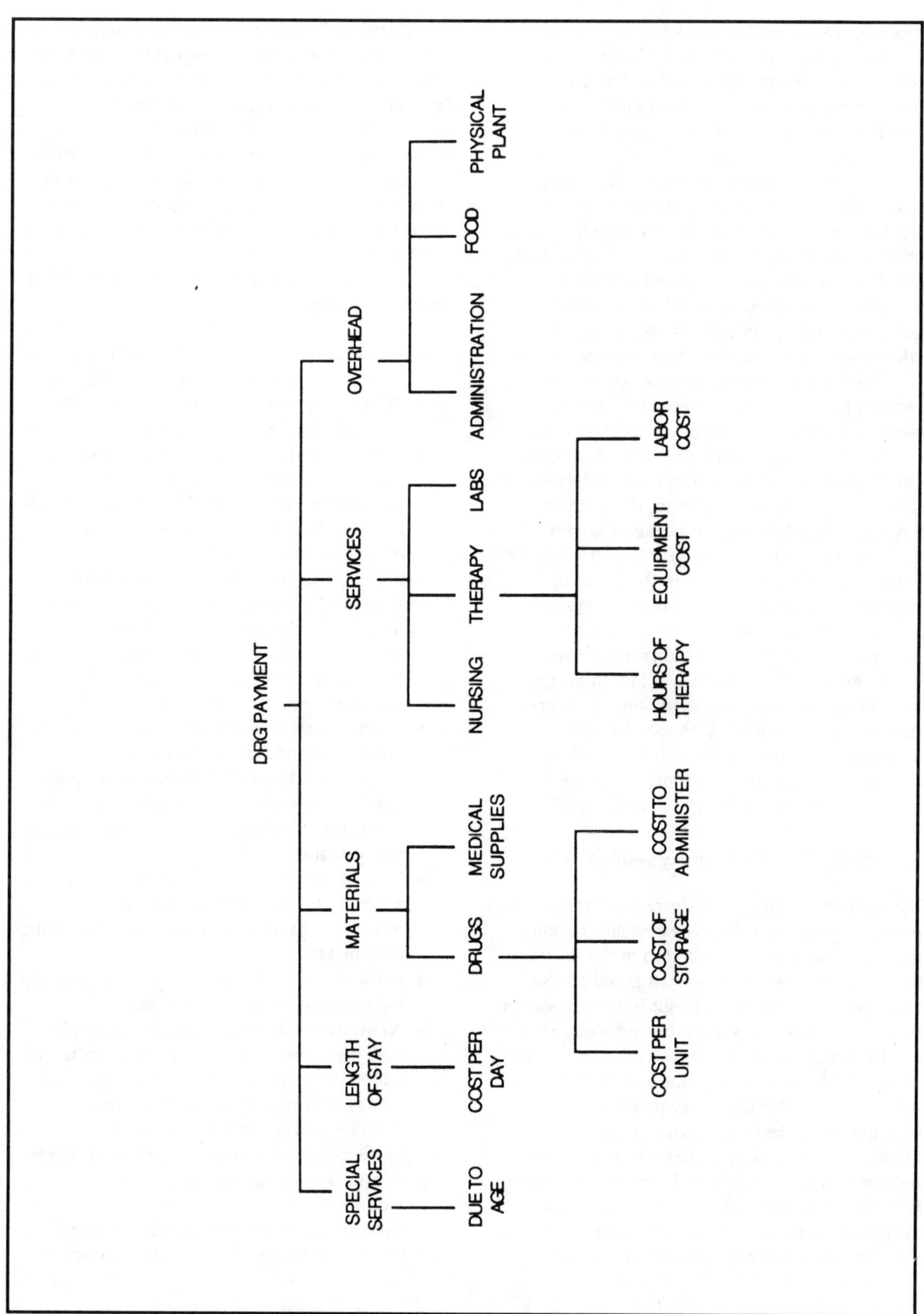

Figure 6. A generic DRG classification model.

represents a unique instantiation of a model, some of the DRG models would be very complex and involve many variables. Even a small number of patient cases would generate a volume of data too great for efficient manual processing.) Most hospitals already maintain computer-based patient records so the marginal cost of data entry to provide a system such as we describe would be small. The payoff, on the other hand, would be tremendous. The system effectively would put the patient records to work for the hospital. Instead of passively generating billing statements, the records would take on an active role in hospital administration.

These example applications demonstrate two key points. First, the initial formulation in terms of linear models does not severely limit the immediate application of the methodology. On the contrary, linear accounting models are ubiquitous in business. Second, the methodology supports a learning process by the user. By building more intelligence into the software, the system could begin to share in the learning process. In the health care example, a system might be able to monitor the DRG case data automatically, deduce commonalities either within or across the DRG cases, and then suggest corrective measures whenever cost overruns appeared imminent. Since problem diagnosis is not unique to the health care industry, we believe this approach has potential for equal success in other industries as well.

Summary and Future Research

To summarize, the system described in this paper supports aspects of the decision-making process from problem finding to problem structuring and diagnosis. When triggered by the monitor, the problem processor initiates a search for relevant assertions from the knowledge base (via the process control subsystem) and dynamically clusters these into causation trees representing potential explanatory problem hypotheses. To test the validity of these hypotheses, the system constructs an arithmetic representation of each branch and retrieves data from the data base to compute values based on the model. If the computed values are "close" to observed values, the user's mental model is validated and the problem's causes have been located. If the model fails to explain the problem, the user's model apparently is deficient and the system may be used to alter and retest the model. If a better model is found, the knowledge base is updated and used in future diagnoses. In this manner, the user and the system learn together about the underlying structure of the problem domain as models are tested and refined.

Our work extends that of Bouwman [23] in numerous ways:

- It operationalizes his model within the context of ongoing managerial diagnostic activity and provides a system specifically designed for decision support;
- It integrates Bouwman's approach with a data-base management system and provides for the construction of mathematical models to support ongoing quantitative diagnosis of problems;
- It integrates Bouwman's approach with structural modeling and permits the maintenance of user-specified relationships in a knowledge base that can be modified as the user learns about the organizational problem domain;
- It permits the use of digraph analysis techniques such as matrix powering, pulse analysis, and other techniques to support not only diagnosis but also prediction and analysis (including "what if..." analysis, the sine qua non of DSS modeling);
- It includes a memory of successful diagnoses in the EKB, permitting the formal diagnostic process to be bypassed in certain circumstances;
- It allows generation of information concerning causal cues via the EKB; and
- As shown by Paradice and Courtney [88] [89], it permits direct extension to statistical techniques that may be used in numerous ways to support the acquisition, maintenance, and use of organizational knowledge and also permits the inclusion of noncausal relationships and certainty factors [90].

Future efforts will be directed to several activities. First, formal techniques of causal modeling and path analysis [7] will be incorporated into the system to test the validity of user-asserted relationships and to search for missing links in the model. Second, attempts will be made to incorporate other kinds of relationships in the knowledge base, such as "*A* is an upper bound for *B*," as well as strictly qualitative relationships. Efforts will be made to use these relationships to generate models automatically that will support subsequent phases of the decision process. Issues of model validation such as those described by Gass [50] and DeMillo, Lipton, and Perlis [38] may be addressed. Finally, laboratory studies may be conducted to determine the system's ability to influence cognitive biases such as those described by numerous researchers [31] [45] [85] [74] [109] [110] [111] [59] [60] [98] [2] [87] [108] [101] [12].

References

[1] Ackoff, R. L. Towards a system of systems concepts. *Management Science*, 1971, *17*, 661-671.

[2] Ackoff, R. L. The future of operational research is past. *Journal of the Operations Research Society*, 1979, *30*(2), 93-104.

[3] Ackoff, R. L. *Creating the corporate future*. New York: Wiley, 1981.

[4] Ackoff, R. L. Beyond prediction and preparation. *Journal of Management Studies*, 1983, *20*(1), 59-69.

[5] Ackoff, R. L., & Sasieni, M. W. *Fundamentals of operations research*. New York: Wiley, 1968.

[6] Adams, D., Courtney, J. F., & Kasper, G. M. Evaluation of DSS modeling software: A methodology and some results. In *Proceedings of the Twentieth Hawaii International Conference on Systems Sciences*. North Hollywood, CA: Western Periodicals, 1987.

[7] Asher, H. B. *Causal modeling*. Beverly Hills, CA: Sage, 1983.

[8] Ata Mohammed, N. H. *A knowledge based decision support system for managerial problem recognition and diagnosis*. Unpublished Ph.D. dissertation, Texas Tech University, 1985.

[9] Austin, L. M., & Burns, J. R. *Management science: An aid for managerial decision making*. New York: Macmillan, 1985.

[10] Averill, R. F., Kalison, M. J., Sparrow, D. A., & Owens, T. R. How hospital managers should respond to PPS. *Healthcare Financial Management*, 1984, *14*(3), 72-74, 76, 82, 84, 86.

[11] Axelrod, R. M. (Ed.). *The structure of decision*. Princeton, NJ: Princeton University Press, 1976.

[12] Barnes, J. H. Cognitive biases and their impact on strategic planning. *Strategic Management Journal*, 1984, *5*, 129-137.

[13] Basden, A. On the application of expert systems. *International Journal of Man-Machine Studies*, 1983, *19*, 461-477.

[14] Berry, L. E. A new treatment for health care cost. *Management Accounting*, 1984, *65*(10), 58-61.

[15] Blanning, R. W. Management applications of expert systems. *Information and Management*, 1984, *7*, 311-316.

[16] Blanning, R. W. An entity-relationship approach to model management. *Decision Support Systems*, 1986, *2*(1), 65-72.

[17] Blum, R. L. Discovery, confirmation, and incorporation of causal relationships from a large time-oriented clinical data base: The RX project. *Computer and Biomedical Research*, 1982, *15*,164-187.

[18] Bonczek, R. H., Holsapple, C. W., & Whinston, A. B. Computer based support of organizational decision making. *Decision Sciences*, 1979, *10*, 268-291.

[19] Bonczek, R. H., Holsapple, C. W., & Whinston, A. B. The integration of network data base management and problem resolution. *Information Systems*, 1979, *4*(2), 143-154.

[20] Bonczek, R. H., Holsapple, C. W., & Whinston, A. B. The evolving roles of models in decision support systems. *Decision Sciences*, 1980, *11*, 337-356.

[21] Bonczek, R. H., Holsapple, C. W., & Whinston, A. B. Future directions for developing decision support systems. *Decision Sciences*, 1980, *11*, 616-631.

[22] Bonczek, R. H., Holsapple, C. W., & Whinston, A. B. *Foundations of decision support systems*. New York: Academic Press, 1981.

[23] Bouwman, M. J. Human diagnostic reasoning by computer: An illustration from financial analysis. *Management Science*, 1983, *29*, 653-672.

[24] Brown, A. Expert systems and PROLOG. *IEEE Videoconference Seminars via Satellite.* Produced by the Institute of Electrical and Electronics Engineers, Inc., and the Learning Channel, 1985.

[25] Brown, J. S., Burton, R., & deKleer, J. Pedagogical and knowledge engineering techniques in SOPHIE I, II, and III. In D. H. Sleeman & J. S. Brown (Eds.), *Intelligent tutoring systems.* London: Academic Press, 1982.

[26] Burns, J. R., & Winstead, W. H. An input/output approach to the structural analysis of digraphs. *IEEE Transactions on Systems, Man, and Cybernetics,* 1982, *SMC-12,* 15-24.

[27] Burns, J. R., & Winstead, W. H. M-labeled digraphs and Forrester-style causal models. *Management Science,* 1985, *31,* 343-357.

[28] Chandrasekaran, B. Towards a taxonomy of problem solving types. *A1 Magazine,* 1983, *4*(1), 9-17.

[29] Chandrasekaran, B., & Mittal ,S. Deep versus compiled knowledge approaches to diagnostic problem solving. *International Journal of Man-Machine Studies,* 1983, *19,* 425-436.

[30] Chorba, R. W., & New, J. L. Information support for decision maker learning in a competitive environment: An empirical study. *Decision Sciences,* 1980, *11,* 603-615.

[31] Churchman, C. W. *The design of inquiring systems.* New York: Basic Books, 1971.

[32] Courtney, J. F., DeSanctis, G. R., & Kasper, G. M. Continuity in MIS/DSS research: The case for a common gaming simulator. *Decision Sciences,* 1983, *14,* 419-439.

[33] Davis, R. Expert systems: Where do we go from here? *AI Magazine,* 1982, *3*(2), 3-22.

[34] Davis, R. Reasoning from first principles in electronic troubleshooting. *International Journal of Man-Machine Studies,* 1983, *19,* 403-423.

[35] Davis, R., Austin, H., Carlbom, I., Frawley, B., Pruchnik, P., Sneiderman, R., & Gilreath, J. The dipmeter advisor: Interpretation of geologic signals. In *Proceedings of the International Joint Conference on Artificial Intelligence.* Menlo Park, CA: American Association for Artificial Intelligence, 1981.

[36] Davis, R., Shrobe, H. E., Hamscher, W., Wickert, K., Shirley, M., & Polit, S. Diagnosis based on description of structure and function. In *Proceedings of the American Association for Artificial Intelligence,* Menlo Park, CA: AAAI, 1982.

[37] deKleer, J. A qualitative physics based on confluences. *Artificial Intelligence,* 1984, *24*(1-3), 7-83.

[38] DeMillo, R. A., Lipton, R. J., & Perlis, A. J. Social processes and proofs of theorems and programs. *Communications of the ACM,* 1979, 22, 271-280.

[39] Dhar, V. On the plausibility and scope of expert systems in management. In *Proceedings of the Nineteenth Hawaii International Conference on Systems Sciences.* North Hollywood, CA: Western Periodicals, 1986.

[40] Doremus, H. D. A reimbursement system that limits the costs of hospital care. *Healthcare Financial Management,* 1983, *13*(4), 86-91.

[41] Einhorn, H. J., & Hogarth, R. M. Prediction, diagnosis and casual thinking in forecasting. *Journal of Forecasting,* 1982, *1*(1), 23-36.

[42] Elam, J. J. *Model management systems: A framework for development* (Technical Report 79-02-04). Unpublished manuscript, University of Pennsylvania, 1979.

[43] Elam, J. J., & Henderson, J. C. Knowledge engineering concepts for decision support system design and implementation. *Information & Management,* 1983, *6*(2), 109-114.

[44] Elam, J. J., Henderson, J. C., & Miller, L. W. Model management systems: An approach to decision support in complex organizations. In *Proceedings of the First International Conference on Information Systems.* Chicago, IL: Society for Management Information Systems, 1980.

[45] Feather, N. *Expectancy, incentive, and action.* Hillsdale, NJ: Lawrence Erlbaum, 1981.

[46] Fedorowicz, J., & Williams, G. D. Representing model knowledge in a logic-based DSS. *Decision Support Systems,* 1986, *2*(1), 3-14.

[47] Feigenbaum, E. A., & McCorduck, P. *The fifth generation: Artificial intelligence and Japan's computer challenge to the world.* Reading, MA: Addison-Wesley, 1983.

[48] Forbus, K. Modeling motion with qualitative process theory. In *Proceedings of the National Conference on Artificial Intelligence.* Menlo Park, CA: American Association for Artificial Intelligence, 1982.

[49] Gaschnig, J. Preliminary evaluation of the performance of the PROSPECTOR system for mineral exploration. In *Proceedings of the International Joint Conference on Artificial Intelligence.* Los Altos, CA: Morgan Kaufmann, 1979.

[50] Gass, S. I. Decision-aiding models: Validation, assessment, and related issues for policy analysis. *Operations Research,* 1983, *31,* 603-631.

[51] Gentner, D., & Stevens, A. L. (Eds.). *Mental models.* Hillsdale, NJ: Lawrence Erlbaum, 1983.

[52] Harary, F., Norman, R. Z., & Cartwright, D. *Structural models: An introduction to the theory of directed graphs.* New York: Wiley, 1965.

[53] Hart, P. E. Direction of AI in the eighties. *SIGART Newsletter,* 1982, No. 79, 11-16.

[54] Henderson, J. C., & Martinko, M. J. Cognitive learning theory and the design of decision support systems. *DSS-81 Transactions.* Atlanta, GA: Execucom Systems Corp., 1981.

[55] Hogarth, R. M., & Makridakis, S. Forecasting and planning: An evaluation. *Management Science,* 1981, *27,* 115-138.

[56] Hudetz, W. A graphical interactive system simulation program for minicomputers. In H. Bossel (Ed.), *Concepts and tools of computer-assisted policy analysis.* Basel, Switzerland: Birkhauser, 1977.

[57] Hunt, R. G., & Sanders, G. L. Propaedeutics of decision-making: Supporting managerial learning and innovation. *Decision Support Systems,* 1986, 2(2), 125-134.

[58] Janis, I. L., & Mann, L. *Decision making: A psychological analysis of conflict, choice, and commitment.* New York: Free Press, 1977.

[59] Johnson, W. *People in quandaries: The semantics of personal adjustment.* New York: Harper & Bros., 1946.

[60] Judson, A. J., & Cofer, C. N. Reasoning as an associative process: I. Direction in a simple verbal problem. *Psychological Reports,* 1956, 2, 469-473.

[61] Kane, J. A primer for a new cross-impact language—KSIM. *Technological Forecasting and Social Change,* 1972, 4, 129-142.

[62] Kasper, G. M. The effect of user-developed DSS applications on forecasting decision-making performance. *Journal of Management Information Systems,* 1985, 2(2), 26-39.

[63] Kasper, G. M., & Cerveny, R. P. A laboratory study of user characteristics and decision-making performance in end-user computing. *Information and Management,* 1985, 9(2), 87-96.

[64] Keen, P. G. W. MIS research: Reference disciplines and a cumulative tradition. In *Proceedings of the First International Conference on Information Systems.* Chicago, IL: Society for Management Information Systems, 1980.

[65] Kolb, D. A. *Applications of experiential learning theory to the information sciences* (working paper). Unpublished manuscript, Case Western Reserve University, 1978.

[66] Konsynski, B., & Dolk, D. Knowledge abstractions in model management. *DSS-82 Transactions.* Atlanta, GA: Execucom Systems Corp., 1982.

[67] Kruskal, J. B. Multidimensional scaling and other methods for discovering structure. In K. Enslein, A. J. Ralston, & H. S. Wilf (Eds.), *Statistical methods for digital computers.* New York: Wiley, 1977.

[68] Kruzick, P. G. *KSIM techniques for evaluating interaction among variables* (Technical note OED-16). Menlo Park, CA: Stanford Research Institute, 1973.

[69] Kuipers, B. Commonsense reasoning about causality: Deriving behavior from structure. *Artificial Intelligence,* 1984, *24*(1-3), 169-203.

[70] Kuipers, B. Qualitative simulation. *Artificial Intelligence,* 1986, *29,* 289-338.

[71] Langhorst, F. E. *Computer graphics aided interpretive structural modeling: A tool for conceptualizing complex design problems.* Unpublished Ph.D. dissertation, Purdue University, 1977.

[72] Lenard, M. L. Treating models as data. *Journal of Management Information Systems,* 1986, 2(4), 36-48.

[73] Lendaris, G. G. Structural modeling—A tutorial guide. *IEEE Transactions on Systems, Man, and Cybernetics,* 1980, *SMC-10,* 807-840.

[74] Locks, M. O. The logic of policy as argument. *Management Science*, 1985, *31*, 109-114.

[75] Loy, S. L. *An experimental investigation of a graphical problem-structuring aid and nominal group technique for group decision support system.* Unpublished Ph.D. dissertation, Texas Tech University, 1986.

[76] McLean, J. M. Getting the problem right—A role for structural modeling. In H. A. Linstone & W. H. C. Simmonds (Eds.), *Future research: New directions.* Reading, MA: Addison-Wesley, 1977.

[77] McLean, J. M., & Shepherd, P. The importance of model structure. *Futures*, 1976, *18*(1), 40-51.

[78] McLean, J. M., Shepherd, P., & Curnow, R. *Techniques for analysis of system structure* (SPRU Occasional Paper Series No. 1). Sussex, England: University of Sussex, Science Policy Research Unit, 1976.

[79] Meador, C. L., Guyote, M. J., & Keen, P. G. W. Setting priorities for DSS development. *MIS Quarterly*, 1984, *8*(2), 117-129.

[80] Messmer, V. C. Methods that can be applied to DRG classifications. *Healthcare Financial Management*, 1984, *38*(1), 44-48.

[81] Michie, D. High road and low road programs. *AI Magazine*, 1982, *3*(1), 21-22.

[82] Minch, R. P., & Burns, J. R. Conceptual design for decision support systems utilizing management science models. *IEEE Transactions on Systems, Man and Cybernetics*, 1983, *SMC-13*, 549-557.

[83] Mintzberg, H., Raisinghani, D., & Théorêt, A. The structure of "unstructured" decision processes. *Administrative Science Quarterly*, 1976, *21*, 246-275.

[84] Mitroff, I. L., & Featheringham, T. R. On systemic problem solving and the error of the third kind. *Behavioral Science*, 1974, *19*(6), 383-393.

[85] Mitroff, I. I., Mason, R. O., & Barabba, V. P. Policy as argument—A logic for ill-structured decision problems. *Management Science*, 1982, *28*, 1391-1404.

[86] Mylopoulos, J., Shibahara, T., & Tsotsos, J. Building knowledge-based systems: The PSN experience. *IEEE Computer*, 1983, *16*(10), 83-89.

[87] Newell, A., & Simon, H. A. *Human problem solving.* Englewood Cliffs, NJ: Prentice-Hall, 1972.

[88] Paradice, D. B., & Courtney, J. F. Controlling bias in user assertions in expert decision support systems for problem formulation. *Journal of Management Information Systems*, 1986, *3*(1), 52-64.

[89] Paradice, D. B., & Courtney, J. F. SmartSLIM: A DSS for controlling biases during problem formulation. In *Proceedings of the TAMU Human Factors in MIS Conference.* Norwood, NJ: Ablex, 1986.

[90] Paradice, D. B., & Courtney, J. F. Causal and non-causal relationships and dynamic model construction in a managerial advisory system. *Journal of Management Information Systems*, *3*(4), 39-53.

[91] Patil, R. Szolovits, P., & Schwartz, W. Causal understanding of patient illness in medical diagnosis. In *Proceedings of the International Joint Conference on Artificial Intelligence.* Menlo Park, CA: American Association for Artificial Intelligence, 1981.

[92] Pople, H. Heuristic methods for imposing structure on ill-structured problems. In I. DeLotto & M. Stefanelli (Eds.), *Artificial intelligence in medicine.* New York: North Holland, 1985.

[93] Pounds, W. F. The process of problem finding. *Industrial Management Review*, 1969, *11*(1), 1-19.

[94] Pracht, W. E. *An experimental investigation of a graphical interactive structural modeling aid for decision support systems.* Unpublished Ph.D. dissertation, Texas Tech University, 1984.

[95] Pracht, W. E. GISMO: A visual problem-structuring and knowledge-organization tool. *IEEE Transactions on Systems, Man and Cybernetics*, 1986, *16*, 265-270.

[96] Pracht, W. E., & Courtney, J. F. *The effects of an interactive graphics based DSS to support problem structuring* (working paper). Unpublished manuscript, Texas A&M University, Business Analysis and Research Department, 1986.

[97] Raiffa, H. *Decision analysis.* Reading, MA: Addison-Wesley, 1968.

[98] Reitman, W. R. Heuristic decision procedures, open constraints, and the structure of ill-defined problems. In M. W. Shelly II & G. L. Bryan (Eds.), *Human judgments and optimality.* New York: Wiley, 1964.

[99] Roberts, F. S. Building and analyzing an energy demand signed digraph. *Environment and Planning*, 1973, *5*(3), 18-29.

[100] Roberts, F. S. *Graph theory and its applications to problems of society*. Philadelphia, PA: Society for Industrial and Applied Mathematics, 1978.

[101] Rowe, A. J. How do senior managers make decisions? *Business and Economics*, Winter 1977, pp. 17-20.

[102] Sage, A. P. Behavioral and organizational considerations in the design of information systems and processes for planning and decision support. *IEEE Transactions on Systems, Man, and Cybernetics*, 1981, *SMC-11*, 640-678.

[103] Schueller, J. K., Slusher, R. M., & Morgan, S. M. An expert system with speech synthesis for troubleshooting grain combine performance. *Transactions of the American Society of Agricultural Engineers*, 1986, *29*, 342-344.

[104] Sen, A., & Biswas, G. Decision support systems: An expert systems approach. *Decision Support Systems*, 1985, *1*(3), 197-204.

[105] Shortliffe, E. *Computer-based medical consultations: MYCIN*. New York: American Elsevier, 1976.

[106] Simon, H. A. *The new science of management decisions*. New York: Harper & Row, 1960.

[107] Stefik, M., Aikens, J., Balzer, R., Benoit, J., Birnbaum, L., Hayes-Roth, F., & Sacerdoti, E. The organization of expert systems, A tutorial. *Artificial Intelligence*, 1982, *18*, 135-174.

[108] Taylor, I. A. A retrospective view of creativity investigation. In I. A. Taylor & J. W. Getzels (Eds.), *Perspectives in creativity*. Chicago, IL: Aldine, 1975.

[109] Tversky, A., & Kahneman, D. Belief in the law of small numbers. *Psychological Bulletin*, 1971, *76*(2), 105-110.

[110] Tversky, A., & Kahneman, D. Availability: A heuristic for judging frequency and probability. *Cognitive Psychology*, 1973, *5*, 207-232.

[111] Tversky, A., & Kahneman, D. Judgement under uncertainty: Heuristics and biases. *Science*, 1974, *185*, 1124-1131.

[112] Tversky, A., & Kahneman, D. The framing of decisions and the psychology of choice. *Science*, 1981, *211*, 453-458.

[113] Wakeland, W. QSIM2: A low budget heuristic approach to modeling and forecasting. *Technological Forecasting and Social Change*, 1976, *9*, 213-229.

[114] Waller, R. J. Comparing and combining structural models of complex systems. *IEEE Transactions on Systems, Man and Cybernetics*, 1979, *SMC-9*, 1120-1128.

[115] Wang, M. S., & Courtney, J. F. Design and implementation of the MAGIC/ROC decision support systems generator. *DSS-82 Transactions*. Atlanta, GA: Execucom Systems Corp., 1982.

[116] Wang, M. S., & Courtney, J. F. A conceptual architecture for generalized DSS software. *IEEE Transactions on Systems, Man and Cybernetics*, 1984, *24*, 701-710.

[117] Warfield, J. N. *Structuring complex systems* (Monograph No. 4). Columbus, OH: Battelle Memorial Institute, 1974.

[118] Warfield, J. N. *Societal systems: Planning, policy and complexity*. New York: Wiley-Interscience, 1976.

[119] Weiss, S. M., Kulikowski, C. A., Amarel, S., & Safir, S. A model-based method for computer-aided medical decision making. *Artificial Intelligence*, 1978, *11*(2), 145-172.

[120] Yadav, S., & Korukonda, A. Management of Type III error in problem identification. *Interfaces*, 1985, *15*(4), 55-61.

Comax: An Expert System for Cotton Crop Management

Hal Lemmon

Today three bales of synthetic fibers are milled for every bale of cotton. Further, the synthetic fiber industry has recently adopted a vigorous research program to produce fibers at still lower cost. For cotton to survive, research to lower production costs is imperative (1).

An expert system, Comax (COtton MAnagement eXpert), has been developed that advises cotton growers on crop management at the farm level. The expert system is integrated with a computer model, Gossym (from *Gossypium* and simulation), that simulates the growth of the cotton plant (2). This is the first integration of an expert system with a simulation model for daily use in farm management.

Gossym

Researchers began developing Gossym in 1973. The program was developed over 12 years with contributions from ten scientists at four institutions (3) in two countries. It simulates the growth and development of the entire cotton plant on an organ-by-organ basis: roots, stems, leaves, blooms, squares, and bolls. It also simulates soil processes such as the transfer of water and nutrients through the soil profile. For Gossym to accomplish this, it needs data from mechanical and chemical soil analyses of the farm field to which it is being applied. Such analyses can be performed by state-owned soil test laboratories, the Soil Conservation Service, or commercial laboratories. The specific data required are soil hydrologic properties, soil fertility, soil impedance (resistance to root growth), water release curves, and bulk density.

The model is driven by weather variables. It requires, on a daily basis, such data as the maximum and minimum temperatures, solar radiation, and rainfall. It was developed with SPAR (Soil-Plant-Atmosphere-Research) units, where cotton is grown under highly controlled conditions and the various rate processes can be determined, but it was extensively tested and validated against field data.

Gossym is capable of running on most computers, including microcomputers. A complete simulation, from emergence to harvest, can be done in 6 to 8 minutes on a VAX 750 computer, in 60 to 90 minutes on a microcomputer (an IBM PC, or equivalent, with a math coprocessor), and in 20 to 30 minutes on an advanced microcomputer (an IBM PC-AT, or equivalent, with a math coprocessor).

The development of microcomputers has expedited the movement of Gossym to the farm to assist in crop management. In 1984 a project to use Gossym on cotton farms was initiated by the USDA Agricultural Research Service in cooperation with the National Cotton Council, and microcomputers were provided for a 6000-acre farm in the Mississippi Delta (4) and a 1000-acre farm in the South Carolina Coastal Plain (5). In 1985 Comax was tested on the 6000-acre farm.

In the research laboratory, a multidisciplinary team of cotton experts provides Gossym with input and interprets its output. Comax was developed to provide the input and to perform the analyses when Gossym is used for practical, on-farm decision making. This is the first attempt I am aware of to integrate an expert system with a simulation model with the objective of optimizing crop production.

Comax

An expert system is a computer system with the capability of performing at the level of human experts in some particular domain. It is possible to build expert systems that perform at

Reprinted with permission from *Science*, vol. 233, July 1986, 29-33.

remarkable levels (6). While there are several methods for designing expert systems, rule-based systems have emerged as the popular architecture. Deriving their knowledge from relatively easily understood facts and rules, rule-based systems offer surprising power and versatility (7).

Comax is a rule-based expert system that operates Gossym the way a human expert would to determine three factors: irrigation schedules, nitrogen requirements, and the crop maturity date.

As shown in Figure 1, Comax consists of a knowledge base, an inference engine, Gossym, a weather station, and data (for example, the seeding rate and soil parameters). The knowledge base is a set of rules and facts written in near-English. The inference engine examines the rules and facts to determine what is to be done. It prepares data files accordingly to hypothesize the weather and to hypothesize applications of water and nitrogen. Then it calls Gossym, which reads the data files prepared by the inference engine and simulates the growth of the cotton plant under the conditions specified in those files. Results from the simulation (such as the day the simulated crop goes into water stress) are saved as facts in the knowledge base.

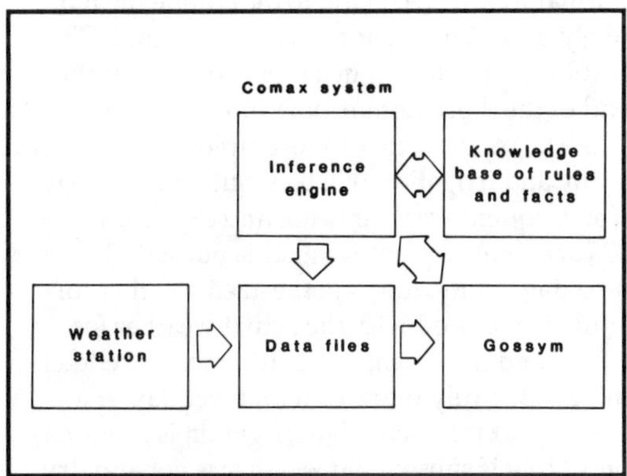

Figure 1. The Comax components. The four components to the right reside in a microcomputer located at the grower's farm.

The inference engine program and the Gossym program change little if at all. The knowledge base continuously changes as researchers and growers improve management strategies or observe the impact of different strategies.

Software, Hardware, and Data

The software components of Comax are the inference engine and Gossym. The inference engine is written in the LISP computer language, and Gossym is written in FORTRAN. The computer languages were selected on the basis of appropriateness for the task to be performed, LISP being appropriate for an expert system but inappropriate for simulation. The knowledge base, so far, has about 50 rules, the inference engine about 6000 lines of code, and Gossym about 3000 lines of code.

Comax was developed on a Symbolics 3670 computer and is down-loaded, unchanged, to the PC computers where it runs under Common LISP, offered by Gold Hill Computers. Gossym was developed on the VAX 750 computer and is also down-loaded, unchanged, to the PC computers and compiled using the FORTRAN 77 compiler offered by Ryan-McFarland.

The cotton grower who used Comax has a microcomputer (an IBM PC or equivalent) with a math coprocessor and a dot-matrix printer in his office. The system can automatically call the weather station daily by telephone but, if a phone line is not practical, the data may be entered into the computer manually. The microcomputer costs $4000 to $7000, depending on the configuration selected. The cost of the weather station is $4000, which includes solar panels to provide power. Hardware for telephone connection is $1200.

Comax Rules

Figure 2 shows some of the facts and one of the rules used in Comax. This rule, "find-water-stress-day," is one of the set of rules used to determine the optimum irrigation schedule. The rule is true if every term in the "if" part of the rule matches a term in the facts base. In this case, (run-number *?number*) of the rule matches the fact (run-number 1) if *?number* is assigned the value 1, and (hypothesized-weather *?weather*) matches the fact (hypothesized-weather hot-dry) if *?weather* is assigned the value hot-dry. Entries that begin with a question mark, such as *?number*, are treated as variables by the inference engine and are assigned values, as needed, to cause a match.

In the case shown in Figure 2, the rule is true, and the inference engine will proceed with the actions in the "then" part of the rule. It first prints on the computer screen a message describing the action. Next, it runs the Gossym program using the hot-dry weather scenario. When Gossym is finished, the inference engine examines the results of the run and places new facts into the facts base. One of the new facts will be, for example, (w-stress-day 236), where 236 represents the day of the year the crop went into water stress.

```
FACTS
   (run-number 1)
   (hypothesized-weather hot-dry)
   (irrigation amount 1)
   (irrigation application-time 4)
   ...

RULE find-water-stress-day
  IF
    (run-number ?number)
    (hypothesized-weather ?weather)
  THEN
    (printout "Finding water stress day")
    (run-gossym ?number ?weather)
    (assert (set-hypothesized-irrigation)
```

Figure 2. Four of the facts and one of the rules used in Comax.

The final action of the inference engine is to assert a new fact, (set-hypothesis-irrigation), into the facts base. The purpose of this new fact is to cause another rule, which is called "set-up-hypothesized-irrigation" and is not shown in the figure, to be true. That rule, a lengthy one, determines the day that irrigation should be applied. Conceptually, it does this by taking the water stress day, subtracting the application time given in the fact (irrigation application-time 4), determining the amount of water to be applied from the fact (irrigation amount 1), and asserting a new fact (hypothesized-irrigation 232 1). However, there are actually other considerations, such as how soon to harvest and how many days since the last irrigation, which this rule also considers.

Comax recomputes the optimum management scenario each day, prints a daily report that recommends crop management procedures and, if it is desired, summarizes the intermediate simulations to explain the basis for the recommendations. Comax can show the results of simulations either by tabular reports or by graphs on the dot-matrix printer.

Operating Comax on the Farm

Comax is designed to run continuously throughout the crop year on a dedicated microcomputer. Each day it computes the expected irrigation date, the expected date and amount of fertilization, and the expected date of crop maturity. These are computed daily because, as the hypothesized weather for each day is replaced by the actual weather for that day, the computed dates change.

Determining Irrigation Requirements

Comax begins each day by determining the expected irrigation date. It does this by running Gossym with a hypothesized weather scenario, noting the date the crop goes into water stress and subtracting the number of days it takes to apply the irrigation. Some irrigation systems, the center-pivot type, for example, take several days to apply water. Comax uses three different types of hypothesized weather scenarios: (i) normal weather, (ii) hot-dry weather, and (iii) cold-wet weather. The weather scenarios are specific to each farm. Comax first runs Gossym with the hypothesized hot-dry weather scenario. This establishes the earliest date that irrigation would be required. Comax then runs Gossym with the normal weather scenario to determine the most likely date that irrigation will be required. The results are presented in a report printed at the end of the daily Comax operation.

The report states, for example, that today is 1 July and irrigation will be required on 10 July if subsequent weather is hot and dry or on 17 July if subsequent weather is normal. The next day, 2 July, the hypothesized weather for 1 July is replaced with the actual weather for 1 July, and the irrigation requirement is redetermined. If 1 July was a cold and wet day, the new report may state that irrigation is required on 12 July if subsequent weather is hot and dry (instead of 10 July as reported the day before) or on 19 July if the subsequent weather is normal (instead of 17 July). Conversely, if 1 July is actually a hot and dry day, the irrigation date for hot-dry weather will still be 10 July, but the irrigation date for the normal weather hypothesis will be earlier, perhaps 15 July instead of 17 July.

Determining Nitrogen Requirements

With cotton, it is important not to overfertilize, not only because of the obvious economic waste but also because overfertilization can cause the plant to be in an undesirable state at time of harvest. To determine the nitrogen requirements, Comax first ensures that there is no water stress by calculating an additional series of irrigation dates. After each calculation Comax determines the day the simulated crop went into water stress and, on the basis of the assumption that the grower would irrigate to relieve that stress, it hypothesizes a date and amount of irrigation. It then runs Gossym again to determine the next date that the crop will be in water stress. This process is repeated until the end of the season is reached, and the result is an hypothesized irrigation schedule that should prevent the crop from ever being in water stress. This schedule is only for use in determining nitrogen requirements and is never followed. The actual irrigation schedule to be followed is determined as described in the previous section.

Comax is now ready to determine the minimum amount of nitrogen that can be safety applied. It does so by making a series of Gossym runs with the cold-wet weather scenario, to simulate the minimum plant growth and thus to estimate the minimum nitrogen requirement. Comax again makes a series of these Gossym runs and, after each run, the day the crop went into nitrogen stress is noted. Comax then enters into the calculation a predetermined amount of nitrogen, and runs Gossym again. If nitrogen stress occurs again, the amount of nitrogen hypothesized is increased. When too much nitrogen is applied, there will be an undesirable effect: after the bolls are mature, the plant will begin to grow vigorously. If such undesirable growth (shown in Figure 3, row 4, third graph) occurs, Comax reduces the amount of nitrogen. This process is repeated until Comax has determined the amount of nitrogen just sufficient to relieve nitrogen stress. This value is printed in the Comax daily report and represents the minimum amount of nitrogen the grower should apply.

The process is repeated with the normal weather scenario. This tells the grower the most probable nitrogen requirement. Finally, the process is repeated a third time with the hot-dry weather scenario, and the result tells the grower the maximum nitrogen requirement. From these three figures and from his own assessment of the weather the grower decides the amount of nitrogen to apply.

The grower's safest strategy is to assume the cold-wet weather scenario will hold and apply the minimum amount of nitrogen. If the weather turns out to be better than this, the grower can apply additional amounts of nitrogen later in the season. The penalty for underestimating the nitrogen requirement is only the cost of applying the additional nitrogen. The penalty for overestimating the nitrogen requirement is the cost of the excess nitrogen plus, at harvest, the loss from its undesirable effects, which can be substantial.

There is an additional risk that nitrogen applied too early in the season can be lost because of leaching. Such a loss varies with soil conditions, rainfall, and irrigation. Gossym is capable of identifying the amount of nitrogen lost in this way.

Farms that do not have irrigation systems are handled in a different, simpler manner. Farms with trickle irrigation require a different set of rules, a problem which will be addressed this year.

Determining Harvest Date

Comax also informs the grower when the cotton is mature so he can apply defoliants and boll openers. This is particularly important in such locations as the Mississippi Delta, where early rains can physically damage the cotton, induce boll rot, and make the ground so muddy that the mechanical cotton pickers cannot operate. Near the end of each season the grower must decide either to wait until it is certain the cotton has reached its maximum yield or to proceed with the harvest before the rains begin. With Comax, the farmer knows weeks in advance when his crop will mature. This can only be an approximation because of uncertainty in the weather; but as each day passes, the hypothesized weather is replaced by the actual weather, and the projected maturity date becomes more reliable.

Comax in Operation

An example of the operation of Comax as it selects nitrogen and irrigation schedules is shown in Figure 3. The graphs in each row are the results of a Gossym simulation run by Comax. In the first graph of each row, the

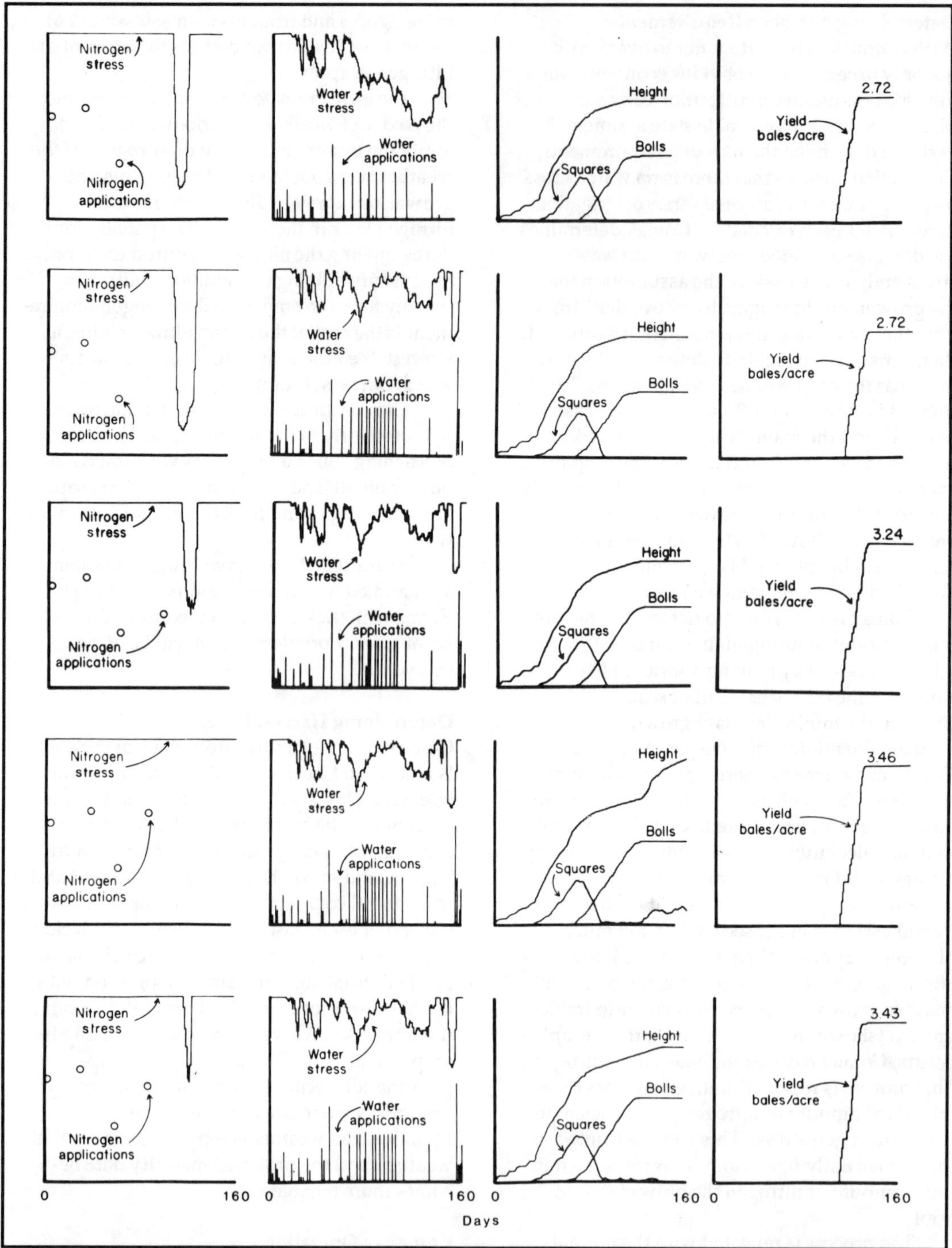

Figure 3. Graphs produced by Comax from the results of Gossym simulations, showing the process whereby Comax reduces the water stress and then the nitrogen stress, as described in the text.

circles represent nitrogen applications. The first three applications are actual, but the fourth application (on the first graph of rows 3, 4, and 5) is hypothesized by Comax. On this farm the grower has applied 55, 60, and 30 pounds of nitrogen per acre at the time of planting and at

33 and 63 days after the plants emerged, respectively. The line shows the nitrogen stress, computed as the ratio of the nitrogen used to the nitrogen needed by the plant for full growth of all organs. In the second graph of each row, the jagged line represents a measure of water stress in the plant, and the vertical bars indicate the amount of water applied or that is expected to be applied by either rain or irrigation. The third graph of each row shows the height of the plant, the number of squares (unpollinated flower buds), and the number of bolls. The number of squares increases with time and then decreases as some squares are shed (because of stress) and others turn to bolls. The fourth graph of each row shows the development of the predicted yield. The final yield, in bales per acre, is printed above the curve.

The first row of graphs were produced by Comax just after the third application of nitrogen. The second row of graphs is the last of a series of Gossym runs in which Comax has directed its attention to the water stress problem and hypothesized a heavier irrigation schedule with no additional nitrogen. The second graph of this row shows that increased irrigation resulted in reduced water stress and in intensified nitrogen stress. With increased water, the simulated plant has the capacity for increased growth, and therefore it needs even more nitrogen. Even though irrigation is increased, there is no increased yield.

In the third row, Comax has hypothesized an application of 30 pounds of nitrogen per acre. The nitrogen stress is reduced, and the yield is increased.

In the fourth row, Comax has hypothesized an additional 60 pounds of nitrogen per acre. The nitrogen stress is eliminated, and the yield has increased correspondingly. However, the third graph of this row shows that, after the bolls have all matured, the cotton plant has had a spurt of new growth and that it has started adding new squares that will never mature. At the point where the yield levels off, the crop should be harvested since no more cotton would be expected and delay would increase the risk of harvest losses due to inclement weather. To harvest cotton with modern equipment, it is necessary to apply a defoliant; however, this model plant would be so robust that the defoliant would not be as effective as it should be. The rules of Comax will cause this hypothesis to be rejected.

In the last row, Comax has selected 40 pounds of nitrogen per acre in conjunction with the indicated irrigation applications. This provides the maximum yield subject to the constraint of no secondary growth.

Constraints, such as irrigation capacity and the time required to irrigate, are provided for in the knowledge base. For example, on a field with pivot irrigation a typical constraint may be that 1 inch of water can be applied in 4 days. Constraints are considered on a farm-by-farm basis; as a consequence, the knowledge base varies somewhat from farm to farm.

Results from a Pilot Test

Comax was tested on the Mitchener farm (4) so that we could acquire experience in its practical operation under realistic conditions (8). In mid-July 1985 Comax predicted the need for nitrogen at the rate of 50 pounds per acre, as shown in the last row of Figure 3. As a result, the grower, who had not planned to apply any additional nitrogen, applied 20 pounds per acre throughout the farm except on a 6-acre test plot where no nitrogen was applied on alternate eight-row strips. Comax predicted an additional 200 pounds of cotton lint on the cotton treated with nitrogen, with no delay in the date of maturity. At the end of the season, the test plots were picked, some by hand and some by machine. Although cotton is no longer picked by hand for commercial purposes, some rows of the test plot were so picked to obtain a precise figure to compare with the yield predicted by Comax. The hand-picked rows showed a net increase of 180 pounds per acre of cotton, and the machine-picked rows a net increase of 115 pounds per acre. The additional cotton (machine-picked) had an economic value of about $71 per acre, the cost of the nitrogen was $4 per acre, and the cost of application was $5 per acre. Allowing for the cost of processing the additional cotton, there was a net gain of over $60 per acre on this 6000-acre farm.

The grower believes, however, that it is the system's ability to pinpoint the day the crop is mature that is its most valuable feature. In the previous year (1984), the system predicted a maturity date of 1 September for the crop. Instead, the grower elected to use the widely accepted rule that a crop is not mature until 60% of the bolls are open and delayed harvesting until

21 September. Rain began on 6 October, and it was not possible to complete the harvest until November, which resulted in a loss of both yield and quality. The grower now believes that the maturity date of 1 September was correct and that, if the harvest had begun on that date, cotton production would have increased by approximately 4.3 million pounds and the quality would have been improved by an amount worth an additional $0.11 per pound.

Future Outlook

During the coming crop year (1986), testing and development of Comax is continuing with 15 growers in five states and with a total cultivation of over 50,000 acres of cotton.

In the United States, there are 10 to 12 million acres (varying from year to year) of cotton on 30,000 farms. Approximately 1300 farms (4%) are of 1000 acres or more and account for 33% of the cotton, whereas 4000 farms are of 500 acres or more and account for 58% of the production (9). The former are obvious candidates for Comax; the latter are probable candidates.

References and Notes

1. R. J. Kohel and C. F. Lewis, Eds. *Cotton* (American Society of Agronomy, Madison, WI, 1984), pp. xi-xii.
2. D. N. Baker, J. R. Lambert, J. M. McKinion, *S.C. Agric. Exp. Stn. Tech. Bull. 1089* (December 1983).
3. The scientists and their institutions are: D. N. Baker, J. M. McKinion, R. E. Fye, USDA Agricultural Research Service, Mississippi State, MS; F. D. Whisler, J. A. Landivar, D. R. Reddy, S. G. Kharche, A. Ben-Porath, Mississippi State University, Mississippi State, MS; J. R. Lambert, Clemson University, Clemson, SC; and A. Marani, Hebrew University of Jerusalem, Rehovot, Israel.
4. Mitchener farm, Sumner, MS.
5. McCoy farm, Sumter, SC.
6. R. O. Duda and E. H. Shortliffe, *Science* 220, 261 (1983).
7. R. Davis, *ibid.* 231, 957 (1986).
8. F. Mitchener, *Cotton Grower* 2, 42 (1986).
9. A. Jordan, National Cotton Council, Memphis, TN, personal communication.

Review Questions

III. Applications

Accounting

Dungan and Chandler

1. The development approach used in AUDITOR employed interviews, multiple experts, and iterations through prototype versions. How does this approach compare to the methodology described in the article by Freiling et al.? Be specific. What was better and what was worse?
2. The authors spend little time on the validation of AUDITOR. Do the procedures they performed show internal or external validity? Discuss. How convinced are you that AUDITOR works? What specific additional procedures for validation, if any, would you suggest?
3. The authors extensively discuss the evaluation of AL/X as a development tool. What do you consider the most important advantage and disadvantage of AL/X, and why? Judging from the presentation, do you see any other problems with the AL/X environment? Describe modifications to the AL/X system that would overcome the stated disadvantages.
4. Discuss the authors' use of multiple experts. Were multiple experts necessary? Are there unique aspects of business decisions that make use of multiple experts advantageous?

Hansen and Messier

1. Discuss the advantages and disadvantages of the authors' approaches to knowledge acquisition.
2. How reliable are the results of the subjects' evaluations? Does the procedure lead them to their result, or does it allow them to make unbiased evaluations? Discuss.
3. Comment on the subjects' evaluations of expert systems. Are their evaluations unique to accounting, or can they be generalized to other business fields?
4. Discuss the impact of the expert system on the subjects' control judgments. Is this a beneficial goal or a detrimental side effect?
5. Are there other electronic data processing audit decisions that you feel could benefit from expert systems support? Discuss.

Shpilberg and Graham

1. The goal of ExperTAX℠ is quite different from that of most expert systems: it is to provide advice on the means, as opposed to the end, of decision making. For the decision under consideration by ExperTAX℠, corporate tax planning, which area is more beneficial to support, information acquisition or decision making? Discuss.
2. Coopers & Lybrand's simulative approach to knowledge acquisition is unique in all expert systems development projects. Evaluate this approach against more conventional expertise acquisition approaches. Was their decision unique, requiring a unique approach, or could this approach be generalized to any expert system development project?
3. Compare the authors' simulative approach to automated knowledge acquisition approaches such as induction (see the Braun and Chandler article).
4. ExperTAX℠ had unique problems regarding expertise. Experts were needed on the process and on the result of that process, and these experts were distributed throughout the firm. Is this a problem with all business decisions, or just with Coopers & Lybrand's tax problem? Must one broaden the scope of the business decision domain to make it cost beneficial?

Steinbart

1. The number of experts used in building an expert system is an issue. The author uses one expert to construct the initial knowledge base and then six to refine it. Evaluate this composite approach in light of the Prerau (1987) and Dungan and Chandler articles. Discuss the author's parting comments about the lack of consensus on the general expert system design problem.
2. AUDITPLANNER's validation and refinement phase by six senior auditors resulted in 8 out of 13 acceptable responses and a consensus that AUDITPLANNER possessed "a general level of competence... as a decision aid." Do you think "a general level of competence" is sufficient for learning about information effects? Does the qualified nature of the assessment detract from the author's claims about decision making?
3. The typical expert system is designed to aid the end of decisions. This expert system was built to help understand the means of decisions, i.e., the decision making process itself. Does this change the nature of the expert system and the expert system development process? If so, what characteristics take on more, or less, importance?
4. Evaluate the use of expert systems as a tool to understand decision making. Could the same results have been discovered through means other than expert systems? What, if any, unique characteristics do expert systems bring to the study of human information processing?

Financial Planning

Mui and McCarthy

1. Most expert systems have dealt with reasoning. This project stresses the familiarization phase over the reasoning phase. Given that the domains of many expert systems must be very narrow to be practical, would developing AI-based preprocessors to reduce the scope of complex decisions for "human reasoners" help in decision support? Discuss the implications for both decision support systems and expert systems.
2. What other business decisions could benefit from an intelligent preprocessor? Select one and define an example schema similar to the example shown for FSA.
3. Could you replicate this study from the details given in the article? If yes, how? If not, what additional data would you need? Be very specific.

Kastner et al.

1. How is this system development project different from other expert systems projects?
2. How does the decision domain of financial marketing offer both research and application possibilities?
3. Comment on the user friendliness of the FAME design. Does using a language over a shell help or hurt this process?

Urness

1. Is the Underwriting Advisor an expert system, a decision support system, or some other category of system? Discuss.
2. Discuss the problem that decision makers may have about developing or using a system that may think for them. How did the company in this article overcome this problem?
3. Of the benefits described at the end of the article, how many are unique to an expert system application?
4. Describe three other potential expert systems applications in the insurance field.

Braun and Chandler

1. Discuss the authors' validation phase. Are there methods for establishing external validity other than the one cited in the paper? Could they be applied here? How effective and reliable is their approach to internal validity? What other approaches are there, and would they be applicable?
2. Is the authors' "main question," i.e., accurate prediction of stock movements, really the most important issue? That is, can one gain more from a "learning-from-example" approach to prediction than from other approaches? For example, if both an LFE approach and discriminant analysis (DA) predicted better than an expert, and each was equally good, would you use LFE or DA? Justify your choice.
3. Evaluate the development of this expert system using the guidelines set out in the Prerau (1985) paper. Which guidelines apply and which do not? Discuss each of the major categories of properties. Does this system have a chance of becoming a commercial success?
4. If you were given the task of replicating this study, how would you design it? What would you do differently or the same? Why? Do you think the design of the study biased the result? Why or why not?

Manufacturing

Bruno et al.

1. Describe the nature of the scheduling problem and explain why an expert systems approach is appropriate for production scheduling.
2. The rule-based system described in the article has two major components: a rule-based scheduler and an algorithm-based evaluator. Why are both needed? How can they be integrated? What implementation problems could occur in this system?
3. How was the system evaluated? What other approach may be appropriate for evaluating this system? Why?

Malmborn et al.

1. Why is selecting a truck type an appropriate decision for an expert system? What other decision support approaches might also be applicable?
2. Contrast the complexity of the sample rules in Tables 2 through 6 with the simplicity of Table 7.
3. The authors used the extant literature as their basis for knowledge acquisition. Is this sufficient, given the authors' argument on the unstructured nature of truck selection?
4. The authors criticize expert systems in general for having "shallow justifications for their recommendations, since they simply point to the specific rules used in developing a recommendation when explaining their reasoning." Is this true of all expert systems, or is it a function of the individual expert system design?
5. Suppose you had to develop an expert system to select a car for yourself. Draw up a list of data categories similar to those in Table 1 and justify the inclusion of each category. Also suppose that there are three types of cars: sports car, family car, and recreational vehicle. Make up lists of sample rules (as in Tables 2 through 6) for each type of car.

Mertens and Kanet

1. Evaluate the completeness of the authors' taxonomy of production management activities.
2. Inventory management is the only decision area that does not have a single expert task identified. Why is this so? Is it a particular decision environment for which typical operations research models apply and there is no need for an expert systems approach, or is it too complex? Discuss.
3. Discuss the authors' assessment procedure.
4. In the last section of the article the authors state, "Only expert systems with limited scope have a good chance of realization and acceptance." Later in that section, they state that "successful expert systems of the future might well be ones that take a broader perspective." Are the authors contradicting themselves? If not, then resolve the apparent difference of opinion. Discuss.

Management

Steinberg and Plank

1. Evaluate the match between expert systems and the sales management function.
2. Is SELL! SELL! SELL! really an expert system? Discuss.
3. Does the combination of SELL! SELL! SELL! and the performance monitoring system (PMS) create a decision support system or an expert system? If either combination is deficient, then what features should be added to make them complete?
4. Discuss the impact of "the lack of lawlike generalizations" on the development of marketing expert systems. Is this lack unique to the marketing discipline or is a general problem for all business domains?

Sathi et al.

1. How many tasks are involved in project management? Why are classical approaches to project management inadequate?
2. What is activity management? How does Callisto handle activity management?
3. What is configuration management? How does Callisto handle configuration management?
4. What is constraint-directed negotiation? Can an optimization model be developed to improve the efficiency of the process?
5. Criticize the approach the authors used to evaluate Mini-Callisto.

Courtney et al.

1. Discuss the role of diagnosis in problem solving. Relate your discussion to the six expert systems tasks identified by Stefik et al.
2. How was Bouwman's study different from previous studies?
3. Describe structural modeling. How does it relate to the organization of a knowledge base?
4. How does an experiential knowledge base differ from a traditional knowledge base?
5. Describe two other business diagnosis problems, not discussed in the article, that could benefit from an expert systems approach.

Lemmon

1. COMAX interacts with and operates another software system, GOSSYM. Comment on the broader question of an expert system automatically initiating action based on its own reasoning.
2. Is the relationship between COMAX and GOSSYM essentially automatic learning? Discuss.
3. COMAX is aimed at the agri-technical aspects of cotton growing, but its proof lies in its economic impacts. Are there other areas of business where an expert system could attack a purely technical problem and have economic implications?

IV. PERSPECTIVES

This final section takes an objective look at expert systems applications. Friedenberg and Hensler discuss issues that are relevant to those who want to start and operate their own expert systems development firms. The new and fuzzy area of legal liability of expert systems is presented clearly by Frank. The last two articles represent a counterbalance to the glowing reports of the applications section. Expert systems development is not without its problems and limitations. Successful applications in the future must learn from the mistakes as well as the successes of the past. Dreyfus and Dreyfus, long-time critics of artificial intelligence, raise some fundamental philosophical questions about applying expert systems. Partridge takes a more practical view of the limitations of expert systems, essentially producing a research and development agenda for the future. All the articles in this section raise some interesting questions that may move the reader to reread previous articles.

Strategy and Business Planning for Artificial Intelligence Companies: A Guide for Entrepreneurs

Robert A. Friedenberg and Ralph L. Hensler

Like most consultants, we have developed certain paradigms that we use to help our clients. We have worked with both entrepreneurs starting small technology-oriented business and with sources of venture capital. Frequently, we find that there is a gap between these two groups created by vastly different goals and objectives as well as diverse communication styles. The unfortunate result of this gap is the difficulty many startups experience in obtaining capital.

We do not intend to provide a comprehensive review of business theory, to contrast our methodology with others, or to provide a historical perspective on venture capital. We also ignore a large body of reference material to instead focus on the more pragmatic topic of what actual entrepreneurs do that is right and that is wrong. The concepts in this article are not restricted to the field of artificial intelligence; they are equally applicable to other technology-driven entrepreneurial, or intrapreneurial, efforts.

Development and Implementation of a Corporate Strategy

Often, the long-term considerations of strategic planning and the tactical concerns of a startup operation seem to be at odds with each other. This is unfortunate because strategic planning is essential to a small firm, spin-off, or new ventures group even if the corporate planning document (not to be confused with a business plan for seeking capital!) is not.

Hi-Tech Venture Consultants frequently uses a simple model we call a Z-Plan to sort out these strategic planning issues for smaller companies and startups (see Figure 1). The steps in the Z-Plan are similar to those in the standard scientific, engineering, and business review that larger companies perform. We have endeavored to recast these reviews into a form more suitable for a smaller organization that doesn't have the time, resources, or need for weighty planning tomes. Additionally, we find the Z in the Z-Plan to be a useful guide for relating technical-and business-planning issues, a step most larger companies perform poorly, if they try at all.

The basic premise of the Z-Plan is that both the formation and the execution of a new business or product require a separate review of scientific, engineering, and business issues in order to develop stable goals and objectives. These reviews should involve the entrepreneur, seed capital investors, and independent consultants and should result in a consensus about the directions that everyone's efforts should take. Usually, we find that it's best to have thought all of these issues through before seeking substantial amounts of financing. In fact, the Z-Plan makes a natural precursor to developing any formal documentation, that is, a business plan for use in approaching sources of capital.

Reprinted with permission from *AI Magazine*, vol. 7, no. 3, August 1986, 111-118.

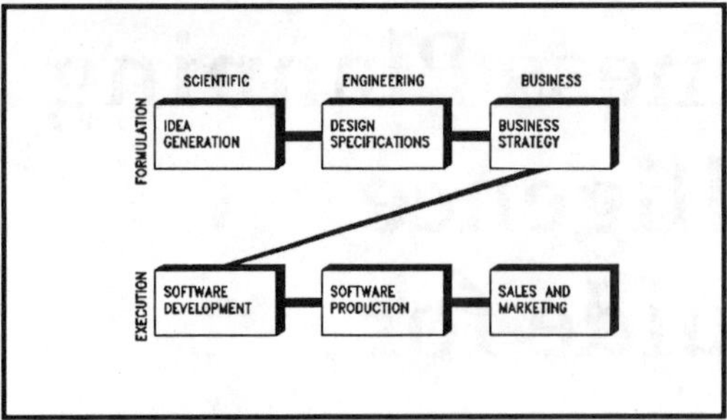

Figure 1. The Z plan.

The important components of a Z-Plan are idea generation, design specifications, business strategy, software development, software production and beta testing, and sales and marketing.

Idea Generation
This is the realm of the entrepreneur. By the time there is something to plan about, the idea has been hatched.

Design Specifications
Frequently, we find that although the product has been thought out conceptually, the nuts and bolts impact of the software engineering was not thoroughly thought out during the idea-generation stage. An unforeseen design aspect can alter the funding or timing requirements of the project. Some questions you should consider follow.

How might the product fail in a real-world environment, and how will it be serviced or upgraded? For products still requiring substantial R&D, careful consideration must be given to how the product will be superseded by you or by others.

Are standard rules for software and hardware design being followed to the maximum extent possible? It is often difficult to choose between preserving a proprietary technique and isolating yourself from the marketplace.

Is there a costly implementation process that can be replaced by something less exotic? (For example, is it possible to integrate an expert system with existing database and communications software?) Your clientele might perceive the cost-quality trade-offs differently from you, for example, focusing more on compatibility with existing hardware and converting existing files than on the subtle points of knowledge representation and expert simulation. (See Example 1.)

Example 1. A financial institution only considers AI applications that do not require AI hardware, even as a "knowledge server." The institutions perceive of it as too brittle. In addition, the institution considers it the AI vendors' responsibility to fit software into their financial institution's current environment, using existing client files, online quotes, and so on. The vendors' skills in these conventional areas turned out to be the most important factor in the purchase decision.

Business Strategy
The development and implementation of a business strategy is a critical process for any new venture. In essence, it is a model of the major elements of the business for next five (or however many, but this is a figure the venture capital community likes) years. This strategy represents all aspects of the business, including suppliers, operations, consulting, marketing, and accounting and not just R&D, sales, and product development. Some things to think about follow:

What activities are going on other than R&D, marketing and product development? These activities and their associated costs need to be included in order to ascertain the correct amount of capitalization.

What are the key developmental milestones? Are they small enough steps to quickly indicate whether the project is ahead of or behind schedule, or over or under budget? These milestones make you credible to investors as well as provide a basis for project management.

How much time, salary, and equity will it take to attract the type of human resources required to transform an idea into a company? This requires a hard look at the differences between creating and maintaining a new venture. (See Example 2.)

Example 2. A company with a voice-vision telephone product discovered as a strategic model was being built that, rather than dealing primarily in manufacturing, the company would be dominated by sales and marketing in terms of expenditures and personnel. In order to keep its new venture lean, the company entered into a strategic joint venture with more established telecommunications companies in order to obtain sales and customer service help.

We are ignoring a rather large topic called an environmental or macroeconomic review. Larger corporations usually pay more attention to the environment than smaller corporations. This is probably not a critical area for an AI start-up company. Just be careful to avoid getting caught by surprise like the solar energy industry, where deregulation of natural gas prices hurt many companies badly.

Software Development

We find that most new ventures are very clear about the ultimate goal of their R&D efforts. They are also aware of the resources required for direct support, given the project runs smoothly. Less thought, however, is given to how these resources interrelate and how the entire project is to be managed. Neglecting these issues can result in both the direct and indirect costs of a project getting out of hand. Although there are formalized techniques to assist with project management (Pert charts or the critical path method), we generally prefer to use a simpler process:

Start with the well-defined goal, and work backward. The end product of an R&D project is dependent on the completion of a number of tasks, each of which is dependent on the completion of a number of preliminary tasks, and so on back to the definition of the goals. All of these tasks should be listed or drawn on a chart.

Make a note of which tasks have less certain timetables and which tasks have the greatest number of other tasks dependent on them.

Judge critical to your development effort those tasks whose time to completion are difficult to estimate and which have many other tasks dependent upon their conclusion. If many aspects of your effort depend on any tasks, these tasks need to be carefully controlled to avoid delaying the completion of your product. Standalone tasks with uncertain timetables present localized risk but shouldn't endanger the entire project.

Software Production and Beta Testing

Once the research is completed, product development begins. As part of the Z-Plan, you should consider:

Does the idea fit neatly into one product, or does it appear to have multiple uses? If so, do all of the potential clients need the same version, or should there be several variations (for example, an application generator that could be sold as either a generic product or as a variety of applications)? This should be considered as part of the business strategy, but our experience has shown us that this issue pops up again at this point in the development process.

What incremental product-line extensions can be made? Are there variations of the basic concept that can lead to new products in order to sustain the new venture? (See Example 3.)

Example 3. A firm making microcomputer firmware packages to teach the sciences expanded its product line as one might expect to include all the basic sciences. While producing these packages, it occurred to the firm that it could use the same basic software and peripherals for entertainment products. The addition of this new product line reduces investor risk and is expected to make it far easier for the firm to obtain capital.

Sales and Marketing

Most new ventures have thought about who they would like to target as customers and how they would like to distribute their product. From a more strategic standpoint, you should also consider the following:

What product are you hoping to replace and what advantages do you offer? Every technology has a predecessor and a successor.

What product might replace you, and what are you doing about it?

How do both of these issues look from your customers' perspective? Frequently there are barriers to converting from one technology to another, especially when yet another technology is on the horizon.

Finally, you should have learned from this discussion that you are the one who should be pursuing your own technology's successor most vigorously. As a result, by the time you execute all the steps in the Z-Plan, you might be ready to start a new one.

Production of Appropriate Documentation

The appropriate documentation for any new company is a business plan. This plan must describe a business, not a product or a technology. This is the most common fatal flaw in the business plans that we review. Also, venture capital firms tell us that the major reason they reject a plan is not because of a new venture's technology but because of an unconvincing marketing and management presentation.

We strongly recommend that every startup get assistance in writing and promoting its business plan. The reason for this is that the entrepreneur has been living and breathing AI software for a substantial period of time. Even if you have a good background in strategy, marketing, financial analysis, and management, you are likely to have difficulty sorting out the issues you believe are critical from those potential investors believe are critical; you are too close to the day-to-day tactical problems. Many consultants will work out an arrangement for compensation based on stock or on cash from a company's capitalization, so that there is little or no initial cost to the startup.

Depending on the type of capital being sought (partnership, seed money, startup, first stage, second stage, initial public offering, joint venture), various sections of the business plan are modified to include legal and accounting sections. We recommend that a document strictly containing the business issues be circulated (with suitable disclaimers) prior to any official offering document. This modified document is less expensive to produce and is an excellent marketing tool that can be distributed to potential investors to provide some feedback.

A typical table of contents for the business plan of an AI software firm is shown in Figure 2. Some of the key issues in writing a business plan are:

Acme Expert Systems
Preliminary Business Plan
Table of Contents

Summary
- The Company
- Product and Service Description
- Marketing
- Management Team
- Financial Requirements

Description of AI Technology
- Predecessor Technologies/Methods
- Successor Technologies/Methods

Acme Expert Systems Product Description
- Initial Product
- Product Line Extensions
- Potential New Products

Market Analysis
- Definition of Potential Market
- Market Penetration Strategy
- Market Research Program
- Distinctive Competence
- Competitive Analysis/Risk Factors

Distribution Strategy

Financial Analysis
- Five Year Projection
- Assumptions
- Use of Capital

Appendix
- Background of the Principals
- Relevant Articles
- Audited Financials (if available)

Figure 2. Sample business plan table of contents.

Executive Summary

This is by far the most important section of a business plan. You have perhaps five minutes to capture the interest of a potential investor or a screener of business plans at a venture capital firm. If you do not hit all of the critical points in that amount of time, your plan is not read further. Some of the key issues to keep in mind when writing the summary include the following:

The executive summary must be totally self-sufficient. In all likelihood, the person, if any, who reads the body of the plan is not the same person who reads the executive summary.

The summary should contain absolutely no jargon. Even if the person reading the plan has a technological background, the plan is also usually circulated to nontechnical people. Rummage through some AI articles in *BusinessWeek* to get an idea of the level of sophistication to use.

Include key financial numbers and graphs. Do not be concerned about redundancy between the summary and the body of the plan, even if text is repeated verbatim. This is actually a good educational technique.

Description of AI Technology

The purpose of this section is to educate potential investors who are unfamiliar with artificial intelligence. We usually take a somewhat historical approach, focusing on the development and validation of the projected market. A good level of sophistication to use in this section is that used in *High Technology* magazine. In this section list predecessor and successor technologies and methods.

Predecessor Technologies and Methods. Describe relevant software concepts that fulfilled more or less the same role in the eyes of the consumer. Do not attempt to portray your program as unique; if nothing else, there is a noncomputer way of performing a similar service (later, there is a discussion of distinctive competence for selling unique benefits). It should also contain relevant success stories and notable failures.

Successor Technologies and Methods. A look ahead at emerging technologies is often overlooked in the general technology review. In this section, you can evaluate what the expected life of your product or service might be and what product or service might succeed it. This is an important section; without it potential investors tend to assume that a technological product, especially software, will become obsolete before they can recover their investment. One need only look at the recent commercialization of expert systems to sympathize with this perspective (see Example 4).

> **Example 4.** A firm is selling turnkey photovoltaic cell factories. When asked about the successor to the technique, the firm revealed it was the leader in research in this area. Adding a description of its research to the offering document assisted this firm with its second public offering.

Product or Service Description

It is extremely important that you describe your product or service and not your technology. First, decide if you are selling a product or a service. With software, there can be a subtle difference. Concentrate on what the end user is buying in terms of tangibles, features, functions and services. Some sections to include are descriptions of the initial product and product-line extensions (see Example 5).

> **Example 5.** A firm is marketing energy management equipment that is produced by others for commercial use. This firm hired us at the behest of its investors to explore alternative types of equipment for the same market (product-line extensions) and to find other residential and industrial energy management products that it could also market (new products).

Initial Product. Describe the initial product. Be careful that you are not blurring several products into one.

Product-Line Extensions. If there are variations to your product that you might sell in the near future, include them as product-line extensions. This could include "new and improved" versions of your software or versions for different applications.

Potential New Products. Here you can include new applications of your basic programming technology, for example, a new shell in which to build applications. Every product has a finite life cycle. Evidence that you've given thought to new products makes investors feel they are investing in a company rather than a product.

Market Analysis

This is the next most important section to the executive summary. Now that you have let a potential investor understand your software and its place in the larger world, you must address the questions of how many dollars are in your market, how you plan to go after them, who is competing with you and how you plan to deal with them. We generally break this rather formidable task into five smaller areas: potential market definition, market penetration strategy, market research program, distinctive competence, and competitive analysis and risk factors.

Definition of Potential Market. The total of all the expenditures that could be made for your product or service must be defined. This is not to say that all of these customers will buy your product or even buy competitive products, but the universe must be defined. For example, if you developed a customer-service expert system for banks that sells for $1000.00, your potential market is

Banks x # Customer Service Terminals per Bank x $1000.

This figure should be far in excess of what you actually plan to sell on a cumulative basis so that you are not thought to be saturating your market and should also reflect potential growth. There is always suitable market-size information available, although it can be difficult to dig up. Try phoning your competitors and the market research firms referenced in business periodicals and trade journals if you are having difficulty (consultants can be particularly helpful in this area because they are considered neutral). We recommend that you always try to reach line engineers and researchers as opposed to salespersons. State your desire to get nonproprietary background information and references. Make it clear when dealing with a research firm that you are not a potential client and that you are seeking a few leads and not information contained in their reports. Finally, build a network of contacts. Ask every person you call for the names of others you should talk to. (In our discussion of marketing, we give an example of how we obtained market size and competitive information for a small market.) Finally, you must also segment this potential market either by type of potential client or by geographic region. If you have more than one product or service, this segmentation must be developed as a matrix for each product line.

Market Penetration Strategy. Here you must describe how you will approach the potential market that you previously outlined. Some important considerations are what your position is (low-cost producer, high-quality producer, specialty product); which products will be pursued first and for what market segments; what type of sales force will be used; how customer service will be handled; what existing companies will be used for joint sales, marketing and distribution and what types of promotions will be used.

For a startup, we believe that the market-penetration strategy should not focus on unknown detail. Writing volumes on pricing strategy, for example, is more appropriate for established companies selling established products in established markets than for a start-up. An investor would probably rather hear about why a potential customer would find enough value in your product to pay more than it cost you to provide. We have found this to be no small issue with regard to expert systems.

Market Research Program. On an ongoing basis, any startup needs to keep track of competitors and, more importantly, feedback from customers. It is always a good idea to formalize a tracking system as part of a program in order to give potential investors confidence.

Distinctive Competence. All of the factors that you believe will make you succeed in a new market with a new product must be listed here. Be sure to discuss your product or service, technical skills, AI experience, management experience, marketing skills, subject matter expertise and anything else that you do well and might relate to your new venture. Attach an organizational chart here if you are a startup (have a separate section on management if you are an operating company). It is critical that you make your management levels appear as deep as possible. This can be accomplished by having your key shareholders and business advisers on a board of directors and your technical advisers and subject-matter experts on a board of advisers.

Competitive Analysis/Risk Factors. We recommend a three-level approach to competitive analysis. The first level is products that are directly competitive with you (for example, other AI software). The second level is other types of products and services that currently fulfill the same need in the marketplace that you propose to fulfill. The third level is companies that can easily compete with you if they desire to (see Example 6).

There are also three levels of risk factors. There is the internal risk that your product will never operate as anticipated or that you will fail to deliver it at the promised cost in the promised time frame. There is the external risk that the demand will be lower than expected or that a competitor will gain the market share and squeeze you out. Finally, there is the technology risk that as AI software advances, your product could experience a much shorter life cycle than necessary to please investors.

Financial Analysis

The financial analysis should include a five-year projection and the assumptions on which all your figures are based.

Five-Year Projection. Pay attention to accounting conventions, styles, and formats when you develop financial projections. Being clear isn't good enough. Always keep key schedules on one page, and use supporting schedules if necessary. At a minimum, you should have a monthly schedule of operating profit for the first year, an annual income statement for the first five years, a balance sheet for the first five years, application of capital proceeds, and

Example 6. We refer once again to the voice-vision telephone firm. We followed specific procedures to obtain background, market-size, and competitive information. Using Dow Jones News Retrieval, we downloaded encyclopedia information about AT&T's original vision phone and teleconferencing product. We did a text search of teleconferencing and vision joined with "telephone" in the online version of the *Wall Street Journal.* The nonelectronic analogs to these steps are fairly straightforward. This process revealed the names of several small firms, usually with their location, with new products in the area. Telephone calls to these firms resulted in product literature, annual reports, and other company's efforts in the voice-vision telephone area. Some of these brochures referred to trade magazines we were unaware of and compared different products and technologies by specification and product function. By continuing this networking, we had a good feel for the industry in a few weeks at almost no cost and in spite of the fact that this area is not really covered as yet by stock market analysts, market researchers, and the like.

revenue breakdown by product and market segment for the first five years. The more supporting and detailed information you have the better, but put it in an appendix. The potential investor doesn't want to see it (although the investor's accountant might) and it is this person who is your target audience. As a final note of advice, include graphs whenever possible.

Assumptions. For every line possible on every schedule, state explicitly the assumptions being made. If you estimate a number because you have supporting data, reference it clearly. State any depreciation and amortization lifetimes used, the average payable and receivable periods assumed and why, and any inflation assumptions. Be careful about overusing statements such as "Management's Estimate."

Other Sections

Depending on the product or service, other sections are frequently needed. Some examples of these include manufacturing strategy (not likely for software!), distribution strategy, and joint venturing strategy. If a factor you consider critical to your firm is not included in our guideline, by all means create a section. Be very careful to review your plan. Be sure that the reader doesn't need to know facts for section A that aren't defined until section C. Although this might sound obvious, we find that the liberal use of cold readers (people unfamiliar with the company or even the technology) always produces some surprising errors in continuity.

Appendix

Include in the appendix any information on the principals, articles from business publications that might be relevant, an operating history if available, and any other supporting information that you consider important but too detailed to be included in the body of the report.

Background of the Principals. A brief resume of each officer, director, and adviser should be included. Please remember that this is not a forum for convincing readers you are smart or well published or have had an interesting career. Strip everything away that doesn't contribute to the narrow goal of making your company credible. We recommend a maximum description length of one-half page for the key technical person and the president and less for all others. Make sure all of the resumes are in the same format.

Relevant Articles. First, get any articles in business publications (for example, *BusinessWeek* and *High Technology*) relevant to your market. Second, include any review articles on the appropriate AI technology. Third, include any technical articles, especially those written by the principals of your firm (the potential investor will almost certainly want an independent review of your product, and you should make that as easy as possible). Last, include literature from any competitors, especially that from any company with conventional software or a noncomputer technique you expect to replace. If your product is truly superior, there is no better way to deal with the competition than to let the competition describe its product in its own words.

Audited Financials. If you have an operating history, make it easily available to potential investors.

Approaching Sources of Capital

Although much can be said (and has been—contact the small business unit of any of the "Big 8" accounting firms) on the mechanics of seeking capital, we contain our discussion to some stylistic issues—such as placing a value on your company, doing your homework, defining your role and being professional, and being flexible—that are frequently "deal killers."

Valuing Your Company

One of the things that you must do before anything else is to value your company. We approach the valuation process from the perspective that the value derived from the process is a secondary result of the more important process of deciding how large a percentage of the ownership of your firm you must give up in order to get the capital you require. This is not a mathematical calculation but a complex process involving many issues such as the following:

Dilution and Control. If an investor puts $1,000,000 into your startup and gets 30% of the stock, the investor's shares are worth $300,000 book value. At the same time, the investor has created an implicit market value for your company of $3,333,333. If you owned 50% of the stock prior to this investment, you now own 35%. You must establish how much control you are willing to give up in this round of capitalization and still remain sensitive to the investor's perspective.

Return on Investment. Many venture capital firms have a minimum acceptable return on investment. Your five-year projections must show a decent return on investment in order to justify the investment on a value basis. To continue with the previous example, if the original capital plus the retained earnings (assuming no dividends) was $15,000,000 by the end of year 5, our hypothetical investor's $1,000,000 investment is worth 30% of $15,000,000 or $5,000,000 which is a return on investment of about 38% per year.

Use of Proceeds. Even if the dilution and the return on investment are acceptable, any potential investor will be concerned over how efficiently the proceeds of his investment are utilized. The best way for him to increase his return on investment is to invest less. It is common for a startup to find that they cannot get all of the capital they believe they need from an investor regardless of the percent of ownership they are willing to give up.

Homework. Before you send any business plan around, ask some potential investors (or better yet have a neutral party such as a consultant call) to identify the right individual in each firm you approach. Then, call this individual and tell him about your business and see if they would like to review the plan. This can keep your document out of the large pile that sits on every potential investor's desk.

Roles. Your role in your own corporation will change as a result of an infusion of capital, and any investor is unlikely to provide capital without a role in the company's management. This is often difficult for an entrepreneur to deal with. Our advice is to decide if your ultimate role is to be technical, marketing or managerial (only one!) and relinquish the other responsibilities to new additions to your firm. A corollary of this is that very few successful entrepreneurial ventures are controlled by the entrepreneur, but rather the founder will become chief scientist and/or have a strategic role. Day to day management is left for managers. Many investors we talk to will avoid any product, no matter how promising, if they feel the founder won't relinquish control of certain business issues. We have had dealings with a firm in the waste to energy business that has had enormous difficulty getting capitalized due to their desire to limit outside investors' managerial role. They perceived of venture capital as some sort of bank with higher interest rates, while venture capital sources perceived of them as uncooperative and too risky to deal with.

Professionalism. The business world has its own culture, jargon, mannerisms, etc. Entrepreneurs who appear to function better in their environment are generally felt to be more professional whether or not this feeling is justified. The principals of the waste-to-energy firm previously mentioned did not volunteer certain information to potential investors because they believed the information would reflect unfavorably upon the company. Although the entrepreneurs didn't avoid any direct questions, their lack of communication contributed to the unfavorable perception investors had.

Working Flexibly
Frequently, an investor will want to team you up with other companies he or she knows of, to introduce new suppliers, to develop new products, or to pursue new markets. By all means consider these alternatives. (See Example 8.)

> **Example 8.** We are in the process of introducing a firm with a handheld online terminal to a competitor with what is perhaps a better technology and another firm with home energy controllers to a similar firm that could fill in a gap in its product line.

Who to Send It To
Everybody. We generally find that concepts and early startups (those looking for seed capital) do better with industry support. Many companies you perceive as suppliers, distributors and even competitors might be sources of capital. The companies generally would perceive you to be a cheaper and faster alternative to an internal development effort. Formed companies that are ready to begin operations (looking for startup or first-stage capital) will appeal to the venture capital community and affluent individuals. Operating companies (looking for first-stage or second-stage financing) should consider the venture capital groups of larger financial institutions, public offerings such as a "Reg D," or even project financing. These guidelines are very loose, however.

What the Investor Is Looking For
Different potential investors might be looking for different things from your company. These different goals can impact the type of deal they seek and the level of control they want. Some books, such as *The Guide to Venture Capital Sources,* or *Venture Magazine* give this information, but you can always ask the investor. Some goals they aim for follow:

Return on Investment. This is by far the most common investment goal of the venture capital community. The investor will want to be involved in all managerial, financial, and marketing decisions in order to have your company grow as rapidly as possible. Technical areas will be impacted less.

Risk Diversification. Sometimes, it is not only return on investment that matters but how the risk of your company might relate to the risk of other startups. This concern is particularly true with venture capital funds or partnerships. These types of investments enable retail and institutional investors who are not venture capitalists to invest in these areas.

Strategic Partnering. A company that is a potential client of yours or a potential supplier to you might perceive you as an opportunity for vertical integration. A larger competitor might perceive you as an opportunity for horizontal integration. Partnering presumes that your company is left intact as either a subsidiary or a division of the acquiring firm. The strategic partner can be relatively uninvolved or can be intimately involved with your firm.

Technology Transfer. As opposed to integration, a company might invest merely to get access to technology in a less expensive manner than it would through internal development. Because the technology is an AI company's only real asset, this could leave your startup in poor shape. The problem is that you usually can't tell in advance if your suitor is interested in integration or in technology transfer. The investing company might not even know itself.

Strategic Venture Capital Pools. This concept is a blend of the risk diversification idea and the integration idea. A company will create a pool of capital to invest in several opportunities for investment purposes, then screen the candidate startups to choose those which are working on technologies that might have long-term strategic value for them. The best-known company to use this strategy is General Motors.

Summary

In summary, entrepreneurs must look beyond their own experiences when proposing to turn a concept into a business and capitalize it. This applies to each of the three phases of forming a business we have described in this article—the development of a corporate strategy, the production of documentation, and seeking capital.

What AI Practitioners Should Know about the Law

Steven J. Frank

Although recent computer-related disputes have involved a variety of legal issues — breach of contract specifications, misrepresentation of performance capability, and outright fraud, to name a few — it is the threat of tort liability that continues to strike the greatest fear in the heart of mighty industrialist and struggling start-up alike.

Once inside the courtroom, what role can the computer assume in its own defense or in the service of some other litigant? The law of evidence, developed to govern the testimony of human witnesses, must continually evolve to accommodate new, nonhuman sources of information. At the same time, developers of intelligent computer systems will have to achieve a great deal of communicative power before their machines will be given a day in court. These two topics — tort liability, and the computer as witness — are the focus of this paper.

Tort Liability

The system of tort compensation exists to provide victims of injury — physical, economic, or emotional — with the means to seek redress in the form of monetary damages. The purpose of the damage award is to "make the plaintiff whole" by compensating for all losses flowing from the defendant's wrongful act. Although this concept seems straightforward, damage awards have been known to vary enormously, even for identical injuries. The host of subjective factors that appear in the calculus of compensation precludes accurate forecasts in most cases, leading some defendants to financial ruin and others to surprised relief. However, injury alone does not guarantee recovery. Rules of tort liability mediate between the victim's need for recompense and the defendant's right to remain free from arbitrarily imposed obligation.

Although sensational cases involving large recoveries tend to generate the greatest alarm, the magnitude of damages in a particular case is actually far less important than the availability of any damages in similar cases. Potential tort defendants are primarily interested in their overall liability exposure, as determined by the evolving structure of case precedent. For software developers, expenditures for debugging, design safety analysis, and quality control assurance are necessarily affected by the extent of perceived vulnerability to tort actions.

More so than in any other legal field, the boundaries separating human from machine will be forced into focus by questions of tort liability. In addition to compensation, another function of tort law is to project proper standards of care in the conduct of activities that might cause harm. When the agent of injury is a tangible device or product, attention is currently directed toward three sets of possible culprits: manufacturers (Was the product designed or manufactured defectively?), sellers (Was the product sold in a defective condition?), and purchasers (Was the product used improperly?). Absent from the lineup is the injury-producing item itself, whose existence is relevant only insofar as it pertains to the conduct of human beings. As "devices" come to include electronic systems capable of judgment and behavior, they too will become objects of direct inquiry. Naturally, financial responsibility will ultimately rest with a human being or a corporation possessing a bank account; but the standards by which humans and machines are judged will begin to merge as the tasks they perform grow similar.

The question of whether liability accrues in a given instance invariably reduces to the

Reprinted with permission from *AI Magazine*, vol. 9, no. 2, Summer 1988, 109-114.

application of two legal variables: the standard of care expected of the defendant and the requirement that a causal link exist between the defendant's substandard conduct and the plaintiff's injury. The existence of a valid tort cause of action means that someone has suffered loss. This much is beyond change. The function of the liability standard is to allocate loss among all parties involved based on considerations of fairness, efficiency, and accepted behavioral norms. The terms of the standard prescribe the level of vigilance expected of individuals who conduct a particular type of activity. Although variations exist, most formulations derive from the fault-based concept of negligence: If the defendant failed to act in the manner of a reasonably prudent person under all circumstances, the loss falls on him or her. A special relationship between plaintiff and defendant or the performance of an unusual activity can prompt a court to adjust the standard. Innkeepers, for example, have been held liable to guests for the "slightest negligence" because of the high degree of trust placed in their hands. Certain activities have been identified as so inherently dangerous or unfamiliar that no degree of care can adequately prevent mishap. For these "strict liability" activities, the loss falls on the defendant, regardless of fault, as a cost of doing business.

This choice of liability standard calls for a decision based on public policy. Although through less obvious means, the parameters of causation are ultimately shaped by similar considerations. A scientific view of deterministic causality provides only a starting point for the legal notion of causation. Judges have recognized that too many events are logically interrelated for liability to rest solely on logic. Fairness to defendants requires that a line be drawn at some level of remoteness, and the location of this line reflects a policy-oriented value judgment. Liberal tests of causation shift a greater amount of loss toward tort defendants by including more distant effects of liability-producing conduct within the range of potential recovery. These tests generally focus on the existence of a chain of events, such that causation is based on proof of an unbroken progression of occurrences; the outer limits of connectedness are typically bounded only by the reluctance to impose liability for the extremely unpredictable. Restrictive tests of causation focus directly on the defendant's ability to foresee the possible harm arising from particular actions and reverse the shift in favor of the plaintiffs.

Returning to liability issues, the rule applied to parties engaged in commercial trade depends heavily on what is being sold. Providers of services have traditionally been held to a negligence standard based on reasonably prudent practice within a given area of specialization. In contrast, sellers and manufacturers of tangible commodities face strict liability for injuries to individual consumers caused by defects in their wares. The reason for the distinction does not lie in any perceived disparity of associated danger, but rather in the fact that product sellers are viewed as economically better able to spread a loss over a large number of users through price adjustments.

Courts have had difficulty fitting computer programs into this bifurcated world of products and services. Software can be supplied in a variety of forms, some more tangible than others. Programmers might write software for mass distribution, tailor an established package to the needs of a particular user, or design from scratch a custom system for an individual client. Although no court has yet faced this issue in the precise context of tort liability, most commentators (including this writer) believe that characterization as product or service is most properly determined by the supplier's degree of involvement with the customer. Greater availability of technical assistance and support make the overall transaction appear more like a service.

Because implementation of the high-level tasks performed by commercial AI software requires extensive immersion in the field of application, initial development contracts call most clearly for treatment as service arrangements. If the finished program proves suitable for an entire class of users, however, subsequent sales might appear to involve a product. Ambiguity is inevitable where the uncertain intrinsic character of software diverts attention to its mode of supply for purposes of tort liability.

The question of causation raises a different set of issues — those chiefly related to the manner in which the computer program actually makes contact with the end user. The factors that evoke a clear liability rule for mass-marketed software likewise provide the strongest link between defect and injury. Simple sales transactions force the consumer to rely solely on the purchased item for effective performance, and thus, any harm suffered can be traced directly to improper program operation. It seems doubtful, however, that AI programs will reach consumers through such direct market channels any time soon. The simplest current reason is cost: AI software is enormously expensive to produce. A longer-range consideration is the likely reluctance of human experts to relinquish control over the provision of their expertise. Professions shielded by licensure requirements, for example, have shown themselves to be well equipped to defend against unauthorized practice. For the foreseeable future, then, the most likely role for many applied knowledge programs is as an aid to the human expert.

Although perhaps depriving AI developers from access to the consumer market, such restrictions also relieve developers of a great deal of potential liability. The law will not treat an appurtenant factor as a causal agent of injury unless it materially contributes to this injury; yet material contribution is precisely what is prohibited by restrictions on unauthorized practice. For example, if a physician were to attempt to lay blame on a diagnostic expert system for improper treatment, the physician would thereby admit to allowing the computer to perform as a doctor. The price of limiting the practice of a profession to a select group of peers is accepting complete responsibility for professional misjudgment.

Of course, if the source of the physician's error were indeed traceable to the expert system, the physician might sue the software developer to recover the money that must be paid to the injured patient. This possibility leads to the question: How should the law of product liability be applied to the creator of a device whose domain-specific capabilities might match or exceed those of human experts? The first step in any such lawsuit (whether based on strict liability or negligence) is to demonstrate that the product contains a defect. Should defectiveness be inferred from the mere fact of incorrect diagnosis? Human physicians are certainly not judged this harshly; their diagnoses must only be "reasonable." Separating programming errors from legitimate mistakes of judgment falling within professional discretion will indeed prove formidable.

A second, more practical obstacle facing this hypothetical physician is that a strict liability standard would probably not apply, regardless of whether the program is viewed as a product. Courts generally permit strict liability recovery only in actions for physical injury and property damage; economic loss is insufficient to trigger the doctrine. Unlike the hapless patient, the physician has personally suffered only financial impairment. The physician's tort suit, therefore, must be based on negligence. If the software developer has exercised reasonable care in debugging and packaging the product, including some statement warning of the system's limitations, the negligence burden might prove a difficult one to carry. The appropriate level of resources devoted to debugging efforts and the scope of the necessary warning depends on actual reliability and system design. For example, deep expert systems can generally be expected to deliver acceptable results over the entire useful range of the underlying causal model. Courts will undoubtedly expect greater vigilance from developers of shallow systems (or deep systems based on models that are not robust) simply as a consequence of the diminished reliability implied by program design.

To be sure, not all applications of AI techniques involve roles currently occupied by organized professions, nor must computer output actually touch consumers in order to affect their lives. The degree of contact necessary to trigger liability is once again determined by the nature of the commercial relationship. Personal interaction comprises an inherent feature of consultative service transactions, and a causal gap is probably inevitable unless the computer somehow communicates directly with the injured consumer; otherwise, the intervention of human judgment is likely to prove a sufficient superseding event to interrupt the nexus. Sales transactions, in contrast, are characteristically impersonal. The path of causation is likely to be far more direct if the computer's role involves assisting in the fabrication of a product. Any modicum of assistance not filtered through independent human oversight can furnish a link between computer operation and injury caused by defective manufacture. Hence, developers of computer-aided manufacturing (CAM) systems can expect increasing exposure to liability as their software assumes control over a greater portion of the manufacturing process.

Product design occupies a status somewhere between service and manufacture. Although the ultimate goal might be the production of a usable product, the design process involves early-stage development decisions of a far more basic and creative nature than those involved in automating production. The collaboration of computer-aided design programs with human engineers seems likely to persist for a much longer time than might be anticipated for CAM systems, which reduce design to actual practice, maintaining a greater opportunity for events that sever the chain of causation.

Increased trustworthiness inevitably results in heightened liability. As the role played by computers expands from passive assistant to independent practitioner, and as tasks delegated to computers begin to encompass a greater dimension of injury-producing activity, their owners will find themselves increasingly responsible for mishap traceable to improper operation.

Computers in the Courtroom

As AI research produces systems capable of real-time communication, computers can be expected to ascend from their present courtroom role as sidelined objects of legal controversy to active participation in the trial process itself. To lawyers, a computer serving as an expert witness offers unique potential advantages when compared to its human counterpart: quicker and more accurate responses to questions, greater capacity for immediately accessible domain-specific knowledge, and complete indifference to the charged atmosphere of a heated trial or the unnerving interrogation of a skilled attorney. For computer scientists, the specialized vocabulary and rules that govern judicial proceedings offer a relatively structured environment for developing knowledge-based systems capable of genuine interaction.

An initial issue confronting the introduction of computer testimony would be veracity: The law demands that witnesses give some assurance of truthfulness. The traditional oath-taking ceremony is no longer an indispensable feature of trial procedure, but all courts require that witnesses provide some form of affirmation backed by the threat of punishment for perjury. Could a machine furnish such an affirmation? No, not at present, because no contrivance yet devised is capable of anything resembling voluntary moral choice. Some human — programmer, user, or the litigant propounding the computer witness — must accept direct responsibility for the truth of testimonial output.

If the oath requirement presents some administrative inconvenience, restrictive rules of evidence stand as a far more formidable obstacle to the witness chair. As they currently stand, these rules bar today's computers from most courtroom affairs. Not only are current systems forbidden to act as witnesses, but their output often cannot even be introduced as substantive evidence. This impasse is created by a much-popularized but highly complex precept of evidentiary doctrine — the hearsay rule.

The rule owes its origin to the unfortunate judicial experience of Sir Walter Raleigh. In 1603, the legendary English adventurer, statesman, and author was accused of plotting to commit treason against King James I and forced to stand trial. The primary evidence introduced against Raleigh was a sworn statement made by his alleged co-conspirator, Lord Cobham, and a letter written by Cobham. Raleigh insisted that Cobham had recanted his statement and sought to question him directly. The prosecutor, Sir Edward Coke, refused to produce Cobham. Instead, he called a boat pilot who testified that while in Portugal he had been told, "Your king [James I] shall never be crowned for Don Cobham and Don Raleigh will cut his throat before he come to be crowned." Raleigh again protested, objecting that "this is the saying of some wild Jesuit or beggarly priest; but what proof is it against me?" Lord Coke replied, "It must perforce arise out of some preceding intelligence, and shows that your treason had wings." On this evidence, Raleigh was convicted and eventually beheaded.

Contemporaries considered the trial and its outcome cruelly unjust, and continued outrage ultimately resulted in the rule against the introduction of *hearsay*, that is, evidence whose source is not present in court for cross-examination. Unless a computer is capable of independently responding to questions, therefore, its output is unalterably hearsay and presumptively inadmissible.

The modern hearsay rule is not ironclad, however. Centuries of application have resulted in dissatisfaction with a doctrine that withholds so much highly informative evidence from the jury's consideration, and various exceptions have been introduced to mitigate its broad sweep. Computer output sometimes gains entry through one or more of these "loopholes." In particular, one widely recognized hearsay exception permits the introduction of routine business records; hence, the output of software that merely automates office functions often bypasses hearsay objection. Furthermore, the definition of hearsay is not all-encompassing: Only evidence introduced for the truth of its content falls within its terms. If a supposedly mute witness is heard to utter, "I can speak!" the content of these words is no more relevant than if this witness had said, "Banana." The ability to speak can be inferred from the act of speech itself. Similarly, a litigant is permitted to introduce computer output as proof that a computer was in fact employed (if such is an issue in the case), even if its content remains inadmissible.

What remains flatly barred is a computer's appearance as a witness, unless it possesses adequate communicative ability. In this regard, the demands of the hearsay rule are closely aligned with the objectives pursued by designers of natural language-processing systems: An acceptable witness must be able to understand questions posed by counsel for both sides and express responses in a manner graspable by judge and jury. The interactive processes implicated by this description can be decomposed into three consistent segments:

- Mechanical translation of speech signals into digital code,
- Interpretive analysis of the encoded text to derive meaningful information that can be acted upon, and
- The formulation of coherent expressions of properly identified knowledge.[1]

Of these three segments, decoding speech signals is undoubtedly the least essential. Courts are often called on to accommodate the deaf and the mute; written questions and answers, shown to the witness and read aloud to the jury, satisfy courtroom protocol. Nonetheless, the ability to interact vocally with a witness is considered a highly valuable rhetorical asset by attorneys. Particularly when the subject matter is technical, juries are far less likely to fall asleep when observing a genuine interchange than when listening to a lecture delivered secondhand.

Researchers in this phase of speech-recognition technology have been more successful eliminating transcription errors at the intake stage than creating software to assign meaning to the correctly recognized words. Neither facet, however, has attained the level of verbal dexterity necessary to facilitate truly interactive exchange. Template-matching techniques of word recognition must remain flexible enough to accommodate the acoustic patterns of a variety of speakers yet retain sufficient discriminatory power to decipher their messages accurately. Recognition difficulties are further heightened when speech consists of a continuous stream of utterances rather than isolated words. Disaggregating conjoined groups of words, whose individual pronunciation frequently depends on the surrounding phonetic signals, requires context-oriented analysis and the knowledge of allowed syntactic structures in order to cut through the ambiguity.[2]

"Understanding" the content of speech, which from an operational point of view might be defined as locating the appropriate internally represented knowledge in response to a question and fashioning an answer, represents the central focus of much current natural language research. Computer scientists are experimenting with a number of instructive models, but the greatest obstacles have been recognized for decades.[3] Vast amounts of subliteral inference contribute to the attribution of meaning in human communication, and an effective knowledge search requires precise characterization of this meaning. Contriving a satisfactory approach for bringing such soft concepts within the processing abilities of computer systems remains an elusive goal. Perhaps the recurring sequences of action and dialogue that take place in all legal proceedings can provide a basis for reducing the amount of world knowledge necessary for drawing the proper inferences. In particular, techniques based on scripts might prove useful as a means of formalizing courtroom discourse into patterns of expectable and, hence, more readily understandable verbal interchange.

Formulating a comprehensible response to a question once the appropriate knowledge is located requires more than simply translating it back into a natural language. In order to communicate effectively, additional features become necessary. A computer witness must be able to determine the level of detail and complexity appropriate for the audience (either autonomously or through external human calibration) and adjust its output accordingly. Answers perceived as unclear might need to be rephrased. Achieving the fluent command of language necessary to perform these tasks will demand a vocabulary of considerable richness and a highly sophisticated expressive capability. Once again, although numerous researchers have devised methods of generating limited semantic representations of linguistically unorganized data, systems possessing advanced cognitive faculties have yet to be developed.

These three phases of speech processing describe the ingredients necessary for basic voice communication; yet, while comprehensibility itself is a technologically formidable goal, it nevertheless describes only the surface of communicative ability. A satisfactory witness must be able to do more than interact. Especially where expertise in a particular field is claimed, the jury expects sound conclusions supported by adequate explanation. Attempts to implement the necessary reasoning processes will entail a great deal of structural planning at the level of knowledge representation. For purposes of witness testimony, the contours of required informational support are shaped largely by the proclivities of trial lawyers. Cross-examination is viewed by attorneys and judges as the acid test of witness credibility. When the witness is subjected to the cynical scrutiny of an experienced advocate, it is at least hoped that insincere assertions, erroneous convictions, and specious reasoning are exposed to the jury. Cross-examining attorneys rely on four principal avenues of investigative inquiry: witness qualification and experience, vulnerabilities in the witness's factual assumptions or scientific premises, the cogency of the ultimate opinion, and possible sources of bias.

The first of these areas is merely descriptive. The second requires some sort of recursive ability, such that conclusions can be traced to their origin; an attorney might wish to challenge the sufficiency of factual predicates or the respect accorded scholarly sources by the scientific community. The persuasiveness of an expert opinion is often tested by varying specific assumptions to determine whether alternative scenarios might produce indistinguishable conclusions. Thus, the computer witness's inferential processes will need to be capable of operating at real-time speed in order to maintain the pace of courtroom dialogue. The final aspect of the lawyer's inquisitory prerogative, a search for possible bias, engages some of the most difficult types of knowledge to implement in a computer's range of response. Bias is based on personal predilection. For an expert in a technical field, it can take such ill-defined forms as disdain for a particular scientific school of thought or a preferred method of approaching problems. The process of transferring expert knowledge to computer-based reasoning systems not only fuses individual experts' inclinations into the representational scheme, but can result in additional sources of bias as a consequence of programming design. The organization of a production system's control structure, for example, can involve conflict-resolution choices that tend to favor certain groups of rules.

These obscure sources of influence will remain beyond the reach of cross-examination unless the computer program is equipped to defend its own programming logic. If knowledge is simply gleaned from human sources and shuttled directly into a system of fixed rules, the computer will remain ignorant of the foundations underlying its expertise. True, this extraneous information might be painstakingly introduced into the computer's knowledge base solely to facilitate cross-examination, or perhaps, human experts could stand ready to provide supporting testimony. Either solution would render the computer a most ungainly witness. It appears that only those future "metaknowledgeable" systems capable of developing and maintaining their own knowledge structures could feasibly maintain sufficient familiarity with chosen sources of intelligence. However, independent evaluation, selection, and absorption of raw information implies extraordinary computing power and currently represents a distant goal of AI research.

It is difficult to predict which phase of communicative capacity — comprehensibility or intellectual sufficiency — will prove the more intractable to develop. The measure of progress necessary for access to the courtroom is not solely a technological issue, however. As computers become recognized as authoritative sources of valuable knowledge, pressure will mount to permit greater use of their capabilities in judicial contests. Diminishing skepticism and the desire to produce the fairest verdicts will undoubtedly increase the tolerance for less than perfect communication skills, and prompt judges to allow sophisticated computer systems to take the stand.

Notes

[1]Voice synthesis would also comprise a useful, although not essential, element of the system. Because numerous commercial synthesizers capable of delivering perfectly acceptable speech output currently exist, it was not considered necessary to explore this aspect.

[2]*See* 1 A. Barr and E. Feigenbaum, *The Handbook of Artificial Intelligence* 323 (1981).

[3]An overview of current research directions can be found in Waldrop, "Natural Language Understanding," *Science*, April 27, 1984, at 372. A recent example is described in Glasgow, "YANLI: A Powerful Natural Language Front-End Tool," *AI Magazine*, Spring 1987, at 40.

Why Expert Systems Do Not Exhibit Expertise

Hubert and Stuart Dreyfus

Scientists who stand at the forefront of artificial intelligence have long dreamed of autonomous "thinking" machines that are free of human control. And now they believe we are not far from realizing that dream. As Marvin Minsky, a well-known AI professor at M.I.T., recently put it: "Today our robots are like toys. They do only the simple things they're programmed to. But clearly they're about to cross the edgeless line past which they'll do the things we are programmed to."

Encouraged by such optimistic pronouncements, the U.S. Department of Defense is sinking millions of dollars into developing fully autonomous war machines that will respond to a crisis without human intervention. Business executives are investing in "expert" systems whose wisdom they hope will equal, if not surpass, that of their top managers. And AI entrepreneurs are talking of "intelligent systems" that will perform better than we can — in the home, in the classroom, and at work.

But no matter how many billions of dollars the Defense Department or any other agency invests in AI, there is almost no likelihood that scientists using the conventional approach to artificial intelligence can develop machines capable of making intelligent decisions. After 25 years of research, AI has failed to live up to its promise, and there is no evidence that it ever will. In fact, rule-following, symbol-manipulating machine intelligence will probably never replace human intelligence simply because we ourselves are not "thinking machines." Human beings have an intuitive intelligence that "reasoning" machines simply cannot match.

Military and civilian managers may see this obvious shortcoming and refrain from deploying such "logic" machines. However, once various groups have invested vast sums in developing these machines, the temptation to justify this expense by installing questionable AI technologies will be enormous. The dangers of turning over the battlefield completely to machines are obvious. But it would also be a mistake to replace skilled air-traffic controllers, seasoned business managers, and master teachers with computers that cannot come close to their level of expertise. Computers that "teach" and systems that render "expert" business decisions could eventually produce a generation of students and managers who have no faith in their own intuition and expertise.

We wish to stress that we are not Luddites. There are obvious tasks for which computers are appropriate and even indispensable. Computers are more deliberate, more precise, and less prone to exhaustion and error than the most conscientious human being. They can also store, modify, and tap vast files of data more quickly and accurately than humans can. Hence, they can be used as valuable tools in many areas. As word processors and telecommunication devices, for instance, computers are already changing our methods of writing and our notions of collaboration; expert systems, which we prefer to call competent systems, have already found a place in business and industry.

However, we believe that trying to capture more sophisticated skills within the realm of logic — skills involving not only calculation but also judgment — is a dangerously misguided effort and ultimately doomed to failure.

Acquiring Human Know-how

Most of us know how to ride a bicycle. Does that mean we can formulate specific rules to teach someone else how to do it? How would we explain the difference between the feeling of falling over and the sense of being slightly off-balance when turning? And do we really know, until the situation occurs, just what we would do in response to a certain wobbly feeling? No, we don't. Most of us are able to ride a bicycle because we possess something called "know-how," which we have acquired from practice and sometimes painful experience. That know-how is not accessible to us in the form of facts and rules. If it were, we could say we "know that" certain rules produce proficient bicycle riding.

There are innumerable other aspects of daily life that cannot be reduced to "knowing that." Such experiences involve "knowing how." For example, we know how to carry on an appropriate conversation with family, friends, and strangers in a wide variety of contexts — in the office, at a party, and on the street. We know how to walk. Yet the mechanics of walking on two legs are so complex that the best engineers cannot come close to reproducing them in artificial devices.

This kind of know-how is not innate, as is a bird's skill at building a nest. We have to learn it. Small children learn through trial and error, often by imitating those who are proficient. As adults acquire a skill through instruction and experience, they do not appear to leap suddenly from "knowing that" — a knowledge guided by rules — to experience-based know-how. Instead, people usually pass through five levels of skill: novice, advanced beginner, competent, proficient, and expert. Only when we understand this dynamic process can we ask how far the rule-following computer could reasonably progress.

During the novice stage, people learn facts relevant to a particular skill and rules for action that are based on those facts. For instance, car drivers learning to operate a stick shift are told at what speed to shift gears and at what distance — given a particular speed — to follow other cars. These rules ignore context, such as the density of traffic or the number of stops a driver has to make.

Similarly, novice chess players learn a formula for assigning pieces point values independent of their position. They learn the rule: "Always exchange your pieces for the opponent's if the total value of the pieces captured exceeds that of pieces lost." Novices generally do not know that they should violate this rule in certain situations.

After much experience in real situations, novices reach the advanced-beginner stage. Advanced-beginner drivers pay attention to situational elements, which cannot be defined objectively. For instance, they listen to engine sounds when shifting gears. They can also distinguish between the behavior of a distracted or drunken driver and that of the impatient but alert driver. Advanced-beginner chess players recognize and avoid overextended positions. They can also spot situational clues such as a weakened king's side or a strong pawn structure. In all these cases, experience is immeasurably more important than any form of verbal description.

Like the training wheels on a child's first bicycle, initial rules allow beginners to accumulate experience. But soon they must put the rules aside to proceed. For example, at the competent stage, drivers no longer merely follow rules; they drive with a goal in mind. If they wish to get from point A to point B very quickly, they choose their route with an eye to traffic but not much attention to passenger comfort. They follow other cars more closely than they are "supposed" to, enter traffic more daringly, and even break the law. Competent chess players may decide, after weighing alternatives, that they can attack their opponent's king. Removing pieces that defend the enemy king becomes their overriding objective, and to reach it these players will ignore the lessons they learned as beginners and accept some personal losses.

A crucial difference between beginners and more competent performers is their level of involvement. Novices and advanced beginners feel little responsibility for what they do because they are only applying learned rules; if they foul up, they blame the rules instead of themselves. But competent performers, who choose a goal and a plan for achieving it, feel responsible for the result of their choices. A successful outcome is deeply satisfying and leaves a vivid memory. Likewise, disasters are not easily forgotten.

Intuition of Experts

The learner of a new skill makes conscious choices after reflecting on various options. Yet in our everyday behavior, this model of decision making — the detached, deliberate, and sometimes agonizing selection among alternatives — is the exception rather than the rule. Proficient performers do not rely on detached deliberation in going about their tasks. Instead, memories of similar experiences in the past seem to trigger plans like those that worked before. Proficient performers recall whole situations from the past and apply them to the present without breaking them down into components or rules.

For instance, a boxer seems to recognize the moment to begin an attack not by following rules and combining various facts about his body's position and that of his opponent. Rather, the whole visual scene triggers the memory of similar earlier situations in which an attack was successful. The boxer is using his intuition, or know-how.

Intuition should not be confused with the reenactment of childhood patterns or any of the other unconscious means by which human being come to decisions. Nor is guessing what we mean by intuition. To guess is to reach a conclusion when one does not have enough knowledge or experience to do so. Intuition or know-how is the sort of ability that we use all the time as we go about our everyday tasks. Ironically, it is an ability that our tradition has acknowledged only in women and judged inferior to masculine rationality.

While using their intuition, proficient performers still find themselves thinking analytically about what to do. For instance, when proficient drivers approach a curve on a rainy day, they may intuitively realize they are going too fast. They then consciously decide whether to apply the brakes, remove their foot from the accelerator, or merely reduce pressure on the accelerator. Proficient marketing managers may intuitively realize that they should reposition a product. They may then begin to study the situation, taking great pride in the sophistication of their scientific analysis while overlooking their much more impressive talent — that of recognizing, without conscious thought, the simple existence of the problem.

The final skill level is that of expert. Experts generally know what to do because they have a mature and practiced understanding. When deeply involved in coping with their environment, they do not see problems in some detached way and consciously work at solving them. The skills of experts have become so much a part of them that they need be no more aware of them than they are of their own bodies. Airplane pilots report that as novices they felt they were flying their planes, but as experienced pilots they simply experience flying itself. Grand masters of chess engrossed in a game are often oblivious to the fact that they are manipulating pieces on a board. Instead, they see themselves as participants in a world of opportunities, threats, strengths, weaknesses, hopes, and fears. When playing rapidly, they sidestep dangers as automatically as teenagers avoid missiles in a familiar video game. When things are proceeding normally, experts do not solve problems by reasoning; they do what normally works.

We recently performed an experiment in which an international chess master, Julio Kaplan, had to add numbers at the rate of about one per second while playing five-second-a-move chess against a slightly weaker but master-level player. Even with his analytical mind apparently jammed by adding numbers, Kaplan more than held his own against the master in a series of games. Deprived of the time necessary to see problems or construct plans, Kaplan still produced fluid and coordinated play.

As adults acquire skills, what stands out is their progression *from* the analytic behavior of consciously following abstract rules *to* skilled behavior based on unconsciously recognizing new situations as similar to remembered ones. Conversely, small children initially understand only concrete examples and gradually learn abstract reasoning. Perhaps it is because this pattern in children is so well known that adult intelligence is so often misunderstood.

This is not to say that deliberative rationality has no role in intelligence. Tunnel vision can sometimes be avoided by a type of detached deliberation. Focusing on aspects of a situation that seem relatively unimportant allows another perspective to spring to mind. Or a decision maker, after deliberation, may decide to reject a compelling intuition because changes in the environment have rendered past experiences irrelevant.

Thinking with Images, Not Words

Experimental psychologists have shown that people actually use images, not descriptions as computers do, to understand and respond to some situations. Humans often think by forming images and comparing them holistically. This process is quite different from the logical, step-by-step operations that logic machines perform.

For instance, human beings use images to predict how certain events will turn out. If people know that a small box is resting on a large box, they can imagine what would happen if the large box were moved. If they see that the small box is tied to a door, they can also imagine what would result if someone were to open the door. A computer, however, must be given a list of facts about boxes, such as their size, weight, and frictional coefficients, as well as information about how each is affected by various kinds of movements. Given enough precise information about boxes and strings, the computer can deduce whether the small box will move with the large one under certain conditions. People also reason things out in this explicit, step-by-step way — but only if they must think about relationships they have never seen and therefore cannot imagine.

At present, computers have difficulty recognizing images. True, they can store an image as a set of dots and then rotate the set of dots so that a human designer can see the object from any perspective. But to know what a scene depicts, a computer must be able to analyze it and recognize every object. Programming a computer to analyze a scene has turned out to be very difficult. Such programs require a great deal of computation, and they work only in special cases with objects whose characteristics the computer has been programmed to recognize in advance.

But that is just the beginning of the problem. Computers currently can make inferences only from lists of facts. It's as if to read a newspaper you had to spell out each word, find its meaning in the dictionary and diagram every sentence, labeling all the parts of speech. Brains do not seem to decompose either language or images this way, but logic machines have no choice. They must break down images into the objects they contain — and then into descriptions of those objects' features — before drawing any conclusions. However, when a picture is converted into a description, much information is lost. In a family photo, for instance, one can see immediately which people are between, behind, and in front of which others. The programmer must list all these relationships for the computer, or the machine must go through the elaborate process of deducing these relationships each time the photo is used.

Some AI workers look for help from parallel processors, machines that can do many things at once and hence make millions of inferences per second. But this appeal misses the point: that human beings seem to be able to form and compare images in a way that cannot be captured by any number of procedures that operate on descriptions.

Take, for example, face recognition. People can not only form an image of a face, but they can also see the similarity between one face and another. Sometimes the similarity will depend on specific shared features, such as blue eyes and heavy beards. A computer, if it has been programmed to abstract such features from a picture of a face, could recognize this sort of similarity.

However, a computer cannot recognize emotions such as anger in facial expressions, because we know of no way to break down anger into elementary symbols. Therefore, logic machines cannot see the similarity between two faces that are angry. Yet human beings can discern the similarity almost instantly.

Many AI theorists are convinced that human brains unconsciously perform a series of computations to perceive such subtleties. While no evidence for this mechanical model of the brain exists, these theorists take it for granted because it is the way people proceed when they are reflecting consciously. To such theorists, any alternative explanation appears mystical and therefore anti-scientific.

But there is another possibility. The brain, and therefore the mind, could still be explained in terms of something material. But it does not have to be an information-processing machine. Other physical systems can detect similarity without using any descriptions or rules at all. These systems are known as holograms.

Is the Mind Like a Hologram?

In our view, the most important property of holograms is their ability to detect similarity. For example, if we made a hologram of this page and then made a hologram of one of the letters on the page, say the letter *F*, shining a light through the two holograms would reveal an astonishing effect: a black field with bright spots wherever the letter *F* occurs on the page. Moreover, the brightest spots would indicate the *F*s with the greatest similarity to the *F* we used to make our hologram. Dimmer spots would appear where there are imperfect or slightly rotated versions of the *F*. Thus, a hologram can not only identify objects; it can also recognize similarity between them. Yet it employs no descriptions or rules.

We take no stand on the question of whether the brain functions holographically. We simply want to make clear that the information-processing computer is not the only physical system that can exhibit mindlike properties. Other devices may provide closer analogies to the way the mind actually works. The digital computer is so powerful that it already is being used to simulate holistic devices. The "new connectionists," building devices and writing programs that operate somewhat like neural nets, are creating systems that can recognize patterns and detect similarity and regularity without using inferences or isolated features at all. For example, a parallel distributed processing model developed by James McClelland and David Rumelhart has been able to learn the past tenses of both regular and irregular English verbs from repeated examples without being given or creating any general rules or lists of exceptions.

Given the above considerations, what level of skill can we expect logic machines to reach? Since we can program computers with thousands of rules combining hundreds of thousands of features, machines can become what might be thought of as expert novices. As long as digital computers' ability to recognize images and reason by analogy remains a vague promise, however, they will not be able to approach the way human beings cope with everyday reality.

Despite their failure to capture everyday human understanding in computers, AI scientists have developed programs that seem to reproduce human expertise within a specific, isolated domain. The programs are called expert systems. In their narrow areas, such systems perform with impressive competence.

In his recent book on "fifth-generation" computers, Edward Feigenbaum, a professor at Stanford, spells out the goal of expert systems: "In the kind of intelligent systems envisioned by the designers of the Fifth Generation, speed and processing power will be increased dramatically. But more important, the machines will have reasoning power: they will automatically engineer vast amounts of knowledge to serve whatever purpose human beings propose, from medical diagnosis to product design, from management decisions to education."

The knowledge engineers claim to have discovered that all a machine needs to behave like an expert in these restricted domains are some general rules and lots of very specific knowledge. But can these systems really be expert? If we agree with Feigenbaum that "almost all thinking that professionals do is done by reasoning," and that each expert builds up a "repertory of working rules of thumb," the answer is yes. Given their speed and precision, computers should be as good as or better than people at following rules for deducing conclusions. Therefore, to build an expert system, a programmer need only extract those rules and program them into a computer.

Just How Expert Are Expert Systems?

However, human experts seem to have trouble articulating the principles on which they allegedly act. For example, when Arthur Samuel at IBM decided to write a program for playing checkers in 1947, he tried to elicit "heuristic" rules from checkers masters. But nothing the experts told him allowed him to produce master play.

This checkers program is one of the best expert systems ever built. But it is no champion. Samuel says the program "is quite capable of beating any amateur player and can give better players a good contest." It did once defeat a state champion, but the champion turned around and defeated the program in six mail games. Nonetheless, Samuel still believes that checkers champions rely on heuristic rules. Like Feigenbaum, he simply thinks that the champions are poor at recollecting their compiled rules: "The experts do not know enough about the mental processes involved in playing the game."

Internist-1 is an expert system highly touted for its ability to make diagnoses in internal medicine. Yet according to a recent evaluation of the program published in *The New England Journal of Medicine*, this program misdiagnosed 18 out of a total of 43 cases, while clinicians at Massachusetts General Hospital misdiagnosed 15. Panels of doctors who discussed each case misdiagnosed only 8. (Biopsies, surgery, and postmortem autopsies were used to establish the correct diagnosis for each case.) The evaluators found that "the experienced clinician is vastly superior to Internist-1, in the ability to consider the relative severity and independence of the different manifestations of disease and to understand the ... evolution of the disease process." The journal also noted that this type of systematic evaluation was "virtually unique in the field of medical applications of artificial intelligence."

In every area of expertise, the story is the same: the computer can do better than the beginner and can even exhibit useful competence, but it cannot rival the very experts whose facts and supposed rules it is processing with incredible speed and accuracy.

Why? Because the expert is not following any rules! While a beginner makes inferences using rules and facts just like a computer, the expert intuitively sees what to do without applying rules. Experts must regress to the novice level to state the rules they still remember but no longer use. No amount of rules and facts can substitute for the know-how experts have gained from experience in tens of thousands of situations. We predict that in no domain in which people exhibit holistic understanding can a system based on heuristic rules consistently do as well as experts. Are there any exceptions?

At first glance, at least one expert system seems to be as good as human specialists. Digital Equipment Corp. developed Xcon to decide how to combine components of VAX computers to meet consumers' needs. However, the program performs as well as humans only because there are so many possible combinations that even experienced technical editors depend on rule-based methods of problem solving and take about 10 minutes to work out even simple cases. It is no surprise, then, that this particular expert system can rival the best specialists.

Chess also seems to be an exception to our rule. Some chess programs, after all, have achieved master ratings. However, these programs have an Achilles' heel. Although designed for the world's most powerful computers, capable of examining up to 30 million possible positions in choosing each move, they can see only about four moves ahead for each player. So fairly good players, even those whose chess rating is somewhat lower than the computers', can win by using long-range strategies such as developing a queen's side pawn majority. When confronted by a player who knows its weakness, the computer is not yet a strong master-level player, although with enough speed it might someday overcome its strategic blindness by tactical accuracy and become one.

In every domain where know-how is required to make a judgment and brute force cannot substitute for understanding, rule-based computers cannot deliver expert performance, and it is highly unlikely that they ever will. Restricted to behaving like competent human beings at best, they produce performance often evaluated as being about 75 to 85 percent as good as experts.

Those who are most acutely aware of the limitations of expert systems are best able to exploit their real capabilities. Sandra Cook, vice president of expert systems at MAD Intelligent Systems, is one of these enlightened practitioners. She cautions prospective clients that expert systems should not be expected to perform as well as human experts, nor should they be seen as simulations of human expert thinking.

Cook lists some reasonable conditions under which expert, or rather "competent," systems can be useful. For instance, such systems should be used for problems that can be satisfactorily solved by human experts at such a high level that somewhat inferior performance is still acceptable. Processing of business credit applications is a good example, because rules can be developed for this task and computers can follow them as well and sometimes better than inexperienced humans. Of course, there are some exceptions to the rules, but a few mistakes are not disastrous. On the other hand, no one should expect expert systems to make stock-market predictions because human experts themselves cannot always make such predictions accurately.

Expert systems are also inappropriate for use on problems that change as events unfold. Advice from expert systems on how to control a nuclear reactor during a crisis would come too late to be of any use. Only human experts could make judgments quickly enough to influence events.

It is hard to believe some AI enthusiasts' claim that the companies who use expert systems will dominate all competition. In fact, a company that relies too heavily on expert systems faces a genuine danger. Junior employees may come to see expertise as a function of the large knowledge bases and masses of rules on which these programs must rely. Such employees will fail to progress beyond the competent level of performance, and the company may ultimately discover that its wells of true human expertise and wisdom have gone dry.

We are in danger of becoming a society that confuses computer-type rationality with true expertise. If we fail to put logic machines in their proper place, as aids to human beings with expert intuition, then we shall end up servants supplying data to our competent machines. Should calculative rationality triumph, no one will notice that something is missing, but now, while we still know what expert judgment is, let us use that expert judgment to preserve it.

The Scope and Limitations of First Generation Expert Systems

Derek Partridge

It is now clear that current expert system's technology (CEST), which has given us the first generation of expert systems and is focused on modular knowledge bases in conjunction with efficient logical inference strategies, is one development of AI that has enormous commercial potential. The potential for the commercialization of this technology appears to be almost limitless. But there are some nagging problems: the incremental development of knowledge bases, especially as they become large; the automatic generation of meaningful explanations of unanticipated behaviors; etc.

These may be relatively self-contained problems that will, in due course, be solved or circumvented within the current paradigm. On the other hand, these problems may be the first manifestations of some fundamental limitations of CEST. It is this latter possibility that I shall put forward. Furthermore, I shall use these problems as a basis for an attempt to sketch out the scope and limitations of CEST.

Are expert system harbingers of things to come? Yes, and no. Yes, they are a first taste of the fruits of AI research as practical software, but not one that is smoothly extendible to the full potential of what expert systems, in a more general sense, may have to offer. Figure 1 is a diagrammatic representation of a hopeful (perhaps popular) view of the expected invasion of software engineering by expert systems, together with a prediction of the future as suggested in this paper. In Figure 1a we are currently a little way up the slope with our expert systems. The way ahead is on and up to more powerful implementations as we construct bigger and better expert systems.

In Figure 1b the continuous line traces the progress supported by CEST — logical-proof-based reasoning over non-adaptive collections of context-free knowledge units. There will soon be a levelling out in terms of the size of manageable knowledge bases as well as the quality of expertise producible, and we shall find that certain domains of human expertise do not yield at all to the current technology. In fact, I believe that we can already see the first signs of having reached this plateau in the guise of some of the generic problems that expert system's developers are facing. For example, the knowledge acquisition problem and the resurgence of interest in machine learning — the knowledge bases that support expert systems are proving to be resistant to incremental upgrading, they are demanding an inordinate amount of high quality knowledge-engineer expertise, and not performing much the better for it. The dashed line in Figure 1b represents my contention that work in AI, outside of expert systems proper, has some fundamental problems, such as that of machine learning, to solve (to some degree) before expert system's technology can incorporate these techniques which are necessary for its own advancement.

Other criticisms are beginning to appear, and they provide some degree of balance in an area that is prone to overstatement. Thus Van de Riet [18] deals with the question of whether the current situation around expert systems is a healthy one. He focuses largely on the R1 system [10], and in particular on the maintenance problems which include the now-acknowledged phenomenon of "unrepairable failures."

Reprinted with permission from *Future Generation Computer Systems*, vol. 3, 1987, 1-10.

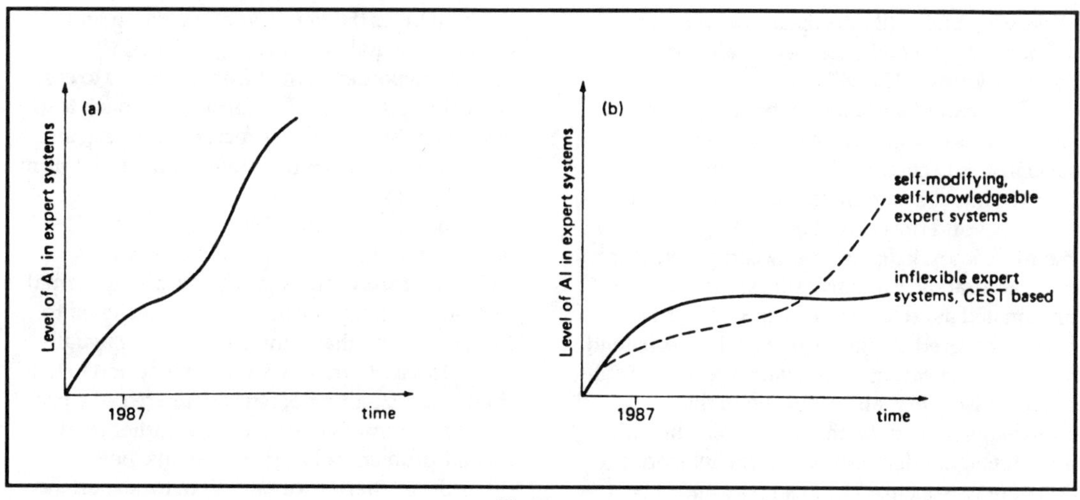

Figure 1.

Martins [8] supports my general claim, but from the standpoint that expert system technology is composed of largely old ideas. Of course, there is nothing wrong with old ideas except that the ones that form the basis of expert systems (such as table-driven processes) have long been known to embody severe limitations. Yet these limitations are being glossed over in the rush to market this "new technology." I agree with these sentiments, and in this paper I shall try to go further and begin to map out these limitations.

I shall consider two general problems that I feel are particularly instructive in regard to the task that I have set myself. The two problems are: the need for explanation capabilities in expert systems, and the problem of incrementally upgrading incomplete knowledge bases. But first let us review and consider the fundamental assumptions that underlie this first generation expert system's technology, and at the same time we can consider other related criticisms.

The Basic Assumptions and the Criticisms

The basic assumptions upon which CEST rests are:

- That the necessary knowledge can be represented as a collection of more or less independent rules; and
- That intelligent decision making can be implemented as a logical, truth-derivation mechanism.

And both of these assumptions are true — to some extent. Consider the language PROLOG, which is an important facet of CEST: PROLOG is, of course, perfectly fitted to the implementation of CEST-based systems; it is an efficient, machine-executable implementation of just these assumptions — thus it also has limitations that parallel those of CEST.

The above two assumptions are particularly reliable in domains of abstract, technical expertise. Domains such as mathematics, geology, chemistry, medical diagnosis, configuring computer systems, game playing and puzzle solving. Domains that are, of course, the areas of success with CEST.

Examples of domains in which these assumptions are particularly weak are: natural language processing; intelligent tutoring; self-explanation of behavior; and house-cleaning robots.

Another assumption that is implicit in my division of domains of applicability and inapplicability of the current technology is that the knowledge is relatively static: it does not change with time to any appreciable degree, and new knowledge does not invalidate the old. The need for this assumption rests in part on the current absence of sufficiently powerful, robust and reliable algorithms for machine learning (and as we shall see machine learning appears to be necessary to combat the knowledge acquisition problem even in domains of relatively static knowledge). It also rests on the monotonicity of currently viable logics. Work on both machine learning and non-monotonic logics is well underway, but until appropriate results are forthcoming the exclusion of domains of dynamic knowledge will continue.

Thus expert systems can be constructed to analyze mass spectrograms as well as a specialist PhD chemist. But the technician who runs the mass spectrometer has 'expertise' that is well beyond the current technology. The PhD chemist's knowledge is largely composed of (or, more accurately, can fairly successfully be approximated as) static, context-free units that, once discovered (a significant task in itself), tend to retain their validity largely irrespective of subsequent discovery, and inclusion in the knowledge base, of further such units. In addition, intelligent decisions about the interpretation of mass spectrograms can reasonably be expected to be forthcoming from a logical proof type of process: the construction of a relatively complete case for, or against, a hypothetical interpretation. The reasonableness of this expectation derives from the fact that mass spectrogram analysis is an abstract intellectual procedure that has been developed as a logic-like reasoning process.

The technician, on the other hand, the chap who operates the mass spectrometer, has to deal with the chemicals and their containers, the mass spectrometer itself, the power supply, the air conditioning, etc. In sum, he has to base his decisions on knowledge that is dynamic, diverse, inherently incomplete, most probably inconsistent, and not always (seldom?) subject to any logic-like reasoning procedure. The expertise of the technician is beyond the pale of CEST.

Hewitt [6] questions the adequacy of current logic programming methods for developing the intelligent systems of the future. Of particular relevance to my current argument is his alternative to logical proof as a reasoning mechanism. He states that "In the presence of conflicting information and contradictory beliefs, logical proof is inadequate as a reasoning mechanism. Instead we need *due-process reasoning* that investigates different sides of beliefs, goals, and hypotheses that arise."

Thus if a mass spectrogram of compound X, which has been entirely used up, has some characteristics that do not fit well with expectations based on other knowledge of X, then it might be necessary to 'open up' the decision process. Is this really a mass spectrogram of X? Is the mass spectrometer malfunctioning, etc.? Intelligent decisions about these sorts of questions are more likely to be forthcoming from weighing and debating partial evidence for and against various hypotheses, than from attempts to construct logical proofs. The former approach to decision making is due-process reasoning, and as Hewitt says, "is fundamentally different from logical proof."

Coombs and Alty (1984) suggest that CEST is misaimed: human technical experts, they claim, are rarely required to perform the formal decision-making role that CEST is designed to fill. They claim that human experts are usually asked to assist other experts to refine and extend their understanding of a problem area — a procedure that involves educational rather than formal-problem-solving skills. Thus they describe an alternative paradigm for expert systems, and one that does not have the luxury of well-defined, abstract problems.

With respect to inconsistency in knowledge bases, Hewitt offers "the Conjecture of Inconsistency: The axiomatization of the human knowledge of all physical systems are uniformly inconsistent in practice." The decision making of the mass spectrometer technician has to accommodate such inconsistency; but the PhD chemist reasoning in the abstract domain of mass spectrograms and chemical structure can largely avoid the problem. We see again the limitation of CEST to abstract domains, and the exclusion of current logic-based reasoning from domains that involve the physical world to some significant degree.

In their attempt "to demonstrate that human intelligence extends far beyond factual knowledge and abstract reasoning" and hence to question much of current AI, Dreyfus & Dreyfus (1986a, 1986b) present an extensive critique of CEST. They discuss "structured" problem areas in which the presuppositions of mainstream AI hold. The presuppositions are that:

- Symbols represent objective, context-free features;
- Such symbols can be combined into abstract symbolic descriptions;
- Relationships can be expressed in terms of strict rules;
- Logical inference can be used to generate new states of affairs.

They contrast structured problems, which may be adequately characterized by the above four points, with "unstructured" problem areas. "Such areas contain a potentially unlimited number of possibly relevant facts and features, and the ways those elements interrelate and determine other events is unclear. Management, nursing, economic forecasting, teaching, and all social interactions fall into that very large class."

There are clear parallels between the Dreyfus & Dreyfus characterization of CEST and my own; there are also significant differences. They are attacking current AI and attempting to demonstrate what they believe to be fundamental misconceptions in the field. I am attempting nothing so radical; my arguments are focussed on CEST and, although I see non-trivial changes as necessary if certain problems are to be solved, the next generation expert system's technology could well fit comfortably within the general paradigm that Dreyfus & Dreyfus are questioning. Let us now look more closely at the 'explanation' and knowledge acquisition problems.

Explanations and Context Sensitivity

Context-sensitivity is a feature of AI that helps to distinguish AI that is currently viable in practical software, and AI that is not. The critical test, I argue, is how context-free or loosely-coupled to its context an AI problem is. Tightly-coupled context-sensitivity characterizes the empty set of practical AI software.

Science thrives on context-free problems: problems that can be solved irrespective of the context in which they occur. Thus the square root of an integer is calculatable in a predetermined and correct way no matter where the integer originated nor to what use the answer will be put. Contrast the problem of understanding natural language, when, for example, the human user and expert system participate in a dialogue to determine the type of explanation required: the meaning of a sentence may depend more upon who is saying it and why they are saying it, than it does upon the actual words used to construct the sentence. Truly context-free problems are, in fact, somewhat scarce; abstract scientific domains are the major preserve of these objects. The question of interest then becomes: to what extent our context-free abstraction can adequately account for the corresponding phenomena in the empirical world. Simon [21] has an interesting argument to support his contention that although many real-world systems, such as you and I, are not collections of context-free subsystem, they do tend to have the property of "near decomposability." In my terminology near decomposability is loosely-coupled context sensitivity. Systems that possess this property can be treated as collections of context-free modules, to a first approximation; tightly-coupled context-sensitive problems cannot.

In his exploration of the possibilities for AI, Haugeland [7] characterizes formal systems as "self-contained; the 'outside world' is strictly irrelevant," they are also "digital," which implies that such formal systems are independent of any particular medium — chess (a formal system) can be played with bedknobs or broomsticks, but football (not a formal system) is critically dependent on certain necessary characteristics of the ball, as well as many other things. CEST certainly exploits such formal domains and the syntactic manipulation of the representations used (commonly termed, a lack of 'deep knowledge'), which is all that is necessary in a formal system; semantics, as meaning, necessarily relates to the 'outside world.' In Haugeland's terminology: the extent to which we can successfully ignore the outside world in problem solving is a measure of the possibilities for automation in general, which, of course, includes CEST. With tightly-coupled, context-sensitive problems meaning, in his sense, cannot be ignored and CEST is not applicable because the assumption of context-free knowledge units does not hold.

Another useful dimension along which we can view context-sensitivity is with respect to its tendency to change — at the crudest level, is it static or dynamic? I shall argue below that many AI problems are characterized by tightly-coupled and dynamic context-sensitivity. Then a need to take complex and dynamic relationships into account for decision making leads us inexorably on to a need for machine learning.

To some extent context sensitivity can be internalized in the function and we have a context-free, but larger, function. Some of the knowledge encapsulated by AI implementations is internalized context.

The most realistic approaches to intelligent computer-aided instruction (CAI), for example, include a model of the user. The most important context sensitivity in this problem is that between the machine and the human being under instruction — the system user. By generating and maintaining a model of each user the computer system has internalized the crucial context sensitivity of the problem.

Apart from the problem of maintaining up-to-date models or knowledge of the relevant aspects of an AI program's domain (i.e. machine learning, the topic of the next section), an important question in AI is: how much context do we need to internalize?

It all depends on the scope of our AI system. It is clear that a useful level of expertise can be achieved in limited domains as a result of an internalization of a severely limited collection of knowledge; expert systems exhibit some AI on the basis of a narrow domain-specific knowledge base.

What is not clear is: how much can the AI in expert systems be upgraded and extended (e.g. to include a sophisticated explanation component) within the current framework for such systems — inflexible and highly limited context sensitivity?

If we are aiming for a more general AI system, not necessarily one with the full capabilities of you or I, but say an expert system that takes people into account — their aims, objectives, hopes and fears, all with respect to the particular expertise of the AI system — then the context sensitivity must be both broadened and made dynamic.

You and I have internalized a model of the world within which models of specific subworlds are developed to differing degrees dependent upon their relative importance in our lives. We can behave sensitively, and thus have a basis for intelligent responses, to a wide range of phenomena. It is clear that our intelligence is founded upon a lot of knowledge; it is also clear that we do not know anything approaching all that there is to know. But what we do have is the ability to learn and dynamically internalize new knowledge (develop a new or expanded context sensitivity), whenever it is in our interest to do so.

In principle the state of any given person's knowledge at a given time could be fed into a computer and the computer system could behave just as intelligently as the original person although it has no learning capability whatever. But for how long would it remain intelligent? The answer depends upon how static or dynamic is the knowledge upon which the intelligent behavior is founded.

Expertise in, say, pure mathematics could be expected to endure for long periods of time; the basic knowledge is well established and not subject to major changes. But intelligent interaction with respect to current affairs, or with any given individual, is liable to degrade rapidly — both contexts are dynamic. Out-of-date knowledge will soon reduce this static system to a pathetic anachronism.

So we'll just update the system's knowledge whenever necessary — every day, or every hour, or even every minute — there is still no necessity for machine learning? I think that there is, but this is an argument for the next section.

Domain-specific knowledge may be relatively static, as in the above example of pure mathematics. The implementor of an expert system, who spends an inordinate amount of time modifying the system's knowledge base, might well want to challenge that statement. But compared to knowledge of the empirical world (who and what are where, and doing what), knowledge of chemical structure, and knowledge of geological formations, and knowledge of the associations between symptoms and diseases, are decidedly static.

The fact that even with these static knowledge bases the knowledge engineer is largely preoccupied with modifying the knowledge base is a danger signal for the way knowledge-engineer intervention will escalate when more dynamic contexts are attempted, if we fail to incorporate self-adaptivity.

In describing XSEL, a front end to the R1 expert system, McDermott [11] singles out the context-free nature of XSEL's three main tasks. He says, "The most striking characteristic of these subtasks is that for all three the decisions to be made are relatively independent both of prior and of subsequent decisions." And although a significant amount of knowledge is required to achieve performance adequacy, "the fact that the component selection task can be recognition driven [i.e. context free] makes XSEL conceptually quite simple."

The explanation task, he continues, is quite different. In reference to the knowledge-based programs of recent years, he says, "for the most part, these programs do not treat explanation as a task that requires intelligence." As a first approximation to the user-context sensitivity necessary for good explanations, XSEL has five kinds of information from which to generate an explanation. The adequacy of this fixed, five-point, discrete approximation to the continuum of user context remains to be seen.

My argument is not that such discrete simulations cannot support the rich and continuous context sensitivity within user-and-system interaction — such would be one of the well-known Dreyfus fallacies. What I am saying is that however sophisticated the discrete approximation becomes it will need to be self-adaptive in order to exhibit the explanation capabilities of an average human being. Again we return to the question of: are the capabilities of an average human being necessary? Clearly, in some very practical sense, they are not, but to achieve anything like the full potential of the promise of expert systems a surprising amount of such capabilities will be necessary.

An analogous argument based on the reasoning capabilities of current expert systems is given by Wos et al. [24]. They state, in their text on automated reasoning, that current expert systems rely largely on "focused reasoning" (i.e. reasoning with known procedures that can be well-controlled). They argue that "unfocused reasoning" (i.e. no well-defined procedure is known that will directly yield the answer) must be used or else we will overlook many possible applications. In their words, "many significant applications will require unfocused reasoning."

Returning to the specific limitations of system rigidity, Boden [1], for example, also discussing expert systems, states that, "Current systems are relatively simple and inflexible, and restricted to very narrow domains. They can be incrementally improved, but only up to a point." She also sees machine learning as a pressing problem for the future. "If a program cannot learn for itself, its development is limited by the time and ability of the programmer to provide it with new information and ideas."

Clearly Boden's ideas are supportive of my argument although she does not seem to view machine-learning as playing quite the same unique and crucial role as I do. Nevertheless, this brings us on to the question of the need for, or necessity of, machine-learning in expert systems. I will argue that it is a necessity in practice if not in principle; the alternative is a severely limited application of expert system's technology in practical software.

Updating Knowledge Bases and Machine Learning

"To be blunt, an AI program that doesn't learn is no AI program at all." [20] I wouldn't go that far (and neither would he at other times, I suspect), but even neglecting the hyperbole, Schank is clearly with me in spirit. Although we agree on the importance of learning, I am happy with the term AI software as applied to adequate implementations of complex, open-ended problems even though they make no pretensions to learn.

And although not so dramatic, my point is somewhat harder to substantiate. I would agree with Schank that, "Learning is, after all, the quintessential AI issue." But it does not necessarily follow that expert systems must involve machine learning. The result of a learning behavior can always, in principle at least, be simulated by periodic updating of the system by some outside agency.

In practice we are already witnessing a renewal of interest in machine learning as a strategy for alleviating the problems generated by the knowledge bases used in expert systems — problems of both construction and maintenance of large and complex, but relatively static, collections of information. We find this point made in the review of AI chaired by Waltz (1983), and in almost every other mention of the knowledge acquisition problem.

Michie [14], for example, in his review of the state-of-the-art in machine learning, sees a practical need for machine learning in terms of increasing programmer productivity. He then focuses on a semi-automated scheme for knowledge acquisition — he calls this scheme "structured induction."

Waltz's committee, in their state-of-the-art report on AI, cite "the ability to learn from experience" as one of a small number of "important characteristics that such machines would have to have before AI could be said to have succeeded" [23]. They do not single out machine learning as I would, but to my mind the other characteristics that they list — such as, common sense, and the ability to deal appropriately with natural language input — all imply a prerequisite machine learning ability. This would seem to cast the machine learning characteristic in a more fundamental role than they appear to accord it.

From his long perspective on the AI scene, Samuel [19] singles out natural-language communication and learning as the two basic problems of AI. He goes on to say "that the desired progress in man-machine communication will not be made until it is treated as a learning problem.... In fact, I look on learning as the central problem of AI research." So it seems that I am in good company with my extreme view.

I think that it is clear that, in practice at least, there is general agreement that machine learning is an important research problem that still needs to be solved to some reasonable degree.

The limits of non-adaptive expert systems are those problems that involve interaction with neither people nor any other aspect of the empirical world, except in a very subsidiary role. This is clearly a characterization that is closely akin to the earlier ones based on loosely-coupled context sensitivity and static contexts.

The possibility of having a knowledge-based AI system that behaves intelligently without a self-adaptive capability will only be viable in the domains of relatively static knowledge. That restriction largely excludes intelligent interaction with people and the domains of everyday such as house cleaning. It is a limitation to intellectual expertise in largely theoretical domains — there's clearly lots of scope for current expert systems technology there, but it is also a domain of applicability that excludes many aspects of human endeavor, aspects that we might expect to be suitable targets for expert system's technology.

Remember that I am not arguing that CEST cannot go any further without non-trivial machine learning. There may be decades of useful and exciting expansion of the applications of non-learning expert systems. I am making the case that without sophisticated machine learning our options will always be limited; large and important sections of potential application areas will be excluded, and the full potential of expert systems as practical software will not be achieved.

Even if we can agree that sophisticated adaptivity will be necessary in certain expert systems that still leaves the question of, to what degree will the system have to be self-adaptive? A given need to assimilate information may be implemented in many ways. In particular there is a spectrum of possibilities from totally automated discovery to a fairly trivial ability to accept from a human tutor mentally predigested information. This latter possibility does not really qualify to be called non-trivial machine learning, but there are many strategies, intermediate between these two extremes, that do qualify (see [12] for a thorough coverage of the current state of the art in machine learning).

It may be possible to implement the necessary sophisticated adaptivity in terms of a fairly simple program, and a smart and dedicated human tutor — and this is a valid approach to take when researching the problem. But for commercial AI it falls foul of all of the previous arguments for the necessity of machine learning — i.e. human beings will be doing all of the difficult work, and this onerous task will be different for every individual copy of the software.

For non-trivial machine learning a lot of knowledge concerning the program's organization and goals and objectives must be available somewhere — either in the program itself or in the human tutor. The main point underlying the necessity for machine learning is that no human being has to maintain, at his finger-tips, all of this knowledge about the program (and remember, each copy of the program is an individual) such that he can accurately modify it at the drop of a new significant fact.

So although the necessity for machine learning does mean that the machine and not the human should indeed be shouldering the burden, it is again not at all clear how far we can go with AI into dynamic contexts by sharing the load to some extent. Indeed, the real power of AI may reside in an intimate man-machine relationship — a symbiotic superintelligence. But I do not believe that this partnership will work if all of the learning and adaption has to come through the organic partner.

It is clear that incrementally upgrading non-trivial knowledge bases presents formidable complexity problems. In their first book on machine learning Michalski et al. [12] state that one need for automated learning is that humans quickly become incapable of upgrading AI systems because they cannot maintain an understanding of the system to the necessary logical depth. The requirement that the machine bears the burden of the learning is a specific measure to lessen the complexity that the associated humans have to manage. This is true even in the relatively static domains where expert systems currently promise to be effective. For even in these relatively static domains the concept of a complete knowledge base is not seriously entertained. Incremental upgrading is an intrinsic feature of the use of such systems, not just of their development. Rather than a developmental nuisance that will go away as soon as we learn to specify our knowledge bases properly, incremental upgrading must be countenanced for the life of the system — it is part of what makes an AI system rather than a conventional software engineering system. I have argued elsewhere, at length in [16] and more succinctly in [15], that incremental development of a machine-executable specification, throughout the life of a system, is a fundamental feature of the AI domain. It is not just the code hacking syndrome that AI will divest itself of as soon as it becomes sufficiently mature. Code hacking is prevalent in AI, and it should be discouraged, but what it should give way to is a disciplined development of the Run-Understand-Debug-Edit cycle (the RUDE paradigm). AI problems are typically not amenable to complete prior specification, thus the goal of AI system development should not be the Specify-Prove-Implement-Verify based paradigm (the SPIV paradigm) that conventional software science aspires to (this viewpoint is argued in [17]). If we then consider possible applications in dynamic environments, such as house cleaning, domains outside of the relatively fixed, abstract domains of medical diagnosis and mass spectrogram analysis, the incremental upgrading problem leaps in difficulty by at least an order of magnitude.

Conclusions

In sum, I claim that the "explanation problem" associated with current expert system's technology is a manifestation of the fact that this technology is inherently limited to the relatively static and relatively context free domain of abstract technical expertise. The problem of incrementally upgrading knowledge bases also partly derives from the context sensitivity typically associated with the AI domain. But it is also indicative of the incremental system development paradigm needed in AI (which to some extent is itself due to the context sensitivity feature). In addition, this necessity for continual knowledge base updating, even in these relatively static domains, suggests that some reasonable level of solution to the problem of machine learning will be required in order that these limitations on current expert system's technology may be overcome.

The point is that these two types of problem do not appear to be individual problems that will be solvable within the current expert system's technology; they are symptoms of inherent limitations within the technology. Some indication that current limitations are not generally acknowledged as fundamental challenges to the presuppositions of CEST can be found, for example, in [22]. Steels offers a characterization of "Second Generation Expert Systems," "a substantial jump forward in expert systems technology" that touches on "the nature of the potential problem domains, the type of reasoning being performed, the explanation capabilities, and most importantly the way knowledge acquisition is performed." A grand manifesto and one that leads us to expect that either much of my earlier analysis is incorrect (because the explanation problems, etc. have been solved within CEST), or my characterization of CEST is outdated (because these second generation systems employ a new technology that is not subject to the limitations of CEST). Neither of these implications is correct. In fact the assumptions of CEST are not challenged but in addition we are promised "expert systems [that] can learn new rules by examining the results of deep reasoning."

The reality turns out to be exhaustive backchaining search of a complete causally-linked (i.e., A causes B; B causes C; etc.) set of rules; this procedure is called "deep reasoning." The claimed "causal" knowledge is of exactly the type that has been exposed as simplistic in the extreme by Chandrasekaran & Mittal (1983), and the use of the term "deep reasoning" is a blatant over-glorification of a trivial process (McDermott [9] exposed this pernicious trend in AI many years ago). Worse than this, the non-innovative suggestions will not work in practice because success is predicated upon having a *complete* causal network. If the "deep reasoning" exhausts the network without finding a reason for the current problem then it concludes that the reason is, for example, a faulty internal component in the physical system being diagnosed — this presupposes that no causal rule is missing, i.e., that the knowledge is complete. This requirement is very surprising because one of the features that makes expert systems AI rather than conventional software engineering is that we must abandon the luxury of completeness: one thing that we know for certain about any knowledge base is that it does not contain all potentially relevant knowledge whatever the domain — i.e., knowledge bases are necessarily incomplete.

When the learning of new rules is explained, we see that it consists of the addition of a direct 'anomaly-causes-problem' rule where the particular anomaly and problem are those linked by the prior deep reasoning process. It is a new manifestation of the "memo function" feature explored in the language POP-2 [13]. In effect a look-up table of previously computed results is maintained to provide a faster response than recomputing the result for subsequent accesses to the knowledge base with repetitions of earlier diagnosed problems. The many problems associated with this simple idea have been well-known for a long time, and although Steels demonstrates an awareness of some of the limitations of this mechanism, he offers no solutions that might transform the memo-function idea into a machine learning mechanism that will be useful in practice.

So, I would maintain, the first generation of expert systems technology is still very much the CEST that I have attempted to characterize above. Can we begin to circumscribe the scope and limitations of CEST? I think that we can begin to do so. Ernst [5], for example, has provided an analysis of the scope of practical utility of CEST with respect to business knowledge based systems. And even though I am by no means convinced that I have identified the most critical inherent limitations with great accuracy. There are, as one referee pointed out, other, largely independent and equally pressing, limitations of CEST: for example, reasoning with uncertainty, and the inability to employ spatial and isomorphic representations. Nevertheless, I am sure that efforts to define some aspects of the scope and limitations of this new technology will be beneficial. It will help to counterbalance the usual oversell. It will help to locate the problems that need to be tackled. And, in the meantime, it will serve to guide future applications into those domains where success is most likely.

I am not trying to be alarmist, and I don't see this paper as defeatist. But I do believe that many of the problems that beset the expert system developer will not be solved by a few more rules in the knowledge base, or any such fix within the current expert system technology. If this is true it does not mean that expert systems are doomed, or severely limited forever; it means that when these problems are solved (as part of mainstream AI research) then the new, or expanded, resultant expert system technology can be applied to extend both the domain and efficacy of expert systems. But before they can be solved they must be recognized as fundamental problems outside the scope of current expert system technology.

References

[1] Boden, M.A. (1984) Impacts of Artificial Intelligence, *AISB Quarterly*, No. 49, pp. 9-14.

[2] Coombs, M., & Alty, J. (1984) Expert Systems: an alternative paradigm, *Internat. J Man-Machine Studies*, 20, p. 21-43.

[3] Dreyfus, H.L., & Dreyfus, S.E. (1986a) *Mind over Machine*, Free Press/MacMillan.

[4] Dreyfus, H.L., & Dreyfus, S.E. (1986b) Competent Systems: the only future for inference-making computers, *Future Generations Computer Systems*, 2 (1986), pp. 233-244.

[5] Ernst, M.L. (1986) Business Applications of Artificial Intelligence Knowledge Based Expert Systems, *Future Generation Computer Systems*, 2.

[6] Hewitt, C. (1985) The Challenge of Open Systems, *BYTE*, April, pp. 223-242.

[7] Haugeland, J. (1985) *Artificial Intelligence, the very idea*, MIT Press: Cambridge, Mass.

[8] Martins, G.R. (1984) The Overselling of Expert Systems, *Datamation*, 30, 18.

[9] McDermott, D. (1976) Artificial Intelligence meets Natural Stupidity, *SIGART Newsletter*, No. 57, pp. 4-9.

[10] McDermott, J. (1981) R1: The formative years, *AI Magazine*, 2, 2, pp. 21-29.

[11] McDermott, J. (1982) XSEL: a computer sales person's assistant, in *Machine Intelligence* 10, J.E. Hayes, D. Michie, and Y-H Pao (eds), Ellis Horwood: Chichester, UK, pp. 325-337.

[12] Michalski, R.S., Carbonell, J.G., and Mitchell, T.M. (1983, 1986) *Machine Learning*, vols. I and II, Morgan Kaufmann, CA.

[13] Michie, D. (1968) 'Memo' functions and machine learning, *Nature* 218, pp. 19-22.

[14] Michie, D. (1982) The State of the Art in Machine Learning, in *Introductory Readings in Expert Systems*, D. Michie (ed), Gordon and Breach: London, pp. 208-229.

[15] Partridge, D. (1985) Design, like AI system development, is an incremental and an exploratory process, *The AI Magazine*, 6, 3, pp. 48-51.

[16] Partridge, D. (1986) *AI: Applications in the Future of Software Engineering*, Ellis Horwood/Wiley: Chichester, UK.

[17] Partridge, D. & Wilks, Y. (1987) Does AI have a methodology different from software engineering?, *AI Review Journal*, Vol. 1, no. 2, pp. 111-120.

[18] van de Riet, R.P. (1987) Expert Systems in Trouble, *Future Generation Computer Systems* (to appear).

[19] Samuel, A. (1983) AI, where has it been and where is it going? *Proc. IJCAI-83*, Karlsruhe, W. Germany, pp. 1152-1157.

[20] Schank, R.C. (1983) The Current State of AI: One Man's Opinion, *The AI Magazine*, Winter/Spring, pp. 3-8.

[21] Simon, H.A. (1962) The Architecture of Complexity, *Procs. American Phil. Soc. 106*, 6, pp. 467-482.

[22] Steels, L. (1985) Second Generation Expert Systems, *Future Generations Computer Systems*, 1, 4, pp. 213-221.

[23] Waltz, D. (1983) Artificial Intelligence: an assessment of the state-of-the-art and recommendations for future directions, *The AI Magazine*, Fall, pp. 55-67.

[24] Wos, L., Overbeek, R., Lusk, E., and Boyle, J. (1984) *Automated Reasoning*, Prentice-Hall: NJ.

Review Questions

IV. Perspectives

Freidenberg and Hensler

1. Discuss the major steps in developing a corporate strategy. Why is it important for an AI company to develop a corporate strategy?
2. What information should be included in a good business plan?
3. What issues need to be considered in seeking capital for an AI firm?
4. Suppose you are developing a software package that integrates the power of spreadsheet software and the reasoning capabilities of rule-based expert systems. Prepare a market analysis for such a product.

Frank

1. To prove negligence in tort liability cases, the software developer must be shown to have not "exercised reasonable care" in developing the product. In the development of an expert system, what tasks would you consider necessary to demonstrate "reasonable care"? Discuss. Given the current variability in validating expert systems (discussed in the articles by O'Leary and O'Keefe et al.), how safe is expert systems development? Should expert systems developers wait for more rigorous approaches?
2. An assumption of the product liability framework is that the vendor has the ability to spread losses over many users. How does this assumption fit with the expert systems market? Are expert systems more risky than other software products, or are they immune from this legal approach?
3. The author implies that "deep" expert systems are safer (legally) than "shallow" ones. Discuss deep versus shallow expert systems. Do you agree or disagree with the author? Why or why not?
4. The author mentions that the direct link of CAD/CAM to product design to consumer product establishes a strong basis for liability. There are many expert systems, called program traders, that monitor stock behavior and automatically generate buy/sell orders. Such systems received significant attention in the stock market crash of October 1987. Is this the same kind of direct link identified by the author? Discuss.
5. Based on the author's description of the characteristics of an expert witness, answer the following questions: What can an expert system do now? What will an expert system be able to do soon? What will an expert system never be able to do?

Dreyfus and Dreyfus

1. What is the thesis of this article? Why do the authors argue that "There is no likelihood that scientists using the conventional approach to artificial intelligence can develop machines capable of making intelligent decisions"? Comment on the authors' statement.
2. What is the nature of "know-how"?
3. What limitations may expert systems have? Given these limitations, how can expert systems contribute to enhanced human decision making?
4. Expert systems may be different from human beings in many ways, including knowledge representation, reasoning, and uncertainty processing. Given this understanding, would you develop and use expert systems? Why or why not?

Partridge

1. How does business decision making stack up against the author's two assumptions of CEST? Does it fit or not?
2. Are first-generation expert systems aimed at decisions that are too rigid and built with mechanisms that are too exact? Has this affected the growth of business expert systems?
3. Are business decisions context-sensitive or context-free? Discuss the implications for expert systems.
4. Where do you think business expert systems should go in the near future? Should they continue with first-generation technologies, with the potential for forcing a second-generation decision into a first-generation solution, just to get a solution now? Or should they hold off and wait for expert systems technology to catch up?